Consumer Behavior for Marketing Managers

Edited by

Ian Fenwick
York University

John A. Quelch
Harvard University

Consumer Behavior for Marketing Managers

Allyn and Bacon, Inc.

Boston London Sydney Toronto

Library of Congress Cataloging in Publication Data

Fenwick, Ian, 1949–
Consumer behavior for marketing managers.

1. Consumers. I. Quelch, John A. II. Title.
HF5415.3.F38 1984 658.8′342 83-27526
ISBN 0-205-08120-7

Printed in the United States of America

10 9 8 7 6 5 4 3 2 1 88 87 86 85 84

CONTENTS

Preface *ix*

Introduction 1

CHAPTER ONE
Fundamentals of Consumer Behavior

1. Formal Models of Consumer Behavior: A Conceptual Overview 13
J. R. Bettman and J. Morgan Jones

2. Multiattribute Models in Marketing: A Bicentennial Review 26
R. J. Lutz and J. R. Bettman

3. Some Internal Psychological Factors Influencing Consumer Choice 34
W. J. McGuire

4. Memory Factors in Consumer Choice: A Review 55
J. R. Bettman

5. Hemispheral Lateralization: Implications for Understanding Consumer Behavior 75
F. Hansen

CHAPTER TWO
Influences on Consumer Behavior

6. Psychographics: A Critical Review 93
W. D. Wells

7. Interpersonal Influence on Consumer Behavior: An Attribution Theory Approach 115
B. J. Calder and R. E. Burnkrant

8. An Investigation of Situational Variation in Brand Choice Behavior and Attitude 127
K. E. Miller and J. L. Ginter

9. Behavioral Learning Theory: Its Relevance to Marketing and Promotions 142
M. L. Rothschild and W. C. Gaidis

CHAPTER THREE
Consumer Decision-Making Processes

10. Consumer Decision Making—Fact or Fiction? 155
R. W. Olshavsky and D. H. Granbois

11. "Consumer Decision Making—Fact or Fiction?" Comment 165
M. Ursic

12. Rejoinder 168
R. W. Olshavsky and D. H. Granbois

13. Decision Making within the Household 170
H. L. Davis

14. The Information Overload Controversy: An Alternative Viewpoint 194
N. K. Malhotra, A. K. Jain, and S. W. Lagakos

15. An Appraisal of Low-Involvement Consumer Information Processing 207
F. S. DeBruicker

CHAPTER FOUR
Consumer Behavior and Market Segmentation

16. Issues and Advances in Segmentation Research 219
Y. Wind

17. Some Practical Considerations in Market Segmentation 244
S. Young, L. Ott, and B. Feigin

18. Person-Situation: Segmentation's Missing Link 254
P. R. Dickson

19. Market Segmentation by Personal Values and Salient Product Attributes 265
A. S. Boote

CHAPTER FIVE
Consumer Behavior and Product Development

20. Identification of Determinant Attributes: A Comparison of Methods 277
M. I. Alpert

21. Positioning Your Product 287
D. A. Aaker

22. New Way to Measure Consumers' Judgments 295
P. E. Green and Y. Wind

23. Customer-Oriented Approaches to Identifying Product-Markets 306
G. S. Day, A. D. Shocker, and R. K. Srivastava

CHAPTER SIX
Consumer Behavior and Pricing Policy

24. An Experiment in Brand Choice 321
P. Charlton and A. S. C. Ehrenberg

25. A Theoretical and Empirical Evaluation of Price Deals for Consumer Nondurables 331
R. C. Blattberg, G. D. Eppen, and J. Lieberman

26. Repeat Rates of Deal Purchases 346
R. W. Shoemaker and F. R. Shoaf

27. Consumer Response to In-Store Price Information Environments 355
V. A. Zeithaml

CHAPTER SEVEN
Consumer Behavior and Communications Programs

28. Perception and Advertising 373
I. A. Horowitz and R. S. Kaye

29. Subliminal Advertising: What You See Is What You Get 380
T. E. Moore

30. Fear: The Potential of an Appeal Neglected by Marketing 392
M. L. Ray and W. L. Wilkie

31. An Experimental Investigation of Comparative Advertising: Impact of Message Appeal, Information Load, and Utility of Product Class 402
S. Goodwin and M. Etgar

32. Consumer Initial Processing in a Difficult Media Environment 416
P. H. Webb

CHAPTER EIGHT
Managing Consumer Research

33. Designing Research for Application 433
B. J. Calder, L. W. Phillips, and A. M. Tybout

34. Making Marketing Research Accountable 447
J. Gandz and T. W. Whipple

35. Four Subtle Sins in Marketing Research 456
J. A. Martilla and D. W. Carvey

36. Decision Support Systems for Marketing Managers 465
J. D. C. Little

PREFACE

Consumer behavior is one of the fastest growing areas of business education and research. Virtually unrecognized twenty years ago, consumer behavior now occupies a central position in almost all management education programs, and its principles are applied in a wide range of management decisions. The managerial importance of consumer behavior stems directly from the marketing concept. When consumers and their requirements are the focus of the business, consumer behavior has to be a cornerstone of marketing strategy. As acceptance of the marketing concept becomes commonplace, so an understanding of consumer behavior becomes a fundamental management tool.

Consumer behavior is essentially multidisciplinary. Theories, concepts, and techniques are borrowed from many sources, particularly from psychology, sociology, and economics. This has several implications for marketing users of consumer behavior. First, the literature is scattered. Key findings are reported in a wide variety of sources, many not readily accessible. This book collects, in a single source, readings that effectively summarize the major themes and findings of consumer research.

A second consequence of consumer behavior's relatively recent emergence is a tendency to emphasize theory over practice. Although theory was comparatively easy to borrow, it has proved difficult to adapt and apply to a business environment. In many areas practical applications are only now being realized, and it is fair to say that only a minority of the research conducted to date has involved applications. This is typical of the early stage of development of any field. Practical application of consumer behavior principles is being made; applications-oriented research is being conducted. The trend is for these areas to grow. However, it is easy for a manager, or a practical-minded student, to lose sight of applications in the morass of theory that dominates the more academic journals.

This volume of readings is based on a systematic review of a wide range of journals, and draws heavily from the latest published findings. The readings selected are purposely skewed toward applications wherever possible. Our aim is not to ignore theory, but to use application and managerial relevance as the justification for the theories and conceptual frameworks presented. Before you can apply consumer behavior principles, you must understand them; to be motivated to understand them requires confidence that application is indeed possible. The long-term measure of the value of studying consumer behavior must be its contribution to management decision making.

We are grateful to Professor Russell W. Belk of the University of Utah, Professor Sharon Banks Beatty of the University of Oregon, Professor George E. Belch of San Diego State University, Professor Pradeep K. Korgaonkar of Wayne State University, and Professor James H. Leigh of Texas A&M University, who reviewed our outline and made many helpful suggestions.

Consumer Behavior for Marketing Managers

INTRODUCTION

Consumer behavior covers a tremendously wide range of topics. From the consumer's first (internal) recognition of a need, through the external influences of people, information, and products, to the decision to purchase (or not) and its subsequent effects—all these events and processes come under the heading of consumer behavior. The first challenge in producing a set of consumer behavior readings is to structure the available material in a meaningful fashion.

We have elected to use the classic market planning framework. Chapters 1, 2, and 3 examine the basic building blocks of consumer behavior. In Chapter 4 these building blocks are applied to market segmentation and the selection of target markets. Each element of the marketing program is then analyzed in turn. Chapter 5 looks at the contribution of consumer behavior to product development; Chapter 6 at its contribution to pricing; and Chapter 7 at its contribution to marketing communications. Interestingly, in our view, the fourth element of the marketing program, distribution, has not yet attracted sufficient attention from consumer researchers to warrant separate inclusion. Finally, Chapter 8 examines the design and implementation of a successful, practical consumer research program within the corporate framework.

Chapter Summaries

Chapter 1: Fundamentals of Consumer Behavior

Chapter 1 summarizes the basics of consumer behavior. It aims to show where consumer behavior comes from, and where it is headed. Without a doubt, many more papers could have been included in this section. What we present is the bare basics. The material in this chapter is of necessity less applied than that appearing later in the book. However, bear with it. Virtually all the theory here is applied in subsequent readings, or is the subject of current applications. You should make a point of referring to the readings in this chapter as you proceed through the book. When you have completed the book, try to match the theory presented here with the application topics of later chapters. Try to identify the theoretical areas that have not yet been applied to management problems. What applications can you suggest for them?

The first reading, by Bettman and Jones (1972), provides an overview of the consumer behavior models most frequently applied in the business context. This article summarizes what are probably the most crucial foundations for the application of consumer behavior in marketing. Subsequent readings in this volume build on, extend, and apply the models discussed here, so be sure to review them carefully.

The next two papers, by Lutz and Bettman (1977), and by McGuire (1976), are strongly oriented to psychology's contribution to understanding consumer behavior. Although parts of both papers are heavily theoretical, they represent the essential basis for many applications. While reading these papers, particularly McGuire (1976), consider how the principles discussed can be applied. Think about the company you work for, or a case with which you are familiar. How can marketing management use the concepts presented to better understand the consumer? What marketing decisions will be affected?

The attitudinal models discussed by Lutz and Bettman (1977) have been a major concern of consumer behavior researchers. These models underlie many of the product positioning and marketing communications applications presented later in this volume. The paper summarizes the research findings to date. It also examines the process of borrowing theory, formulating models, testing them empirically, and refining both models and theory, that has characterized research on consumer behavior. The next paper, by Bettman (1979), summarizes psychological research and theory on memory, emphasizing findings of special relevance for marketers. In particular, Bettman analyzes the implications of memory research for promotional decisions. This article is a good example of the way theoretical work in another discipline (psychology) can contribute practical insights for marketing management.

The final paper in Chapter 1, Hansen (1981), illustrates the most recent application of this borrowing, adaptation, and refinement process. It is too soon to say whether brain lateralization will find a lasting place in the marketing manager's pantheon, but as Hansen points out, the concept has many potential applications. It has also aroused the interest of many marketing and advertising executives. An important lesson of this paper is that even the most unlikely sounding developments in other disciplines can have major applications to practical management decisions.

Chapter 2: Influences on Consumer Behavior

This chapter deals with the internal and external factors that affect the ways in which consumers act. Wells (1975) reviews the state of the art of measurement of individual lifestyles, a field that he helped to develop. Lifestyle analysis recognizes that the most important differences between individuals may not be their demographic characteristics (age, education, income, etc.) but the ways in which they live their lives. Individual interests, attitudes, opinions, and outlooks have been found extremely useful in explaining consumer decision making, offering insights that can be directly incorporated into marketing program design. Wells discusses the development and application of lifestyle analyses and provides a useful bibliography for those who wish to pursue this topic.

The next reading, by Calder and Burnkrant (1977), examines the ways in which individual consumers affect one another. The authors identify situations in which interpersonal influence is most likely to occur; determine why consumers choose personal information sources; and analyze the internal processes involved. Although this article seems to have an academic orientation, it is most definitely of practical importance. Knowledge of the ways in which consumers choose and use reference groups can be important to market segmentation decisions. Similarly, an understanding of the type of information that consumers seek from interpersonal sources, and their reasons for seeking information there rather than from media sources, can help marketing managers design more effective communication programs.

The next paper, by Miller and Ginter (1979), looks at the effects of situational variables on buying decisions. So far we have considered the effects of individual attitudes, values, and lifestyles; now we examine the effect of the context in which buying takes place. Your own experiences, both as consumers and marketers, probably suggest that the situations in which products are bought and used influence brand choice. This paper shows that a model that includes situational variables does indeed provide a better understanding of consumer behavior than traditional, nonsituational models.

The final paper in Chapter 2, by Rothschild and Gaidis (1981), describes behavioral learning theory, summarizing the major findings and drawing implications for marketing decisions. As the authors point out, behavioral learning theory offers a simple but elegant framework within which to structure many marketing decisions.

Chapter 3: Consumer Decision-Making Processes

Chapter 3 examines the ways in which consumers make purchase decisions, with particular reference to their use of information. That consumers do in fact follow some sort of decision-making process is a basic tenet of almost all consumer behavior analyses. The first reading in this chapter, by Olshavsky and Granbois (1979), challenges this faith. The authors review the evidence for a decision-making process and conclude that, although many purchases are preceded by some sort of decision-making process, some are not; and for those that are, the "process" may be less complex than the name implies. This reading is an important antidote to the more formal models presented by other authors—for example, the models reviewed by Bettman and Jones, 1972, in Chapter 1—and to the analyses of information overload presented below. Management must be careful not to over-rationalize the consumer. It is easy to assume that the consumer weighs a purchasing decision just as carefully as management weighs its marketing decisions. For many products, particularly those purchased frequently or involving limited choices, consumers may in fact purchase with little or no decision making. Notice the comment by Ursic (1980) and the rejoinder by Olshavsky and Granbois (1980).

Davis (1976) reviews findings on the effect of the family on decision making. While many traditional theories have emphasized the consumer as a single unit, in practice individuals rarely buy alone. They are influenced not only by the factors discussed in Chapter 2, but by the household in which they live and their family roles. As Davis points out, where the influence of the family has been considered, analysis has rarely moved beyond studies of husband and wife. The influence of other family members is little understood; in particular, their influence before the actual shopping trip has not been well analyzed. From a practical applications viewpoint, this reading provides more of a caution than a prescription: although we do not yet understand the influences exerted by other family members, we can be sure that they exist.

The next reading deals with consumers' use of information. Buyers are subjected to a barrage of data on products' characteristics and performance, presented through mass media advertising, product labels, salespersons, and in-store displays. Some public authorities and marketers believe that the result is counterproductive: consumers simply tune out and make decisions based on little or no information. Malhotra, Jain, and Lagakos (1982) review the existing research on information load and reanalyze several studies, using a new technique. Unless you have a specific interest in data analysis, it is not necessary to have a detailed understanding of the method used, although the outline should be understood (for those who wish to look at the analysis technique in more detail, the authors provide a bibliography. The reference to Green, Carmone, and Wachpress, 1977, is probably the most useful).

The final reading in this chapter, DeBruicker (1979), reviews low involvement consumer decision making. Marketers have recognized that, in many buying situations, consumers do not display the careful attention that traditional models of consumer behavior imply. They are not involved in the buying decision. This paper reviews theoretical and empirical evidence on low involvement, and draws implications for planning marketing communications.

Chapter 4: Consumer Behavior and Market Segmentation
This is the first chapter completely oriented to applications, and it deals with one of the most important tasks facing marketing management—definition of appropriate target markets. The readings show how consumer behavior findings may be applied to segmenting the market and to identifying suitable target segments. The first paper, by Wind (1978), reviews the progress and the problems of segmentation research. It provides a systematic review of the segmentation field, and the many methods available for market segmentation, together with a comprehensive bibliography. It is a worthwhile project to pick a segmentation topic that is of particular interest to you, and to use the bibliography to develop a paper on that topic.

The second reading in this section, Young, Ott, and Feigin (1978), develops some of the practical problems faced in market segmentation. The authors present some useful guidelines on when and how to segment, and illustrate their analysis with three real-life applications.

The next paper, by Dickson (1982), looks at the use of situational factors as the bases for market segmentation. Before reading this article you should review the paper on situational variables by Miller and Ginter (1979) in Chapter 2. Dickson supplies a clear, practical framework for segmentation by product use situation, and the advantages of such a segmentation.

The final reading in this chapter, Boote (1981), uses personal values as the basis for market segmentation. He finds that personal values identify more distinctive segments than does demographic analysis, and can be applied to the design of advertising appeals and the development of new products.

Chapter 5: Consumer Behavior and Product Development
This chapter examines the application of consumer behavior findings to product marketing decisions: product positioning, product adaptation (or repositioning), and new product development. The first reading, Alpert (1971), presents the important concept of "determinant attributes," or product features that actually affect consumers' preferences and purchases. The paper compares alternative methods of identifying determinant attributes. Although the sample used is small and nonrandom, the analysis is a useful guide to applying the methods and to the principle of cross-validation.

Aaker (1982) reviews the aims and methods of product positioning. This article is relevant to any application of product positioning. Green and Wind (1975) discuss conjoint, or trade-off, analysis. This method of analyzing the effects of product characteristics on consumers has found wide use over the last five years. The presentation is nonmathematical and highly applied. Try to devise some applications of trade-off analysis. Can you see any limitations to its use?

The final paper in this chapter, by Day, Shocker, and Srivastava (1979), takes a more strategic view of the use of consumer behavior findings. The basic problem discussed is the identification of product-market boundaries. Definition of the market in which a product competes is fundamental to almost all marketing decisions. Yet such a definition is not easily obtained. The authors compare methods and discuss their usefulness for particular management decisions. Next time you see a reference to a market-based measure (for example, market share, or number of competitors), ask how the market was defined. Was the most appropriate definition used? Would the results be different if another method of market definition was applied?

Chapter 6: Consumer Behavior and Pricing Policy

Because of the objective nature of price information, consumer researchers are showing increasing interest in the effects of price changes on brand choice behavior.

The study by Charlton and Ehrenberg (1976) examines the effects on brand choice of price differentials, a price promotion, and other marketing program adjustments. Over a twenty-five-week period, members of a consumer panel were given the opportunity each week to buy one pack of detergent and tea from among a set of brands. The experiment was conducted under what the authors call "semi-laboratory conditions," representing a compromise between internal and external validity. According to the authors, the approach is useful in tactical decision making—"not for assessing absolute levels or for deciding whether promotions are generally more effective than advertising, but for comparing two or more relatively similar promotional devices and determining which works better." The approach makes no claims beyond those which may legitimately be made for consumer research as a whole. Very little consumer research can be applied by marketing managers at the strategic, as opposed to the tactical, level.

A second important feature of the Charlton and Ehrenberg experiment is its longitudinal nature. The authors do not examine consumer behavior at a single point in time; they investigate consumer purchasing patterns over a period of time. Since marketing managers have to deal with the dynamics of the marketplace, longitudinal studies using consumer panels can provide more valuable guidelines for marketing action than one-shot laboratory experiments. The increasing use of electronic scanning devices in supermarkets makes longitudinal testing of tactical marketing programs more feasible.

The next two articles, by Blattberg, Eppen, and Lieberman (1981) and Shoemaker and Shoaf (1977), also analyze consumer panel data to throw light on retailer and consumer responsiveness to temporary price deals. Promotion expenditures of price nature now exceed advertising expenditures in the brand budgets of many consumer markets. Blattberg et al. argue that retailers implement price deals in order to shift the burden of inventory carrying costs to households. The authors also examine whether or not price deals accelerate the timing of consumer demand and/or the quantity of product purchased. They provisionally confirm the existence of these effects. Shoemaker and Shoaf establish that a repeat purchase is less likely among consumers who purchase a brand on deal rather than at regular prices.

Our final pricing article examines a practical issue of concern to public policymakers. Will the disappearance of individual item price marking caused by scanning checkout systems in supermarkets lower consumer awareness of prices and make price comparison shopping harder? Zeithaml (1982) examines the relative effectiveness of different penetration formats in communicating price information to consumers at the point-of-purchase. She measures consumer response at the cognitive, attitudinal, and behavioral stages of the hierarchy of effects, one of the basic concepts used by marketers and policymakers in developing communications programs.

Chapter 7: Consumer Behavior and Communications Programs

We have seen, in Chapter 3, the emphasis that consumer researchers continue to place on understanding how consumers acquire and process information in order to make purchase decisions. Since the goal of marketing communications policy is to influence consumer information processing and the decision-making process, a disproportionate number of consumer research studies have addressed questions related to the communications policy element of the marketing mix.

In the lead article in this chapter, Horowitz and Kaye (1975) argue that both the personal characteristics of a consumer and the attributes of a product—both experienced and communicated—influence a consumer's product perceptions. Managers can develop communications programs that aim to influence these product perceptions. For example, the product may be advertised in a manner that encourages the target consumer to identify the product image with his ideal self-image. Moreover, product perceptions may be influenced by marketing communications after the purchase as a result of cognitive dissonance.

Moore's (1982) article also deals with perception—this time, subliminal perception. Subliminal advertising is alleged to alter consumer preferences and behaviors subconsciously. The author finds no empirical support for the alleged power of subliminal advertising and, furthermore, indicates that the concept is incompatible with established theories of perception and motivation. The article illustrates the value of consumer research in debunking a claim frequently made by advertising's critics.

The next two articles deal with two specific types of advertising message—the fear appeal and the comparative advertisement. Ray and Wilkie (1970) review evidence from the social psychology literature on the impact of fear appeals, and explain why moderate rather than overly strong fear appeals may be most effective in marketing communications. The authors relate consumer personality traits to responsiveness to fear appeals, and discuss the impact of fear on message exposure, consumer learning, attitude change, and consumer behavior.

In introducing their experiment, Goodwin and Etgar (1980) note that marketers do not yet know whether comparative advertising is more appropriate for functional products or for psychic ego-intensive products. In developing copy for a comparative advertising campaign, they need guidance on the type of comparative claim that should be made and on the extent of comparative attribute information that should be included. Although the authors found that comparative advertising was less effective than expected, their experiment indicates how effective consumer research can help to fine tune the formulation of advertising messages.

Webb's (1979) concern is the media environment of an advertising message, rather than the content of the message itself. He attempts to identify the relative impact of different factors on a viewer's attention to and comprehension of a television commercial. These factors include the position of a commercial within a string of advertisements and within a program, the length of the commercial break, and the frequency of such breaks. The optimal timing of commercial exposures is of obvious concern to the marketer who seeks to maximize the impact of his or her advertising expenditures.

Chapter 8: Managing Consumer Research

This chapter examines how to develop and direct research to produce practical, usable findings. The readings discuss the criteria for "good" research and the management issues involved, and review the successes and failures of past research.

The first article, by Calder, Phillips, and Tybout (1981), discusses the effect of research purpose on research design. In particular, the authors distinguish between research conducted to develop theoretical understanding and that conducted to obtain information that can be directly applied to the marketing situation. These different research purposes require distinct research designs.

The next reading, by Gandz and Whipple (1977), presents a method of evaluating research expenditures. Research, like other activities, will be accepted within the organization only when its effects on profit can be demonstrated. Strangely, this is a problem that few research studies choose to address. The authors trace a research project from development to execution, analyzing the financial implications at each stage.

The next article focuses on market research, but is equally applicable to research on consumer behavior. Martilla and Carvey (1975) identify and explain five problems that frequently occur in marketing (and consumer) research. This paper is important, both to those who conduct research and to those who apply its findings. The problems they discuss seem deceptively simple, but can, in fact, be found even in very sophisticated research projects.

The last reading in this volume looks forward to the methods, models, and techniques that will be used routinely by marketing managers of the future. Little (1979) outlines the components of what he terms "Decision Support Systems." These use the models and findings we have read about in this book in conjunction with powerful computer software to provide the manager with timely, relevant analyses—not merely a regurgitation of data, but analyses designed to assist in problem solving and strategic planning. Many ideas discussed by Little are already in use; others will undoubtedly follow. However, it is important to remember that the output from a decision support system is only as good as the models that it contains. It will still be necessary to evaluate the models used, and to understand which are most appropriate for the application on hand. Such evaluations will invariably rest on an understanding of the principles of consumer behavior.

CHAPTER ONE

Fundamentals of Consumer Behavior

READING 1

Formal Models of Consumer Behavior: A Conceptual Overview

James R. Bettman and J. Morgan Jones

Introduction

In the last ten years, there has been a great increase in building formal models of consumer behavior. By formal models we mean those models with an explicit structure, normally either mathematical or computer, as opposed to verbal models. These models have proliferated very rapidly and exist in a bewildering array of forms. The purpose of this paper is to give an overview of the field of formal consumer models and provide a framework for understanding the field and placing the many model types in perspective. Accordingly, the paper is much more conceptual than technical in nature.

We start by outlining a rough classification of model types, and describing these types. Next, the conceptual bases of the various model types are discussed and compared. This discussion considers such topics as the general world view of the modelers, necessary data properties, individual differences and aggregation, and model uses. Potentially useful interactions between model types are then discussed. Finally, prospects and problems for each model type are considered, and overall conclusions are drawn.

Classes of Formal Models of Consumer Choice

Formal models of consumer behavior may be roughly classified into four broad types: information-processing models, stochastic models, experimental and other linear models, and large-system models. The characteristics of models in each of these classes will be discussed in this section.

The discussion in this section is *not* intended as a literature review. Several good reviews already exist. The object of this section is to discuss the essential features of models in the various classes, in order to set the stage for the comparative discussions which follow.

Stochastic Models[1]

A stochastic model generally consists of two important components—a model of individual behavior and a "rule" for aggregating these individual models. The individual model describes some aspect (e.g., brand choice, interpurchase time) of an individual consumer's purchase behavior. This behavior is made an explicit function of a few (zero to two) of the *major* determinants of this aspect of behavior. All other determinants are accounted for by making the model stochastic. For example, in models of brand-choice behavior, the *probability* of purchasing brand *A* is modeled as a function of such determinants as the brand purchased last time, external time effects, the past history of purchases, or some combination of effects.[2] Other factors—for example, price—are not usually explicitly considered by the model.[3] However, since what is modeled is the *probability* of purchase, rather than the purchase outcome itself, such factors are implicitly considered because the model is stochastic.

The aggregation rule for these models usually takes one of two forms. The most straightforward

Reprinted from the *Journal of Business* (1972): 544–562, by James R. Bettman and J. Morgan Jones, by permission of the University of Chicago Press.

approach is to assume that every individual is the same in all aspects of behavior. However, following some pioneering work by Morrison,[4] many of the current models assume that individuals are different with respect to some aspect of their behavior. That is, different individuals will react somewhat differently when subject to the same set of stimuli. The aggregation problem becomes more difficult in this case, and it is usually this difficulty which restricts the number and complexity of allowable individual differences. (This problem will be discussed further in the section on aggregation.)

Hence, stochastic models are characterized by (1) a willingness to use stochastic elements to handle behavioral complexity; (2) a concentration on broad, general determinants of behavior; and (3) a concern for aggregation to populations.

Information-Processing Models of Consumer Choice

One recent trend in formal models of consumer decisions has been the emergence of information-processing models. These models make the basic assumption that man receives continual information input from his environment and processes this information as an integral part of making choices. In particular, an individual has certain rules by which he processes and manipulates information, and these rules specify his decision processes. It is deemed essential by the theory to actually model all of the detailed rules used.

Much of the early work in this field was done in psychology and computer science. Newell, Shaw, and Simon[5] assert that the basic components of information-processing models are (1) a number of memories containing symbolic information; (2) a number of simple primitive information processes, which are building blocks for more complicated processes; and (3) definite rules for combining simple processes to yield whole programs, or coherent wholes, of processing. This program then generates observable behavior.

In contrast with the stochastic consumer models, information-processing models assume that the rules they contain can be formulated deterministically, without probabilistic notions. Also, information-processing models take as their province the particular individual. Each subject requires a possibly different model. These models are obtained by having each subject think out loud while he is performing the behavior being modeled. Such a record is termed a protocol. Thus, Bettman had his subjects think out loud as they were in the actual process of shopping in order to collect his data.[6] Given these data, a model of how the subject processes the data from the environment to make a choice is constructed. All of the detailed processes that can be inferred are modeled, if possible. This inference process from the protocol is a difficult task, and only recently have structured and formal methods been proposed.[7]

Particular information-processing models of consumer choice are few. Bettman modeled two consumers' choices for grocery products.[8] Alexis, Haines, and Simon modeled women's clothing decisions,[9] and Haines also modeled raincoat choices.[10] King developed an information-processing framework for consumer choice.[11] Recently, Russ has developed models of choices of several subjects for small durable goods in a laboratory setting.[12] Finally, Clarkson modeled a trust investment officer's stock purchases.[13]

In summary, the major facets of information-processing models are (1) an assertion that individuals actively process information when making choices and that the processing rules used are to be modeled in as much detail as possible; (2) the belief that deterministic models are appropriate models of choice processes (rather than having probabilistic phenomena subsume detail, the detail itself is modeled); and (3) a concentration on models of particular individuals by using protocol data. Thus studies in this area use very small numbers of subjects (one or two, usually), and the models developed are highly idiosyncratic.

Experimental and Other Linear Models

The models which we include in this classification are dissimilar with regard to content but have a common formal mathematical structure. Many experimental studies have been conducted on various aspects of consumer behavior. Because of a strong tradition of linear relationships imbedded in the statistical theories of multivariate analysis, several of these studies implicitly contain a linear model of behavior. In addition, other studies have explicitly stated a linear model.

We shall use a broad definition of linear relationships in this paper, such as $\log x + e^{v}$. Strictly speaking, these are additive separable relationships. We include these because the data are often transformed to obtain the best-fitting model. Mathematically, the model might be described as

$$f(y) = \sum_i g_i(x_i) + \epsilon,$$

where y is the dependent variable (aspect being modeled), the x_i are the independent variables (one or more other factors), and ϵ is a random element. This ϵ is included to account for the other factors which affect y but are not explicitly considered in the formulation. Most of these models are designed to represent the *market,* rather than the individual consumer.

Without close inspection, it is difficult to separate the studies containing implicit models from the set of all experimental models. Generally, these models describe one aspect of consumer behavior (e.g., market share of the brand) as a linear function of one or more other factors. One set of explicit linear models is the Fishbein-Dulany approach to predicting behavior and attitudes.[14] These models incorporate some data on individuals' inner states to predict behavior. This approach has been recently applied to marketing problems.[15] Day presents other linear attitude models.[16] A second major set of explicit linear models consists of models of purchasing behavior using demographic and personality test scores as independent variables.[17] Finally, a third type of linear model is one in which independent variables are marketing variables, and sales or purchases are the dependent variable.[18] This brief characterization of linear models certainly does not exhaust the field, but it gives an idea of the range of models which have been developed. Note that these linear models are basically descriptive and are designed to represent the *market* or *population,* not the individual.

The main characteristics of these linear models are then (1) linear model structure, (2) inclusion of a stochastic error factor, and (3) subsuming of individual differences in a population or market orientation.

Large-System Models of Consumer Choice

The class of large-system models contains those models of consumer choice characterized by a broad general structure of postulated interrelationships, usually verbal, with a somewhat simplified formal model fit within this framework. Three main models of this type are considered in this paper: Amstutz; Farley and Ring's linear realization of the Howard-Sheth model; and Nicosia.[19] There is more formal mathematical diversity within this class of models than within the other model types. The modeling techniques themselves differ among all three models—they are, respectively, simulation, simultaneous linear regression equations, and a system of differential equations. The major coherence for this class is in the comprehensiveness of the underlying conceptual system, to which the model is a first approximation. These conceptual systems are all heavily based on the results of linear experimental models, used as data points for induction. Because the models differ, we will give a brief overview of each.

Amstutz's consumer-behavior model is a microanalytic simulation. By this is meant that there is a detailed specification of individual decision processes, which are aggregated. His consumer-choice model is rather involved, including marketing factors, attitudes, media communications and word of mouth, and several other components. The model is probabilistic, with the response-probability generation functions being simple linear or exponential forms, for the most part. Amstutz also does not attempt to fit his individual models to specific consumers, but uses his population of individual models to attempt to fit aggregate data. Thus, like information-processing models, detailed models of the individual are developed. However, Amstutz's model differs sharply from information-processing models in the use of probability mechanisms and in developing generalized models of an individual rather than specific models for given individuals.

The Howard-Sheth verbal theory of buyer behavior[20] represents an extremely complicated theoretical system. Farley and Ring have developed a system of eleven simultaneous regression equations as a first empirical test of the theory. Thus they have built a simple formal model within the Howard-Sheth framework. Particular attention was paid to modeling the endogenous variables from the theory (e.g., attention, stimulus ambiguity, brand comprehension), although exogenous marketing and demographic variables were also included. Their linear model is probabilistic in the sense of including probabilistic error terms, and is a model for populations rather than for individuals. In the empirical test carried out, the findings for the endogenous variables were satisfactory, but the exogenous variable relationships and the overall goodness of fit were not. Much of the difficulty is attributed to problems of precise specification of complex variables and problems in measurement.[21]

Nicosia first develops a verbal and flow-chart model based on four fields, or building blocks.[22] Then he develops a system of differential equations whose variables represent the inputs and outputs of his four fields; thus the equations comprise a reduced formal model of his comprehensive scheme. Nicosia analyzes a system of four linear differential equations in some detail.[23] The variables involved are buying behavior, motivation, attitude, and advertising. Nicosia analyzes properties of the solutions of the system, both in equilibrium and over time. The model is deterministic rather than probabilistic. It is unclear what the model is intended to depict. It appears to model an average or generalized consumer. Nicosia has not attempted to apply the model to actual data. Measurement problems would seem to be severe in trying to apply the model.

In summary, the large-system models are characterized as formal models (1) corresponding to reductions of large and comprehensive verbal schemes of consumer choice processes, (2) having substantial measurement and estimation problems due to the abstraction and generality in their variables, and (3) being more heterogeneous than the other model types.

Given this overview of classes of formal consumer models, we now turn to an examination of their underlying properties and concepts.

Underlying Concepts of the Formal Models

An attempt will now be made to outline some of the conceptual framework underlying the building of formal models, and to compare the model types outlined above according to this framework. Four basic areas are considered: (1) the general "world view" espoused by the model builders, (2) the type of data used and the method of collection, (3) how the problems of heterogeneity (individual differences) and aggregation of individuals are handled, and (4) how the models are intended to be used.

General World View

In this section many contrasts could be made. Only a limited subset will be examined here. All of these contrasts are interrelated, but we discuss them separately for the sake of convenience.

A somewhat subtle comparison can be made regarding the basic approach to model building espoused by the various formal consumer modelers. It is similar to the inductive versus deductive classification, but not the same. Information-processing modelers and large-system modelers take as given more a philosophy of model building than any particular model structure. Information-processing modelers consider the basic ideas of man as an information processor, and large-system modelers hold the concepts of system components and interrelations as their basic tenets. These philosophies then guide examination of data, and a particular model structure emerges. Many stochastic modelers, on the other hand, see modeling from a more formal structural point of view. A set of formal mathematical structures exists, and modeling problems become structural concerns such as parameter estimation and goodness of fit.[24] Some stochastic modelers, particularly Ehrenberg, object to this view and tend to let structure emerge from the data.[25] This difference, of course, is probably to some extent confounded with stage of development and model complexity. Information processing and large-system models are much more recent and complex, and hence a foundation of particular formal structures has not been developed.

A second major consideration is whether the modeler, for the purpose of his models, sees behavior as being probabilistic or deterministic. As mentioned briefly above, information-processing models assume that decision rules can be expressed by deterministic models. Nicosia also assumes no probability element in his differential-equation model. Stochastic models, of course, assume a basic probabilistic nature. The probabilistic element enters because not all factors are intended to be included by the modeler, particularly situational factors. Also, to some extent, it subsumes differences between individuals. Linear models, including the formal Farley and Ring realization of the Howard-Sheth model, also have a probabilistic element in that error terms are included to handle factors not accounted for by the model. Finally,

Amstutz's models are in essence probabilistic, using simple stochastic response functions and a Monte Carlo procedure.

Another consideration is whether the individual or some population is the unit of analysis for any particular model. Here we have a clear split, as information-processing models consider the individual, whereas the other model types all consider populations. Amstutz considers generalized individuals, but his main interest is to fit aggregate population data. Related to this is the question of what processes are considered for inclusion in a model. In general, because of the interest in the individual, information-processing models are concerned with any decision rule that can be characterized, no matter how idiosyncratic. On the other hand, the other model types limit themselves to a selection of one or a few (most stochastic models) or several (large-system and linear models) rather general processes assumed to be universally present. Note that this contrast is rather deeply interconnected with general philosophies of model analysis—to use well-defined tools of analysis such as the stochastic and linear models employ, the models must be kept reasonably simple.

The time frame of reference varies for the model types. Most stochastic models and the Amstutz and Nicosia models are connected with behavior that occurs over time. They are in essence dynamic models. On the other hand, most linear models deal with a single experiment or at most a one-time change. Information-processing models also deal with the structure of decision rules at a given point in time. Although decision rules change, no attempt has been made to model change over time for consumer-decision-process models, although dynamic information-processing models have been developed in other domains.[26]

One final contrast may be briefly drawn. Information-processing, stochastic, the Nicosia, and the Amstutz models share a concern with the form of choice processes. For example, stochastic model builders concern themselves with the existence of purchase-event feedback and with the time span of memory (e.g., what past purchases affect the current purchase). Amstutz considers the form of his response functions.[27] Nicosia is concerned with the structure of feedback involving motivation, attitude, and behavior.[28] On the other hand, linear model builders do not envision consumers calculating linear model coefficients in their heads. Linear models are simply useful for predicting outcomes or for performing hypothesis tests. Matching actual choice processes is to some extent irrelevant.

Data Considerations

Data collection is deeply entwined with the "world view" held, so the present discussion will amplify that of the last section to some extent.

Depending upon the model type, the level of detailed data required varies. Most stochastic models require only data on overt purchase responses. Some linear models also require only reasonably objective data.[29] However, some attitude models—particularly the Fishbein-Dulany models, the Farley and Ring linear realization of the Howard-Sheth model, Nicosia's model, and Amstutz's—require more subjective data on inner feelings and states. Finally, information-processing models require the most detailed data base. Not only are data on inner states required, but the sequential aspects of data are very important for inferring decision rules. Thus protocol data are very fine grained compared with data for other model types.

Another consideration as to type of data gathered concerns the content of the data. Most stochastic models do not include the effects of marketing variables, although there are exceptions.[30] On the other hand, some linear models,[31] information-processing models, and large-system models in general try to determine how marketing variables affect decisions. Hence, this type of data on marketing variables is required.

Time considerations are also important in data collection. Data can be taken on a one-time basis or over time. This is obviously closely related to the static or dynamic character of the models discussed in the last section. Stochastic models require data collected over time for the same individual, as found on panel data. The Amstutz model and the linear realization of the Howard-Sheth model also use over-time panel data.[32] Finally, although it has not been fit to actual data, the Nicosia model would certainly need data collected over time to fit its differential equations. Most linear models use only one-time measurements, as do most information-processing models.[33]

The structure inherent in the collection procedure offers a clear contrast. Information-processing models use protocol data, collected in a very unstructured manner (the subject is merely instructed to "think out loud" while making choices). Data for the other models are obtained from structured questionnaires or panel diaries. There has been some controversy in the psychological literature as to whether protocols represent behavior. Information-processing theorists have strenuously defended the process: "But if we had not recorded the things the subject said he was considering along with the things he actually did, the task would be hopeless. It is actually easier to simulate the person's spoken thoughts than to simulate only the decisions that appear in his behavior. Since thinking aloud permits more of the person's thought processes to project through the plane of perception, it helps to limit the variety of conceivable descriptions to a handful that are reasonably accurate."[34]

Individual Differences and Aggregation

As mentioned above, the model classes are differentiated by their assumptions about the individual. Information-processing models are designed to represent, in great detail, the decision processes of a single individual. On the other hand, most experimental and linear models never consider an individual per se, but only the collective behavior of all individuals in the market. Somewhere between these two extremes are stochastic models and large-system models. This section is devoted to a further discussion of these aspects for each group of models, and to some of the philosophical and practical questions which are raised by these differences.

Some model types may not be intended to model market behavior. However, if models which describe individual behavior *are* to be used for modeling market behavior, they must be aggregated in some way. Hence, let us now discuss the three major types of aggregation, since the type of aggregation used has strong implications for the way the modeler views individuals.

The most widespread aggregation technique is to assume that all individuals are homogeneous in their behavior. That is, the model which represents the behavior of consumer *A* can represent the behavior of consumer *B* equally well. Under this assumption the model of the population is essentially the same as the model of the individual.

The second technique for aggregation is that of microaddition. In this technique a (supposedly heterogeneous) population is divided into relatively homogeneous subgroups. Then representative individual models are developed for each subgroup. Presumably these representative models differ across subgroups. Aggregation then consists of combining the representative models, taking into account the relative sizes of the subgroups.

The third technique we shall call probabilistic aggregation. It assumes that individual models are heterogeneous in some aspect and that this heterogeneity is distributed over the population according to some probability distribution. For example, some parameter in the model may be assumed to have a beta distribution across individuals in the population.[35] This is, in a very real sense, a generalization of the microaddition technique, since it assumes that there will be a number of individuals with essentially the same model of behavior. *However,* unlike the microaddition technique, probabilistic aggregation can be applied to any given population. Microaddition, on the other hand, requires defining the subgroups which are to have representative models.

Having outlined the types of aggregation possible, let us now consider how the various model types aggregate consumers. To date, information-processing models have only been applied to individuals. No effort has been made to aggregate across individuals. One can wonder, of course, whether such aggregation would ever be possible, if every individual is truly different from every other individual. Some work has been done on measuring the similarity of decision nets.[36] This technique could be applied to a large-scale study of individuals, in an effort to develop relatively homogeneous subgroups to use with microaddition techniques. Perhaps some of the heterogeneity techniques would also be applicable here, although the technical problems of application seem very difficult.

At the other end of the spectrum are the experimental and linear models. Most of these ignore any consideration of individuals, and the few that consider a model of individual behavior also make the homogeneity assumption, so that there is basically no distinction between the market model and the individual model. Thus, these models are truly *market* models, with essentially no consideration of individuals.

The stochastic models represent a strange anomaly. Although they are treated as models of individual behavior which are aggregated over the population, few studies[37] make any attempt to verify the model of the individual. All others test only the model of the market obtained through the aggregation process. A serious question is thus raised as to whether these models truly represent aggregated individual behavior or merely a market whose model is obtained by a complicated process. Until such verification is obtained, one should be cautious about the inferences of individual behavior which can be obtained from these models.

The large-system models vary in their aggregation techniques. Amstutz uses basically a microaddition approach. He assumes different parameters for individuals but does not use a theoretical distribution over those parameters. Farley and Ring, with their linear model, assume homogeneity; and it is not clear how Nicosia would handle aggregation. It appears microaddition would be used.

Model Uses

There are generally three potential uses for a model: description, prediction, and understanding. Let us now turn to each group of models to determine their main area of use.

The information-processing models currently are most useful for describing and understanding *individuals* but, because of their aggregation problems, least useful for prediction in large markets. There appear to be two potential uses of such models: (1) as a basis of understanding in building better macromodels, and (2) in modeling situations where the total market consists of a very few individuals (some industrial marketing situations, for instance). Thus, information-processing models would be useful for describing the behavior of *small* groups and in furthering the development of the more macromodels. Information-processing modelers, at this point in time, do not see large-market prediction as a legitimate function for their models.

Experimental and linear models stand at the opposite end of the spectrum. In terms of a few "gross" variables, they can describe the behavior of a market or population as a whole. As mentioned above, the advantages of these models are that they can be immediately applied to the market. On the other hand, they *cannot* be used to infer any type of individual behavior. Therefore they add little to the continuing development of models. (This is not necessarily true of some of the more micro experimental and linear models such as the Fishbein-Dulany models.) They are useful for *describing* market behavior, but the modeler must be careful in any *prediction* application because of the danger of misrepresentation due to a change in the market. Without understanding, prediction in a changing environment is a hazardous undertaking.

It is uncertain to what extent stochastic models are useful. Several have been used as predictive models and have proven themselves powerful and accurate. On the other hand, because of the philosophical question raised in the previous section, of whether these are truly individual models and not merely market models, their ability to provide understanding of individuals is in question. At the level of the market, of course, they are good descriptive and predictive models.

Finally, large-system models present a similar question, although the verification of the market model is much more complicated. For example, although the Amstutz model is based upon elaborate representations of the consumer, which are then aggregated by microaddition, there has been little effort beyond face validity to verify the complex interrelations in these individual models (although Amstutz did try to verify some model components).[38] Also, it is not at all clear that the Farley and Ring and especially the Nicosia models could even be used to predict market behavior at this stage of their development. The main use of these models may be in attempting to understand behavior rather than predict it. In any case, unlike the stochastic models, at the market level it is very difficult to verify the output of the large-system models. Because verification of large-system models at both the individual *and* market levels is problematical, one must ask what these models really represent. That has not been adequately resolved to date. Certainly such a question should be considered by the potential user of such a model!

If one takes as his goal the modeling of a market (and, as we have seen, this may not necessarily be the case), it is important to determine which model fits the situation best. To a large extent this depends upon the market. If the market consists of only five consumers, it would probably be best to represent each by an information-processing model. On the other hand, one of the other techniques should be used on a market which consists of a million individuals.

In addition to the above consideration, the practitioner should realize that there are two aspects of modeling which are generally incompatible with each other—ease of use and realism. Generally, a model is able to describe a situation more realistically as it becomes more complex. Unfortunately, increased complexity implies an increased effort to estimate parameters for and obtain results from the model. On the other hand, simplistic models may not adequately represent all situations to which they are applied. Thus, the practical user must consider the realism-cost trade-off when deciding which model to use in a specific situation.

This problem is complicated further by the fact that model realism itself is hard to assess. Many models may fit the same set of data reasonably well. Also, the fact that a particular model works very well

TABLE 1
Properties of Model Types

				LS		
	S	*IP*	*EL*	*A*	*FR*	*Ni*
World view:						
Approach to model building:						
philosophy (P) or structure (S)?	S	P	S	P	P&S	P
Probabilistic (P) or deterministic (D)?	P	D	P	P	P	D
Unit of analysis: individual (I)						
or population (P)?	P	I	P	P	P	P
General (G) or particular (P) processes?	G	P	G	G	G	G
Static (S) or dynamic (D) time frame?	D	S	S	D	S	D
Interest in process (P) or output (O)?	P	P	O	P	P	P
Data:						
Overt (O) or inner states (I)?	O	I	O&I	I	I	I
Marketing variables included?	N	Y	Y	Y	Y	Y
One-time (O) or longitudinal (L)?	L	O	O	L	L	L
Collection structured (S) or						
unstructured (U)?	S	U	S	S	S	S
Aggregation:						
Type of aggregation:						
homogeneous (H),						
microaddition (M),						
probabilistic aggregation (P)?	P	M	H	M	H	M
Uses:						
Understanding:						
Individual?	?	Y	N	?	N	?
Market?	Y	?	N	Y	?	?
Prediction:						
Individual?	N	Y	N	?	N	?
Market?	Y	?	?	Y	?	?
Description:						
Individual?	?	Y	N	?	N	?
Market?	Y	?	Y	Y	Y	?

Note: S = stochastic, IP = information processing, EL = experimental and linear, LS = large system, A = Amstutz, FR = Farley and Ring, Ni = Nicosia. N = no, Y = yes.

for the coffee market does not mean it will work well for the beer market. More empirical work is needed to compare model types for many product classes.[39]

We have now discussed many properties and concepts relating to formal consumer models. Table 1 attempts to summarize the basic ideas of the above sections. This overall view of the model types highlights the many contrasts and similarities.

In the next sections, we step back somewhat and consider the future of formal models of consumer choice. We first consider how work on each of the various types can benefit research on the other model types.

Interactions Between Model Types

Findings for each of the various model types can certainly be used as input to the development of other model types. This section briefly discusses how such interactions between pairs of model types could be beneficial.

Stochastic Models and Information-Processing Models

Information-processing models can benefit stochastic models by suggesting new structures or variables with which to enrich stochastic models.[40] For example, if information-processing models suggest perceived risk of a product type as an important variable,[41] then a stochastic model might fruitfully include a perceived-risk variable which has a distribution over the population. One could then hypothesize different stochastic choice processes depending upon the particular realization of the risk variable. Another type of input from information-processing models is insight into the feedback structure of purchase events—does purchase-event feedback occur in information-processing models, and how many past purchases are involved? Finally, information-processing ideas can be useful in providing behavioral rationales for mathematical models.[42]

Stochastic models can also provide beneficial inputs to information-processing models. Of particular relevance is insight into what types of effects occur over time, since most information-processing models are static and need to be extended to take account of dynamic effects.

Stochastic Models and Linear Experimental Models

As with other interaction situations involving linear models, stochastic models can benefit from linear models if testable linear hypotheses can be proposed for stochastic models. At least one of these has already been completed by Carman (n. 2 above). In addition, the linear models may detect important variables which should be included in stochastic models. For example, a more process-oriented stochastic model might be developed from the preliminary linear model of Farley and Ring.

Stochastic Models and Large-System Models

A fascinating possibility that remains largely unexplored is to use stochastic models as components for large-system models. One could conceivably use one stochastic model—for example, a linear learning model—as a model of one population subgroup, and another model—say, a Markov model—as a model of a second subgroup. Then one would aggregate not only within each subgroup but across subgroups, combining stochastic model types. This approach has not yet been tried, to our knowledge.

Information-Processing Models and Linear Experimental Models

An unresolved problem in the psychological literature is that of linear versus configural models.[43] Linear models of choice often fit well, but subjects claim they are using patterns of data, not merely linear terms. Analysis of information-processing models can help to interpret this problem and suggests that perceptual-expectations phenomena are important here.[44] Thus, information-processing models can aid in interpreting linear models.

Linear experimental models can be helpful in validating information-processing models. Process models often imply certain relations between stimuli, structural or otherwise. These relations can generate hypotheses which can be checked in a laboratory setting by an appropriate linear model. This aids in confirming information-processing microstructure which has been derived from protocols.

Information-Processing Models and Large-System Models

There is a two-way interaction that can aid both information-processing and large-system models.

Analysis of information-processing models can yield generalized paradigms based on an information-processing point of view that suggest large-system models. Bettman has performed such an analysis,[45] and the general model developed bears very close resemblance to the verbal Howard-Sheth paradigm. In a similar manner, large-system models can give insights into the general structure one might expect in inferring generalized information-processing models using specific individuals' models as instances.

Linear Experimental Models and Large-System Models

Again we have a two-way general interaction. Linear models form the building blocks from which many large-system models are induced. Thus linear models can stimulate elaboration of large-system models. Also, large-system models often generate testable hypotheses that can be considered linear experimental models.

Formal Consumer-Choice Models: Problems and Prospects

Formal models of consumer choice have an intense if short history. In this section problems facing each model type are outlined, and prognoses for future progress are discussed.

Stochastic Models

The promise of stochastic models looks bright. The philosophy of modeling is sound—model the individual consumer and aggregate across consumers. However, some serious problems stand between these models and their widespread adoption.

One aspect of most of the brand-choice models in this category is that they collect all brands other than the brand of interest into a single artificial "all other" brand.[46] While, in a market of many brands, it might be reasonable to consider several similar brands as a single competitor, it seems unwise to collect *every* other brand into a single group. Fortunately, most Markov models[47] do not suffer from this problem. Also, progress is being made on alleviating this problem in other promising models.[48]

Another problem in this class of models is the lack of integration among the brand-choice, interpurchase-timing, and quality-purchased models. Clearly if market sales are to be modeled, all three factors should be combined into a single model. Researchers have just begun to turn their attention to this problem, and it (we hope) will be resolved shortly.

A final problem with these models is that, because of their mathematical complexity, they have not included many marketing variables in their formulation. While this will continue to be a problem, new and more powerful mathematical and computational techniques should help to alleviate it in the future. As these mathematical problems are solved, it can also be expected that more micro process variables will be included.

On the positive side, stochastic models seem to provide the best prospects for modeling large-scale market behavior at the current time. It looks as though linear models are not comprehensive enough, while large-system models seem to be, at best, difficult to apply.

Information-Processing Models

As mentioned earlier, one of the major problems confronting information-processing models is the idiosyncratic nature of the models developed, due to the emphasis on depicting actual decision rules. If each individual needs a separate model, this is little consolation to the consumer-choice theorist. For the information-processing approach to be viable, some generalizations must become apparent. Thus, individual models become data points from which a more general model may be induced.

For this generalization to occur, several developments seem necessary. First, more models of individuals must be built, in more types of situations. Second, models of the same individual over time must be studied. Finally, it would be most helpful for making generalizations if methods for comparing information-processing models could be developed. One such method has been proposed, and if it proves viable, it can be used to cluster individuals and develop process-oriented typologies useful for generalization.[49]

It has been noted that building information-processing models of more individuals would be helpful in leading to generalized models. However, a second problem with information-processing models is that data collection and analysis are extremely time consuming. Methods for formalizing protocol analysis would be very helpful. Some work on such methods is underway[50] but is progressing slowly. Methods such as AID[51] that infer tree structures from data might also be tried, with the idea that inferring an information-processing model from detailed data can in fact be constructed as a complicated form of parameter estimation. Hence, developing tree structures using a formalized procedure could be thought of as a parameter-estimation technique. One would certainly need to carefully compare the estimated models with models inferred directly from the protocols to see if the idea were practical.

Finally, much work needs to be done on building learning processes into information-processing models. Most information-processing models are constructed for subjects who have *already* learned. However, using naïve foreign subjects[52] might yield data on actual learning procedures. An information-processing model of a subject playing a business game shows that such learning strategies are extremely hard to characterize.[53]

Experimental and Other Linear Models

The formulation of these models is probably not realistic of the situations being modeled, but they are easy to solve. As a result, they will undoubtedly continue to be used and may be valuable to formal consumer model building, since the potential exists for pointing out additional variables which need to be included in other models.

On the other hand, the linear models seem to be too restrictive in their form to represent the market very adequately. Also, the assumption of homogeneity implicit in most linear models seems to be grossly inadequate. As a consequence, these models can probably best be used as exploratory tools to aid in formulating other, more complicated models.

Large-System Models

One problem facing the Amstutz microsimulation models, the linear realization of the Howard-Sheth model, and the Nicosia model is measurement. Extremely subtle and nontransparent constructs are involved, and developing questionnaire measures to gather data for model testing is very difficult. Farley and Ring have discussed such difficulties in the Howard-Sheth model.[54] However, psychometric techniques have made great strides in the last few years and may help with these problems.

A problem particularly inherent in simulation models such as those proposed by Amstutz is that of model validation. It is still unclear how to compare simulation results with actual results analytically, although spectral analysis has been proposed.[55] Also, estimation of parameters in simulation models has been a very hard theoretical problem.

Finally, reasonable models should be testable.[56] With broad, general models it is often hard to develop critical empirical tests that allow for model rejection. This does not seem to be so much the case for present large-system models but may cause problems with further generalizations.

Thus the main problems with large-system models are brought about by their sheer size, unwieldiness, and generality. These properties make constructs hard to specify and measure and validation difficult.

Conclusions

There are many different ways in which the various models of consumer behavior can be compared. It is important for the modeler who is engaged in this activity to be aware of these differences, since they imply quite different philosophical approaches to formal consumer models. The various types of models have been discussed within a comparative conceptual framework, in an effort to make the differences more clear to the reader.

In addition to the modeler, the practitioner also should become involved in these questions, for they have strong implications for the applicability of a particular model in a particular situation.

Endnotes

1. For a good review of particular stochastic models, see William F. Massy, David B. Montgomery, and Donald G. Morrison, *Stochastic Models of Buying Behavior* (Cambridge, Mass.: M.I.T. Press, 1970).
2. Examples of these model types are Frank Harary and Benjamin Lipstein, "The Dynamics of Brand Loyalty: A Markov Approach," *Operations Research* (January–February 1962), pp. 19–40, and Donald G. Morrison, "Testing Brand Switching Models," *Journal of Marketing Research* (November 1966), pp. 401–9 (brand purchased last time); David B. Montgomery, "A Stochastic Response Model with Application to Brand Choice," *Management Science* (March 1969), pp. 323–27 (external time effects); James Carman, "Brand Switching and Linear Learning Models," *Journal of Advertising Research* (June 1966), pp. 23–31, and Alfred A. Kuehn, "Consumer Brand Choice–A Learning Process?" *Journal of Advertising Research* (December 1962), pp. 10–

17 (past history of purchases); and, finally, J. Morgan Jones, "A Dual-Effects Model of Brand Choice," *Journal of Marketing Research* (November 1970), pp. 458–64 (combination of effects).

3. For an exception, see L. G. Telser, "The Demand for Branded Goods as Estimated from Consumer Panel Data," *Review of Economics and Statistics* (August 1962), pp. 300–324.
4. Morrison.
5. Alan Newell, J. C. Shaw, and Herbert A. Simon, "Elements of a Theory of Human Problem Solving," *Psychological Review* (May 1958), pp. 151–66.
6. James R. Bettman, "Information Processing Models of Consumer Behavior," *Journal of Marketing Research* (August 1970), pp. 370–76.
7. Alan Newell, "On the Analysis of Human Problem Solving Protocols" (working paper, Carnegie-Mellon University, 1966).
8. Bettman, "Information Processing Models."
9. Marcus Alexis, George Haines, and Leonard Simon, "Consumer Information Processing: The Case of Women's Clothing," *Proceedings of the American Marketing Association*, ser. 28 (1968), pp. 197–205.
10. George Haines, "Information and Consumer Behavior" (working paper, University of Rochester, July 1969).
11. Robert H. King, "A Study of the Problem of Building a Model to Simulate the Cognitive Processes of a Shopper in a Supermarket," in *Consumer Behavior: Learning Models of Purchasing*, by George Haines (New York: Free Press, 1969), pp. 22–67.
12. Frederick A. Russ, "Consumer Evaluation of Alternative Product Models" (Ph.D. diss., Carnegie-Mellon University, 1971).
13. Geoffrey Clarkson, *Portfolio Selection: A Simulation of Trust Investment* (Englewood Cliffs, N.J.: Prentice-Hall, Inc., 1962).
14. Martin Fishbein, "Attitude and the Prediction of Behavior," in *Readings in Attitude Theory and Measurement*, ed. M. Fishbein (New York: John Wiley & Sons, 1967), pp. 477–92.
15. For examples, see Flemming Hansen, "Consumer Choice Behavior: An Experimental Approach," *Journal of Marketing Research* (November 1969), pp. 436–43; and Peter Sampson and Paul Harris, "A User's Guide to Fishbein," *Journal of the Market Research Society* 12, no. 3 (July 1970): 145–64.
16. George S. Day, *Buyer Attitudes and Brand Choice Behavior* (New York: Free Press, 1970).
17. Work in this area is well represented by William F. Massy, Ronald E. Frank, and Thomas Lodahl, *Purchasing Behavior and Personal Attributes* (Philadelphia: University of Pennsylvania Press, 1968).
18. For an example of this type of model, see Ronald E. Frank and William F. Massy, "Shelf Position and Space Effects on Sales," *Journal of Marketing Research* (February 1970), pp. 59–66.
19. Arnold E. Amstutz, *Computer Simulation of Competitive Market Response* (Cambridge, Mass.: M.I.T. Press, 1967); John U. Farley and L. Winston Ring, "An Empirical Test of the Howard-Sheth Model of Buyer Behavior," *Journal of Marketing Research* (November 1970), pp. 427–38; and Francesco Nicosia, *Consumer Decision Processes: Marketing and Advertising Implications* (Englewood Cliffs, N.J.: Prentice-Hall, Inc., 1966).
20. John A. Howard and Jagdish N. Sheth, *The Theory of Buyer Behavior* (New York: John Wiley & Sons, 1969).
21. Farley and Ring, pp. 434–36.
22. Nicosia, pp. 155–57.
23. Nicosia, pp. 208–37.
24. The comparison made here is somewhat similar to the distinction in operations research between dynamic programming as a modeling philosophy and linear programming as a class of structurally well-defined models.
25. M. Bird, C. Channon, and A. S. C. Ehrenberg, "Brand Images and Brand Usage," *Journal of Marketing Research* (August 1970), pp. 307–14; and A. S. C. Ehrenberg, "Models of Fact: Examples from Marketing," *Management Science* (March 1970), pp. 435–45.
26. Geoffrey Clarkson, "Decision Making in Small Groups—A Simulation Study," *Behavioral Science* (July 1968), pp. 288–305; and Edward A. Feigenbaum, "The Simulation of Verbal Learning Behavior," in *Computers and Thought*, ed. E. A. Feigenbaum and J. Feldman (New York: McGraw-Hill Book Co., 1963).
27. Amstutz, pp. 386–91.
28. Nicosia, p. 197.
29. For example, Frank and Massy (n. 18 above).
30. See Massy, Montgomery, and Morrison (n. 1 above), pp. 428–40; and Telser (n. 3 above).
31. For example, Frank and Massy; or P. McClure and E. West, "Sales Effects of a New Counter Display," *Journal of Advertising Research* (March 1969), pp. 29–34.
32. Amstutz, pp. 383–85; Farley and Ring, pp. 437–38.
33. However, Bettman uses measurement over time for his information-processing models.
34. George Miller, Eugene Galanter, and Karl Pribram, *Plans and the Structure of Behavior* (New York: Holt, Rinehart & Winston, 1960).
35. Morrison (n. 2 above).
36. James R. Bettman, "A Graph Theory Approach to Comparing Consumer Information Processing Models," *Management Science*, pt. 2 (December 1971), pp. 114–28.
37. Ronald E. Frank, "Brand Choice as a Probability Process," *Journal of Business* (January 1962), pp. 43–56; and William F. Massy, "Order and Homogeneity of Family Specific Brand-Switching Processes," *Journal of Marketing Research* (February 1966), pp. 48–54.
38. Amstutz, pp. 386–93.

39. For beginnings in this area, see J. Morgan Jones, "A Comparison of Three Models of Brand Choice," *Journal of Marketing Research* (November 1970), pp. 466–73; and David B. Montgomery, "Stochastic Consumer Models: Some Comparative Results," in *Applications of Management Science in Marketing*, ed. D. B. Montgomery and G. Urban (Englewood Cliffs, N.J.: Prentice-Hall, Inc., 1970), pp. 99-113.
40. For a similar viewpoint from cognitive psychology, see Paul Slovic and Sarah Lichtenstein, "Comparison of Bayesian and Regression Approaches to the Study of Information Processing in Judgment," *Oregon Research Institute Research Monograph*, vol. 10 (December 1970).
41. Bettman, "Information Processing Models of Consumer Behavior" (n. 6 above).
42. Private communication with Prof. A. Tversky, Stanford University, indicates work on a hierarchical elimination-choice model for which a lexicographic satisficing process rationale can be developed.
43. Louis Goldberg, "Simple Models or Simple Processes? Some Research on Clinical Judgments," *American Psychologist* (July 1968), pp. 483–96.
44. James R. Bettman, "The Structure of Consumer Choice Processes," *Journal of Marketing Research* (November 1971), pp. 465–71.
45. Ibid.
46. For example, Carman; Jones, "A Dual-Effects Model of Brand Choice"; Montgomery, "A Stochastic Response Model with Application to Brand Choice"; and Morrison (see n. 2 above).
47. Harary and Lipstein (n. 2 above).
48. Private communication with Mr. Jack Bieda, Procter and Gamble Co., Cincinnati, indicates significant progress on a multi-brand linear learning model.
49. Bettman, "A Graph Theory Approach to Comparing Consumer Information Processing Models" (n. 36 above).
50. Newell (n. 7 above); and William C. Farrell, "A Simulation Model of Decision Making in a Management Game" (M.S. thesis, Graduate School of Business Administration, University of California, Los Angeles, 1971).
51. J. Sonquist and J. Morgan, *The Detection of Interaction Effects*, Monograph 35 (Ann Arbor, Mich.: Survey Research Center, University of Michigan, 1964).
52. Jagdish N. Sheth, "How Adults Learn Brand Preferences," *Journal of Advertising Research* (September 1968), pp. 25-36.
53. Farrell.
54. Farley and Ring (n. 19 above), pp. 435–38.
55. George Fishbein and Philip Kiviat, "The Analysis of Simulation Generated Time Series," *Management Science* (March 1967), pp. 525–57.
56. Geoffrey Clarkson, *The Theory of Consumer Demand: A Critical Appraisal* (Englewood Cliffs, N.J.: Prentice-Hall, Inc., 1963).

READING 2

Multiattribute Models in Marketing: A Bicentennial Review

Richard J. Lutz and James R. Bettman

Multiattribute models of attitude have been prominent in marketing and consumer behavior literature only in recent years, and the following reasons explain, in varying degree, the increasing importance of these models.

1. *The Diagnostic Tool.* Multiattribute models are not only a means for measuring consumer attitudes but also for diagnosing these attitudes and suggesting attitude change strategies. That is, by careful analysis of consumers' perceptions of product attributes, the manager can alter his market offering (most notably the promotion element) to favorably influence attitudes and behaviors toward his product. The most cogent statements of this rationale can be found in Boyd, Ray and Strong (1972), and Cohen (1974).
2. *Intuitive Appeal.* It makes good sense that consumers select products that possess desirable attributes and reject those which do not. Kotler's (1967) definition of a product was couched in these terms: "a bundle of physical, service and symbolic particulars expected to yield satisfactions or benefits to the buyer" (p. 289). Substitution of the word attributes for particulars in this definition does little to change its meaning but does clarify the centrality of product attributes in marketing theory.
3. *Industry Acceptance.* Although more practitioners have published psychographic studies than is the case with the multiattribute model, it is still unusual to find a major marketing survey questionnaire that does not have a section on perceptions of brand attributes. Increasing acceptance by industry encourages further application and refinement of the multiattribute model.
4. *Research Pragmatics.* Data conforming to a multiattribute model are easy to collect and susceptible to analytical techniques ranging from simple to extremely sophisticated ones. Unfortunately, the pragmatics of publishing and/or perishing dictate the interest of many researchers in this model.
5. *Theoretical Relevance.* A final reason for the popularity of multiattribute models is their linkage to basic psychological processes of the individual and to the earlier works in psychology by Fishbein (1963) and Rosenberg (1956). These theories in turn are closely related to even earlier thinking by Lewin (1938). Thus a strong research tradition underlies these models as explanatory constructs that can help in yielding insights into consumer behavior.

The major purpose of using multiattribute models is one of prescription. Before prescriptions for changing behavior can be made, there must be an adequate explanation for that behavior and, to reach the desired goal of prescribing attitude change strategies, it must first be demonstrated that the theory underlying the multiattribute model is reasonably valid.

This paper will review selectively the recent literature on multiattribute models, focusing on those studies aimed at testing the theory.

The Multiattribute Model in Marketing: Its Origins

At least two forms of the multiattribute model have bases in psychological theory, namely the Fishbein and Rosenberg models. A third approach, and the most common to date, encompasses a wide range of various model types and has been called, for present purposes, the intuitive approach. Each of these major model types is described briefly below.

The Fishbein Model

Working within the tradition of behavioristic learning theory, Fishbein (1963) developed a theory of attitude formation and change, which can be summarized by the following equation:

$$A_O = \sum_{i=1}^{n} b_i a_i \qquad (1)$$

where A_O is the attitude toward (i.e., affect for or against) any psychological object; b_i is the belief (i.e., the subjective likelihood) that object O possesses some attribute i; a_i is the evaluation (i.e., goodness or badness) of attribute i; and n is the number of salient attributes. Thus affect is seen as the multiplicative summation of salient beliefs about a brand, weighted by the value of those beliefs.

Theoretically then, attitude toward a brand could be influenced by modifying either beliefs about brand attributes or the evaluations of these attributes, or by adding a new salient attribute(s).

Since 1972, a number of studies have appeared that have investigated the Fishbein model (e.g., Ahtola 1975a; Bettman, Capon & Lutz 1975a–d; Nakanishi & Bettman 1974; Mazis, Ahtola & Klippel 1975; Lutz, 1975a, b; Tuncalp & Sheth 1975; Raju, Bhagat & Sheth 1975). Of interest also is the growing literature on Fishbein's (1967) extended model for the prediction of specific behaviors, which is an outgrowth of his earlier attitude model. This research has recently been reviewed by Ryan and Bonfield (1975; see also Anderson (1976) for a set of papers dealing with this topic).

The Rosenberg Model

While Fishbein focused on learning theory to explain initial attitude formation, Rosenberg (1956) worked within the framework of consistency theory to explain how attitudes change. Equation 2 summarizes Rosenberg's model:

$$A_O = \sum_{i=1}^{m} PI_i VI_i \qquad (2)$$

where A_O is affect for or against an object; PI_i is the *perceived instrumentality* of that object in leading to or blocking the attainment of a particular value i; VI_i is the *value importance* of the ith value, expressed as the degree of satisfaction or dissatisfaction felt by the individual with respect to that value; and m is the number of salient values. Thus Rosenberg's model is one of cognitive-affective consistency. Several applications in marketing have used Rosenberg's basic measurement procedures but have substituted product attributes for the deeper values used by Rosenberg (e.g., Hansen 1969; Mazis, Ahtola & Klippel 1975).

Again, several earlier multiattribute studies in marketing purported to use the Rosenberg model (e.g., Sheth & Talarzyk 1972) but mistakenly measured respondents' stated "importance" of attributes rather than degree of satisfaction-dissatisfaction, as specified by Rosenberg (1956). Thus most of the early "Fishbein-Rosenberg" studies in marketing may be viewed as pertaining to the intuitive approach outlined below.

The Fishbein and Rosenberg models share the following properties:

1. Basis in psychological theory
2. Clearly specified constructs and measurement procedures
3. Theoretically derived attribute combination rules (i.e., multiplication and summation).

The above properties combine to allow meaningful testing of the two models and the construction of a body of empirical evidence which can be brought to bear on the models. That is, explanatory power of the above models can be examined for the purpose of building prescriptions for attitude change.

The Intuitive Approach

The intuitive approach to multiattribute models in marketing is represented by a conglomeration of model forms and measurement procedures. Perhaps the easiest way to characterize this approach is by the following equation:

$$S = f(B,I) \tag{3}$$

where S is a summary measure of approach tendency toward a brand (e.g., attitude, preference, intention, choice), B is a measure of consumers' beliefs regarding the brand's possession of various attributes; and I is the importance (or salience) of these attributes in the mind of the consumer.

In contrast to the Fishbein and Rosenberg models, the intuitive approach rests on no theoretical foundation; nor does it specify measurement procedures or algebraic manipulations in a rigorous manner. More significantly, the dependent variable in the model is not invariant across applications, so generalizations are virtually impossible.

The bulk of marketing research applications fall under the intuitive approach. Virtually all the studies reviewed by Wilkie and Pessemier (1973) and the vast majority of those published since 1973 are in this category. Unfortunately, few if any of these studies add to the body of knowledge surrounding the multiattribute model as a diagnostic device.

In their review, Wilkie and Pessemier (1973, p. 439) concluded that three areas needed further research: model conceptualization, component measurement, and testing methods. While they did not explicitly define the boundaries of these three issues (and there is a certain degree of overlap among them), attention is now directed at recent research to determine what progress, if any, has been made in these domains since 1973.

Component Definition and Measurement

The two major areas considered below are how many constructs should be included in the model, and how to operationalize the constructs that are included.

The standard multiattribute model, as shown above, has two components, or constructs: a belief measure, and a weighting for each belief. For Fishbein models, beliefs as to the likelihood of outcomes are used, and the weights are evaluations of the outcomes. A typical study under the intuitive approach uses degree of possession belief measures and importance as the weight (e.g., Bass & Wilkie 1973). The most prevalent question in examining whether only one construct might be used rather than two has been whether a "beliefs only" model, where the importance or evaluation term is dropped, is adequate (e.g., Sheth & Talarzyk 1972; Cohen & Ahtola 1971; Beckwith & Lehmann 1973; Bettman 1974; Nakanishi & Bettman 1974; Bruno & Wildt 1975). The general finding has been that dropping the weighting term has little effect on obtained correlations. Explanations of this result have been offered that range from lack of variation in the weights (Cohen & Ahtola 1971) to psychological interpretations (Bettman 1974).

Dawes and Corrigan (1974) contend, however, that the tasks studied in applying linear models have an important effect. The situation demands behavior approximately like that implied by a unit weighting or beliefs-only model if the behavior is to be appropriate (Simon 1969). In many applications of the multiattribute model in marketing, the task is evaluation of product classes where most attributes included are inherently desirable. Hence the measured weights obtained from subjects tend to be positive in the great majority of cases. This type of task would lead to good predictions for a model that simply dropped the weights from the equation. However, Feldman (1974), using the Fishbein model, showed that when several negatively evaluated outcomes are included, simply dropping the a_i term can lead to poor predictions, since the direction of the relationships of beliefs to the criterion is then incorrect. Correlations were obtained between $\Sigma a_i b_i$ and five criterion variables and between Σb_i and the same five criteria. In all five cases, dropping the a_i term substantially reduced the correlation obtained (e.g., from .68 to .18 in one case). Of course, one might argue that unit weights could be used which are +1 or −1 depending upon the direction of the relationship of each variable to the criterion. If this were done, good predictive results would probably be obtained. However, the crucial issue for theoretical development of the multiattribute model seems to be whether the weights are psychologically meaningful. Individuals hold evaluations of different outcomes and claim that these evaluations can be distinguished in both direction and magnitude.

If the beliefs-only model performs well because it is appropriate for the tasks to which it has been applied, one may argue that for other types of tasks the weighted model may be needed even for good predictive results. Research delineating the properties of tasks for which the weighted or unweighted models will perform well is needed.

Several authors have also suggested that additional constructs should be added to the multiattribute model. For example, Hackman and Anderson (1968) added "relevance" (R_i) of each belief for the criterion used in the Fishbein model; Feldman (1974) examined adding a certainty component, C_i, to the Fishbein model; and Bennett and Harrell (1975) similarly postulated that confidence in beliefs (c_i) might be added to form terms $a_i b_i c_i$. Finally, Holbrook and Hulbert (1975) tested a model with belief, evaluation, and salience (importance) components. In all cases, the two-component model performed at least as well as the three-component alternatives using degree of fit as the measure of performance. Thus, adding a third component directly to the model does not seem to be a fruitful approach. However, Bennett and Harrell (1975) found that if their sample was segmented on overall confidence in their belief ratings, the standard two-component model fit better for the high confidence segment, indicating that a moderator variable approach rather than a direct inclusion approach may be valuable.

Given that a two-component model seems appropriate, the question of how to operationalize these components arises. Bettman, Capon, and Lutz (1975a) argue strongly for operationalization of components as suggested by Fishbein, with one component a belief about the likelihood (likely-unlikely) of an outcome and the second an evaluation (good-bad) of each outcome, with each component measured on bipolar (e.g., -3 to $+3$) scales. Bettman, Capon and Lutz compared this operationalization to the major competing scheme, the so-called "adequacy-importance" model, where belief is measured as degree of possession of an atrribute (high-low) and importance is used as the weighting term (important-unimportant).

Students were presented with "profiles" of information about one attribute of a brand. Some subjects received profiles based on the Fishbein scales (e.g., likely to have a good attribute), others profiles based on adequacy-importance scales (e.g., high in an important attribute). Subjects rated their attitude toward using the brand based only on the information in the profile. The hypothesis, based upon the formulation of the models, would be that the components should be multiplied and scaled in bipolar fashion by those subjects performing the Fishbein rating task or unipolar fashion (e.g., 1 to 7 scaling) for those subjects performing the adequacy-importance task. The analysis of variance results showed that most subjects performing the Fishbein task appeared to combine the components in the expected manner, but that the adequacy-importance components resulted in much heterogeneity in responses across subjects. In particular, many subjects receiving the adequacy-importance scales did not treat the importance component as unipolar but as bipolar. Treatment of the importance component seemed to be quite variable and was the major problem underlying the adequacy-importance model results. Thus Bettman, Capon and Lutz (1975a) conclude that evaluation should be used rather than importance as the weighting term.

Ahtola (1975a) argues that the measure of beliefs used by Fishbein confounds belief strength and content of the belief, that operationalization of belief mixes up what is believed and how strongly beliefs are held. To avoid this problem, Ahtola proposes partitioning the dimension to be rated into categories. Then, using a probability scale, the individual would rate the probability of each category being true for a brand (which would sum to one over categories, and an evaluation of each category. Thus the model would become

$$A_k = \sum_{i=1}^{n} \sum_{j=1}^{g(i)} b_{ijk} a_{ij} \qquad (4)$$

where A_k is attitude toward brand k; b_{ijk} is the probability that category j of dimension i is associated with brand k; a_{ij} is the evaluation of category j of dimension i; $g(i)$ is the number of categories for dimension i; and n is number of salient dimensions.

This model would make the belief rating more precise, at the cost of increasing the complexity of the model. Also, note that Ahtola assumes that individuals treat belief as a unipolar probability measure; and the task he uses to measure b_{ijk}, distributing 10 poker chips among the possible categories, forces subjects to rate in terms of such a measure. The Bettman, Capon and Lutz (1975a) results, using a different task, suggest that individuals conceptualize belief in a bipolar fashion. Further research is needed to examine how individuals form belief concepts and the nature of these concepts.

The results cited above imply that evaluation is best measured on good-bad scales. In the model as formulated, evaluation is postulated to depend on the outcome alone, not on the attitude object evaluated. That is, evaluation is measured for each outcome, but not for each brand-outcome combination. Miller (1974) and Parker and Dyer (1975) propose that perhaps evaluations should be measured for object-outcome pairs. However, Miller's results show little or no improvement in degree of fit for predictions of preference, and Parker and Dyer's results, which show differences in measures of a_i for two different objects, seem to be dealing with different situations, that is, attitudes toward the same objects in different situations, not toward different objects in the same situation. The latter is the appropriate scenario for typical applications of multiattribute attitude models in marketing. Differences in situation may well elicit different levels of intensity on the various attitude components.

Two final issues relating to component conceptualization and operationalization need brief discussion. First, normalization of belief and weighting scores has been shown to improve degree of fit greatly (Bass & Wilkie 1973; Ginter 1974).[1] Theoretically, however, why it should work is unknown, beyond explanations at the level of individual response biases (Bass & Wilkie 1973). Perhaps there is no deeper theoretical import, but effects of such magnitude might cause speculation that some systematic factor is at work. A final issue relates to the dependent variable appropriate for multiattribute models. A great variety of criterion variables have been used, ranging from preference to behavior. Fishbein (Fishbein & Ajzen 1975) specifically notes that attitude models predict affect, not behavior; other components, such as normative factors, are needed to predict intentions, which then predict behavior. Thus a good-bad, evaluative dependent variable seems most appropriate. Finally, attitude toward a specific act in a specific situation should be the focus, not a general attitude toward an object when behavioral prediction is the ultimate goal (Ryan & Bonfield 1975).

1. Normalization as defined by Bass and Wilkie (1973) is not well suited to the Fishbein model. For example, Bass and Wilkie define a normalized belief score, bn_{ij}, as $bn_{ij} = b_{ij}\Sigma_j b_{ij}$. The sum in the denominator can be negative or zero for models such as Fishbein's where bipolar scales are used. To circumvent the problem, a constant can be added to each b_{ij} to make it positive, but this yields a nonlinear transformation on bn_{ij}, which can change resulting correlation levels (Schmidt & Wilson 1975).

Model Conceptualization

A major form of the multiattribute model under the intuitive approach has been a linear combination of attribute perceptions (weighted or unweighted by importance) which is used to predict attitude (e.g., Cohen & Ahtola 1971). Several authors have suggested that various alternative combination rules might be more applicable under some conditions. For instance, Einhorn (1970) discussed conjunctive, disjunctive and lexicographic models, while Russ (1971) employed various combinations of lexicographic, lexicographic semiorder, and satisficing models.

These models are all based on the premise that individuals do not compare attributes in the compensatory fashion assumed by the linear model. That is, poor performance on one attribute may be compensated in the linear model by good performance on one or more other attributes. This is not the case with noncompensatory models where, for example, decisions may be based on the most important attribute only (lexicographic) or on some minimum cutoff values (conjunctive).

Bruno and Wildt (1975) examined the complementarity of five forms of the multiattribute model to determine the degree of overlap in predictive power. The overlap among the models ranged from a low of 45.6% to a high of 92.5%, while correlations among the predictions from the five model types ranged from .39 to .98. Thus there appears to be a good deal of shared variance among the compensatory and noncompensatory models.

Future research in this area will likely follow the lead of Wright's (1974) paper, which examines the impact of situational factors on the form of the consumer decision process.

Investigations of the Fishbein Model

Ahtola attracted attention to the confounding of belief content and strength, and his initial test of the revised model (labeled the "vector" model) showed it to be somewhat better than the Fishbein model. This would appear to be a promising direction for future research, and Ahtola (1975b) has applied similar thinking to the normative component in Fishbein's extended model for the prediction of behavioral intention. The only major obstacle to the development of this approach is the complex measurement procedure required to operationalize the model.

Two important assumptions in the Fishbein model (Equation 1) are that the b_i and a_i terms multiply within attributes and that the resultant products add across attributes. Studies I and II (Bettman, Capon & Lutz 1975a,b) were directed at testing the multiplicative assumption, which was upheld in most cases although individual differences appeared.

Study III (Bettman, Capon & Lutz 1975c) showed that $b_i a_i$ products typically combine in an additive fashion across attributes, but this study was unable, due to its design, to distinguish between adding versus equal-weight averaging. Consequently, a fourth study (Bettman, Capon & Lutz 1975d) was conducted which indicated that averaging across attributes was more common than adding across attributes. This finding awaits replication, particularly via other methods, but it does suggest an important modification of the basic Fishbein model.

To summarize, there is an increasing amount of research directed at the issue of model conceptualization, at least as represented by the specification of the cognitive "rules" by which attributes are combined to yield overall attitude and/or choice. One trend seems to be toward explicit recognition and identification of individual and situational differences in cognitive processing strategies. Thus representative sampling of both people and situations would seem to be an important concern in future research.

Testing Methodologies

Up to 1973, virtually all tests of the multiattribute model had taken a static, correlational approach wherein attributes were combined in some manner and then related to a dependent variable. This approach is useful for establishing the predictive validity of the multiattribute model, and the body of evidence accumulated thus far does provide fairly strong support for the model. However, this approach is incapable of speaking to the construct validity of the model. To establish the multiattribute model as a diagnostic and prescriptive device, it must be shown that changes in brand attribute perceptions or importances lead to, or cause, changes in brand attitudes. Correlational designs can assess only predictive power, not the explanatory power necessary to conclude that the model is useful for the purposes for which it has been adopted.

A recent approach to validating multiattribute models is analysis of variance that allows the only really unambiguous test of the multiplicative assumption in the Fishbein and Rosenberg models, for example (Schmidt & Wilson 1975).[2] Use of analysis of variance method also permits the researcher to vary cognitive elements (e.g., attribute ratings) and observe directly the effects of these variations on attitude. Thus the causal influence of attributes on attitude can be assessed, a crucial bit of evidence in the quest for model validation.

Multimethod approaches are also becoming more common in the literature. For example, Bettman, Capon and Lutz (1975b) used cross-sectional correlation, individual level correlation, and analysis of variance to investigate three different multiattribute model formats. Park and Schaninger (1976) used both structured and unstructured protocol procedures and statistical modeling to identify attribute processing rules. In both studies different results were obtained under the various methods, although a good deal of convergence was observed.

Yet another approach to model validation has been the use of attitude change paradigms. That is, rather than simply measuring attributes and attitudes as they exist at a particular moment, the researcher can attempt to modify certain attributes (or their evaluations) and examine the resultant impact on attitude. The three studies reported to date that have used this approach (Lutz 1975a,b; Olson & Dover 1976) have found a fair degree of support for the model.

Based on these few studies, it appears that the attitude change strategy of belief modification rather

2. Schmidt and Wilson (1975) note that if interval scale measures of belief and evaluation components are obtained, then for a model such as the multiattribute attitude model, where the components are multiplied, correlations with the dependent measure vary, depending upon the particular interval scaling used. Thus degree of fit can be changed by making allowable (under the interval scaling assumptions) transformations of the scaling of the components, rendering conclusions based on degree of fit useless. Schmidt and Wilson, however, incorrectly state that within individual applications do not suffer from this problem; it can be shown that within individual correlational analyses, belief measures may be interval-scaled but evaluation measures must be ratio-scaled to obtain invariant correlation results. If belief measures are interval, interval-scaled evaluation measures can be used only if the sum of the belief measures across attributes is the same for all brands, a highly artificial restriction.

than evaluation modification is more promising. The strategy of adding more attributes into salient cognitive structure is yet to be tested.[3] Clearly, more studies of this type need to be conducted before firm conclusions can be reached.

A final development in the testing of multiattribute models is the use of causal-correlational techniques determining if a body of data conforms to the causal structure hypothesized to underlie consumer decision processes. Recent papers by Beckwith and Lehmann (1975), Ryan (1975), and Lutz (1975d) illustrate this approach, although the latter two papers investigated the extended Fishbein model rather than the multiattribute model of principal interest here.

In general the results of these initial studies have been supportive of the causal patterning presumed to operate in these models, although the Beckwith and Lehmann (1975) paper does not explicitly recognize this. The promise of these models is great for future studies of the multiattribute model as well as in other domains of consumer behavior.

Further Considerations

Another aspect of choice rules is the form of processing implied by such a rule. In one case, each brand is processed and evaluated as a whole, and a choice is then made based on these overall evaluations. This may be called processing by brand. A second form of processing involves comparison of all brands on a single attribute, followed by comparisons on a second attribute, and so on. This may be called processing by attribute. The compensatory formulation of the multiattribute attitude model, whether adding or averaging formulations are used, assumes processing by brand. Other models do not make such an assumption.[4]

This distinction about form of processing affects the attitude notions presented above. If processing by attribute is used, a rule may function to yield an overall evaluation for each alternative, but in a different manner than implied by most attitude models. For example, alternatives may be eliminated after the first attribute has been examined. This group of eliminated alternatives may form one evaluation class, with further classes formed as the process continues. It is not clear whether this derived evaluation has any relation to what the consumer does in forming overall evaluations for each brand, however. If processing by attribute is performed in a manner where elimination is not used, it is difficult to specify how (or even if) evaluations are assigned to specific alternatives. For example, if differences between alternatives are utilized, as in the additive difference model (Tversky 1969), only a difference in evaluation may be available.

Thus the notion of an evaluation process and of an attitude seem based on a view of processing where each alternative is evaluated and evaluations are then compared (processing by brand). However, recent research supports the view that humans often use processing by attribute (Russo & Dosher 1975; Bettman & Jacoby 1976; Russ 1971; Wright & Barbour 1975; and Russo & Rosen 1975). Tversky (1969) argues that the presentation format of the data has important effects. If alternatives are displayed sequentially (e.g., in advertisements), processing by objects is encouraged. If information on dimensions of several alternatives is available simultaneously, people show strong tendencies to process by attribute. This factor appears implicit in the above studies. The information displays (mostly visual arrays) used by almost all of the studies make attribute and object processing equally easy, and subjects prefer attribute processing. Svenson (1974), on the other hand, used individual booklets for each alternative and found more object processing. Presumably it was more difficult for subjects to use dimensional strategies, particularly when the number of alternatives was large. After an elimination phase, his subjects did seem to use more processing by attribute. Supermarket shelves are organized by brand, as are most commercials products. Also, some consumer choice research (Bettman & Jacoby 1976; Jacoby, Szybillo & Busato-Schach 1974) has demonstrated the importance of brand name as a chunk of information—an organized, familiar unit of data that summarizes a great deal of

3. The adding versus averaging issue is critical when this strategy is being considered. See Bettman, Capon and Lutz (1975c).

4. Eight major models of combination rules have been presented in the consumer choice literature: affect referral (Wright & Barbour 1975); linear compensatory; conjunctive; disjunctive, lexicographic; elimination by aspects (Tversky 1972); lexicographic semiorder (Russ 1971; Tversky 1969); and additive difference (Tversky 1969). Of these eight models, only affect referral and linear compensatory require brand processing. Conjunctive and disjunctive models can use either brand or attribute processing, and the remaining four models require processing by attribute.

information (Simon 1974). Over time, a brand name itself may come to summarize configurations of attributes rather than simply serving as a label for some detailed attribute list in memory. To the extent that consumers use brand name as a summary construct in this way, processing by brand would be facilitated. Thus processing by brand may be required to a great extent in actual consumer environments.

Failure to recognize processing by attribute as a form of processing has led to an emphasis on brand processing that may be unwarranted. If many consumers use processing by attribute, the notion of choice rules as directly yielding attitudes may be inadequate. Some form of affective measure may be developed in conjunction with the processing of alternatives, but it does not seem to be directly related to the processing steps implied by several rules (e.g., conjunctive, lexicographic). Thus more thought should be given to conceptualizing the meaning of attitude as an evaluation of a brand (or more precisely, of the act of buying a brand) in light of the findings discussed above. Studies of the form of processing used in actual, as opposed to laboratory, task settings need to be carried out, particularly since most consumer tasks may be carried out in environments that hinder processing by attribute and encourage processing by brand, as noted above. The concept of attitude and the form of processing implied by this concept must be congruent with research findings of form of processing.

The multiattribute models seem to have problems in situations where objective data or discrete points on a dimension are used. Objective data could emanate from public policy decisions on provision of information, since objective ratings would be provided (Wilkie 1975). Discrete attributes, such as number of bedrooms in a house examined by a prospective home purchaser, also arise. For such cases the standard model has difficulty with the belief measure, since degree of possession (high-low) or degree of likelihood (likely-unlikely) do not seem to apply. It seems unrealistic and forced to transform the number of bedrooms example to one where a consumer evaluates amount of bedroom space (high-low) or belief that the house is spacious (likely-unlikely). It seems more congruent with what consumers probably do to measure the evaluation of three bedrooms directly and then weight that evaluation. A general information integration model is proposed by Anderson (1971).[5]

$$R = C + \sum_{i=1}^{n} w_i s_i \qquad (5)$$

where R is some overt response, say an attitude rating; C is a constant; s_i is the scale value for piece of information i (say, its evaluation); and w_i is the weight of piece of information i.

Thus, for objective data, each piece of information may be evaluated directly rather than indirectly as a judgment of belief. This general model seems to be a realistic approach to the case where objective or discrete data utilize the standard model contrived.

The form of processing and objective data issues are important ones for the multiattribute model. The ultimate validation of any theory or model is its usefulness. To the extent that the multiattribute model can be adapted to solve these and other "real-world" problems, it becomes a useful contribution to the understanding of consumer behavior.

---

5. The model presented above is additive. An averaging model could also be proposed, where $R = C + \Sigma_i w_i s_i / \Sigma w_i$.

READING 3

Some Internal Psychological Factors Influencing Consumer Choice

William J. McGuire

The directive, information-processing aspects of the personality are described in terms of eight successive steps: exposure, perception, comprehension, agreement, retention, retrieval, decision making, and action. Each of these steps is illustrated by recent psychological research. The dynamic, motivational aspect of human personality is described more briefly in terms of 16 basic human motives that have received attention in recent psychological research.

Introduction

Consumer psychology has been depicted in a recent paper (Jacoby, 1975) as including the whole range of social psychology; my inclination is to be even more ecumenical and describe it as embracing all of psychology. As psychologists, we study how people's behavior and conscious experience can be described, predicted, and influenced. The domain of behavior and experience surely includes consumers' decisions regarding products and their perceptions of and feelings toward these products. Of all the external forces acting on the person, and all the dynamic and directive aspects of human nature regulating the person's responses to such forces, there are few that do not also operate in this area of consumer choice. Hence, in carrying out my assignment here of describing what psychology can tell us about the condition and problems of the person as consumer, I find it difficult to decide where to begin and nearly impossible to determine where to end. To be sure, some aspects of psychology are more relevant to consumer issues than others, and my own unequal knowledge of the various areas of psychology provides a further (and more embarrassing) basis for selectivity, but at many points in the passages that follow, I shall have to be fairly arbitrary in eliminating topics and truncating discussions.

In a fuller version of this paper (McGuire, 1976), I have surveyed the psychology of consumer choice from three different perspectives: the external factors influencing consumer choice, the internal directive factors, and the internal dynamic factors. Those interested in a discussion of the external factors can find a review of this topic in the fuller publication, which deals with the effects on the consumers' decisions of product-relevant communications received from other persons (through face-to-face contacts and the mass media), their own past experiences with the product, and their point-of-purchase experience with the product.

The discussion here is confined to the recent psychological work on the internal characteristics of the person that affect exposure to and influence by these outside factors when he or she is making purchase and consumption decisions. We divide this internal psychological makeup of the consumer into a traditional distinction (no less respectable for its age) between the directive aspect and the dynamic aspect of personality. The first, longer part of this paper deals with the directive aspect, that is, the structural characteristics of one's personality that channel the information processing of one's own experiences and of communications from other people through successive steps of exposure, perception, comprehension, agreement, etc., to the ultimate purchasing act and

Reprinted with permission from the *Journal of Consumer Research,* 2:4 March 1976, 302–319.

consumption behavior. The second section deals with the dynamic aspects of personality, that is, the energizing components of human personality—the motivational forces that activate and sustain this information processing and account for its termination. Reflecting the recent flourishing of cognitive psychology and the relative quiet on the frontier of motivational psychology, this survey of recent psychological advances relevant to consumer psychology will be fuller in the first section on the directive, information-processing aspects of the person than in the second section on the dynamic, motivational aspects.

Directive Aspects of Personality Structure: Information Processing in Consumer Decision Making

In discussing the directive aspects of human personality, we assume that the person is structured in a way that channels internal and external forces through successive stages, which we call "information processing" in accord with popular current jargon (although "information" has an unfortunately narrow intellectualistic ring). This personality structuring presumably developed through phylogenetic and ontogenetic experience in helping the species and the individual cope with the customary environment. (It must be recognized, of course, that nonadaptive aspects of personality structure may develop as the result of a change in the environment from that with which the organism was prepared to cope, because of accidental malfunctions, a stress level beyond the organism's ability to cope; but it is a useful working hypothesis that people's characteristic modes of behavior are adaptive, considering the demands on the individual and the individual's capacities.)

We break down the information-processing aspect of personality into a series of steps, the points of division being somewhat arbitrary but necessary if we are to have manageable topics with which to deal. Various analytic schemes are possible; the one singled out for discussion here happens to be the one that we find most provocative. Choice of alternative divisions would probably make little difference in the discussion at the level of precision that we can employ here in applying psychological knowledge to consumer decision making. We shall divide the process into eight successive steps, each of which we shall discuss in a separate subsection.

The first step, which we call *exposure*, deals with the habits of the person that determine the kind of information to which he or she will be exposed. The second, *perception*, deals with the determination of what part of the information to which a person is exposed he or she effectively receives. We shall deal here with processes such as attention, sensation, and selectivity. The third step is *comprehension*, which deals with what and how the received material becomes encoded and entails notions such as meaning and information storage. The fourth step we call *agreement* (though it might alternatively be thought of as acceptance or yielding) and involves decisions on what portion of the information that is comprehended the person accepts as a valid and appropriate basis for changing his or her attitudes and actions. The fifth step is *retention* of this immediate impact through storage in memory. Sixth comes *retrieval* from the cognitive system of information bearing on the decision at the point when the consumer must make it. The seventh step is *decision making* on the basis of the retrieved information and involves choice and integration of this retrieved material. Finally comes the eighth step of taking *action* to carry out the decision, presumably about purchasing.

This information-processing approach is very fashionable for both psychological and consumer research. In basic psychology, it is the gist of the cognitive psychology that has replaced S-R reinforcement theory (or behaviorism) as the dominant view. A key book originally defining this field is Neisser's (1967). Briefer and more digestible presentations are found in Lindsay and Norman (1972), Posner (1973), and B. F. Anderson (1975). A reading of any of these last three volumes would be a feasible and provocative experience for a consumer researcher who wishes to learn about recent developments in basic research on information processing for possible application to consumer decision making.

In consumer research itself, it is currently fashionable to depict the consumer who is making a buying choice largely as an information-processing machine suitably represented as something approximating the "flow diagram" that one draws prior to writing a computer program. Indeed, the consumer researcher does proceed to write an appropriate computer program (or more likely hires a more technically skilled person to do so) and then tests and perfects the model by processing real or simulated data through it in search of plausible (and even valid) outcomes. Intriguing examples of this approach can be found in the work of Howard and his associates (Farley, Howard, and Ring, 1974; Holbrook and Howard, 1976; Howard and Sheth, 1969) and in the "consumenoid" model of Moran (1973).

In the remainder of this section, we shall consider successively the eight steps in information processing mentioned earlier.

Exposure to Information

Getting information to the consumer is the concern of various constituencies, including marketing people trying to increase demand for their product or to encourage the choice of their brand over competing ones, public agencies interested in getting information to the consumer about the nutritional or safety characteristics of products, and ecology advocates seeking to decrease the desire for products or to clarify their polluting or energy-consuming characteristics. Such organizations and individuals can transmit a great deal of information pertinent to their aims; but for the information to have any effect on the consumer's choice, the consumer must be exposed to it. Behavioral science research gives a variety of insights into the characteristics of the social structure and personal proclivities that determine the individual's information exposure. Here we touch only briefly on examples from the social and personal categories.

Social Structuring of Information Exposure. We can partition the population on several demographic dimensions—age, sex, social class, ethnicity, geographic location (regional and urban-rural), etc.—each of which divides the population into segments that differ in both their information exposure habits and their consumption styles. Recognition of this fact has produced a contemporary fad in the marketing and advertising sector called "market segmentation" that has given employment to computer modelers and provides a basis for distributing the advertising dollar among the media. The idea that different segments of the population have different media exposure habits has drastically influenced the flow of the advertising dollar, even to the extent that magazines and television shows which seemed to be highly popular in terms of absolute numbers of receivers have been abandoned by advertisers and have gone out of business because studies (or intuition) suggested that they had the wrong kind of readers or viewers, with low buying potential for widely advertised products. The conventional wisdom in this area tends to become a "self-fulfilling prophecy" when advertisers flee from print to electronic media on the basis of such suppositions. The results are a growing number of one-newspaper towns, the failure of magazines that provided entertainment or information for many, and the dropping of enjoyable television shows because the audiences proved to be too old or too sophisticated or too uninterested in frequently advertised products or too hard to influence by typical commercials.

Both the intended impact on consumer choice and the unintended side effects just mentioned derive from presumptions about exposure habits and purchasing potential that are extrapolations beyond the data. More seriously still, they are probably based on an exaggerated notion of the extent to which this first step of exposure is critical in determining the final, eighth step of actual purchasing. People in the public sector who want to communicate nutritional information, encourage medical checkups for hypertension, urge obedience to the speed limit or the use of seat belts, or discourage the misuse of cigarettes, alcohol, and other drugs should think carefully about taking this exposure differential into consideration. Such public service people should utilize the exposure information as is done in market segmentation studies, but they should not be misled by overly simplistic decision making on the basis of exposure data. It may be that teenage targets for information against drug abuse constitute most of the audience of certain rock-and-roll radio stations, so that many of the desired targets could be exposed to the commercials on these programs; but the context of the exposure on such stations might be particularly inappropriate for the information to have its desired impact. Again, the audience of sports programs may be heavy beer drinkers, so that beer advertising on these programs would get high exposure to the appropriate sector of the population. However, while the sports-oriented husband may drink the beer, it may be the sports-bored wife who buys it. We need more information about household decision making (see Davis's article in this issue) before we can be sure. In this connection, we also need further studies on time budgeting, uses of leisure time, and media consumption habits along the lines of the Szalai (1972) study, and on different life styles, especially as they affect media exposure habits and consumption patterns (see chapter on life styles by Wells and Cosmas in the final volume of this project [Ferber, 1976]).

Personal Characteristics Affecting Exposure. Besides one's demographic characteristics and social situation, one's individual proclivities have an effect on both media exposure habits and consumption patterns. Here we touch only briefly on personal determinants of exposure to information. Early in the history of communications research, Klapper (1949) suggested that a fundamental discovery of the field is the selective-exposure hypothesis, that people tend to expose themselves to information with which they are likely to agree and to avoid exposure to dissonant information. This idea has received wide acceptance, but there is reason to reject the selective-avoidance hypothesis. McGuire (1968b) has pointed out that there are many plausible reasons, supported by evidence, why people would want to acquaint themselves with opposition arguments. In most actual situations, any tendency to avoid dissonant information would be overridden by other considerations. Even cynics who regard other people as essentially uninteresting would have to work a bit to imagine a general population so dull that they would only want to hear what they already know. Novelty, surprises, controversy, etc., also have their appeal. A number of studies have demonstrated that people seek out information that is adaptive and novel, each enhancing the likelihood of exposure to dissonant information. Those wishing to convey information about the nutritional value of food or the wisdom of giving up cigarettes need not be over-concerned that those given to eating non-nutritious foods or smoking a great deal may actively avoid the message. But for continued tuning in by such relevant targets, the message should not be a high-fear communication stressing the dangers, but rather should stress solutions such as alternative foods that provide the same gratifications with higher nutritional value than the habitual undesirable ones or ways of cutting smoking and the health benefits of stopping. People do not have to be convinced that cancer is a bad thing but instead must be taught how, by means available to them, they can avoid it.

Perception of the Information Presented

The world is too much with us. It is, as William James pointed out, a big, booming, buzzing confusion, and we must learn to cope with it by selectively ignoring a great deal of the information impinging on us. Hence, of the mass of information to which the structure of our physical and social environment and our personal proclivities have exposed us, we effectively receive only a small subset. This second information-processing step, the selective reception process, is outlined here by briefly discussing psychological research usually considered under the rubrics of attention, sensation, and perception.

Attention Levels. Interest in attention has produced a vast literature, old and new; brief presentations are found in Norman (1969) and Posner (1973), while more detailed discussions can be found in Bakan (1966), Moray (1969), Mackworth (1970), and Kahneman (1973). The person has a general level of attention, or activation or arousal level, which fluctuates across individuals and circumstances. To convey relevant information to which the consumer will not only be exposed but will attend, we need to know much more about how the attention level for commercials or public health measures is affected by their being in certain kinds of material. Leaving aside the question of whether advertisers shun very interesting programs because they distract from the commercials, the question remains whether certain kinds of material of high interest or certain types of excitement detract from attention paid to the interspersed material. We do not know, for example, whether attention paid to such material is higher at the beginning or at the end or when intermingled with the entertainment material.

The span of attention is another issue that has been much studied but still needs to be applied more skillfully to this area: Given that a certain amount of time can be co-opted for communication to the consumer, should this time be partitioned into numerous short segments or a few long ones? The issues of divided attention need to be explored further in this context; for example, does a driver listening to a car radio pay less attention to the material than the same person would when sitting quietly at home in front of a television set?

Sensory Modalities. Scientific psychologists began with the study of sensation, and ever since have been telling us more than most other people really want to know about receptor processes. Nor have the physiologists been lax in studying this topic. Those persons with a deep interest and a long life expectancy might catch up with what is known about this field through the massive handbook of sensory physiology, most appropriately in its recent volume on psychophysics of vision (Jameson and Hurvich, 1972), or through the three-volume *Handbook of Perception* (Carterette and Friedman, 1973, 1974), but the busier executive might try Cornsweet (1970) for a broader and briefer review of what is known about visual perception. The *Annual Review of Psychology* averages two or more chapters each year on one or another sensory modality.

Our heart grows faint at the task of choosing, out of this vast area of inquiry, a few examples bearing on this issue of the role of sensation in consumer choice. There are, for example, issues dealing with the various modalities—whether information conveyed via the eye or the ear is more likely to be received. This is also the interesting issue of across-modality sensation, synesthesia, whereby characteristics in one modality map into others. For example, Stefflre (1968) has pointed out possibilities of mapping the taste and aroma of coffee or scotch whisky into packaging whose shape, colors, and design will communicate these taste characteristics via eye and ear. The recent trend that is most relevant here is the great leap forward in multidimensional scaling, the general contours of which can be found in Shepard, Romney, and Nerlove (1972), with its special relevance to the consumer area more explicitly treated in Green and Carmone (1970).

Selective Perception. Of the many energies in the universe, our own limits and habits preserve us from exposure to all but a relative few. But even among those energies falling on our appropriate sensors, we effectively perceive only a small portion. One can perform an informal experiment to experience this point by looking at one's environment, then closing one's eyes and trying to answer detailed questions about the scene just viewed; one finds oneself unable to answer many questions about the scene that one would have no difficulty answering had they been posed in advance. What determines the subset of the information reaching our appropriate sensors that gets effectively perceived? Information on selective perception is found in many of the volumes on cognition, attention, and sensation cited earlier. We shall attempt here our own summary of the general strategies that a person employs in selecting from the information to which he or she is exposed. We need not belabor the relevance to consumer choice of this issue of what is singled out for perception among all the information to which the consumer is exposed.

To deal with sensory overload, we use at least seven strategies that result in our perceiving a subset of all the information that reaches our receptors. One such strategy is lumping or chunking. Faced with too many trees and too many waves to grasp effectively, we tend to refocus to a larger grain size, so that we see a forest and an ocean rather than trees and waves. A second strategy is to grasp more through rapid shifts in perception, alternating between one and another part of the scene. A third strategy is temporary storage, such as in short-term memory, allowing us to put part of the present information into some kind of push-down list for at least a few moments so that we can deal with the information in what we hope is a less hectic future moment. A fourth strategy is to distribute our attention less sharply but more broadly, or alternating between sharp and broad attention, such as when we shift from a sharp attention on the foveal image to a broader, less acute perception of the total retinal image. Fifth, there may be some possibility of parallel processing that allows us to attend simultaneously to materials in two different modalities, such as through audition and vision. A sixth strategy assumes that perception is not a zero-sum game; rather we can draw some cognitive capacity from other activities at moments of need and concentrate it more completely on perception of the current sensory information, such as in an emergency when we may withhold thought for a moment from what we shall do next and concentrate all our cognitive resources on listening for new information from the environment. Finally, we may exercise some kind of selectivity, effectively perceiving some aspects of the current sensory information while ignoring others.

Each of these seven strategies deserves full treatment in its own right, but here we shall examine further only the last, selectivity. Perceptual selectivity is exercised on a number of bases, each of which has implications for designing communications to convey information to consumers so that they will maximize the probability that the critical information will be selectively perceived. We shall describe seven bases of selectivity, itself only one of seven modes of coping with sensory overload. Stimulus intensity is one determinant of perceptual selectivity, in that we are more likely to notice loud noises than soft ones and bright lights more than dim ones. Past reinforcement is a second determinant; that is, a person can be made to notice some aspects of the environment rather than others by prior training that associates noticing these aspects with rewards. Dimensional dominance or prepotency is a third determinant; for example, there are interesting individual differences and developmental trends as regards noticing the color versus the form of physical objects.

Other determinants of perceptual selectivity are more in the person than in the stimulus, but these internal states themselves are amenable to influence. The person's transient need states constitute a fourth determinant, in that people are more likely to notice aspects of their environment that are relevant to the satisfaction of their current needs. A fifth factor is the person's persisting values; people tend to notice aspects of the environment that are relevant to those aspects of the world they evaluate highly. A sixth factor is the person's present expectation (which goes under a variety of other names such as set, familiarity, context, or availability), such that the person tends to notice in the environment what he or she expects to find there. A seventh determinant—in some ways peculiarly opposed to the sixth—is distinctiveness (or novelty or unpredictability), such that the person tends to notice the incongruous or surprising aspects of the environment.

We have here merely named the seven sons of a seventh son. Those who wish to travel far through consumer choice should visit the whole galaxy and stay awhile with each of these sons. Each is highly suggestive regarding effective communication to the consumer.

Comprehension of What Is Perceived

Given that the message is adequately perceived in the second step in information processing (so that, for example, it can on a subsequent occasion be accurately identified), in the next step it must be meaningfully comprehended in order to have further impact. For one to grasp the import of some message dealing with consumer behavior, one must go beyond mere perception and effectively encode the information in one's meaning system so that one can grasp its import. Involved here are constructs such as abstraction and encoding and meaning systems.

Abstraction. From the beginning of Western thought in the Hellenic world, philosophers have struggled with the process of abstraction and its yield of universal concepts. How do we abstract from the specific experiences that make up our perceptions the general classes that constitute the categories to which we assimilate our subsequent specific experience, while at the same time adjusting these preformed mental categories to accommodate the new experience? Piaget (1952) has dealt with the ontogeny of the process, and anthropologists such as Lévi-Strauss (1963) and Colby (1975) have dealt with it in cross-cultural perspective. In the laboratory, the work has been pursued under such rubrics as concept acquisition, concept formation, and probability learning. Recent work in this area is summarized in Neimark and Santa (1975), and a more digestible review is found in Johnson (1972).

Encoding. The issue of comprehension obviously is intricately related to language. Indeed, it had until very recently been orthodox to assume that we could understand or comprehend what we perceived only to the extent that we could linguistically encode it. Lately there has been more recognition that encoding can also take place in imagery (Pollio, 1974). Hence, much of the research in psycholinguistics (see reviews in Blumenthal, 1970; Deese, 1970; and Slobin, 1971) is relevant to this issue of comprehension, especially work under such rubrics as "meaning" and "language and cognition." Recent work on the theory of encoding into language, from the point of view of both cognitive simulation and artificial intelligence, is available in Schank and Colby (1973).

Since, in the previous era of psychology when behaviorism and psychoanalytic theory were in the ascendance, it was customary to equate consciousness and language, we should make it explicit here that current wisdom makes comprehension much broader than consciousness. We may well be effectively encoding in the language system, and especially in the imagery systems, material that has not reached the conscious level. Those who feel that the unexamined life is not worth living must be driven to believe that we would all be better off dead, since current theorizing (Bem, 1970) stresses how little of our own reactions come to our conscious attention, unless under explicit pressure. If information about the nutritional value of food were communicated to consumers, it is likely that they would take in a considerable amount of this information and could be shown subsequently to have acted on the basis of it without even being aware of or able to report the basis for their actions.

Agreement with What Is Comprehended

Even when their copy research shows that their messages are being correctly understood, public health advocates of nutritional or safety practices, as well as advertisers and their clients extolling the virtues of a product, must not, of course, assume that they are having the desired impact on the consumer. It must be ascertained further whether the recipients agree with what they have comprehended. A variety of constructs are involved in this fourth step, although here we shall mention only a few that fall under the rubrics of credibility and attitude change.

Credibility. Given that it is adequately understood, the believability of information derives from many aspects of the communication. For example, the perceived source of the message adds to its acceptance to the extent that this person is recognized as expert and trustworthy. To a lesser extent, the source's perceived attractiveness and power also contribute to believability. The contents of the message, including the type of appeal used, the structure, the argument, the style, etc., all have their impact. Even the media through which the message is communicated affects the elicitation of agreement, since the different media have different credibility ratings for their receivers. Again, credulity varies with such characteristics of the receiver as age, sex, personality, and ability. This literature has been analyzed by McGuire (1968a, 1969) in general terms and with application to this area of consumer choice (McGuire, in press).

Attitude Change. The area of attitude change is the largest single body of research in social psychology, with over 5 percent of the 25,000 articles and books summarized each year in the *Psychological Abstracts* being devoted to this topic, even when a strict criterion of relevance is used. Useful summaries of the literature appear in the works by McGuire just cited. In addition, three detailed summaries of the theoretical and empirical research of attitude change are found in Kiesler, Collins, and Miller (1969), Triandis (1971), and Fishbein and Ajzen (1975). Four briefer volumes that stress possible applications include Zimbardo and Ebbesen (1969), Bem (1970), Mehrabian (1970), and Miller and Burgoon (1973). A précis of the most recent material can be found in Kiesler and Munson (1975).

Since our own expertise is identified with the area of attitude change, cutting out a few segments for discussion here leaves us in an emotional state more like the true mother than like Solomon. We can bear to make only a couple of passing remarks. First, we have the impression that practitioners in the consumer area view people as constituting a more hostile audience than is the case. The people to whom one wants to transmit some message urging a change in eating habits, whether in behalf of their improved health or the improved health of one's firm, are frequently viewed as set in their ways, suspicious of one's purposes, and predisposed to reject what is said. On the contrary, research suggests that one's audience is generally favorably predisposed to accept what one has to say, although somewhat uninterested in paying much attention to it and a bit opaque about seeing its implications for their own decisions as consumers. Hence, the source often wastes time, space, and effort to convince an audience that is already favorably predisposed, while neglecting attention-holding devices and the need to make clear the implications of the arguments for the consumer's behavior. For example, if one wants to induce the audience to move toward a diet lower in sugar and fat, it is probably rather wasteful using time to stress the dangers of obesity and tooth decay (which, indeed, the audience may already fear excessively). It would be better to spend the communication time making clear what foods or preparation method should be avoided and how comparable gratifications can be obtained through alternate diets.

A final point that we shall mention in connection with the agreement step in persuasion is that even in those cases where inducing the person to agree with what has been comprehended presents an appreciable problem, communicators tend to exaggerate the importance of this step in mediating the persuasive impact of the message on the consumer's behavior. To illustrate this point by an example taken once again from the nutritional area, if for proprietary or public health reasons one wishes to induce consumers to improve the nutritional quality of their eating habits, the issue may arise of using negative appeals such as inducing fear of heart attacks if they continue their current diet. Concentrating exclusively on this step of inducing acceptance of the information, it may seem appropriate to use a very high threat appeal to instill the fear of God in the consumer with regard to his or her current diet. However, it is quite possible that these high-fear appeals interfere with reception and comprehension of the message, so that the message impact suffers more through decreasing the information processing via the preceding steps than it adds through enhancing acceptance (McGuire, in press).

Retention of What Is Accepted

The firth step in information processing is retention of that portion of the comprehended information that the person accepts as valid. Campaigns mounted to inform or convince the consumer usually have as their target not some immediate impact but rather a purchasing decision to be made some time subsequent or on a continuing basis. Perhaps, in rare cases, an immediate impact is sought, such as when a public health spot is presented on the late late show to induce the midnight snacker to cut a smaller piece of cheesecake, or when a beer commercial induces the viewer to put another six-pack in the refrigerator. However, these are exceptional cases, and the cost of advertising campaigns can usually be justified only insofar as there is a continuing impact on purchasing behavior.

It becomes appropriate to ask how much a persuasive message, even after it is accepted, will continue to be influential on those later occasions when the consumer has to make purchasing decisions. The study of memory, retention, forgetting, etc., is almost as old and frequent within psychology as the topic of sensation, which, as we marveled earlier, has continued to interest so many researchers. We are now almost at the centennial of Ebbinghaus' *Gedächtnis,* and yet the practitioners, at least, show no signs of being bored to this day.

Research in the memory area is sufficiently heavy to merit treatment in the *Annual Review of Psychology* in alternate years, most recently by Postman (1975). An intermediate way of keeping up with the literature, between the detail of the journal articles and the compression of these annual reviews, is to follow the series of volumes called *Psychology of Learning and Motivation,* brought out every two years or so by Academic Press. Murdock (1974) provides an up-to-date and solid summary of the state of the art. Using once again a Draconic selectivity such as we have employed earlier, we shall discuss here only two topics from this literature: forgetting and delayed processing. The first deals with retention over time of what was initially comprehended, and the second deals with further processing of the initially comprehended material as time passes. Even after narrowing ourselves down to these two topics, we shall have to be highly selective within them.

Forgetting. Recent work on forgetting has shown the importance of distinguishing between a short-term, active memory, which is measured in seconds or fractions of seconds, and long-term memory storage (Deutsch and Deutsch, 1975). Our division into steps of what is actually a continuous information processing, like any other analysis, must draw lines somewhat arbitrarily. In our division, when we are dealing with the reception step, we group what is usually called "short-term memory" with perception. We are concerned here with longer-term memory storage, currently called (somewhat inadequately) "semantic memory."

Commonsense observation and formal experimentation agree that forgetting is a general phenomenon; that is, material stored in memory tends to decay or become inaccessible as time passes (leaving aside somewhat exotic "reminiscence" phenomena where apparent recall might grow for a time after active rehearsal ceases). The basic nature of forgetting has always been controversial, the issue being whether it is passive decay or occurs only because of retroactive inhibition, that is, the learning of some kind of interfering material in the interim. Whether it accounts for all of forgetting, interference is evidently a major contributor to decreasing retention over time, a consideration that has drastic and discouraging implications for communicators who would make any lasting change in consumer behavior. Material about the nutritional qualities of food or the special qualities of one's product must decay rather rapidly considering the similar materials likely to be communicated about similar products, thus constituting optimal conditions for retroactive inhibitions. As the amount of nutritional information communicated about products continues to grow (whether by consumer demand, government policy, or distributor's or processor's initiative), this problem becomes increasingly serious.

Without pretending that there is one exactly describable forgetting function that fits all people, conditions, and material, we do feel that it is a reasonable summary of the findings to say that in general the forgetting curve is negatively accelerated; that is, most decay of memory occurs soon after learning, with successively less in absolute terms being forgotten during successive equal time intervals. Forgetting seems to approach its asymptote at an exponentially, negatively accelerated rate; also, the asymptote may be greater than zero, so that even after an indefinitely long period of time, there may still be some small residual recall. Many conditions affect the rate of forgetting, including individual and group differences in memory capacity, the type of material, the way in which the original learning took place, and the conditions of the postlearning interval. Many of these relationships have implications for how information can be communicated to consumers with more lasting effects; the reader is referred to the sources on cognition and learning mentioned earlier, with somewhat more focused recent reviews to be found in Norman (1970), Greeno and Bjork (1973), Kausler (1974), and Gregg (1974).

A caution that must be kept in mind by those wishing to apply these findings about "long-term" memory to consumer information programs is that it may be possible to generalize many of the findings only to the first few hours after learning. The longer periods that would particularly interest us with respect to consumer behavior are dealt with in other literatures dealing with such rubrics as permanent semantic storage systems and concept formation, which we shall discuss later. Also, the retention studies have, for the most part, concentrated on linguistically encoded material. It may well be that we have a second storage system involving imagery material. In these days when so much of the information presented to consumers comes via television and therefore involves pictorial as well as verbal messages, the information is probably encoded both semantically and in imagery.

Delayed Processing. There is much evidence that in the period subsequent to the initial exposure to the information, considerable change occurs in cognitive content, not only through forgetting and the learning of new material but also by constant reprocessing of the material already in memory storage. We are all aware that people mull over and rethink the past with some frequency, resulting in both mental anguish and better subsequent coping. This reprocessing also goes on at the unconscious level and, indeed, even during sleep, as we know from the confusion states that result from sleep deprivation. This is perhaps particularly the case when people are wakened during the rapid eye movement periods that are thought to be associated with dreaming, a process that seems important in cognitive recoding.

Elsewhere, we have reviewed the evidence that induced attitude change tends to be more persistent than the retention in memory of the informational content that may initially have produced it (McGuire, 1969). In contrast to the monotonically declining memory curves for content, there is a prevalence of delayed-action effects as regards the persuasive impact of communications. A number of alternative mechanisms seem able to produce the gradually increasing persuasive impact during a period of hours or days after the persuasive communication has been received. One of these mechanisms, the "sleeper effect" or "discounting-cue" explanation, has been increasingly questioned in recent analyses (Capon and Hulbert, 1973; Gillig and Greenwald, 1974). It is not surprising that the postexposure decay of memory for content and the postexposure persistence of induced attitude change should show different temporal decay curves, considering that the relationship between initial learning and initial attitude change is only moderate (Eagly, 1974; Greenwald, 1968; Watts and McGuire, 1964).

Not only are comprehension and acceptance of communication content rather independent as regards both their initial relationship and their temporal decay curves, but also the effect of given independent variables on learning scores differ somewhat from their effect on attitude change. This relative independence suggests several caveats to copy researchers testing the relevant efficacy of various messages for communicating information to consumers or otherwise influencing them. First, evaluations of the copy on the basis of its effectiveness for producing learning may give only a noisy indication of its relative effectiveness in producing attitude change (and an even noisier indication of its ultimate impact on consumer behavior). Second, the relative effectiveness of different copy formats in terms of their immediate attitude-change effects may be different from their relative long-term effectiveness. Copy testing is usually done in terms of immediate impact, while the intended payoff typically comes in the long term, so that misleading interpretations can be made in copy selection and adjustments if we do not take into account the differential decay rates.

We have pointed out elsewhere (McGuire, 1960) that communications do have remote ramifications on other parts of the belief system, but typically with a spatial and temporal inertia. For example, communications to consumers about a whole class of products would tend to filter down to specific types of products within the class or to specific brands only after the passage of a certain amount of time; the impact might also spread to related classes of products, but again only after a period of time had passed for subsequent cognitive processing. Hence, in determining at what level of generality to communicate to the consumer, there must be a trade-off between gradual and low-level effects over a wide range of products and a more sizable immediate effect on the specific product on which we might concentrate. An implication of this research on remote cognitive implications is that the more general communication, while it may have little immediate impact on specific products, does tend to spread to them as time passes. This work on remote cognitive impact of communications has been reviewed in detail by Wyer (1974).

Information Search and Retrieval

Given that the information intended for consumers has reached them and been retained in their cognitive systems, we now deal with the sixth step in information processing—the active search or passive emergence of this information so that it has some impact on their decision at a subsequent critical occasion. To indicate current psychological knowledge on these issues, we shall touch on recent work dealing with the structure of the cognitive storage systems and with the search strategies used to retrieve information from such systems.

Structure of Cognitive Storage Systems. To understand how past information is brought to bear on a current decision, it is obviously important to know how this past information is stored in the memory system. Much ingenious work has been done in recent years on how the memory system is structured or organized and how information in it is tagged for retrieval. The cutting edge of this research can be found in several volumes of collected contributions, including Bower (1972), Tulving and Donaldson (1972), and Melton and Martin (1972). Those who are interested less in traveling with the first wave than in finding a more royal road to this knowledge might prefer the briefer and better digested presentations in Norman (1969) and Posner (1973).

The fact that we have highly organized memory systems which classify our information in given domains is indicated not only by the psychological research just cited but also by anthropological analyses showing that people in preliterate societies have very complex pictures of the world in various domains such as kinship, aesthetics, and ethical systems. For example, the ethnobotany of an apparently simple society may be very different from the scientific classification used in Western society, but may turn out to be equally elegant and adaptive (Berlin, Breedlove, and Raven, 1974; Colby, 1975). The results and the methods of psychological and anthropological structural analyses offer valuable lessons to those concerned with consumer information processing and consumer behavior. It is our observation that people working in the consumer area have very naive concepts and little curiosity about how the person organizes the cognitive space in which experience with and communications about products are stored and from which considerations affecting purchasing choices are drawn. The "motivation research" fad of a decade or two ago raised some questions about this topic (or at least proposed some a priori answers to it) but yielded only Freudian-derived generalities about the deeper meaning of certain products or the unconscious gratifications involved in purchasing them. Psychological and anthropological research suggest appropriate methods for defining the organization and contents of the cognitive space surrounding various products and their use; more understanding of this topic would, we believe, allow consumer researchers to reformulate in a much more sophisticated and useful manner the questions that they are currently asking about getting information to consumers.

Search Strategies. To understand the retrieval process we need to know, besides how the storage system is organized and the information in it tagged, how individuals go about searching memory storage to aid their decision making in the consumer area. The relevant psychological research is found under such rubrics as concept identification, heuristics, problem solving, and search strategies. Besides the general works listed earlier, recent volumes that give particular mention to this topic include Nilsson (1971), Newell and Simon (1972), and Wickelgren (1974). As with other aspects of information processing, these search procedures are not necessarily conscious and deliberate; we are interested in uniformities in search patterns that can be inferred from behaviors, whether or not the consumer is conscious of and able to report what information is brought to bear or how it was retrieved.

The topic of search tactics that retrieve from memory information bearing on choices deals with what is sometimes called "divergent thinking," in keeping with Guilford's (1967) analysis of the structure of intellect. We are concerned here with the processes that generate response options or multiple considerations among which the consumer chooses in arriving at a decision. We stress this aspect of human thought because it tends to be neglected in the currently fashionable thinking in the administrative, management, and organizational sciences. Research in these sciences is currently overly preoccupied with a subsequent stage in information processing, namely, decision making. The research on decision making (to which we turn in the next section) focuses on the issue of how, given the alternatives or options, one chooses among them. Neglected in these management sciences with which most workers in the consumer area are identified is the issue of how these multiple considerations and response options are derived.

The consumer's search strategy will, to some extent, be tailored to the type of structure in which cognitions are stored; thus, the previous issue and the current one are intertwined. Depending on whether the cognitive domain surrounding the consumer product is organized into a tree diagram, a matrix, push-down lists, or whatever, we can expect differences in the type of search strategies that the person will and should use to bring this informational domain to bear on a given purchasing choice. Wickelgren (1974) suggests seven possible search strategies that can be utilized in problem solving of the type often involved in consumer purchases, thus providing suggestive leads to the student of consumer behavior, even though a couple of the proposed strategies are more concerned with the subsequent selection among options than with the initial generation of them, and even though he offers them prescriptively rather than descriptively. At this moment in history, however, it is our feeling that the student of consumer behavior would do better to invest energy in describing the organization of memory than in examining the strategies used to retrieve from it. Once the organization is made clear, one can meaningfully deal with such issues as whether search strategies go deeply or broadly over a structure, whether there are parallel searches in different memory systems, and how the person monitors the search to determine whether it is getting close, "hot," "cold," etc.

Deciding among the Available Options

The previous section was devoted to discussing how the information to which the consumer had previously been exposed and had encoded is, at the time when a purchasing decision must be made, brought to bear on that choice. Assuming that more than one consideration must be taken into account because of what has been retrieved from the cognitive system and of what the consumer's current environment presents, the consumer must put it all together by deciding which considerations will be taken into account and how the information will be weighted and integrated so as to yield a decision regarding whether to purchase or which product to purchase. As illustrative research issues in this area, we shall consider here choice strategies and information integration. More detailed discussion of this area can be found in the Lancaster and Hansen chapters in the final volume of this project (Ferber, 1976).

Choice Strategies. The research relevant to the topic of choice strategies can be found under such rubrics as judgmental processes and decision making. Useful reviews of the topic on a somewhat simple level can be found in Lee (1971) and at a more demanding and penetrating level in Rapoport and Wallsten (1972) and Slovic and Lichtenstein (1971).

The consumer is typically operating in a situation of uncertainty where information is lacking or ambiguous for many dimensions, and it is far from clear what optimal weightings need to be given to the various considerations. The work of Tversky and Kahneman (1974) on the heuristics used in thinking under conditions of uncertainty and the biases in judgment that result is particularly suggestive. They present evidence that when forced to make a choice in a situation involving uncertainty, people tend to use heuristics that are highly economical and reasonably effective but introduce systematic errors under certain conditions. For example, when having to make a decision on which of several classes a product belongs to, people tend to choose the class whose characteristics are most embodied in the product without taking into account the relative class frequencies. People's judgments introduce systematic biases because they tend to select the most available evidence rather than to sample the evidence more representatively, and because they start by assuming an initial anchoring value and adjusting from this (possibly biased) anchor on the basis of further information. For an area of research characterized by abstruse and arcane issues, the Tversky and Kahneman (1974) paper offers a high yield per page of ideas regarding consumer choice, although the separate decision-making heuristics that they report cry for integration into a broader theoretical picture.

Another relatively simple idea suggested by the very technical body of decision-making research is that the person, having to choose among items on the basis of a number of characteristics, may choose by using an "elimination-by-aspects" strategy. As an example, consider the case where a consumer must decide among competing brands by taking into account nutritional value, taste, convenience of preparation, and price. The more conventional matrix decision model has the consumer in effect weighting each of these four dimensions to reflect its personal importance to him or her, and then estimating a scale value on each of the four dimensions for each of the brands under consideration. Each brand then obtains a choice score equal to the sum-of-products of dimensional importance times the scale value, which sum-of-products scores determine the consumer purchasing choice among brands.

The alternative "one-dimension-at-a-time" model depicts the consumer as making the choice by a considerably easier process. Among the four dimensions, the consumer first considers the one that he or she judges most important (for example, price) and eliminates the one or more brands that score quite poorly on this dimension; then he or she considers the next most important (for example, nutritional value), and among the remaining brands eliminates the one or more that fail to meet a sufficing criterion on this dimension, etc., until only one brand remains. This presents the consumer with a much simpler (presumably unconscious) arithmetic than does the matrix, sum-of-products model, and typically yields the same result. However, under certain circumstances the simpler procedure is not as adaptive to the consumer's needs, such as when certain brands that were eliminated on an earlier dimension would have won out in the long run if they had remained in contention because they would have scored very highly on subsequent dimensions.

Besides the relevance to consumer decision making of the descriptive approaches just mentioned, the prescriptive approaches also offer contributions to this area. Work by Dawes (1971) on how decision making by judges involved in personnel selection can be improved by various boot-strapping techniques is also relevant for improving consumer's judgments of which products or brands to buy. A program of consumer education should take into account the biases introduced by the normally adaptive heuristics used in thinking under uncertainty, such as we discussed earlier, and the boot-strapping technique suggested by Dawes. The methods are of a complexity and type that would more appropriately be introduced in the classroom, such as in elementary and high school courses on consumer behavior or in adult education courses. With educator ingenuity, it may be that some of these improvements could be taught through magazine articles or pamphlets made available to citizens. However, it does not seem likely that education could be achieved by point-of-purchase posters or addenda to advertisements.

Information Integration. How a person puts together the various pieces of retrieved and externally presented information about each brand in arriving at a choice among them is an area of study to which much can be contributed by the current work on information integration (N. H. Anderson, 1974a; Rosenberg, 1968). Various alternative models, often of considerable elegance, that have been described and tested are suggestive of how consumers arrive at decisions. Of interest here are such questions as how the different pieces of information are weighted, how overlap between them is handled, and whether the items of information are simply summated or averaged. This last issue can be critical, such as in a situation where the consumer knows three very good things about a product and then learns a fourth thing that is only moderately good. If the person uses an additive rule of information integration, this new information of a moderately good product characteristic would increase the perceived attractiveness of the brand; but if the person is using an averaging rule of information integration, the new information of an only moderately good characteristic would decrease the brand's attractiveness. Current research suggests that an averaging rule is used (N. H. Anderson, 1974b), although the issue remains somewhat in doubt (Fishbein and Ajzen, 1975).

Another question of considerable relevance to consumer decision making concerns what we might call "mental arithmetic." On this topic, unlike the previous ones we have considered, current psychological research offers us very little established knowledge that is waiting to be applied to consumer behavior. In this case, the issue is an important one for understanding and improving consumer behavior, but it is for the consumer area to stimulate research in basic psychology to a higher level than has thus far been reached. We are concerned here with issues such as how the consumer, faced with the problems of choosing among different brands on the basis of their varying prices for different-sized packages, carries out the necessary mental computations. Comparable tasks arise when the consumer must decide the extent of the economy of scale offered by purchasing the economy, jumbo size. The consumer's task in this regard has recently been somewhat eased by unit pricing and the growing ubiquity of the hand calculator, but the need still often arises. In these difficult computational situations, people are quite likely to use simplifying heuristics such as rounding off to the nearest ten, using more familiar rather than the exact divisors, or using "ball-park" summation approximations, because there is a gigantic difference between how our hand-held calculators have been wired for the sole purpose of carrying out precise mathematical computations like the idiot-savants that they are, and the way the wiring of our brain evolved not only to carry out these computational tasks (in a rough-and-ready way) but also to cope with vast varieties of other problems.

Cross-cultural work on differences in thought patterns arising in different human environments, as summarized by Cole and Scribner (1974), are suggestive regarding how such investigations should be done and about what they might yield in this specific area of the consumer's approximate arithmetic. As we learn more about these heuristics, we shall know better how to improve consumer education in this area. It is interesting to note that after living through the old math and the new math, there now seems to be emerging on the educational scene a new, new math where arithmetic is being taught in a way that encourages the use of these simplifying approximations (for example, in the new public television "Count Us In" educational program prescribing such rough-and-ready, easy math). It should be noted that as we gain more insight into the use of this approximate arithmetic, we shall increase the potential for "mischievous" pricing and sizing practices that capitalize on the characteristic errors introduced by these approximations by setting these numbers at levels which maximize decisions in favor of a given brand.

Acting on the Basis of the Decision

One of the many scandals of social psychology is the low correlation between attitudes and actions. Individual differences in attitudes toward objects are surprisingly poor in predicting individual differences in overt behavior toward those objects, and variables that relate in a given way to attitude change often relate quite differently to the relevant behavioral change. Hence, it is appropriate to continue our analysis of information processing beyond the previous step of decision making and determine the extent to which this choice of action is actually carried out. It should be noted, however, that the scandal is more pervasive than this issue of the relationship between the seventh step of decision making (for example, buying intention) and the eighth step of actual purchasing action. Similar questions could have been asked about each of the successive steps considered previously. We already adverted to findings that the amount of comprehension of communication content and the amount of attitude change induced by it are not closely related. One would expect an even noisier relationship between more distant steps, such as between the comprehension and the action steps.

Although this scandal is neither subtle nor hidden, it needs to be brought emphatically to the attention of those in the consumer behavior area. Those who make their living in marketing are often concerned with evaluating alternative packaging or doing copy research to test the relative efficacy of different advertisements whose payoff presumably entails increasing the sales of the product. However, these evaluation studies often test effectiveness in terms of a step far back in the information-processing chain. For example, copy or packaging is often evaluated in terms of a perceptual criterion (such as amount of looking or amount of recognition), or in terms of recall or of changed attitude toward the product. It must be emphasized that the further back in the information-processing chain we go from actual purchasing, the poorer these criteria predict the payoff action.

Those interested in consumer education should likewise realize that if they rely on current marketing evaluation practices, they will be testing techniques for conveying information about the nutritional value of foods by using comprehension tests and the like, which bear a noisy relationship to effectiveness in terms of the ultimate behavioral target. They should also realize that not only do differences between alternative techniques tend to disappear as we go from an earlier step to later ones, but relationships are sometimes reversed, so that the approach which seems better in terms of comprehension might be less good in terms of attitude change. McGuire (in press) discusses the psychodynamics in such situations. As a gesture toward doing justice here to this demoralizing but important topic, we shall first index the literature on attitude-action relationships and then examine the actual versus the conscious bases of action.

Attitude-Action Relationships. There is an extensive literature on the question of attitude-action relationships that has grown rapidly of late. We have recently prepared an analytic review on the topic (McGuire, 1975). There are three recent collections of readings, each pulling together a variety of studies (somewhat overlapping) from among the scattered journal articles on this topic (Deutscher, 1973; Liska, 1974a; Thomas, 1971). The Deutscher volume is particularly rich in giving interpretive material, although the other two volumes also offer some original editorial commentary. Analytic reviews of the attitude-behavior relationship are available in Ehrlich (1969), Calder and Ross (1973), and Liska (1974b). Fishbein and Ajzen (1972) devote much of their long chapter on attitude change to this topic, as they do also in their more recent book (Fishbein and Ajzen, 1975). A somewhat pessimistic appraisal of the possibilities of predicting behavior from attitudes is found in Wicker (1969), while Fishbein (1973) offers a more optimistic view.

Having recently completed a long analytic review of this topic (McGuire, 1975), we shall not review the matter once again here. In the present context, the communicator seeking to improve the nutritional value of the public's diet should develop persuasive material that maximizes the likelihood of evoking each of the steps in information processing from exposure, reception, comprehension, etc., down to the ultimate step of action. All too often those seeking to communicate effectively become preoccupied with just one or two of the eight steps (for example, concentrating simply on attention getting to ensure reception, or on clarity to maximize comprehension, etc., or on believability to maximize acceptance) and design communications to maximize that step to the neglect of other steps and even at the cost of introducing components whose unintended side effects decrease ultimate impact by interfering with the other steps in information processing (McGuire, 1975, in press). Rather than this simplistic thinking, the communicator should design the communications with components that maximize effective transmission through each of the necessary steps of information processing and that interfere with other steps as little as possible.

Conscious and Unconscious Bases of Action. We have mentioned several times in this discussion of the information-processing steps that the person is often unconscious of what he or she is doing and when explicitly questioned is unable to give an adequate explanation of how the information was handled or the decision reached. At other times, the person can report how the decision was arrived at, but analytic techniques allow us to determine that in actuality the processing that the person describes (presumably in good conscience) was not actually employed (Hammond et al., in press).

Even people in highly rational enterprises who make decisions of great personal importance to them (such as investment counselors advising a client on the appropriate makeup of a stock portfolio or university faculty members choosing which graduate students to admit) are often unaware of the bases of their own decisions or, still worse, think that they use bases for deciding which actually they do not employ. This happens even where the decision making occurs frequently, with considerable opportunity for feedback. It seems likely that consumers are still less aware of the true bases for their purchasing actions, even when they think that they know the reasons for their choice, since consumers are less likely on the average than the professionals mentioned above to place a high evaluation on rationality, to have so explicit a set of bases for choosing, or to have such opportunities for correcting errors through quantitative and continuing feedback. Those interested in the bases of consumer behavior should be familiar with this literature in order to determine how one can check the extent to which one can take at face value the consumers' self-reports of bases for decision, and how one can test alternative hypotheses about the bases of choice.

Conclusions Regarding Human Information Processing

We have traced the internal processing of information from its initial presentation through eight steps culminating in the ultimate purchasing (or nonpurchasing) action. We discussed each of the eight steps by citing summaries of current psychological research and sketching some illustrative examples of what the area may offer to those interested in consumer behavior. We typically discussed the examples in terms of a public service agency wishing to convey usable information to the consumer regarding the nutritional value of food. In the space available, we have obviously had to be very selective in presenting these examples. In compensation, for those interested in pursuing each of the topics further, we provided a detailed guide to current literature, citing where possible both briefer and more extended discussions of the topic. We also included elementary, well-digested discussions as well as technical current reviews of the still-contested issues at the cutting edge of the field. Our treatment of information as a successive-step routine has neglected a consideration of cognitive executive functions that would admit more flexible control into the system.

This review of the directive, information-processing aspect of human personality must be supplemented by a review of the dynamic aspects of personality, that is, the motivational, driving aspects of the person that energize this information processing and determine its instigations, continuations, and terminations. The next major section of this paper touches on these dynamic aspects.

Dynamic Aspects of Personality: The Motivational Factors behind Consumer Decisions

Having considered the directive components of personality that channel information processing, we turn here to the dynamic aspects of personality which motivate that processing. Thus, our discussion of the "hows" of the consumers' handling of information that leads to their purchases is followed by a discussion of the "whys" behind this processing. What are the motivational aspects of human personality that energize or drive the individual, initiating each of these information-processing steps, continuing them in one or another direction, and finally terminating the process?

Recent Trends in Motivational Theory

The 1970s find psychological research on the directive, information-processing aspects of personality in a much more flourishing state than research on the dynamic, motivational aspects. The latter area has not been completely neglected; it is unthinkable that so important an aspect of human personality would not have its students. However, nothing has happened recently in the motivational field of a magnitude comparable to the "cognitive-revolution," which during the 1960s replaced behaviorism and S-R reinforcement theory as the paradigmatic guiding orientation of Establishment psychology with the new notion of the human as an information-processing machine and a heavy leaning on the computer as analogue. At most, we might say that the psychoanalytic and behavioristic reinforcement models of human motivation that have dominated psychological thinking about the driving aspect of human personality ever since the first quarter of this century have been somewhat augmented by humanistic theories of personality and by the spillover of cognitive theory from the dynamic to the directive aspects of drives.

Current Thinking on Human Motivation. Of the writing of books—and especially of articles—on human motivation, there is no end. Those wishing to know the current state of psychological theorizing about motivation can find it in recent volumes by Weiner (1972, 1974) and Madsen (1974) or in briefer, if slightly less trendy, form in Cofer (1972). In addition, the *Annual Review of Psychology* in alternate years contains review chapters on basic drives (most recently in the 1973 volume) and on derived drives (most recently in 1974). Each year a new volume of the *Nebraska Symposium on Motivation* is devoted to recent advances in this area, the most recent volume (the 21st in the series) having been edited by Cole and Dienstbier (1974).

The two most notable recent trends in motivational theory are the increasing emphases on humanistic and on cognitive orientations. Examples of the humanistic approach are Maslow's (1970) hierarchical theory of human motivation, which stresses how, on the basis of fundamental biological needs, cognitive, aesthetic, and self-actualization needs are built. More influential still is Erikson's (1963) extension of the biologically oriented Freudian system of psychosexual development into later stages of the life span, when more mature human needs and forces evolve. In general, these approaches stress the person's ego-growth and self-actualizing and integrative needs. Those concerned with consumer behavior might wonder whether such profundities about the search for total ego integration has much relevance to the consumer's choice among alternative brands of tuna fish. However, before we dismiss them as irrelevant to the present issues, we should entertain the possibility that in some purchasing domains (and not only for the big-ticket items), the consumer is driven by ego needs to form a favorable self-image as well as by biological or economic necessities.

In regard to the other recent trend, the growing stress on cognitive aspects of motivation, we must admit that this is almost a contradiction in terms considering the classical division in Western thought between the cognitive, the affective, and the conative (or perhaps we can call them knowing, feeling, and acting). But interest in the cognitive area has been so heavy that it has overflowed into the affective, so that we now have "cognitive" components of motivation. Dember (1974) reviews this cognitive revolution in motivation theory, and the Weiner (1972, 1974) and Madsen (1974) volumes heavily emphasize these cognitive aspects of motivation, as does Zimbardo (1969).

With regard to current thinking on motivation, the reader familiar with psychoanalytic theory and behavioristic or stimulus-response reinforcement theory—knowledge of which has diffused widely among the educated laity since mid century—will have a fairly good grasp of the current wisdom. It remains for us here to call attention to the new thinking on the topic that stresses the cognitive and humanistic aspects of motivation. Our discussion will be truncated since we have recently published a review (McGuire, 1974) that outlines current thinking about human motivation and applies it specifically to the area of communication gratification (that is, how the motivational complexities of persons help to explain why so much of their time is spent in mass media consumption). With a little imagination, it is easy enough to reapply this analysis to the area of consumer behavior. We shall discuss briefly some classifications of human motives, and then discuss in more detail eight cognitive motives and eight affective motives that have lately received considerable research attention.

Classifications of Human Motives. The vastness of our linguistic wealth in describing human motivation is intimidating. Allport and Odbert (1936), working through an unabridged English dictionary, found in the neighborhood of 18,000 words that described personality trait names. Although not all these words were motivational in their connotation, a great proportion were, and they need additional grouping and organization before the dimensions of motivational space can be meaningfully grasped. Probably the most frequently used system of human motivation is the one worked out by Murray et al. (1938), which lists 20 basic psychological needs, including such well-known ones as achievement, affiliation, power, and abasement, and groups them into six classes. Maslow's (1970) hierarchical theory of human motivation provides a still more inclusive and structured list.

We also need to consider systematizations of domains not called "motives" but conceptually related to them, such as McDougall's (1923) list of instincts, Bridges' (1932) list of emotions, or lists of values such as those proposed by Allport, Vernon, and Lindzey (1951) or more recently by Rokeach (1973). Even more appropriately included are the various multidimensional personality systems, since the factors that are usually called personality traits can alternatively be thought of as motives. Systems such as those provided by Jung (1923), Cattell and Eber (1957), and Eysenck (1962) for measuring personality in multidimensional terms could equally well be called descriptions of the motivational makeup of the individual. Indeed, the Murray need system mentioned earlier has given rise to a number of commonly used personality inventories, including the Edwards (1959) Personal Preference Schedule, Jackson's (1967) Personality Research Form, and the Gough-Heilbrun (1965) adjective checklist.

A Contemporary System for Classifying Human Motives

In recognition of recent developments of motivational theory in both the cognitive and the humanistic direction, we outline here a classification system for human motives that emphasizes these two recent trends and identifies within a meaningful structure the currently growing points of the psychological research on motivation. Hence our basic division among the motives will be between the more recently stressed cognitive type and the more traditional affective type. The cognitive motives are those driving aspects of human personality that stress the person's need for being adaptively oriented toward the environment and for achieving a sense of meaning. The affective motives stress more the individual's need to reach satisfying feeling states and to attain emotional goals. We subdivide both cognitive and affective motives into those that stress the individual as striving to maintain equilibrium versus those that deal with the person's need for further growth (the latter being the type stressed by the humanistic movement).

Putting these two dichotomies (the cognitive–affective and the preservation–growth) into conjunction yields four classes of motives. We divide each of these classes on the basis of two further dichotomous dimensions. The third basis for division is whether the person's behavior is actively initiated or represents passive response to circumstances. The final, fourth dichotomy is based on whether the motives are directed toward achieving a new internal state or a new external relationship to the environment. These four dichotomies generate a matrix of 16 cells. In a recent chapter (McGuire, 1974), we considered at length 16 human motives, each fitting into one of the cells and each being the subject of considerable recent psychological research. This system of 16 motives is shown in Table 1.

Each of these 16 motives can be regarded as a partial view of the human personality, abstracting one aspect of the dynamic forces that drive us on, any one of them playing a relatively large role in determining our behavior in some areas and a relatively insignificant role in other areas. The individual researcher, typically preoccupied with one of these motivational forces, tends to stress its importance by choosing aspects of behavior in which it is a dominant drive, so that the researcher's discussion often sounds as if this is the only or the most important aspect of the human motivational system. When we are interested in studying some particular domain of human behavior, however, such as consumer decision making, it is wise to take a more eclectic view and consider how each of a wide range of human motives (such as the set mentioned here) affects the consumer behavior in question.

We should therefore consider each of the 16 motives in turn, sketching the fundamental concept of the person that it encapsulates, identifying its contemporary advocates and research sources, and considering its implications for consumer behavior. Instead, because of the limited space available here, we refer the reader to McGuire (1974) for a discussion of the first two points—the basic concept of human personality encapsulated in each motive and an indication of the current research being done on it. This information will allow interested readers to carry out the third step of applying each of these 16 partial views of human nature to the motivation of consumer behavior. Working through the 16 motives with the information provided in McGuire (1974) not only will suggest how consumers are influenced by each of

TABLE 1
A Structuring of 16 General Paradigms of Human Motivation

	Initiation	*Active*		*Passive*	
Mode	*Orientation and Stability*	*Internal*	*External*	*Internal*	*External*
Cognitive	*Preservation*	1. Consistency	2. Attribution	3. Categorization	4. Objectification
	Growth	5. Autonomy	6. Stimulation	7. Teleological	8. Utilitarian
Affective	*Preservation*	9. Tension-Reduction	10. Expressive	11. Ego-Defensive	12. Reinforcement
	Growth	13. Assertion	14. Affiliation	15. Identification	16. Modeling

Source: McGuire (1974, p. 172).

the classes of external forces operating on them, as discussed in the fuller version of this paper (McGuire, 1976), but also will clarify how the consumer's information processing is guided through the directive aspects of their personalities, which we described earlier in this paper.

Conclusion

We have already adverted to the vast outpouring of psychological research at the present time. In each of the recent years, no fewer than 25,000 books and articles have been described in each annual edition of *Psychological Abstracts.* It would be absurd to suggest that we have done justice to this outpouring; indeed, an appreciable portion of this outpouring cries for mercy rather than for justice. What we have tried to do here is simply sweep through these recent advances in psychological theorizing and findings from several different directions, hoping to sketch out for the reader a wide variety of points where bridges can be built between the basic psychological work and the applied area of consumer behavior, bridges over which some interesting intellectual stimulation could pass.

In the course of these sweepings across the field, we have pointed to a wide variety of psychological topics, each of which we feel has substantial implications for a better understanding of consumer behavior, but most of which have not so far been adequately exploited. We have not attempted to draw explicitly all the implications involved. Rather, with each topic we have tried to show where it fits into a broader depiction of the person and where information (at various degrees of depth) can be found regarding current research on the topic; and we have given an illustrative example or two of implications it might have for aspects of consumer behavior that are relevant to current public policymaking (for example, increasing the consumer's awareness and utilization of health-relevant information about products, such as the nutritional quality of food). We cannot claim to have done more than sketch out a map of where the treasure might lie; it remains for the practitioners in the consumer behavior area who would find that purportedly embedded gold mine of information to follow the routes indicated and dig in for themselves.

References

Allport, G. W. and H. S. Odbert. "Trait-names: A Psycholexical Study," *Psychological Monographs,* 47 (1936), No. 211.

Allport, G. W., P. E. Vernon, and G. Lindzey. *The Study of Values.* (Rev. ed.) Boston: Houghton Mifflin, 1951.

Anderson, B. F. *Cognitive Psychology: The Study of Knowing, Learning, and Thinking.* New York: Academic Press, 1975.

Anderson, N. H. "Algebraic Models in Perception," in E. C. Carterette and M. P. Friedman, eds., *Handbook of Perception.* Vol. 2. *Psychophysical Judgment and Measurement.* New York: Academic Press, 1974a, 215–98.

——. "Cognitive Algebra: Integration Theory Applied to Social Attribution," *Advances in Experimental Social Psychology,* 7 (1974b), 1–101.

Bakan, P., ed. *Attention: An Enduring Problem in Psychology.* Princeton: Van Nostrand, 1966.

Bem, D. J. *Beliefs, Attitudes, and Human Affairs.* Belmont, Calif.: Brooks/Cole, 1970.

Berlin, B., D. E. Breedlove, and P. H. Raven, eds. *Principles of Tzeltal Plant Classification: An Introduction to the Botanical Ethnography of a Mayan-speaking People of Highland Chiapas.* New York: Academic Press, 1974.

Blumenthal, A. L. *Language & Psychology: Historical Aspects of Psycholinguistics.* New York: Wiley, 1970.

Bower, G. H., ed. *The Psychology of Learning and Motivation.* Vol. 6. *Advances in Research and Theory.* New York: Academic Press, 1972.

Bridges, K. M. B. "Emotional Development in Early Infancy," *Child Development,* 3 (December 1932), 324–41.

Calder, B. J. and M. Ross. *Attitudes and Behavior.* Morristown, N.J.: General Learning Press, 1973.

Capon, N. and J. Hulbert. "The Sleeper Effect—An Awakening," *Public Opinion Quarterly,* 37 (Fall 1973), 333–58.

Carterette, E. C. and M. P. Friedman, eds. *Handbook of Perception.* 3 vols. New York: Academic Press, 1973, 1974.

Cattell, R. B. and H. W. Eber. *The Sixteen Personality Factor Questionnaire.* Champaign, Ill.: Institute for Personality and Ability Testing, 1957.

Cofer, C. N. *Motivation and Emotion.* Glenview, Ill.: Scott, Foresman, 1972.

Colby, B. N. "Cultural Grammars," *Science,* 187 (March 14, 1975), 913–19.

Cole, J. K. and R. Dienstbier, eds. *Nebraska Symposium on Motivation, 1973: The Complexities of Sexual Script.* Vol. 21. Lincoln: University of Nebraska Press, 1974.

Cole, M. and S. Scribner. *Culture and Thought: A Psychological Introduction.* New York: Wiley, 1974.

Cornsweet, T. N. *Visual Perception.* New York: Academic Press, 1970.

Dawes, R. M. "A Case Study of Graduate Admissions: Application of Three Principles of Human Decision Making," *American Psychologist,* 26 (February 1971), 180–88.

Deese, J. E. *Psycholinguistics.* Boston: Allyn and Bacon, 1970.

Dember, W. N. "Motivation and the Cognitive Revolution," *American Psychologist,* 29 (March 1974), 161-68.

Deutsch, D. and J. A. Deutsch, eds. *Short-term Memory.* New York: Academic Press, 1975.

Deutscher, I. *What We Say/What We Do: Sentiments and Acts.* Glenview, Ill.: Scott, Foresman, 1973.

Eagly, A. H. "Comprehensibility of Persuasive Arguments as a Determinant of Opinion Change," *Journal of Personality and Social Psychology,* 29 (June 1974), 758-73.

Edwards, A. L. *Personal Preference Schedule: Manual.* (Rev.) New York: Psychological Corporation, 1959.

Ehrlich, H. J. "Attitudes, Behavior, and the Intervening Variable," *American Sociologist,* 4 (February 1969), 29-34.

Erikson, E. H. *Childhood and Society.* New York: Norton, 1963.

Eysenck, H. J. *Maudsley Personality Inventory.* San Diego: Educational and Industrial Testing Service, 1962.

Farley, J. U., J. A. Howard, and L. W. Ring. *Consumer Behavior: Theory and Application.* Boston: Allyn and Bacon, 1974.

Ferber, R., ed. *A Synthesis of Selected Aspects of Consumer Behavior.* Washington, D.C.: National Science Foundation, 1976.

Fishbein, M. "The Prediction of Behaviors from Attitudinal Variables," in C. D. Mortensen and K. K. Sereno, eds., *Advances in Communication Research.* New York: Harper & Row, 1973, 3-31.

Fishbein, M. and I. Ajzen. "Attitudes and Opinions," *Annual Review of Psychology,* 23 (1972), 487-544.

——. *Belief, Attitude, Intention, and Behavior. An Introduction to Theory and Research.* Reading, Mass.: Addison-Wesley, 1975.

Gillig, P. M. and A. G. Greenwald. "Is It Time to Lay the Sleeper Effect to Rest?" *Journal of Personality and Social Psychology,* 29 (January 1974), 132-39.

Gough, H. G. and A. B. Heilbrun. *The Adjective Checklist Manual: ACL.* Palo Alto, Calif.: Consulting Psychologists Press, 1965.

Green, P. E. and F. J. Carmone. *Multidimensional Scaling and Related Techniques in Marketing Analysis.* Boston: Allyn and Bacon, 1970.

Greeno, J. G. and R. A. Bjork. "Mathematical Learning Theory and the New 'Mental Forestry,'" *Annual Review of Psychology,* 24 (1973), 81-116.

Greenwald, A. G. "Cognitive Learning, Cognitive Response to Persuasion, and Attitude Change," in A. G. Greenwald, T. C. Brock, and T. M. Ostrom, eds., *Psychological Foundations of Attitudes.* New York: Academic Press, 1968, 147-70.

Gregg, L. W., ed. *Knowledge and Cognition.* New York: Wiley, 1974.

Guilford, J. P. *The Nature of Human Intelligence.* New York: McGraw-Hill, 1967.

Hammond, K., T. R. Stewart, B. Brehmer, and D. Steinman. "Social Judgment Theory," in M. Kaplan and F. Schwartz, eds., *Human Judgment and Decision Processes: Formal and Mathematical Approaches.* New York: Academic Press, in press.

Holbrook, M. B. and J. A. Howard. "Consumer Research on Frequently Purchased Nondurable Goods and Services," in R. Ferber, ed., *A Synthesis of Selected Aspects of Consumer Behavior.* Washington, D.C.: National Science Foundation, 1976.

Howard, J. A. and J. N. Sheth. *The Theory of Buyer Behavior.* New York: Wiley, 1969.

Jackson, D. N. *Personality Research Form Manual.* Goshen, N.Y.: Research Psychologists Press, 1967.

Jacoby, J. "Consumer Psychology as a Social Psychological Sphere of Action," *American Psychologist,* 30 (October 1975), 977-87.

Jameson, D. A. and L. M. Hurvich, eds. *Visual Psychophysics.* New York: Springer-Verlag, 1972.

Johnson, D. M. *Systematic Introduction to the Psychology of Thinking.* New York: Harper & Row, 1972.

Jung, C. G. *Psychological Types.* New York: Harcourt, Brace, 1923.

Kahneman, D. *Attention and Effort.* Englewood Cliffs, N.J.: Prentice-Hall, 1973.

Kausler, D. H. *Psychology of Verbal Learning and Memory.* New York: Academic Press, 1974.

Kiesler, C. A., B. E. Collins, and N. Miller. *Attitude Change: A Critical Analysis of Theoretical Approaches.* New York: Wiley, 1969.

Kiesler, C. A. and P. A. Munson. "Attitudes and Opinions," *Annual Review of Psychology,* 26 (1975), 415-56.

Klapper, J. T. *The Effects of Mass Media.* New York: Bureau of Applied Social Research, Columbia University, 1949.

Lee, W. *Decision Theory and Human Behavior.* New York: Wiley, 1971.

Lévi-Strauss, C. *Structural Anthropology.* New York: Basic Books, 1963.

Lindsay, P. H. and D. A. Norman. *Human Information Processing: An Introduction to Psychology.* New York: Academic Press, 1972.

Liska, A. E., ed. *The Consistency Controversy: Readings on the Impact of Attitude on Behavior.* New York: Wiley, 1974a.

——. "Emergent Issues in the Attitude-Behavior Consistency Controversy," *American Sociological Review,* 39 (April 1974b), 261-72.

McDougall, W. *Outline of Psychology.* New York: Scribner's, 1923.

McGuire, W. J. "A Syllogistic Analysis of Cognitive Relationships," in C. I. Hovland and M. J. Rosenberg, eds., *Attitude Organization and Change: An Analysis of Consistency among Attitude Components.* New Haven: Yale University Press, 1960, 65-111.

——. "Personality and Susceptibility to Social Influence," in E. F. Borgatta and W. W. Lambert, eds., *Handbook of Personality Theory and Research.* Chicago: Rand McNally, 1968a, 1130–87.

——. "Selective Exposure: A Summing Up," in R. P. Abelson et al., eds., *Theories of Cognitive Consistency: A Sourcebook.* Chicago: Rand McNally, 1968b, 797–800.

——. "The Nature of Attitudes and Attitude Change," in G. Lindzey and E. Aronson, eds., *The Handbook of Social Psychology.* Vol. 3. *The Individual in a Social Context.* (2nd ed.) Reading, Mass.: Addison-Wesley, 1969, 136–314.

——. "Psychological Motives and Communication Gratification," in J. G. Blumler and E. Katz, eds., *The Uses of Mass Communications: Current Perspectives on Gratifications Research.* Beverly Hills, Calif.: Sage Publications, 1974, 167–96.

——. "Concepts of Attitudes and Their Relations to Behavior." Unpublished paper, Department of Psychology, Yale University, April, 1975.

——. "Psychological Factors Influencing Consumer Choice," in R. Ferber, ed., *A Synthesis of Selected Aspects of Consumer Behavior.* Washington, D.C.: National Science Foundation, 1976.

——. "An Information-Processing Model of Advertising Effectiveness," in H. L. Davis and A. J. Silk, eds., *Behavioral Management Sciences in Marketing.* New York: Ronald Press.

Mackworth, J. F. *Vigilance and Attention: A Signal Detection Approach.* Harmondsworth, Middlesex, England: Penguin Books, 1970.

Madsen, K. B. *Modern Theories of Motivation: A Comparative Metascientific Study.* New York: Wiley, 1974.

Maslow, A. H. *Motivation and Personality.* (2nd ed.) New York: Harper & Row, 1970.

Mehrabian, A. *Tactics of Social Influence.* Englewood Cliffs, N.J.: Prentice-Hall, 1970.

Melton, A. W. and E. Martin, eds. *Coding Processes in Human Memory.* New York: Wiley, 1972.

Miller, G. R. and M. Burgoon, eds. *New Techniques of Persuasion.* New York: Harper & Row, 1973.

Moran, W. T. "Consumenoid." Unpublished paper, Lever Brothers, New York, November, 1973.

Moray, N. *Attention: Selective Processes in Vision and Hearing.* London: Hutchinson Educational Ltd., 1969.

Murdock, B. B. *Human Memory: Theory and Data.* New York: Wiley, 1974.

Murray, H. A. et al. *Explorations in Personality: A Clinical and Experimental Study of Fifty Men of College Age.* New York: Oxford University Press, 1938.

Neimark, E. D. and J. L. Santa. "Thinking and Concept Attainment," *Annual Review of Psychology,* 26 (1975), 173–205.

Neisser, U. *Cognitive Psychology.* New York: Appleton-Century-Crofts, 1967.

Newell, A. and H. A. Simon. *Human Problem Solving.* Englewood Cliffs, N.J.: Prentice-Hall, 1972.

Nilsson, N. J. *Problem-Solving Methods in Artificial Intelligence.* New York: McGraw-Hill, 1971.

Norman, D. A. *Memory and Attention: An Introduction to Human Information Processing.* New York: Wiley, 1969.

——, ed. *Models of Human Memory.* New York: Academic Press, 1970.

Piaget, J. *The Origins of Intelligence in Children.* (2nd ed.) New York: International Universities Press, 1952.

Pollio, H. R. *The Psychology of Symbolic Activity.* Reading, Mass.: Addison-Wesley, 1974.

Posner, M. I. *Cognition: An Introduction.* Glenview, Ill.: Scott, Foresman, 1973.

Postman, L. "Verbal Learning and Memory," *Annual Review of Psychology,* 26 (1975), 291–335.

Rapoport, A. and T. S. Wallsten. "Individual Decision Behavior," *Annual Review of Psychology,* 23 (1972), 131–76.

Rokeach, M. *The Nature of Human Values.* New York: Free Press, 1973.

Rosenberg, S. "Mathematical Models of Social Behavior," in G. Lindzey and E. Aronson, eds., *The Handbook of Social Psychology.* Vol. 1. *Historical Introduction/Systematic Positions.* (2nd ed.) Reading, Mass.: Addison-Wesley, 1968, 179–244.

Schank, R. C. and K. M. Colby, eds. *Computer Models of Thought and Language.* San Francisco: Freeman, 1973.

Shepard, R. N., A. K. Romney, and S. B. Nerlove, eds. *Multidimensional Scaling: Theory and Applications in the Behavioral Sciences.* 2 vols. New York: Seminar Press, 1972.

Slobin, D. I. *Psycholinguistics.* Glenview, Ill.: Scott, Foresman, 1971.

Slovic, P. and S. Lichtenstein. "Comparison of Bayesian and Regression Approaches to the Study of Information Processing in Judgment," *Organizational Behavior and Human Performance,* 6 (November 1971), 649–744.

Stefflre, V. J. "Market Structure Studies: New Products for Old Markets and New Markets (Foreign) for Old Products," in F. M. Bass, C. W. King, and E. A. Pessemier, eds., *Applications of the Sciences in Marketing Management.* New York: Wiley, 1968, 251–68.

Szalai, A., ed. *The Use of Time: Daily Activities of Urban and Suburban Populations in Twelve Countries.* The Hague: Mouton, 1972.

Thomas, K., ed. *Attitudes and Behaviour: Selected Readings.* Harmondsworth, Middlesex, England: Penguin Books, 1971.

Triandis, H. C. *Attitude and Attitude Change.* New York: Wiley, 1971.

Tulving, E. and W. Donaldson, eds. *Organization of Memory.* New York: Academic Press, 1972.

Tversky, A. and D. Kahneman. "Judgment under Uncertainty: Heuristics and Biases," *Science,* 185 (September 27, 1974), 1124–31.

Watts, W. A. and W. J. McGuire. "Persistence of Induced Opinion Change and Retention of the Inducing Message Contents," *Journal of Abnormal and Social Psychology,* 68 (March 1964), 233–41.

Weiner, B. *Theories of Motivation: From Mechanism to Cognition.* Chicago: Markham, 1972.

——, ed. *Cognitive Views of Human Motivation.* New York: Academic Press, 1974.

Wickelgren, W. A. *How to Solve Problems: Elements of a Theory of Problems and Problem Solving.* San Francisco: Freeman, 1974.

Wicker, A. W. "Attitudes vs. Actions: The Relationship of Verbal and Overt Behavioral Responses to Attitude Objects," *Journal of Social Issues,* 25 (Autumn 1969), 41–78.

Wyer, R. S., Jr. *Cognitive Organization and Change: An Information Processing Approach.* New York: Wiley, 1974.

Zimbardo, P. G. *The Cognitive Control of Motivation: The Consequences of Choice and Dissonance.* Glenview, Ill.: Scott, Foresman, 1969.

Zimbardo, P. G. and E. B. Ebbesen. *Influencing Attitudes and Changing Behavior: A Basic Introduction to Relevant Methodology, Theory, and Applications.* Reading, Mass.: Addison-Wesley, 1969.

READING 4

Memory Factors in Consumer Choice: A Review

James R. Bettman

This paper reviews research and theory on human memory, emphasizing key findings and concepts of importance to marketing and consumer choice. Several implications for promotional decisions are discussed. It is hoped that this review will stimulate further research on, and applications of, memory principles in marketing.

Memory plays a major role in consumer choice. The specific inferences drawn by consumers from product stimuli, advertising, word of mouth, and other sources of product-related information are heavily dependent upon what data are in memory and how they are organized. Important questions to which research on consumer memory can contribute insights include (a) What is remembered from an advertisement or a product-related conversation; (b) Under what conditions do consumers tend to emphasize information on packages or stored in memory when they are in the store; (c) How much time is necessary for consumers to learn some piece of information from an ad; (d) How many repetitions are needed before a consumer can remember a piece of information; (e) What can be done to facilitate in-store recognition of a brand by consumers; and (f) What types of new information, claims, and so on are easier for consumers to remember, given their current knowledge about a product.

Despite its potential importance, research on consumer memory is a relatively neglected area. The purpose of this paper is to present a survey of the literature on the structure and operation of memory and some implications of the memory principles uncovered by the survey (see Olson 1978b for another review of memory notions as related to consumer choice).

Reprinted by permission of the American Marketing Association from the *Journal of Marketing,* Spring 1979, 37–53.

Overview

One concept of memory that recently has been very influential is the multiple-store approach. It is postulated that there are different types of memory storage systems, each with different functions and properties. A typical model of this type hypothesizes a set of sensory stores (SS), a short-term memory store (STS), and a long-term store (LTS) (Atkinson and Shiffrin 1968).

In the basic processing sequence, information passes from the sense organs to the appropriate sensory store which is hypothesized to be very short-lived, losing information within fractions of a second unless the information is further processed (i.e., unless attention is allocated to the stimulus). If the information is attended to and processed, it is transferred to the STS. The STS has a limited capacity and information can be kept active in it by further processing. Information which is active in the STS can be retrieved quickly and almost automatically. Information in the LTS may be brought into the STS as needed to interpret the input information. Thus the STS is the locus of current processing activity, where information from the sense organs and long-term memory can be brought together and processed. Finally, a portion of that information, if adequately processed (a discussion of the meaning of "adequate" in this context is given below), can be transferred to the LTS which is hypothesized to be essentially unlimited in capacity and a permanent repository of information. Although the above discussion, if taken literally, implies that there are several physically distinct memory stores, the separate *functions* of these are the crucial element of the multiple-store viewpoint.

In addition to this characterization of the basic structure of memory, one must also consider how individuals *use* memory. Individuals have various strategies for how and what to process, for what to store in long-term memory and how to store it, and for how to retrieve information from long-term memory. Such strategies are often called control processes (Atkinson and Shiffrin 1968). Although in many cases, storage of and access to items in memory may be nearly automatic, retrieval and storage also can be involved and difficult processes.

In consumer choice there is an *external* memory, in many cases, where information is available without needing to be stored in the consumer's memory. Package information, shopping lists, buying guides, or ads clipped out by the consumer and brought to the store are part of this external memory system.

Thus there is a memory system and a set of control processes which can be used to interact with that system. In general, two very basic kinds of memory usage occur. In one case, information which is currently in long-term storage or external memory must be retrieved *from* the memory to be used in interpreting incoming information or in current processing. In the second case, incoming information is processed and stored *in* memory for later use. These two functions are, of course, not independent: they simultaneously occur at almost all times.

Some basic memory concepts are now presented in more detail: multiple store and other views of memory, control processes; properties of short-term and long-term memory, and the impact of different types of consumer choice tasks on memory usage. In examining memory research, one general caveat should be considered. Much of the experimental research studies situations where individuals are *trying* to memorize (for texts which review this research, see Loftus and Loftus 1976; Crowder 1976; Norman 1976). Consumers also may deliberately try to remember things at times, but in many situations what consumers remember may be incidental rather than deliberate. This difference needs to be considered in attempting to apply any experimental results, and suggests that future research on consumer memory might emphasize incidental memory (McLaughlin 1965; Postman 1975).

Basic Concepts of Memory

Multiple Store and Other Approaches to Memory

As noted above, one prevalent view of memory is the multiple-store view. However, recent research has begun to cast doubt on the strict interpretation of this concept, particularly the distinction between the LTS and the STS as separate memories. Postman (1975) provides a thorough and critical summary of the evidence and concludes that the distinction is not well supported. Other conceptions of memory have been advanced which do not postulate separate multiple stores.

Craik and Lockhart (1972) propose that individuals have limited processing capacity which can be allocated to processing incoming information. In particular, they argue that capacity can be allocated to yield various *levels of processing* which might range from simple sensory analysis (e.g., noting that the information is printed in red type) to more complex semantic and cognitive elaborations of the information (e.g., relating it to other information in memory and seeing how it fits with previous beliefs). Presumably the "lower" levels of processing (e.g., sensory analyses) would require less allocation of capacity than the "higher" or "deeper" levels (e.g., semantic analyses). It is then hypothesized that the level of processing attained determines the future retention of the information. In particular, "deeper" levels of processing (and hence greater use of processing capacity) are hypothesized to be associated with more elaborate and longer lasting memory for the information. For example, consumers who only process an advertisement's sensory features (e.g., a waterfall, a pretty scene, or a well-dressed spokesperson), without processing the semantic information in the ad and relating it to what they know about the product category, presumably will not recall the claims presented when they attempt to make a choice. In that sense, advertisements can err in actually *encouraging* sensory rather than semantic processing by their very nature (i.e., the "background" of the ad may divert attention from the message). Although this issue of background diversion is not new, examining it from the viewpoint of research on memory can suggest approaches for studying such diversion—researching which parts of an ad are processed, and with what degree of elaboration; and what information, images, and reactions to the various parts of the ad are stored in memory after exposure.

Since there is a limited overall processing capacity to be allocated, only a small amount of information can be processed in depth at any one time. Rather than postulating several distinct memories, the levels of processing theory assumes one memory, an overall processing capacity, and the ability to engage in different levels of processing. Although this theory is quite provocative, it also has some serious problems. Some have suggested that *spread* of processing (i.e., the degree of elaboration used in coding the information) is more important than depth alone (Craik and Tulving 1975). Others note that there is a substantial problem with measuring depth of processing in some a priori and independent fashion (Nelson 1977; Baddeley 1978). Most research simply uses types of processing that seem intuitively to differ in depth, without attempting any formal measure of depth. These critics are quite persuasive, so the fate of levels of processing approaches is not clear at present, although research continues (Jacoby, Bartz, and Evans 1978; Saegert 1979; Seamon and Virostek 1978; Cermak and Craik 1978). Until these problems are resolved, however, this approach might best be regarded with caution.

Another general conception of memory which does not require multiple stores is the activation model. In this model, there is one memory store, but only limited portions of that store can be activated at any one time. Only the activated portion can be used for current processing. Activation is temporary and will die out unless further effort is devoted to maintaining it. The exact nature of activation is typically unspecified; however, the concept is one of rate or intensity. Therefore, notions of effort (Kahneman 1973) or allocation of processing capacity also can be viewed as concepts of activation. A general model of this type is outlined by Collins and Loftus (1975) and considered in more detail below. The limited capacity for dealing with incoming information which led to postulation of the STS is thus handled in this model by the limitation on total amount of activation.

The three models described to this point, multiple-store, levels of processing, and activation, do not seem incompatible. The multiple-store theories do not strictly require that there by physiologically separate stores; the *functions* of each store are important. Shiffrin and Atkinson (1969, pp. 179-180) note that their system is "equally as consistent with the view that stores are separate physiological structures as with the view that the short-term store is simply a temporary activation of information permanently stored in the long-term store." Bower (1975) makes the same point. Thus, the multiple-store model can be viewed as an activation model. A liberal view of the Craik and Lockhart (1972) model also allows it to be viewed as an activation approach, since the allocation of processing capacity is a major mechanism of the model.

It seems that all three models of memory are consistent with the principles of a limited processing capacity and a single memory store with allocations of that capacity to the processing of incoming information. The phenomena of the limited STS seem perfectly explainable in these terms, since there is a limitation on the total amount of processing capacity available for allocation. In examining the properties of memory below, the terminology of short-term memory (STM) and long-term memory (LTM) will be utilized to escape from the notion of separate stores, rather than defining new terms for the currently activated portion of memory and the entire memory itself. These terms are to be understood in the light of the above discussion.

As noted above, external memory devices ranging from package information to detailed shopping check lists are often available. The presence of an external memory can serve to reduce the burden on the consumer's internal memory. That is, both internal memory and external memory can be viewed functionally as sources of information. In some cases, it may be easier to encode and process information from a package when making product comparisons than to try to retrieve and process these same data, perhaps fallibly, from internal memory. The consumer also may not try to store complex data internally if these data are available in external memory. The use of information in internal memory may be necessary to interpret such externally available data when they are processed, of course, but overall the burden on internal memory seems smaller if an external memory exists. Thus, the availability of external memory in any particular choice situation can be an important characterizing factor.

Memory Control Processes

Memory control processes are the strategies used by humans to control the flow of information in and out of memory (Atkinson and Shiffrin 1968). These processes can be under the active control of the individual. There are certainly many habitual, nearly automatic processes used by individuals in inputting and outputting information. However in some cases, such conscious decisions are made, so an understanding of the strategies involved is important. In the following, several such strategies are discussed.

Rehearsal. After a stimulus has entered short-term memory, processing effort, called rehearsal, may be needed to further analyze it. The two roles usually assigned to rehearsal are maintenance of information (keeping it activated) in the STM and ultimate transfer of information to the LTM.

The initial concept of rehearsal was that of rote repetition of the information in STM, usually verbal in memory experiments. That is, the individual was viewed as silently repeating the information being considered. Retention in LTM was postulated to be a direct function of the amount of time spent in rehearsal. However many studies have shown that retention in LTM does not necessarily vary directly with amount of rehearsal time. Instead, retention can vary with the form of the rehearsal itself (Woodward, Bjork, and Jongeward 1973; Postman 1975), whether mere repetition (less retention) or more detailed analysis (more retention). Thus, rehearsal can probably best be characterized as allocation of processing capacity, which will be done in accordance with the goals of the individual and the requirements of the task at hand. For example, consumers may remember a price or the value of some other product attribute not so much by rote repetition of the attribute value to themselves, but by mentally relating the value to what they already know (e.g., this price is a few cents more than the cost of my regular brand).

Coding. Coding refers to the way the individual *structures* information for rehearsal. It is now well known that subjects in verbal learning studies use mnemonics, associations, images, and many other strategies of encoding the inputs received to facilitate memory (Bower 1970; Reitman 1970). In attempting to remember the name of a new brand from an ad, the consumer may also associate the brand name with some mental image that suggests that name. For example, a consumer may remember Autumn margarine by associating it with a fall scene. The ads for this margarine use such scenes to try to encourage this process (see Lutz and Lutz 1977).

Transfer. A third control process is the transfer process which governs *what* is stored in memory and the form in which it is stored. Information which is important for attaining goals and/or easily stored is likely to be given highest priority (Shiffrin and Atkinson 1969). These properties need not coincide; that is, information needed for goals may be difficult to process. For example, a consumer may be very interested in nutritional information, but may not be able to store USRDA ratings. Trade-offs must be made in such a case, with the consumer perhaps only attempting to store whether or not the food is basically nutritious.

What is to be stored and the form of storage will thus depend on what the individual expects to do with the information, if such expectations are present. More or less detail may be required depending upon the task to be performed when the information will be used. If the individual plans to compare foods on nutritional content in the store using package information, then only the brands to be compared need be put into memory. However, if the information is presented in an ad and not on the package, the consumer may put more into memory. In situations where individuals do not have firm expectations about how the information will be used, the easiest transfer strategy will probably be used. Events which are surprising, novel, inconsistent with expectations, and so on will often be given priority for processing and storage (e.g., a new price may be stored).

Placement. Placement deals with where an element is stored. This depends upon the existing organization of memory and the particular associations utilized in coding the item. In this sense, the "where" question does not refer to a physical location, but the association structure developed when the item was processed. This structure is affected by the context of presentation: for example, if words are presented in categories, recall tends to be grouped by those same categories (Bower 1970). The importance of the placement decision is that later retrieval may depend upon the likelihood that the particular placement strategy can be reconstructed. In addition, a placement decision may lead to *reorganization* of a portion of memory.

Retrieval. Retrieval of items from memory is a crucial control process. Retrieval processes can range from almost immediate access for familiar items to involved problem solving search processes for other items. The control processes discussed above interact with retrieval. If the basis used for coding, transfer, and placement cannot be retrieved, the item itself may not be accessible. Forgetting is seen, in light of the permanence of the LTM, as a failure of the retrieval process rather than a decay or loss of items. The basic underlying notion can be best seen intuitively by considering cases where an item cannot be remembered, and then some event occurs which gives the "clue" needed to immediately retrieve the item. For example, a consumer may remember needing some item not on his/her shopping list, but not the item itself. While in the store, the item or a related product may trigger remembrance. This retrieval problem is of course central to disputes over the definition of impulse purchases.

Such phenomena imply that the correct retrieval strategy just could not be found at first. Failure of the retrieval process may result from searching in the wrong "part" of memory (i.e., in the wrong set of associations), running out of time to perform the search, or losing one's place in the search. This latter possibility reflects the limited capacity for STM which may result in one's not being able to keep track of one's place in a complex search for a hard to retrieve item (Olshavsky 1971). Use of some external device (e.g., paper and pencil) as a memory aid is often tried by individuals in such cases.

Response Generation. A final control process is response generation. Many theorists view remembering as a constructive process where items are reconstructed from memory. Partial recollections are used as the basis for reconstructing what "must have been." Items are *not* stored in memory exactly as they were entered and aroused in toto when desired. Neisser (1967, pp. 285–86) calls this latter view the "reappearance hypothesis," and rejects it in favor of a constructive approach: "The present proposal is, therefore, that we store traces of earlier cognitive acts. . . . The traces are not simply 'revived' or 'reactivated' in recall; instead the stored fragments are used as information to support a new construction." Jenkins (1974) and Cofer (1973) summarize research supporting the constructive approach. This view implies that memory may be subject to biases, since reconstructions will be based partly on what was and partly on individuals' expectations or schemes for what "must have been" (D'Andrade 1974). A consumer may not remember the actual details of an interaction with a salesperson, for example, but may decide that there "must have been" deceptive statements if he/she is not pleased with a purchase.

Properties of Short-Term Memory

Properties fall into two major categories: capacity and the times needed to transfer information to LTM.

Capacity. As discussed above, the STM is of limited capacity.[1] Miller (1956) first formulated the hypothesis that STM was limited, and reviewed evidence showing that approximately seven chunks of information could be processed at any one time. The number of items is limited because the attention or processing capacity necessary to rehearse these items is limited. Recent evidence (Simon 1974) suggests that a four- or five-chunk capacity seems more likely. A chunk was defined as a configuration that was familiar to an individual and could be manipulated as a unit, in essence an organized, cognitive structure that could grow as information is integrated into it.[2] For example, a brand name can summarize a good deal of more detailed information for a consumer familiar with that brand, hence the name and all it stands for can be thought of as a chunk. The actual amount of underlying material that can be processed simultaneously can be expanded by formation of larger chunks (e.g., by associating several attributes with a brand name so that the mere mention of the name elicits an entire "gestalt"), although the consumer

1. The notion of the STM as a "box" with a fixed number of "slots" has also been used, but is rejected on the basis of the arguments above denying the need for the distinction between the long-term and short-term stores.

2. Bower (1975) points out that this definition is circular: a chunk is something that can be processed as a unit, and the capacity of STM is inferred from examining units of information that are processed, which units are then called chunks.

may presumably reach a point where he or she is unable to further expand a chunk due to difficulties in dealing with more and more complex configurations of information or other factors.

This notion of a capacity for chunks is consistent with a memory model where the constraint is on processing capacity or amount of activation if the assumption is made that the processing capacity needed to manipulate a chunk is independent of its size. That seems to be the essence of the chunking concept; it is the organization of the chunk that allows for ease in processing.

The capacity of STM is lowered if other processing demands are made. This follows immediately from the notion of the limits on STM as processing capacity limits. If part of total capacity must be used for another task, that leaves less for processing chunks of information. The normal capacity may be reduced to a capacity of two or three chunks if other tasks are undertaken simultaneously (see Newell and Simon 1972).

Transfer Times. Another property of STM concerns the amount of time required to transfer an item from STM to LTM, assuming suitable processing is performed (i.e., if the type of coding needed to allow retention in LTM is performed, or if the form of rehearsal leads to retention, as discussed above). Simon (1969, pp. 35–42) and Newell and Simon (1972, pp. 793–96) cite evidence that suggests that approximately five to 10 seconds are required to fixate one chunk of information in LTM if one must later *recall* it. If only *recognition* is required, two to five seconds may be needed (Simon 1969, p. 39; Shepard 1967). This task difference follows from the fact that for recognition, only discrimination of the item from others is needed, not reconstruction of the information. The times above are rough guides rather than precise estimates, and refer to deliberate rather than incidental learning.

If information is not rehearsed at all, it is lost from STM is about 30 seconds or less (Shiffrin and Atkinson 1969). Whether this loss is due to decay or displacement by new items is still under debate (Postman 1975).

Properties of Long-Term Memory

The LTM is hypothesized to be an essentially unlimited, permanent store with semantic and some auditory and visual storage. The basic properties of LTM are the types of elements stored and the organization of that storage.

Elements in Long-Term Memory. There seems to be some agreement that an important part of what is stored in LTM are semantic concepts and the associations among them (e.g., Quillian 1968; Anderson and Bower 1973). Concepts may include events, objects, processing rules, and attributes of objects and events. Underwood (1969) particularly emphasizes that various attributes of objects and events, such as temporal sequence information, spatial aspects information, modality through which the information was obtained (e.g., audio, visual, smell, etc.), affective data, and contextual data, potentially can be stored. This notion of contextual data, particularly time context, has been suggested by several authors (Russo and Wisher 1976; Hintzman and Block 1970). Such timeline memory is essentially similar to Tulving's (1972) notion of episodic memory—memory for past episodes and events.

Another important type of information in memory, related to chunks, is memory schemata. A schema is "an internal structure, developed through experience with the world, which organizes incoming information relative to previous experience" (Mandler and Parker 1976, p. 39). Thus it is an organized pattern of expectations about the environment. One might have schemata about what salespeople are like or how various product attributes interrelate. These schemata can obviously play a powerful role in how consumers perceive the events in their environment. Abelson (1976) considers the related notion of scripts, expectations about how various types of events will unfold (see Wyer and Srull 1979).

Processing rules also are elements of LTM. Newell and Simon (1972) hypothesize that processing rules can be stored in the memory data base and operated on and activated like any other type of information in memory. In addition to memory for semantic concepts, there is substantial memory for visual images and auditory events in LTM, but the mechanisms are currently not well understood (Paivio 1975).

The Structure of Long-Term Memory. There is also general agreement on the structure of the storage of semantic information in LTM. This storage is thought to be organized as a network of nodes and links between nodes, with the nodes representing concepts and the links denoting relationships among concepts; or as some organization which is structurally equivalent to a network formulation (Frijda 1972).[3]

Collins and Loftus (1975) present a network model, originally based on Quillian's (1968) work, in which there are nodes representing concepts and several links between concepts. Each link has a strength corresponding to how essential it is to the meaning of the concept. Processing a concept corresponds to activating the node corresponding to it with activation spreading through the network along the links. Collins and Loftus (1975) show how the theory can explain results on the effects of perceptual set and other data. Anderson and Bower (1973) also see memory as a network of nodes interconnected by associations and use the notion of activation. Finally, within the marketing literature, Nakanishi (1974) proposed a contiguous retrieval model. In this model, concepts are stored in clusters rather than in lists. Their retrieval is based upon their closeness of association or contiguity in the cluster. This model is essentially equivalent to the Collins and Loftus (1975) model, in that the cluster of concepts can be defined by nodes and links, with the notion of closeness or contiguity being modeled by the strength of the links.

Other models also have been proposed, but they can be viewed as equivalent to network models. Newell and Simon (1972) see memory as an organization of list structures (a list whose elements can also be lists). A list structure can be transformed into an equivalent network. Smith, Shoben, and Rips (1974) present a set-theoretical model where concepts are described by a set of features or properties. As Hollan (1975) points out, their model also can be reduced to a network model. (See Smith 1978 for a more detailed discussion of theories of semantic memory.)

In network models, new information is integrated by developing a configuration of links between the new concept and already stored concepts, or by adding links to already existing concepts. Also, inferences can be made by following paths of links and nodes. Such inferences allow us to construct responses and test inputs for consistency with what we already know.

Such models can be extremely important for understanding consumer choice because they imply that consumers have organized systems of concepts related to various brands, ads, stores, and so on. The particular concepts included and the relationships among them can have a powerful effect on the inferences made by consumers based on these concepts (Olson 1978a). For example, if a ballpoint pen has an ultra-fine point, and a consumer links the ultra-fine point with greater writing effort, that consumer may infer that the pen requires greater writing effort and not purchase it, even if in fact greater effort is not required. Also, the inferences underlying the price-quality relationship have been studied a great deal in consumer research (Olson 1977). Thus, studying what concepts are in consumers' memories and exactly how they are linked can be extremely important for understanding consumer responses to products. This type of insight is one benefit of adopting a network view of memory, which provides a framework for *systematically* exploring the contents and interconnections in consumer memory.

Consumer Choice Tasks and Memory

The range of choice tasks performed by consumers is very broad, with decisions not only being made at many levels (save vs. spend, trade-offs among attributes, store, and brand), but in very different task environments, ranging from reading *Consumer Reports* to watching television commercials, ordering from a catalog, or searching through a supermarket. There may also be great differences across tasks in the availability of external memories (e.g., store displays) and their usage. Such factors complicate the examination of memory research, since in general the results are specific to the type of task performed. Therefore, understanding what parts of the memory literature are most relevant for understanding consumer choice requires some notion of what consumer tasks are to be considered. In general, this notion of *task analysis* is important. Newell and Simon (1972) argue that a thorough task analysis yields a great deal of knowledge about how behavior must be structured to adapt to that task environment. Particular tasks impose particular constraints on the processing needed to perform them. Hence, a limited and brief view of some important consumer tasks is presented below, with particular emphasis on the areas of memory research implicated. This task analysis is limited to retail-outlet shopping situations, to some major types of tasks performed outside of the store environment, and to some major types of tasks performed in

3. Wyer and Srull (1979) propose a content-addressable bin model of memory which departs somewhat from these network approaches.

the store. The specific tasks considered were chosen because they seemed most closely related to consumer choice processes.

Tasks Performed Outside the Store. We consider three of the main types of tasks that may be carried out outside the store environment: receipt and processing of information, formation of rules or strategies for weighting attributes, and choice of an alternative.

The consumer receives information outside of the store from many sources, including commercials on television, advertisements, and word of mouth. This information may be presented to the consumer or may be sought by him/her. Important questions relative to the memory component are whether or not the information is stored, and if so, what is stored. Whether or not information can be stored may be in large part a function of not only the consumer's interest in the information, but also of how easy the information is to process. Factors impacting ease of processing include the organization of the information processed, the sheer amount of information presented, and any competing activities carried out while the information is presented (e.g., a consumer is talking while a television commercial is being shown.) Competing activities may have less impact for print ads or for conversations where the consumer has some control over the rate of processing required, than for television or radio where such control is lacking. Finally, the modality of information presentation, visual versus auditory, and the amount of information repetition may impact degree of retention, since these factors also effect ease of processing.

What information is stored may depend in large part on the use, if any, to which the consumer intends to put it. The consumer may wish to use the information as a reminder of something when in the store, such as a brand, which implies that recognition of that brand on the shelf suffices. On the other hand, the consumer may want to decide before arriving at the store, so that recall will be required. An individual difference variable, the degree to which prior planning outside of the store and in-store decision making are used, may greatly influence the type of memory needed, whether for recognition or for recall.

A second out-of-store task considered is the formation of rules or strategies for weighting attributes. Formation of such rules requires information on attributes and the trade-offs among them. Information relevant for developing strategies may be obtained from such sources as ads, family members, product testing magazines, or friends. However, rules for weighting attributes seem to require recall more than recognition, since the rules per se are not usually found explicitly stated in the shopping environment. Thus, recall of evaluative and belief information from memory may be necessary, particularly recall of the rules for combining that information.

Finally, a third out-of-store task is choice of an alternative. As discussed above, the degree to which this occurs out of the store may be an individual difference variable. Choice in the store also occurs, probably more frequently. However, if choice outside the store is carried out, it may involve recall in matching brands against criteria, particularly if the matching is done incrementally as ads or other pieces of information are received. Such an incremental process may require at the very least a recall of the current stage of the process or the operations necessary to reconstruct that stage. In addition, how attribute and evaluative information is stored in memory can be important, since this can affect how alternatives are compared (i.e., whether information is recalled by attribute, across brands; or by brand, across attributes). Finally, external memory can be a factor for choice outside of the store if a display of information such as that in a *Consumer Reports* table is available. Such displays might ease the need for recall of properties of the alternatives, but recall of factors relevant to weighting attributes might still be necessary.

Tasks Performed Inside the Store. One basic feature that characterizes the in-store environment as a task environment is the external memory it provides. Brands are available for inspection, values for various attributes (e.g., price, nutrition) can be obtained from the package, displays may be available, and so on. Within this environment, two basic tasks are considered: formation of rules or strategies for weighting attributes and choice of an alternative.

As noted above, formation or usage of rules for weighting attributes seems to involve mainly recall, since such rules are not normally directly available in the external memory to be recognized. There can be some recognition component, in that examination of packages may remind the consumer of criteria to be used, but recall seems to be the major memory mechanism involved.

A second major in-store task is the choice of an alternative. Here the level of prior experience may be important. In a simple, habitual response situation, the consumer need only recognize what was bought previously, and may very well recall it. At the other extreme is extensive problem solving (Howard and Sheth 1969; Howard 1977), where weights for attributes are developed and processed in some detail. The discussion that follows is not as relevant for the habitual response case, but rather is more suited to decisions involving some problem solving.

Processing alternatives in the store may involve memory only to the extent of recognition of those brands to be processed further from some larger set of brands. However, some recall is probably involved. The particular product class being processed also will have an influence on use of recall versus recognition, since the completeness of the attribute information on the package varies over product classes. If little information is available from the external memory, recall may be more heavily implicated. Also, if no brands are known previously, then recall of information relevant to rules may be necessary. The type of decision being made, whether a choice between product classes or brands within a product class, may also influence use of recognition versus use of recall. For a choice between product classes, the physical setup of the store (e.g., the product classes are probably physically separated) implies that the external memory cannot be relied upon exclusively. Also, more abstract criteria may need to be developed and applied for choice among product classes than for choice among product brands within a product class (Howard 1977). Thus recall may become relatively more important than recognition in choice among product classes. Finally, the context of the original learning about the brand is important, in that recognition or recall may be affected if the context in the store differs from the original learning context.

Thus, the major factors affecting memory involved in in-store tasks are the distinction between recognition and recall, and the effects of differences in context between receipt and attempted retrieval of information. This brief, simplified analysis of typical consumer choice tasks shows the complexity that rapidly arises in attempting to characterize task properties. It also points up the need for a systematic classification or taxonomy of consumer choice tasks, rather than the ad hoc scheme used here.[4] This is an important area for future research. Despite the limitations, several areas of memory research that seem particularly relevant for consumer choice are identified:

- Factors differentially affecting recognition and recall
- Organization of information when received by the consumer
- Effects of a difference in context between the receipt of and attempted retrieval of information
- Form of coding and storage for objects in memory
- Effects of total processing load on the individual
- Memory for rules and operations
- Effects of the modality of information presentation
- Effects of repetition of information

Before turning to a discussion of each of these areas, some perspective on the implications of this research should be given. The problems studied in memory research are often simplistic and narrowly focused, using digits, letters, nonsense syllables, or words as stimuli. As Wright (1974) notes, this research is deficient as far as being directly applicable to consumer research problems in the simplicity of the stimuli and the fact that the responses studied are not evaluative. Reitman (1970) also points out that humans outside the laboratory do not often deliberately rehearse and attempt to memorize items, and that laboratory tasks attempt (with limited success)

4. The concept of a task analysis seems somewhat different from the recent work on situational factors in consumer choice (Belk 1975). Belk (1975, p. 158) defines situational factors to be roughly those factors which are not inherent properties of the individuals or stimuli of interest. Within the context of this definition, task analyses are in some respects more narrow and in some ways more broad than research on situational factors. The task analysis notion is more narrow in the types of situational factors considered, with particular emphasis being placed upon those situational factors which will influence the type of information processing carried out. Thus, the situational factors considered in task analyses are a relatively circumscribed area within the broad range of factors one might consider. In addition, some factors important in performing task analyses may be properties of stimuli (e.g., how many attributes there are for brands in a product class, or the medium through which a particular piece of information is propagated), and hence would not be considered situational factors by Belk's definition. Thus task analyses are more broad in this sense than research on situational impacts alone.

to decouple the study of memory from the strategies people typically use to remember. These strategies, of course, are of great interest for understanding how consumers make real-life decisions. Thus, the results to be presented below should be taken as *indications* of how various processes operate and should raise issues to be considered in the consumer research context. Actual applications of the results might require new research examining the relevant issues in more realistic consumer choice settings.

More Detailed Memory Concepts

Factors Differentially Affecting Recognition and Recall

In the following discussion, the focus is upon differences between recognition and recall. It has been noted above that recognition is in some sense "easier" than recall. Also, the tasks of recognition and recall differ in the basic type of processing that leads to effective performance. To recognize a stimulus from among a set of distracting stimuli, information allowing one to *differentiate* or *discriminate* the previously encountered stimulus is necessary. In recall, however, information allowing one to *reconstruct* the stimulus is required, since the stimulus itself is not present. This distinction between discrimination and reconstruction is implicated again and again in the findings discussed below.

Frequency of Occurrence of Stimuli. Words with low frequency of occurrence in normal text seem to be recognized better than words of high frequency, whereas the reverse is true for recall (Kintsch 1970; Shepard 1967; however, see Goldin 1978 for some contradictory evidence for visual stimuli—chess positions). This finding can be explained by noting that low frequency words, being unusual, are easier to discriminate from others; high frequency words, being familiar, are easier to reconstruct.

This could have implications for the types of brands chosen, depending upon whether choice is guided by recognition (e.g., in-store) or recall (e.g., planning outside of the store). A less frequently seen brand, even if attractive, might be chosen less frequently in the out-of-store situation (recall) relative to the in-store situation (recognition), with the reverse true for more frequently seen brands.

Plans for Learning in Recognition and Recall. The *plans for learning,* or how subjects go about the task, appear to differ between recognition and recall. Given the difference in the tasks themselves, with discrimination required for recognition and reconstruction for recall, this difference in plans should be expected if humans adapt to the task environment (Newell and Simon 1972). Subjects have been shown to encode information differently and to have different levels of recall and recognition accuracy depending upon whether they expected a recall or recognition task (Eagle and Leiter 1964; Tversky 1973).

Thus, the learning plans of the subject may be a function of expected task requirements, and effective plans may *differ* for recall and recognition. The consumer may encode incoming information with some task in mind. This may imply that in some cases the expectation of using recall or recognition procedures in shopping is set a priori, that consumers make this decision at the time of encoding. Since the learning plans may differ depending upon these task expectations and may influence how effectively information is processed, empirical study of this assumption of prior task expectations is desirable. Of course, an alternative hypothesis to setting expectations about use of recognition or recall a priori would be that the task itself determines whether recall or recognition is used, particularly the degree of difficulty involved. Simple tasks may stimulate more use of recall, and more complex tasks may lead to greater use of recognition.

Rehearsal and Transfer Times. Rehearsal may effect recognition and recall differently, although the research results to date are mixed. As noted above, rehearsal can vary from rote repetition to semantic elaboration. Woodward, Bjork, and Jongeward (1973) found that rote repetition rehearsal could improve recognition, but had no effect on recall. However, Chabot, Miller, and Juola (1976) and Nelson (1977) found improvements for recall as well. As noted above, the rough guide for the time required for transfer of a chunk of information to LTM differs for recognition (two to five seconds) and recall (five to 10 seconds). Thus, communications to consumers, particularly in the case of television or radio commercials where the consumer cannot control the rate of information presentation, may have very different effects depending upon whether recognition or recall is attempted.

Effects of Arousal Level. A final factor which may differentially affect recognition and recall is the level of arousal at the time the desired information is to be retrieved from memory (Eysenck 1976). This factor can be important for consumer choice in that arousal (defined by Eysenck 1976, p. 389 as "some elevated state of bodily function") may be characteristic of high time pressure or high conflict choice situations. Eysenck hypothesizes that high arousal may lessen the difficulty of retrieving readily accessible information, but increase the difficulty of retrieving less accessible information. Eysenck then argues that a recognition task, by providing the subject with the item, which then must be judged "old" (recognized) or "new" (not recognized) involves in general more accessible information than a recall task. He summarizes research results which show, as predicted, that under high arousal recognition response speeds are facilitated, but recall response speeds are hindered. These findings could be important for consumer choice, since consumers who tend to use recall may be less able to operate effectively under time pressure or conflict than those who tend to use recognition. Perhaps, on the other hand, consumers choose to rely on either recall or recognition adaptively, choosing recognition more in situations where they feel time pressure, conflict, or some other source of arousal, and recall more for less demanding choice tasks.

Organization of Information Input

In tasks for which recall is the focus, subjects given instructions to recall as much as possible have been consistently shown to use memory strategies which concentrate on organizing, associating, and grouping together the items to be learned (Bower 1970; Buschke 1976). If groupings are already present in the materials to be learned, then this can greatly facilitate recall (Bower et al. 1969).

However, the effects of organization in the input may only be beneficial if this organization *corresponds* to the rules subjects might normally use to group the data. If the groupings or chunks in the input do not match those usually used by subjects in organizing their own memories, the input groupings may hinder recall performance (Bower and Springston 1970). The implication is that if an advertisement is to present information which is already "chunked" or "grouped" for the consumer, whether that structuring is helpful to the consumer or not will depend upon how consumers group or would tend to group the information.

Effects of Context

The role of context has been investigated in memory studies. The encoding specificity hypothesis states that no context, even if strongly associated with a particular item or event, can be effective in aiding retrieval for that item or event *unless* the item or event was originally encoded in terms of that context (Thomson and Tulving 1970). Many studies have shown, for both recognition and recall, that changes in context are associated with poorer performance (e.g., Thomson 1972; Thomson and Tulving 1970). Although information may be *available* (in memory), in the wrong context it can be *inaccessible.*

Such effects of the relationship of the context at memory input to that when memory is to be accessed have not been specifically studied in consumer research. However, advertisements present information in a particular context which very often does not match the in-store context. Perhaps information usage, usage of particular attributes as criteria, or even recognition of brands is influenced by the degree to which the context posed in the ad is present in the actual choice situation. Thus, if in-store recognition is desired, the package should be shown in the advertisement. In one case, a cereal (Life) with a very powerful commercial (the "Mikey" commercial) ingeniously put a scene from the commercial on the front of the package.

Form of Coding and Storage of Objects in Memory

A series of research studies has examined whether encoding and memorization of properties of objects are easier if all the attribute values of one object are presented at one time (object coding or brand coding), or if all the values on a particular attribute for the set of objects under study are presented at one time (dimension coding or attribute coding). Haber (1964) used a brief presentation (1/10 second) of cards portraying stimuli which varied along three dimensions, one of which was emphasized to the subjects as being important. Some subjects were instructed to use object coding, while others were instructed to use dimension coding. Haber found that dimension coders were slower and less accurate in recalling unemphasized dimensions. Lappin (1967) used different stimuli, again with three dimensions, and did not instruct his subjects on coding schemes. Rather, he tested recall by objects and dimensions. He found better recall for the three dimensions of each object than for the same dimension over three objects. Montague and Lappin (1966) found, in a replication of Haber's (1964) results, that object coding was faster than dimension coding. However, they did not find differences in accuracy, contrary to Haber's results. Johnson and Russo (1978) found that subjects tended to store information in the form it was presented to them, whether by object (brand) or by dimension (attribute). However, they did not find differences in time or accuracy depending upon the organization of the input. Thus, there is mixed support for the notion that when inputting data, coding by objects may be more effective for later recall.

Effects of Processing Load

Studies cited earlier have shown that the effective capacity of STM is a function of the total processing load on the individual. If processing capacity is required for some activity which competes with a memory task, less capacity is available for memory processing. In addition, there may be task effects on memory processing. That is, the information input rate characteristic of a task or the processing rate required in performing that task may affect memory. Seibel, Christ, and Teichner (1965) assert that the rate of incoming information itself is not the critical factor, but rather the rate of internal processing the task requires in analyzing and transferring the information into memory, in interaction with this presentation rate. This is completely congruent with a capacity allocation theory of memory. In this view, it is not the presentation rate per se that requires capacity, but the task to be performed. Thus, the more processing required by the task in a limited time period, the greater the effects on memory performance. If the tasks of monitoring and processing the incoming data are not demanding, high input rates may be tolerable.

Since the tasks involved in consumer choice differ greatly across situations, the above considerations may be quite important for consumer choice. If advertisements presenting a great deal of information per unit time are shown to consumers, memory performance may depend upon what is required of consumers in processing the ad. For example, whether recall or recognition is used could be important. Recognition might be less affected by presentation rate than recall, since forming associations and other strategies for recall may require more effort than analyzing a single item for later recognition. Also, if a consumer is processing an ad by looking to see if certain elements are above a threshold (e.g., does this product have at least 25% of the U.S. Recommended Daily Allowance of vitamin C) this may be much easier than attempting to comprehend and learn actual parameters (e.g., 30% of the USRDA for vitamin C).

Memory for Rules and Operations

In judging alternatives, consumers may combine evaluations on various attributes. The rules for combining evaluations are thus important aspects of the choice process. There are very few studies that examine memory for such rules. Dosher and Russo (1976) and Russo and Wisher (1976) show that in mental arithmetic tasks, memory for sequences of operations and intermediate processing details is better than memory for the actual original numbers comprising the arithmetic task. For example, intermediate subtotals in an addition and subtraction task are recognized, but the original numbers are not.

Johnson (1978), in an initial test of the impact of decision processes on consumer memory, used recall reaction times to study similar issues. His results resembled those noted above: final outcomes and intermediate processing results were recalled faster than the original data on the alternatives used. It is clear that more research is needed before any confident statements about consumer memory for rules and operations can be made.

Effects of Input Modality

There is a great deal of research on differences in memory as a function of the sensory modality of the input (e.g., visual versus auditory). The findings have shown that for simple stimuli such as series of digits or numerals, there are modality effects on STM, but *not* on LTM. Penney (1975) reviews this research in some detail. The findings show that there consistently has been better short-term recall of auditory input, particularly for the most recently presented items. For lists where auditory and visual presentations are mixed, recall tends to be organized by modality of the input, and auditory recall is better. Recall performance is best when the initial presentation and test are in the same modality. When auditory and visual tasks compete in a mixed situation, the auditory task seems to have priority (Penney 1975). These findings, although based upon a great deal of research, may not be too applicable to consumer choice because of their emphasis on simple stimuli and STM phenomena. However, some ads may use simple digit stimuli (e.g., nutritional ratings) and the findings can serve as a source of hypotheses to be examined in a consumer context. For example, the notion that competing audio and visual portions of an ad will lead to downgraded recall of the visual information could be quite important for understanding the effects of proposals for presenting visual nutritional information in ads with competing audio portions (Bettman 1975). Also, the notion that the modes at presentation and at test should coincide may imply that points should be made visually that relate to in-store aspects of choice.

Although the above findings can serve as a source of hypotheses, they differ drastically from research involving more complex stimuli. Several authors have noted the powerful beneficial effects on memory of forming visual images involving the input stimuli (see Paivio 1971). Lutz and Lutz (1977) demonstrated such effects of visual imagery using advertisements as stimuli. In addition, Shepard (1967) demonstrated humans' remarkable recognition memory for pictures. Shepard used many ads for stimuli and found that subjects recognized, from a series of about 600 pictures, 96.7%, 99.7%, 92%, 87%, and 57.7% at test delays of zero, two hours, three days, seven days, and 120 days respectively. Finally, Rossiter (1976) shows that visual memory of the package may be quite important in children's cereal choices, and may also be important for adults. He found that cereal preferences assessed visually by using a drawing task differed from preferences assessed verbally.[5] Paivio (1975) argues that in general there is a dual coding system in memory—an imagery system that deals with nonverbal information, and a verbal system that deals with semantic concepts. Depending upon the task requirements, either or both systems may be utilized (other theorists do not subscribe to this view; see Kieras 1978 for a review and model of imagery effects). The nonverbal imagery system needs more research to determine its impact on consumer choice processes, as most research has concentrated on the verbal concept system (see Lutz and Lutz 1978).

5. Rossiter (1975) also found that musical imagery (jingles, songs in ads) was important for children.

Effects of Repetition

One of the oldest notions in the memory literature is that repeated exposure to a stimulus enhances future recall or recognition of that stimulus. Most of the work on the effects of repetition has involved a passive view of human learning, with repetition serving to "stamp in" an item, to increase the strength of that item's memory trace. This research will be briefly reviewed and then the implications of viewing man as a more "active" learner are discussed.

Sawyer (1974) presents a good summary of the effects of repetition as related to marketing phenomena. The basic findings are that recall and recognition increase as a function of presentation frequency and that there are decreasing increments in memory performance as repetition increases (i.e., later exposures appear to add less and less to performance). Even rote repetition without more elaborative processing may improve recognition or recall (Chabot, Miller, and Juola 1976; Nelson 1977). Finally, for single series of stimuli, it has been shown that recall performance is better when a given number of repetitions is spaced or distributed rather than massed (Postman 1975, pp. 316–18). Zielske (1959), in a classic study in marketing, showed that for final level of recall, distributed presentation was better than massed presentation, but noted that the amount of final retention may not be the relevant criterion for the marketer. If maximum temporary response is desired, massed presentation may be better; if maximum average exposure is desired, distributed presentation was better.

This view of repetition ignores the notion of man as an active processor governed by plans and goals. In several studies cited above, it was noted that memory performance may depend upon the learning plans formed by the consumer. Krugman (1972) points this out, and rejects the notion that the effects of learning must be through "practice" alone. He asserts that the presence of interest or involvement is important, i.e., that the consumer has some plan or need for using the information in the ad. He then claims that three repetitions are enough: the first evokes a "What is It?" response, with a preliminary decision about whether the ad is of any use or interest; the second generates more detailed evaluative responses and planning for future actions if the preliminary decision was favorable; and the third becomes the reminder to carry out any plan formed in the second. Most people may screen out ads at the first exposure; however, if later an interest in the product category or brand is present, the person may see an ad for the 23rd time, but process it as if it were their *second* exposure (Krugman 1972, p. 13). Thus, for group data, different levels of interest in a product over time could lead to gradually increasing curves of response to repetition (because with increased repetition, the odds that someone who is interested would have had the first "What is It?" exposure increase), even though for the individual the response was in some sense more rapid. Goldberg and Gorn (1974) offer evidence consistent with Krugman's general notion, in that exposure to one commercial affects children's attitudes toward a toy and their persistence at a task to obtain the toy. However, an increase to three exposures did not change either attitude or persistence beyond the initial effect of the first exposure.

While the specific mechanisms and numbers of exposures proposed by Krugman may be debated, there may be a strong component of active planning and assessment in human learning. If an ad is seen as useful based upon interests, future choice tasks expected, or other factors, then consumers may use the information in the ad to generate partial plans for choice (e.g., "check this brand," "look at this new attribute in my decision," and so forth).[6] The important question then becomes whether sheer repetition has an effect on this process of forming plans, or functions solely to make sure information is available at the relevant time, when needed.

At this point, the evidence seems to be that both processes operate. As Krugman (1965) himself notes, low and high involvement learning may be governed by different processes. For low involvement learning, sheer repetition may have effects, particularly if recognition rather than recall is involved (Woodward, Bjork, and Jongeward 1973; Chabot, Miller, and Juola 1976; Nelson 1977; Postman 1975, p. 303). For learning under higher involvement, more elaborate and focused processing may ensue. (For some recent research on the kinds of processing which occur for different levels of involvement, see Gardner, Mitchell, and Russo 1978.)

6. Of course, even when the consumer is trying actively to learn the information contained in an ad, if there is a great deal of information a number of repetitions may be necessary before the consumer can learn that information. Thus, the number of repetitions necessary for the consumer to carry out plans for learning may vary as a function of the information load in the ad.

Implications for Marketing

The following discussion emphasizes some selected implications of memory principles for promotional decisions. (For further implications, see Bettman 1979, Chapters 10 and 11, particularly for discussion of the effects of the organization of information by brand or by attribute.) In the presentation below, factors influencing *where* and *how* to present information are emphasized.

It is necessary, before discussing these questions, to briefly consider the type of processing characterizing certain consumer decisions, since where and how to present information can depend upon the type of processing used. It has been hypothesized (Bettman 1979) that where consumers have little prior knowledge or experience or where the decision is difficult for some other reason, they will tend to process information in the store and use recognition rather than recall. Consumers with a good deal of experience or for whom the choice is easy will tend to process outside of the store environment and use recall. The basic reasoning behind these hypotheses is that consumers will only be *able* to recall information and make choices outside of the store where the choice is easy and familiar. For difficult choices, attempting to use recall or process outside of the store may be too hard. It should be noted that these hypotheses are speculative and greatly in need of empirical research. However, they seem plausible and are utilized in the following discussion.

Where Information Should Be Provided

Presentation of information in the store (on the package or through various forms of point-of-purchase displays) and presentation of information out of the store (television, radio, print, billboards) may in general have very different properties. In particular, the types of memory processing necessary for consumers to use the information may differ.

Provision of Information in the Store. One of the most salient features of providing information in the store is that the information on packages or other displays can serve as an external memory for the consumer allowing him/her to simply recognize rather than recall various pieces of information. A second characteristic of in-store information provision is that there may be more time available for processing the information, unlike radio or television advertising where there is limited processing time. Finally, it may be easier for consumers to make detailed comparisons among brands if information is provided on packages in the store than to compare brands using memory for the information presented in television advertising, for example.

Given these characteristics, under what conditions might the marketer wish to present information in the store? As noted above, consumers may tend to process in the store for decisions where they have little previous experience or knowledge or where the decision is difficult. Thus, a marketer of a product class characterized by low levels of consumer experience or by difficulty in choice might concentrate to a greater extent on in-store, point-of-purchase information displays or on greater amounts of package information. Even if consumers do have experience, the marketer may wish to encourage comparison of the product with others in the store, if it is a new brand or is believed to have some differential advantage, for example. Comparing package information is easier than making internal memory comparisons. Thus if the marketer feels consumers are processing in the store or wishes to encourage such processing, in-store information provision is needed.

Provision of Information Outside the Store. Presenting information outside the store may require the consumer to rely on his or her own memory to a greater extent. Although print ads can provide an external memory device (by clipping the ad), television, radio, and billboards do not provide an easy external memory aid.

The conditions under which marketers might wish to concentrate on presenting information outside of the store would tend to be the opposite of those for in-store presentation. In general, consumers may process outside the store for product classes where the choice is easy and they have a good deal of experience. Thus a marketer with a brand in a product class where consumers have a good deal of experience might concentrate more on out-of-store and less on in-store activity, since consumers will tend to decide outside of the store. Note that these prescriptions refer to the emphasis which might be appropriate for the marketer. It is not suggested that either the in-store or out-of-store method be used exclusively. Consumers will vary in their degree of prior experience, and the in- and out-of-store methods have different properties, so some combination of approaches will, in most cases, be the best strategy.

How Information Should Be Provided

In the following, two aspects of how to provide information are presented: facilitating use of recognition or recall, and how memory research can help in presenting information to special groups of consumers.

Facilitating Use of Recognition or Recall. Since consumers may attempt to use recognition more often in the store, the external memory provided by packages and in-store displays is a crucial consideration. Use of recognition presupposes some earlier presentation of information, with later recognition of that information. Therefore, in general there may be some out-of-store presentation, with recognition cued by the package or display in the store. This implies that the information on the package or display should be the same or nearly the same as that presented in the out-of-store advertising. One typical method for ensuring this match is to show the package in the advertisement (if visual information can be presented, as for television and billboards). This need not be the only method, however. In the Life cereal case noted above, a scene from an ad was placed on the front of the cereal package, thus bringing the context of the commercial into the store. For radio commercials, either descriptions of the package ("Look for the red and yellow box") or slogans which would be repeated on the package might be used. Finally, if the marketer wishes to have particular claims recognized, they should be presented in the store on the package or in a display, as well as in the advertisement. Although the information on the package may trigger recall of associated information from memory, there is no guarantee that any particular claim will be recalled in this fashion.

For the consumer to use recall, the information presented should be relatively simple and congruent with what consumers know. Recall will tend to be used for familiar choice situations, so the consumer will attempt to fit the new information into an existing set of beliefs about the product class. As noted above, different modes of information presentation can affect the ease of recall of that information. For example, use of visual imagery is often a good way to enhance recall. Lutz and Lutz (1977) show that recall of brand names is higher for advertisements using certain types of visual imagery.

Whether consumers use recall or recognition, the ease with which the information presented can be processed will affect later usage. A general principle is that the amount of information which can be assimilated is a function of the time available for processing. For example, if recall is used, then the research on transfer speeds from short- to long-term memory (cited above) implies that roughly five to 10 seconds of time is required to memorize one chunk of information for later recall. Thus, the feasibility of processing the information and recalling it depends upon the amount of information presented relative to the time available for processing, and the ability of the consumer to organize the information into chunks. For example, if there are 15 seconds available for processing the information and capacity is fully allocated to that processing, perhaps two or three chunks could be recalled at a later time. For recognition, the transfer speeds are on the order of two to five seconds per chunk, so perhaps as many as eight chunks of information could be recognized later after a 15-second presentation.

Thus, the amount of information which may be acquired during the limited time available in a television commercial depends upon the ability of the consumer to chunk the information provided. The degree of chunking possible may depend largely upon the organization of the information in the ad and the degree of the consumer's prior knowledge and interest in it. If information is prechunked for the consumer by the way the ad is designed *and* if these chunks are consistent with the way the consumer categorizes, then "larger" chunks and hence more information could be processed per unit time. Also, if the individual has prior knowledge related to the information presented, so it can be integrated meaningfully with the existing knowledge, then more information in the ad can perhaps be chunked and processed per unit time. Therefore, there is a great effect on memory of the size of the "vocabulary" of chunks in memory. The greater the number of such chunks, the faster information can be processed.

The time available for processing can thus have important effects. For media where the time available for processing is limited (television or radio), the amount of information which can be presented may also be limited. For cases where the marketer wishes to present large amounts of information, or where the information is complex, either media which do not limit the time available for processing should be used (print, in-store), or the time given for processing should be expanded to meet processing needs.

Presenting Information to Special Groups of Consumers. In some cases, marketers may wish to present information to special groups of consumers such as children or the elderly. Such groups may be characterized by different memory properties which must be understood in order to present information effectively.

For example, research on the information processing characteristics of the elderly has tended to focus on memory abilities. Several studies have compared the abilities of groups of differing ages on various memory tasks, and have found that the groups of older subjects (generally over 60) performed less well than the younger subjects (generally in their 20s). These memory findings may have implications for the choice processing of the elderly. First, the elderly appear to have difficulties in making shifts in search (Welford 1962, p. 337) and difficulties in recall (Craik 1971). This may imply that attempting to make choices between product classes by recall would be more difficult for them. Second, tasks requiring rapid processing (e.g., viewing of television commercials which present a great deal of information) may be harder for older subjects due to their slower memory and visual search speeds (Anders and Fozard 1973; Chiang and Atkinson 1976). Finally, tasks where distraction is likely to be present (e.g., viewing television commercials) would probably be difficult (Broadbent and Heron 1962). These findings may suggest greater use of in-store displays or print ads in communicating to elderly consumers, since these methods do not limit processing time and may facilitate use of recognition memory rather than use of recall (see Phillips and Sternthal 1977, for similar arguments).

Directions for Future Research

It is obvious from the above that there is an enormous amount we do not know about consumer memory. However, certain areas seem to be of higher research priority. Basic information on what consumers have in memory and how it is organized is a high priority. As noted above, clarifying the "networks" of concepts and interrelations among them can have many implications for understanding consumer reactions to products. In addition, determining the "vocabulary" of chunks and schemas consumers use would be extremely helpful in addressing other issues, such as how rapidly consumers can process the information contained in ads and how the information in ads can best be organized for consumers. Current research on memory schemas (Markus 1977; Clary, Tesser, and Downing 1978; Kintsch 1978; Wyer and Srull 1979) may be helpful in attacking these issues.

A second major priority is analysis of the properties of various consumer choice tasks, particularly those affecting memory processing. Such factors as the extent of external memory available, time pressure, the organization of available information, and so on might be very relevant. As stated earlier, however, one major factor whose effect should be studied is whether the consumer is trying deliberately to memorize or is remembering items incidentally. Much of the research surveyed studied deliberate memorization. Future research should include studies carried out in consumer settings without explicit instructions to memorize to ascertain whether the conclusions of this prior research still hold.

Finally, research on when consumers use recognition or recall seems very important, since the properties of recognition and recall and the implications for how to present information differ. Thus, knowledge of consumer memory is important for both theoretical and pragmatic reasons. There are many issues to be investigated and work in these areas should be strongly encouraged.

References

Abelson, Robert P. (1976), "Script Processing in Attitude Formation and Decision Making," in *Cognitive and Social Behavior,* John S. Carroll and John W. Payne, eds., Hillsdale, NJ: Lawrence Erlbaum, 33–45.

Anders, Terry R. and James L. Fozard (1973), "Effects of Age Upon Retrieval from Primary and Secondary Memory," *Developmental Psychology,* 9, 411–415.

Anderson, John R. and Gordon H. Bower (1973), *Human Associative Memory,* Washington, D.C.: Winston.

Atkinson, R.C. and R.M. Shiffrin (1968), "Human Memory: A Proposed System and Its Control Processes," in *The Psychology of Learning and Motivation: Advances in Research and Theory,* Volume 2, K.W. Spence and J.T. Spence, eds., New York: Academic Press, 89–195.

Baddeley, Alan D. (1978), "The Trouble with Levels: A Reexamination of Craik and Lockhart's Framework for Memory Research," *Psychological Review,* 85 (May), 139–152.

Belk, Russell W. (1975), "Situational Variables and Consumer Behavior," *Journal of Consumer Research,* 2 (December), 157–164.

Bettman, James R. (1975), "Issues in Designing Consumer Information Environments," *Journal of Consumer Research,* 2 (December), 169–177.

—— (1979), *An Information Processing Theory of Consumer Choice,* Reading, MA: Addison-Wesley.

Bower, Gordon H. (1970), "Organizational Factors in Memory," *Cognitive Psychology,* 1 (January), 18–46.

—— (1975), "Cognitive Psychology: An Introduction," in *Handbook of Learning and Cognitive Processes,* Volume 1, William K. Estes, ed., Hillsdale, NJ: Lawrence Erlbaum, 25–80.

——, Michael C. Clark, Alan M. Lesgold, and David Winzenz (1969), "Hierarchical Retrieval Schemes in Recall of Categorized Word Lists," *Journal of Verbal Learning and Verbal Behavior,* 8, 323–343.

——, and Fred Springston (1970), "Pauses as Recoding Points in Letter Series," *Journal of Experimental Psychology,* 83, 421–430.

Broadbent, D.E. and Alastair Heron (1962), "Effects of a Subsidiary Task on Performance Involving Immediate Memory by Younger and Older Men," *British Journal of Psychology,* 53, 189–198.

Buschke, Herman (1976), "Learning Is Organized by Chunking," *Journal of Verbal Learning and Verbal Behavior,* 15, 313–324.

Cermack, L.S. and F.I.M. Craik, eds. (1978), *Levels of Processing and Human Memory,* Hillsdale, NJ: Lawrence Erlbaum.

Chabot, Robert J., Timothy J. Miller, and James F. Juola (1976), "The Relationship Between Repetition and Depth of Processing," *Memory and Cognition,* 4, 677–682.

Chiang, Alice and Richard C. Atkinson (1976), "Individual Differences and Interrelationships Among a Select Set of Cognitive Skills," *Memory and Cognition,* 4, 661–672.

Clary, E. Gil, Abraham Tesser, and Leslie L. Downing (1978), "Influence of a Salient Schema on Thought-induced Cognitive Change," *Personality and Social Psychology Bulletin,* 4 (Winter), 39–43.

Cofer, Charles N. (1973), "Constructive Processes in Memory," *American Scientist,* 61 (September-October), 537–543.

Collins, Allan M. and Elizabeth F. Loftus (1975), "A Spreading-Activation Theory of Semantic Processing," *Psychological Review,* 82, 407–428.

Craik, Fergus I.M. (1971), "Age Differences in Recognition Memory," *Quarterly Journal of Experimental Psychology,* 23, 316-323.

——, and Robert S. Lockhart (1972), "Levels of Processing: A Framework for Memory Research," *Journal of Verbal Learning and Verbal Behavior,* 11, 671-684.

——, and Endel Tulving (1975), "Depth of Processing and the Retention of Words," *Journal of Experimental Psychology: General,* 1, 268-294.

Crowder, Robert G. (1976), *Principles of Learning and Memory,* Hillsdale, NJ: Lawrence Erlbaum.

D'Andrade, Roy G. (1974), "Memory and the Assessment of Behavior," in *Measurement in the Social Sciences,* H.M. Blalock Jr., ed., Chicago: Aldine, 159-186.

Dosher, Barbara Anne and J. Edward Russo (1976), "Memory for Internally Generated Stimuli," *Journal of Experimental Psychology: Human Learning and Memory,* 2 (November), 633-640.

Eagle, Morris and Eli Leiter (1964), "Recall and Recognition in Intentional and Incidental Learning," *Journal of Experimental Psychology,* 68, 58-63.

Eysenck, Michael W. (1976), "Arousal, Learning, and Memory," *Psychological Bulletin,* 83 (May), 389-404.

Frijda, Nico H. (1972), "Simulation of Human Long-Term Memory," *Psychological Bulletin,* 77 (January), 1-31.

Gardner, Meryl P., Andrew A. Mitchell, and J. Edward Russo (1978), "Chronometric Analysis: An Introduction and an Application to Low Involvement Perception of Advertisements," in *Advances in Consumer Research,* Volume 5, H. Keith Hunt, ed., Chicago: Association for Consumer Research, 581-589.

Goldberg, Marvin E. and Gerald J. Gorn (1974), "Children's Reactions to Television Advertising: An Experimental Approach," *Journal of Consumer Research,* 1 (September), 69-75.

Goldin, Sarah E. (1978), "Memory for the Ordinary: Typicality Effects in Chess Memory," *Journal of Experimental Psychology: Human Learning and Memory,* 4 (November), 605-616.

Haber, Ralph N. (1964), "Effects of Coding Strategy on Perceptual Memory," *Journal of Experimental Psychology,* 68 (November), 357-362.

Hintzman, Douglas L. and Richard A. Block (1970), "Memory Judgments and the Effects of Spacing," *Journal of Verbal Learning and Verbal Behavior,* 9, 561-566.

Hollan, James D. (1975), "Features and Semantic Memory: Set Theoretic or Network Model?" *Psychological Review,* 82, 154-155.

Howard, John A. (1977), *Consumer Behavior: Application of Theory,* New York: McGraw-Hill.

——, and Jagdish N. Sheth (1969), *The Theory of Buyer Behavior,* New York: John Wiley and Sons.

Jacoby, Larry L., Wayne H. Bartz, and James D. Evans (1978), "A Functional Approach to Levels of Processing," *Journal of Experimental Psychology: Human Learning and Memory,* 4 (July), 331-346.

Jenkins, James J. (1974), "Remember That Old Theory of Memory? Well, Forget It!" *American Psychologist,* 29 (November), 785-795.

Johnson, Eric J. (1978), "What Is Remembered About Consumer Decisions," unpublished manuscript. Pittsburgh: Department of Psychology, Carnegie-Mellon University.

——, and J. Edward Russo (1978), "The Organization of Product Information in Memory Identified by Recall Times," in *Advances in Consumer Research,* Volume V. H. Keith Hunt, ed., Chicago: Association for Consumer Research, 79-86.

Kahneman, Daniel (1973), *Attention and Effort,* Englewood Cliffs, NJ: Prentice-Hall, Inc.

Kieras, David (1978), "Beyond Pictures and Words: Alternative Information-Processing Models for Imagery Effects in Verbal Memory," *Psychological Bulletin,* 85 (May), 532-554.

Kintsch, Walter (1970), "Models for Free Recall and Recognition," in *Models of Human Memory,* Donald A. Norman, ed., New York: Academic Press, 331-373.

—— (1978), "Comprehension and Memory of Text," in *Handbook of Learning and Cognitive Processes,* Volume 6: *Linguistic Functions in Cognitive Theory.* W.K. Estes, ed., Hillsdale, NJ: Lawrence Erlbaum.

Krugman, Herbert E. (1965), "The Impact of Television Advertising: Learning Without Involvement," *Public Opinion Quarterly,* 29 (Fall), 349-356.

—— (1972), "Why Three Exposures May Be Enough," *Journal of Advertising Research,* 12 (December), 11-14.

Lappin, Joseph S. (1967), "Attention in the Identification of Stimuli in Complex Visual Displays," *Journal of Experimental Psychology,* 75 (November), 321-328.

Loftus, Geoffrey R. and Elizabeth F. Loftus (1976), *Human Memory: The Processing of Information,* Hillsdale, NJ: Lawrence Erlbaum.

Lutz, Kathy A. and Richard J. Lutz (1977), "Effects of Interactive Imagery on Learning: Application to Advertising," *Journal of Applied Psychology,* 62 (August), 493-498.

——, and —— (1978), "Imagery-Eliciting Strategies: Review and Implications of Research," in *Advances in Consumer Research,* Volume 5, H. Keith Hunt, ed., Chicago: Association for Consumer Research, 611-620.

Mandler, Jean M. and Richard E. Parker (1976), "Memory for Descriptive and Spatial Information in Complex Pictures," *Journal of Experimental Psychology: Human Learning and Memory,* 2 (January), 38-48.

Markus, Hazel (1977), "Self-Schemata and Processing Information About the Self," *Journal of Personality and Social Psychology,* 35 (February), 63-78.

McLaughlin, Barry (1965), "'Intentional' and 'Incidental' Learning in Human Subjects: The Role of Instructions to Learn and Motivation," *Psychological Bulletin,* 63, 359-376.

Miller, George A. (1956), "The Magical Number Seven, Plus or Minus Two: Some Limits on Our Capacity for Processing Information," *Psychological Review,* 63, 81-97.

Montague, William S. and Joseph S. Lappin (1966), "Effects of Coding Strategy on Perceptual Memory," *Journal of Experimental Psychology,* 72 (November), 777–779.

Nakanishi, Masao (1974), "Decision Net Models and Human Information Processing," in *Buyer/Consumer Information Processing,* G. David Hughes and Michael L. Ray, eds., Chapel Hill, NC: University of North Carolina Press, 75–88.

Neisser, Ulric (1967), *Cognitive Psychology,* New York: Appleton-Century-Crofts.

Nelson, Thomas O. (1977), "Repetition and Depth of Processing," *Journal of Verbal Learning and Verbal Behavior,* 16, 151–171.

Newell, Allan and Herbert A. Simon (1972), *Human Problem Solving,* Englewood Cliffs, NJ: Prentice-Hall, Inc.

Norman, Donald A. (1976), *Memory and Attention: An Introduction to Human Information Processing,* 2nd Ed., New York: John Wiley and Sons.

Olshavsky, Richard W. (1971), "Search Limits As a Function of Tree Size and Storage Requirements," *Organizational Behavior and Human Performance,* 6, 336–344.

Olson, Jerry C. (1977), "Price as an Informational Cue: Effects on Product Evaluations," in *Consumer and Industrial Buying Behavior,* Arch G. Woodside, Jagdish N. Sheth, and Peter D. Bennett, eds., New York: North Holland, 267–286.

—— (1978a), "Inferential Belief Formation in the Cue Utilization Process," in *Advances in Consumer Research,* Volume 5, H. Keith Hunt, ed., Chicago: Association for Consumer Research, 706–713.

—— (1978b), "Theories of Information Encoding and Storage: Implications for Consumer Research," in *The Effect of Information on Consumer and Market Behavior,* Andrew Mitchell, ed., Chicago: American Marketing Association, 49–60.

Paivio, Allan (1971), *Imagery and Verbal Processes.* New York: Holt, Rinehart, and Winston.

—— (1975), "Perceptual Comparisons Through the Mind's Eye," *Memory and Cognition,* 3, 635–647.

Penney, Catherine G. (1975), "Modality Effects in Short-Term Verbal Memory," *Psychological Bulletin,* 82 (January), 68–84.

Phillips, Lynn W. and Brian Sternthal (1977), "Age Differences in Information Processing: A Perspective on the Aged Consumer," *Journal of Marketing Research,* 14 (November), 444–457.

Postman, Leo (1975), "Verbal Learning and Memory," *Annual Review of Psychology,* 26, 291–335.

Quillian, M.R. (1968), "Semantic Memory," in *Semantic Information Processing,* M. Minsky, ed., Cambridge, MA: The MIT Press, 216–270.

Reitman, Walter R. (1970), "What Does It Take to Remember?" in *Models of Human Memory,* Donald A. Norman, ed., New York: Academic Press, 469–509.

Rossiter, John R. (1975), "Cognitive Phenomena in Contemporary Advertising," paper presented at the 1975 Conference on Culture and Communication, Temple University, March.

—— (1976), "Visual and Verbal Memory in Children's Product Information Utilization," in *Advances in Consumer Research,* Volume III, Beverlee B. Anderson, ed., Chicago: Association for Consumer Research, 523–527.

Russo, J. Edward and Robert A. Wisher (1976), "Reprocessing as a Recognition Cue," *Memory and Cognition,* 4 (November), 683–689.

Saegert, Joel (1979), "A Demonstration of Levels-of-Processing Theory in Memory for Advertisements," in *Advances in Consumer Research,* Volume 6, William L. Wilkie, ed., Miami: Association for Consumer Research.

Sawyer, Alan G. (1974), "The Effects of Repetition: Conclusions and Suggestions about Experimental Laboratory Research," in *Buyer/Consumer Information Processing,* G. David Hughes and Michael L. Ray, eds., Chapel Hill, NC: University of North Carolina Press, 190–219.

Seamon, John G. and Susan Virostek (1978), "Memory Performance and Subject-Defined Depth of Processing," *Memory and Cognition,* 6 (May), 283–287.

Seibel, Robert, Richard E. Christ, and Warren E. Teichner (1965), "Short-Term Memory Under Work Load Stress," *Journal of Experimental Psychology,* 70, 154–162.

Shepard, Roger N. (1967), "Recognition Memory for Words, Sentences, and Pictures," *Journal of Verbal Learning and Verbal Behavior,* 6, 156–163.

Shiffrin, Richard M. and R.C. Atkinson (1969), "Storage and Retrieval Processes in Long-Term Memory," *Psychological Review,* 76, 179–193.

Simon, Herbert A. (1969), *The Sciences of the Artificial,* Cambridge, MA: The MIT Press.

—— (1974), "How Big Is a Chunk?" *Science,* 183 (February), 482–488.

Smith, Edward E. (1978), "Theories of Semantic Memory," in *Handbook of Learning and Cognitive Processes,* Volume 6: *Linguistic Functions in Cognitive Theory.* W.K. Estes, ed., Hillsdale, NJ: Lawrence Erlbaum.

——, Edward J. Shoben, and Lance J. Rips (1974), "Structure and Process in Semantic Memory: A Featural Model for Semantic Decisions," *Psychological Review,* 81, 214–241.

Thomson, Donald M. (1972), "Context Effects in Recognition Memory," *Journal of Verbal Learning and Verbal Behavior,* 11, 497–511.

—— and Endel Tulving (1970), "Associative Encoding and Retrieval: Weak and Strong Cues," *Journal of Experimental Psychology,* 86, 255–262.

Tulving, Endel (1972), "Episodic and Semantic Memory," in *Organization of Memory,* Endel Tulving and W. Donaldson, eds., New York: Academic Press, 381–403.

Tversky, Barbara (1973), "Encoding Processes in Recognition and Recall," *Cognitive Psychology,* 5 (November), 275–287.

Underwood, Benton J. (1969), "Attributes of Memory," *Psychological Review,* 76, 559–573.

Welford, A.T. (1962), "On Changes of Performance with Age," *Lancet* (February 17), 335–339.

Woodward, Addison E. Jr., Robert A. Bjork, and Robert H. Jongeward Jr. (1973), "Recall and Recognition as a Function of Primary Rehearsal," *Journal of Verbal Learning and Verbal Behavior,* 12, 608–617.

Wright, Peter L. (1974), "Analyzing Media Effects on Advertising Responses," *Public Opinion Quarterly,* 38, 192–205.

Wyer, Robert S., and Thomas K. Srull (1979, forthcoming), "The Processing of Social Stimulus Information: A Conceptual Integration," in *Person Memory and Encoding Processes,* R. Hastie, E. Ebbeson, T.M. Ostrom, R.S. Wyer, D.L. Hamilton, and D.E. Carlston, eds., Hillsdale, NJ: Lawrence Erlbaum.

Zielske, Hubert A. (1959), "The Remembering and Forgetting of Advertising," *Journal of Marketing,* 23 (January), 239–243.

READING 5

Hemispheral Lateralization: Implications for Understanding Consumer Behavior

Flemming Hansen

This paper reviews the findings of studies on hemispheral lateralization, and argues that most models of consumer behavior imply brain functioning normally associated with the left brain. It is proposed that several misunderstood aspects of consumer behavior can be explained, making use of recent findings on the functioning of the right brain. Special methodological problems associated with the study of hemispheral lateralization are also pointed out.

Interest in hemispheral lateralization is increasing among psychologists (Lindzay and Norman 1977), brain researchers (Wittrock 1977), and psychiatrists (Wexler 1980). It has been found that humans specialize in the use of the right and left hemispheres of their brain. Whereas the left hemisphere is primarily responsible for traditional cognitive activities relying on verbal information, symbolic representation, sequential analysis, and the ability to be conscious and report what is going on, the right brain—without the individual being able to report verbally about it—is more concerned with pictorial, geometric, timeless, and nonverbal information.

Students of consumer behavior are beginning to speculate about the implications of the specialized functioning of the brain. For instance, it is proposed that even when attention—in the sense it is normally referred to in advertising research—is not present, it is still possible for the individual to receive and store information. Moreover, it is proposed that this process is particularly efficient with pictorial material, and that the information is stored in a holistic, unedited, nonverbal fashion very different from the way we normally store verbal and similar information (Krugman 1977).

Likewise, the provocative findings by Zajonc (1968) regarding the effects of "mere exposure" are interesting. It is possible that the increased liking he observes resulting from repeated exposures could be explained as a result of predominantly right brain information processing. In the discussion of the effects of advertising on society, it is claimed that advertising has unfortunate long-run effects in addition to the more immediate effects that can be identified (Ottesen 1980; Packard 1957).

It is, however, hard to see how such secondary effects can be explained by means of the conceptual framework underlying existing advertising research, and it is even more difficult to imagine how such effects could be identified with the measurement tools used by the advertising researcher. Here, also, contemporary brain research may contribute. The growing understanding of hemispheral lateralization suggests that individuals may be able to receive and to store information in ways very different from those normally assumed to be at work.

Before these and other implications are covered in more detail, parts of the research on left/right brain functioning are reviewed. This is done by describing a few properties of the human brain, which are necessary prerequisites for understanding this type of research. Following this, some of the more important research findings are presented. Research methodologies are then described, and, implications of hemispheral lateralization for selected areas within

Reprinted with permission from the *Journal of Consumer Research,* 8:1 June 1981, 23-36.

consumer behavior are considered. The implications for understanding long-run effects of advertising and other types of mass communication are evaluated, and, finally, research needs in the area are discussed.

Some Properties of the Human Brain

Hemispheral lateralization has been known for many years. It is well established (Wittrock 1977) that impressions from the left field of view, left ear, and left side of the body are transmitted to sensory areas in the right side of the brain, and vice versa. However, that the left and right half of the brain may treat information very differently is a more recent observation. In spite of the fact that fundamentally different processes seem to be involved, this has remained unobserved by neurophysiologists for many years.

Before the implications of this research are discussed, however, it is necessary to review briefly

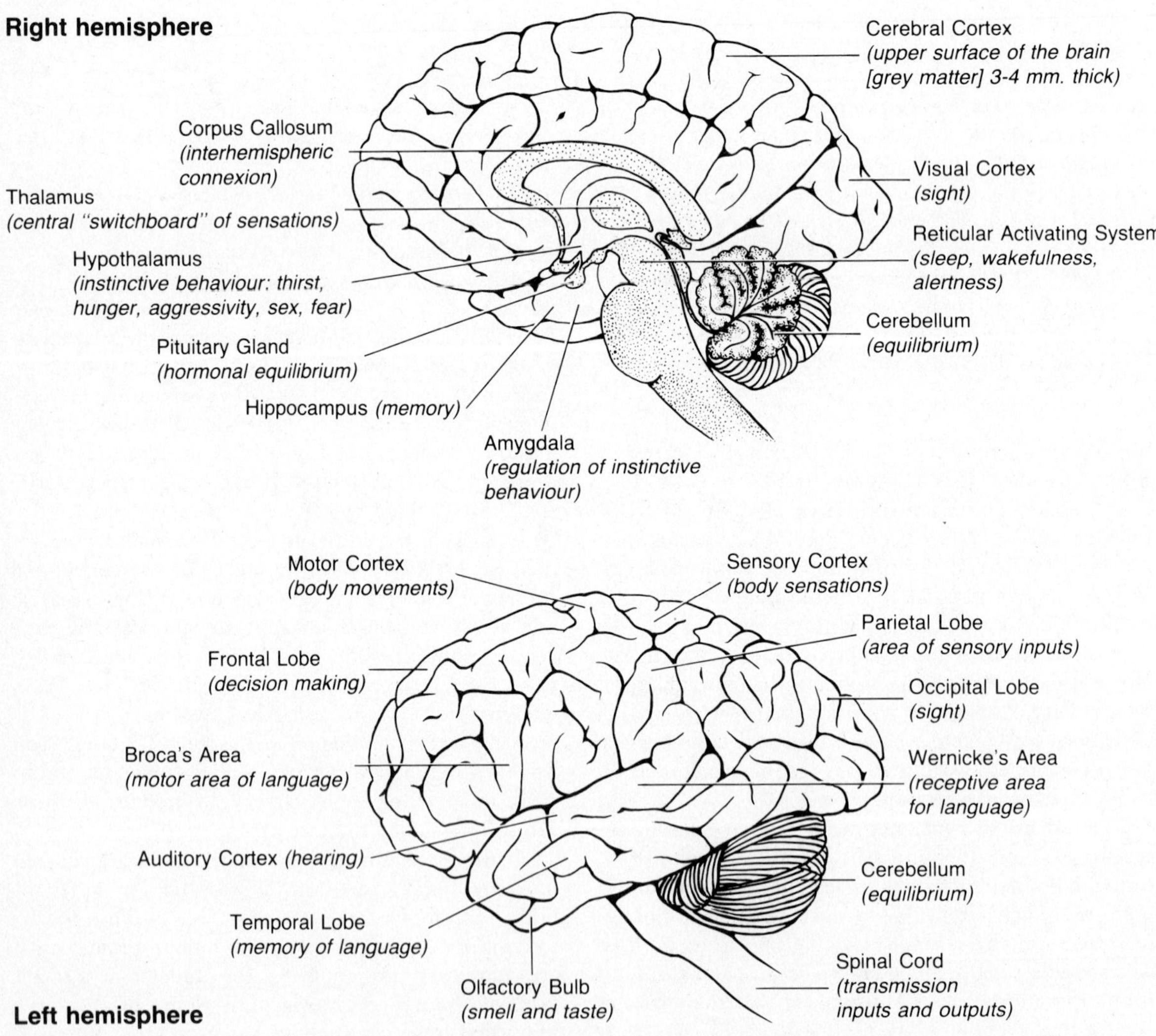

FIGURE A
Major Functional Areas of the Brain (Reproduced with permission of The Unesco Courier 1976)

some properties of the human brain. As illustrated in Figure A, the human brain is composed of two almost identical halves. Much is currently known about the special functions of the various areas of the brain, and some of this knowledge is summarized in Figure A. In the present context it is the cerebral cortex in particular that is of interest. The control of the senses and of sensory inputs are located in these areas, and thought processes and decision making in particular activate these parts.

An important feature of this almost symmetrically structured brain is the way in which the two brain halves are related to each other. This connection first occurs through the corpus callosum (Figure A), which is a tissue of millions of nerve cells with widely spread connections in the left as well as in the right hemisphere. In animal experimentation and, in some instances, with man, this interconnection can be disrupted. When that is done, it becomes possible to study the specialized functioning of the two hemispheres.

It has been known for many years that sensual impressions received from the environment are dealt with in a hemisphere-specialized fashion. Most of what is received through the right ear or what is felt with the right hand is transmitted to the left hemisphere, and in the same way responses made with the right hand or other parts of the right side of the body are controlled by processes occurring in the left brain. A somewhat similar specialization relates to the eyes; however, rather than having the left eye connected with the right brain, and the right eye with the left brain, the specialization is such that all information streaming from the left part of the visual field (defined as what is on the left of the fixation point) is transmitted to the right brain, and vice versa. This specialization of sensual processes is important because it makes it possible in an experimental setting to control what side of the brain receives the information being transmitted.

In dealing with brain lateralization, a peculiar complication arises, because in some instances of left-handedness the hemispheral specialization is more or less reversed. It is estimated that in approximately one-fourth of the cases of extreme left-handedness, the right brain performs the same functions as those by the left half of the brain in right-handed individuals. It is not known to what extent this reversal is inherited or to what extent it is acquired in early childhood. The phenomenon, however, does give rise to research complications, which sometimes have been avoided by securing right-handed subjects only.

Sources of Information

As described before, the corpus callosum is the major connecting link between the left and the right hemispheres. Certain extreme cases of epileptic diseases have been successfully treated by cutting through the corpus callosum and, thereby, disconnecting the two brain halves. Most patients who have undergone this kind of surgery seem to function normally afterwards. More thorough examination, however, reveals remarkable differences.

Some of the earliest cases of this kind of surgery were carried out by Bogen and Vogel (1962); studies of the patients' hemispheral, psychological lateralization were carried out by Sperry (1973) and his coworkers. They found, for example, that if a pair of scissors was presented to the right visual field (Figure B), and the individual was asked what was seen, the person answered "scissors." If, on the contrary, the pair of scissors was presented to the left hand or to the left visual field, the patient was not able to report anything back. If, however, the pair of scissors was presented to the left visual field, and the respondent was asked to pick up, with his left hand, a similar item among the several items placed within reach of his left hand, he would easily pick up the scissors.

Moreover, if the item presented was a wristwatch, and the respondent was asked to select, with his left hand, an item from several that did not include a wristwatch, but included an alarm clock, the respondent would pick up the clock in favor of other items with shapes more similar to the wristwatch. The conclusion from this observation has been that the right brain—being nonverbal—is able to carry out some symbolic information handling.

The observations by Sperry (1973) and Gazzaniga (1977) on patients with intersected brain halves have been of extreme importance to the study of hemispheral lateralization. Morover, these observations have largely been confirmed by findings from patients with more or less extensive damage to the left and/or to the right brain. Similar observations have been made with patients whose left or right brain has momentarily stopped functioning, either due to drugs or by means of electrical inhibition.

A wealth of interesting findings are reported by Deglin (1976) from Russia. Electroconvulsive therapy (ECT) is a treatment occasionally applied to psychotic patients. By this action, part of the brain is momentarily set out of function by an electric shock. It can be done with the left or right brain, so that it

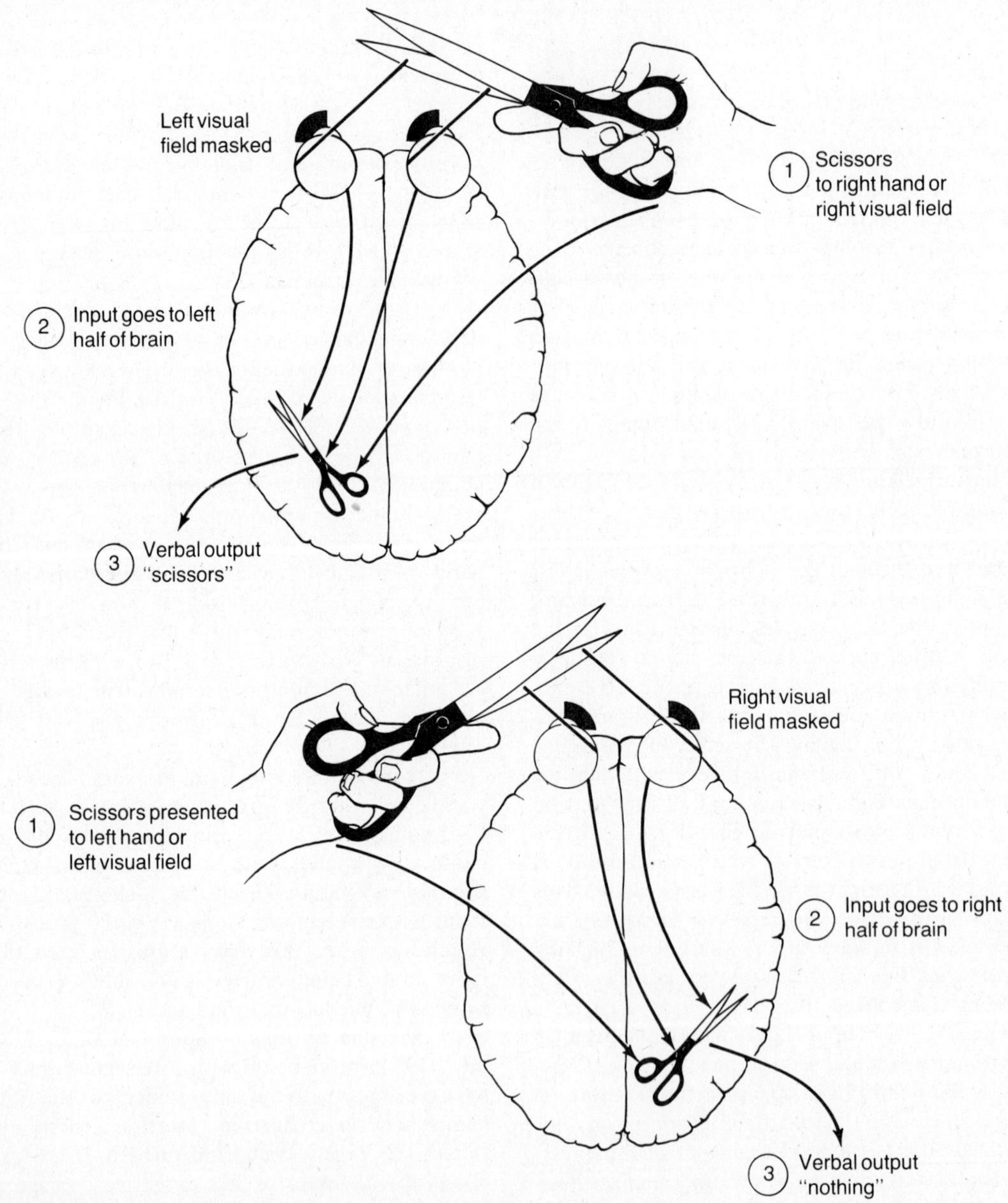

FIGURE B
Presentation of Identical Stimulation to Left and Right Hemisphere with Disconnected Corpus Callosum (Reproduced with permission from Lindzay and Norman 1977)

is possible to study the behavior of the patient with only half of the brain functioning. From research on such patients Deglin concludes, regarding the "left-brain person":

> *A deterioration has occurred in those aspects of his mental activity which underlie imaginal thinking. Those aspects of his mental activity which underlie abstract, conceptual thinking have been retained and even improved. This stratification of the psyche is accompanied by an optimistic emotional outlook (p. 10).*

Regarding the "right-hemisphere person" Deglin writes:

> *The right hemisphere person manifests an impairment in those aspects of mental activity which are the basis of abstract, conceptual thinking while those aspects linked with imaginal thinking have been retained and even improved. This type of stratification of the psyche is accompanied by a negative emotional outlook (p. 13).*

A third approach to the study of lateral specialization relies on control of stimulation transmitted to normal individuals, that is, research on persons with intact corpus callosum and normal interaction between the two brain halves. This research has provided findings corresponding to those resulting from the two first approaches. However, it has also been found that in normal individuals the interaction between the two brain halves is extremely strong. It is not that either of the brain halves monopolizes the handling of the various kinds of information, rather it seems to be a matter of relative dominance.

In a review of this research, Kimura (1973) finds that when it comes to visual information the left brain dominates the handling of letters and words, whereas the right brain is superior in tasks, such as location of points in two dimensions, enumeration of dots and forms, matching of slanted lines, and depth perception. Similarly, with regard to auditory information, Kimura reports that the left brain is superior with words, nonsense syllables, and backward speech, whereas the right hemisphere is superior with regard to musical patterns and non-speech sounds.

Among manual tasks, the left-brain dominance has been observed in connection with skilled movements and free movements during speech. The right brain, on the other hand, has been found superior in locating items that cannot be seen.

Nature of Hemispheral Specialization

Throughout history, many psychologists, philosophers, and others have pointed at a possible dichotomic structure of the human mind. Some of these dichotomies—with the left-brain term mentioned first—have been pointed out by Bogen (1977):

- Rational versus metaphoric (Bruner)
- Active versus receptive (Deikman)
- Secondary versus primary (Freud)
- Realistic versus impulsive (Hilgaard)
- Directed versus free (John Hobbes)
- Differential versus existential (William James)
- Positive versus mythic (Lévi-Strauss)
- Rational versus intuitive (Maslow)
- Sequential versus multiple (Neizer).

Compare these with some of the major differences between right- and left-brain processes as suggested by Ornstein (1973), who maintains that the left brain works sequentially, temporally, verbally, intellectually, causally, logically, and argumentatively, in contrast with the right-brain processes that are more diffuse, spatial, intuitive, and musical.

In summary, the following are some of the major differences between left- and right-brain processes (Lundsgaard 1978):

- The human brain—in contrast with the brain of all other species—is significantly more laterally specialized.
- The lateral specialization accounts for the flexibility of the human brain, including its ability to use language and symbolic representations.
- The left cerebral hemisphere in normal individuals controls speech, arithmetic, and symbolic information handling.
- The right hemisphere controls visual as well as auditory (and musical) impressions.
- Normally both hemispheres are active together, interacting through the connecting corpus callosum; this may account for the richness of human mental abilities.
- Some people are left-brain dominated and others are right-brain dominated.
- The extent to which a person becomes left- and/or right-brain dominated depends partly on inherited

factors and partly on the kind of training, i.e., stimulation, received during childhood.

- Left-brain dominated persons tend to rely more heavily on traditional verbal, symbolic problem-solving processes, and right-brain dominated persons are more influenced, and possibly controlled, by spatial, imaginative impressions.

Thus, some individuals are more likely to rely on verbal elements, whereas others may act directly on pictorial representations, storing complete pictures of events and sequences of events that are then utilized in later situations.

What Can Be Measured?

Students of hemispheral lateralization have relied on a number of measurement approaches normally not used by the consumer researcher. One reason for this is the complicated methodological problems associated with the study of hemispheral specialization.

An important methodological question is whether relative hemispheral dominance is an individual trait characterizing a person's overall way of approaching and handling information, or is situational, in that different informational inputs lead to more or less dominating left- or right-brain processes. If the first is true, one may expect to find stable patterns in the way in which different individuals make decisions and apply information–patterns that occur across different situations–though such individual differences need not be invariant through the entire life span of the individual. If, on the other hand, situational differences determine the relative dominance of the left versus right hemisphere, the individual must have the ability to rely on the left as well as on the right brain type of information processing, and some mechanism in the specific situation determines which will occur. This is in line with Hansen (1977), who proposes that consumers can make choices in very different ways depending on situational factors and on the nature of the problem.

Another methodological problem relates to the interaction that occurs between the two brain halves in normal individuals. This interaction makes it difficult to be sure that experimental manipulations aimed at providing information to either of the two brain halves have been successful, and it forces the researcher to use special techniques to ensure that separate right- or left-brain responses are being measured. The hardware used in such studies is, therefore, often complicated. Some approaches require instruments making it possible to control the information transmitted to the experimental subject in a much more minute manner than is normally done in studies of communication effects. Other approaches rely on highly complicated electronic measurements.

Still other methodological problems follow from the interaction between treatment, measurement, and individual differences. Some methodologies are characterized by the measurements they apply. This is especially so with some of the more "hardware-requiring" methodologies. Here variations in measurement may be studied either among different individuals, or by making several observations of the same individual to study the effect of different treatments. Other methodologies are characterized by their distinctive treatment of the stimulation. Here it becomes possible to study effects of controlled stimulation with a varicty of dependent measures. Still other approaches utilize subjects with known individual differences. Patients with known brain damage are extreme cases, but in recent studies individuals with other, less dramatic, differences have been studied. Some of these approaches are discussed below.

Tachistoscope Technique. In the earliest studies of split-brain patients, a tachistoscope was used for presentation of information either to the left or to the right visual field of the patient. Several devices have been invented for this purpose. Today the most commonly used is illustrated in Figure C. By means of a one-way mirror, it is possible to show pictures in the left or in the right visual field after the respondent has fixed his attention on a particular point. This tachistoscope is also used in the study of normal individual brain functioning.

The technique can be used either for identification of individual differences in the respondent's use of left- versus right-brain processing, or it can be used to study how different pieces of information give rise to different responses, depending on whether they are presented in the left or in the right visual field.

Dichotic Listening. This is similar to the tachistoscope procedure, except that it uses auditory stimu-

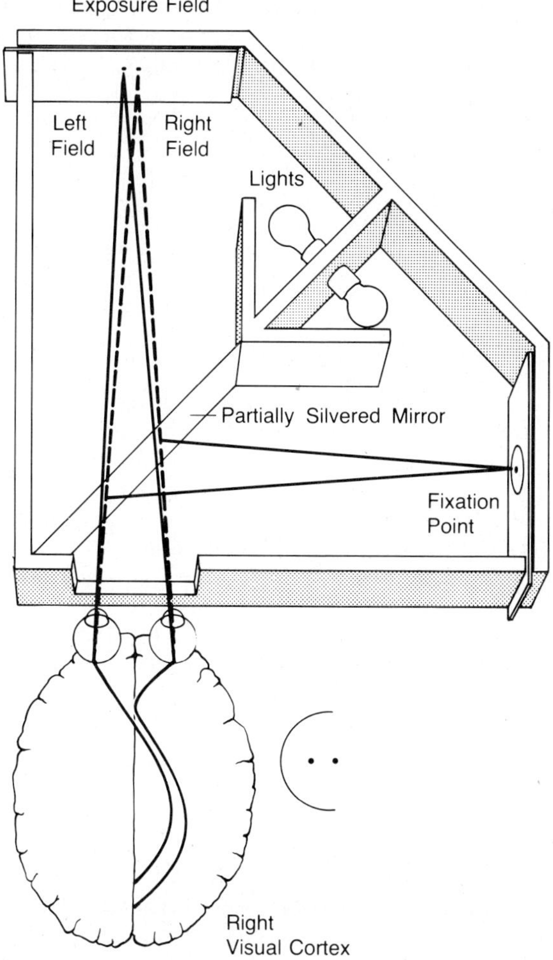

FIGURE C
Two-Field Tachistoscope (Reproduced with permission from Kimura 1973)

The two-field tachistoscope is used for the study of visual perception. When the fixation field is lighted, an observer sees a reflection of the field in the partially silvered mirror. He is asked to fixate on a point in the center of the field. Then the fixation-field light is turned off and the exposure-field light is simultaneously turned on for a few milliseconds. The image on the exposure field passes through the partially silvered mirror and is briefly seen by the observer. At the end of the exposure, the fixation-field light comes on and the exposure-field light goes off. By placing the exposure image in the left or right visual field, as desired, the experimenter can selectively stimulate either the right or the left visual cortex.

lation. In one use of the technique, two different soundtracks send different messages to the left and to the right ear. This can be done with the use of two earphones and stereo equipment with completely separate left and right soundtracks. For example, two different melodies can be played, one to the left ear and the other to the right ear, and from the respondent's report of what is being heard, the dominating brain half can be identified. Alternatively, one can use words, sentences, nonsense syllables, or figures as signals.

Two procedures are used to eliminate the problem of different individuals having different hearing capacities with the left and right ears. In the first approach, prior to the experiment, the individual adjusts the loudness of the two soundtracks, until s/he judges them to be equal. In the other approach, the same word pairs (or other stimuli pairs) are presented in reverse order to both ears. Following this, the number of correctly identified messages to the right (x) ear and the number of correct words identified by the left ear (y) are counted. A ratio indicating the degree of right- versus left-ear dominance is then computed:

$$\frac{(x-y)}{(x+y)} \cdot 100.$$

The larger this ratio is, the more prominent is the right ear, i.e., the left brain.

Like the tachistoscope technique, dichotic listening can be used to identify individual differences, as well as to identify differences in the way in which various kinds of information is handled.

Electroencephalogram (EEG). Whereas the tachistoscope and the dichotic listening techniques control incoming stimulation, the EEG technique is unique in terms of the measurements it applies. The EEG measures the amount and pattern of electrical activity in the cerebral cortex, with the use of electrodes placed on the surface of the skull. For a normal relaxed individual, stable (8–13 per second) fluctuation (alpha waves) can be observed. When the individual is activated, for instance by looking at an interesting picture, faster and lower amplitude waves are observed (beta waves).

When EEG is used to study hemispheral differences, the concern is with the pattern of alpha and beta waves in the two hemispheres. The measurements from the side of the right brain are obtained by connecting an electrode at a point a little below the top of the skull to a point at the neck of the right side of the skull. Similarly, information about the left brain is obtained with electrodes located on the left side of the skull.

By studying the frequency with which alpha waves occur in the left and in the right hemisphere, it is possible to learn about the relative use of the two hemispheres when the individual is engaged in different tasks. This procedure has been applied by Appel, Weinstein, and Weinstein (1979) in an attempt to test right/left brain processing when watching commercials. Several problems are connected with the technique, however. First, the results may differ depending on the precise location of the electrodes on the skull. Moreover, this may interact with the type of message being transmitted. Second, it can be extremely difficult to relate the measured fluctuations to more specific aspects of the message being presented. Imagine EEG measures being taken while a 30-second commercial is being aired. Should one compare the average of the left- and right-brain activities during the entire commercial, or should one compare the brain activities occurring while different sections of the commercial are being aired? The latter would relate brain processes to different parts of the commercial, which could have diagnostic value. However, the activity at any given time may be a function of the information received at the same time, or it may be a function of what was received at some earlier point in time.

Also, this technique can be used to study individual, as well as situational, differences. So far, applications have concentrated on identifying different ways of handling incoming information, although findings (Appel, Weinstein, and Weinstein 1979) suggest that individual differences may be established in this fashion.

Emisionstomgraph Technique. When brain activities increase, blood circulation in that part of the brain also increases. When radioactive material is added to the blood, it is possible to measure variations in the intensity of the blood streaming through various parts of the surface of the brain. This emisionstomgraph technique has been developed by Lassen, Ingvar, and Skinhøj (1978) to study blood circulation and brain defects. The technique provides dynamic colored pictures of the intensity of the activity in various aspects of the brain, and may have promising implications for the study of hemispheral specialization.

Wechsler Adults Intelligence Scale (WAIS). The most frequently used intelligence test for adults is WAIS (Freeman 1962). The test, almost half a century old, has been modified several times. It has two parts, verbal and performance. Although the original purpose of this test was not to measure differences in levels of activity on the two brain halves, it has been suggested that the test does measure aspects of left- as well as right-hemispheral activities.

Some of the test items included in the WAIS battery are particularly suited for testing left-brain abilities, such as, a test measuring verbal ability abstraction, a vocabulary test, and a test measuring arithmetic abilities. Similarly, several items from the performance score are particularly suitable for testing right-brain activities. Among these are the picture completion item (measuring visual abilities), the cube test (measuring visual-spatial abilities and memory), and a puzzle test (measuring visual-synthetic abilities).

Testing for Brain Damage. This is widely used among psychologists. Tests used for this purpose attempt to reveal the extent to which an individual suffers from organic damage to the cortex, resulting in symptoms such as reduced memory, reduced ability to learn, slow thinking, emotional retardedness, unrest, sleepiness, increased disorientation, and inability to make judgments. Some test items used for this purpose are primarily aimed at identifying left-brain activities (Theilgaard 1979).

Tests particularly suited for measuring left-brain capabilities are the "word-pair test," which measures the ability to imprint words by recording how fast and how many word pairs an individual is able to learn, the "copy retention test," and "the subtraction test," the latter measuring arithmetic abilities. Test items suitable for identifying right-brain capabilities are the Goldstein-Scheerer cube test, measuring the ability to handle abstract visual-spatial patterns, and Andersen's ability gestalt test, measuring visual imprinting and memory.

Stroop Test. In this test the individual is confronted with a perceptual conflict. Thus, if an individual is asked how many figures there are in the square below, the correct answer would be five:

44444

To arrive at this answer one would have to rely extensively on left-brain activities, whereas the answer "four" would indicate right-brain activities. Similar conflicts can be constructed between colors and names of colors, and naming of high and low musical pitches. When a sequence of such tests is carried out, individuals may reveal right- or left-brain dominance in their handling of the information. Like the WAIS and the brain-damage tests, it can be used primarily to identify individual differences. Cohen and Martin (1975) have applied this procedure successfully in an attempt to study left- versus right-brain conflicts in interpreting musical impressions.

Conjunctive Lateral Eye Movements (CLEM). These have been proposed by several authors as a measure of the extent to which the right or the left brain dominates information processing. The background for this is an observation made in studies of eye movements in response to electrical stimulation of the brain. The findings show that the eyes move to the right when the left hemisphere is stimulated, whereas they move to the left when the right half is stimulated. It has been suggested that this can be used to identify differences in hemispheral activity by observing to what side the respondent most frequently looks when thinking over an issue. There is, however, strong disagreement over the validity of the method (Ornstein 1973; Theilgaard 1973). Part of the problem is that the direction in which the eyes are moving may be a function of a very complex interaction among the two brain halves, as well as of the particular test situation.

As discussed earlier, the right hemisphere is not constrained by traditional logic; rather, it is artistic or creative in its way of dealing with impressions. In contrast, the left brain is analytical and systematical. With this background, it is natural to suggest that creativity tests may reveal whether an individual relies more or less on right versus left brain information processing. There is also evidence (Cropley and Field 1969) that what is being measured with creativity tests is very different from what is being measured with traditional IQ tests. So far, however, these measurement techniques have not been used in the study of hemispheral specialization, where they have a potential for identifying individual differences.

The individual's use of the left or right hand in gesticulating during conversation has been suggested to relate to brain dominance (Kimura 1973). Again, however, validation is lacking.

Measurements of the pupil size (pupillometrics) have been used to indicate brain activities (Watson and Gatchel 1979), but not to study differential effects. What is being measured is most frequently believed to be involvement, activity, or engagement in the issue (Hess 1972).

As suggested earlier, many psychologists have proposed dichotomies that more or less directly reflect the kinds of differences found between the specialized functions of the left and of the right brain. Therefore, it is not surprising to find that many personality, aptitude, and similar tests include dimensions that may relate to the phenomena discussed here. These tests may provide valuable sources for the researcher trying to develop questionnaire items through which individual differences can be identified.

Implications for Consumer Research Behavior

The findings on hemispheral lateralization of the human brain have implications for the study of consumer behavior. In the following sections of this paper, some of the more obvious implications are discussed—attention processes, pictorial communication, effects of mere exposure, involvement, and individual differences.

Attention Processes

Attention has been studied by observational procedures, such as observation of eye movements and the pupillometer, or based on measures of recall and recognition after tachistoscope exposure. In an excellent review, Broadbent (1977) concludes:

> *For what is is worth, therefore, there seems to be sketchy evidence for at least two stages of perceptual selection. The early global, or the low frequency stage packages information from*

the environment into different segments, each of which can then be attended or rejected. . . .

A later inquiry, or verification stage, works with more detailed information from the original package or segments, and is perhaps more affected by semantic context, by the pleasantness of a word, by co-occurrence probability of detailed features such as sequential probability of letters in words.

One may speculate that the "early global" or "low frequency stage" is predominantly a right-brain process, whereas the later inquiry, or verification stage, implies that the left brain also becomes involved. Moreover, it seems that, whereas the left-brain type of attention can only be maintained for a limited amount of time, the right-brain type of attention is not subject to the same timing process (Kimura 1973). Thus, one can imagine that only if sufficient psychic energy–involvement–is generated, will the extensive inquiry or verification stage occur. In other cases, however, only the first stage is reached, and information is received only in the sense that it gets "packed into different segments."

This suggestion is also in line with the observation by Krugman (1977) that when right hemispheral processes dominate (as in primary attention) recognition is possible, whereas recall requires the involvement of the left-hemispheral type of processes. That is, recognition requires that stored images become activated, whereas recall requires a much higher level of verbal and cognitive activity.

A mechanism like the one just described could, among other things, explain aspects of advertising effects hitherto not understood. The effects of brand names, trade marks, and the like could result primarily from such an elementary unedited storage of total impressions–effects that could be almost proportionate with the number of exposures.

In this connection, one may ask in what form do the informational images formed in the first stage of the attentional process get stored? Under what conditions does this occur? And, how and when can the information influence subsequent behavior? Additionally, questions must also be answered about the role of forgetting. Do such "unedited" impressions last only a short time? Do they disappear, if they are not reinforced? How frequent are reinforcements needed in order to maintain them?

Pictorial Communication

Very little is understood about the role of pictorial (and musical) material in the communication process. Similarly, the role of design and layout has been only scarcely researched (Hubert and Holbrock 1980; Mitchell 1980). A better understanding and theories of these processes are needed.

Linked to Broadbent's two-step theory of perception and interpreted in terms of hemispheral specialization, a hierarchical theory of picture perception could imply:

Step 1: As in Broadbent's first step of attention, pictorial material is perceived and primarily treated in a holistic fashion in the right hemisphere, where a complete image is stored.

Step 2: a) During interaction between the left and right hemispheres, holistically perceived images are decoded, and information relating to relevant attributes is processed and stored, or
b) The images are stored holistically and unedited.

Step 3: In subsequent decisions, the individual may, depending on the situation, rely upon:
a) the encoded–image-like–information stored in the right brain, or
b) the coded attributional information of the left brain.

In Step 3b, choice processes like those assumed in multiattribute models occur (Hansen 1977). In Step 3a, behavior may have great similarity with routinized response behavior (Howard 1977). This suggestion is hypothetical, and much more complicated, or different, brain processes may be involved. Nevertheless, the specialization of the right brain in noncognitive, nonverbal, pictorial, holistic gestalt perception, and of the left brain in verbal, cognitive, symbolic, attributional information processing suggests that the right brain plays a critical role, especially in connection with pictorial information.

Choice Behavior

The previous section has primarily dealt with the special role of right-hemispheral processes in connection with information exposure. There are problems also with regard to the way in which the specialization expresses itself in choice behavior. In this connection, it is worth noting that Olshavsky and Granbois (1979), after reviewing the literature on decision making, conclude: "For many purchases a decision process never occurs, not even on the first purchase."

And, looking for alternative ways in which choices can be explained, they write:

> *. . . , they can be made on the basis of surrogates of various types; or they can even occur on a random or superficial basis. Further research, free of the prepurchase decision assumption, may identify still other ways.*

Basically, what they are saying is that we can observe choices being made with little or no awareness, seemingly influenced by past information, and without the occurrence of cognitive processes of the kind associated with left-brain activities. Such choices are particularly found in areas where brand loyalty can be observed. Such loyalty occurs where choices are frequently repeated, problems are few, and the individual is not much concerned with a single choice. These, however, are the kinds of conditions discussed before, and the choices may be made primarily based on right-hemispheral activities, where simple recognition of an alternative elicits the choice.

If this proposition is valid, the question arises of how information, received holistically and stored as images, may influence such choices. Here the communication model proposed by Zajonc (1968) is of interest. In his "mere exposure" hypothesis, he suggests that with repeated exposure, stimuli will become more positively evaluated. Further, he maintains that this positive evaluation may result from repeated exposure alone. He compares the evaluations of more and of less frequently used words, and finds a strong positive correlation between exposure and liking, with the more frequently used words being the most positively evaluated. However, as Zajonc points out, it is not clear whether the most frequently used words are positively evaluated because they are frequent or whether they are used more frequently because they are positively evaluated. Consequently, he turns to studies where exposures have been experimentally manipulated, and shows that subjects' liking of nonsense words, figures resembling Chinese characters, and photographs increases with the number of exposures.

It may be that "mere exposure" is a dominant factor when new and uninvolving concepts are at stake. The conditions under which Zajonc has shown the principle to work may very well be where right-brain processing dominates. When involvement is stronger and when stimuli are familiar, stimuli will become associated with known concepts and cognitive processes may take over, which in turn may counteract the "mere exposure effect."

Zajonc (1980) has also shown that positive evaluation following from mere exposure can be established under conditions where we would expect right-brain processes to dominate. Exposing subjects very briefly to stimuli prior to a sorting task, he finds that even though the stimulation is so short that respondents are not aware of its occurrence, they, in the subsequent sorting task, prefer those stimuli to which they had previously been exposed.

The role of emotional conditioning, as discussed by Kroeber-Riel, Hemberle, and von Keitz (1979), may also be seen in this light. They suggest that in some areas:

> *The consumer is not interested in the substantial properties such as the ingredients contained in soup or vermicelli. In general, he will rely upon the fact that the soup purchased comes up to a normal standard of quality, and his attitude towards the product is influenced only very little by means of product specific information and the cognitive attitudinal component.*

In these areas, the evaluation of the product is more likely to be controlled by emotional appeals, which can be established by having the product associated with positively loaded images, persons, situations, etc. These are images established in communication situations of low involvement, and images that exert their influence predominantly under the control of right-hemispheral processes.

The Role of Involvement

As early as the 1960s, Krugman (1965) suggested that consumers received information differently depending on whether or not they are involved in the situations in which the information is received. In terms of hemispheral specialization, this should imply that in low-involvement situations right-brain processes dominate, whereas higher degrees of involvement give rise to left-brain processes (Krugman 1977). Therefore, under high-involvement conditions, information processing and deliberate choice making occur, as described in models of decision making and information processing.

Under low-involvement conditions, on the other hand, information is received holistically; pictorial material is received and stored without verbal or similar coding, and possibly emotional impressions are involved. Similarly, in low-involvement situations, choices are made—without any high degree of awareness—based on similarity with situations in the past. Thus, involvement may be a critical variable determining whether left- or right-brain processes dominate. Unfortunately, however, there is no general agreement as to the nature of involvement.

A major question is whether involvement is an enduring characteristic of the individual, describing his/her overall relationship with certain items, products, or groups of items, or whether it is a specific stage of the organism, present in various degrees in different situations. Authors like Lastovicka (1978) and Robertson (1976) discuss involvement in the first sense. They try to identify how individuals are more or less involved with different product categories, assuming that this involvement is relatively stable over time. They also discuss various questionnaire techniques that may be used to quantify this kind of involvement. Sherif, Sherif, and Nebergall's (1965) involvement concept is also of this nature. They assume that under low-involvement conditions, people are willing to accept information that deviates more from their own stand than they are willing to accept under high-involvement conditions.

In the second sense, variations in involvement reflect the extent to which the individual is more or less motivated toward a specific piece of information, product, or the like. Here it can be difficult to distinguish between specific motivation, arousal, and involvement. But, it is implied that with high involvement more psychic energy is released for handling incoming information, sorting it out, and making choices. This is the way in which the concept is used by Kroeber-Riel (1979) and by Mitchell (1980).

In the present context, the concept of involvement can be useful as a measure of the degree of individual motivation in a particular information-acquisition or choice situation, and as a determinant of the extent to which left-brain processing will dominate. It has been proposed by Kassarjian and Kassarjian (1979) and Rothschild (1979) that information processing under low-involvement conditions has implications for message frequency. The number of exposures needed before a sufficient amount of learning has occurred may be greater when right-brain processes dominate. Similarly, in instances where involvement is low, it may be advantageous to rely on media that create lower involvement. Television and movies have been suggested to have such properties (Krugman 1965).

Furthermore, when the planned message is not expected to create involvement to any significant degree, an attempt to communicate with long and complicated messages requiring high involvement on the part of the receiver is wasteful. In general, message context may have to differ depending on the extent to which the marketer is communicating with the right and/or the left brain. The use of pictorial material, the use of extensive copy, the complexity of the message, the number of informational items contained in the message, etc., may have to be adjusted depending on the degree of involvement and the nature of the information-handling process.

Individual Differences

Information processing under low-involvement, right-brain dominated attention processes, pictorial-information processing, and mere exposure effects may occur, to varying degrees, for the same individual in different situations. One may, however, also imagine that individuals differ in the extent to which they, under the same circumstances, rely on right-brain processes. Such individual differences are, in extreme degrees, believed to exist in a number of clinical cases. For instance, schizophrenia has been suggested to be related to extensive right-brain activities; also cases of reduced mental ability related to old age, extensive alcohol abuse, etc., may occur with only little observable damage to right-brain faculties (Wexler 1980).

Others have speculated that qualitative variations in intelligence, and particularly in creativity (Lindzay and Norman 1977), may relate to individual differences in hemispheral lateralization. Here, creativity, intuitive problem recognition, and problem solving are thought to be controlled by right-hemisphere activities.

Eventually, four, rather than two, individual types may exist. One can imagine individuals with more or less extensive left-brain processing, and individuals with more or less extensive right-brain processing. Thereby, four, rather than two, cases arise. With extensive left-brain processing and less extensive right-brain processing (Case 1) versus extensive right-brain processing and limited left-brain processing (Case 2), the dichotomy discussed so far emerges. However, the possibility of simultaneously extensive left- and right-brain processing (Case 3) and simultaneously limited left- and right-brain processing (Case 4) also exists:

Right brain	*Left brain* *Active*	*Left brain* *Less active*
Active	Case 3	Case 2
Less active	Case 1	Case 4

Right-brain dominance influences the reception of information for information storage and for choice behavior. Right-brain dominated persons would act more along the lines discussed in the preceding sections: low-involvement information processing and choice behavior would be more frequent, primary attention processes would occur more often, and there would be a tendency to rely more extensively on musical and pictorial impressions.

An Alternative to the Effect Hierarchy Models

The preceding discussion highlighted various aspects of consumer behavior that, when brought together, may constitute an alternative to the traditional decision-making/effect-types of hierarchy models. This can be summarized by the following hypotheses:

H1: Hierarchy-of-effect types of information processing is a typical left-brain phenomenon.

H2: Traditional decision-making behavior as implied in most models of consumer behavior relies primarily on left-brain information processing.

H3: Exposure without awareness or deliberate attention is possible, and is right-brain controlled.

H4: Information storage after exposure without awareness is holistic, with complete images being stored in an uncoded fashion.

H5: Pictures are always (and sometimes only) perceived as a right-brain process.

H6: Repeated exposures without awareness build up attraction or positive tendencies to act toward the object to which one is exposed.

H7: Right-brain processes become more frequent with decreasing involvement and fatigue.

H8: Some individuals are more likely than others to rely on right-brain processes.

Implications for Understanding the Role of Advertising

If it is confirmed that even with very low levels of attention some information can still be received, our view of how advertising works must then change. It is possible that a considerable amount of the advertising material to which a person is exposed, and which we normally conclude has no effect, may still be extremely important in forming habits, behavior, and attitudes. This may be a kind of long-run, secondary effect of advertising, the existence of which could support the proposition that the value structure of the messages, more or less unconsciously, is adopted by the receivers, and that this is done almost automatically by consumers, as the defense mechanisms are passive in the low-involvement situations where exposure occurs.

An important question relates to the possible occurrence of individual differences. Can two different personality types be identified, some with dominating right-brain activity and others with dominating left-brain activity? Or should four different types of individuals be considered: some who can use both kinds of information fully, some who are very poor at both kinds, and some who are left- or right-hemispherically specialized? Thus, if consumers differ in relying on left- versus right-brain processes, this could have a dramatic influence on communication strategies. Adaptation to the kinds of information processing and choice behavior that consumers in different segments apply may be very important.

At the extreme, in some product areas a relatively large number of consumers may be left almost untouched by commercial messages. These messages often rely on more extensive left-brain processing, whereas the consumers in question may be much more likely to rely on right-brain informational processing.

With regard to public policy issues, individual differences may also be important. Most political information and much information from the public sector is complex, verbal, and not suited for a right-brain dominated type. If such people are numerous, the fact that they rely on completely different kinds of information gives television and the "illustrative" print media an important influence.

Other questions need to be addressed as well. For example, to what extent do the different abilities people have for handling the imaginative versus symbolic depend on the different opportunities they have had for applying different information-processing modes? That is, are some people more thoroughly trained in imaginative information processing, and, if so, does this determine their subsequent personality and their relationship with mass communication?

One may speculate on whether the introduction of the public educational system and the cultural trend in western societies toward verbal, symbolic, and arithmetic information has caused a general change in the extent to which people rely on left- rather than right-brain information processing. If so, what role will television and other pictorial mass communications play in the future? Will they cause a reversal shift toward more right-brain dominated behavior, and will this, in turn, cause a change away from that largely symbolic and verbal culture that has characterized the Western World for the last two decades?

Another important implication is concerned with education. In an era where inductive learning has been emphasized by educators at all levels, the traditional lecture has been considered almost the only way of teaching students. In recent years, however, deductive methods have come into focus. Learning by doing and problem-oriented interdisciplinary group teaching have gained widespread interest, and are seen among some educators as the only possible way of teaching. To the extent that the deductive informal teaching process primarily relates to the right brain and the more traditional inductive teaching process primarily communicates to the left brain, it is important to emphasize the need for a mixture of the two approaches (Bogen 1977).

Future Research Strategies

In a previous section, tentative hypotheses were suggested specifying the more precise nature of the effects of hemispheral specialization. Although these hypotheses are supported by the findings of brain researchers and by those dealing with information handling and choice behavior in other areas, further proof is still needed. It is necessary to derive testable hypotheses from the more complex suggestions discussed in the preceding pages, and to develop methodologies for their testing.

The measurement techniques discussed previously can be used to identify individual differences in the degree to which people rely on the left versus the right hemisphere. Because most of these techniques can be applied only in an experimental setting and with considerable cost associated with each single observation, it is necessary to devise less expensive and less demanding measurement devices. This could be done using elements from the WAIS and from brain-damage testing procedures, in combination with self-rating items, either selected from existing personality and aptitude tests, or constructed with the major differences between right- and left-brain functioning in mind. Such tests, again, could be cross validated with tachistoscope measures, dichotic listening, EEG, and measures of individual differences in lateralization.

The most obvious way of measuring the extent to which different stimuli result in more or less right-brain processing seems to be with the use of EEG measures. Alternatively, measurements could rely on gestures or on the observation of eye movements. As discussed previously, neither of these approaches has been very successful (Ornstein 1973). Thus, the possibility of measuring the dominance of left- or right-brain processes in a specific situation is somewhat less promising than the possibility of identifying individual differences. To overcome this problem, however, one could use a two-step procedure:

- Study the same message (for instance, a combination of pictorial and verbal material) influences of traditional communication-effect measures, such as recognition, recall, learning, attitude, change preference, and change with left- versus right-brain dominated individuals.
- Study how different messages (combination of pictures and verbal material) give rise to different response patterns in terms of traditional communication-effect measures. Following this, compare the observed response patterns with those established to be typical for "left-brain receivers" versus "right-brain receivers."

This would make it possible to study differential effects of picture-dominated and verbal-dominated messages, with variations in involvement, as well as other message-related variables.

References

Appel, Valentine, Weinstein, Sidney, and Weinstein, Curt (1979), "Brain Activity and Recall of TV Advertising," *Journal of Advertising Research,* 19, 7–15.

Bogen, Joseph E. (1977), "Some Educational Implications of Hemispheric Specialization," in *The Human Brain,* ed. M. C. Wittrock, New York: Prentice-Hall, Inc., pp. 133–52.

——, and Vogel, Philip J. (1962), "Cerebral Commissurotomy in Man," *Bulletin of the Los Angeles Neurological Society,* Bulletin No. 27–8, 169–72.

Broadbent, Donald E. (1977), "The Two Processes of Attention," *American Psychologist,* 32, 109–18.

Cohen, Gillian, and Martin, Michael (1975), "Hemisphere Differences in an Auditory Stroop Test," *Perception and Psychophysics,* 38, 79–83.

Cropley, Al J., and Field, Tate W. (1969), "Achievement in Science and Intellectual Style," *Journal of Applied Psychology,* 53, 132–5.

Deglin, Vadim L. (1976), "Journey Through the Brain," *Unesco Courier,* January, 4–14.

Freeman, Frank S. (1962), *Psychological Testing,* New York: Holt, Rinehart and Winston.

Gazzaniga, Michael S. (1977), "Review of the Split Brain," in *The Human Brain,* ed. M. C. Wittrock, New York: Prentice-Hall, Inc., pp. 89–96.

Hansen, Flemming (1977), "Psychological Models of Consumer Choice," in *A Synthesis of Selected Aspects of Consumer Behavior,* ed. R. Ferber, Washington, DC: U.S. Government Printing Office, pp. 33–67.

Hess, Eckard H. (1972), "Pupillometrics: A Method of Studying Mental, Emotional and Sensory Processes," in *Handbook of Psychophysiology,* eds. N. S. Greenfield and R. A. Sternbach, New York: Holt, Rinehart and Winston.

Howard, John F. (1977), *Consumer Behavior: Theory and Applications,* New York: McGraw-Hill Book Co.

Hubert, Joel, and Holbrock, Morris B. (1980), "The Determinants of Esthetic Value and Growth," in *Advances in Consumer Research, Vol. 7,* ed. Jerry C. Olson, Ann Arbor, MI: Association for Consumer Research.

Kassarjian, Harold H., and Kassarjian, Waltraud M. (1979), "Attitudes under Low Commitment Conditions," in *Attitude Research Plays for High Stakes,* eds. John C. Maloney and Bernard Silverman, Chicago: AMA.

Kimura, Doreen (1973), "The Asymmetry of the Human Brain—Recent Progress in Perception," *Scientific American,* 232, 246–54.

Kroeber-Riel, Werner (1979), "Activation Research: Psychobiological Approaches in Consumer Research," *Journal of Consumer Research,* 5, 240–50.

——, Hemberle, Gerhard, and von Keitz, Wolfgang (1979), "Product Differentiation by Emotional Conditioning—A Successful Marketing Strategy in Spite of the Critical Consumer?" working paper, International Series, University of the Saarland, Saarbrücken, West Germany.

Krugman, Herbert E. (1965), "The Impact of Television Advertising: Learning without Involvement," *The Public Opinion Quarterly,* 29, 349–56.

—— (1977), "Memory without Recall, Exposure without Recognition," *Journal of Advertising Research,* 17, 7–12.

—— (1980), "Sustained Viewing of Television," paper presented at The Conference Board, Council on Marketing Research, New York.

Lastovicka, John L. (1978), "Questioning the Concept of Involvement Defined Product Classes," in *Advances in Consumer Research, Vol. 6,* ed. William L. Wilkie, Ann Arbor, MI: Association for Consumer Research, pp. 174–9.

Lassen, Niels A., Ingvar, David H., and Skinhøj, Erik (1978), "Brain Function and Blood Flow," *Scientific American,* October, 50–9.

Lindzay, Peter H., and Norman, Donald A. (1977), *Human Information Processing,* New York: Academic Press.

Lundsgaard, Niels E. (1978), "Psykologiske Funktioners Asymmetriske Representation i den Menneskelige Hjerne," unpublished Ph.D. dissertation at the Copenhagen University, Copenhagen.

Mitchell, Andrew A. (1980), "Using Information Processing Theory to Understand Advertising Effects," in *Advances in Consumer Research, Vol. 7,* ed. Jerry C. Olson, Ann Arbor, MI: Association for Consumer Research.

Olshavsky, Richard W., and Granbois, Donald H. (1979), "Consumer Decision Making—Fact or Fiction?" *The Journal of Consumer Research,* 6, 93–100.

Ornstein, Robert E. (1973), *The Nature of Human Consciousness,* San Francisco: The Viking Press.

Ottesen, Otto (1980), "Behavioural Paradigms in Advertising Research," working paper, The Copenhagen School of Business Administration and Economics.

Packard, Vance (1957), *The Hidden Persuaders,* New York: Longmans, Green & Co.

Ray, Michael L. (1976), "Marketing Communication and the Hierarchy of Effects," in *New Models for Communication Research,* ed. P. Clark, New York: Sage Publications, Ltd.

Robertson, Thomas S. (1976), "Low Commitment Consumer Behavior," *Journal of Advertising Research,* 16, 19–24.

Rothschild, Michael L. (1979), "Advertising Strategies for High and Low Involvement Situations," in *Attitude Research Plays for High Stakes,* eds. John C. Maloney and Bernhard Silverman, Chicago: American Marketing Association.

Sherif, Carolyn W., Sherif, Muzafer, and Nebergall, Roger E. (1965), *Attitude and Attitude Change,* Philadelphia: W. B. Saunders, Inc.

Sperry, Roger W. (1973), "Lateral Specialization of Cerebral Function in the Surgically Separated Hemispheres," in *The Psychophysiology of Thinking*, eds. F. J. McGuigan and R. A. Schoonorer, New York: Academic Press, Inc., pp. 209–29.

Theilgaard, Alice (1973), "Psykologiske Funktioners Repræsentation i Hjernen," *Nordisk Psykiatrisk Tidsskrift*, 7, 418–26.

—— (1979), "Demens–Psykologisk Set," *Nordisk Psykiatrisk Tidsskrift*, 33, 398–413.

Watson, Paul J., and Gatchel, Robert J. (1979), "Autonomic Measuring of Advertising," *Journal of Advertising Research*, 19, 15–24.

Wexler, Bruce E. (1980), "Cerebral Laterality and Psychiatry: A Review of the Literature," *The American Journal of Psychiatry*, 137, 279–89.

Wittrock, Merlin C. (1977), *The Human Brain*, Englewood Cliffs, NJ: Prentice-Hall, Inc.

Zajonc, Robert B. (1968), "Attitudinal Effects of Mere Exposure," *Journal of Personality and Social Psychology*, 9, monograph issue.

—— (1980), "Time and Functions of Mind," *IRS Newsletter* (Spring), Ann Arbor, MI: The University of Michigan, pp. 3–5.

CHAPTER TWO

Influences on Consumer Behavior

READING 6

Psychographics: A Critical Review

William D. Wells

This article presents case histories of five somewhat different uses of psychographic research, and it critically reviews the status of research in this field.

Among the standard fixtures in marketing research, the demographic profile is probably the most familiar. Age, income, education, and other indications of position in life space have so much influence on so many kinds of consumer behavior that users of a product or a brand, viewers of a TV program, or readers of a magazine are virtually certain to differ from the rest of the population on one or more of the common demographic dimensions. Marketing researchers collect demographics as a matter of routine, and marketers feel comfortable using them.

But demographic profiles, essential though they may be, have not been deemed sufficient. Especially since the end of World War II researchers have engaged in a continuous search for new, more comprehensive and more exciting descriptions. It is as though demographics provided only a nodding acquaintance, and marketers wanted to know their customers much better.

Until recently this search has followed two somewhat different directions. Starting with the classic study by Koponen [74], investigators have repeatedly tried to correlate consumer behavior with scores obtained from standardized personality inventories. And, starting with Dichter's innovative studies of consumers' motivations [31], students of the consumer's mind have tried to apply the concepts and methods of clinical psychology to virtually every aspect of marketing.

From Koponen's study on, the work with personality inventories has been judged "equivocal" [65]. The correlations have almost invariably been low, and the relationships uncovered have often been so abstract that they could not be used with confidence in making real-world marketing decisions.

Motivation research has fared much better. In spite of severe criticisms on both ethical and methodological grounds, motivation research enjoyed a tremendous vogue; in its current form—the small scale "qualitative study"—it still has many busy practitioners. It is somewhat ironic that the more rigorous of these two approaches has proved relatively sterile, while the sloppier methodology continues to produce results that intelligent people judge to be of great value.

Sometime during the 1960s a blend of these two traditions began to take shape. Variously called "life style" [102, 104], "psychographic" [29, 89, 90 91, 95, 109], or "activity and attitude" [54, 55] research, this blend combines the objectivity of the personality inventory with the rich, consumer-oriented, descriptive detail of the qualitative motivation research investigation. This new blend has attracted considerable attention, both among "academics" and among "real-world" marketers. It has also attracted its share of criticism, and its share of skeptical questions as to its true usefulness and value [26, 33, 45, 86, 110, 120, 124, 142].

This review attempts to take stock of the present status and future prospects of psychographic research, including consumer-oriented research with standardized personality inventories. It begins with a definition of the field. It continues with examples of five somewhat different approaches to psychographic

Reprinted by permission of the American Marketing Association, from the *Journal of Marketing Research,* 12:2 May 1975, 196–213.

analysis. And it concludes with a critical discussion of the reliability, validity, and usefulness of psychographic measurements.

Definitions

Although the need for a common definition of psychographics is obvious, no single definition has met with general approval. Twenty-four articles on psychographics contain no less than 32 definitions, all somewhat different [29, 30, 33, 45, 53, 68, 79, 83, 89, 92, 95, 100, 105, 108, 109, 110, 111, 119, 120, 134, 140, 142, 143, 146], and each new publication seems to produce still another version of what psychographic research is or is not. Within this diversity, however, certain common elements are clearly visible.

Something More Than Demographics

All psychographic researchers have attempted to move beyond demographics into areas that are relatively untried and unfamiliar. Depending upon the investigator's objectives and to some extent upon his taste, the added dimensions have run from one or two [11, 23, 44, 67, 80] to several hundred [1, 102, 125, 136, 145] and have embraced a wide range of content, including activities, interests, opinions, needs, values, attitudes, and personality traits. In some cases the variables have been "homemade," and in others they have been borrowed from standardized attitude scales or personality inventories. In all cases, however, the common theme has been that demographic attributes alone are not enough.

Quantitative, Not Qualitative

Second, most psychographic researchers have employed precoded, objective questionnaires that can be self-administered or administered by ordinary survey interviewers. Precoding makes the data amenable to complex multivariate statistical analysis; ease of administration encourages—or at least permits—use of large, representative samples. Both practices distinguish psychographic studies from studies in the qualitative motivation research tradition.

Operationally, then, psychographic research can be defined as quantitative research intended to place consumers on psychological—as distinguished from demographic—dimensions. Because it goes beyond the standard and the accepted, it offers the possibility of new insights and unusual conclusions. Because it is quantitative rather than discursive, it opens the way to large, representative samples of respondents, and to multivariate statistical analysis of findings.

Five Examples

A Psychographic Profile Based on General "Life-Style" Dimensions

The need for good descriptions of consumers is well expressed in the following comment by an advertising copy writer:

> *. . . Imagine that I've got to write an ad on a Sunday afternoon, and I want to feel sure I'm on the right track. I want to double check myself that people will understand it/react to it/remember it, plus a few subtleties like will they like it, dislike it, etc.*
>
> *So, I trudge all the way around the block, talking to the neighbors, and forty houses later I have a slight idea of what will happen to my ad when it reaches the world. That's what I understand Research does, only a lot more intelligently and a lot more thoroughly and in a lot more neighborhoods.*
>
> *A writer writes out of his personal collection of life experiences and his knowledge of people, and he imagines and projects them and he tries to translate them into his viewer's or his reader's terms. But he's feeding off himself. He's just one person. He can't afford to trust just his own experience. Research extends the writer. Information is his life blood. He can't write out of thin air. Anything that adds to his storehouse of information is necessary and vital [75].*

Similar needs are felt by all others who must create products, services, or messages for customers they cannot meet in person. Just as the writer knows that he cannot feed only off himself, so also the product designer and the marketing manager know that they run grave risks when they rely solely on their own assumptions. Almost all of marketing is communication; marketers are most effective when they know their audiences.

As an example of the descriptive value of psychographic dimensions, consider the somewhat esoteric problem of communicating with consumers who are heavy users of shotgun ammunition. Persons of this sort would be of special interest to anyone who manufactures, markets, or advertises shotguns, ammunition, or associated hunting paraphernalia; to operators of hunting lodges and private hunting areas; to publishers of hunting magazines; and to government officials who promote or regulate this form of recreation.

TABLE 1
Psychographic Profile of the Heavy User of Shotgun Ammunition

	Percent Who Spend $11+ per Year on Shotgun Ammunition (141)	*Percent Who Don't Buy (395)*
Age		
Under 25	9	5
25–34	33	15
35–44	27	22
45–54	18	22
55+	13	36
Occupation		
Professional	6	15
Managerial	23	23
Clerical-Sales	9	17
Craftsmen	50	35
Income		
Under $6,000	26	19
$6,000–$10,000	39	36
$10,000–$15,000	24	27
$15,000+	11	18
Population Density		
Rural	34	12
2,500–50,000	11	11
50,000–500,000	16	15
500,000–2 million	21	27
2 million+	13	19
Geographic Division		
New England–Mid-Atlantic	21	33
Central (N, W)	22	30
South Atlantic	23	12
E. South Central	10	3
W. South Central	10	5
Mountain	6	3
Pacific	9	15

Source: [107].

A demographic profile of the heavy user of shotgun ammunition appears in Table 1. The man who spends at least $11 per year on shotgun shells differs from the nonbuyer in that he tends to be younger, lower in income and education, and more concentrated in blue-collar occupations. He is also more apt to be living in rural areas, especially in the South.

Now reflect upon the implications of this pattern. Hunting is a risky sport. Is the hunter a risk taker? Is he likely to follow rules on his own, or does he require external control? Hunting is a violent sport. Is the hunter attracted by violence in general? What other products would make good tie-in sales with hunting equipment? Is the hunter also a fisherman or a camper? Is he especially interested in food? Is he a regular newspaper reader? Is he a regular patron of discount stores? From the demographic profile alone, a marketer with a thorough knowledge of young, blue-collar, nonurban life styles might be able to guess the answers to at least some of these questions, but few would guess them all.

The data in Table 2 show how psychographic information can put flesh on demographic bones. These data came from a general life-style study that happened to contain a question about shotgun ammunition along with questions about approximately 100 other products and services. The questionnaire also contained questions about a wide range of activities, interests, and opinions; about reading of major magazines; and viewing of a large number of television programs. The study was not designed around shotgun users, or around the users of any other single product.

In spite of this lack of focus, the data in Table 2 show some interesting patterns. First, it is obvious that hunting is not an isolated phenomenon but rather is associated with other rugged outdoor endeavors. Shotgun shell buyers not only like to hunt, they also like to fish and to go camping. They even like to work outdoors. These relationships are interesting and useful because they suggest activities and settings, other than hunting scenes, that might be appropriate for shotgun ammunition advertising. They suggest products that might be especially appropriate for joint promotions or other cooperative marketing ventures, such as displaying shotgun ammunition near camping or fishing equipment in retail outlets.

TABLE 2
Psychographic Profile of the Heavy User of Shotgun Ammunition

Base	*Percent Who Spend $11+ per Year on Shotgun Ammunition (141)*	*Percent Who Don't Buy (395)*
I like hunting	88	7
I like fishing	68	26
I like to go camping	57	21
I love the out-of-doors	90	65
A cabin by a quiet lake is a great place to spend the summer	49	34
I like to work outdoors	67	40
I am good at fixing mechanical things	47	27
I often do a lot of repair work on my own car	36	12
I like war stories	50	32
I would do better than average in a fist fight	38	16
I would like to be a professional football player	28	18
I would like to be a policeman	22	8
There is too much violence on television	35	45
There should be a gun in every home	56	10
I like danger	19	8
I would like to own my own airplane	35	13
I like to play poker	50	26
I smoke too much	39	24
I love to eat	49	34
I spend money on myself that I should spend on the family	44	26
If given a chance, most men would cheat on their wives	33	14
I read the newspaper every day	51	72

Source: [107].

Table 2 also shows that ammunition buyers are apt to be do-it-yourselfers, which suggests that hunters are apt to be buyers of hardware and tools.

Items in the third group in Table 2 suggest some hypotheses about the psychological makeup of the shotgun ammunition buyer. Compared with the nonbuyer he is definitely more attracted by violence, suggesting that detective, war, and violent Western TV programs ought to draw audiences with disproportionate numbers of shotgun users, and that action and adventure magazines ought to be considered when placing advertising associated with hunting. Relationships between product use and media exposure are always best documented by direct cross-tabulation, but when these data are not available (and they often are not) relationships suggested by life-style patterns can provide helpful direction.

The relatively high levels of agreement with the fourth section of Table 2 suggest that the hunter is generally less risk-averse than is his nonhunting counterpart. To policy makers charged with keeping hunters from shooting themselves and each other, this willingness to accept risk would suggest that sober warnings about the dangers of firearms may well be ineffective. Lest this conclusion seem hopelessly naive, let it be noted that sober warnings about the dangers of firearms are exactly what some policy makers have attempted.

The relatively high levels of agreement with the fifth section suggest a combination of self-indulgence and lack of internal control that seems congruent with the attitude toward risk just noted. If the hunter is in fact self-indulgent and relatively conscienceless, it would seem unwise to rely on appeals to fair play and conservation to regulate his activities. Again, such appeals have been tried with less success than expected.

The level of agreement with "I love to eat" and the hunter's professed willingness to spend money on himself suggest markets for premium foods designed to be taken along on hunting expeditions. These two findings also suggest the suitability of game-preparation recipes for hunting magazines, and they indicate that quantity and quality of food should get particular attention from proprietors of hunting lodges. Hunters don't mind roughing it, but they want it to be a well-fed roughness.

Finally, the relatively low level of agreement with "I read the newspaper every day" should serve as a warning to shotgun ammunition advertisers. This is not to assert that media decisions, positive or negative, should ever be based on responses to a single survey item. Rather, it suggests that any shotgun ammunition advertiser who is spending his budget in newspapers should think twice about alternatives.

This brief example shows how a psychographic profile obtained almost incidentally in the context of a large, general life-style survey can provide suggestions and hypotheses that bear on a wide range of marketing and policy decisions. A demographic profile alone would perhaps have provided some of these inferences, but surely not all of them.

This example also shows how a psychographic profile can help the marketer avoid some traps a demographic profile would have set for him. Knowing that heavy users of shotgun ammunition tend to be younger, more in blue-collar occupations, and less urban than nonusers might suggest that they would be heavier users of beer, more interested in television, more interested in spectator sports, more prone to use credit, and more apt to shop at discount stores. Yet buyers of shotgun ammunition do not differ significantly from nonbuyers on any of these dimensions.

Other psychographic life-style profiles that have appeared in the literature include carryout foods [130]; eye makeup, shortening, oranges, and lemons [133, 136]; beer [103, 127]; mouthwash [127]; heavy duty hand soap [103]; bank charge cards [102]; department stores [83]; and air travel [11]. They also include profiles of the readers of magazines [117, 128] and of viewers of various television programs [104, 128]. In all these cases the psychographic data have provided rich, descriptive detail that could not have been inferred from demographics. See also [1, 47, 50, 58, 77, 118, 132, 136, 138].

A Product-Specific Psychographic Profile

In the previous example, the psychographic profile was drawn from a large set of general life-style items. Because the item list was large and diverse, some of the items happened to be related to consumption of shotgun ammunition. When a psychographic study is devoted to a single product category, it is not necessary to depend on item diversity to get useful relationships. Rather, the investigator can focus upon a limited set of relevant, product-related dimensions.

An excellent example of this use of psychographics is provided in a report by Young [144] on the "positioning" of the Ford Pinto. According to Young, the introductory Pinto advertising portrayed the car as "carefree, small (and) romantic." The strategy was "to sell to small car prospects; to compete against imported small cars; to say that the car was carefree, touble free, beautifully styled, and economical" [144, p. 15].

As the introduction of the Pinto proceeded, psychographic research disclosed that potential Pinto buyers had a less romantic orientation toward cars and driving. They endorsed statements like "I wish I could depend on my car more," "I am more practical in car selection," "A car offers me a chance to tinker with machinery," "I like to feel how powerful my car is" and "The only function for a car is transportation." They rejected statements like "The kind of car you have is important as to how people see you" and "Taking care of a car is too much trouble."

As a result of this research, the Pinto was repositioned (in advertising, by its new agency) as "The epitome of function, exemplifying basic economical transportation, trading on Ford's heritage of the Model A." Consequently, "Today Pinto is the largest selling subcompact, outselling Volkswagen by a sizeable margin" [144, p. 15].

Now it is admittedly farfetched to assume that all (or maybe even most) of Pinto's success was due to this change in position. But it does seem reasonable to believe that emphasis on economy and practicality appealed to the salient needs of potential subcompact buyers, and that the revised message communicated ideas that potential customers would find most persuasive.

Personality Traits as Descriptors

A report on "Ecologically Concerned Consumers: Who Are They?" [72] provides a third example of psychographic analysis. In this report the dependent variable was an "index of ecological concern" that included both attitudes toward ecological issues and conservationist behavior. The independent variables were 7 demographic characteristics, 12 personality traits taken from standardized personality inventories, and a variable called "perceived consumer effectiveness." This attribute was measured by degree of disagreement with "It is futile for the individual consumer to try to do anything about pollution."

The 20 independent variables were first screened by analysis of variance to determine which of them discriminated between respondents who were high and respondents who were low in ecological concern. The 10 variables that survived the screening were then input to Multiple Classification Analysis to "predict" the degree of ecological concern expressed by each respondent. To avoid confusion it should be noted that in this study, as in most psychographic studies, the term "predict" cannot be taken literally. Since the data were all collected at the same point in time, "prediction" really means correlation.

The MCA coefficients for the "factors that were found to be most significant" in "predicting" ecological concern are shown in Table 3. The coefficients show how much the members in each category differ in ecological concern from the total sample. Thus, respondents who were low in perceived consumer effectiveness were 2.49 points below average in ecological concern, respondents who were medium were 4.04 points below average, and so on.

This study differs from the ammunition study and the Pinto study in two important ways. First, in the ammunition and Pinto studies the descriptions of the target groups were developed by considering *all* the psychographic items that discriminated between the target group and the remainder of the population. In this study, on the other hand, the answers that respondents gave to the personality scale questions were summed to produce higher level, more abstract scores on "tolerance," "understanding," and "harm avoidance." This procedure had the effect of eliminating much of the rich descriptive detail that might have been provided by the individual questions. We do not know what answers produced high scores or low scores on the personality dimensions.

Second, in the ammunition and Pinto studies the profiles were developed by cross-tabulating *all* of the psychographic items with the dependent variable. In this study, the independent variables were linked to the dependent variable by a type of multiple regression. Like all other forms of multiple regression, MCA suppresses variables that are closely related to variables that are allowed to enter the equation. As a result, variables closely related to each other could not all have entered the description of the ecologically concerned consumer, even though they might have discriminated sharply in a cross-tabulation.

Many other examples of this general approach are to be found in the literature. In one of the earliest psychographic studies, Koponen regressed Edwards

TABLE 3
MCA Profile of the Ecologically Concerned Consumer

Factor	*Level*	*Regression Coefficient*
Perceived consumer effectiveness	Very low	–
	Low	−2.49
	Medium	−4.04
	High	−1.04
	Very high	2.54
Tolerance	Very low	.15
	Low	− .79
	Medium	− .39
	High	− .04
	Very high	1.00
Understanding	Very low	− .92
	Low	− .81
	Medium	.22
	High	.27
	Very high	1.25
Harm avoidance	Very low	− .59
	Low	.13
	Medium	.27
	High	.73
	Very high	−1.22
Annual family income	Under $5,000	− .39
	$5,000 to $6,999	− .24
	$7,000 to $9,999	.10
	$10,000 to $14,999	− .15
	$15,000 and over	.74

Mean = 11.31.
R^2 = .28.

Personal Preference Schedule scores on consumption of cigarettes and readership of several magazines [74]. A group of investigators from the Advertising Research Foundation regressed the same set of independent variables against consumption of toilet paper, with predictable and poetically just results [5]. Frank, Massy, and Lodahl did the same for coffee, tea, and beer [41]. Wilson [139] factor analyzed an activity, interest, and opinion inventory and regressed various AIO factors against consumption of a list of products that included soft drinks, lipstick, and stomach remedies. And Darden and Reynolds [27] used scales representing fashion interest, fashion venturesomeness, cognitive style, information seeking, relative popularity and relative self-confidence to "predict" fashion opinion leadership. See also [21, 25, 39, 46, 69, 85, 87, 100, 123].

In all these cases a large set of descriptive items was reduced to a smaller number of more abstract scores, and this reduced set of independent variables was then linked to the dependent variable by means of some form of multiple regression. The descriptions thus provided were therefore more abstract and less redundant than the descriptions that would have been provided by simple cross-tabulation of the uncondensed raw data.

A General Life-Style Segmentation Study

A report of a major study by the Newspaper Advertising Bureau [109] provides an example of still another approach to psychographics. In this study a national sample of approximately 4,000 respondents completed questionnaires containing 300 psychographic questions, several dozen questions about product use, and questions about exposure to various media. The psychographic questions were reduced to a smaller set of scales by R-type factor analysis, and the resulting factor scores were input to Q-type factor analysis to place the respondents into relatively homogeneous groups. Condensed descriptions of the eight male groups are given in Figure 1.

This study differs from the first three in that it did not assume that members of any target group are all very similar. Instead of attempting to discover what hunters, Pinto buyers, or ecologically concerned consumers have in common, this study admitted the possibility that users of a product might fall into several quite different segments.

The wisdom of this approach is illustrated in Table 4. There it can be seen that the heavy users of several products and several brands, the readers of some magazines and the viewers of some TV programs tend to be concentrated in two or more segments that differ quite significantly from each other. When that is the case, any attempt to discover the characteristics of an undifferentiated target group—e.g., "the heavy beer drinker," "the user of Brand X deodorant," "the *Playboy* reader," or "the TV news viewer"—whether by simple cross-tabulation or by multiple regression—will be sure to underestimate the importance of the attributes upon which the segments differ. In extreme cases, when one segment of the target group is above average on a particular attribute and another segment is below average, merging the two segments into one target group can make the target group appear to be not different from the remainder of the population. (See [54, 55] for a neat example of this phenomenon.)

A Product-Specified Segmentation

In the preceding example, the segmentation was based on general—as opposed to product related—psychographic items. When the investigation is devoted to one product, the investigator can focus upon product-related material. An example of the latter approach is given in a report by Pernica [95] of a stomach remedy segmentation. Pernica developed a list of 80 items that included symptom frequency, end benefits provided by different brands, attitudes toward treatment, and beliefs about ailments. Items tapping general personality traits were recast so as to be product specific. For instance, "I worry too much" was translated into "I seem to get stomach problems if I worry too much."

The 80 product-specific items were reduced to 13 factors by R factor analysis, and scores on the 13 factors were input into Q factor analysis to assign the respondents to homogeneous groups. The segments were described both in terms of the variables that went into the segmentation and in terms of personality traits, life-style attributes, and demographic characteristics (Figure 2). The ability of this procedure to discriminate among the brands in this product category is shown in Table 5.

Note that the discrimination produced by the product-specific approach is somewhat sharper than the discrimination produced by the more general segmentation. This outcome is common. When the segmentation is based upon the dimensions upon which brands differ, it is almost certain to discriminate more sharply among brands than when it is based upon more general considerations [54, 55, 143, 146]. Other examples of the product-specific approach can be found in [12, 30, 42, 52, 145-8].

This case history, and the four that precede it, provide five different examples of psychographic analysis. Collectively they show how psychographics can supplement demographics in interesting and useful ways. Individually they show the range of capabilities of these techniques, and they provide previews of some problems and ambiguities. We now turn to critical discussion of the problems that have arisen in the application of psychographic methods.

FIGURE 1
Eight Male Psychographic Segments

Group I. *"The Quiet Family Man"* (8% of total males)

He is a self-sufficient man who wants to be left alone and is basically shy. Tries to be as little involved with community life as possible. His life revolves around the family, simple work and television viewing. Has a marked fantasy life. As a shopper he is practical, less drawn to consumer goods and pleasures than other men.

Low education and low economic status, he tends to be older than average.

Group II. *"The Traditionalist"* (16% of total males)

A man who feels secure, has self-esteem, follows conventional rules. He is proper and respectable, regards himself as altruistic and interested in the welfare of others. As a shopper he is conservative, likes popular brands and well-known manufacturers.

Low education and low or middle socio-economic status; the oldest age group.

Group III. *"The Discontented Man"* (13% of total males)

He is a man who is likely to be dissatisfied with his work. He feels bypassed by life, dreams of better jobs, more money and more security. He tends to be distrustful and socially aloof. As a buyer, he is quite price conscious.

Lowest education and lowest socio-economic group, mostly older than average.

Group IV. *"The Ethical Highbrow"* (14% of total males)

This is a very concerned man, sensitive to people's needs. Basically a puritan, content with family life, friends, and work. Interested in culture, religion and social reform. As a consumer he is interested in quality, which may at times justify greater expenditure.

Well educated, middle or upper socio-economic status, mainly middle aged or older.

Group V. *"The Pleasure Oriented Man"* (9% of total males)

He tends to emphasize his masculinity and rejects whatever appears to be soft or feminine. He views himself as a leader among men. Self-centered, dislikes his work or job. Seeks immediate gratification for his needs. He is an impulsive buyer, likely to buy products with a masculine image.

Low education, lower socio-economic class, middle aged or younger.

Group VI. *"The Achiever"* (11% of total males)

This is likely to be a hardworking man, dedicated to success and all that it implies, social prestige, power and money. Is in favor of diversity, is adventurous about leisure time pursuits. Is stylish, likes good food, music, etc. As a consumer he is status conscious, a thoughtful and discriminating buyer.

Good education, high socio-economic status, young.

Group VII. *"The He-Man"* (19% of total males)

He is gregarious, likes action, seeks an exciting and dramatic life. Thinks of himself as capable and dominant. Tends to be more of a bachelor than a family man, even after marriage. Products he buys and brands preferred are likely to have "self-expressive value," especially a "Man of Action" dimension.

Well educated, mainly middle socio-economic status, the youngest of the male groups.

Group VIII. *"The Sophisticated Man"* (10% of total males)

He is likely to be an intellectual, concerned about social issues, admires men with artistic and intellectual achievements. Socially cosmopolitan, broad interests. Wants to be dominant, and a leader. As a consumer he is attracted to the unique and fashionable.

Best educated and highest economic status of all groups, younger than average.

TABLE 4
Product and Media Use by Psychographic Group

	Psychographic Group[a] Percentages							
	I	*II*	*III*	*IV*	*V*	*VI*	*VII*	*VIII*
Drink beer	45	56	57	51	75	59	80	72
Smoke cigarettes	32	40	40	29	54	42	51	38
Air travel outside U.S.	4	4	6	7	5	8	12	19
Air travel, domestic	14	15	14	26	19	32	20	42
Use Brand X deodorant	7	7	6	8	14	10	9	12
Used headache remedy in past four weeks	53	60	66	61	61	64	65	67
Read current issue of:								
Playboy	8	11	8	13	25	27	36	30
National Geographic	21	13	11	30	13	28	16	27
Time	17	8	7	16	9	26	17	29
Newsweek	17	14	8	20	11	18	13	22
Field & Stream	10	12	14	8	12	9	13	3
Popular Mechanics	11	6	9	9	9	9	8	6
Viewed in past week:								
Sanford & Son	32	35	29	19	26	25	27	23
Sonny & Cher	17	24	22	19	14	24	30	22
Marcus Welby	26	25	26	23	20	16	20	18
Rowen & Martin	21	23	17	15	22	20	23	21
New Dick Van Dyke	19	15	16	13	11	8	10	12

a. Described in Figure 1.

Critical Discussion

Questions about psychographics can be classified under four major headings: reliability, validity, applications to real-world marketing problems, and contributions to the study of consumer behavior. These topics will be discussed in turn, with special reference to the five case histories just given.

Reliability of Individual Items and Scales

Here the term "reliability" is used in the restricted technical sense—i.e., freedom from *random* error [84, 93]. Although reliability of this sort is quite important, it is far from being the sole determinant of what a marketer is likely to be thinking about when he asks, "Can I rely on this study to guide my actions?" The other factors involved in that difficult and much more general question will be discussed in subsequent sections of this article.

When assessing reliability, it is important to distinguish between two major uses for psychographic measurements. One use is as a public opinion poll. An investigator might want to know, for example, how many people agree with "There should be a gun in every home," "Television commercials put too much emphasis on sex," or "I consider myself to be a member of the silent majority." In this use, when samples are of the size typically found in marketing surveys, *random* errors tend to cancel, and overall averages and percentages tend to be quite stable.

The other use of psychographics is in relation-

TABLE 5
Brand Use of Stomach Remedy Segments (Percent Use Brand Most Often)

Brand	*Severe Sufferers*	*Active Medicators*	*Hypochondriacs*	*Practicalists*
A	6	3	1	1
B	32	23	10	8
C	16	17	12	5
D	16	19	24	8
E	5	29	37	51

FIGURE 2
Segmentation of Stomach Remedy Users

The Severe Sufferers
The Severe Sufferers are the extreme group on the potency side of the market. They tend to be young, have children, and be well educated. They are irritable and anxious people, and believe that they suffer more severely than others. They take the ailment seriously, fuss about it, pamper themselves, and keep trying new and different products in search of greater potency. A most advanced product with new ingredients best satisfies their need for potency and fast relief, and ties in with their psychosomatic beliefs.

The Active Medicators
The Active Medicators are on the same side of the motivational spectrum. They are typically modern suburbanites with average income and education. They are emotionally well adjusted to the demands of their active lives. They have learnt to cope by adopting the contemporary beliefs of seeking help for every ill, and use remedies to relieve even minor signs of ailments and every ache and pain. In a modern product, they seek restoration of their condition and energy, mental recovery, and a lift for their active lives. They are influenced by a brand's reputation and by how well it is advertised. They tend to develop strong brand loyalties.

The Hypochondriacs
The Hypochondriacs are on the opposite side of the motivational spectrum. They tend to be older, not as well educated, and women. They have conservative attitudes toward medication and a deep concern over health. They see possible dangers in frequent use of remedies, are concerned over side effects, and afraid of remedies with new ingredients and extra potency. To cope with these concerns, they are strongly oriented toward medical authority, seeking guidance in treatment, and what products they should use. They hold rigid beliefs about the ailment and are disciplined in the products they use, and how frequently. They want a simple, single-purpose remedy, which is safe and free from side effects, and backed by doctors or a reputable company.

The Practicalists
The Practicalists are in the extreme position on this side of the motivational spectrum. They tend to be older, well educated, emotionally the most stable, and least concerned over their ailment or the dangers of remedies. They accept the ailment and its discomforts as a part of life, without fuss or pampering. They use a remedy as a last resort, and just to relieve the particular symptom. They seek simple products whose efficacy is well proven, and are skeptical of complicated modern remedies with new ingredients and multiple functions.

---

ships, either in cross-tabulations—as in the shotgun and Pinto examples—or in "predictions" of dependent variables like ecological concern. Reliability is particularly important in studies of relationships because unreliable measurements can, in and of themselves, make strong relationships appear to be weak [84, 93].

Very little has been published on the reliability of "homemade" psychographic items and scales. In a review of the evidence available in 1971, Pessemier and Bruno [16, 98] reported a range of six-month test-retest reliability coefficients for individual items from "under .30" to "over .80" with a median between .60 and .69. And they reported reliability coefficients for multi-item scales ranging from .64 to .90, with a median of about .80. More recently, Darden and Reynolds [28] reported split-half reliabilities for 13 psychographic dimensions ranging from .60 to .89, with a median of .80.

Authors of standardized personality scales, like the scales used to identify the ecologically concerned consumer, normally provide evidence on scale reliability in their test manuals. Additional reliability data can often be found in *The Mental Measurements Yearbook* [18] and in literature reviews in such journals as *Psychological Bulletin.* These sources show that the standardized scales most often used by psychographic researchers have reliabilities that run from about .70 to about .90—somewhat higher than the reported reliabilities of homemade variables.

What all this says is that both homemade and standardized psychographic measurements *can* have reliability high enough to support fairly strong relationships. However, it also says that the reliability of some psychographic measurements—especially some individual homemade items—may well be low enough to put a rather severe limitation on accuracy of "prediction."

Reliability of Dependent Variables

The maximum possible correlation between two variables is fully as dependent upon the reliability of what is being predicted as it is upon the reliability of the predictor [84, 93]. In psychographic studies, where the dependent variable is normally some form of consumer behavior, this means that strong relationships cannot be obtained unless the consumer behavior itself is measured accurately, no matter how reliable the psychographic measurements may be. This limitation is compounded by the fact that some kinds of consumer behavior—such as choice of a specific brand on a given occasion or exposure to a particular television program—may be so unstable that accurate prediction is virtually impossible, quite apart from any random measurement errors. Indeed, Bass [9] has gone so far as to assert that individual brand choice is so unstable that it can *never* be accurately predicted, by psychographics or by anything else.

With a few exceptions, psychographic researchers have not investigated the reliability of dependent variables. Successful prediction implies (but does not certify) adequate reliability. But unsuccessful prediction leaves the researcher in a quandary. Unsuccessful prediction can be due to unreliability in the psychographic measurements, to unreliability in the dependent variables, to lack of any "real" relationships between the psychographics and the behavior in question, or to some combination of all three. In the absence of reliability data it is impossible to determine which is the case.

Reliability of Relationships

In psychographic studies, as in other forms of marketing research, it is normal to find painstaking analysis of relationships that may be due at least in part to chance. In the shotgun ammunition study, for example, it is not possible to be sure that the same differences between buyers and nonbuyers would be found in a new sample drawn from the same population of respondents. Similarly, one cannot be sure that the same attitudes would identify subcompact car buyers if the Pinto study were repeated; or that, on replication, ecologically concerned consumers would differ from people in general as indicated by the data in Table 3. In the ecology study, some of the findings are particularly suspect. It does not seem at all likely that ecological concern really increases with income up to $10,000, drops between $10,000 and $14,999 and then resumes its upward climb. A much more probable explanation for that peculiar irregular relationship is some chance quirk in the data.

The only sure safeguard against being deceived by chance relationships is replication. When replication is impossible, the best procedure is to divide the sample into random parts, complete the analysis on one part, and then determine whether the same conclusions would have been reached via an identical analysis of the holdout group [6, 7, 14, 22, 34, 94, 141]. It is indeed unfortunate that this procedure has been the exception rather than the rule.

Reliability of Structure

Closely related to the question of reliability of relationships is the question of reliability of structure: do psychographic variables relate to each other in much the same way from study to study? In their reliability review Pessemier and Bruno compared factor analysis results from five large-scale studies, including one conducted in Canada. They concluded that "the wide range of variables employed and the constructs to which they relate appear to be sufficiently reliable for both practical and theoretical purposes" [98, p. 397]. This conclusion is encouraging because it asserts that items tend to hang together in much the same way when studies are repeated. If that were not the case, it would be hard to put much credence in their relationship to anything else.

A further and more difficult question concerns the stability of the segments produced by various clustering procedures. If the Newspaper Advertising Bureau's general life-style segmentation or Pernica's segmentation of stomach remedy users were repeated on new samples of consumers, would the same conclusions be reached as to segment content and segment size? The answer to that question is of the utmost practical importance. If segments vary greatly in size, or disappear altogether, from one analysis to another, it makes no sense at all to develop products, messages, or media schedules on the assumption that the segments are real.

In a caveat that has gone largely unheeded, Appel and Warwick noted in 1969 that: "Although Q-analysis is capable of reliably classifying people into relatively homogeneous groups based on psychographic data, there is a real question as to how many such groups can be reliably specified. . . . Unless the analyst is able to certify the reliability of the Q-group designations, the study findings are in serious question" [4, p. 25].

In the same vein, Johnson has more recently stated, "It has been the sad experience of many researchers that cluster analysis has produced interpretable groups differing dramatically in meaningful ways—and then subsequent analysis of new data has obtained equally convincing but entirely unrelated results. There are some uses of cluster analysis with which this would not be troublesome; but more frequently it would be an indication that neither solution is to be trusted" [62, p. 8].

The reliability of segments produced by empirical clustering procedures depends on several factors. First, and probably most important, reliability depends upon whether sharply differing, relatively homogeneous groups of consumers actually exist in the respondent population. The more segmented the population really is, the more the segmentation will be influenced by real structure, and not by adventitious bleeps [57]. Second, reliability will be influenced by the number of variables used, the size of the respondent sample, the accuracy with which the respondents answered the questions, and anything else that influences the stability of the correlations upon which the segmentation is based. Reliability will be influenced by the number of segments extracted. The larger the number of segments, the less likely they are to be reproducible [4]. And finally, reliability will depend upon the segmentation technique employed. Hierarchical clustering [61], a technique that has been used in a number of proprietary studies, may be much less reliable than alternative methods.

At this point in the development of psychographics, techniques for deriving segments are still primitive. We need to know much more about the conditions under which they succeed and the conditions under which they fail. We know for sure, however, that cluster solutions can be quite unstable, especially when the number of clusters is large. For this reason, it is especially important to compute the analysis on randomly selected halves of the sample and to reject solutions that do not match. This minimum requirement has often not been met. (See, for example [3, 12, 25, 39, 42, 76, 100].)

Reliability Summary

The available data indicate that psychographic measurements and analytic procedures can have satisfactory reliability. But, generally satisfactory reliability does not imply adequate reliability in all cases, and it may well be that some of the failures to find useful relationships between psychographics and consumer behavior have been due to instability in the measurements themselves. This may be especially true of the dependent variables, which can be unreliable both in the sense that they contain substantial amounts of random error, and in the sense that the behavior being measured is intrinsically unstable.

Unreliability also reduces the confidence one can place in relationships revealed by cross-tabulations or regressions, and the confidence one can place in clusters, both as to content and as to size. When important decisions are to be made on the basis of psychographics, it is essential that cross-tabulations, regressions, or clusters be cross-validated against holdout samples. It is all too easy to overanalyze findings that may be partially due to chance.

Validity

The term "validity" is used here in the traditional way. That is, a measurement is "valid" to the degree that it really does measure what it was intended to measure. Like other measurements, psychographic measurements can be reliable without being valid. They can be relatively free of random error but so full of irrelevancies and biases that conclusions based on them are partly (or even completely) false.

The question of the validity of psychographics is difficult and complex and cannot be answered simply. Here it is pursued under four headings: (1) construct validity of "homemade" psychographic variables, (2) construct validity of standardized scales, (3) construct validity of segments, and (4) predictive validity.

Construct Validity of Homemade Psychographic Variables

The construct validity of a measurement is established by showing that it relates to other variables to which it should be related, and does not relate to other variables to which it should not be related [19, 48, 93]. The process of establishing construct validity is normally spread out over time. It involves gradual accumulation of evidence, often by independent investigators, rather than a single finding of valid or not.

Pessemier and Bruno's review of the stability of certain psychographic constructs [16, 98] provides some evidence that bears upon the construct validity question. The fact that similar factors did indeed emerge when similar sets of items were answered by independent samples of respondents provides some assurance that individual psychographic items tend to relate to each other in internally consistent ways. While that finding is far from conclusive evidence of construct validity, it is a beginning. It shows that items which should go together do go together, while items that should not do not.

Further evidence of internal consistency can be found in the relationships between psychographics and demographics. Frequently one finds that the relationship between demographic and psychographic variables makes perfectly good sense. The evidence is not always conclusive, but when young people differ from old people in expected ways, or when more college graduates than nongraduates agree with "most of my friends have had a college education," the responses to the psychographic items seem right.

Beyond internal consistency, evidence for the construct validity of homemade items and scales is hard to find. The most general practice is to assume, unless there is evidence to the contrary, that the respondent is reporting accurately. Stated this baldly, the assumption sounds naive, but it is common in marketing research. When respondents are asked about brand preferences, exposure to media, or consumption of products, the general practice is to take answers at face value, even though it is known that such answers are sometimes wrong.

Much stronger evidence on construct validity would come from painstaking item-by-item and scale-by-scale convergent and discriminant validation [19]. That process has scarcely even begun, and it is so vastly complex that it will surely never be completed. In the meantime, users of homemade variables must be content with the assumption that respondents' answers contain a useful amount of valid information.

The Construct Validity of Standardized Scales

The psychographic researcher who uses standardized scales is less dependent upon face validity than is the researcher who assembles his own set of independent variables. Almost all published attitude scales and personality inventories are accompanied by at least some validity data, and in some instruments are accompanied by quite a lot. If the scale has been widely used, the results of construct validity studies can be found in the *Mental Measurements Yearbook* and in reviews in psychological journals.

It is virtually impossible to make a valid generalization about the construct validity of standardized personality and attitude scales. Indeed, it often seems that the more a scale is investigated the less agreement there is as to its true meaning. (See for example [36, 38].)

It is safe to say, however, that the information that is available has frequently been ignored. In a recent review of personality inventories in consumer research, Kassarjian observed, "Typically a convenient, available, easily scored, and easy-to-administer personality inventory is selected and administered along with questionnaires on purchase data and preferences. The lack of proper scientific method and hypothesis generation is supposedly justified by the often-used disclaimer that the study is exploratory" [65, p. 415]. He followed that observation with a quote from Jacoby that also bears repeating ". . . in most cases, no *a priori* thought is directed to *how*, or especially *why*, personality should or should not be related to that aspect of consumer behavior being studied. Moreover, the few studies which do report statistically significant findings usually do so on the basis of post-hoc 'picking and choosing' out of large data arrays" [60, p. 244].

Failure to make sensible use of construct validity data has been all too common. Its implications will be discussed in the next to the last section of this review.

The Construct Validity of Segments

Anyone who makes policy decisions on the basis of segmentations like those shown in Figures 1 and 2 must necessarily assume that relatively homogeneous groups of consumers fitting those descriptions actually exist. As noted in the reliability discussion, one way to check on this assumption is to determine whether the segments hold up under cross-validation with a held out sample of respondents. If segments disappear or change dramatically in size from one sample to another, the notion that the segments are "real" would appear to be tenuous indeed.

But even when segments hold up under cross-validation, there is still the question of how accurately the descriptions fit each member of each group. The "Traditionalist" described in Figure 1 is said to represent 16% of the adult male population—about 10 million people. How many of these 10 million really do differ from other consumers in all of those ways?

At present, questions about the reality of psychographic segments have no good answers, and with rare exceptions [40, 61, 62, 63, 81, 82, 86], such questions have scarcely even been approached. Few aspects of psychographics are more in need of basic research.

Predictive Validity

In econometrics, the validity of a model is established by its ability to predict the summed or averaged behavior of large numbers of individuals. In psychometrics, the validity of a test is established by its ability to predict the behavior of separate individuals. This distinction is important because the degree of accuracy that can be expected of predictions at the aggregate level is much higher than the degree of accuracy that can be expected of predictions at the individual level. One can predict with virtual certainty that there will be a traffic jam on the George Washington Bridge on a pleasant summer Friday afternoon; but one cannot be sure Arbuthnot will be in it.

The results of individual level predictions with psychographic instruments have paralleled the experience in research on personality. In the absence of good reason to believe that the psychographic construct would be closely related to the specific consumer behavior being studied, correlations have usually run between +.20 and −.20, with many close to zero [5, 15, 41, 49, 51, 70, 73, 76, 87, 88, 99, 100, 101, 131, 137]. When the psychographic constructs have been clearly relevant to the behavior being studied, individual correlations have been in the .20s and .30s [13, 20, 27, 102, 128]. And when relevant dimensions have been linked together in multiple regression, multiple correlations have been in the .50s and .60s [2, 43, 69, 96, 139].

Whether this record is good or bad depends greatly upon one's point of view. Many critics have declared that low correlations are of no practical value and have dismissed them out of hand [5, 7, 35, 64, 66]. But, as Bass, Tigert, and Lonsdale [10] have cogently argued, accounting for differences among groups of consumers, rather than explaining the variance in individual behavior, is often the real object of psychographic analysis. From that standpoint, the record looks much better.

The data in Table 2 are typical of the group differences that can be produced by psychographic items. Some of the differences are quite large, and many of them are larger than the differences produced by the demographic variables in Table 1. The data in Table 3 are typical of the discriminating power of more abstract general personality traits. The differences produced by the personality traits are rather small; but, as in the shotgun example, the differences produced by psychographics are larger than the differences produced by demographics.

Other comparisons of psychographics and demographics can be found in reports by Wilson [139], Good and Suchland [46], King and Sproles [69], Nelson [89], Pessemier and Tigert [96], and Berger and Schott [17]. These reports all show that the predictive validity of psychographic variables is likely to be substantially higher than the predictive validity of the demographic attributes that have long been accepted as good, true, and beautiful in marketing research.

Validity Summary

It is difficult to give a concise answer to the question: "Are psychographic measurements valid?" The answer would depend greatly upon exactly what type of validity the questioner had in mind. Even within a single type of validity the answer would vary greatly from study to study. The evidence does show that psychographic variables generally relate to each other, to demographics, and to use of products and media in ways that make perfectly good sense. That is not a very strong statement, but at least it says that the patterns in the data are consistent with what we believe to be true about consumer behavior.

The evidence on predictive validity shows that psychographic variables seldom account for large portions of the variance of individual behavior. However, this evidence also shows that psychographic variables are capable of producing substantial differences between groups of consumers, and that these differences are often larger than the differences produced by the standard demographic profile.

From a policy point of view, the most immediately pressing question concerns the reality of psychographic segments. Marketers who make important decisions on the basis of segmentation studies urgently need ways to determine when the products of cluster analysis or Q factor analysis represent real groups of real consumers, and when they represent figments of the computer's imagination.

Applications to Marketing Problems

The last two sections of this review bear upon usefulness—first in the context of real-world marketing problems, then in the context of present and potential contributions to a more general understanding of consumer behavior. The real-world discussion will argue that reliability and validity are neither necessary nor sufficient to insure that psychographic data can be used. The remainder of the discussion will argue that psychographic methods have already made significant contributions to the understanding of consumer behavior, and these contributions are likely to become more important as time goes on.

How to Get Valid, Useless Results

The results of psychographic research can be reliable and valid, and still not useful, when relationships that should not have been expected fail to appear. This may seem like a perfectly obvious observation, yet—as Kassarjian and Jacoby have already indicated—the literature is full of attempts to predict consumer behavior from personality test scores in the absence of any good reason to believe that the two should be related [59]. Perhaps the classic example of this shot-in-the-dark approach is an early psychographic effort in which scales from The Edwards Personal Preference Schedule—scales intended to measure such needs as autonomy, dominance, order, and endurance—were correlated with purchases of single- and double-ply toilet tissue [5]. Even if it were true that all of the measurements in this study were perfectly reliable and perfectly valid, the failure to find a significant correlation between need for dominance, for example, and purchase of toilet paper, could hardly come as much of a surprise. The same general comment applies to Evans's finding that the Edwards scales cannot separate Ford owners from Chevrolet owners [37]; to Robertson and Myers's finding that California Psychological Inventory scores do not account for much of the variance in innovativeness or opinion leadership [116]; to Kollat and Willett's finding that a set of general personality traits including optimism, belief in fate, and belief in multiple causation of events did not predict impulse purchasing [73]; and to many other negative findings that have not been published. The general proposition is: when one has no reason to believe that the psychographic constructs should be related to the consumer behavior in question, a negative finding—even though all the measurements may be highly reliable and highly valid—is not worth much.

Another way to circumvent usefulness is to be too abstract. A grand example of abstraction carried to extremes is provided in a study by Sparks and Tucker [122]. This study found that a latent canonical root with heavy positive loadings on sociability and emotional stability, and a heavy negative loading on responsibility, accounted for much of the variance of a dimension that represents heavy consumption of alcoholic beverages, cigarettes, and shampoo. The study also found that a second latent dimension represented by a heavy positive loading on emotional stability and a heavy negative loading on cautiousness accounted for much of the variance of a dimension that represents heavy consumption of after-shave lotion, light consumption of headache remedies, light consumption of mouthwash and coffee, and disinclination to adopt new fashions. Assuming for the moment that this finding is both reliable and valid, just what does one do with it?

Third, psychographic measurements may be reliable and valid but so close to the behavior being studied that the relationship is essentially redundant. In Table 2, the best predictor of shotgun ammunition use is "I like to hunt." In Table 3, the best predictor of low ecological concern is agreement with "It is futile for the individual consumer to try to do anything about pollution." In Darden and Reynold's study of men's fashions [27], the best predictors of fashion opinion leadership were two scales measuring "fashion interest" and "fashion venturesomeness." Findings of this sort are useful in the very restricted sense that they point to the construct validity of the psychographic items, but they are hardly likely to be greeted by marketing managers as world-shaking revelations.

To be useful in making real-world marketing decisions, psychographic data must be in some middle range between being almost totally redundant and being entirely unrelated to the behavior being studied. They must contain just the right amount of surprise. When that is the case, they can be very useful indeed, even when correlations are not high and even when questions about reliability and validity cannot be completely answered. This principles applies to profiles and to segmentations, for the same basic reason.

Why Psychographic Profiles Are Useful

To see why psychographic profiles are useful even in the absence of assured reliability and validity, it is necessary to consider the alternatives. Consider, for example, the copy writer quoted toward the beginning of this review. Confronted with a deadline for creating an advertisement, he could sit in his office and imagine his audience. But he might be wrong. As he said, he can't afford to trust just his own experience. He might do his own informal psychographic study—trudge all the way around the block talking to the neighbors. But to the degree that his neighbors are different from his customers, this informal research might easily be misleading.

The copy writer might depend upon a qualitative motivation study. If he did, he would be looking at findings from the small unrepresentative sample, and he would be depending upon the subjective judgment of the motivation research analyst. He might examine a demographic profile obtained from a large-scale quantitative market survey. But, as the shotgun study illustrates, he would almost surely miss some valid relationships, and he would almost surely make some false inferences. Given these alternatives, it is easy to see why psychographic profiles have seen wide use in spite of legitimate questions as to reliability and validity. The copy writer cannot wait for convergent and discriminant validation. He must produce an advertisement, and to do that, he must use whatever information he can get.

The same basic problem confronts product designers, package designers, product managers, and media analysts. What product features will fit the life style of the potential customer? To what sort of person should the package be designed to appeal? Is the customer for this product or service unusually price conscious? Fashion conscious? Concerned about pollution? Concerned about his health? What are consumers' attitudes and opinions about what appears in magazines, newspapers, radio, and TV? All of these questions are regularly answered by some combination of intuition and quantitative and qualitative research. In many cases psychographic profiles add information that would not otherwise be available.

Why Psychographic Segmentations Are Useful

General segmentations like the Newspaper Advertising Bureau study offer the opportunity to tailor new products and services to the needs of different groups within the consumer population. It is easy to see that the "Quiet Family Man," the "Traditionalist," the "Ethical Highbrow," and the "Pleasure Oriented Man" (Figure 1) ought to have quite different requirements in automobiles, entertainment, vacations, insurance policies, food, and clothing. The life-style descriptions show those need patterns in considerable detail, and the media data normally collected in such studies show how to reach each group [121].

Product-specific segmentations like the stomach remedy study offer the opportunity to position and reposition existing brands. They show what needs the product meets within each group, and which brands are best at meeting them. With this information the marketer can appeal directly and efficiently to those groups most apt to find his brand appealing, and he can create new brands to fit need patterns his brand cannot satisfy. Parallel values accrue to marketers of services.

But the question remains—are the descriptions of the segments reliable and valid? Do real groups of real consumers fitting these descriptions actually exist? If the answer is yes, the user of a psychographic segmentation has at his disposal a new and superior way of understanding his customers. If the answer is no, the marketer who takes a segmentation study seriously is marketing to a family of fictions.

In view of the reservations already expressed as to the reliability and validity of segmentation procedures it might seem that the wisest course would be to ignore psychographics until the procedures have been thoroughly validated. But again, one must consider the alternatives. Marketers know that the customers for a product or a service are frequently not much alike. They know that empirical segmentation procedures hold out the possibility of new insights into how consumers may be divided into groups. And they know that the reliability and validity of segmentation procedures have not been established beyond all doubt. Given that dilemma, many marketers have elected to conduct and to use segmentation studies even when fully aware of the art's imperfections.

Understanding Consumer Behavior

Finally, psychographic methods have contributed to more general knowledge of consumer behavior in at least three ways. Psychographic profiles have shed new light on some of the familiar and recurring topics in consumer research. Trend data now becoming available have shown how consumers are changing and how they are not. And general segmentations of the consumer population have created new typologies within which consumer behavior might be more efficiently described and better understood. This review concludes with brief descriptions of studies in each of these fields.

Profiles

Psychographic profiles have already contributed to our understanding of opinion leadership [69, 113, 126], innovativeness [23, 32, 60, 97, 126], retail outshopping [114], private brand buying [17], social class [129], consumerist activism [56], catalog buying behavior [112], store loyalty [115], differences between Canada and the United States [8], differences between French-speaking and English-speaking Canadians [125], and concern for the environment [71, 72]. In all these cases the value added by the psychographic profile was much the same as the value added to the description of the shotgun ammunition buyer. Sometimes psychographics confirmed the existence of attributes that might have been inferred from demographic profiles. Sometimes they revealed the existence of attributes that a demographic profile did show. And sometimes they disconfirmed inferences that would have been incorrect. It seems certain that the trend toward psychographic descriptions of interesting groups of consumers will continue, and that such descriptions will become accepted as necessary components of studies of this kind.

Trend Data

As studies are repeated, it becomes possible to accumulate trend data that show how consumers are changing and how they are not changing. Such data are particularly valuable in an era when every other observer is prepared to describe "the changing consumer" and to make predictions about the effects of these changes upon markets for goods and services. In monitoring trends, the task of empirical psychographic analysis is to separate the changes that are actually happening from the changes that are not [24, 106].

New Typologies

The third application of psychographics to the study of consumer behavior is just now beginning to take shape. General segmentations, like the Newspaper Advertising Bureau study and the series of life-style studies conducted by the Leo Burnett Company [24, 92, 105, 106], have begun to produce the outlines of a new consumer typology. As groupings like those shown in Figure 1 are identified and confirmed by independent sets of investigators, it is at least possible that marketers will begin to think routinely in terms of segments marked off by common sets of activities, interests, needs, and values, and to develop products, services, and media schedules specifically to meet them.

At present, agreement among general segmentation studies is pretty far from complete. Differences in item content, sampling procedure and analytic technique have produced different sets of findings, each claiming to be real. Yet, even though the segments produced by various general segmentation studies differ in a number of ways, there is enough similarity among them to suggest that eventual consensus is not a vain hope. If consensus eventually is reached, there will be a new way of thinking about consumers as life-style groups.

Summary of Uses

To the marketing practitioner, psychographic methods have offered a way of describing consumers that has many advantages over alternative methods, even though much work on reliability and validity remains to be done. To researchers with more general interests, psychographic methods have offered new ways of looking at old problems, new dimensions for charting trends, and a new vocabulary in which consumer typologies may be described.

From the speed with which psychographics have diffused through the marketing community, it seems obvious that they are perceived as meeting a keenly felt need. The problem now is not so much one of pioneering as it is one of sorting out the techniques that work best. As that process proceeds, it seems extremely likely that psychographic methods will gradually become more familiar and less controversial, and eventually will merge into the mainstream of marketing research.

References

1. *A Psychographic View of the Los Angeles Marketing Area.* Los Angeles, Calif.: Los Angeles Times, 1972.
2. Ahmed, Sadrudin A. "Prediction of Cigarette Consumption Level With Personality and Socioeconomic Variables," *Journal of Applied Psychology,* 56 (October 1972), 437–8.
3. Alpert, Mark I. "Personality and the Determinants of Product Choice," *Journal of Marketing Research,* 9 (February 1972), 89–92.
4. Appel, Valentine and Kenneth Warwick. *Procedures for Defining Consumer Market Targets.* New York: Grudin/Appel Research Corporation, 1969.
5. *Are There Consumer Types?* New York: Advertising Research Foundation, 1964.
6. Armstrong, J. Scott. "Derivation of Theory by Means of Factor Analysis, or Tom Swift and His Electric Factor Analysis Machine," *American Statistician,* 21 (December 1967), 17–21.
7. Arndt, Johan. *Market Segmentation.* Bergen, Norway: Universitetsforlaget, 1974.
8. Arnold, Stephen J. and Douglas J. Tigert. "Canadians and Americans: A Comparative Analysis," paper delivered at the Annual Convention of the American Psychological Association, Montreal, Canada, 1973.
9. Bass, Frank M. "The Theory of Stochastic Preference and Brand Switching," *Journal of Marketing Research,* 11 (February 1974), 1–20.
10. ——, Douglas J. Tigert, and Ronald F. Lonsdale. "Market Segmentation: Group Versus Individual Behavior," *Journal of Marketing Research,* 5 (August 1968), 264–70.
11. Behavior Science Corporation. *Developing the Family Travel Market.* Des Moines, Iowa: Better Homes and Gardens, 1972.
12. Bernay, Elayn K. "Life Style Analysis as a Basis for Media Selection," in Charles King and Douglas Tigert, eds., *Attitude Research Reaches New Heights.* Chicago: American Marketing Association, 1971, 189–95.
13. Birdwell, Al B. "A Study of the Influence of Image Congruence on Consumer Choice," *Journal of Business,* 41 (January 1968), 76–88.
14. Bither, Steward W. and Ira J. Dolich. "Personality as a Determinant Factor in Store Choice," *Proceedings.* Third Annual Conference, Association for Consumer Research, 1972, 9–19.
15. Brody, Robert P. and Scott M. Cunningham. "Personality Variables and the Consumer Decision Process," *Journal of Marketing Research,* 5 (February 1968), 50–7.
16. Bruno, Albert V. and Edgar A. Pessemier. "An Empirical Investigation of the Validity of Selected Attitude and Activity Measures," *Proceedings.* Third Annual Conference, Association for Consumer Research, 1972, 456–74.
17. Burger, Philip C. and Barbara Schott. "Can Private Brand Buyers Be Identified?" *Journal of Marketing Research,* 9 (May 1972), 219–22.
18. Buros, Oscar K. *The Seventh Mental Measurements Yearbook.* Highland Park, N.J.: The *Gryphon* Press, 1972.
19. Campbell, Donald T. and Donald W. Fiske. "Convergent and Discriminant Validation by the Multitrait-Multimethod Matrix," *Psychological Bulletin,* 56 (March 1959), 81–105.
20. Carman, James M. "Correlates of Brand Loyalty: Some Positive Results," *Journal of Marketing Research,* 7 (February 1970), 67–76.
21. Claycamp, Henry J. "Characteristics of Owners of Thrift Deposits in Commercial Banks and Savings and Loan Associations," *Journal of Marketing Research,* 2 (May 1965), 163–70.
22. Cooley, W. W. and P. R. Lohnes. *Multivariate Procedures in the Behavioral Sciences.* New York: John Wiley, 1962.
23. Coney, Kenneth A. "Dogmatism and Innovation: A Replication," *Journal of Marketing Research,* 9 (November 1972), 453–5.
24. Coulson, John S. "How Much Has The Consumer Changed?" paper presented at the Meeting of the American Association for Public Opinion Research, 1974.
25. Cunningham, William H. and William J. E. Crissy, "Market Segmentation by Motivation and Attitude," *Journal of Marketing Research,* 9 (February 1972), 100–2.
26. Danzig, Fred. "Int'l Marketing Congress Hears Psychographics Criticized, Defended," *Advertising Age,* 3 (June 1969), 104–5.
27. Darden, William R. and Fred D. Reynolds, "Predicting Opinion Leadership for Men's Apparel Fashions," *Journal of Marketing Research,* 9 (August 1972), 324–8.
28. ——. "Backward Profiling of Male Innovators," *Journal of Marketing Research,* 11 (February 1974), 79–85.
29. Demby, Emanuel. "Psychographics: Who, What, Why, When, Where and How," in Charles King and Douglas Tigert, eds., *Attitude Research Reaches New Heights.* Chicago: American Marketing Association, 1971, 196–9.
30. ——. "Psychographics and From Whence It Came,"

in William D. Wells, ed., *Life Style and Psychographics.* Chicago: American Marketing Association, 1974, 9–30.

31. Dichter, Ernest. *Handbook of Consumer Motivations.* New York: McGraw-Hill, 1964.
32. Donnelly, James H., Jr. "Social Character and Acceptance of New Products," *Journal of Marketing Research,* 7 (February 1970), 111–3.
33. Dorny, Lester R. "Observations on Psychographics," in Charles King and Douglas Tigert, eds., *Attitude Research Reaches New Heights.* Chicago: American Marketing Association, 1971, 200–1.
34. Einhorn, Hillel J. "Alchemy in the Behavioral Sciences," *Public Opinion Quarterly,* 36 (Fall 1972), 367–78.
35. Engel, James F., David T. Kollat, and Roger D. Blackwell. "Personality Measures and Market Segmentation," *Business Horizons,* 12 (June 1969), 61–70.
36. Entwisle, Doris R. "To Dispel Fantasies about Fantasy-Based Measures of Achievement Motivation," *Psychological Bulletin,* 77 (June 1972), 377–91.
37. Evans, Franklin B. "Psychological and Objective Factors in the Prediction of Brand Choice: Ford vs. Chevrolet," *Journal of Business,* 32 (October 1959), 340–69.
38. Fiske, Donald W. "Can A Personality Construct Be Validated?" *Psychological Bulletin,* 80 (August 1973), 89–92.
39. Frank, Ronald E. "Predicting New Product Segments," *Journal of Advertising Research,* 12 (June 1972), 9–13.
40. Frank, Ronald E. and Paul E. Green. "Numerical Taxonomy in Marketing Analysis: A Review Article," *Journal of Marketing Research,* 5 (February 1968), 83–94.
41. Frank, Ronald E., William F. Massy, and Thomas M. Lodahl. "Purchasing Behavior and Personal Attributes," *Journal of Advertising Research,* 9 (December 1969), 15–24.
42. Frank, Ronald E. and Charles E. Strain. "A Segmentation Research Design Using Consumer Panel Data," *Journal of Marketing Research,* 9 (November 1972), 385–90.
43. Fry, Joseph N. "Personality Variables and Cigarette Brand Choice," *Journal of Marketing Research,* 8 (August 1971), 298–304.
44. Gardner, David M. "An Exploratory Investigation of Achievement Motivation Effects on Consumer Behavior," *Proceedings.* Third Annual Conference. Association for Consumer Research, 1972, 20–33.
45. Garfinkle, Norton. "The Value and Use of Psychographic Information in Decision Making," in Charles W. King and Douglas Tigert, eds., *Attitude Reaches New Heights.* Chicago: American Marketing Association, 1971, 206–10.
46. Good, Walter S. and Otto Suchsland. *Consumer Life Styles and Their Relationship to Market Behavior Regarding Household Furniture.* East Lansing, Mich.: Michigan State University Research Bulletin, No. 26, 1970.
47. Gottlieb, Morris J. "Segmentation by Personality Types," in Lynne H. Stockman, ed., *Advancing Marketing Efficiency.* Chicago: American Marketing Association, 1959, 148–58.
48. Green, Paul E. and Donald S. Tull. *Research for Marketing Decisions,* second edition. Englewood Cliffs, N.J.: Prentice-Hall, 1970.
49. Greeno, Daniel W., Montrose S. Sommers, and Jerome B. Kernan. "Personality and Implicit Behavior Patterns," *Journal of Marketing Research,* 10 (February 1973), 63–9.
50. Grubb, Edward L. and Gregg Hupp. "Perception of Self, Generalized Stereotypes and Brand Selection," *Journal of Marketing Research,* 5 (February 1968), 58–63.
51. Gruen, Walter. "Preference for New Products and Its Relationship to Different Measures of Conformity," *Journal of Applied Psychology,* 44 (December 1960), 361–4.
52. Heller, Harry E. "Defining Target Markets by Their Attitude Profiles," in Lee Adler and Irving Crespi, eds., *Attitude Research on the Rocks.* Chicago: American Marketing Association, 1968, 45–57.
53. "How Nestle Uses Psychographics," *Media Decisions* (July 1973), 68–71.
54. Hustad, Thomas P. and Edgar A. Pessemier. "Segmenting Consumer Markets with Activity and Attitude Measures," Institute Paper No. 298, Krannert Graduate School of Industrial Administration, Purdue University, 1971.
55. ——. "The Development and Application of Psychographic, Life-Style and Associated Activity and Attitude Measures," in W. D. Wells, ed., *Life Style and Psychographics.* Chicago: American Marketing Association, 1974, 31–70.
56. ——. "Will the Real Consumer Activist Please Stand Up: An Examination of Consumers' Opinions About Marketing Practices," *Journal of Marketing Research,* 10 (August 1973), 319–24.
57. Inglis, Jim and Douglas Johnson. "Some Observations on, and Developments in, the Analysis of Multivariate Survey Data," *Journal of the Market Research Society,* 12 (April 1970), 75–98.
58. Jacobson, Eugene and Jerome Kossoff. "Self-Percept and Consumer Attitudes Toward Small Cars," *Journal of Applied Psychology,* 47 (August 1963), 242–5.
59. Jacoby, Jacob. "Personality and Consumer Behavior: How Not to Find Relationships," Purdue Papers in Consumer Psychology, No. 102, 1969.
60. ——. "Personality and Innovation Proneness," *Journal of Marketing Research,* 8 (May 1971), 244–7.
61. Johnson, Richard M. "How Can You Tell if Things Are

'Really' Clustered? paper read at a joint meeting of the New York chapters of the American Statistical Association and American Marketing Association, New York, 1972.

62. ——. *Using Q Analysis in Marketing Research.* Chicago: Market Facts, Inc., 1974.

63. Joyce, Timothy and C. Channon. "Classifying Market Survey Respondents," *Applied Statistics,* 5 (November 1966), 191–215.

64. Kassarjian, Harold H. "Social Character and Differential Preference for Mass Communication," *Journal of Marketing Research,* 2 (May 1965), 146–53.

65. ——. "Personality and Consumer Behavior: A Review," *Journal of Marketing Research,* 8 (November 1971), 409–18.

66. ——. "Personality and Consumer Behavior: A Way Out of the Morass," paper presented at the 1973 meeting of the American Psychological Association.

67. Kay, Herbert. *Important News About Prime-Prospect Service.* Montclair, N.J.: Herbert Kay Research, Inc., 1969.

68. King. Charles W. "Social Science, Pragmatic Marketing Research and Psychographics," in Charles W. King and Douglas J. Tigert, eds., *Attitude Research Reaches New Heights.* Chicago: American Marketing Association, 1971, 228–31.

69. —— and George B. Sproles. "The Explanatory Efficacy of Selected Types of Consumer Profile Variables in Fashion Change Agent Identification," Institute Paper No. 425, Krannert Graduate School of Industrial Administration, Purdue University, 1973.

70. King, Charles W. and John O. Summers. "Attitudes and Media Exposure," *Journal of Advertising Research,* 11 (February 1971), 26–32.

71. Kinnear, Thomas C., James R. Taylor, and Sadrudin A. Ahmed. "Socioeconomic and Personality Characteristics as They Relate to Ecologically-Constructive Purchasing Behavior," *Proceedings.* Third Annual Conference, Association for Consumer Research, 1972, 34–60.

72. ——. "Ecologically Concerned Consumers: Who Are They?" *Journal of Marketing Research,* 38 (April 1974), 20–4.

73. Kollat, David T. and Ronald P. Willett. "Customer Impulse Purchasing Behavior," *Journal of Marketing Research,* 1 (September 1960), 6–12.

74. Koponen, Arthur. "Personality Characteristics of Purchasers," *Journal of Advertising Research,* 1 (September 1960), 6–12.

75. Kuelper, Robert. "The Pit and the Pendulum," internal memo, Chicago: Leo Burnett Company, 1970.

76. Lessig, V. Parker and John O. Tollefson. "Market Segmentation Through Numerical Taxonomy," *Journal of Marketing Research,* 8 (November 1971), 480–7.

77. *Life Style of the WWD Subscriber.* New York: Women's Wear Daily, 1971.

78. "Life Style Portrait of the Hunter," *Journal of Leisure Research,* in press.

79. Lovell, M. R. C. "European Developments in Psychographics," in W. D. Wells, ed., *Life Style and Psychographics.* Chicago: American Marketing Association, 1974, 257–76.

80. Lunn, J. A. "Psychological Classification," *Commentary,* 8 (July 1966), 161–73.

81. ——. "Empirical Techniques in Consumer Research," in D. Pym, ed., *Industrial Society: Social Sciences in Management.* Baltimore: Penguin Books, 1968, 401–25.

82. Massy, William F., Ronald E. Frank, and Yoram Wind. *Market Segmentation.* Englewood Cliffs, N.J.: Prentice-Hall, 1972.

83. May, Eleanor G. "Psychographics in Department Store Imagery," Working Paper P-65. Cambridge, Mass.: Marketing Science Institute, 1971.

84. McNemar, Quinn. *Psychological Statistics,* second edition. New York: John Wiley & Sons, 1955.

85. Michaels, Peter W. "Life Style and Magazine Exposure," in Boris W. Becker and Helmut Becker, eds., *Combined Proceedings: Marketing Education and the Real World and Dynamic Marketing in a Changing World.* Chicago: American Marketing Association, 1973, 324–31.

86. Monk, Donald. "Burnett Life Style Research," *European Research: Marketing Opinion Advertising,* 1 (January 1973), 14–19.

87. Montgomery, David B. "Consumer Characteristics Associated With Dealing: An Empirical Example," *Journal of Marketing Research,* 8 (February 1971), 118–20.

88. Myers, John G. "Determinants of Private Brand Attitude," *Journal of Marketing Research,* 4 (February 1967), 73–81.

89. Nelson, Alan R. "A National Study of Psychographics," paper delivered at the International Marketing Congress, American Marketing Association, June 1969.

90. ——. "New Psychographics: Action-Creating Ideas, Not Lifeless Statistics," *Advertising Age,* 1 (June 28, 1971), 34.

91. ——. "Psyching Psychographics: A Look at Why People Buy," in Charles W. King and Douglas J. Tigert, eds., *Attitude Research Reaches New Heights.* Chicago: American Marketing Association, 1971, 181–8.

92. *New Information on Sugar User Psychographics.* Chicago: Leo Burnett, 1972.

93. Nunnally, Jum C. *Psychometric Theory.* New York: McGraw-Hill, 1967.

94. Overall, J. E. and C. J. Klett. *Applied Multivariate Analysis.* New York: McGraw-Hill, 1971.

95. Pernica, Joseph. "The Second Generation of Market

Segmentation Studies: An Audit of Buying Motivation," in W. D. Wells, ed., *Life Style and Psychographics.* Chicago: American Marketing Association, 1974, 277-313.

96. Pessemier, Edgar A. and Douglas J. Tigert. "A Taxonomy of Magazine Readership Applied to Problems in Marketing Strategy and Media Selection," Institute Paper No. 195, Krannert Graduate School of Industrial Administration, Purdue University, 1967.

97. Pessemier, Edgar A., Philip C. Burger, and Douglas J. Tigert, "Can New Product Buyers Be Identified?" *Journal of Marketing Research,* 4 (November 1967), 349-54.

98. Pessemier, Edgar A. and Albert Bruno. "An Empirical Investigation of the Reliability and Stability of Activity and Attitude Measures," Reprint Series No. 391, Krannert Graduate School of Industrial Administration, 1971.

99. Peters, William H. and Neil M. Ford. "A Profile of Urban In-Home Shoppers: The Other Half," *Journal of Marketing,* 36 (January 1972), 62-4.

100. Peterson, Robert A. "Psychographics and Media Exposure," *Journal of Advertising Research,* 12 (June 1972), 17-20.

101. —— and Allan L. Pennington. "SVIB Interests and Product Preferences," *Journal of Applied Psychology,* 53 (August 1969), 304-8.

102. Plummer, Joseph T. "Life Style Patterns and Commercial Bank Credit Card Usage," *Journal of Marketing,* 35 (April 1971), 35-41.

103. ——. "Learning About Consumers as Real People: The Application of Psychographic Data," paper presented to the Montreal Chapter, American Marketing Association, November 1971.

104. ——. "Life Style Patterns: A New Constraint for Mass Communications Research," *Journal of Broadcasting,* 16 (Winter 1971-72), 79-89.

105. ——. "The Theory and Uses of Life Style Segmentation," *Journal of Marketing,* 38 (January 1974), 33-7.

106. ——. "Life Style and Social Change: Evolutionary—Not Revolutionary," paper read at the 20th Annual AMA Management Seminar, Toronto, 1973.

107. ——. "Life Style Portrait of the Hunter," *Journal of Leisure Research* (in press).

108. ——. "Applications of Life Style Research to the Creation of Advertising Campaigns," in W. D. Wells, ed., *Life Style and Psychographics.* Chicago: American Marketing Association, 1974, 157-69.

109. *Psychographics: A Study of Personality, Life Style, and Consumption Patterns.* New York: Newspaper Advertising Bureau, 1973.

110. Reiser, Richard J. "Psychographics: Marketing Tool or Research Toy?" *Chicago Marketing Scene* (October 1972), 8-9.

111. Reynolds, Fred D. *Psychographics: A Conceptual Orientation.* Research Monograph No. 6. Athens, Ga.: Division of Research, University of Georgia, College of Business Administration, 1973.

112. ——. "An Analysis of Catalog Buying Behavior," *Journal of Marketing,* 38 (July 1974), 47-51.

113. —— and William R. Darden. "Mutually Adaptive Effects of Interpersonal Communication," *Journal of Marketing Research,* 8 (November 1971), 449-54.

114. ——. "Intermarket Patronage: A Psychographic Study of Consumer Outshoppers," *Journal of Marketing,* 36 (October 1972), 50-4.

115. —— and Warren S. Martin. "The Store Loyal Consumer: A Life Style Analysis," *Journal of Retailing,* in press.

116. Robertson, Thomas S. and James H. Myers. "Personality Correlates of Opinion Leadership and Innovative Buying Behavior," *Journal of Marketing Research,* 6 (May 1969), 164-8.

117. Roper, Elmo and associates. *Movers and Shakers.* New York: Harper-Atlantic Sales, 1970.

118. Ross, Ivan. "Self-Concept and Brand Preference," *The Journal of Business,* 44 (January 1971), 38-50.

119. Segnit, Susanna and Simon Broadbent, "Life Style Research," *European Research: Marketing Opinion Advertising,* 1 (January 1973), 6-13.

120. Simmons, W. R. "Overall Impressions of Psychographics," in Charles W. King and Douglas J. Tigert, eds., *Attitude Research Reaches New Heights.* Chicago: American Marketing Association, 1971, 215-9.

121. Skelly, Florence and Elizabeth Nelson, "Market Segmentation and New Product Development," *Scientific Business,* 4 (Summer 1966), 13-22.

122. Sparks, David L. and W. T. Tucker. "A Multivariate Analysis of Personality and Product Use," *Journal of Marketing Research,* 8 (February 1971), 67-70.

123. Summers, John O. "The Identity of Women's Clothing Fashion Opinion Leaders," *Journal of Marketing Research,* 7 (May 1970), 178-85.

124. Teleki, Margot. "The Research Go-Round," *Media-Scope* (March 1970), 27-32, 38-40.

125. *The Lifestyles of English and French Canadian Women.* Toronto: Vickers and Benson Ltd., Marketing Services Department, 1972.

126. Tigert, Douglas J. "Psychometric Correlates of Opinion Leadership and Innovation," unpublished working paper, University of Chicago, 1969.

127. ——. "A Research Project in Creative Advertising Through Life Style Analysis," in Charles W. King and Douglas J. Tigert, eds., *Attitude Research Reaches New Heights.* Chicago: American Marketing Association, 1971, 223-7.

128. ——. "Life Style Analysis as a Basis for Media Selection," in W. D. Wells, ed., *Life Style and Psychograph-*

ics. Chicago: American Marketing Association, 1974, 171-201.

129. —— and William D. Wells. "Life Style Correlates of Age and Social Class," paper presented at the First Annual Meeting, Association for Consumer Research, Amherst, 1970.

130. Tigert, Douglas J., Richard Lathrope, and Michael Bleeg. "The Fast Food Franchise: Psychographic and Demographic Segmentation Analysis," *Journal of Retailing,* 47 (Spring 1971), 81-90.

131. Tucker, W. T. and John J. Painter. "Personality and Product Use," *Journal of Applied Psychology,* 45 (October 1961), 325-9.

132. Vitz, Paul C. and Donald Johnston. "Masculinity of Smokers and the Masculinity of Cigarette Images," *Journal of Applied Psychology,* 49 (June 1965), 155-9.

133. Wells, William D. "Segmentation by Attitude Types," in Robert L. King, ed., *Marketing and the New Science of Planning.* Chicago: American Marketing Association, 124-6.

134. ——. "Life Style and Psychographics: Definitions, Uses and Problems," in W. D. Wells, ed., *Life Style and Psychographics.* Chicago: American Marketing Association, 1974, 315-63.

135. —— and Arthur D. Beard. "Personality and Consumer Behavior," in Scott Ward and Thomas S. Robertson, eds., *Consumer Behavior: Theoretical Sources,* Englewood Cliffs, N.J.: Prentice-Hall, 1973, 141-99.

136. Wells, William D. and Douglas J. Tigert. "Activities, Interests, and Opinions," *Journal of Advertising Research,* 11 (August 1971), 27-35.

137. Westfall, Ralph. "Psychological Factors in Predicting Product Choice," *Journal of Marketing,* 26 (April 1962), 34-40.

138. "What's Their Life Style?" *Media Decisions* (September 1969), 34-35, 70, 72.

139. Wilson, Clark L. "Homemaker Living Patterns and Marketplace Behavior—A Psychometric Approach," in J. S. Wright and J. L. Goldstucker, eds., *New Ideas for Successful Marketing.* Chicago: American Marketing Association, 1966, 305-47.

140. Wind, Yoram and Paul E. Green. "Some Conceptual, Measurement, and Analytical Problems in Life Style Research," in W. D. Wells, ed., *Life Style and Psychographics.* Chicago: American Marketing Association, 1974, 97-126.

141. Wind, Yoram, Paul E. Green, and Arun K. Jain. "Higher Order Factor Analysis in the Classification of Psychographic Variables," *Journal of the Market Research Society,* 15 (October 1973), 224-32.

142. Yoell, William. "Causes of Buying Behavior: Mythology or Fact?" in Mernard A. Morin, ed., *Marketing in a Changing World.* Chicago: American Marketing Association, 1969, 241-8.

143. Young, Shirley. "Psychographics Research and Marketing Relevancy," in Charles A. King and Douglas J. Tigert, eds., *Attitude Research Reaches New Heights.* Chicago: American Marketing Association, 1971, 220-2.

144. ——. "Research Both for Strategic Planning and for Tactical Testing," *Proceedings.* 19th Annual Conference, Advertising Research Foundation, New York, 1973, 13-16.

145. ——. "The Dynamics of Measuring Unchange," in Russell Haley, ed., *Attitude Research in Transition.* Chicago: American Marketing Association, 1972, 49-82.

146. Ziff, Ruth. "Psychographics for Market Segmentation," *Journal of Advertising Research,* 11 (April 1971), 3-10.

147. ——. "Closing the Consumer-Advertising Gap Through Psychographics," *Combined Proceedings: Marketing Education and the Real World and Dynamic Marketing in a Changing World.* Chicago: American Marketing Association, 1973, 457-61.

148. ——. "The Role of Psychographics in the Development of Advertising Strategy," in W. D. Wells, ed., *Life Style and Psychographics.* Chicago: American Marketing Association, 1974, 127-55.

READING 7

Interpersonal Influence on Consumer Behavior: An Attribution Theory Approach

Bobby J. Calder and Robert E. Burnkrant

Attribution theory is used to develop a new approach to interpersonal influence. As a first step in investigating this approach, an experiment explores how people infer personal dispositions from observing a consumer's behavior. The results illustrate the value of the attribution approach but suggest the need for extending existing attribution theory.

Interpersonal influence is widely recognized as a major determinant of consumer behavior. It is typically considered at the sociological level of group membership (social class, subcultures, etc.). Psychological studies at the individual process level have been less common. In fact, there seem to have been only three types of studies at the process level. One type has examined the relationship between direct group pressure and product evaluations (e.g., Burnkrant and Cousineau 1976; Cohen and Golden 1972; Stafford 1966; Witt 1969; Witt and Bruce 1970). A second type of study has focused on more indirect social influence (e.g., Grubb and Hupp 1968; Jacobson and Kossoff 1963; Ross 1971). Interpersonal determinants are construed to be perceived attributes of the product (status, masculinity, etc.). A third type of study has arisen in connection with the normative beliefs component of Fishbein and Ajzen's (1975) attitude model. Normative beliefs contain information about what other people think the consumer ought to do, i.e., social norms. These beliefs determine behavior along with attitude. Ryan and Bonfield (1975) have further proposed that normative beliefs are related to a construct they term "social compliance." This construct represents the individual's readiness to be influenced by others by virtue of social rewards and costs.

None of these three lines of work provides an integrative psychological approach to interpersonal influence. Each attacks a different aspect of the problem. The group pressure and product attribute studies deal with specific social influence effects. The Extended Fishbein Model suggests a psychological basis (beliefs) for the influence of social norms. A more general approach is needed—an approach that (1) conceptualizes the consumer as a social actor linked to others through a variety of role relationships, all of which are specific sources of influence as well as indirect normative influence, and (2) accounts for influence in psychological terms applicable to both the consumer and the influencer. This paper develops such an approach using attribution theory.

"Attribution" is a psychological construct referring to the cognitive processes through which an individual infers the cause of an actor's behavior. Studies of attribution have relied heavily on two theoretical perspectives, one due to Kelly (1967, 1971, 1972) and the other to Jones and Davis (1965). Both perspectives dwell on conditions which determine whether a behavior is attributed to internal, personal causes or to external forces. In general, individuals are biased toward internal attributions. That is, they tend to see the dispositions (traits, preferences, etc.) of an actor as causing the actor's behavior.

Internal attributions are not automatic, however. Individuals consider external factors as alternative explanations. Kelley suggests an "analysis of vari-

Reprinted with permission from the *Journal of Consumer Research,* 4:1 June 1977, 29–38.

ance" analogy. An individual analyzes the covariation between observed behaviors and a possible dispositional cause. There are four dimensions of possible covariation. One dimension is the "distinctiveness" of the behavior. If an observer tends to attribute a certain disposition to everyone (low distinctiveness), a self-attribution external explanation is ruled out, and an internal attribution to the actor is plausible. The plausibility of an internal attribution also increases if there is "consistency" over time and place in the observations of the actor's behavior. Such consistency eliminates possible confounds with nonpersonal factors. Finally, the plausibility of an internal attribution increases if there is a consensus among other people that a behavior reflects a disposition. Thus, to the extent that an actor's behavior exhibits distinctiveness and consistency over time, place, and the reactions of others, it is accepted as evidence of a personal disposition. Otherwise, the behavior is discounted and attributed to external factors.

Jones and Davis' perspective is formulated somewhat differently. They pose the question of how an observer can be sure that the language he uses to describe an actor's behavior is also descriptive of the personal dispositions of the actor. Their term for the match between observed behaviors and inferred dispositions is "correspondence." The problem for the observer is whether the actor's dispositions correspond to the observer's description of the actor's behavior. Jones and Davis explicitly include the "effects" produced by a behavior as well as the behavior itself in their analysis. Correspondence depends on the number of "noncommon effects" produced by a choice act.

The theory postulates that observers construe behavior as a choice between either explicit or implicit alternatives. A chosen alternative is associated with a set of observed effects; each of the unchosen alternatives is associated with a set of hypothetical consequences which would have been the effects had it been chosen. The chosen alternative may or may not have effects in common with the unchosen alternatives. Noncommon effects indicate the basis of choice more clearly than do common effects. Common effects reflect external, situational constraints. To the extent that a choice results in noncommon rather than common effects, it yields a stronger inference of correspondence. Moreover, the inference is stronger the fewer the number of noncommon effects, for a few noncommon effects indicate the actor's intentions more precisely than a larger number.

Jones and Davis also hold that correspondent inference depends on the "assumed social desirability" of effects. If most people would not have preferred a chosen alternative, the effects of that choice should be more descriptive of the uniquely personal characteristics of the actor than of external factors. "To learn that a man makes the conventional choice is to learn only that he is like most other men" (Jones and Davis 1965, p. 227). The lower the social desirability of a chosen alternative, the stronger is the inference of correspondence.

Most social psychological research has treated the concept of correspondent inference as equivalent to that of a strong internal attribution. Internal attributions are typically measured by asking observers to rate the extent to which an actor possesses a disposition, e.g., rating the actor's honesty on a semantic differential scale. Confidential ratings are sometimes used, more in keeping with the notion of correspondence, to assess the overall strength of internal attribution.

Attribution theories, as we shall see, are by no means fully developed. Even so, our position is that these ideas suggest a general approach to interpersonal influence. In purchasing and using products, the consumer is a social actor whose behavior is largely open to observation by others. The consumer's behavior is informational input for the attribution processes of observers. Observers infer the consumer's personal dispositions from his or her behavior. Our argument is that attributions underlie interpersonal influence. Attributions amount to judgments about the consumer. These judgments shape the observer's actions with respect to the consumer. The observer's actions may directly affect the consumer's behavior. Attributions thus provide a psychological basis, or reason, for the actions of influencers, something that is missing from "group pressure" studies.

Influence of a more indirect kind is accomplished if the consumer is sensitive to the attributions others make, or to those he expects them to make, or to those "generalized others" might make, and he acts so as to produce the attributions he desires. That is, the consumer engages in behaviors which he believes will lead observers to make attributions which he considers desirable. Conceptualizing such indirect influence as operating through perceived product attributes is potentially misleading. The influence does not stem from the product itself but from the consumer's beliefs about the attributions others make from observing his behavior. This is a far more dynamic process than product-attribute social-influence conceptualizations imply.

We propose a paradigm for research rather than a full-blown model. This paradigm is diagrammed in Figure A. The research reported in this paper deals with a fundamental aspect of this paradigm, shown as Relationship (1) in Figure A. This is the functioning of the attribution process itself: how an observer infers personal dispositions from a consumer's behavior. In order to pursue the full paradigm, it is necessary, as a first step, to investigate this relationship, to explore the applicability of existing attribution theory to observations of consumer behavior.

There are, however, two other aspects of the full paradigm (see Figure A). One is the accuracy of the consumer's knowledge of the attributions observers make from his behavior. We refer to this as the consumer's attributional sensitivity.[1] The other aspect of the full paradigm is how the consumer's attributional sensitivity affects his own subsequent behavior.

Attribution theory thus provides an integrative approach to the study of interpersonal influence. This approach encompasses the concerns of previous influence studies. Relationship (2) in Figure A, between the observer's attributions and the actor's sensitivity to these attributions, can involve overt pressure by the observer or the mere presumption of an attribution by the actor. Relationship (3), between the actor's attributional sensitivity and his subsequent behavior, necessarily involves the question of how this sensitivity is represented psychologically (e.g., normative beliefs?) and how it affects other determinants of behavior such as attitudes. Though directed more at normative influence, the approach can be generalized to informational influence as well: In assessing the adequacy of his behavior, the consumer may be sensitive to the attributions others make about his competence.[2]

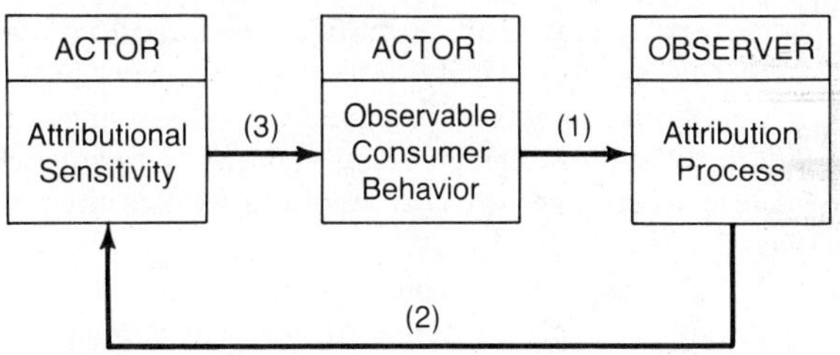

FIGURE A
An Attribution Paradigm for the Study of Interpersonal Influence

Let us further consider how people make internal attributions from observing consumer behavior—the fundamental aspect of the proposed influence paradigm. The basic principle emerging from Kelley's and Jones and Davis' work is that *a person is more likely to attribute an internal disposition or personal characteristic to an actor when there are no plausible external, alternative explanations for an act.* This "discounting principle" may be further operationalized in terms of two variables which we believe are especially significant for the consumer context. The first variable is suggested by Jones and Davis' hypothesis that the strength of an internal attribution varies inversely with the assumed social desirability of a choice. If most other people would not have made the choice, the actor is less likely to have been forced into the choice by external constraints. In Kelley's terms, the choice is highly distinctive if most people would not have made it. Applied to the context of consumer behavior, assumed social desirability is closely linked to brand advertising. One of the major purposes of advertising is to generate a consumer franchise for a brand, to create the impression that a brand is prestigious and widely purchased. With the cosmetic products used in this study, a heavily

1. It is of interest to note that recent work in the social psychology literature has examined how accurate observers are in inferring the dispositions of actors (e.g., Calder, Ross, and Insko 1973), but there has been no work on the problem posed here—how sensitive actors are in their knowledge of observer attributions.

2. Note that our approach applies to circumstances which might at first seem removed from the actor-observer attribution paradigm. Situational advertisements, for example, portray an actor-observer scenario for the consumer. For many products, attributional sensitivity may stem from vicarious exposure to the attributions manifested by these fictitious observers. Also, attribution theory deals with the actor's observation of his own behavior. Thus, attributional sensitivity need not depend on observers, real, generalized, or fictitious, but on the actor's own "self-perception" (Bem 1972).

advertised manufacturer's brand (Revlon) should be perceived as more widely desired than a private-label manufacturer's brand (Walgreens).[3] Observing the purchase of the Walgreen brand may thus be expected to lead to stronger internal attributions than the purchase of the Revlon brand.

The second variable operationalizes the discounting principle in terms of the structure of the choice situation observed. A high-choice situation is one in which an actor is observed to select from a variety of different alternatives: a low-choice situation is one in which he selects from fewer, more similar alternatives. In the high-choice situation, the actor is less constrained by the alternatives present. The chosen alternative is likely to be associated with noncommon effects. In the low-choice situation, the alternatives are likely to have common effects. The high-choice situation implicitly indicates distinctiveness. This logic implies that internal attributions are stronger under high choice than low choice.[4]

It may be argued, however, that an actor's consideration of only a few alternatives in a low-choice situation indicates a prior choice, a choice of these alternatives from a wider consideration class or evoked set. Accordingly, both the prior choice of the alternative set and the terminal choice act may provide a basis for attributions. This argument is particularly applicable to consumer choices which frequently entail shopping decisions as well as purchasing decisions. An actor who shops at a store providing a low-choice situation, when there are different, alternative stores available, has indeed made two choices, in which case an observer might not construe the overall situation as one of low choice. An observer might take into account both choices in making attributions about the actor.

It should be noted that Jones and Davis explicitly contend that prior choices have no effect on attributions.

> *If we observe that a man leaves his chair, crosses the room, closes the door, and the room becomes less noisy, a correspondent inference would be that he intended to cut down the noise. One might ask whether the inference that the man intended to reach the door is not also a correspondent inference since "reaching the door" is an effect of crossing the room. But the subordinate parts of a meaningful action sequence do not have to be confused with the effects of an action. In this case, the perceiver is likely to "organize" the action in his mind as beginning with the decision to leave the chair and ending with the closing of the door. It is the effects of the terminal act in a meaningful sequence, then, that provide the grist for our theory. (Jones and Davis 1965, p. 225)*

While the effects of prior choices have not been empirically ruled out, most attribution theory research does support the prediction of stronger internal attributions under high rather than low choice (cf. Calder, Ross, and Insko 1973). This study tests this prediction in a consumer context in which prior choices may be more salient than in previous research. If prior choice is salient, low choice may well yield stronger attributions than high choice.

The present study thus seeks to demonstrate that people make attributions from observing consumer behavior in accordance with the discounting principle. In addition to whether the product chosen was a Walgreen or Revlon brand and whether the situation was one of high or low choice, two other variables were included to explore the generality of the discounting principle. One variable was the product usage situation. Belk's (1974) research suggests the importance of different situations for consumer behavior. He conceives of the situation as everything which exists at a point in time that is not a property of the product or the consumer. He defines the situation in terms of observable aggregate effects that are susceptible to external verification without reference to any psychological state. This objective approach is employed here to examine how different situations modify attributions made about a consumer. The two situations investigated differ, at a minimum, in the

3. The greater social desirability of the Revlon over the Walgreen brand name is an assumption of this research. While this assumption was suggested by preliminary interviews before the study, we have no pilot data to support it.

4. This logic assumes that the low-choice situation results in no noncommon effects. According to Jones and Davis' theory, low choice would result in a stronger attribution than high choice if there were some noncommon effects but fewer than under high choice. While this does not seem the more likely possibility in this case, and for this reason the high-choice prediction is stated here, it illustrates the difficulty of developing attribution theory predictions. Note that the high-choice prediction is bolstered by Kelley's (1967) distinctiveness hypothesis.

extent to which the use of the chosen product is public and involving, or more or less private and less involving.

This situational difference seems particularly relevant to attribution theory, though existing theories do not make clear predictions. Certainly, public involvement is more likely to reflect external constraints, thereby hindering attributions. Sometimes, however, a publicly involving situation of use also conveys stronger behavioral evidence of commitment to the choice, which might lead to a stronger attribution than would private usage. In any event, the two situations are less important for theoretical prediction than for assessing the cross-situational generality of the two discounting variables. For this, it is only required that the situations differ in a way that might be expected to affect attributions.

The other variable included for generality was the product itself. Two cosmetic products, mascara and deodorant, were employed. They were selected because usage of mascara is more observable and conspicuous than usage of deodorant. As with the situations of use variable, it is of interest to determine whether attributions are made in a parallel manner for objectively different products.

Method

Subjects

One hundred twenty-four female subjects participated in this study. They were students at the University of Illinois at Urbana-Champaign enrolled in home economics courses. The study was conducted during the scheduled sessions of five classes. No communication was allowed between subjects, and subjects in each class received all the experimental treatments.

Independent Variables

The independent variables were manipulated by asking subjects to take the role of observers while reading written scenarios portraying a consumer's behavior. The choice situation varied according to whether the consumer chose a brand of a given product from two similar brands (low choice) or from four, more dissimilar brands (high choice). Also varied was whether the consumer chose a heavily advertised manufacturer's brand (Revlon) or a private-label brand (Walgreens). In the low-choice condition, the consumer chose Revlon after considering Revlon and Max Factor or chose Walgreens after considering Walgreens and K-Mart. In the high-choice condition, the consumer chose Revlon after considering Revlon, Max Factor, Walgreens, and K-Mart or chose Walgreens after considering all four brands.

The two variables included for generality were manipulated by changing the situation of use and the product described in the scenarios. The situation of use was either to wear on an evening out with people the consumer considered important (public and involving use) or to keep in the lounge at the consumer's place of work (more private and less involving use). The product was either mascara or deodorant.

Procedure

These variables were manipulated in a 2 X 2 X 2 X 2 between-subjects factorial design. Each subject received a description of a typical consumer situation that could well face a young woman similar to herself. The specific description read as follows:

> *A young woman about 20 years old is going to college and working part-time in a medium-sized midwestern city. She works in a small office with one other female employee. The woman shops fairly regularly at one of the larger local shopping centers. There are two women's specialty shops, a Walgreens, and a K-Mart that she goes to. On one such occasion, one of the items she intends to buy is deodorant [mascara]. As she has noted on her shopping list, she wants the deodorant [mascara] for everyday use. In fact, she would like to keep it in her compartment in the women's lounge at work to freshen up occasionally [for a special occasion. In fact, she has been invited out to dinner with several people whom she likes and for whom she is especially anxious to be at her best].*
>
> *On this particular trip, the woman looks at the following brands of deodorant [mascara] displayed at the cosmetic counters in these stores: Revlon deodorant [mascara], Max Factor deodorant [mascara], Walgreen deodorant [mascara], and K-Mart deodorant [mascara]. These are the only brands she considers buying on this trip. [In the low-choice condi-*

tion, only two brands were provided: either Revlon and Max Factor or Walgreens and K-Mart.]

After looking at these brands, the woman chooses the Walgreen [Revlon] deodorant [mascara] to keep in the women's lounge at work for her private use [to wear out to dinner with her friends].

Subjects were contacted in the normal classroom environment. After being introduced by the instructor, the researchers informed the subjects that they would be given a brief questionnaire in which a typical consumer situation would be followed by a series of questions about the person described in that situation.

Each questionnaire contained one of the sixteen possible descriptions. The questionnaires were distributed to subjects in each classroom so that descriptions were assigned at random. After reading the brief description of the consumer situation, subjects were asked to evaluate the shopper's personality. They were instructed to "think back to the person described on the previous page and try to determine the personality traits she might have."

Dependent Variables

Consistent with previous attribution research, two types of dependent variables were assessed—semantic differential ratings of the consumer on twenty-seven personality traits and a rating on a ten-point scale of confidence in these personality ratings. An internal attribution, the extent to which the consumer is seen to have a given disposition, is indicated by the extremity of the trait ratings. Both positive and negative extremes on the bipolar adjectives indicate strong internal attributions. The confidence ratings measure the overall extent to which observers believe that their attributions correspond to the actor's actual internal dispositions. Higher confidence ratings indicate that observers are more sure that they learned something about the consumer.

The personality traits were selected to represent a broad spectrum. The two discounting variables are predicted to affect all traits which are perceived as potential causes of the consumer's behavior. In the absence of any theory about which traits might be relevant as potential causes, it was necessary to select traits on a representative basis. Null-hypothesis results, as usual, are uninformative: the absence of experimental effects could be due to inadequacy of the discounting principle or to failure to include appropriate traits. The existence of the predicted effects for the selected traits, however, provides evidence for the discounting principle.

Results

Since the personality traits were selected on a representative basis, it would be capitalizing on chance to analyze the effects of the independent variables for each trait separately. It was thus necessary to determine the interrelationships among traits. To do this, a within-cells correlation matrix was computed for the twenty-seven personality trait ratings. The correlation between each pair of elements in such a matrix is adjusted to remove treatment effects. The within-cells correlation matrix thus reflects the general structure of the subjects' attributions without being affected by the independent variables. To uncover this structure, the matrix was submitted to a principal-components analysis.

Two factors clearly emerged from this analysis (Table 1). Limiting a factor pattern to those variables with more than 25 percent of their variation involved in a pattern (a loading greater than .50), reveals in Table 1 that the variables composing Factor 1 might be labeled "social evaluation" and those for Factor 2 "personal effectiveness." Scores on these variables were summed to yield two derived dependent variables, one for each factor. The remaining analyses were conducted for the summed (raw score) social evaluation and personal effectiveness variables and the seven separate personality traits not included in either factor. Table 2 presents the means for all but two of these variables.

An exact least-squares analysis of variance was performed on each of the variables in Table 2. As shown in Table 3, there was a highly significant main effect for Walgreens versus Revlon and a significant product by Walgreens-Revlon by public-private use interaction for the social evaluation dependent variable. In general, subjects' social evaluation attributions were more positive with Revlon than Walgreens. (Note that 44 is the objective midpoint of this scale.) The triple interaction, however, adds further information and is displayed in Figure B. For the mascara product, there is a sharper increase in social evaluation from Walgreens to Revlon with private use than with public use. On the other hand, for the deodorant product, there is a sharper increase with public use. Subjects infer a more positive social evaluation from the choice of Revlon, especially for the private use of mascara and the public use of deodorant.

TABLE 1
Factor Matrix for Personality Ratings[a]

	Orthogonally Rotated Factors[b]	
Variable	*1*	*2*
Rugged/delicate[c]	(.59)	−.06
Unattractive/attractive	(.77)	.18
Low status/high status	(.73)	−.07
Inferior/superior	(.66)	.18
Insincere/sincere	.22	.41
Unsociable/sociable	(.70)	.18
Insecure/secure	.41	.37
Introvert/extrovert	(.68)	.14
Masculine/feminine	(.73)	.16
Foolish/wise	.45	(.58)
Worthless/valuable	.48	(.64)
Unhappy/happy	(.69)	.50
Awkward/graceful	(.73)	.39
Submissive/dominating	.37	.49
Unpopular/popular	(.70)	.50
Extravagant/economical	−.20	(.77)
Immature/mature	.30	(.74)
Unsuccessful/successful	(.55)	(.58)
Uninformed/informed	.32	(.72)
Dull/interesting	.50	(.66)
Conformist/nonconformist	−.13	(.65)
Cautious/impulsive	.41	.04
Critical/tolerant	.30	.37
Frivolous/serious	−.15	(.63)
Quiet/talkative	.43	.42
Sloppy/neat	(.65)	.35
Ungenerous/generous	.49	.48
Percent Total Variance	55.7	44.3

a. Loadings greater than an absolute value of .50 are shown in parentheses.
b. Varimax rotation.
c. The order of the adjectives represents the order in which they were scored from one to seven (for some the order was reversed on the questionnaire).
NOTE: These results are based on a principal components/principal axis factor analysis of the within-cells correlation matrix. The factors are not affected by the experimental treatment conditions.

The analysis of variance for the personal effectiveness variable revealed a significant product by Walgreens-Revlon interaction. The form of this interaction is quite simple (see Figure C): There is no difference between Walgreens and Revlon for mascara but a large difference for deodorant. Attributions of personal effectiveness lie at the objective midpoint of the scale for mascara. For Walgreens deodorant, however, personal effectiveness is rated positively. For the Revlon deodorant, it is rated negatively. Apparently, subjects felt the consumer to be wiser, more informed, etc., for buying the Walgreen brand deodorant and not so wise for buying the Revlon brand deodorant, while the brand made no difference for mascara in terms of personal effectiveness.

The seven personality traits not included in either the social evaluation or personal effectiveness variables were analyzed individually. A significant product by Walgreens-Revlon by public-private use interaction was obtained for the insincere/sincere trait ($F = 3.97$, $p < .049$). For mascara, there is an increase in sincerity from Walgreens to Revlon for private use but not for public use. Using Revlon mascara in a more private situation seems sincere as well as positive in social evaluation. On the other hand, for deodorant, the brand makes no difference in sincerity for public use; but, for private use, Walgreens yields high sincerity ratings, while Revlon gives rise to low sincerity. Evidently, using Revlon deodorant in private, unlike mascara, seems phony. It is the Walgreens deodorant used in private which reflects sincerity. A fairly similar product by Walgreens-Revlon by private-public use interaction pattern is displayed by the ungenerous/generous variable ($F = 5.03$, $p < .027$), except that the Revlon deodorant increases the attribution of generosity under public use, while it does not increase the attribution of sincerity in this case.

Of particular interest is the attribution of the quiet/talkative trait. Verbal participation has been strongly implicated in a number of social processes such as leadership and, in itself, serves as an important informational cue (Calder and Whetzel 1976). There were three significant effects for the quiet/talkative variable, a Walgreens versus Revlon main effect ($F = 4.92$, $p < .029$), a private-public use main effect ($F = 4.38$, $p < .039$), and a product by choice interaction ($F = 5.86$, $p < .017$). Subjects inferred that the consumer was more talkative about the Revlon brand than the Walgreens brand and also

TABLE 2
Means for Personality Factors, Separate Traits, and Confidence

	Mascara							
	Low Choice				High Choice			
	Walgreens		Revlon		Walgreens		Revlon	
Variable	*Private*	*Public*	*Private*	*Public*	*Private*	*Public*	*Private*	*Public*
Social evaluation[a]	40.89	49.29	59.89	58.13	48.71	56.00	58.13	53.57
Personal effectiveness[b]	31.89	37.43	38.00	10.67	36.86	40.43	34.88	35.57
Insincere/sincere	5.44	3.86	4.33	3.00	4.57	5.71	5.25	3.57
Cautious/impulsive	3.33	4.14	4.78	4.25	4.57	4.00	4.50	4.29
Critical/tolerant	2.89	2.57	4.00	3.38	2.57	2.71	3.38	3.57
Quiet/talkative	3.00	3.57	4.56	4.50	3.14	3.86	4.00	4.14
Ungenerous/generous	3.00	3.71	4.22	4.00	3.57	5.00	4.00	5.43
Confidence	3.11	4.00	4.44	4.50	3.86	3.14	4.88	4.14
n	9	7	9	8	7	7	8	7

	Deodorant							
	Low Choice				High Choice			
	Walgreens		Revlon		Walgreens		Revlon	
Variable	*Private*	*Public*	*Private*	*Public*	*Private*	*Public*	*Private*	*Public*
Social evaluation[a]	51.50	48.12	60.14	56.89	52.63	43.43	58.12	59.57
Personal effectiveness[b]	41.38	38.50	35.71	34.56	44.25	35.14	30.52	34.28
Insincere/sincere	6.88	6.00	7.43	5.56	5.12	6.14	2.88	5.29
Cautious/impulsive	5.00	3.75	3.86	3.89	5.75	4.86	3.75	4.43
Critical/tolerant	2.75	2.25	4.00	3.58	2.25	2.71	3.88	4.14
Quiet/talkative	4.00	2.13	4.29	3.89	4.00	4.14	3.00	4.00
Ungenerous/generous	4.25	4.00	4.14	4.44	3.25	3.43	3.88	4.43
Confidence	4.12	4.00	4.14	4.67	4.37	3.57	3.12	4.71
n	8	8	7	9	8	7	8	7

a. Average of eleven semantic differentials from Factor 1.
b. Average of nine semantic differentials from Factor 2.

more talkative about public than private use. The former result fits the greater social evaluation ratings under Revlon and, in fact, may be implied by this evaluation. The latter effect probably reflects the import of the woman going out to dinner. The interaction is more intriguing. Under low choice, the deodorant product revealed a stronger attribution of talkativeness but under high choice the mascara was stronger.

There was a main effect for Walgreens versus Revlon on the cautious/impulsive variable ($F = 17.61$, $p < .001$). Subjects always attributed more impulsiveness to the subject purchasing the Revlon brand. Similarly, there was a choice by Walgreens-Revlon interaction on the critical/tolerant variable ($F = 5.61$, $p < .020$), so that buying the Revlon brand was seen as less critical under high choice. In short, subjects saw the purchase of the Revlon brand

TABLE 3
Analyses of Variance for Personality Factors and Confidence

Source[a]	*Social Evaluation F's*	*Personal Effectiveness F's*	*Confidence F's*
Product (*P*)	<1	<1	4.95[b]
Choice (*C*)	<1	<1	<1
Walgreens-Revlon (*WR*)	22.60[c]	2.84	2.65
Public-private use (*U*)	<1	<1	<1
P X *C*	<1	<1	4.65[b]
P X *WR*	<1	4.46[b]	<1
P X *U*	2.28	2.52	1.08
C X *WR*	1.26	2.56	<1
C X *U*	<1	<1	4.13[b]
WR X *U*	<1	<1	<1
P X *C* X *WR*	2.35	<1	<1
P X *C* X *U*	<1	<1	<1
P X *WR* X *U*	4.12[b]	2.61	<1
C X *WR* X *U*	<1	<1	<1
P X *C* X *WR* X *U*	<1	<1	1.75

a. Each source has one degree of freedom.
b. Significant at .05 level.
c. Significant at .01 level.

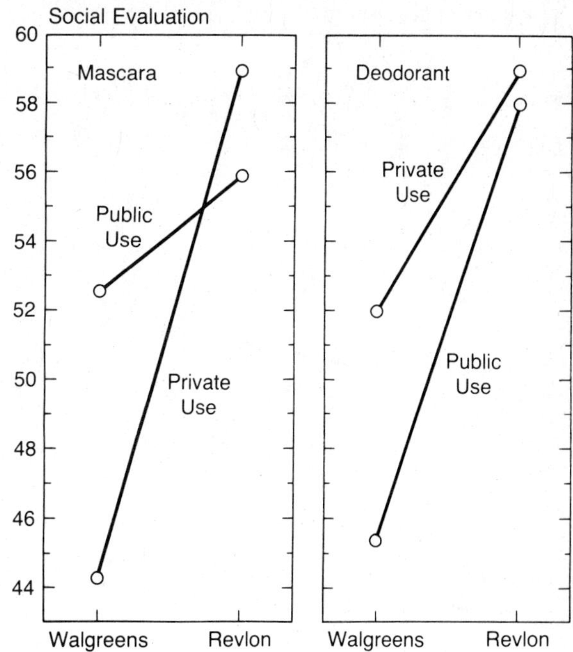

FIGURE B
Mean Social-Evaluation Scores for the Product by Walgreens-Revlon by Private-Public Situation of Use Interaction

as being impulsive and, if there were a wide choice, as reflecting less critical attention. There were no significant effects for the insecure/secure or submissive/dominating judgments.

The mean confidence ratings of subjects in their personality attributions are shown in Table 2 and the analysis of variance in Table 3. There were two significant interactions, a choice by private-public use effect ($F = 4.13$, $p < .045$) and a choice by product effect ($F = 4.65$, $p < .033$) (see Figure D). Subjects were more confident under low choice and private use and under high choice and public use. Similarly, subjects were more confident under low choice and the deodorant product and under high choice and the mascara product. As indicated by Figure D, a high-choice purchase is clearly more revealing for mascara and a low-choice purchase for a private-use situation.

Discussion

The major results for the personality traits can be summarized as follows. The Revlon brand implied more positive social evaluation than the Walgreen brand, this effect being even greater for the private use of mascara and the public use of deodorant. In contrast, for the deodorant purchase, the Revlon brand indicated less personal effectiveness than the Walgreen brand. (Personal effectiveness was not affected for the mascara product.) Thus, purchase of the Revlon deodorant implied a socially popular but not especially competent person. In addition, the Revlon brand led to greater attributions of sincerity and generosity, except for the private use of deodorant. Buying the Revlon brand suggested that the consumer was more talkative, more impulsive, and, under low choice, less critical. Again, the Revlon brand implied the consumer was socially positive but not very thoughtful.

Whereas brand was the central factor affecting personality attributions, the strength of subjects' general propensity to make internal attributions, as reflected by their confidence ratings, depended mainly on choice. For private use, the low-choice situation led to greater confidence. For mascara, the high-choice situation generated more confidence.

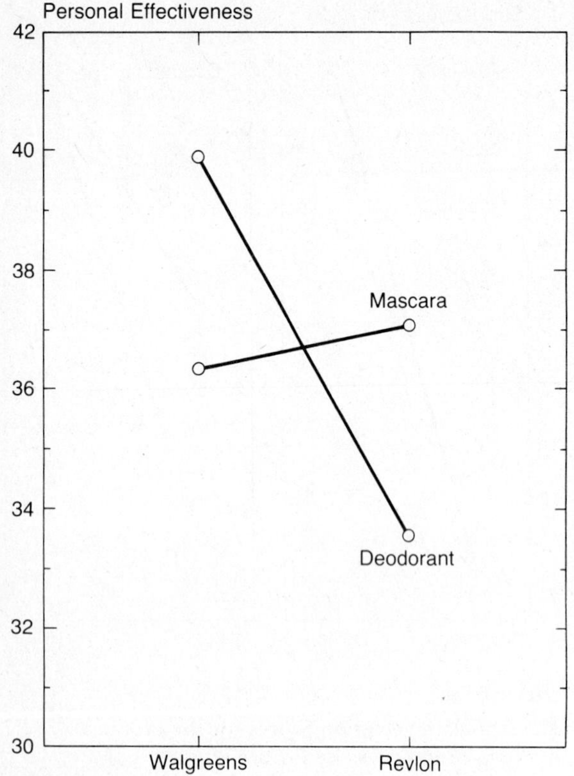

FIGURE C
Mean Personal Effectiveness Scores for the Product by Walgreens-Revlon Interaction

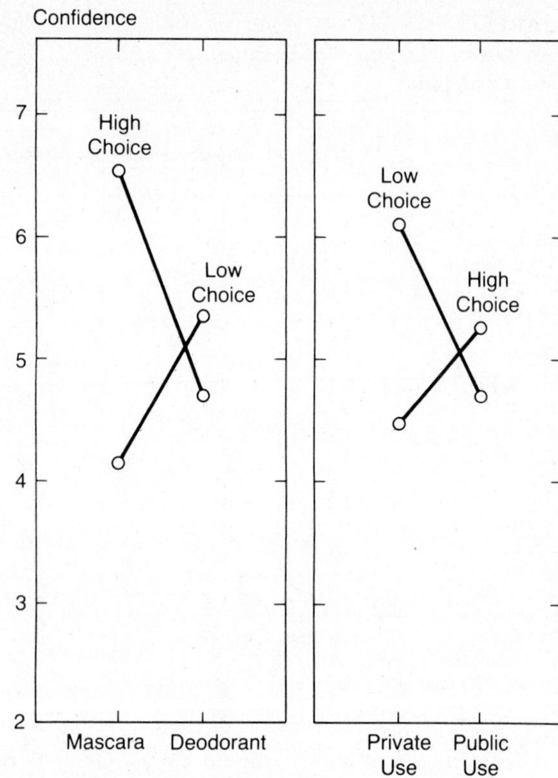

FIGURE D
Mean Confidence in Attributions for the Choice by Product Interaction (Left) and the Choice by Private-Public Situation of Use Interaction (Right)

What do these results mean for the applicability of attribution theory to the consumer context? Recall that the private-label Walgreen brand was expected to lead to stronger internal attributions than the Revlon brand on the basis of its lower assumed social desirability and higher distinctiveness. To the contrary, however, the Revlon brand yielded the stronger attributions across both situations of use and both products. (Except for the deodorant product, these attributions were in the positive direction.) This unpredicted finding casts doubt on the adequacy of existing attribution theory. The discounting principle, or at least common operationalizations of it, is not sufficient as an explanation of how attributions are made.

The Revlon versus Walgreens result suggests what is lacking. Attribution theorists have failed to consider fully the differential significance of choices for observers. Observers may expect some choices to be more revealing than others because actors implicitly or explicitly attach special importance to them. A special case of such importance is when an actor is thought to engage in a behavior at least partly for the reason of expressing, i.e., revealing, himself. It should be noted that Jones and Davis predict more correspondent inferences as the worth (hedonic relevance) of a choice increases. This is another special case of the choice's perceived importance to the actor. In general, observers may believe that a choice which is important to an actor, for any reason, is more closely linked to specific intentions of the actor than one which is unimportant. For these significant choices, observers may pay less attention to plausible external, situational explanations, thereby not conforming to the discounting principle.

The consumer context provides a likely setting for variations in the significance of choices. In terms of our results, the choice of a Revlon brand may have indicated to the observers that the purchase was important to the consumer. The greater social desirability of the Revlon brand implies that the consumer choosing it must be more concerned about the product than one who buys the Walgreen brand. The significance of the Revlon choice would explain the stronger internal attributions with Revlon than Walgreens.

Further evidence regarding the discounting principle comes from the choice variable. Choice affected the global confidence ratings rather than, with one exception, the specific trait attributions. Most interesting is that the effects of choice depended on both the situation of use and the product. Confidence was not always higher in the high-choice situation. This result may reflect the prior choice problem discussed earlier. With the private-use situation and the deodorant product, the purchase might have seemed more routinized to the observers under low than high choice, indicating a history of prior choices. Observers may have interpreted the low choice-private use and low choice-deodorant conditions as actually reflecting a higher degree of choice than the corresponding high-choice conditions. This would explain the stronger internal attributions under low choice.

The results involving the situation of use and product variables confirm the desirability of investigating attributions in different settings. Both of these variables affected the degree to which Revlon yielded stronger attributions than Walgreens. Evidently, the situation of use can have either of the effects postulated: with mascara, public use may have indicated external constraints while, with deodorant, public use may have indicated a stronger behavioral commitment. As discussed previously, these variables may also have altered observers' interpretation of the choice variable.

The present results are useful in two ways. For one, they attest to the need for an attribution approach to interpersonal influence. Most interesting in this regard is the finding that the Revlon brand implied a socially positive but not very competent consumer. Suppose that our observers were linked to our hypothetical consumer through actual role relationships. Their influence would depend on the consumer's attributional sensitivity (Figure A). Assuming that the observers' behavior reflected their attributions, if the consumer were most sensitive to social evaluation attributions, the observers' influence would be to support the Revlon choice. But, if the consumer were most sensitive to personal effectiveness attributions, the observers' influence would be to undermine the Revlon deodorant choice. *Interpersonal influence is only to be accounted for in terms of the psychological processes which underlie it.*

This study illustrates the importance of understanding the variables which affect observers' internal attributions and the consumers' sensitivity to them. If subsequent research confirms that heavily advertised brands engender stronger internal attributions, the marketers of such brands would want to increase their attention to interpersonal influence in their advertising strategies. They would particularly want to counteract negative internal attributions such as the personal effectiveness attribution associated in this study with the use of Revlon deodorant.

The present results are also useful in suggesting the need for extending existing attribution theory. Although attribution theory is presently one of the most active areas of social psychological thinking, almost all of this work is guided by the discounting principle. Our results, however, indicate that the discounting principle is not sufficient to explain attributions made in a consumer context. It appears necessary, at a minimum, to consider the importance observers believe consumers attach to a choice (the significance of the choice) and the assumptions observers make about prior choices.

Attribution theorists have, in general, neglected people's expectations about the meaning of observed behaviors. In addition to discounting, it is necessary to consider the role of "typicality" in making attributions (Calder 1974a, 1974b, 1977). Typicality refers to the observer's intuitive beliefs about the internal characteristics that are usually associated with a given behavior. To make an internal attribution, apart from discounting situational causes of the behavior, an observer must believe that certain characteristics are typical of the behavior. The choice of Revlon must mean something to an observer. We have suggested that it means that the particular product is important to the consumer. However, the choice of Revlon may imply other characteristics which are thought to be typical of Revlon users as well.

Just as it is plausible that choosing Walgreens may mean that the particular product is not important to the consumer, it may be that the choice of Walgreens means less in general. Observers may have weaker beliefs about the characteristics typical of choosing Walgreens than about those typical of choosing Revlon. Although nonpersonal influences can be discounted more easily with the choice of Walgreens, this may be outweighed by the stronger beliefs about the characteristics typical of the Revlon choice. Thus, the present findings of stronger attributions with Revlon than Walgreens may depend more on typicality than discounting.

In developing an attribution approach to interpersonal influence, it will be necessary to clarify the roles of discounting and typicality. While both are probably important in the attribution process, for consumer behavior, the question boils down to which kind of choices yield stronger attributions: choices for which nonpersonal causes can be discounted or choices for which people have strong beliefs about the internal characteristics typical of the choice?

References

Belk, R. W. (1974), "An Exploratory Assessment of Situational Effects on Buyer Behavior," *Journal of Marketing Research*, 11, 15-63.

Bem, D. (1972), "Self-Perception Theory," in *Advances in Experimental Social Psychology, Vol. 6*, ed. L. Berkowitz, New York: Academic Press.

Burnkrant, R., and Cousineau, A. (1975), "Informational and Normative Social Influence in Buyer Behavior," *Journal of Consumer Research*, 2, 206-15.

Calder, B. (1974a), "Informational Cues and Attributions Based on Role Behavior," *Journal of Experimental Social Psychology*, 10, 121-5.

—— (1974b), "An Analysis of the Jones, Davis, and Gergen Attribution Paradigm," *Representative Research in Social Psychology*, 5, 55-9.

—— (1977), "An Attribution Theory of Leadership," in *New Directions in Organizational Behavior*, eds. B. Staw and G. Salancik, Chicago: St. Clair Press.

——, Ross, M., and Insko, C. (1973), "Attitude Change and Attitude Attribution: Effects of Incentive, Choice, and Consequence," *Journal of Personality and Social Psychology*, 25, 84-99.

——, and Whetzel, C. (1976), "Attribution and the Rate of Participation in Ongoing Interaction," submitted for publication.

Fishbein, M., and Ajzen, I. (1975), *Belief, Attitude, Intention, and Behavior*, Reading, Mass.: Addison-Wesley.

Grubb, E., and Hupp, G. (1968), "Percept of Self, Generalized Stereotypes, and Brand Selections," *Journal of Marketing Research*, 5, 58-63.

Jacobson, E., and Kossoff, J. (1963), "Self-Percept and Consumer Attitudes Toward Small Cars," *Journal of Applied Psychology*, 47, 242-5.

Jones, E., and Davis, K. (1965), "From Acts to Disposition: The Attribution Process in Person Perception," in *Advances in Experimental Social Psychology, Vol. 2*, ed. L. Berkowitz, New York: Academic Press.

Kelley, H. (1967), "Attribution in Social Psychology," *Nebraska Symposium on Motivation*, 15, 192-238.

—— (1971), *Attribution in Social Interaction*, New York: General Learning Press.

—— (1972), *Causal Schemata and the Attribution Process*, Morristown, N.J.: General Learning Press.

Ross, I. (1971), "Self-Concept and Brand Preference," *Journal of Business*, 44, 38-50.

Ryan, M., and Bonfield, E. (1975), "The Fishbein Extended Model and Consumer Behavior," *Journal of Consumer Research*, 2, 118-36.

Stafford, James E. (1966), "Effects of Group Influence on Consumer Brand Preferences," *Journal of Marketing Research*, 3, 68-75.

Witt, Robert E. (1966), "Informal Social Group Influence on Consumer Brand Preferences," *Journal of Marketing Research*, 6, 473-7.

——, and Grady, D. Bruce (1970), "Purchase Decisions and Group Influence," *Journal of Marketing Research*, 7, 535-7.

READING 8

An Investigation of Situational Variation in Brand Choice Behavior and Attitude

Kenneth E. Miller and James L. Ginter

Empirical evidence is presented which supports the explicit consideration of situational factors in the study of consumer behavior. Situational variation of brand choice behavior and attitude is identified. The use of situation-specific measures in an attribute-based attitude model is found to increase the ability of the model to predict subsequent brand choice behavior as reported in a multiple wave survey.

Recent marketing literature contains reports of several studies in which the affective component of consumer attitudes is modeled on the basis of product attributes and the resultant measure used to predict preference or behavior (Johnson, 1974; Lehmann, 1971; Wildt and Bruno, 1974; Wilkie and Pessemier, 1973). One of the reasons for the popularity of this approach to the study of consumer behavior is the diagnostic value which the attribute-based model holds for the marketing manager. Explicit consideration of situation-related variables that are specific to the consumer's decision-making context may reduce the unexplained variance and increase the managerial value of the research for product positioning decisions.

Researchers recently have considered only broad product categories in investigating the situational variation of preference for product types (Belk, 1974; Sandell, 1968). The emphasis has been placed on the situational variation of primary demand for the product types. The marketing manager, however, typically is concerned with the secondary demand for his brand as it competes with other brands of the same product type. Marketing strategies for specific brands are related to their relative strengths and weaknesses. The concept of situation becomes managerially important if these relative strengths and weaknesses differ by situation, i.e., if the effect of situation is not the same for all brands. In addition to the greater managerial importance of studying the situational variation in purchase of brands rather than general product classes, the use of brands provides a more conservative test of the influence of situations. For example, it is less impressive to show that a person's choice of dining out in an expensive restaurant rather than in a fast food franchise is related to the nature of the eating occasion than to show that choice of one fast food franchise over another is related to eating occasion.

Previous studies have not examined differential situation effects across brands. Another characteristic of previous studies of situation is that they have relied on measurement of preference within specified situational scenarios, instead of situational variation in observed or reported brand choice behavior.

The research reported here is designed to address each of these issues and to assess whether situation-specific measures improve the measured relationship between attitude and behavior (consistent with suggestions by Wicker, 1969). Specifically, the authors extend previous research by: (1) using competing brands in a narrowly defined product category, and (2) considering self-reports of behavior rather than preference, thus allowing examination of situational attitude-behavior congruence.

Reprinted by permission of the American Marketing Association, from the *Journal of Marketing Research,* 16:1 February 1979, 111-123.

Background

Situational variation of stated preference for specific product types within a general product class has been established empirically. Belk (1974), for example, found that 19.7% of the variance in preference for snack products (e.g., potato chips, popcorn, cookies, fruit, ice cream) and 34.3% of the variance in preference for meat products (e.g., hot dogs, steak, chicken, hamburgers, fish) were explained by main effects of situation and the interaction of situation with other variables. The appeal of the concept of situational variance in consumer behavior has led to a discussion of adequate and generalizable methods of defining and measuring situations (Belk, 1974; Lutz and Kakkar, 1975).

Belk (1974) defines situation as "all those factors particular to a time and place of observation which do not follow from a knowledge of personal (intra-individual) and stimulus (choice alternative) attributes, and which have a demonstrable and systematic effect on current behavior." This definition separates the influences of the person, the situation, and the stimulus object (brand) on consumer behavior. It therefore establishes situation as external to the individual's psychological nature. Though other researchers (Lutz and Kakkar, 1975) have argued that situation should be defined psychologically in terms of how the individual transforms the situational input to behavioral output, the primary managerial value of the concept appears to lie in its generalizability. Situation may interact with individual characteristics to determine response, but a greater benefit can be derived from objective specification of commonly occurring situations. Such specification allows for their description, isolation, and control in relation to the consumers' actual responses toward the brands. The advantage, in managerial terms, is that situations are identified across individuals, and brand-related decisions specific to these situations can be made.

Bearden and Woodside (1976) augmented measures of attitude with generalizable situation descriptors and found an improvement in accuracy of prediction of behavioral intention for specific brands. Their framework, however, involves the assumption that attitudes do not vary with situation. The managerial value of the situation concept is enhanced if attitudinal variations over situations exist and if diagnosis of these situation-specific attitudes can be used in development of situation-oriented marketing programs. The investigation of situational variation of attitudes is an integral part of this study.

No previously reported research has examined the situational variation of measures of attitude toward specific brands. This research focuses on the issue of managerial relevance in that the situational variation of importances, perceptions, and self-reported behavior is examined. The relationship between situation-specific attitudes and situation-specific brand choice behavior is also investigated.

The research issues were examined through testing of the following hypotheses:

H1: Purchase levels of specific brands vary differentially across situations.

H2: Attribute importances vary differentially across situations.

H3: Perceptions of specific brands vary differentially across situations.

H4: Situation-specific measurement of attribute importances and perceptions improves prediction of brand choice over general (nonsituational) measurement.

Method

The elements of the multiattribute attitude model were measured within specific situational scenarios. The use of situation-specific measures to analyze or predict behavior is meaningful if the values of the dependent measure and the explanatory measures vary across situations. That is, lack of a situational component of variance in the measures would suggest use of a more general model. The existence of situational variance in brand choice behavior, attribute importances, and perceptions was tested. In addition, the use of explanatory elements measured in a nonsituational format was compared with the use of elements measured within specific situational contexts in terms of ability to predict self-reported subsequent brand choice.

Selection of Product and Attributes

The product category of fast food restaurants was chosen for analysis. This product category was narrowed to include primarily those fast food restaurants oriented toward hamburgers. Inclusion of different types of products could have led to emphasis on differences between brands selling different types of products and masking of differences between brands selling the same type of product. This definition of the product category also seemed consistent with that which would be used by one of the brand managers in identifying the closest competitors. The following eight fast food restaurants were used in the study.

- Arby's
- Borden Burger
- Burger Chef
- Burger King
- Hungry Herman's
- McDonald's
- Wendy's
- White Castle

Seven of the eight brands specialize in hamburgers, and Arby's offers roast beef sandwiches. Hungry Herman's is a local operation with only one location, and Borden Burger is a local chain with more locations in the city than any other brand at the time of the study. The other brands have broad regional or national distribution.

According to preliminary investigation, these brands were frequently used by much of the local population and permitted consideration of a series of choices. The use of a set of choices provided a richer measure of behavior than a single choice because the effects of factors unique to any one choice were reduced. Moreover, each choice in this setting could be affected by the situational context. The selection of the fast food market also made brand-specific analysis possible. Preliminary investigation indicated that this local market had some degree of benefit segmentation. White Castle, for example, was perceived to be lowest in price, whereas Wendy's was seen as offering a higher quality product at a higher price, and Borden Burger was seen to have a wide variety of menu and to be very convenient. The fact that different brands were perceived as being most favorable on different attributes would tend to reduce "halo" effects, whereby the preferred brand is seen as the best on all attributes.

Six group interviews of six to eight persons were conducted to determine the criteria on which consumers differentiate fast food restaurants and decide which restaurant(s) to frequent. The following attributes were elicited.

- Speed of service
- Variety of menu
- Popularity with children
- Cleanliness
- Convenience
- Taste of food
- Price

These attributes are consistent with those suggested by Becknell and Maher (1962), who conducted a factor analysis of image items for food retailers and found that the five most important factors were related to food quality, cleanliness, price, service, and unique features.

Selection of Situations

The external definition of situation was used in this study because of its managerial advantage, and situation was operationalized as different eating occasions. The eating occasions were chosen on the basis of two criteria: (1) they should be encountered frequently by customers so that an adequate number of observations could be obtained for each situation, and (2) they should be perceived by respondents as clearly different so that variation between them could be measured.

Group interviews resulted in selection of the following four eating occasions.

- Lunch on a weekday
- Snack during a shopping trip
- Evening meal when rushed for time
- Evening meal with the family when not rushed for time

The eating occasions appear to contrast on dimensions discussed by Belk (December 1975): physical surroundings, time frame, interpersonal surroundings, mood, and goal direction. The proportion of respondents indicating that they frequented fast food restaurants in each of the situations is shown in Table 1. These findings suggest that the eating occasions selected met the criteria established for the study.

Data Collection

Data were collected over a three-month period from a mail panel residing in Columbus, Ohio, by a five-wave questionnaire. The panel was constructed by a solicitation letter to a random sample of 2,800 residents whose names appeared in the Columbus telephone directory. A total of 950 fast food users initially

TABLE 1
Proportion of Respondents Who Frequented Fast Food Restaurants in Each Situation

Situation	*Percentage*
Lunch on a weekday	79.2
Snack during a shopping trip	70.4
Evening meal when rushed for time	55.0
Evening meal with the family when not rushed for time	47.7

agreed to participate in the study. Introductory instructions for each questionnaire specified that the same household member was to respond each time, and demographic checks were made to assure the consistency of respondents. Compensation for completing all five questionnaires consisted of five dollars and a small gift.

The data relevant to the research were collected on each questionnaire. Each respondent indicated attribute importances and perceived locations of brands in a nonsituational format. In addition, attribute importance, perceived convenience of each brand, and self-reported purchase behavior were collected within eating occasion from each respondent in every questionnaire wave.

The number of usable responses from each of the five questionnaire waves is shown in Table 2. Demographic features and initial attitudes of respondents who dropped out of the study werç compared with those of respondents who completed all five questionnaires. The two groups were different ($\alpha =$ .05) on only three of 96 explanatory variables considered. Tests also were conducted to ascertain whether participation in the study influenced attitudes or behavior. Five days after the mailing of the fourth questionnaire, a similarly generated independent sample received the same questionnaire (76 fast food users returned the questionnaire in usable form). Comparison of these responses with those from wave four of the panel showed that the panel members were more familiar with some of the brands. The increased familiarity may have been caused by the study's use of some fast food restaurants which were not very well known (e.g., Hungry Herman's). Attitudinal differences between the groups were minor (near the level of chance), and behavioral differences were nonexistent. Also, situational usage frequency was not significantly different. Respondents were asked to identify the objectives of the research project on the fifth questionnaire, and six individuals were excluded from further analysis because of their insight.

TABLE 2
Number of Usable Responses

Questionnaire Wave	*Number of Responses*[a]
1	742
2	622
3	502
4	487
5	440

a. Original mailing 950.

Attitude Measures

Attribute-based models of affect have taken several forms. Some have been shown to be well suited to the study of individual actions, whereas others have been developed for the analysis of choice among alternative brands (Bass, 1972). A primary concern in the managerial setting is the relative positions of competitive brands in a single product category. Therefore, attitude toward each brand is expressed in this study as a function of attribute importance and the perceived performance of the brand on each of the attributes.

Attribute importances and perceptions on one attribute (convenience) were measured within eating occasion scenarios. The situational measurement of perception on convenience only was based on the notion that the relevance of eating occasion may not be the same for perceptions on all attributes. Beliefs on some attributes may be tied directly to the brand and invariant across situations, and beliefs on other attributes may be related to the eating occasion for which the brand is considered. Belk (December 1975) also made the distinction between characteristics which are "lasting and general" features and those which are specific to "time and place." Perceptions of convenience of the brands were expected to vary across the eating occasions, because differences in the respondents' general locations for different occasions could have caused differences in the relative perceived proximity of the alternative fast food establishments. Because perceptions on the other attributes were not expected to vary across the eating occasions considered and questionnaire length was an important consideration, these perceptions were not measured within the situational contexts.

The situational measures of brand choice behavior, attribute importances, and perceived convenience were used in testing for the existence of situational variation of these constructs. Attribute importances and perceptions (on all attributes) also were measured without reference to eating occasion. These nonsituational measures and their situational counterparts were compared in terms of their ability to predict brand choice.

Analysis and Results

Situational Variation of Behavior (H1)

Reported brand choice was the dependent variable in the predictive phase of the study, and its variation across eating occasions was tested. Each respondent's reported choice data over the 12 weeks of the study were used in the analysis (respondents who did not purchase any of the brands on any of the eating occasions were eliminated). The data for each respondent consisted of an eight brand by four eating occasion matrix of number of purchases. The cell means are shown in Table 3.

Significance of differences in the purchase frequencies across brands and situations was tested by a two-way analysis of variance (see Table 4). Because each respondent had a complete data matrix (with some cells containing zeroes if a brand was not purchased on an eating occasion), a completely crossed repeated measures design, with situations X brands X subjects, was used (Myers (1972) refers to this as a two-factor repeated measurements design). The main effects of brands and situations were significant. In addition, the interaction term was significant, thus indicating that the effect of situation on purchase frequencies was different for different brands (H1 was supported). In addition to being a more conservative test of the influence of situation on purchase choice than that used in previous studies of general

TABLE 3
Mean Numbers of Purchases During the Study (n = 391)

Brand	*Sit. A Lunch on a Weekday (Mkt. Share)*	*Sit. B Evening Meal When Rushed for Time (Mkt. Share)*	*Sit. C Evening Meal with Family When Not Rushed for Time (Mkt. Share)*	*Sit. D Snack During a Shopping Trip (Mkt. Share)*
1 Arby's	.24[a]	.11	.06	.05
	(4.8)	(5.4)	(3.7)	(4.2)
2 Borden Burger	.91	.39	.17	.16
	(18.4)	(19.1)	(10.4)	(13.3)
3 Burger Chef	.46	.11	.09	.05
	(9.3)	(5.4)	(5.5)	(4.2)
4 Burger King	.69	.32	.20	.17
	(13.9)	(15.7)	(12.3)	(14.2)
5 Hungry Herman's	.17	.03	.03	.01
	(3.4)	(1.5)	(1.8)	(0.8)
6 McDonald's	1.40	.68	.62	.43
	(28.3)	(33.3)	(38.0)	(35.8)
7 Wendy's	.65	.28	.36	.16
	(13.1)	(13.7)	(22.1)	(13.3)
8 White Castle	.43	.12	.10	.17
	(8.7)	(5.9)	(6.1)	(14.2)

a. The 391 respondents averaged .24 purchases of Arby's on the eating occasion "lunch on a weekday," and this figure represents 4.8% market share in this situation.

TABLE 4
ANOVA of Brand Choice

Source	*d.f.*	*s.s.*	*F*
Brands	7	568.95	44.55[a]
at Sit. A	(7)	431.81	33.89[a]
at Sit. B	(7)	123.66	9.71[a]
at Sit. C	(7)	105.85	8.31[a]
at Sit. D	(7)	45.45	3.57[b]
Brands X Subjects	2730	4980.58	
Situations	3	426.26	49.94[a]
at Br. 1	(3)	9.03	1.06
at Br. 2	(3)	145.57	17.09[a]
at Br. 3	(3)	41.90	4.92[b]
at Br. 4	(3)	68.28	8.01[a]
at Br. 5	(3)	6.66	.78
at Br. 6	(3)	214.08	25.13[a]
at Br. 7	(3)	50.51	5.93[b]
at Br. 8	(3)	28.19	3.31[c]
Situations X Subjects	1170	3328.65	
Brands X Situations	21	137.97	4.50[a]
Brands X Situations X Subjects	8190	11970.38	
Subjects	390	1140.17	
Total	12511	22552.96	

a. $p < .001$.
b. $p < .01$.
c. $p < .05$.
The Geisser-Greenhouse (1958) correction for use of the F distribution in multivariate analysis was used in all tests of significance.
NOTE: The presentation of both sets of simple main effects in this table is somewhat redundant as each of them partitions the interaction term. The analysis of simple main effects of brands at situation, for example, is a partitioning of the main effect of brands and the interaction term. The degrees of freedom of these simple main effects ($4 \times 7 = 28$) is equal to that of the main and interaction effects ($7 + 21 = 28$), and the same is true for sums of squares. Similarly, the simple main effects of situation at brand have degrees of freedom and sums of squares equal to those of the situation main effect and the interaction (24 and 564.23, respectively). The total variance in this analysis is partitioned among the terms adjacent to the left margin, and the degrees of freedom used for tests of simple main effects only are in parentheses. For a more complete explanation of analysis of simple main effects, see Kirk (1968).

product classes (Belk, 1974; Sandell, 1968), this result is potentially very useful in a managerial sense. However, a marketing manager is more interested in knowing the exact loci of the influences. Specifically, he wants to know whether purchase level of a given brand (his or a competitor's) varies significantly across situations. The existence of situational variance of individual brands was examined by analysis of simple main effects of situation at each brand (see Kirk, 1968). These tests showed that purchase levels of six of the brands varied significantly across situations and that the purchase levels of Arby's and Hungry Herman's did not.

The significant interaction term also can be viewed as showing that differences among brands varied by situation. Analysis of simple main effects of brand at situation led to sums of squares indicating that brands were most different on the eating occasion "lunch on a weekday" and least on "snack during a shopping trip." Table 4 notes that the analysis of both sets of simple main effects is somewhat redundant, as each partitions the interaction term. Both sets of analyses are reported, however, because the importance of the research question may depend on one's perspective.

The nature of the interaction can be seen in Figure 1, where mean purchase frequency of each eating occasion is plotted for each brand. The average purchase level of each brand across the four situations is also shown in Figure 1 as a basis for visually assessing the effects of the situations. The general level of the eating occasions is a reflection of the relative frequency shown in Table 1. There are some exceptions to this general trend, however. For example, Tukey's HSD test[1] showed that the mean number of purchases of Wendy's was greater for "evening meal when not rushed" than for "evening meal when rushed" ($q = 3.98$, $p < .01$), whereas the mean number of purchases of the other brands followed the trend of being either equal for these two occasions or greater for the latter. Another exception to the general level of eating occasions was the higher purchase frequency of White Castle for "during a shopping trip" than for "evening meal when not rushed."

If the market shares of the brands as shown in Table 3 were equal across situations, the lines in Fig-

1. This test was used because only the pairs of points in Figure 1 with potential managerial interest were tested for equality.

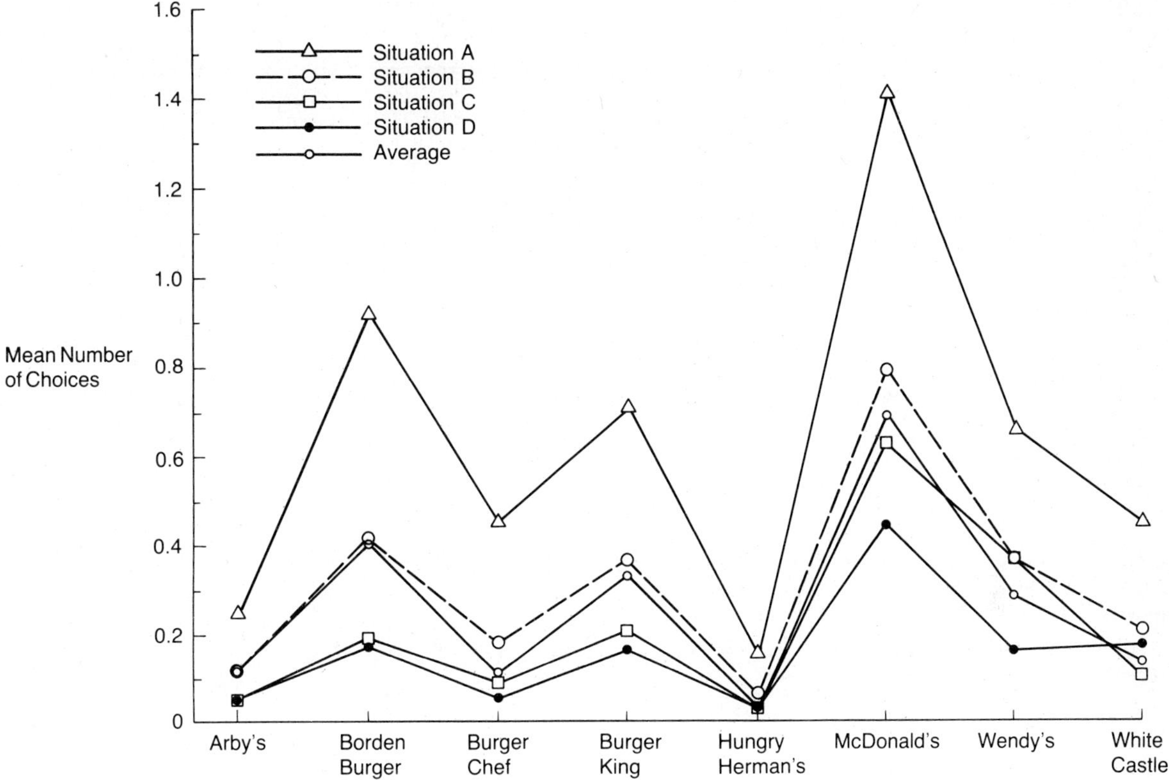

FIGURE 1
Frequency of Choice

ure 1 would be parallel with their shapes determined by the frequency of each eating occasion. Although market share on different eating occasions is not shown directly in Figure 1, changes in market share are reflected by the nonparallel lines. Wendy's, for example, ranked fourth in market share in each of the situations with the exception of "evening meal when not rushed" where it ranked second.

The results of this analysis indicate that purchase levels for specific brands do vary significantly across situations and that these situational differences are not the same for all brands. There are two potential explanations for the observed differences. One is that each of the eating occasions may be most relevant to a different group of respondents with unique preferences. A second is that the respondents purchased on more than one occasion, but their preference varied across the eating occasions. The second possibility is pursued hereafter through investigation of the existence of situational variation in attitudes.

Situational Variance of Attribute Importance (H2)

If the use of situation-specific attribute importances is to improve predictive power of the attitude measure, the values of these measures must show situational differences. The existence of situational variation in attribute importance was tested on data collected from the first questionnaire, on which the number of respondents was greatest. Each respondent had indicated the eating occasions on which he/she used the product and the importance of the attributes for each of these eating occasions. The data for each respondent potentially consisted of a seven attribute by four eating occasion matrix of attribute importances. Table 5 shows the mean attribute importances within

TABLE 5
Mean Attribute Importances (n = 111)

Attribute	*Nonsituational*	*Lunch on a Weekday (Sit. A)*	*Evening Meal When Rushed for Time (Sit. B)*	*Evening Meal with Family When Not Rushed for Time (Sit. C)*	*Snack During a Shopping Trip (Sit. D)*
1 Taste of food	4.76[a]	4.64	4.60	4.72	4.48
2 Cleanliness	4.54	4.32	4.31	4.41	4.35
3 Convenience	3.47	4.32	4.32	3.40	4.23
4 Price	3.64	3.92	3.84	3.83	3.89
5 Speed of service	3.65	4.45	4.45	3.05	3.98
6 Variety of menu	2.83	2.70	2.62	3.43	2.79
7 Popularity with children (n = 62)	2.28	1.95	2.69	3.21	2.58

a. Importances were measured on a scale from 1 = very unimportant to 6 = very important.

each eating occasion. The means of the nonsituational responses, which were used in the general form of the multiattribute model, also are shown. The significance of situational differences in attribute importances was tested by a two-factor repeated measurements analysis of variance design. The use of this analytical design limited the analysis to only those individuals who had reported using the product on all of the eating occasions and who provided complete data (n = 111). The attribute "popularity with children" was eliminated from this analysis because it was relevant only for respondents with children, and its inclusion in the analytical design would have further reduced the number of responses analyzed. A one-way analysis of variance with repeated measures of importance of "popularity with children" showed that it varied significantly across the four eating occasions.

The results of the two-way analysis of variance are shown in Table 6. The main effects of attributes and situations and their interaction were significant in this analysis. The significant interaction term indicates that the difference in importance on various eating occasions was not the same for all attributes and therefore supports H2. The differential effect of situations on attribute importances raises the question of where this influence was strongest. That is, which attributes varied most across situations, and were there attributes whose importance was constant across situations? These questions were investigated by analysis of simple main effects of situation at attribute. The sums of squares indicated that importance of "speed of service" was most different across the situations and that importance of "taste of food," "cleanliness," and "price" did not vary with situation.[2] Another way of viewing the significant interaction term is that differences among attribute importance ratings varied by situation. This view leads to the question of which situations showed greater (or less) difference in importance among attributes. The analysis of simple main effects of attribute at situation showed that attribute importances were most different for "evening meal when rushed for time" and least for "snack during a shopping trip," although attribute importances were significantly different within each of the eating occasions. As in the analysis of purchase level, the investigation of both sets of simple main effects is somewhat redundant as each involves partitioning of the interaction term. Results of both sets of analyses are presented, however, because of the different questions they address.

The nature of the interactions can be seen in Figure 2. Several pairwise comparisons of cell means shown in Figure 2 with potential managerial importance were conducted with Tukey's HSD test. Variety

2. The effect of the reduced sample size, due to the requirement of complete data for all four eating occasions, on these results was examined by testing equality of importance of each attribute in all possible pairs of eating occasions. This step allowed use of data from all respondents who had frequented fast food restaurants in the two situations compared. Results supported findings shown in Table 6.

of menu was more important for "evening meal with family when not rushed for time" than for each of the other situations ($q = 10.43$, $q = 11.55$, $q = 9.13$, respectively, all $p < .01$). Respondents considered convenience to be less important for "evening meal with family when not rushed for time" than for each of the other situations ($q = 13.12$, $q = 13.12$, $q = 11.84$, respectively, all $p < .01$). Speed of service was significantly more important for the occasions of "lunch on a weekday" and "evening meal when rushed for time" than for "evening meal with family when not rushed for time" ($q = 19.97$, $q = 19.97$, respectively, both $p < .01$) or "snack during a shopping trip" ($q = 6.70$, $q = 6.70$, respectively, both $p < .01$).

TABLE 6
ANOVA for Attribute Importance

Source	*d.f.*	*s.s.*	*F*
Attributes	5	774.42	64.68[a]
at Sit. A	(5)	275.90	23.09[a]
at Sit. B	(5)	297.89	24.93[a]
at Sit. C	(5)	232.42	19.45[a]
at Sit. D	(5)	206.29	17.26[a]
Attributes X Subjects	550	1317.08	
Situations	3	24.83	12.89[a]
at Att. 1	(3)	3.41	1.78
at Att. 2	(3)	.75	.39
at Att. 3	(3)	66.38	34.57[a]
at Att. 4	(3)	.62	.32
at Att. 5	(3)	146.16	76.13[a]
at Att. 6	(3)	45.59	23.74[a]
Situations X Subjects	330	212.00	
Attributes X Situations	15	238.08	29.06[a]
Attributes X Situations X Subjects	1650	901.09	
Subjects	110	896.28	
Total	2663	4363.78	
One-way ANOVA for attribute 7 ($n = 62$)			
Situations	3	49.65	13.40[a]
Situations X Subjects	183	226.92	

a. $p < .001$.

Situational Variation of Belief (H3)

Convenience was the only attribute on which perception was measured in a situational format. Responses of individuals who had indicated use of fast food establishments on all four eating occasions and who had provided a complete set of data on perceived convenience were considered ($n = 120$). As in the previous analysis, this limitation of the sample was necessary for the repeated measures design. The data for each respondent consisted of an eight brands by four eating occasions matrix of perceived convenience. Mean situational and nonsituational perceptions of convenience from the first questionnaire are shown in Table 7.

The results of the two-factor repeated measurements analysis of variance are shown in Table 8. Main effects of situations and brands and their interaction were significant. The significance of the interaction term indicates that perceptions of the individual brands varied differentially across the situations and therefore supports H3. As in the previous analyses, this finding raises the question of the location of the situational influence. Analysis of simple main effects of situation at brand showed that perceived convenience of Arby's was most different across situations and that perceived convenience of Wendy's and White Castle did not vary by situation.[3] The interaction term also can be interpreted as showing that differences in perceived convenience among brands varied across situations. Analysis of simple main effects of brand at situation showed that perceived convenience was most different in the situations "evening meal when rushed for time" and "evening meal with family when not rushed for time" and least in "lunch on a weekday," although perceived convenience of the brands was significantly different on each of the eating occasions.

The nature of the interaction of brands and eating occasions for perceived convenience can be seen in Figure 3. Pairs of means depicted in this figure with potential managerial importance were compared. Arby's, Borden Burger, Burger King, and McDonald's were perceived as less convenient for "lunch on a

3. The effect of the reduced sample size was examined in the same manner as for the attribute importance analysis. Results shown in Table 8 were supported.

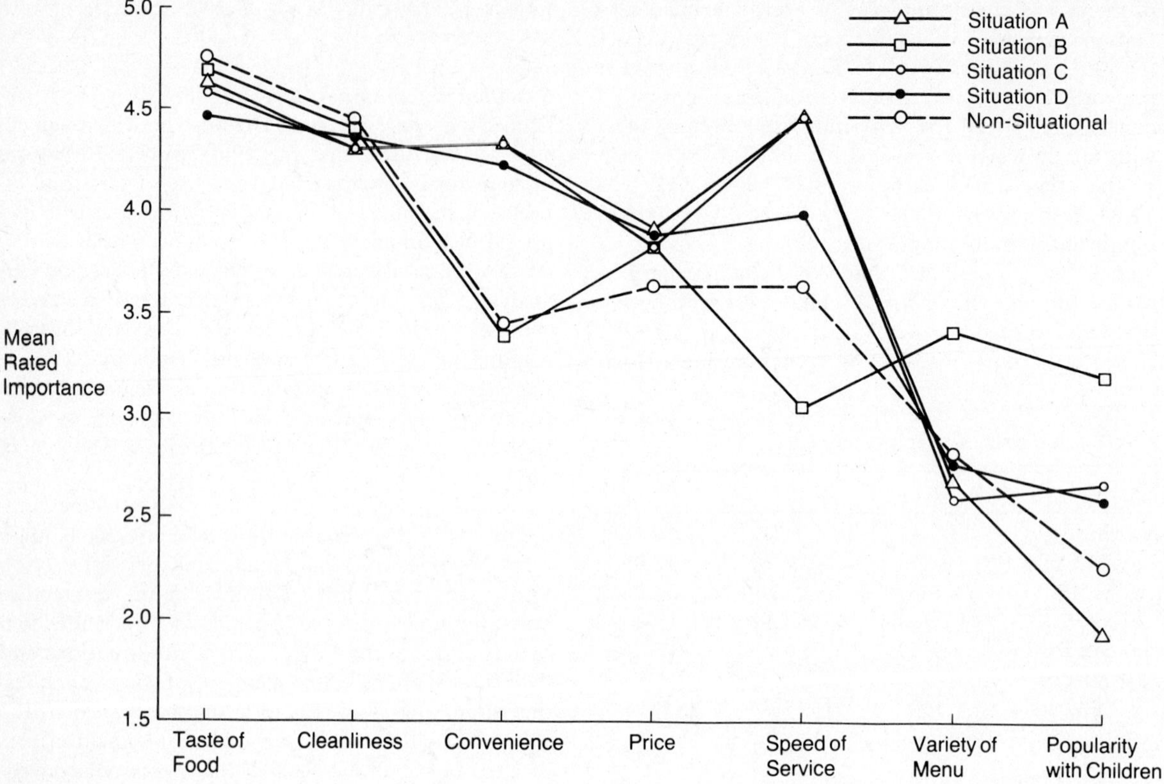

FIGURE 2
Attribute Importance

TABLE 7
Mean Convenience Perceptions (n = 120)

Brand	*Nonsituational*	*Lunch on a Weekday (Sit. A)*	*Evening Meal When Rushed for Time (Sit. B)*	*Evening Meal with Family When Not Rushed for Time (Sit. C)*	*Snack During a Shopping Trip (Sit. D)*
1 Arby's	2.50[a]	1.56	2.09	2.26	2.49
2 Borden Burger	3.64	3.00	3.64	3.67	3.43
3 Burger Chef	2.81	2.04	2.71	2.87	2.53
4 Burger King	2.99	2.89	3.34	3.49	3.64
5 Hungry Herman's	.88	1.24	.69	.74	.87
6 McDonald's	3.75	3.29	3.82	3.82	3.72
7 Wendy's	2.80	2.63	2.74	2.94	2.83
8 White Castle	2.65	2.27	2.18	2.35	2.18

a. Perceptions of convenience were measured on a scale from 1 = out of the way to 6 = close to where I am.

TABLE 8
ANOVA for Perceived Convenience

Source	*d.f.*	*s.s.*	*F*
Brands	7	2752.33	66.48[a]
at Sit. A	(7)	436.39	10.55[a]
at Sit. B	(7)	869.83	21.03[a]
at Sit. C	(7)	843.18	20.38[a]
at Sit. D	(7)	739.20	17.87[a]
Brands X Subjects	833	4926.48	
Situations	3	92.44	11.16[a]
at Br. 1	(3)	56.64	6.84[a]
at Br. 2	(3)	34.75	4.20[b]
at Br. 3	(3)	46.01	5.56[a]
at Br. 4	(3)	37.83	4.57[b]
at Br. 5	(3)	22.22	2.69[c]
at Br. 6	(3)	22.98	2.78[c]
at Br. 7	(3)	5.95	.75
at Br. 8	(3)	2.34	.28
Situations X Subjects	357	985.87	
Brands X Situations	21	136.26	
Brands X Situations X Subjects	2499	2790.42	
Subjects	119	2474.17	
Total	3839	14157.97	

a. $p < 001$.
b. $p < .01$.
c. $p < .05$.

weekday" than for each of the other situations (probability for each of these tests $<.01$). Hungry Herman's, however, was seen as more convenient for "lunch on a weekday" than for each of the other situations ($q = 5.70$, $q = 5.18$, $q = 3.84$, respectively, all $p < .01$). Arby's and Burger King were perceived as more convenient for "snack during a shopping trip" than for "evening meal when rushed for time" ($q = 4.14$, $p < .01$; $q = 2.90$, $p < .05$). These results possibly can be explained by different location strategies of the brands: e.g., close to major shopping centers or near residential areas.

The results of the analyses indicate that, as hypothesized, purchases of specific brands, attribute importances, and perceived convenience varied across the four eating occasions. The ability of situational measurement of attitude to improve prediction of subsequent behavior over that obtained from non-situational measurement was examined by the following analysis.

Prediction of Behavior (H4)

Self-reported behavior within situations was predicted with two forms of the multiattribute model. In the first form, attribute importances and perceptions were measured without situational scenario.

$$A_j = \sum_{i=1}^{n} V_i B_{ij}$$

where: A_j = attitude toward brand j,
V_i = affective importance of attribute i,
B_{ij} = perceived amount of attribute i contained by brand j, and
n = number of attributes considered.

This operationalization is consistent with previous managerial applications of the model, and this form is referred to as the "general" form, or "model G." The predictive power of model G provides a basis for comparison of the performance of the situation-specific multiattribute model.

In the second form of the model, attribute importances and perceptions of one attribute (convenience) were measured within eating occasion scenarios. Perceptions on the other six attributes were measured without reference to eating occasion. This model form is referred to as the "situational" model, or "model S," and can be shown as:

$$A_{js} = \sum_{i=1}^{n} V_{is} B_{ijs}$$

where: A_{js} = attitude toward brand j in situation s,
V_{is} = importance of attribute i in situation s,
B_{ijs} = perceived amount of attribute i contained by brand j, in situation s,
n = number of attributes considered,
s = situation ($s = 1, 2, \ldots, p$), and
p = number of situations considered.

Respondents had indicated number of purchases of each brand within each eating occasion. Brand chosen

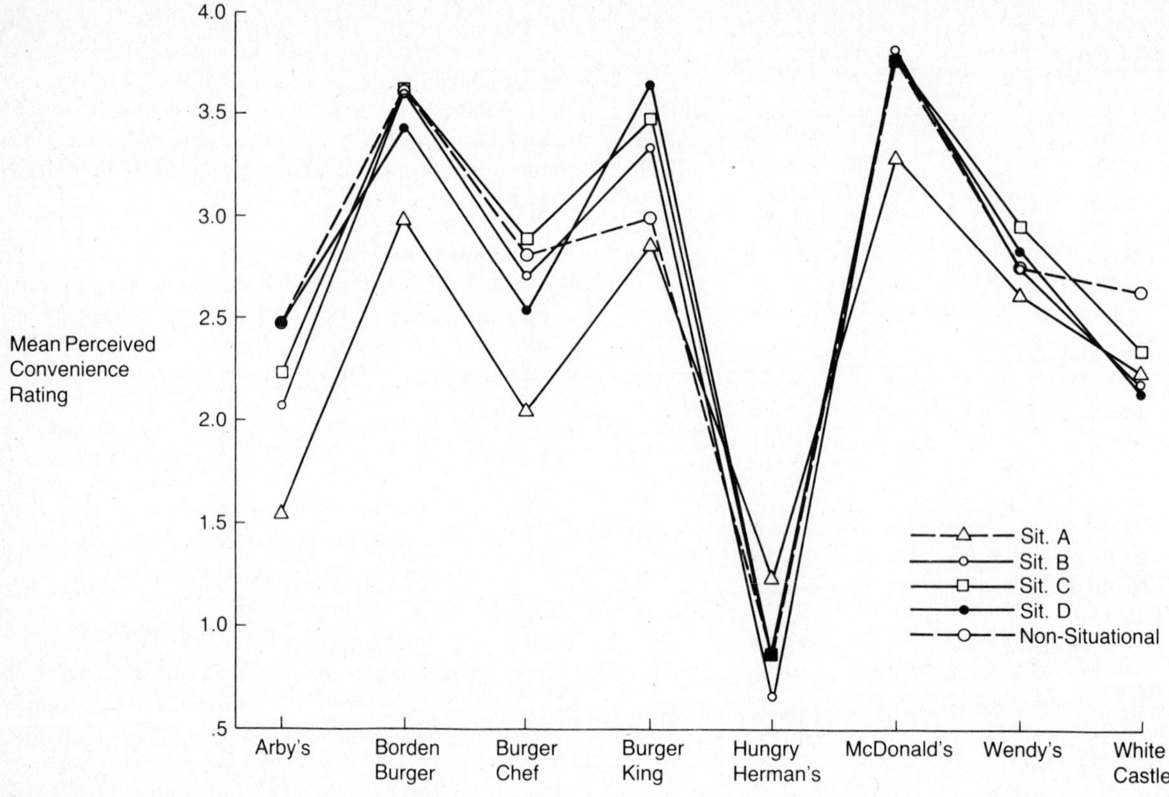

FIGURE 3
Perceived Convenience

within each eating occasion was predicted with model S by using attribute importance and convenience perception data specific to that eating occasion.

The predictive ability of the two forms of the model was compared within each situation to test the hypothesized superiority of model S. For each model form, the attitude data from each questionnaire were used to predict the brand purchased during the subsequent three-week period. The dependent measure in this analysis was the brand (or brands) purchased within the situation during each three-week period. Through this procedure every purchase made by the individual during a three-week period was predicted to be that brand with the most favorable attitude score from the immediately preceding questionnaire. Distribution of purchases across more than one brand during one of the three-week periods lowered the predictive accuracy. The measure of performance of each model was the cumulative proportion of correct predictions during the 12-week course of the study. Predictions were made separately for each of the 440 individuals completing the study who frequented fast food restaurants during the course of the study.

The prediction of subsequently reported behavior avoids many of the methodological problems of previous attempts to predict behavior (see Tittle and Hill, 1967). The potential increase in correlation due to consecutive measurement of attitude and preference or behavioral intention is eliminated. Also, the use of measured attitudes to predict subsequently reported behavior in the field eliminates error due to attitude shifts after purchase. A possible problem with the procedure used in this study arises from an effect of attitude measurement on subsequent behavior. However, the fourth wave comparison of behavior of the panel and the independent sample indicated that the problem did not exist because purchase behavior was similar for the two groups.

TABLE 9
Accuracy of Prediction of Behavior

Situation	n^a	*Mean Proportion Correct* *Model G*	*Model S*	*Mean Difference (s.d.)*	*Z*
Lunch on a weekday	210	.305	.413	.108 (.023)	4.65[b]
Evening meal when rushed for time	159	.386	.440	.054 (.017)	3.05[b]
Evening meal with family when not rushed for time	128	.459	.495	.036 (.021)	1.69[b]
Snack during a shopping trip	94	.316	.347	.031 (.034)	.92

a. Sample size is number of respondents who purchased on each occasion during the course of the study.
b. $p < .05$.

The model forms were compared in each situation by subtracting model G's percentage correct from that of model S for each person. The means and standard deviations of the differences were used to test the hypothesis that model S led to greater predictive accuracy. The results of the comparisons shown in Table 9 indicate that model S led to a significantly greater proportion of correct predictions in three of the four situations. Therefore, H4 was supported for "lunch on a weekday," "evening meal when rushed for time," and "evening meal with family when not rushed for time" and was rejected for "snack during a shopping trip." A possible explanation for the unique finding with respect to "snack during a shopping trip" can be developed from Tables 5 and 7. The attribute importances and perceptions of convenience within this situation appear to be generally closer to the nonsituational values than are the corresponding measures within other situations.

Discussion and Managerial Implications

The tests of situational variation of the attitude and choice measures and comparison of the two model forms led to the following findings for the fast food market.

1. Mean number of purchases varied over the four eating occasions for six of the eight brands.
2. Perceived importance of four of the seven restaurant attributes varied across eating occasions. The significant interaction between attribute and situation indicated that situational differences in importance were not the same for all attributes.
3. Perceived convenience of the restaurants varied according to situational scenario presented. The interaction between situation and brand indicated that situational differences in perceived convenience were not the same for all brands.
4. The use of situation-specific measures of attribute importance and perceived convenience increased the predictive power of the multiattribute model significantly for three of the four eating occasions.

The first three findings are clearly not independent of each other. The results showed situational variation in purchase level, attribute importance, and perceptions, but many attribute-based models assume linkages among these constructs. Lutz and Kakkar (1976), for example, provide a conceptual framework for the ways in which situations may affect attitudes and behavior. These linkages among the constructs lead to the managerial usefulness of situational analysis. The existence of situational variation of behavior in a closely competitive product category was established. The situational advantages (or deficiencies) of those brands exhibiting situational variation can be assessed through measurement of situation-specific attribute importances and perceptions. Consideration of competitive position within situational context, rather than in the general setting, may lead to greater diagnostic precision and, therefore, to additional information for decision making. Wendy's, for example, has a higher mean proportion of purchases for "evening meal with the family when not rushed for time" than for other situations (Table 3). Table 5 shows that speed of service is relatively less important for that situation than for the others. A check of mean perceptions of speed of service indicated that Wendy's was perceived to be about average on that attribute. Management of this brand may be able to increase sales in other situations by increasing speed of service (if necessary) and/or promoting that characteristic.

The variation of attribute importances across situations may have implications for promotional strategy. For example, Table 3 shows that the number of purchases on the eating occasion "lunch on a weekday" was higher than on the other eating occasions ($p < .01$), and Table 5 shows that "convenience" was relatively important in that situation. Yet analysis of Table 7 shows that four brands were perceived as less convenient for "lunch on a weekday" than for any other eating occasion. Managers of these brands may be able to increase lunchtime sales by improving the perceived convenience of their brands for "lunch on a weekday." If a product characteristic is much more important in one situation than in others, it may be beneficial to promote that characteristic in a situational context. The alternative strategy of promoting a product characteristic without reference to situation requires the consumer to associate the message with the setting in which it is important and may be less effective. Because the same consumer may purchase the product in several situations and may have different concerns in each of these situations, a potential strategy is to develop a *set* of situation-specific messages. Each consumer then would be exposed to a set of promotions which would focus on product characteristics most applicable to specific contexts in which the product is purchased.

Many of the managerial implications were developed from the analyses of simple main effects of situation within the other variables. The alternative investigations of the interaction term, analyses of simple main effects of variables within situation, may be of greater interest to the consumer researcher and of less interest to the brand manager. These results show that differences in purchase level among brands, differences in importance among attributes, and differences in perceived convenience among brands varied by situation. Although these differences were statistically significant in each case, those eating occasions on which the differences were greater or less were identified.

Conclusions

The results of the model comparison were consistent with the previously cited proposals for situation-specific measurement of attitude and behavior. Both the significance of the relative predictive power of the situational model and its absolute level of predictive accuracy (49.5% in the best situation) support its use. The procedure of predicting subsequent actual brand choice enhances the credibility of these figures.

The findings of this study support the argument that explicit consideration of situational contexts may contribute to the understanding of consumer behavior. In addition, the use of brands in this study demonstrates that situational influence is not restricted to grossly different product types. As the discussion indicates, the added understanding of influences of behavior can be very helpful to a marketing manager. Use of nonsituational models is equivalent to the aggregation over contexts, and differences among situations then contribute to the unexplained variance of the measures.

One possible avenue of future research is the investigation of the relationship between nonsituational measures and situational measures. A weighted composite of situational measures (perhaps by frequency with which the situations are encountered) may reflect general attitudes and behavior. This approach would be especially relevant to product categories in which one purchase is used in several situations (e.g., durable goods).

References

Bass, Frank M. "Fishbein and Brand Preference: A Reply," *Journal of Marketing Research*, 9 (November 1972), 461.

Bearden, William O. and Arch G. Woodside. "Interactions of Consumption Situations and Brand Attitudes," *Journal of Applied Psychology*, 61, No. 6 (1976), 764–9.

Becknell, J. C. and H. Maher. "Utilization of Factor Analysis for Image Clarification and Analysis," *Public Opinion Quarterly*, 25 (1962), 658–63.

Belk, Russell W. "An Exploratory Assessment of Situational Effects in Buyer Behavior," *Journal of Marketing Research,* 11 (May 1974), 156-63.

——. "Situational Variables and Consumer Behavior," *Journal of Consumer Research,* 2 (December 1975), 157-64.

——. "The Objective Situation as a Determinant of Consumer Behavior," *Proceedings,* Vol. II, Association for Consumer Research, 1975, 427-37.

Geisser, Seymour and Samuel W. Greenhouse. "An Extension of Box's Results on the Use of the *F* Distribution in Multivariate Analysis," *Annals of Mathematical Statistics,* 29 (1958), 885-9.

Johnson, Richard M. "Trade-off Analysis of Consumer Values," *Journal of Marketing Research,* 11 (May 1974), 121-7.

Kirk, Roger E. *Experimental Design: Procedures for the Behavioral Sciences,* Belmont, California: Brooks/Cole, 1968, 263-6.

Lehmann, Donald R. "Television Show Preference: Application of a Choice Model," *Journal of Marketing Research,* 8 (February 1971), 47-55.

Lutz, Richard J. and Pradeep Kakkar. "The Psychological Situation as a Determinant of Consumer Behavior," *Proceedings,* Vol. II, Association for Consumer Research, 1975, 439-53.

—— and ——. "Situational Influence in Interpersonal Persuasion," *Proceedings,* Vol. III, Association for Consumer Research, 1976, 370-8.

Myers, Jerome L. *Fundamentals of Experimental Design,* 2nd ed. Boston: Allyn and Bacon, 1972, 186-8.

Sandell, Rolf G. "Effects of Attitudinal and Situational Factors on Reported Choice Behavior," *Journal of Marketing Research,* 5 (November 1968), 405-8.

Tittle, Charles R. and Richard J. Hill. "Attitude Measurement and Prediction of Behavior: An Evaluation of Conditions and Measurement Techniques," *Sociometry,* 30 (1967), 199-213.

Ward, Scott and Thomas S. Robertson. *Consumer Behavior: Theoretical Sources.* Englewood Cliffs, New Jersey: Prentice-Hall, Inc., 1973, 26.

Wicker, Allan W. "Attitudes Versus Actions: The Relationship of Verbal and Overt Behavioral Responses to Attitude Objects," *Journal of Social Issues,* 25 (1969), 41-78.

Wildt, Albert R. and Albert V. Bruno. "The Prediction of Preference for Capital Equipment Using Linear Attitude Models," *Journal of Marketing Research,* 11 (May 1974), 203-5.

Wilkie, William L. and Edgar A. Pessemier. "Issues in Marketing's Use of Multi-Attribute Models," *Journal of Marketing Research,* 10 (November 1973), 428-41.

READING 9

Behavioral Learning Theory: Its Relevance to Marketing and Promotions

Michael L. Rothschild and William C. Gaidis

Behavioral learning theory has been generally overlooked in the development of marketing thought. The central concept states that behavior that is positively reinforced is more likely to recur than nonreinforced behavior. This runs parallel to the marketing concept and may be a sufficient model for dealing with most low involvement purchase situations. Its greatest value may be in the development of promotional strategies. This paper extends some of the ideas presented in an earlier paper in this journal.

In his 1977 presidential address to the Association for Consumer Research, Kassarjian (1978) called for a return to simpler models of consumer behavior. He felt that most consumer decisions were "unimportant, uninvolved, insignificant (and) minor," and for these "we do not need a grand theory of behavior." Kassarjian felt that a theory that could contribute some degree of parsimony might be behaviorism, also known as behavioral learning theory, instrumental conditioning, behavior modification, or operant conditioning deriving from the work of Skinner (1953) and Thorndike (1911).

Nord and Peter (1980) have recently presented an explication of several such behavioral concepts under the general rubric of a "Behavior Modification Perspective on Marketing." They are to be commended for introducing this paradigm into the marketing literature, and for covering a broad range of materials in a basic exposition. This paper will take the opposite approach and will examine one aspect of behaviorism (and the Nord and Peter paper) in greater depth. The topic dealt with herein is behavioral learning theory. It has been selected because of its philosophical similarity to the marketing concept and because of its strong potential as a contributor to marketing thought.

Reprinted by permission of the American Marketing Association, from the *Journal of Marketing,* 45:2 Spring 1981, 70–78.

An Expanded View of Behavioral Learning Theory

Behavioral learning theory is the paradigm generally referred to when a layperson speaks of "behavior modification." A review of some of its basic concepts can be found in Nord and Peter and will not be reviewed here. Nord and Peter correctly state that behavioral learning occurs when a response behavior precipitates the appearance of a stimulus. This paradigm is not new to marketers: the marketing concept is an example of its principles in that a transaction occurs when purchase behavior (response) takes place and a product (stimulus) is received by the consumer. If the product is pleasing (e.g., meets needs), the probability of repeat behavior will increase. Additionally, one can enhance the pleasingness of the product through appropriate manipulation of price, distribution, and promotional variables. Since the key to successful marketing is closely tied to repeat purchase behavior, the notion of providing positive reinforcement for desired behavior is crucial; therefore, positive reinforcement must be the ultimate goal of the marketer. A more rigorous examination of the principles of behavioral learning theory will allow marketers to take advantage of what behaviorists have learned. Such an examination follows.

Figure 1 shows an overview of the relationships between various common stimuli and responses in marketing. S_1 (advertising) is felt to lead to the responses of awareness and knowledge (R_1). This paradigm is based on the verbal learning model and the power of a repetitive S_1. The concepts of vicarious learning and modeling discussed by Nord and Peter are relevant here.

S_2 (product attribute) is felt to reinforce R_2 (purchase behavior). If S_2 is viewed positively, then the probability of future purchase behavior ($R_{3 \ldots n}$) is increased. If the goal of marketing is to elicit certain long run behaviors, the reinforcement of a good product will be much more powerful than the preceding commercial stimulus. S_1 can promise a benefit and establish a manufacturer's implicit contract with consumers; S_2 must deliver the perceived benefit. Behavioral learning is primarily concerned with the relationship between S_2, R_2 and $R_{3 \ldots n}$.

The present discussion will focus upon five components of the behavioral learning paradigm that are relevant to marketing—shaping, extinction, reinforcement schedules, immediate versus delayed reinforcement, primary versus secondary reinforcers. Of these, shaping and reinforcement schedules were introduced by Nord and Peter and are expanded here. The others represent concepts that have proven to be useful in other fields, would seem to have potential for marketing, and were not discussed by Nord and Peter.

Shaping Procedures

Shaping may be the single most potentially useful concept for marketers. Nord and Peter, though, gave a relatively weak example of shaping; they have reduced what is generally regarded as a multistep process to a one-step process in their illustration.

Shaping is an essential process in deriving new and complex behavior because a behavior cannot be rewarded unless it first occurs; a stimulus can only reinforce acts that already occur. New, complex behaviors rarely occur by chance in nature. If the only behavior to be rewarded were the final complex sought behavior, one would probably have to wait a long time for this to occur by chance. Instead, one can reward simpler existing behaviors; over time, more complex patterns evolve and these are rewarded. Thus, the shaping process occurs by a method of successive approximations.

Shaping is important to marketers since the initial purchase of any new product involves a complex set of behaviors. To elicit repeat purchase behavior is even more complex. One way to reach this final

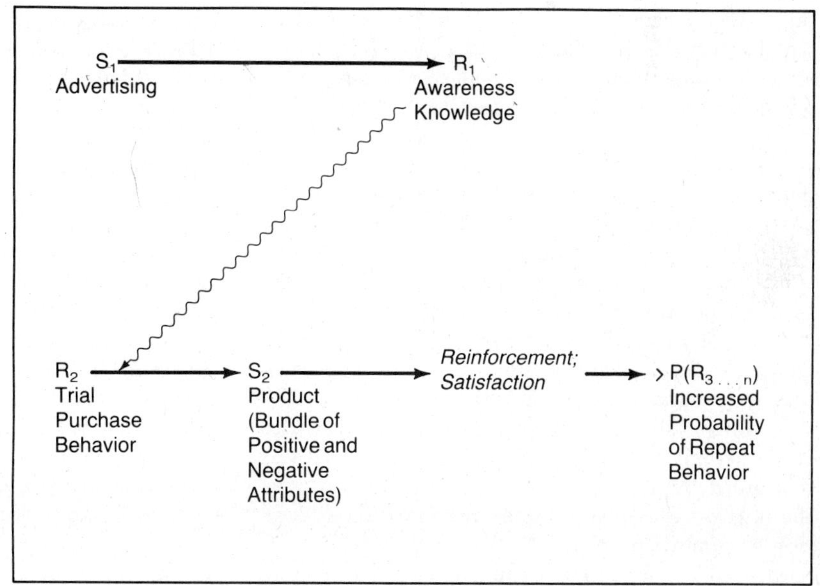

FIGURE 1
Learning Theory in a Marketing Context

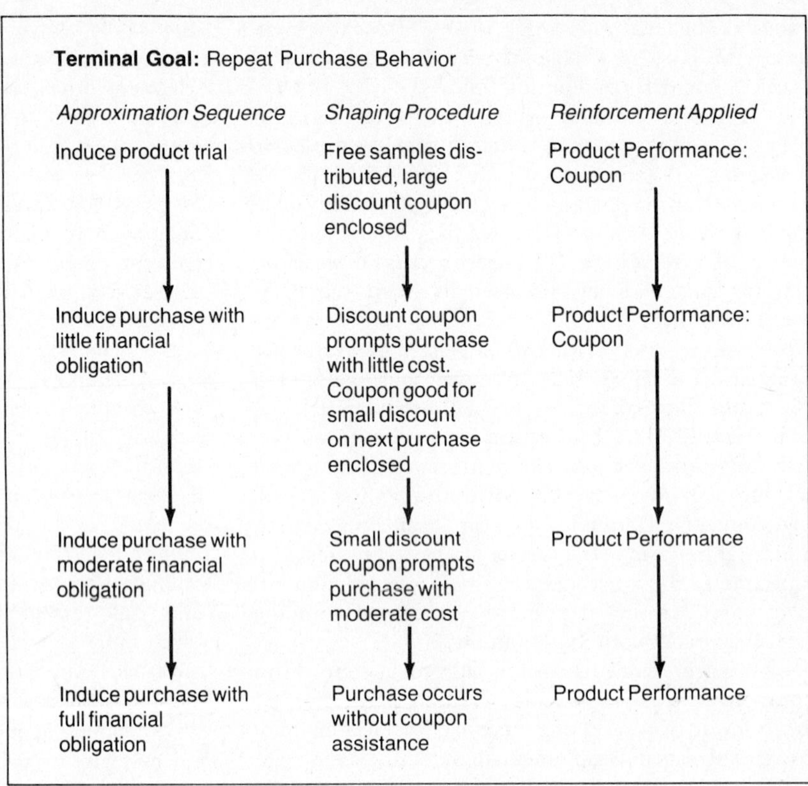

FIGURE 2
Application of Shaping Procedures to Marketing

behavior is through a series of successive approximations. Such a series might begin with the use of a free sample (for a frequently purchased low priced product). A coupon would be included in this sample for a large discount on the first purchase, and in the first purchase the consumer would find a coupon for a smaller discount on later purchases. As these incentives are reduced, the behavior approximates repeat purchase of the product at its full retail price. Soon no artificial reinforcers may be necessary. After the approximate responses have been evoked and firmly established, the arbitrary stimulus supports are "faded" or gradually withdrawn as control is transferred to stimuli likely to function as the major elicitors under naturalistic conditions.

In the above example the sample was given to allow perusal and trial of the product. The trial was reinforced by a good product and a coupon toward the next purchase. The coupon reinforced consideration of product purchase. Each ensuing purchase was reinforced by the product and the enclosed coupon. Each coupon had a lesser value; ultimately, the product was sufficient reinforcement, repeat behavior was achieved, and the coupons (contingent reinforcers) were faded out. In a series of successive approximations, behavior has gone from nothing, to trial without financial obligation, to usage with slight obligation, to repeat usage with financial obligation. Figure 2 summarizes this process. Not only has the desired behavior been accomplished, but the desired behavior is ultimately reinforced by the product itself and not by promotional incentives. A common error in the use of promotional tools for shaping purposes may be the improper fading out of the ancillary incentives. When the incentives are eventually dropped without gradual shaping of approximate behavior and gradual fading out of incentives, sales may drop as consumers revert to the brand used before the incentives were employed.

A second common error may be the tendency to overuse these aids; as a result, purchase may become contingent upon the presence of a promotional tool. Removal of the promotion may lead to the extinction of purchase behavior. If long-term behavior toward the product is desired, promotional tools should not overshadow the product. In a marketing situation, it is paramount that reinforcement for purchase be derived primarily from the product, lest purchase become contingent upon a never ending succession of consumer deals.

As seen from the above, shaping can be a valuable concept in developing strategies concerning promotional tools. Given that expenditures on these tools is now greater than expenditures on advertising in the U.S. marketplace (Strang 1976), a set of guidelines for the use of promotional tools is certainly called for. Shaping procedures may form the basis for such guidelines.

Extinction

Extinction is the removal of a correlation between a response and a reward. This is generally done by removal of the reward or by introduction of rewards not correlated with the response. Since most products attempt to reinforce continuously, lack of reinforcement (poor product performance) will lead to rapid extinction of behavior. This would be especially pronounced in a competitive situation.

In the case of promotional incentives, behavior toward a product may be based primarily on reinforcement caused by the incentive. If this is the case, then removal of the incentive will lead to extinction of behavior. It is important, then, to build behavior toward the product and not toward the promotional incentive. Conversely, the role of the incentive should be to shape appropriate behavior toward the product. Extinction, then, may be the result of improper shaping techniques and an overreliance on incentives that are later removed.

Reinforcement Schedules and Locus of Power

Nord and Peter note that appropriate behavior can be reinforced on a continuous basis or on a variety of intermittent schedules; most of these scheduling notions, though, have limited value for marketing. The concepts of intermittent scheduling work very well in situations where there is an imbalance of power and/or lack of competition. For example, when pigeons are starved to 80% of their normal body weight, they work very hard on an intermittent schedule; factory piece workers work hard on an intermittent schedule in part because they do not perceive themselves as having much power in their employer relationships. (Strong unions do not allow their members to be caught up in a piece work situation.)

In a simultaneous choice situation (such as generally exists in marketing), it is incumbent upon a marketer to maintain continuous reinforcement. If reinforcement becomes intermittent, consumers will shift behavior to the purchase of a competitive product providing continuous reinforcement. Intermittent reinforcement in such a situation may be seen as punishment by the consumer.

Not acknowledging this situational difference may lead, in turn, to the development of an inappropriate reinforcement strategy. For behavioral learning to work most effectively, one party must control the situation. This implies a lack of competition, an imbalance of power, and a closed system. Private sector marketing in competitive situations, therefore, may require reinforcement procedures very different from the noncompetitive examples commonly used in discussions of reinforcement schedules. While there may be few opportunities to use noncontinuous schedules in relation to the product itself, there are many opportunities to use the notions of scheduling with regard to promotional tools.

Immediate Versus Delayed Reinforcers

In almost all cases, a delayed reinforcement is worth less than immediate reinforcement during acquisition of a behavior; delayed reinforcement inhibits learning and will lead to a lower probability of a future occurrence. If the reinforcement is delayed, then irrelevant behaviors will occur between the desired behavior and the reinforcement. As a result, the most recent behavior will be more strongly reinforced than will the desired behavior.

For example, if a consumer collects proof-of-purchase coupons and then mails them to the manufacturer for a premium, the typical time to reinforcement is four to six weeks. When the premium arrives it may strongly reinforce the behavior of opening one's mailbox rather than the behavior of making multiple purchases of the product. If the premium has the qualities of a good reinforcer, it will likely lead to the pursuit of other mail premiums. The goal of the manufacturer, though, is reinforcement of the purchase rather than the pursuit of premiums. Mail premiums are theoretically weak reinforcers of purchase behavior due to this delay in reinforcement.

If purchase behavior is to be reinforced (other than through a quality product), the reinforcing premium should be in or on the package. If repeat purchase behavior is to be reinforced, a multipart premium may need to be included in or on the package.

Primary Versus Secondary Reinforcers

The notion of delayed reinforcement can be extended by considering primary versus secondary reinforcers. Primary reinforcers, loosely defined, have intrinsic utility (the product) while secondary reinforcers (tokens, coupons, trading stamps) have no such utility and must be converted. When, for example, trading stamps are given as reinforcers, delayed gratification results; when they must be collected before redemption (delayed secondary reinforcers), the potential for success of the promotion may be further eroded. Secondary reinforcers have taken on value over time because individuals have learned that they can be converted for primary reinforcers; they are still, theoretically, less powerful than primary reinforcers. Given this relationship, perhaps marketers should concentrate on deals giving more product per unit of price. This focuses on the primary reinforcer (product) and gives immediate reinforcement.

A Review of Some Promotions Literature

Given the above discussion of behavioral learning concepts, it becomes clear that much of the value of these concepts lies in their relationship to promotional tools. A review of relevant literature shows very little work done concerning promotions and none relating promotions to operant conditioning.[1]

Two recent papers considered promotions from the point of view of self perception theory. Scott (1976) found weak repeat behavior in response to a number of different one-time incentives, although some (a discounted trial) did better than others (free trial, free trial plus premium). From a behavioral learning perspective the results are also weak, but serve as a case to support the notion presented earlier that shaping procedures are generally poorly used. In Scott's experiment the treatments were all single incentives where consumers received savings and/or gifts ranging in value from 25¢ to $1 on a 50¢ item.

Since the item (a community newspaper) was a low involvement item,[2] there was low prior awareness, low subscriber level after introduction, and low cost of product; there would be no behavioral reason to suspect a one-time incentive to alter long run behavior. Given a low involvement product, behavior would need to be shaped slowly over time, otherwise any behavior would be due merely to the more highly involving financial incentive. When the high involvement incentive was removed, behavior would be expected to extinguish. This was, indeed, the case.

In Scott's case, the incentive, and not the product, was the primary reward for purchase behavior. When it was withdrawn, the behavior was extinguished. In contrast, if initial purchase were accompanied by a small premium, the product and not the premium would be the primary reward for purchase behavior. When the premium is then withdrawn, purchase behavior may be unaffected. Scott, quite rightly, suggests that incentives may exist upon a continuum and that researchers need to identify the size/impact of various incentive levels. Behavioral learning theory offers marketers a framework to study the impacts of incentives upon purchase behavior. This framework includes consideration of various types of reinforcers (primary, secondary), various types of reinforcement schedules (continuous, intermittent), and the impact of any delay that might occur between a behavior and its reinforcement (immediate or delayed reinforcement). It seems essential, however, that any study of the incentive/purchase behavior relationship employ a shaping paradigm to provide the greatest insight into the impact of consumer deals upon long run behavior.

Dodson, Tybout, and Sternthal (1978) also examined incentives from a self-perception framework, examined one-time incentives (media coupons, cents-off deals, and in-package coupons) for low involvement products (margarine and flour), and found weak but sometimes significant results. In this study there was strong brand switching behavior when dealing

1. There is a large body of work outside the traditional marketing literature that essentially examines promotions and operant conditioning for issues such as transit usage, energy conservation, and curtailing littering. This work, while relevant, was felt to be inappropriate here, since it comprises the body of mainstream behavioral learning research and generally uses noncompetitive situations of limited relevance to marketers.

2. For a general discussion of involvement, see Houston and Rothschild (1978), among others.

occurred, but little follow-up behavior when deals were retracted.

Behavioral learning theory would suggest that deals cause brand switching because the deal is more likely to be reinforcing than the product. In fact the authors found that the greatest switching occurred for the greatest financial incentive; next most switching occurred where there was less financial incentive but great ease of use (the cents-off deal required no prior purchase or coupon clipping). It is reinforcing to save money if little effort needs to be expended.

When they considered repeat purchase the impact of the deals was reversed. Now the in-package coupon outperformed the media coupon and cents-off deal. Operant conditioning would predict poor results from the latter incentives because no shaping had gone on over time. While the in-package coupon also provided poor shaping, it was better than the others in that it provided a two-step process leading to changed behavior. Again self-perception theory may be inappropriate due to the low involvement nature of the products; repeat behavior may not be attained because the one-time incentive was not powerful enough to overcome apathy and inertia.

A consideration of behavioral learning theory would suggest that in both the case of a media coupon and a cents-off deal, the primary reinforcement for purchase behavior was derived from the deal, not the product itself. Hence when the deal was withdrawn, purchase behavior was extinguished. The authors provide some support for this when they suggest a media coupon may be advisable to induce switching when the dealt product is perceived to be superior on some relevant attribute. In this case one presumes that primary reinforcement would be derived from the product itself; the deal would play a secondary role.

It is interesting to note that in the two reviewed papers, self-perception and behavioral learning theories make similar predictions as to the outcome of the one-time incentive, but for different reasons. The two theories, though, suggest different strategies to alleviate the ineffectual one-time incentive. Both theories predict a low level of success, but self-perception predicts this because the most effectual change will come when people attribute their behavior to inner causes rather than external incentives; therefore, incentives should be minimized. Behavioral learning predicts greater behavior change through a shaping process and therefore more incentives would be necessary.

Each theory would seem to have its place. In high involvement situations where complex cognitive activity would seem to take place, self-perception based strategy may be more appropriate. In low involvement cases where little cognitive activity is necessary for adequate decision making, behavioral learning based strategy may be more appropriate. The two cited studies were low involvement cases; and, therefore, the lack of success in each should be more easily remedied by behavioral learning strategies.

In low involvement cases, Kassarjian has called for a return to simple models of behavior explanation. Self-perception and other cognitive theories assume a high level of involvement, since individuals are felt to go through a complex mental activity. If such activity does not take place, then a one-time incentive will not be successful; shaping procedures are needed to avoid early extinction.

Another set of contributing data is from a proprietary study reported by Ogilvy and Mather (n.d.), who found that samples that include a coupon for an initial purchase have a 20% higher initial purchase rate than do samples without coupons. This is a test of a two-step versus a one-step shaping procedure that clearly favors the two-step procedure, and is consistent with the theory.

A final contribution to this discussion comes from Prentice (1975), who divided the common promotional tools into classes: those that contribute to the Consumer Franchise Building effort (referred to as CFB) and those referred to as non-CFB. This work is a report on current industry practice and is not based on any theoretical model. Conclusions include that most promotional deals are too short temporally, and that for a promotion to work, a brand must provide value of its own. Behavioral learning theory would support the following conclusions: Shaping takes time; promotions of short duration cannot do the tasks asked of them; behavior toward a brand of little value will rapidly extinguish, since there is no primary reinforcement.

In separating tools into CFB and non-CFB classes, the author suggests that non-CFB tools do not emphasize product/brand value but rather key on other issues. For example, price-off deals and refund offers stress financial issues, premiums stress other objects, and contests/sweepstakes stress games. CFB tools stress the product. Examples here are samples and coupons. This classification is also intuitively consistent with behavioral learning, which suggests

FIGURE 3
Promotional Effects Predictions Made by the Three Models

Promotional Tool	*Behavioral Learning Theory*	*Self-Perception Theory*	*Consumer Franchise Building Model (CFB) (Prentice 1975)*
Samples	Good, Positively Reinforcing	Poor (Scott 1976)—Free trial did not help	Good, focuses on product value
In-package Coupon	Good since it requires approximate repeat behavior in order to redeem	Good (Dodson, Tybout, Sternthal 1978), Led to repeat purchase	Good, won't be used without product value
Media Coupon	Depends on method—need to use as shaping mechanism	Poor (Dodson, Tybout, Sternthal 1978), Did not lead to repeat purchase	Good
Price-Off Deal	Depends on method—need to use as shaping mechanism	Poor—Did not lead to repeat purchase (Dodson, Tybout, Sternthal 1978) Good—Led to repeat subscription (Scott 1976)	Poor, too much financial emphasis
Premiums	Poor, does not reinforce appropriate behavior	No effect of premium plus free trial (Scott 1976)	Poor, nonproduct emphasis
Contests/ Sweepstakes	Poor, does not reinforce appropriate behavior		Poor, nonproduct emphasis
Refund Offer	Poor, reinforcement is too delayed to be effective		Poor, too much financial emphasis

that secondary reinforcers (money, objects, games) are less likely to lead to appropriate behavior than will good product. The CFB/non-CFB model has not been rigorously tested but is generally consistent with behavioral learning theory. Figure 3 summarizes the relationships between the three models discussed above.

Discussion

It can be seen that modern marketing thought is at least implicitly related to behavioral learning. Since repeat purchase is necessary for survival in the marketplace, behavior must be positively reinforced. Since new products are continuously entering the market, shaping procedures can be used so that trial is more than a random process. In behavioral learning terms, purchase is a behavior, and the product is a positive (or negative) reinforcer. This discussion will consider the theoretical issues emerging from behavioral learning theory, research questions which must be answered before wholesale adoption of these principles can be made, and the potential implications of behavioral learning for marketing strategy.

Theoretical Issues Emerging from Behavioral Learning Theory

As Nord and Peter (1980) point out, there are many areas where benefits to marketing can be derived, and one should consider the differences between cognitive learning and behavioral learning. Cognitive learning (especially as it applies to marketing) takes place without reinforcement, and can, indeed, be forced upon consumers through the judicious use of repetition in advertising (Ray et al. 1973) and can occur as a result of mere exposure.

Behavioral learning occurs through the use of reinforcers. While Ray shows that trial purchase behavior may also occur as a function of advertising repetition, such behavior is often stimulated by the use of promotional devices. Repeat behavior, on the other hand, is certainly based on reinforcement of the trial. Krugman (1965) posits that this reinforcement leads to a positive attitude after the trial. (A behaviorist would not add the hypothetical construct of attitude onto a discussion of these events.)

Two issues emerge:

- Reinforcement is necessary to behavioral learning, especially beyond the trial stage. Advertising (modeling, vicarious learning) can help in behavioral learning, but product, price, and place must be favorable in the long run.
- Cognitive learning focuses on the internalization of messages rather than the learning of behavior patterns. In behavioral learning the message cue announces the upcoming reinforcement opportunity.

Returning to the concept of attitude, the behaviorist feels that since he/she cannot observe any state of consciousness, he/she should merely be concerned with that which is observable (i.e., behavior). This is a very different concept from that held by consumer researchers who use a social psychology model. It is not, though, inconsistent with notions concerning low involvement (Kassarjian 1978). As Kassarjian suggests, perhaps the middle range social psychology theories are best reserved for high involvement cases, and behavioral learning theory should be used in low involvement cases.

In recent years the notion of involvement has become popular in consumer behavior (e.g., Houston and Rothschild 1978). Part of its popularity is due to its intuitive appeal as a simpler model of behavior development for unimportant decisions. It is in these cases of decision making when consumers have low involvement and attempt to satisfice, that behavioral learning theory has its greatest potential. As involvement increases, cognitive processes become more complex; here the middle range theories of cognitive dissonance, attribution, personality, perceived risk, and so on have their value. In low involvement cases, behavioral learning theory may be most relevant for consumer behavior. While economic man may be an appropriate model for high involvement cases, marketing man (Bagozzi 1975) is more the prototype for low involvement cases.

Research Issues Emerging from Behavioral Learning Theory

There are some questions that have not been formally raised by marketers but should be explored before there can be wholesale adoption of behavioral principles. Each of these has been explored in the behavioral learning literature but none has been resolved in a marketing context:

- Behavioral learning works well in the laboratory because the environment can be controlled by the experimenter. In the competitive marketplace the marketer has much less control; hence, research is needed to assess the impact of the low degree of control the marketer can exercise on the predictions of behavioral learning theory. For example, do simultaneous choice situations necessitate the use of continuous reinforcement schedules?
- Is shaping through successive approximation an efficient/effective method for inducing new product trial and long-term purchase behavior? Would the employment of shaping procedures have decreased the attrition rates found by Dodson, Tybout, and Sternthal (1978) and Scott (1976) when deals were used on a one-time basis?
- Are premiums and other promotional devices more effective when based upon primary versus secondary reinforcers? Are premiums and other promotional devices more effective when based upon immediate versus delayed reinforcement? Is there an interactive effect between type of reinforcement (primary, secondary) and the delay between behavior and reinforcement (immediate, delayed)?

Figure 4 dichotomizes both types of reinforcement and delay between behavior and reinforcement. Behavioral learning theory suggests greater long run rates of behavior change will be experienced when respondents are moved through an A → B → D → E or A → C → D → E sequence than when any one treatment is presented in isolation. This test of the greater value of shaping procedures versus a one-time consumer deal was not performed in the studies of Scott or Dodson, Tybout, and Sternthal.

There are also situational types of research questions that can be raised:

- Are there differences in the above questions that are a function of high or low involvement situations?
- Can the issues of behavioral learning theory give insight to increasing survey response rates through the use of behaviorally based incentives for respondents?
- Can sales force compensation schedules be made more effective through the use of behavioral learning theory?

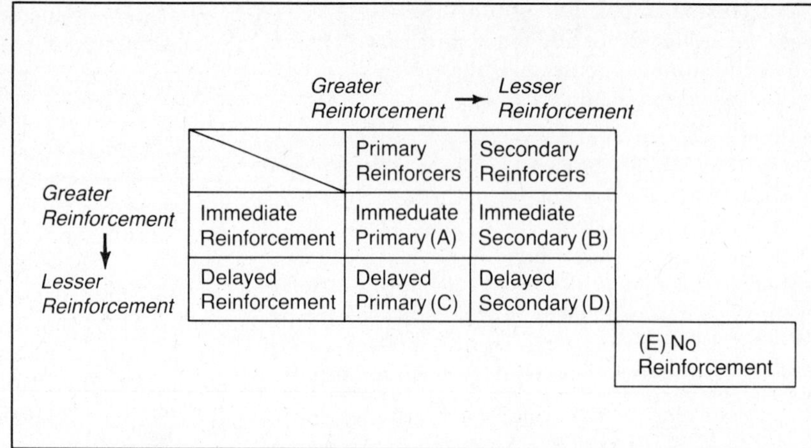

FIGURE 4
The Impact of Reinforcement Type and Reinforcement Delay Within the Context of Behavioral Learning Theory

Application and Strategy Issues Emerging from Behavioral Learning Theory

Turning to a more applied view of behavioral learning, there are a number of concepts discussed above which may lend themselves to the more orderly and efficient development of marketing strategy. The following points are suggested by the literature reviewed above and by Nord and Peter:

Motivation and Meeting Needs. Both the marketing concept and behavioral learning stress meeting needs. Appropriate long run behavior only takes place when the reinforcer meets some need. A reinforcer can't be positive if it does not meet needs.

Controlling the Environment. Behavioral learning works well in the laboratory because the environment can be controlled. In the marketer's world there is much less control; therefore, the 4 Ps must be organized. Due to the lack of total control, those areas where control is possible must be utilized to their fullest.

Shaping Through Successive Approximation. It may be possible to aid consumers in their acquisition of new behaviors through the use of shaping procedures. In cognitive terms, risk is reduced; in behavioral terms, any behavior is a minor change from the preceding one.

Immediate Reinforcement. In addition to creating time utility, in itself reinforcing, immediate reinforcement is strong because it is linked most directly with the appropriate behavior.

The Need for Systematic and Consistent Application. Behavioral learning has worked best in laboratory environments where the world of the subject is orderly and predictable (to the subject). In transferring these principles to the marketplace, behavioral learning theory suggests that reinforcers should be immediate, should be as described in the discriminative stimulus, and should be consistent.

The Use of Promotional Tools. These tools can be used in both the shaping of new behavior and the reinforcement of existing behavior. There is a tendency to overuse these aids; as a result, a dependency develops so that removal of the promotion leads to extinction of behavior. Promotional tools should not overshadow the products they are aiding (if long-term behavior toward the product is desired).

In addition to the similarities between behavioral learning theory and marketing, and the insights that the former can provide to the latter, there are also a number of problem areas which need to be considered. For example, in the controlled environment where behavioral research is generally conducted (e.g., a Skinner box), the experimenter has total control of the situation and absolute power; there are no competitive choices available to the subject. Such a situation rarely exists in the private sector marketplace; as a result, some behavioral notions cannot be transferred.

A Concluding Comment

Behavioral learning theories offer a framework within which to organize and structure marketing and promotional activities, and a simple but elegant model of the generic concept of marketing. In marketing, the desired end is appropriate behavior manipulation and control to further the goals of the organization. The currently recognized most efficient means to these ends is through the use of the marketing concept. By developing reinforcers which meet needs, marketing would seem to have already embraced behavioral learning theory. Behavior is a function of its consequences and environment; by assessing needs, marketers are best able to meet their own needs and control portions of the consumer's environment.

This model may be appropriate for many of the "... unimportant, uninvolved, insignificant, minor decisions that are made in the marketplace everyday..." (Kassarjian 1978, p. xiv). In these situations, consumers have weak cognitive processes, and as a result, behavioral learning theory can offer insightful direction to the marketer.

References

Bagozzi, R. P. (1975), "Marketing as Exchange," *Journal of Marketing,* 15 (October), 32-39.

Dodson, J. A., M. A. Tybout, and B. Sternthal (1978), "Impact of Deals and Deal Retraction on Brand Switching," *Journal of Marketing Research,* 15 (February), 72-78.

Houston, M. J. and M. L. Rothschild (1978), "A Paradigm for Research on Consumer Involvement," working paper, University of Wisconsin, 12-77-46.

Kassarjian, H. H. (1978), "Presidential Address, 1977: Anthroposorphism and Parsimony," in *Advances in Consumer Research,* Volume V., H. K. Hunt, ed., Ann Arbor: Association for Consumer Research.

Krugman, H. (1965), "The Impact of Television Advertising: Learning without Involvement," *Public Opinion Quarterly,* 29 (Fall), 349-356.

Nord, W. R. and J. P. Peter (1980), "A Behavior Modification Perspective on Marketing," *Journal of Marketing,* 44 (Spring), 36-47.

Ogilvy and Mather (n.d.), *How to Create Advertising That Sells,* New York: Ogilvy and Mather.

Prentice, R. M. (1975), "The CFB Approach to Advertising/Promotion Spending," in *The Relationship Between Advertising and Promotion In Brand Strategy,* R. A. Strang, ed., Cambridge: Marketing Science Institute, 75-90.

Ray, M. L., A. G. Sawyer, M. L. Rothschild, R. M. Heeler, E. C. Strong, and J. B. Reed (1973), "Marketing Communications and the Hierarchy of Effects," in *New Models for Mass Communications Research, Volume II, Sage Annual Reviews of Communications Research,* P. Clarke, ed., Beverly Hills, CA: Sage.

Scott, C. A. (1976), "The Effects of Trial and Incentives on Repeat Purchase Behavior," *Journal of Marketing Research,* 13 (August), 263-269.

Skinner, B. F. (1953), *Science and Human Behavior,* New York: The Free Press.

Strang, R. A. (1976), "Sales Promotion—Fast Growth, Faulty Management," *Harvard Business Review,* 54 (July-August), pp. 115-124.

Thorndike, E. L. (1911), *Animal Intelligence.* New York: Macmillan.

CHAPTER THREE

Consumer Decision-Making Processes

READING 10

Consumer Decision Making—Fact or Fiction?

Richard W. Olshavsky and Donald H. Granbois

A synthesis of research on consumers' prepurchase behavior suggests that a substantial proportion of purchases does not involve decision making, not even on the first purchase. The heavy emphasis in current research on decision making may discourage investigation of other important kinds of consumer behavior.

The most pervasive and influential assumption in consumer behavior research is that purchases are preceded by a decision process. Writers who have suggested models of this process have used varying terminology, but all seem to agree that:

1. Two or more alternative actions exist and, therefore, *choice* must occur.
2. Evaluative criteria facilitate the forecasting of each alternative's consequences for the consumer's goals or objectives.
3. The chosen alternative is determined by a decision rule or evaluative procedure.
4. Information sought from external sources and/or retrieved from memory is processed in the application of the decision rule or evaluation procedure.

Virtually every text on consumer behavior includes a verbal or flow chart model of consumer decision processes. Engel, Blackwell, and Kollat (1978) base an elaborate stage model on five steps (problem recognition, search, alternative evaluation, choice, and outcomes) suggested 70 years ago by John Dewey. Howard's (1977) refinement of the concept of routinized response behavior, advanced in Howard and Sheth (1969, p. 9), assumes that even simplified, habitual behavior reflects the earlier application of choice criteria to alternative brands. When situational constraints block the repetition of an earlier choice, a reduced-form evaluation process follows, in which dichotomized criteria are applied to a small evoked set of brands (Howard 1977, pp. 27–30).

Research on decision making currently takes several forms. Multidimensional scaling and conjoint measurement are widely applied measurement tools whose relevance grows out of the "multi-attribute nature of consumer decisions" (Green and Wind 1973, p. 5). Different processing rules, such as compensatory, disjunctive, conjunctive, lexicographic, and various hybrid procedures decision makers might use in multi-attribute problems are being tested in studies where subjects verbalize or report on their thought processes as they perform choice tasks (Bettman and Zins 1977; Lussier and Olshavsky 1974; Payne 1976; Russ 1971). Investigators in other studies observe or photograph the sequence and extent of information utilization by subjects provided with brochures, display boards, labelled packages, etc., containing attribute information for several brands from which a choice must be made (Bettman and Kakkar 1977; Jacoby, Szybillo, and Busato-Schach 1977; Russo and Rosen 1975; van Raaij 1977). Other approaches to the study of decision processes include correlational methods (Scott and Wright 1976) and information integration techniques (Bettman, Capon, and Lutz 1975).

In his presidential address to the Association for Consumer Research, Kassarjian (1978) raised the possibility that we may be attributing choice processes to consumers when no choice processes occur.

Reprinted with permission from the *Journal of Consumer Research*, 6:2 September 1979, 93–100.

Kassarjian was not simply saying that decision processes often are routinized or habitual rather than extended (as Howard and Sheth have already pointed out), but that in some cases no prepurchase process exists. This is a very bold charge, for it implies that much empirical research and theorizing on consumer decision making is less broadly applicable than has been assumed.

Assessing the Evidence

Kassarjian only raised the issue; he presented no supporting evidence. The validity of his position can be assessed in two ways. Applying an evaluation procedure to various alternatives on two or more evaluative criteria requires considerable information, sometimes more than is readily available in memory. Evidence of the circumstances of purchasing behavior occurring in the *absence* of external search, then, helps to establish the *maximum* scope of the nondecision behavior postulated by Kassarjian. Information processing of the sort assumed in alternative evaluation and choice can, of course, be performed with previously acquired and stored information alone. Therefore, the second condition leading to purchase without prior decision process is insufficiency of stored information suitable for alternative evaluation or nonuse of relevant stored information. While the nature of internal processing (or lack of processing) can be studied only indirectly, a convincing case can be made that internal information is frequently either not available, not relevant, or not consulted.[1]

There are several comprehensive reviews of research on consumer prepurchase behavior that provide considerable evidence of external prepurchase information search. These reviews have encompassed surveys in which consumers were asked to describe their prepurchase behavior retrospectively for a recent purchase, or their "usual" behavior, as well as studies of consumers in real-life purchasing situations during which some type of observational method was used to measure the decision process appearing to precede purchase.

It must be recognized that consumer researchers using observation and retrospective questionnaire techniques have probably been influenced by the assumption of decision process behavior, so that their results may reflect a subtle bias overstating the prevalence of decision-making behavior. To some extent, research instruments measure what their designers expect to find. Consumers, too, may overstate the extent of prepurchase deliberation and choice-making behavior, because this may appear desirable as well as expected behavior. What this means, then, is that the research to be cited probably *overstates* the extent of prepurchase behavior for which the decision model is appropriate.

Objectives and Method

The primary purpose of this paper is to assess, through a synthesis of the review articles just mentioned, the apparent scope of consumer behavior not preceded by external search. Additional objectives, secondary only in that less substantial evidence is available for evaluation, include:

- identifying circumstances in which external environmental and situational constraints limit consumers to a single alternative; and
- identifying research in which purchase has been observed to occur without reference to relevant stored information.

Each of the four sections of the paper represents one element of the comprehensive classification of consumer behavior offered by Gredal (1966). These are renamed slightly here, and include: (1) budget allocation (savings/spending and allocation across broad expenditure categories); (2) generic allocation (expenditures for specific products and services); (3) store patronage (shopping and purchasing at specific shopping centers, stores, etc.); and (4) brand purchase.

In each section, conclusions from review articles on prepurchase behavior are cited. Discussion is then directed to why the behavior involved may be subject to influences and constraints precluding an internal evaluation of alternative actions. The principal review articles drawn upon include Ferber (1973) and Ölander and Seipel (1970) on budget allocation, Ferber (1973) on generic allocation, Granbois (1977) on store patronage, and Newman (1977) on brand purchases.

1. Certain "process tracing" techniques, in particular protocol analysis, do permit direct monitoring of internal processing, although to a limited extent. However, when this technique is used, subjects are instructed, implicitly or explicitly, to engage in decision making.

Budget Allocation

Saving Versus Spending

How does the allocation of income between saving and spending come about? In his report of a wide ranging review of research on family economic behavior, Ferber (1973) concluded:

> *Despite its basic importance for the understanding of consumer financial behavior, the role of financial planning within the family—in the sense of explicit consideration of the allocation of expected financial resources between saving and spending—seems to have received very little attention in empirical work, and would seem to be a prime area for future research (p. 34).*

Since Ferber's review, there appears to have been no empirical studies of consumers' information-seeking relative to savings. There are, however, a few studies of consumers' information about alternative forms of savings and their self-assessment of the degree to which "planning" precedes savings. In his review, Ferber reported substantial proportions of households (up to 87 percent) without a "financial plan," although the meaning of "financial plan" was often not clearly defined (Ferber 1973, p. 35).

A review by Ölander and Seipel (1970) also evaluated consumers' knowledge of financial matters, e.g., interest rates, where stocks can be purchased, and tax regulations. One study reviewed reported: "The respondents' knowledge of tax regulations was good in many respects but often did not appear to influence behavior in the direction of using savings and investment forms which were more advantageous from the tax point of view" (p. 68). Further discussion by these reviewers suggests that individual characteristics, such as low achievement motivation, perceived inability to control one's own financial destiny, and very short future time orientation and planning horizon may inhibit planning. Other evidence on the extent of deliberation preceding savings behavior comes from four studies that found the proportion of self-identified systematic savers to be 15 percent, 27 percent, 28 percent, and 40 percent, respectively (p. 31). In another study, 36 percent of respondents predicted very accurately the extent of savings accumulated six months later (p. 33).

Thus, perhaps one-fourth to one-third of all consumers show evidence of some systematic planning and decision making regarding saving; the majority, however, may not be classified as deliberate choosers. An exception may be newlywed couples; Ferber and Nicosia found that half of the couples they interviewed three to six months after marriage reported a definite plan for saving (Ferber 1973, p. 51).

Allocation of Income Across Expenditure Categories

What, if any, type of decision process precedes the allocation of income across the various categories of goods and services, i.e., food/beverage, housing, household furnishings, etc.? We could find no studies of prepurchase behavior relative to household allocation behavior. Clearly, however, purchases within certain categories are nondiscretionary. Income must be allocated to the categories of food/beverage, housing, clothing, and medical care.

Products within certain other categories are not necessary for survival, yet they are essentially nondiscretionary. Certain items of personal care, recreation, and education are very strongly compelled by social pressure. Moreover, purchase of one product or service is often interlocked with other products or services. The purchase of an automobile, for instance, dictates the purchase of gasoline, repair services, and insurance.

Still other expenditures are compelled by consumers' strong preference for a culturally-mandated life style, usually acquired early in life. Most household furnishings, for example, are discretionary, yet 99.9 percent of the electrically wired homes in the United States have a refrigerator. Presumably this is because few American consumers will tolerate the type of life style implied by living without a refrigerator. Many products in the transportation, personal care, household furnishings, and household operations categories are nondiscretionary in this sense; they constitute what Riesman and Roseborough (1955) termed the "standard package," a set of products uniformly represented throughout American society.

Even allocations to categories that seem purely discretionary may not reflect true choice behavior. Tobacco expenditures, for example, are by no means universal; cigarette smoking, the dominant form of tobacco usage, occurs in only 35 percent of United States households [*Adult Use of Tobacco-1975* (1976)]. Studies reveal that smoking behavior is acquired largely in the preteen and teenage years (*Teenage Smoking* 1976), primarily as a result of such "psychosocial factors" as curiosity, imitation, identification with adult roles, status striving, and rebellion (Lawton 1962). Striving for these goals is socially motivated and strongly influenced by the behavior of peers, siblings, and parents. Processes such as identification and imitation perhaps explain expenditures in this category better than does the notion of individual choice (Wohlford 1970).[2]

All this suggests that the manner in which income is allocated across categories is largely nondiscretionary. This is not to say, however, that consumers make no decisions regarding this type of allocation. Clearly, choices could be made concerning the priorities by which needs will be satisfied and the proportion of income spent within each category. One way to estimate the extent of such decision making in household budget allocation is to ask if a plan exists within the household for distributing income. A unique survey of 300 Minnesota families representing three generations found that only seven percent of grandparents, 21 percent of parents, and 24 percent of married children reported such plans, and similar proportions claimed to use procedures for estimating expenses and setting specific amounts aside (Hill 1963, pp. 127–37).

The relatively few empirical studies of household budget allocation have sought to discover the comparative roles of family members (Ferber 1973) rather than the nature, incidence, and extent of the process itself. If joint participation by husband and wife, rather than control over the allocation by one spouse, is more likely to indicate conscious deliberation over alternatives, then evidence presented by Ferber and Lee (1974) that the "family financial officer" role tends to shift from joint to individual performance with increasing length of marriage seems to support the hypothesis advanced earlier by Kyrk (1953) that deliberation over household budgets declines over the life cycle.

2. Following experimental smoking during the "transition phase," those going on to become regular smokers (the "maintenance phase") apparently do so because they develop physiological and/or psychological dependence on cigarettes, and discontinuance becomes very difficult or impossible for most smokers.

Generic Allocation

What, if any, type of decision process precedes the allocation of income within expenditure categories? Ferber summarizes studies showing that from 20 to 25 percent of durable goods and clothing purchases appear to be "impulsive," in that urgency or a special purchase opportunity displaced deliberation and prepurchase planning, or that satisfaction with the product being replaced reduced family discussion and planning (Ferber 1973, pp. 44–5). Up to 50 percent of supermarket purchases and 33 percent of transactions in variety stores and drugstores are "impulsive purchases," in that shoppers do not state intentions to buy these items in store-entrance interviews (Engel, Blackwell, and Kollat 1978, p. 483). Evidence from other studies (e.g., Wells and LoSciuto 1966) suggests that for certain grocery products decision processes do not occur in the store either.

Additional evidence relating to the existence of prepurchase processes within expenditure category comes from studies of the adoption and diffusion of innovations. A general finding from this research is that substantial differences exist across consumers in the amount of prepurchase deliberation that occurs. Rogers and Shoemaker's (1971) review shows that 12 of 14 studies of information seeking found that early adopters sought more information about the innovation than did later adopters (p. 374). Their review also shows considerable evidence that early adopters have significantly greater exposure to change agents, mass media, and interpersonal communication channels (pp. 371–4). This declining intensity of decision making is explained, at least in part, by the "diffusion effect," the increasing social pressure on nonadopters to adopt the innovation as the percentage of adopters increases. Further, Rogers and Shoemaker (1971, p. 122) and Robertson (1971, p. 61) acknowledge that evidence for the existence of "stages" in the adoption decision may be artifactual; both cite evidence that when unstructured questionnaires are used, certain stages are skipped or in some cases no decision process occurs.

Contemporary consumers researchers often overlook differences in the cognitive and motivational patterns associated with the many products and services involved in consumption. An early attempt to categorize these differences recognized products that are primarily hedonic (appealing to the senses), those with important symbolic meaning (ego-involving), and a third category valued primarily in terms of their functional performance (Woods 1961). While many generic products have two or even all three dimensions, prepurchase choice processes are most likely when functional performance dominates.

Sensory preferences are often well established in early childhood, although these may change somewhat with maturation, e.g., increasing preferences for salty and sharp flavors as children enter the teen years (Reynolds and Wells 1977, p. 83). Likes and dislikes for certain tastes, because of their early origins, may be reflected in consumption patterns without deliberation or even awareness by the consumer. Symbolic aspects of products are also often learned in childhood. Moore (1957) points out that eating, like other physiological activities, is especially prone to symbolic elaboration, perhaps because these activities "reach back into infancy, and are complexly patterned long before there is any autonomous intelligence or maturity with which to perceive the difference between the act itself and its accompanying feelings, social circumstances, contradictions, and coincidental motives" (Moore 1957, p. 77). One study of five-, seven-, and nine-year-olds found:

> *Children apparently begin assigning social values to goods around age seven, particularly to elaborate toys. Nine-year-olds also are slightly fashion conscious in the sense that they may express a desire for certain articles of clothing being worn by other children, for example, tennis shoes and skirts . . . Children involve themselves considerably with some durable goods. In discussing automobiles with them, it was found that practically all of them have preferences for certain autos . . . (McNeal 1969, pp. 263, 265).*

These examples suggest that better understanding of the processes leading to early childhood acquisition of taste preferences and symbolic interpretations of products may be more relevant for understanding preferences for "hedonic" and "symbolic" products than research structured on models of choice and decision.

Finally, in many instances consumers have no control over the specific products and services they purchase or consume. In the extreme case, consumers who are institutionalized (e.g., in hospitals, rest homes, or military institutions) typically have little or no control over the type of food, clothing, or furnishings they use. College students who live in dormitories and fraternities are similarly constrained. Apartment dwellers, and in many cases even home buyers, have little control over such items as fixtures, appliances, and floor coverings.

Store Patronage

Analysis of the spatial environment within which most consumers obtain goods and services reveals the potential relevance of choice models in portraying shopping and store patronage behavior. Consumers often find desired products and services to be available in two or more cities or towns within reasonable driving distance, or in numerous local shopping centers or areas, scattered retail outlets, and so forth. Catalogs, mail order, door-to-door sales organizations, telephone ordering services, etc., further expand the range of possible sources. A review of studies on shopping and patronage suggests, however, that extended search and evaluation typically does not precede store patronage (Granbois 1977).

Use of Nonstore Sources

While nonstore shopping sources are important in most product categories, studies of their use have revealed considerable city-to-city variation. One study found high users of mail order also to be high telephone order users; another found heavy in-home buyers also to be active store shoppers. Several studies have found distinctive socioeconomic characteristics associated with heavy use of these modes (Granbois 1977, p. 270). All the findings suggest that a significant subset of all consumers may not even consider sources other than the conventional retail outlets.

Patronage of Urban Areas/ Shopping Centers

Patronage of shopping areas tends to vary directly with assortment size and inversely with distance or effort involved in reaching them. Studies of patronage have firmly established the broad predictive usefulness of simple formal models establishing these relationships. Recent research, however, points to exceptions to, and constraints on, the patterns predicted by these models. For example, attention has been given to the impact of physical barriers, differential behavior of consumers with varying socioeconomic characteristics, and the impact of differing levels of promotion and price differences (Granbois 1977). The existence of limitations on the range of alternative shopping areas is further supported by the findings of "outshopping" studies, seeking determinants of shopping trips to nearby cities. Two studies found distinctive profiles of outshoppers with regard to variables such as income, age, race, sex, and beliefs, suggesting this pattern to be limited to certain market segments (Granbois 1977, p. 287).

Patronage Among and Within Store Types

Studies of shopping activity preceding major durable goods purchases have typically found a high incidence of purchases occurring after a single store visit, despite the fact that the high dollar value, physical complexity, relatively low purchase frequency, and the presence of a significant proportion of first-time purchasers in the samples would seem to indicate more extensive consideration of alternative outlets. The following data illustrate this finding (Granbois 1977, p. 264):

Type of purchase	*Percent of buyers reporting a single store visit*
Black and white television	39
Color television	50
Furniture	22
Carpet	27

Similar studies of soft goods purchases reveal that 75-80 percent of all purchases are made after visiting a single store (Granbois 1977, p. 266).

Deliberation and true choice might be expected to be at a maximum among residents new to an area. Nevertheless, such studies have consistently found that convenience and past loyalty to chains in the previous area are important criteria in making selections, and that new patterns are established quickly—supermarkets selected within three weeks, several other store types picked within five weeks (Granbois 1977, p. 272). These and other results indicate a less-than-full evaluation of alternatives. One study of supermarket shoppers using retrospective accounts of store selection found that nine percent of the sample reported to have made no choice; patronage occurred instead on bases such as personal recommendations or preferences acquired in early childhood (Olshavsky and MacKay 1978).

As in the case of generic product preferences, store preferences developed at an early age may serve as constraints on the range of choice alternatives considered by adults. Evidence of this pattern was also found by McNeal, who writes: "Starting as early as five children show likes and dislikes for certain stores as well as specific types of stores" (McNeal 1969, p. 263).

Brand Purchase

How does brand purchase occur? In his review of research on prepurchase information seeking, Newman (1977) found little evidence of extensive search and some evidence that no search or evaluation occurred in many instances. On sources of information, Newman reports that:

> *One survey found that one-third of the buyers of major appliances received information from only one source . . . A more recent survey found that 15 percent of the buyers of major appliances and automobiles consulted no external source before buying . . . In both surveys source referred to a type or category such as friends and neighbors; books, pamphlets, and articles; advertising; and retail outlets . . . A survey of small electrical appliance buyers found that 10 percent of them could not recall obtaining helpful information in any way other than by visiting a retail store (p. 80).*

On number of alternatives considered, Newman writes:

> *Several studies have shown that many consumers limit their attention to few alternatives. Forty-six percent of the buyers of major household appliances considered only one price range . . . appliance buyers who examined only one brand ranged from 41 percent for refrigerators to 71 percent for vacuum cleaners . . . of the buyers of household appliances and cars, 47 percent considered mainly a single brand at the outset of the decision process . . . These findings are consistent with other evidence that the buyer's "evoked set" of brands . . . is typically small (p. 81).*

Finally, with respect to results based on studies that developed a comprehensive index of information seeking, Newman states:

Using a scale ranging from one for no information seeking to six for very active search, Katona and Mueller reported that 40 percent of the buyers of major appliances had scale values of one or two while 10 percent had values of five or six . . . The results led Katona and Mueller to conclude that 'Any notion that careful planning and choosing, thorough consideration of alternatives, and information seeking accompanied every major purchase was contradicted by the data . . . Rather, it appeared . . . that many purchases were made in a state of ignorance or at least indifference.' In another study of major appliances and automobiles, on a 20-point scale representing out-of-store search (zero meaning none), 49 percent had scores of 5 or less; 38 percent scored from 6 to 11; and 13 percent had scores of 12 to 20 (p. 82).

There are only a few direct studies of the brand choice process, each with strong limitations. Wells and LoSciuto (1966) using an in-store, on-the-spot technique, observed 1,500 supermarket shoppers. Only representative data for cereals, candy, and detergent were presented. In 55 percent of the cases for cereals, 38 percent for candy, and 72 percent for detergent, there was no visible evidence of an in-store prepurchase choice process, such as inspecting two or more packages. In 15 percent of the cases for cereal, 44 percent candy, and 12 percent for detergent, no purchase occurred. Hence, according to these data, in only 30 percent of the cereal, 18 percent of the candy, and 12 percent of the detergent purchases was there even the possibility that an in-store prepurchase process occurred. Unfortunately, the technique used could not observe the mental processes; strong conclusions about the choice process, therefore, cannot be drawn from this study.

In another study of supermarket shoppers (Bettman 1970), a "process tracing" technique was used, which was more likely to reveal any choice processes that occurred. For a period of six to eight weeks, Bettman observed the shopping behavior of two homemakers and asked them to think aloud as they made their purchases. He analyzed these protocol data to obtain insights about the evaluative criteria and evaluation processes used. A similar study of women's ready-to-wear clothing was performed by Alexis, Haines, and Simon (1968).

While these and other studies using process tracing techniques generally find evidence for prepurchase process, the techniques are inherently biased; as Bettman and Zins (1977) point out:

A second bias in the protocols occurs because the consumer is asked to give protocols for choices where in many cases a great deal of learning has already occurred . . . the consumer may have bought the same brand many times, and may not really think much about this type of choice while it is being made. The request from the experimenter to keep talking may then lead to retrospection about why the particular brand was bought in the first place, although such reasoning is not relevant now (p. 82).

In another study of in-store behavior, Olshavsky (1973) analyzed tape recorded conversations between customer and salesman for major appliance transactions, without the customer being aware of the recording. This study provided clear evidence of at least a limited amount of prepurchase processes. At the same time, however, in some cases customers relied entirely upon the salesman's recommendation.

Other studies provide more direct evidence concerning the way brand purchases occur without prior consideration of alternatives. Several studies document that consumers make purchases on the basis of recommendations from either personal or nonpersonal sources. Feldman and Spencer (1965) reported that 75 percent of newcomers to a community selected a physician solely on the basis of a recommendation. Some studies have indicated that brand purchase behavior represents conformity to group norms; this occurs particularly for highly conspicuous products. Venkatesan (1968) demonstrated in a laboratory study the influence of group pressure on selection of men's suits. Also, some evidence suggests that brand preferences are acquired early in life, as part of the general acculturation process (Ward 1974). It has even been found that brand purchases are influenced by such superficial factors as shelf height and shelf facings (Frank and Massy 1970).

Finally, there is some evidence that brand purchases are made on the basis of surrogates or indices of quality, rather than on the basis of a direct evaluation of the brands' attributes. Price, manufacturer's reputation, and packaging are but a few of the indices studied (Monroe 1973; Gardner 1971; McConnell 1968; Brown 1958).

Conclusions and Implications

Our review of studies that provide some evidence, direct or indirect, for the existence of prepurchase processes and our analysis of the constraints and influences on purchasing behavior suggest that Kassarjian is right. A significant proportion of purchases may not be preceded by a decision process. This conclusion does not simply restate the familiar observation that purchase behavior rapidly becomes habitual, with little or no prepurchase processes occurring after the first few purchases. We conclude that for many purchases a decision process never occurs, not even on the first purchase.

How then does purchasing occur if not as a result of some type of decision process? This review identified a number of different ways: Purchases can occur out of necessity; they can be derived from culturally-mandated lifestyles or from interlocked purchases; they can reflect preferences acquired in early childhood; they can result from simple conformity to group norms or from imitation of others; purchases can be made exclusively on recommendations from personal or nonpersonal sources; they can be made on the basis of surrogates of various types; or they can even occur on a random or superficial basis. Further research, free of the prepurchase decision assumption, may identify still other ways.

Another conclusion we draw from this review is that even when purchase behavior is preceded by a choice process, it is likely to be very limited. It typically involves the evaluation of few alternatives, little external search, few evaluative criteria, and simple evaluation process models. There is little evidence that consumers engage in the very extended type of search and evaluation a product testing organization like Consumers Union performs routinely.[3]

It would be an oversimplification, however, to characterize purchasing behavior as either involving predecision processes or not. While this may be an accurate characterization of some purchases, in general, we should allow for combination or "hybrid" strategies whereby choice and nonchoice are used; e.g., personal recommendations can be combined in various ways with limited search and evaluation. Indeed, future research may reveal that such hybrid strategies are the most common type of prepurchase behavior.

These conclusions have important implications for theories of consumer behavior. Certainly any theory whose central thesis is that purchases are preceded by a decision process (Engel, Blackwell, and Kollat 1978; Howard and Sheth 1969) can provide an adequate explanation of only certain types of consumer purchasing behaviors. Theory needs to be developed along at least two separate lines. Wright has argued that a process he calls "affect referral" often describes purchases. Global measures of affect, not attribute-specific information, provide the basis for choice, where either the "best" or the "first acceptable" option thought of is selected (Wright 1976). This first line of development will be particularly fruitful if it entails low involvement learning as part of an ongoing socialization process.

The second line of development is suggested by the work of Lussier and Olshavsky (1974), Payne (1976), and others who have argued for a contingent processing view of decision making. Payne, for example, points out that the various choice strategies (e.g., additive difference, conjunctive, and elimination-by-aspects) are not competing, but complementary.

> *In that regard, the four decision processes discussed in this paper might be conceptualized as different subroutines in a general choice program. The control conditions under which one of these sets of processes might be called would then seem to depend, at least in part, on the characteristics of the decision problem. In that respect, the less cognitively demanding decision procedures, conjunctive and elimination-by-aspects, might be called early in the decision process as a way of simplifying the decision task by quickly eliminating alternatives until only a few alternatives remained as choice possibilities. The subject might then employ one of the cognitively demanding choice procedures, e.g., additive difference model, to make the final evaluation and choice (Payne 1976, p. 385).*

This contingent processing concept needs to be broadened to incorporate other purchasing heuristics of the type identified here, e.g., conformity, imitation, recommendations.

In view of the tremendous interest in consumer

3. This is not to imply that consumers who use *Consumer Reports* could not engage in extensive evaluation of the data presented, but that they do not gather such data themselves. Indeed, in most cases, this cannot be done by the typical consumer because of the time, effort, expense, or expertise involved.

purchasing behavior it is surprising, to say the least, that there have been so few studies of prepurchase processes that involve actual consumers in actual settings using methodologies that permit observation of behaviors contrary to those predicted by models of choice and decision processes. Such research is fraught with difficulties that must be overcome if we are to have a secure empirical foundation for theory construction and testing.

These conclusions also have implications for private and public policy. Clearly, if some purchases are not preceded by any type of prior search and evaluation, then recommendations based on research that incorporates the assumption that they are may be inappropriate. The issue of "information overload," for instance, which has occupied so many pages in marketing journals recently, must be interpreted quite differently if a significant percentage of consumers of particular products or services do not engage in prepurchase activities.

References

Adult Use of Tobacco-1975 (1976), U.S. Department of Health, Education, and Welfare, Public Health Service, Center for Disease Control, National Clearinghouse for Smoking and Health.

Alexis, Marcus, Haines, George H., and Simon, Leonard (1968), "Consumer Information Processing: The Case of Women's Clothing," in *Proceedings*, Chicago: American Marketing Association, pp. 197–205.

Bettman, James R. (1970), "Information Processing Models of Consumer Behavior," *Journal of Marketing Research*, 7, 370–6.

——, Capon, Noel, and Lutz, Richard (1975), "Cognitive Algebra in Multiattribute Attitude Models," *Journal of Marketing Research*, 12, 151–64.

——, and Kakkar, Pradeep (1977), "Effects of Information Presentation Format on Consumer Information Acquisition Strategy," *Journal of Consumer Research*, 3, 233–40.

——, and Zins, Michel A. (1977), "Constructive Process in Consumer Choice," *Journal of Consumer Research*, 4, 75–85.

Brown, Robert L. (1958), "Wrapper Influence on the Perception of Freshness in Bread," *Journal of Applied Psychology*, 42, 257–60.

Engel, James F., Blackwell, Roger D., and Kollat, David T. (1978), *Consumer Behavior*, Hinsdale, IL: The Dryden Press.

Feldman, Sidney P., and Spencer, Merlin C. (1965), "The Effect of Personal Influence in the Selection of Consumer Services," in *Marketing and Economic Development*, ed. Peter Bennett, Chicago: American Marketing Association, p. 440–52.

Ferber, Robert (1973), "Family Decision Making and Economic Behavior: A Review," in *Family Economic Behavior: Problems and Prospects*, ed. Eleanor B. Sheldon, Philadelphia: Lippincott, pp. 29–61.

——, and Lee, Lucy Chao (1974), "Husband-Wife Influence in Family Purchasing Behavior," *Journal of Consumer Research*, 1, 43-50.

Frank, Ronald E., and Massy, William F. (1970), "Shelf Position and Space Effects," *Journal of Marketing Research*, 7, 59–66.

Gardner, David M. (1971), "Is There a Generalized Price-Quality Relationship?" *Journal of Marketing Research*, 8, 241-3.

Granbois, Donald H. (1977), "Shopping Behavior and Preferences," in *Selected Aspects of Consumer Behavior—A Summary from the Perspective of Different Disciplines*, Washington, D.C.: U.S. Government Printing Office, pp. 259–98.

Gredal, Karen (1966), "Purchasing Behavior in Households," in *Readings in Danish Theory of Marketing*, ed. Max Kjaer-Hansen. Copenhagen: Einar Harcks Forlag, pp. 84–100.

Green, Paul E., and Wind, Yoram (1973), *Multiattribute Decisions in Marketing*, Hinsdale, IL: The Dryden Press.

Hill, Reuben (1963), "Judgment and Consumership in the Management of Family Resources," *Sociology and Social Research*, 47, 460-6.

Howard, John A. (1977), *Consumer Behavior: Application of Theory*, New York: McGraw-Hill Book Company.

——, and Sheth, Jagdish N. (1969), *The Theory of Buyer Behavior*, New York: John Wiley & Sons, Inc.

Jacoby, Jacob, Szybillo, George J., and Busato-Schach, Jacqueline (1977), "Information Acquisition Behavior in Brand Choice Situations," *Journal of Consumer Research*, 3, 209–16.

Kassarjian, Harold H. (1978), "Presidential Address, 1977: Anthropomorphism and Parsimony," in *Advances in Consumer Research, Vol. 5*, ed. H. Keith Hunt, Ann Arbor, MI: Association for Consumer Research, pp. xii–xiv.

Kollat, David T., and Willett, Ronald P. (1967), "Customer Impulse Purchasing Behavior," *Journal of Marketing Research*, 4, 21–31.

Kyrk, Hazel (1953), *The Family in the American Economy*, Chicago: University of Chicago Press.

Lawton, M. P. (1962), "Psychosocial Aspects of Cigarette Smoking," *Journal of Health and Human Behavior*, 3, 163–70.

Lussier, Denis A., and Olshavsky, Richard W. (1974), "An Information Processing Approach to Individual Brand Choice Behavior," paper presented at the ORSA/TIMS Joint National Meeting, San Juan, Puerto Rico.

McConnell, J. Douglas (1968), "The Development of Brand Loyalty: An Experimental Study," *Journal of Marketing Research,* 5, 13-9.

McNeal, James U. (1969), "An Exploratory Study of the Consumer Behavior of Children," in *Dimensions of Consumer Behavior,* ed. James U. McNeal, New York: Appleton-Century-Crofts, 255-75.

Monroe, Kent B. (1973), "Buyers' Subjective Perceptions of Price," *Journal of Marketing Research,* 10, 70-80.

Moore, Harriet (1957), "The Meaning of Foods," *The American Journal of Clinical Nutrition,* 5, 77-82.

Newman, Joseph W. (1977), "Consumer External Search: Amount and Determinants," in *Consumer and Industrial Buying Behavior,* eds. Arch G. Woodside, Jagdish N. Sheth, and Peter D. Bennett, New York: North-Holland Publishing Co.

Ölander, Folke, and Seipel, Carl-Magnus (1970), *Psychological Approaches to the Study of Saving,* Urbana, IL: Bureau of Economics and Business Research, University of Illinois.

Olshavsky, Richard W. (1973), "Customer-Salesman Interaction in Appliance Retailing," *Journal of Marketing Research,* 10, 208-12.

——, and MacKay, David B. (1978), "An Empirical Test of Four Alternative Supermarket Choice Models," unpublished working paper, Indiana University, Department of Marketing.

Payne, John W. (1976), "Task Complexity and Contingent Processing in Decision Making: An Information Search and Protocol Analysis," *Organizational Behavior and Human Performance,* 16, 366-87.

van Raaij, W. Fred (1977), "Consumer Information Processing for Different Information Structures and Formats," in *Advances in Consumer Research, Vol. 4,* ed. William O. Perreault, pp. 176-84.

Reynolds, Fred D., and Wells, William D. (1977), *Consumer Behavior,* New York: McGraw-Hill.

Riesman, David, and Roseborough, Howard (1955), "Careers and Consumer Behavior," in *The Life Cycle and Consumer Behavior, Vol. 2,* ed. Lincoln Clark, New York: New York University Press, pp. 1-18.

Robertson, Thomas S. (1971), *Innovative Behavior and Communication,* New York: Holt, Rinehart, and Winston.

Rogers, Everett M., and Shoemaker, F. Floyd (1971), *Communication of Innovations,* New York: The Free Press.

Russ, Frederick A. (1971), "Evaluation Process Models and the Prediction of Preference," in *Proceedings,* Chicago: Association for Consumer Research, ed. David M. Gardner, pp. 256-61.

Russo, Edward J., and Rosen, Larry D. (1975), "An Eye Fixation Analysis of Multi-Attribute Choice," *Memory and Cognition,* 3, 267-76.

Scott, Jerome E. and Peter Wright (1976), "Modeling an Organizational Buyer's Product Evaluation Strategy: Validity and Procedural Considerations," *Journal of Marketing Research,* 13, 211-24.

Teenage Smoking, National Patterns of Cigarette Smoking, Ages 12 through 18, in 1972 and 1974 (1976), U.S. Department of Health, Education and Welfare, Public Health Service, National Institute of Health.

Venkatesan, M. (1966), "Experimental Study of Consumer Behavior Conformity and Independence," *Journal of Marketing Research,* 3, 384-7.

Ward, Scott (1974), "Consumer Socialization," *Journal of Consumer Research,* 1, September, 1-14.

Wells, William, and LoSciuto, Leonard A. (1966), "Direct Observation of Purchasing Behavior," *Journal of Marketing Research,* 3, 227-33.

Wohlford, Paul (1970), "Initiation of Cigarette Smoking: Is It Related to Parental Smoking Behavior?" *Journal of Consulting and Clinical Psychology,* 34, 148-51.

Woods, Walter A. (1960), "Psychological Dimensions of Consumer Decision," *Journal of Marketing,* 24, 15-9.

Wright, Peter (1976), "An Adaptive Consumer's View of Attitudes and Other Choice Mechanisms, as Viewed by an Equally Adaptive Advertiser, in *Attitude Research at Bay,* eds. Deborah Johnson and William D. Wells, Chicago: American Marketing Association, pp. 113-31.

READING 11

"Consumer Decision Making—Fact or Fiction?" Comment

Michael Ursic

Olshavsky and Granbois's article, "Consumer Decision Making–Fact or Fiction?" (1979) suffers from three conceptual difficulties: an inappropriate conceptualization of the prepurchase decision process; a lack of congruence between the evidence presented and the stated purpose of the article; and a lack of correspondence between the implications and the conclusions.

Conceptualization

The purpose of the article was to "assess the apparent scope of consumer behavior not preceded by external search" (p. 98). Yet after citing numerous studies, the authors concluded that a significant proportion of purchases may not be preceded by a decision process. The implication is that external search constitutes the entire prepurchase decision process. This is not the case. The prepurchase decision process is very broad, encompassing problem recognition and evaluation, in addition to search (Engel, Kollat, and Blackwell 1978).

Evidence

The studies that the authors cited do not support the contention that a significant proportion of purchases are not preceded by a search, or the contention that purchases are not preceded by a decision-making process.

Reprinted with permission from the *Journal of Consumer Research*, 7:3 December 1980, 331–333.

Budget Allocation

The section on spending versus savings decisions quotes a Ferber article that stated that most families do not have a financial plan. Yet, it is acknowledged that Ferber never clearly explained the meaning of a financial plan in his article. Thus, the conclusions of the study do not foreclose the possibility that, for most families, the decision to save or invest is preceded by careful thought and by a search for more information. A study by Ölander and Seipel (1970) was referenced, which stated that tax knowledge was not used in most decisions to save or invest. The conclusions of this study certainly do not preclude the possibility of a decision-making process or information search, because other factors, such as risk, could enter into an investment decision. Finally, the authors cite evidence to show that a low percentage of people are systematic savers. However, the act of not saving regularly could be a planned decision preceded by information gathering.

In the section on allocation of income across expenditure categories, the authors contended that because many goods, such as cars and gasoline, are complementary, most of the allocation decisions are nondiscretionary. No studies are cited to indicate the extent of nondiscretionary allocations. Further, because the purchase of such products as gasoline may be nondiscretionary, the quantity of purchase of these items is frequently a discretionary act, preceded by search and evaluation. For instance, a family may consciously plan to allocate less money to gas consumption because the price of this product has drastically increased.

Generic Allocation

The section on generic allocation, or allocation within expenditure category, quotes a Ferber study that said that 20 to 25 percent of durable goods and clothing purchases appear to be on impulse and not require planning and family discussion, because of urgency, a special purchase opportunity, or satisfaction with the present product. A special purchase opportunity or satisfaction with the present product does not preclude a conscious search or decision process. A special purchase opportunity could mean that a family, through continuous searching, found a very high quality product at a very low price so that no extensive planning, discussion, or search was necessary. Satisfaction with the present product probably means that a family at some earlier time went through an extensive search and evaluation process to find that product.

An Engel, Kollat, and Blackwell (1978) study is also quoted, which stated that in 50 percent of the transactions in variety and drugstores, people do not state their intention to buy in an in-store entrance interview. This evidence does not eliminate the possibility of a problem recognition, search, and evaluation process occurring within the store. The authors also cited evidence that showed that shoppers vary in the amount of prepurchase shopping behavior undertaken, but never explained the relevance of this knowledge to the existence of a search and decision process. Finally, it was stated that many tastes and preferences are acquired in childhood. However, such childhood learning does not support the conclusion that a search and evaluation does not occur, as consumers will search and evaluate products based on their acquired preferences.

Store Patronage

The evidence that was referenced in the area of store patronage, such as the positive relationship between mail order users and telephone users, and between in-home buying and active store shopping, does not support the notion that nonstore sources are not used; even if nonstore sources were not used, this would not mean that a prepurchase search and evaluation does not occur. Evidence was also cited to show that a consumer's choice of stores is limited by distance, but this fact does not mean that an evaluation and search process does not occur in choosing a store within a reasonable distance. A study by Granbois (1977) was discussed to indicate that many purchases of expensive durables are made in a single store visit. However, for none of the products mentioned are the percentage of purchase decisions made in one visit excessively high (i.e., over 50 percent). Further, a single store visit does not mean that a search and evaluation process does not occur. Consumers could have shopped extensively by phone, through catalogs, or through advertisements in making a purchase decision. Lastly, the writers stated that new residents tend to maintain store loyalty from their prior place of residence. This does not preclude the possibility that a search and evaluation process occurred initially to find a desirable chain.

Brand Purchase

In the section on brand preference, a study by Newman (1977) was referenced that stated that 15 percent of the buyers of major appliances consulted no external source before buying, and that ten percent of the buyers of electrical appliances could not obtain helpful information in any way other than visiting a retail store. These figures do not mean that a search and evaluation process does not occur in an overwhelming number of cases. The figures in regard to the percentage of consumers who did not consult external sources, and who obtained information exclusively from retail stores are very small—15 and 10 percent, respectively. Also, consumers can obtain large amounts of information concerning small appliances (e.g., price, warranty coverage) from a store visit.

The Newman article quoted a study by Dommermuth that found that in 71 percent of the vacuum cleaner purchases, and in 42 percent of the refrigerator purchases, consumers only examined one brand. This study, however, relied on telephone interviews, rather than on observations. Consumers were asked to *recall* the number of brands examined for any purchase of specified major durables made in the previous two years. The results obtained from such a procedure would be biased as most respondents, due to memory problems, probably underestimated the amount of search undertaken for a purchase made a year or two in the past.

A study by Wells and LoSciuto (1966) was cited that found that in 55 percent of the cases for cereal, 38 percent of the cases for candy, and 72 percent of the cases for detergent, consumers examined only one brand before purchasing. This study does not indicate that prepurchase search and evaluation does not occur in these instances; it is possible that the search and evaluation happened either on a prior visit or outside the store. Wells and LoSciuto stated in their article that their findings showed only that consumers had determined their purchase before entering the store.

Finally, the authors referred to several studies that suggested that consumers were heavily influenced by group norms in making purchase decisions. Even if this were the case, it would not indicate the absence of a search and evaluation process, but merely that consumers consider the views of their peers before making a purchase. Burnkrant and Cousineau (1975) found that much of the motivation to comply with the assessment of a group was not related to a fear of rejection, but to a reliance on the views of others as an indication of a product's quality.

Implications

Even if the evidence that the authors cited supported the conclusion that a significant number of purchases are not preceded by a choice process, the implications that are stated do not follow from this conclusion. The writers stated that noncompensatory strategies and global measures of affect, rather than attribute weighting, provide the basis for choice. Such a view implies the existence of *some* prepurchase decision-making process.

References

Burnkrant, Robert, and Cousineau, Alain (1975), "Informational and Normative Social Influence in Buyer Behavior," *Journal of Consumer Research*, 2, 206–15.

Dommermuth, William (1965), "The Shopping Matrix and Marketing Strategy," *Journal of Marketing Research*, 2, 128–32.

Engel, James F., Blackwell, Roger D., and Kollat, David T. (1978), *Consumer Behavior*, 3rd ed., Hinsdale, IL: The Dryden Press.

Granbois, Donald H. (1977), "Shopping Behavior and Preferences," in *Selected Aspects of Consumer Behavior—A Summary from the Perspective of Different Disciplines*, Washington, D.C.: U.S. Government Printing Office, pp. 259–98.

Newman, Joseph W. (1977), "Consumer External Search: Amount and Determinants," in *Consumer and Industrial Buying Behavior*, eds. Arch G. Woodside, Jagdish N. Sheth, and Peter D. Bennett. New York: North-Holland Publishing Co.

Ölander, Folke, and Seipel, Carl-Magnus (1970), *Psychological Approaches to the Study of Saving*, Urbana, IL: Bureau of Economics and Business Research, University of Illinois.

Olshavsky, Richard W., and Granbois, Donald H. (1979), "Consumer Decision Making—Fact or Fiction?" *Journal of Consumer Research*, 6, 93–100.

Wells, William, and LoSciuto, Leonard A. (1966), "Direct Observation of Purchasing Behavior," *Journal of Marketing Research*, 3, 227–33.

READING 12

Rejoinder

Richard W. Olshavsky and Donald H. Granbois

Ursic's comments (1980) will be addressed in the same order in which they appear in his paper.

Conceptualization

The use of search as an index of the extent of prepurchase decision making is predicated on our statement that "applying an evaluation procedure . . . requires considerable information. . . . Evidence of the circumstances of purchasing behavior occurring in the *absence* of external search, then, helps to establish the *maximum* scope of the nondecision behavior postulation by Kassarjian" (Olshavsky and Granbois 1979, p. 94). In other words, if there were no external search for information (and stored information is either not available or irrelevant) *then the evaluation stage simply cannot occur.* Our focus on only the search and evaluation stages is consistent with the focus of most of the past research on consumer decision making. Moreover, in theoretic formulations of decision making only the evaluation stage is considered (Lee 1971; von Newman and Morgenstern 1947).

Our purpose, it should be remembered, was to assess the degree to which available research did or did not seem to substantiate a five-step process. As most published research has at least implicitly assumed such a process, our review could hardly have been expected to provide validation for any specific alternative processes. The finding that research has found substantial evidence of behavior apparently inconsistent with the prediction of a five-step process model at best suggests the need for new exploratory research *not* biased by assumptions about the nature of the process. Indeed, this was the conclusion we attempted to convey.

Reprinted with permission from the *Journal of Consumer Research*, 7:3 December 1980, 333–334.

Evidence

Ursic states that in several instances the research cited does not preclude the possibility of a prepurchase decision process occurring. We agree. However, we emphasize the two points we made in each of these many decision contexts. First, surprisingly little evidence, direct or indirect, exists to support the assumption of a prepurchase decision process. Second, the evidence that does exist often suggests that decision making may not occur. For instance, the finding by Ferber (1973) that up to 85 percent of the respondents were without a financial plan suggests that deliberation often does not precede saving-spending behavior; certainly the data do not suggest the opposite.

In another type of criticism, Ursic claims that we have overstated our point. For instance, he argues that the quantity of gasoline purchased may be discretionary. We agree that the quantity of gasoline purchased may be discretionary. Indeed, we stated: "This is not to say, however, that consumers make no decisions regarding this type of allocation. Clearly choices could be made concerning the priorities by which needs will be satisfied and *the proportion of income spent within each category*" (p. 95).

Ursic also comments that the extent of search may be underestimated by measures based on recall, particularly when long periods intervene between purchase and recall. Survey research is subject to biases of many kinds, some of which may underestimate and some of which may overestimate the extent of search. It is difficult to know which direction the net bias will be in any particular study. But, we suspect that the extent of search will be typically overstated (as we stated on p. 94).

Finally, in response to Ursic's comment about conformity not precluding prepurchase choice processes, we restate our position that choice and nonchoice purchasing strategies can occur in combination. "It would be an oversimplification, however, to characterize purchasing behavior as either involving prepurchase processes or not. While this may be an accurate characterization of some purchases, in general, we should allow for combination or 'hybrid' strategies whereby choice and nonchoice are used; e.g., personal recommendations can be combined in various ways with limited search and evaluation. Indeed, future research may reveal that such hybrid strategies are the most common type of prepurchase behavior" (p. 99). But, we must also emphasize our basic point that behavior at the generic, store, or brand level can occur exclusively on nonchoice bases, such as conforming to group norms.

Implications

Ursic interprets our two "nonchoice" recommendations for future theory development as implying "choice" processes. We disagree. In an effort to clarify this issue we will elaborate on our two recommendations. First, we stated that theory needs to be developed along lines in which "global measures of affect, not attribute specific information, provide the basis for choice. . . ." We can do no better than to quote Zajonc (1980) on this alternative (nonchoice process) theoretical explanation of affect.

> *Affect is considered by most contemporary theories to be postcognitive, that is, to occur only after considerable cognitive operations have been accomplished. Yet a number of experimental results on preferences, attitudes, impression formation, and decision making, as well as some clinical phenomena, suggest that affective judgments may be fairly independent of, and precede in time, the sorts of perceptual and cognitive operations commonly assumed to be the basis of these affective judgments. . . . It is concluded that affect and cognition are under the control of separate and partially independent systems that can influence each other in a variety of ways, and that both constitute independent sources of effects in information processing (p. 151).*

Second, we stated that theory development should pursue the notion of a contingent processing model "broadened to incorporate other purchasing heuristics of the type identified here, e.g., conformity, imitation, recommendations" (p. 99). What we are suggesting is that the consumer has a repertoire of *purchasing* strategies, some of which involve decision-making processes (compensatory and noncompensatory), some of which do not involve decision-making processes (following recommendations of others, conforming to group norms, etc.) and some of which involve a combination of the two. According to a broadened contingent information-processing model, the type of purchasing strategy used depends on the specific values of the consumer and task environment variables characterizing a particular purchase situation.

References

Ferber, Robert (1973), "Family Decision Making and Economic Behavior: A Review," in *Family Economic Behavior: Problems and Prospects,* ed. Eleanor B. Sheldon, Philadelphia: Lippincott, pp. 29–61.

Lee, Wayne (1971), *Decision Theory and Human Behavior,* New York: John Wiley & Sons, Inc.

von Newman, J., and Morgenstern, O. (1947), *Theory of Games and Economic Behavior,* 2nd edn., Princeton University Press.

Olshavsky, Richard W., and Granbois, Donald H. (1979), "Consumer Decision Making—Fact or Fiction?" *Journal of Consumer Research,* 6, 93–100.

Ursic, Michael (1980), "Consumer Decision Making—Fact or Fiction? Comment," *Journal of Consumer Research,* 7, 331–33.

Zajonc, Robert B. (1980), "Feeling and Thinking: Preferences Need No Inferences," *American Psychologist,* 35, 151–75.

READING 13

Decision Making within the Household

Harry L. Davis

Existing research on household decision making is reviewed in terms of three questions: (1) Which family members are involved in economic decisions? (2) What is the nature of family decision processes? and (3) Are decision outcomes affected by differences in family role structure and decision strategies? Problem areas related to each of these questions are discussed, including an overemphasis on decision roles rather than processes and outcomes, noncomparable and insufficient measures of purchase influence, and marketing's preference for individual-based models of consumer behavior.

Introduction

The literature on consumer behavior contains a growing number of references to the household as the relevant unit for studying consumer behavior. For example, Ferber (1973b) urged economists to incorporate findings about household decision making into their research on aggregate consumption and savings behavior. Six other papers prepared for that interdisciplinary conference on family economic behavior were published in the same volume (Sheldon, 1973). The first four issues of the *Journal of Consumer Research* included four articles related to family roles in consumer behavior (Davis and Rigaux, 1974; Ferber and Lee, 1974; Granbois and Summers, 1975; Munsinger, Weber, and Hansen, 1975). Academic meetings frequented by consumer researchers are now likely to include at least one session on family or multiperson decision making. The second edition of the largest selling textbook on consumer behavior (Engel, Kollat, and Blackwell, 1973) devotes considerably more space to the family than does the 1968 edition.

This paper attempts to review and evaluate this growing area of research interest. Since no overall theories or well-defined concepts have guided this literature, the best approach is to consider several related topics in some reasonable order. These are (1) the involvement of family members in economic decisions, (2) the process by which family decisions are made, and (3) the consequences of different family structures and decision-making styles.

Whether, in fact, the family is the appropriate focus in studying consumer behavior is a key issue that deserves comment from the outset. Casual observation would suggest that the family is a critical decision-making and consumption unit. Major items of consumer spending such as food, shelter, and transportation are often jointly "consumed." A husband may buy a station wagon, given the reality of having to transport four children, *despite* his strong preference for sports cars. Husbands wear ties, underwear, and socks; yet the purchase of these products is often made by wives. A housewife bases product and brand decisions to some extent on orders or requests from family members and on her judgment of what they like or dislike and what is "good for them." Even preferences for products individually consumed are likely to be influenced by feedback from members of the family—e.g., "Gee, Mom! That dress makes you look fat," or "I like the smell of that pipe tobacco." The number of products that an individual always buys for individual consumption must certainly represent a very small proportion of consumer expenditures.

These observations have not escaped some students of marketing. Almost 20 years ago, Converse,

Reprinted with permission from the *Journal of Consumer Research*, 2:4 March 1976, 241–260.

Huegy, and Mitchell (1958) dismissed the wife as the principal consumer and described the family as the "most important business conference in America." Alderson (1957) also devoted considerable attention to the family—i.e., the extent of task coordination and compatibility—as a critical aspect of consumer buying.

Two economists have made similar observations. Arrow (1951, p. 134) draws an analogy between the theory of the firm and consumer behavior: "The unit of the theory of production is not really the individual but the firm, which is an operating organization of individuals. Similarly, the unit of the theory of consumption is really the household, not the individual consumer." Samuelson (1956, pp. 8-9) remarks:

> *Who after all is the consumer in the theory of consumer's (not consumers') behavior? Is he a bachelor? A spinster? Or is he a "spending unit" as defined by statistical pollsters and recorders of budgetary spending? In most of the cultures actually studied by modern economists the fundamental unit on the demand side is clearly the "family," and this consists of a single individual in but a fraction of the total cases.*

Despite these observations, most research in this area has been characterized historically by a preoccupation with consumers as individual decision makers. Although various reference groups have been identified and studied, interest is most often focused on whether and how these groups affect individuals' attitudes and behavior. Questionnaires and interviews frequently ask who "really decided," "had the most to say," or "most often buys" in a given consumption category. Issues of group decision making are thus avoided by these procedures since they assume that decision responsibility can be attributed to one family member.

Researchers trying to develop and test various theories often link, without apparent concern, individual-based, independent variables to group-based, dependent variables. This approach can be no better observed than in studies using personality traits to predict brand choice. A well-known marketing study by Evans (1959) used husbands' personality to predict family ownership of Ford versus Chevrolet. In all the comments and rejoinders generated by this study, no one bothered to question whether husbands actually made the brand-choice decision. Could it be that Evans included a significant number of "wrong" respondents in his analysis?

This same point of view characterizes investigations of brand loyalty and consumer attitudes. Individual characteristics have been used, without much success, to explain differences in brand loyalty measured by panel data (Cunningham, 1956; Farley, 1966; Frank, 1967; Jacoby and Kyner, 1973). Since these data often reflect purchases by several family members as well as their brand preferences, why should one expect the *housewife's* brand attitudes or personality to predict household purchases over time? In a similar fashion, why should one expect an individual's brand attitudes to predict actual purchase behavior if the choice situation involves compromise and other relevant role attitudes, e.g., what a good spouse or parent should do?

By way of overview, this paper will show that recent work on household decision making has not had a noticeable impact in other areas of consumer research. The view of consumers as individual decision makers is still very much alive despite commonsense observations that the family is the relevant decision-making unit and a growing research interest in the field.[1] We further demonstrate that even the relatively simple task of describing which family members are involved in consumer decisions is clouded by a diverse and often noncomparable set of measures and concepts. It is argued that a whole set of group-related constructs, critical to understanding consumer decision making, has been largely ignored. And finally, we describe how researchers have only begun to explore the issue of whether differences in family role structure affect consumer decisions.

Involvement of Family Members in Economic Decisions

Categories of Economic Decisions

Research on which family member is involved in various financial decisions can be grouped roughly into three categories. The first two include spending decisions for frequently purchased goods or services and

1. Two papers prepared for this same project point to the fact that group level analyses have been largely ignored in studies of brand-choice behavior (Wind, 1976) and the diffusion of innovation (Rogers, in this issue).

for durables. Almost without exception, data on the former have been collected by the print media with the objective of showing that husbands have a significant influence on household purchase decisions. Studies of family-member involvement in durable goods buying come from more varied sources, including sociologists and marketing researchers in addition to commercial organizations. Typically, these studies focus on interrelationships among decisions or various determinants of involvement such as social class, life-cycle stages, or the wife's employment status. A third category of economic decisions includes a very small number of published studies about husband-wife involvement in saving and investment decisions, tasks surrounding the family budget, and family planning.

Several examples from each category will be described in the following three sections. This review is not inclusive of all published research on household decision making.[2] Included are studies that sample different decision areas, employ various methodologies, or are frequently cited in the literature.

Frequently Purchased Goods or Services. Three of the earliest studies of male versus female influence were conducted for *True* (*Male vs. Female Influence*, 1948, 1950; Starch, 1958). All were undertaken to dispel that "mythical idea" that 85 percent of every family dollar is spent by women. Products were selected on the basis of the then-current advertisers in *True*.

The first two volumes included information on some 65 product categories, 50 of which were nondurables. In the 1948 survey, questionnaires were returned by 1,376 households in which both husband and wife independently answered questions about "who originally decided on the make or brand" and "who made the most recent purchase." Less than 40 percent of the products studied were mainly husband or wife dominated (defined by 80 percent or more of the respondents in either category). The remainder had substantial proportions in at least two of the categories, i.e., husband, wife, or both. The percentage of respondents reporting "both" was consistently lower in response to "who went shopping" than "who decided on the brand."

The report by Daniel Starch and staff (1958) remains one of the most thorough studies of male versus female influence. The researchers focused on 12 products grouped into eight categories.[3] Among the nondurables studied were beer, liquor, and shaving cream. Using relatively small samples of 100 couples for each product, in-depth interviews were conducted separately with the husband and wife. A wide range of topics was covered, including brand preferences of each spouse, relative involvement of each spouse in brand selection and in shopping, and motivation for involvement. Based on cultural attitudes and patterns of consumption, respondents viewed the three nondurable products as predominantly masculine. In these cases, wives expressed few brand preferences and purchased only those brands that husbands requested. A high level of within-family agreement regarding who influenced the choice of brand was found; i.e., an average of only 8 percent of the couples did not verify each other's answers for the three nondurables.

Undoubtedly, *Life* has sponsored more studies of husband-wife involvement in product decisions than any other publication. Its readership by men *and* women was viewed as attractive to advertisers if it could be demonstrated that brand decisions were frequently made jointly within the family. The products selected, therefore, were frequently purchased items targeted on TV or in print almost exclusively to women.

Two reports prepared for *Life* by Nowland and Company (1964, 1965) were among the earliest efforts to study brand preferences of husbands and wives. In the 1965 study, for example, each spouse in 1,134 households was asked to assess his or her preferred brand for 30 different supermarket products. Information was also collected on who went on the last shopping trip as well as brands actually in the home. The data showed that husbands go on 39 percent of supermarket shopping trips—15 percent alone and 24 percent with their wives. Both studies found an association between husband-wife brand consensus and the presence of that brand in the household. There is an advantage, according to the report, "in preselling both the husband and wife of about eight to five over selling the wife alone."

Jaffe Associates (n.d.) conducted a series of pilot studies for *Life* in 301 households. The 11 products studied included coffee, frozen orange juice,

2. Ferber (1973b), Sheth (1974), and Davis (in press) provide a comprehensive literature review.

3. Product groupings included alcoholic beverages, automotive, clothing, insurance, major appliances, men's toiletries, sporting goods, and transportation.

toothpaste, pet food, and seven durable goods. For each product, husbands and wives were taken through purchase histories in which they identified the role played by themselves and their spouse. The number of stages in the decision process was found to be less for nondurables than for durables. Yet, even for frequently purchased products, the husband's involvement varied by stage. For example, the percentage of husbands who actually purchased coffee (29 percent) was considerably less than the percentage who initiated the purchase or suggested a particular brand (41 percent). Only 16 percent of husbands initiated the purchase of pet food, while 40 percent of them suggested what brand of pet food to buy.

The Learner Marketing Research and Development report (1968) is an in-depth view of family-member involvement when new or different brands are brought into the home. Housewives, husbands, and teenagers from 706 households were asked to describe "critical incidents" surrounding the purchase of 30 supermarket items. In particular, they tried to recall the overall nature of the incident, who was involved, who initiated the change, and the role of advertising, price, and product dissatisfaction. The overall conclusions reinforced a now-familiar theme. Even though wives did most of the grocery shopping, they did so with an awareness of the products and brands that their families liked. Husbands and teenagers were frequently involved in new or different brand incidents, although the extent of their involvement varied significantly by product category. Interestingly, each family member apparently drew upon a different subsample of incidents (their reality?). Conclusions about who was involved were very sensitive to which respondent in the household was interviewed.

A recent survey sponsored by five magazines (Haley, Overholser and Associates, 1975) carried on the tradition of supplying information to advertisers about the relative influence of husbands and wives in specific product categories. Measures of shopping participation, direct and indirect influence at both product and brand levels, were obtained from 2,373 wives and 1,767 husbands on 87 packaged products.[4] Husband involvement was lowest in actual shopping, with men having made an average of 23 percent of all purchases during the preceding month. At the same time, husbands directly influenced an average of 32 percent of the brand and product decisions. Husbands' indirect influence (taking their preferences into account) was even higher; they accounted for an average frequency of 38 percent of indirect influence for the 87 product and brand decisions.

A study for *Sports Illustrated* (Travel Research International, 1968) examined household decisions for pleasure trips involving airlines. Data from over 500 male respondents showed that husbands played the "predominant" role in mentioning the initial idea to take a trip, suggesting a destination, and selecting an airline.[5] The *decision* (as opposed to suggestion) on where to go was a mutual decision, however, in two-thirds of the households.

The nine commercial studies just reviewed have received relatively little attention by academic researchers. This is unfortunate in light of the large samples generally used and the large number of products represented. Moreover, the studies do dispel some of the conventional wisdom that views the world of supermarket purchases to be the exclusive domain of women. Husbands are involved in actual purchasing, although wives clearly predominate. Husbands are aware of brands in many product categories and express brand preferences on questionnaires.

The commercial studies do seem weak, however, in tracing the extent and nature of the purchase influence of husbands. For example, knowledge that a husband and wife have the same brand preference does not indicate whether brands were discussed or when a discussion took place. It does not even reveal whether a wife is aware of her husband's preferences or vice versa. The husband's response to questions about brand preferences could reflect only awareness under the following logic: "I know what brands my wife buys since I see them on the table," or "I have seen ads for instant coffee on TV and it's good to have preferences when filling out questionnaires." Some of the attempts to measure the husband's influence are undoubtedly biased by social desirability. What "good wife" would want to admit that her husband's brand comments were not important to her or

4. Categories with two or more products included beverages, cereals, desserts, frozen specialties, meats, sauces and dressings, snacks, soups, vegetables, drugs, toiletries, cleaning products, paper products, pet foods, alcoholic beverages, health and personal care, and tobacco products.

5. This conclusion masks to some extent the amount of variability in the data. According to their husbands, 35 percent of the wives did make the initial suggestion. Moreover, the choices of airline and travel arrangements were made by wives or travel agents in over 40 percent of the cases.

that she did not take his preferences into account? Finally, the analyses contained in these commercial studies are very limited: Nothing has been published about interrelationships among products in terms of who shops or influences, and little use has been made of predictor variables to explore differences in husband-wife involvement among families.

Durable Goods. Research on family-member influence in durable goods buying is more abundant than that on frequently purchased items. Even a casual observer would probably agree that important, one-time purchases are likely to involve more than one household member. In contrast to nondurables, purchases of durable goods are often preceded by a progression of interrelated decisions and activities through time. Husbands, wives, and children have more opportunities to become involved at one or more steps in the process. One can presume that family members are also more motivated to participate, since the purchase of an automobile, for example, often precludes other acquisitions, given families' budget constraints.

At one extreme in terms of length of the decision process, amount of deliberation, and financial importance is the housing purchase. A number of studies have shown, not surprisingly, a high degree of joint decision making in buying homes (Bernhardt, 1974; Blood and Wolfe, 1960; Cunningham and Green, 1974; Davis and Rigaux, 1974; Hempel, 1974; Munsinger et al., 1975). Those studies that subdivided the purchase into several interrelated decisions found considerable variability in the relative involvement of husband and wife. Bernhardt (1974) reports that husbands' influence was highest for decisions concerning price range and whether to move, while wives' influence was highest in deciding on the number of bedrooms and other house features.

The automobile purchase has been another popular arena in which to study marital roles (Blood and Wolfe, 1960; Brehl and Callahan Research, 1967; Conway/Milliken Research, 1969; Davis, 1970, 1972a; Green and Cunningham, 1975; Haley et al., 1975; Jaffe Associates, n.d.; Starch, 1958). Some researchers have used overall measures of influence on "deciding about buying a new car." Others have focused on husband-wife influence regarding specific product attributes (e.g., make, model, color, interior, accessories, size, performance features), shopping or use characteristics, and budget considerations (e.g., price or when to buy). In contrast to the housing purchase, all these studies have found husbands' influence to be greater than wives'.

Empirical research has also investigated marital roles in the purchase of home furnishings (Davis, 1970; Green and Cunningham, 1975; Jaffe Associates, n.d.; Scott, 1970; Woodside, 1975). Other product categories for which similar data are available include small appliances, major appliances, home entertainment (e.g., TV and stereo), cameras, life insurance, vacation travel, and watches (Green and Cunningham, 1975; Haley et al., 1975; Jaffe Associates, n.d.; Starch, 1958).

Studies of marital roles in durable goods buying represent a very active area of empirical research. Identical measures of purchase influence for the same product categories have been used by different researchers. Even with the small, convenience samples that characterize some of these studies, the results are remarkably consistent. Three studies of automobile buying, for example, all show wives' influence to increase as one moves from the decision on make to that on model and finally on color (i.e., Conway/Milliken Research, 1969; Davis, 1970; Starch, 1958).

These same studies can be criticized, however, on the basis of their rather limited objectives. With few exceptions, researchers have not explored *why* some product categories or subdecisions within product categories are dominated by husbands and others by wives. Since very few studies include more than one product, analyses of roles across product categories within households are rarely made. Little effort has gone into explaining why a single decision usually shows some variability in marital roles among families.

Other Economic Decisions. Although durable and nondurable purchases encompass a multitude of decisions, they have little to do directly with how families manage their overall finances or plan other areas of their life. These areas also require frequent decision making and thus provide opportunities for differing degrees of husband-wife involvement.

Ferber (1973b) has identified and reviewed relevant studies in three related areas of financial management. The first is money management—"an arrangement within the family for the handling of money, payment of bills, budgeting, and keeping accounts" (p. 32). Data from two older studies (Sharp and Mott, 1956; Wolgast, 1958) and a more recent study (Ferber and Lee, 1974) are remarkably consistent in showing considerable variability in the way families handle money and pay bills. These studies reported the percentage of families in which the wife is responsible as 40 percent, 40 percent, and 34 percent, respectively.[6]

A second area identified by Ferber (1973b, p. 33) is saving behavior—"the allocation of available financial resources for a given period between spending and saving, specifically what amount or proportion of these total resources should be allocated to saving and what proportion or amount to spending." Closely related is a third area—asset management. Information about marital roles in both areas is very scarce and generally limited to one question about who takes care of savings or life insurance (e.g., Blood and Wolfe, 1960; Davis and Rigaux, 1974; Green and Cunningham, 1975; Haley et al., 1975; Sharp and Mott, 1956; Wolgast, 1958). More detailed data about marital roles in savings and insurance decisions are contained in the Starch (1958) report and in panel data collected by Ferber and Nicosia (1972).

The reasons why researchers have ignored financial management decisions relative to product-specific decisions are probably numerous. With the exception of financial institutions, there is no constituency for funding such research. The home economics literature has long contained a normative but largely nonempirical discussion of family financial management. It is also true that studies of durable goods buying frequently contain questions relevant to the family budget (e.g., deciding how much to spend and when to make the purchase, handling financing arrangements, or making monthly payments). The view of husband-wife involvement that emerges when these decisions are "piggy-backed" onto product decisions must surely be incomplete, however. Decisions to spend rather than save or to spend money for a new roof instead of a vacation involve "across-product" evaluations that cannot possibly be understood if one focuses only on one or two product categories.

A final area that has major economic consequences for the family concerns decisions about the number and spacing of children. Family planning programs generally assume that the wife is the major influence in a household's decision to use birth control practices. As a consequence, these programs are almost always directed toward women, and research is based almost exclusively on samples of women. The reasons for assuming that family planning is the wife's personal decision are numerous and surprisingly reminiscent of the logic encountered in consumer good studies. Consider the following:

1. Many modern birth control methods (e.g., IUD, pill) are used by women. It is convenient to assume that the person who uses a device will be the one who decides whether or not to adopt it.
2. Women are believed to be more receptive to the family planning concept than men. The day-to-day impact of having children falls more heavily on women. Women are also easier to reach since they are the ones who generally visit birth control or family planning clinics. Since children are presumably evidence of men's power and masculinity, it is often assumed that they want large, not small, families. Why promote a "product" to a market segment whose attitudes are basically neutral or even antagonistic?
3. The cost of reaching both spouses within the household must be weighed against the benefits of reaching more women. Program officials, who are typically evaluated on the basis of their activities rather than lowered birth rates, are likely to opt for reaching 10,000 women instead of 5,000 families.

Despite these "commonsense" reasons, recent studies have shown that husbands play an important, perhaps the major, role in family adoption decisions. In one of the earliest studies on the topic (Dubey and Choldin, 1967), the decision to use an IUD was made by the wife alone in only 7 percent of the cases. Husbands were reported to have made the final decision in 44 percent of the families. Other investigations carried out in both developed and underdeveloped countries confirm the husband's considerable influence in contraceptive use (Lam, 1968; Mercado, 1971; Mullen et al., n.d.; Pillai, 1971).

Some Recurring Findings

Three general findings about husband-wife involvement in consumer decisions continue to emerge from the many studies mentioned above.

Variability by Product Category. Husband-wife involvement varies widely by product category. This

---

6. It is interesting to note that the Ferber and Nicosia sample consisted entirely of young marrieds. Since Wells (1959) found increasing specialization of these tasks with length of marriage, it may be that the difference here is due to the sample composition.

seemingly obvious conclusion contrasts, nevertheless, with discussions about differences in men versus women as consumers without regard to specific products. Wolff (1958), for example, suggested that women more than men take a long time to make up their minds and are more stubborn about changing them. Women were also described as having a different sense of humor, a tendency toward irrational beliefs, and less desire for achievement, domination, or power. Not only have studies failed to document many of these differences, but when this absolute view of roles is applied to household decision making, the results have also led to curious contradictions. Marketing textbooks in the early sixties (Beckman and Davidson, 1962; Phillips and Duncan, 1964) described both the growing involvement of women in family decisions *and* the growing importance of men as buyers!

Variability within Product Category. Husband-wife involvement within any product category varies by specific decisions and decision stages. Early writings often equated purchasing decisions with actual purchasing activities such that the person who went shopping for a product was assumed to have also made the product and brand decision. This view undoubtedly underlies the folklore that women control 80 percent of every family dollar. According to Converse et al. (1958), this "finding" was based on the rather unbelievable fact that someone once counted shoppers in a city department store and found that 80 percent were women. Manufacturers and advertisers have also found it convenient to look for one dominant spouse in each product category. The studies reported earlier, however, demonstrate again and again that family-member participation varies within each product category depending on what is being done or decided. From any point of view, it is a serious oversimplification to talk about a product category as simply husband dominant, wife dominant, or joint.

The automobile purchase illustrates how variable husband-wife involvement really is. According to the Jaffe report (n.d.), wives were as involved as their husbands in gathering relevant information from people. Davis (1970) found 60 percent of couples classified as husband dominant for the decision about make of automobile but only 25 percent for the decision about color. Couples frequently shop together for the car and use the car equally after purchase.

Family-member involvement also seems to vary systematically at different stages in the decision-making process. In the family planning area, wives are found to be more involved than husbands in information seeking in contrast to initiating search or making the final adoption decision (Lam, 1968; Palmore, 1967). Davis and Rigaux (1974) obtained information about marital roles at each of three decision stages (problem recognition, search for information, and final decision) for 25 household decisions. While no significant differences were found in average relative influence across the three stages, the proportion of couples in the "joint" category was significantly less for the information search phase than for either of the other two phases. Similar data were reported by Wilkes (1975). Intercorrelations among relative influence scores in four decision stages (problem recognition, search, final decision, and purchase) were generally low. No significant association was found between "who purchased the major household good" and "who searched for information" ($r = .14$ for husbands; $r = .01$ for wives).

Variability among Families. Husband-wife involvement for any consumer decision is likely to show considerable variability among families. Discussion of marital roles frequently understate the variance that is found even in the case of highly specific decisions. To illustrate, the Starch report (1958, p. 59) concludes that "the husband, as the family 'authority' on mechanical matters, decides upon the make of the new family car." This conclusion was drawn from data showing that the husband decides in 61 percent of the families, the wife in 1 percent, and both in 38 percent. In contrast to the quotation, the data indicate that the decision about make of automobile is not actually the exclusive domain of husbands.

Some variability is even present in product categories characterized by a high degree of role specialization. The survey by Haley, Overholser and Associates (1975) reports the percentage of husbands who made purchases of packaged goods during the preceding seven days and the percentage who actually influenced the product and brand selected. In none of the 87 product categories did husbands make less than 10 percent of the purchases.

Marketing studies that show considerable variation in decision roles are paralleled in sociology. The Parsons and Bales (1955) theory, which predicts family role differentiation according to instrumental and socioeconomic functions, has been criticized. Aronoff and Crano (1975), for example, document that contrary to theoretical predictions, women make substantial contributions to subsistence production in over 800 societies.

Some Recurring Problems

At least four problem areas can be identified in the research dealing with family-member involvement in consumer decisions. It is useful to discuss each area in order to highlight future research priorities.

Choosing Decisions and Tasks. The issue raised here, though not unique to the study of household decision making, is fundamental to all the research just reviewed. Before family-member involvement can be measured, the relevant universe of decisions and decision-related tasks must be determined. Researchers (including the present author) typically select decisions on fairly arbitrary grounds and ignore the implications of these choices.[7]

What decisions should be included in order to measure family roles in a single product or expenditure category? What might first seem like an easy task becomes exceedingly complicated on execution. Consider, for example, grocery shopping. In one family, "going shopping" means walking to the store, picking out a "few things that look good for tonight's dinner," and returning home. In another family, "going shopping" includes preparing a detailed list, driving to the store with two preschool children, cashing a check, looking for store coupons, buying a week's groceries, returning home, and spending a half hour putting things away. Since the meaning of "grocery shopping" differs in the two families, so does the meaning of husband-wife involvement in this activity. It is only possible to interpret answers to such questions once it is clear what *actual* task the respondent is asked to evaluate.

Attempts to specify various stages in the decision-making process are also subject to the same problems. Granbois (1963), as well as Davis and Rigaux (1974), employed traditional formulations of problem-solving behavior—i.e., problem recognition, determination of alternatives via search, and selection from among recognized alternatives. Gredal (1966) divided the purchasing process into a series of four gradual decisions ranging from the initial suggestion to the actual purchase. Specifically, she hypothesized a general purchasing or budgeting decision (how much money can be spent on individual items and how it is to be distributed among these), a concrete purchasing decision (e.g., "Let's buy a new car"), a series of selection decisions (price, quality, brand, store), and finally, a technical purchasing action (placing the order and picking up the product).[8]

Jaffe and Senft (1966) proposed an even more elaborate framework including information seeking (via people and media), a prepurchase stage (initiating, selecting the type and brand, and budgeting), a buying stage (shopping and purchasing), and finally, a postpurchase stage (using and evaluating). All these formulations suffer from the same problem: They *begin* by assuming that households actually go through these stages. The fact that questionnaires are "correctly" filled out does not justify these questions. Is it any wonder that respondents enjoy answering questions that confirm the logic, rationality, and careful thought given to past decisions?

Studies of household decision making may also want to develop an overall measure of decision-making roles rather than limiting the focus to a single product category. While the objectives of such studies are somewhat different, the problem of specifying relevant decisions is exactly the same as just described.

---

7. As an example, it is interesting to note how frequently the Blood and Wolfe (1960) measure of power was used by other researchers simply because the study was widely cited.

8. Partial support for this typology of decisions and activities is found in a study of husband-wife influence in 12 automobile and furniture purchase decisions (Davis, 1970). Using a clustering technique to group decisions together in terms of their similarities on relative influence, two bases for role differentiation were apparent. The first was the product itself—decision roles in the purchase of an automobile were not related to decision roles in the purchase of furniture. Simply stated, knowing the roles played by a husband and wife in buying a car provides little or no information about who makes furniture purchase decisions in the same family. The study also showed that roles were differentiated on the basis of the type of decision being made. Within each product category, relative influence in "product-selection" decisions (what model, make, and color to buy) were unrelated to relative influence in "allocation" or "scheduling" decisions (how much to spend and when to buy the car). The decisions labeled as "product selection" seem very close to Gredal's (1966) selection decision. Moreover, the "allocation" decisions are similar to a general purchasing or budgetary decision. It would be interesting to know if additional questions about who made the initial suggestion and who assumed responsibility for shopping would form the two additional clusters suggested by Gredal.

Families in different situations face a different set of decisions and tasks. A low-income household, for example, is not likely to spend much time considering details of a new home purchase. A family with three young children faces an additional set of decisions not present in a childless family. It is of doubtful validity, then, to compare marital roles across families when the universe of actual decisions and tasks is not the same or the weights attached to the same decision are different.

One possible way to deal with this problem is to obtain time budgets within families. An impressive international study (Szalai, 1972), which included about 30,000 time budgets drawn from 12 nations, illustrates the richness of data stemming from this procedure and shows its relevance to household decision making. Patterns of daily life were recorded in nine categories broken down into 96 specific activities. The 24-hour diaries included not only what activities were performed but also time, place, and duration. Secondary activities that occurred simultaneously with the primary activity were also obtained. Data such as these would provide a basis for defining a family's relevant decision and task universe, which could then be used to measure who is involved.

A second approach to solving this problem is found in emerging typologies of household economic decisions. Ferber (1973b) classified financial decisions into four groups—money management, spending behavior, saving behavior, and asset management. Other writers have suggested product typologies that may explain family-member involvement in spending decisions. Gredal (1966) used the dimensions of durable versus nondurable goods and individual versus collective consumption. Individual decision making was hypothesized to be least important for durable goods collectively consumed and most important for nondurables individually consumed. Lovell, Meadows, and Rampley (1968) suggested a longer list of factors affecting the extent of interhousehold influence, including (1) whether the product is jointly or individually consumed, (2) whether it is consumed by children or adults, (3) whether the brand name is clearly visible during use, and (4) whether the product is changed between purchase and use. They hypothesized greater family influence either for durables jointly consumed by husband and wife or for products individually consumed by adults when the brand was visible during use and unchanged by the housewife after purchase. A typology of family consumption by final product is that suggested by Sheth (1974). He classified consumption by individual members (e.g., razor blades for the husband, lipstick for the wife), the family as a whole (e.g., food), and the household unit (i.e., products used indirectly, such as paint or a lawnmower, for maintaining the physical dwelling).

These typologies have been of limited use to date. With few exceptions, they have been developed on an a priori basis. Whether, in fact, the decisions classified together are similar has not been empirically established. Nevertheless, they represent an important first step toward defining the total universe of a household's economic decisions and specifying common decision characteristics that may influence "who is involved."

Specifying the Relevant Decision-Making Unit. The reader is now painfully aware that the "family" in most studies of household decision making is in reality just the husband and wife. While critics of consumer behavior research might argue that this is at least an improvement over research that "forces" decisions into an individual framework, this perspective is still a partial one.

Researchers have probably been guided by intuition in specifying the husband and wife as the relevant decision-making unit for durable goods buying. Measures of influence become exceedingly complicated if more than two people are involved. It is also likely that the desire for comparability of research has tended to focus attention on the husband-wife dyad.

Whatever the reasons, serious problems do exist. The relevant decision-making unit is specified a priori by the research design rather than by the household. Casual observation suggests that some consumer decisions involve other than a husband-wife dyad, e.g., child-wife for cereals or husband-son for sporting equipment. Parents, as well as friends and relatives, can also participate in "family" decisions. It is also possible that the relevant decision-making unit varies throughout the decision-making process. For example, husband and wife decide together about whether to buy a new car or repair the old one; the husband and teenage son decide about what make to buy.

The solution to this problem is not an easy one. Davis (1972a) used information about who talked to whom regarding specific automobile purchase decisions as a method of verifying if the husband and wife were, in fact, the relevant decision-making unit. The results showed differences by families and decisions. (Husbands discussed what make of car to buy with other people as often as they discussed it with their wives.) Perhaps families and/or decisions should be grouped into common decision units *before* the part played by each member is assessed.

Further complicating this issue is the fact that different measures of influence often point toward a different decision unit as being relevant. Turk and Bell (1972) found that children had power—sometimes substantial—when observational measures were used, but they had no power when the same couples were asked to provide self-reports of decision-making power.

Measuring Involvement. The problems of measuring who participates in household decisions are embedded in the two problem areas already described. Several recurring problems should be mentioned, nevertheless.

Relative Influence versus Total Influence. The great majority of studies make use of a scale that measures the relative influence of husband versus wife. This approach has the advantage of being widely used and thus permitting comparisons across studies. Bernhardt (1974) argued that such scales assume an equal amount of influence associated with each decision, which is then partitioned between husband and wife. In reality, a wife may feel that she exerted substantial influence in some decisions and little influence in others quite *independent* of the part played by her husband. Bernhardt proposed an alternative approach whereby each spouse first assesses how much influence he/she had and then how much the spouse had in various decisions. The result is a measure of both total and relative influence. Thus, four housing decisions—choice of house, of community, and of neighborhood, and architectural style—were classified as joint. The latter decision, however, revealed a low level of husband-wife influence in contrast to the other three.

Response Categories. Researchers have utilized various response formats in order to measure purchase influence. Undoubtedly, the most common measure is a 5-point Likert scale ranging from "husband decided" to "wife decided." Some researchers have used a 3-point scale, which has the effect of increasing the expected level of agreement between husbands and wives as well as possibly altering the proportion of families that fall into the "jointly decided" category. Other studies further divide "equal-influence" responses into syncratic (i.e., always decide together) and autonomic (i.e., sometimes one spouse, sometimes the other) in order to obtain a more sensitive measure of the amount of role specialization. Influence has also been measured by asking each spouse to divide 10 points so as to show "share of husband and wife influence" (Haley et al., 1975). More attention should be given to whether these differing response formats yield comparable results.

Number of Respondents per Family. Two conclusions on how many family members to question can be supported from the literature. If the purpose of a study is limited to describing the relative influence of husband and wife in various decisions, it is sufficient to question only one spouse. Considerable evidence shows that the responses of husbands and wives are very similar when compared on an aggregate basis (Davis, 1970; Granbois and Willett, 1970; Wilkening and Morrison, 1963). If, on the other hand, the researcher wants to use a measure of influence in subsequent analyses (particularly prediction studies), data should be collected from both spouses.

The percentage of couples who agree about the roles played by family members in decision making varies from 30 to 80 percent depending in part on the subject area, the specificity of questions asked, and the skewness of responses. Disagreements are particularly high in areas of communication and decision making—a finding that is worrisome since many studies operationalize the authority relationship between husband and wife in terms of decision-making behavior (Morgan, 1968; Olson, 1969).

A related issue is whether children, particularly adolescents and teenagers, can be used as reporters. An early study by Converse and Crawford (1949) used college students to assess family-member involvement in 19 expenditure categories. Although this study provided no estimate of reliability or validity, Marshall (1963) reported very low intercorrelations when children's and parents' reports about the child's use of money were compared.

Self-reported versus Communication Measures. A lively controversy surrounds the issue whether influence should be measured by self-reports or interaction analysis. Research has shown that when comparing husbands' and wives' responses, global reports about "who is the boss" or "who makes major decisions" are less valid than product-specific reports (Davis, 1971; Wilkes, 1975). Respondents apparently find it easier to recall decisions about specific choices and activities, particularly if a purchase occurred months or years ago. Even here the level of agreement between spouses in response to very specific decisions is far from perfect.[9] Thus, a more fundamental issue regarding self-reports is whether couples can meaningfully think in terms of decision outcomes or power. As Kenkel (1961, p. 159) has remarked:

> *This assumes, of course, that individuals know the relative amount of influence they have, that they are willing to admit it to themselves and others, and that they are able to recall with accuracy how influence was distributed in some past decision-making session.*

Olson and Rabunsky (1972) reported that individuals can more accurately report *what* decisions were made than *who* actually made them. It seems likely that respondents, faced with the tasks of answering questions that have little meaning, will respond in terms of what they consider to be the socially desirable role, namely, who should decide.

Interaction-based measures represent another tradition of research on family decision making (Kenkel, 1963; Mishler and Waxler, 1968; Strodtbeck, 1951). Power is measured in different ways. Kenkel asked families to decide how they would spend an imaginary gift of $300. A spouse's power was measured by the proportion of items "purchased" that were initially suggested by that person. Strodtbeck also used decision outcomes as a measure of power by noting who won a series of revealed-difference discussions. Other studies have focused on aspects of the interaction itself, e.g., the proportion of instrumental acts initiated or the proportion of interruptions initiated by each person.

As is the case with self-reports, these measures also have limitations. Bales' (1950) Interaction Process Analysis excludes nonverbal communication, which is undoubtedly an important indicator of power in long-lasting groups such as the family. The laboratory certainly has an impact on "normal" family interaction: it is a highly reactive environment. The simulated problems given to families by researchers also reinforce the artificiality of the situation. Zelditch (1971) has argued persuasively that one cannot equate a family's laboratory behavior with the behavior of natural families. On the one hand, experiments remove many "place cues" that impinge on families in normal decision-making situations. On the other hand, since families are more complex than the ad hoc small group, it becomes difficult for researchers to study a single phenomenon isolated from other family processes.

These issues aside, it seems clear that self-reports and interaction measures yield differing assessments of who is involved. Turk and Bell (1972) compared eight different measures of power within the same families. The measures were not highly interrelated. Only two associations (out of 36) were greater than .60; .81 percent were in the range of ±.20. Thus, researchers must deal with the problem that characterizing families in terms of power will differ depending on which commonly used measure is employed.

The solution to these problems does not lie principally in methodological improvements—e.g., using more specific questions, specifying the appropriate referent, reducing the lag between decision and data collection, or asking more members within the same family. More important is how decision making itself is conceptualized. It seems likely that measures of *decision outcome* (e.g., who decided or who won) tap a very different aspect of decision making than do measures of the *decision process* (e.g., who initiated the most instrumental acts or interruptions). In this regard, Turner (1970) has suggested that wives are often able to exercise considerable influence in family decisions while at the same time accepting their husbands' superior authority. This is possible because the husband's authority and the wife's centrality in the network may be positively related: the greater the husband's recognized authority is, the fewer will be the direct requests made to him by his children.

As Turner (1970, p. 123) concludes: "An interesting speculation, empirically untested, is the hypothesis that the more unequal the authority of the father in the family, the more powerful the offsetting dominance arising out of the centrality of the

9. Convergent validity for seven automobile and seven furniture purchase decisions was reported as .66 and .61 by Davis (1971). Wilkes (1975) reported correlations ranging between .59 and .79 for specific stages in the decision process. These data show that the maximum variance explained by comparing both spouses' assessment of the same decision is only 56 percent.

mother." Students of consumer behavior have not even begun to consider which orientation (i.e., decision outcome or process) is the most relevant for particular purposes. More attention is given to this issue in the next major section of this paper.

Explaining Variability in Involvement. Researchers have devoted little attention to explaining why, for the same decision, families vary in "who decides." This issue will undoubtedly become more important as efforts are made to "locate" families having particular role patterns. Although a number of theoretical perspectives are available in the sociological and economics literature, these have not been systematically studied in terms of predicting purchase influence within families. Three general conceptions of how tasks and authority are allocated within families are described here.

Cultural Role Expectations. A number of sociologists have suggested that power and task responsibility are built into the roles of husband and wife on the basis of cultural norms and controls (Burgess and Locke, 1960; Parsons and Bales, 1955). Similar to French and Raven's (1959) concept of "legitimate power," a spouse's authority is based on the belief that he or she *should* make a decision or carry out a task irrespective of the actual skills or interest that may be present. The source of a spouse's power is thus external to the family: Power resides in the position rather than in the person. A traditional role ideology specifies large authority differences between husband and wife and a highly differentiated division of labor. A husband will decide what make of automobile to buy and his wife what to serve for dinner when guests are invited, simply because these two decisions *should* be made by husbands and wives, respectively. Sharp distinctions are drawn between "things" that are masculine or feminine.

A companionship ideology, in contrast, prescribes a high degree of joint participation in tasks and decisions. Togetherness is viewed as a desirable end in and of itself. A husband may, therefore, help his wife cook and shop because he wants to spend more time with her. His wife may learn how to ski so that they can spend more of their leisure time together. When authority or tasks are delegated, they are done so only on a temporary and often expedient basis.

Measures of cultural role expectations are either direct or indirect. The direct measures include a large number of scales that ask respondents to agree or disagree about various aspects of the husband's, wife's, and parents' role (e.g., "Marriage is the best career for a woman," "A wife should fit her life to her husband," "I consider the kitchen as the wife's room," or "It is somehow unnatural to place women in positions of authority over men"). Indirect measures attempt to locate categories of families or people that hold a different set of role expectations. Thus, sociologists have found traditional role ideologies more common within families in later stages of the life cycle and among people with no college education, in blue-collar occupations, and with authoritarian personalities.

Comparative Resources. A second conceptualization of the allocation of tasks and authority within families views each marital partner as a source of valued resources to the other (Blau, 1964; Blood and Wolfe, 1960; Scanzoni, 1970). Responsibility for decision making is assigned to the husband and wife on the basis of each one's ability to reward or punish, personal attractiveness, or competence. These "resources," possessed in varying degrees by each spouse, are exchanged for the right to make (or not to make) decisions or to participate (or not to participate) in family activities. Unlike cultural role expectations, exchange theory views the determinants of decision roles to be internal to the family itself. If the resources controlled by either spouse change, their decision and task involvement should also change.

Measures of comparative resources have been developed at both general and specific levels. Resources such as the husband's educational and occupational status are an illustration of the first of these levels. Scanzoni (1970, pp. 147–48) provides an explicit rationale for this relationship:

> *The more the husband fulfills his economic duties . . . , and thus the more the wife defines her status rights . . . [as] being met, the more she will allow her husband to define the norms for . . . decision-making. . . . She . . . gives him power to shape this dimension of the conjugal unit, in exchange for the economic rewards and status benefits he provides for her vis-à-vis the larger community. She is more motivated to "go along" with him, to "give in" to him, to let him "have his way" to the extent that he provides maximum economic rewards.*

If the wife controls resources such as a college education or high occupational status, the husband's "right to govern" is likely to be attenuated. An appropriate measure, therefore, is a score that reflects the difference between the husband's and wife's education or occupational status. Resources also include such specific factors as the time available for decision making. For example, wives have been found to lose influence vis-à-vis their husbands during the child-rearing stage of the family life cycle (Blood and Wolfe, 1960). The reason appears to be the combined effects of having to care for children and of having to give up activities outside the home. Because wives have less time to be involved in decision making and less to contribute in terms of financial resources and information, they become more dependent on their husbands during this period.

Researchers interested in studying the effect of time pressures on household decision making will have to construct indices from sets of background characteristics. In order to construct a measure of the wife's time pressure, one might incorporate the number and ages of children, whether the wife is employed, availability of domestic help, and size of dwelling, among others.

Relative Investment. Closely related to the previous conceptualization is the relative investment that each spouse has in a particular decision domain. Typically, the outcomes of a decision do not fall evenly across all family members. These assessments of the costs and/or benefits associated with particular outcomes should influence whether and how each participates in a given choice situation. Two important differences distinguish the relative-investment and the comparative-resources explanations. First, resources define the *potential* to exert influence while investment defines the *motivation* of a family member to exert influence. Second, relative investment leads to predictions about family-member involvement in specific decisions rather than about the general authority structure of the family.

Two economic theories are relevant to this third conceptualization. Coleman (1966) proposed that when individuals face a sequence of decisions, it is possible for them to give up control over those of little interest for more control over those of greater interest. An individual's power is defined as the ability to obtain outcomes that yield the highest utility. If one family member has control over actions that are important to others, he has a valuable resource that can be explained for the purpose of "getting his way" over actions that are more important to him. Coleman develops a precise algebraic expression for the power of an individual in a system of collective decisions.

Becker's (1973, 1974) "Theory of Marriage" represents another attempt to explain family behavior in economic terms. Spouses are assumed to maximize the consumption of household-produced commodities, which leads to optimal strategies regarding mate selection, love and caring, the incidence of polygamy, etc. The theory predicts that high-wage men will marry low-wage women to gain from the division of labor, that high-income persons marry earlier than low-income persons, and that high-income, high-education people are less likely to divorce than others. Although this framework has not yet been specifically applied to predict family-member participation in decision making and tasks, the extension could certainly be made.

These three conceptualizations need to be tested together as predictors of marital roles. They are probably complementary rather than alternative explanations. French and Raven (1959, p. 155) have drawn attention to the several bases of power in small groups:

> *It is rare that we can say with certainty that a given empirical case of power is limited to one source. Normally, the relation between O [a person, role, norm, or group] and P [a person] will be characterized by several qualitatively different variables which are bases of power.*

They may or may not reinforce each other. In traditional societies, a traditional family ideology is reinforced by the distribution of resources between husband and wife (e.g., women are denied occupational opportunities or family property rights). In modern societies, the stage is often set for conflict since comparative investment or resources may not be consistent with cultural role expectations. Finally, the predictive power of each conceptualization may differ by family and/or product category. Role expectations are likely to be a more important determinant of marital roles during the early years of marriage and less important during the later years. In the same way, role expectations may do a good job of explaining the general division of labor within the household (i.e., whether the wife is employed), while relative investment is a better predictor of involvement in specific product categories.

This discussion should also underline the fact that current efforts to explain this variability are not likely to be successful. Long lists of conventional demographic, attitudinal, or personality variables mechanically regressed against purchase influence reflect neither the appropriate form of the variables (e.g., difference measures between husband versus wife) nor the correct variables themselves (e.g., time pressure or one's stake in the decision).

Process of Decision Making within Families

The problem areas just described are symptomatic of underlying problems with the research to date. Prescribed roles of husband and wife are probably good predictors of "who decides" in stable societies. However, in developed Western societies norms of shared interest, give and take, and companionship are likely to exist. In this situation it is difficult to predict who will win or decide.

Many of the studies already reviewed focus on the outcomes of decision making rather than on the process that has led to these outcomes. The result is that little has been learned about how families actually reach decisions. To use an analogy suggested by Sprey (1971), it is as though one has tried to understand the game of chess by looking only at the outcomes of each game, ignoring entirely the strategies used by each player.

This section describes some issues related to how families make decisions. It is argued that group decision making differs in some important respects from individual decision making. First, group members may not necessarily agree about goals, and agreement is not necessary to reach decisions. Second, families as groups have characteristics that differ from problem-solving groups in organizations or in the laboratory. Third, a repertoire of decision-making strategies is available, with their use depending on what is appropriate to the situation.

There is little research that is relevant to group decision-making processes.[10] The emphasis is still very much on the individual. No theory of household decision making will emerge, nor will research findings build on one another, until the nature of these processes is made explicit.

Decision Making as Consensual versus Accommodative

Using an analogy from organization theory (Thompson and Tuden, 1959), two "ideal" representations of a group making a purchase decision can be proposed. If decision making is consensual, there is either unanimity about what value—i.e., desired outcome—is relevant in the decision or no conflict among group members in the case where several values are relevant. The satisficing criterion (Simon, 1955) would predict that the group will engage in problem solving and will continue to search for alternatives until one is found that satisfies the minimum level of expectations of all members with respect to the value or values perceived as being relevant. If differences between members arise during the search process, the discussion will center only around questions of fact, i.e., whether a particular alternative will really satisfy the value in question. Relying on the judgment of all or a majority of group members, a choice will be made to which all will give equal consent without holding private reservations or resentments about the outcome.

A second "ideal" type of group decision is accommodative rather than consensual; that is, through discussion or observation, group members realize that priorities and preferences are irreconcilable. Even if the group can agree about the likely consequences of each choice, there will be no way that one alternative can be satisfying to all. Bargaining, coercion, and other means may be used to reach an acceptable solution. If the group is successful in this process, the commitment of each person to the solution will be conditional on others carrying out the terms of the compromise. The whole decision area can be reopened for further discussion when, for example, one member perceives that the resulting purchase is not entirely in accord with the agreed-on solution.

While the research evidence is limited, some authors suggest that groups, and particularly families, quite often bargain, compromise, and coerce rather than problem-solve in arriving at decisions. Blood (1960) argues that the involuntary and diffuse character of family relationships and the family's small size and changing developmental tasks lead to a high degree of conflict. Sprey (1969) maintains that treating the family as though the normal state were one of

10. An exception is a paper by Sheth (1974) that applies a modified Howard-Sheth model to family decision making.

agreement and stability is inadequate, since decisions are frequently an on-going confrontation between members having interests in a common situation. It is important, according to Sprey, to understand how conflict management is possible through a set of mutually agreed-on rules. Weick (1971, p. 26) maintains that groups often form around common ends (means interdependencies) rather than common objectives: "In any potential collectivity, members have different interests, capabilities, preferences, and so forth. They want to accomplish different things. However, to achieve some of these diverse ends, concerted, interdependent actions are required."

It is significant to note that it is not necessary for a husband and wife to agree about objectives in order for them to exchange behaviors viewed as mutually rewarding. Weick continues by suggesting that the relationship between means and ends is continuous–i.e., common means will, over time, promote common objectives. One of the initial common objectives is preserving the group itself via the statement and articulation of norms, role specialization, and communication regularity. By preserving the group, members can continue to pursue diverse ends.

Three marketing studies have compared the goals or perceptions of husbands and wives. Project Home (Raymond Loewy/William Snaith, 1967) compared husbands' and wives' "motivations" in home buying within several segments of the market (e.g., first house, upgrade, retiree, two-family home). Substantial disagreements were found between males and females in the upgrade market based on the criteria of privacy, investment, children, and socializing. An apt summary of the differences in the orientation of men and women is as follows: "A man tolerates buying a house for the sake of the woman, while she tolerates the man for the sake of the home" (p. 15). One of the criteria–convenience–was even defined differently by husbands and wives. To women its meaning was functional convenience; men viewed convenience more personally–close to work and/or suitable for relaxation.

Doyle and Hutchinson (1973) presented the results of a multidimensional analysis of automobiles. Although the perceptual spaces were similar, men and women tended to weigh the two dimensions of size and quality (or luxury) differently. Finally, Cox (1975) found a curvilinear relationship between length of marriage and the amount of spousal agreement in preference for new automobile makes. The level of agreement was highest for couples in the intermediate stages of the life cycle.

In the area of family planning, a study by Poffenberger (1969) revealed marked differences in attitudes between husbands and wives regarding low fertility. Husbands emphasized the positive effects of low fertility on living costs and children's educational opportunities. Wives, in contrast, viewed low fertility as an advantage in terms of reducing their work load.

These results suggest that a goal-oriented, problem-solving approach is likely to characterize only a portion of a household's economic decisions. Future research needs to consider the relative frequency of consensual versus accommodative decision making within families. Moreover, little is known about the extent of goal agreement as a function of product category or such family characteristics as social class, race, or the wife's employment status. The accommodative model also points out that each spouse can engage in the same consumption behavior for different reasons. The diversity of ends that can support the same behavior within families needs to be explored.

Group Decision Making versus Family Decision Making

A number of writers have suggested that families, more than other groups, are likely to be "poor" decision makers. This is owing, in part, to the environment in which families decide, the nontask needs that impinge on all decisions, and the interrelatedness of family decisions. Each of these reasons is briefly considered here.

The Environment of Family Decision Making. Laboratory groups are studied under "ideal" environmental conditions. Members are rested, and meetings take place in rooms with good lighting, comfortable temperatures, and seating arrangements that encourage group interaction. Distractions are at a minimum. How does this environment compare with the typical family decision-making session? In the first place, families are often together when energy levels are low –early in the morning or late in the day. Little research has been conducted about decision making under conditions of fatigue although there is a good deal of folklore about the decisions of people "who can't get started in the morning" or "who are too tired to think in the evening." Second, family decision making is undoubtedly subject to distraction. In the morning, the demands of preparing breakfast, or the pressure to leave for work, interfere with concentrated problem solving. The evening contains many of the same distractions—dinner, TV, outside activities. Young children not only make constant demands on their parents throughout the day but also frequently interrupt the parents' conversations.

Although no research on the effects of distraction has been done using families, a laboratory study by Wright (1974) is instructive. He found that distraction (a taped radio program at different volume levels) had the effect of increasing the salience of negative evidence and lowering the number of dimensions on which alternatives were evaluated. It does appear, therefore, that the environment can alter strategies used for making decisions.

The Maintenance Needs of Families. Because of the long-lasting nature of family relationships, actions are frequently taken that assure continuance of the group. This contrasts with the ad hoc laboratory group that exists for a very short period of time. In contrast to a committee or task force, problem situations may be viewed as a threat to the stability of the family, particularly if they are novel or have no obvious solution. One manner of dealing with this situation is to avoid the issue itself and focus instead on group maintenance by minimizing expressions of conflicts and the number of alternatives considered. Aldous (1971, p. 267) suggests that the emphasis within families "tends to be one of reducing the tension-laden situations to an innocuous level rather than submitting the problem to rigorous analysis and assessing the consequences of possible alternative strategies." Legitimate roles can be used to reduce conflict, and this can also have the effect of lowering the quality of decisions. It may be that in the interests of reducing conflict and reaffirming legitimate power (French and Raven, 1959), decisions may be made by a person with less expertise. Weick (1971, pp. 5–6) described this intentional masking of expert power as a "delicate problem of balancing legitimacy with expertness in problem solving procedures" and one that differentiates the family from other decision-making groups.

Results from a series of focus-group interviews (Davis, 1972b) showed that consumers are very much aware of group-maintenance needs in describing their own family decisions. Conflict in at least three areas was described—who should make various purchase decisions, how the decisions should be made (amount of search, reliance on advertising, personal recommendations), and who should implement the decision. Since product-choice situations provide one context in which disagreements arise about appropriate roles in decision making, it is easy for family members to confuse the source of conflict. To the extent that they are confused about the reasons for disagreement, attempts to resolve conflict are likely to be unsuccessful. It is also difficult for the researcher to separate truly product-related disagreements from those relating to family-maintenance needs.

The Interrelatedness of Family Decisions. The typical problem dealt with by committees or laboratory groups is defined and worked on in isolation from other problems. This bypasses a number of questions relevant to the dynamics of family problem solving. Weick (1971, p. 9) succinctly describes the differences as follows:

> *They [laboratory groups] bypass such questions as how one comes to know that a problem exists, what it does to solution adequacy to be working on several different things* concurrently *with problem solving, what it's like to go about solving a felt, intuited problem rather than an explicitly stated consensually validated problem which was made visible to all members at a specific point in time.*

Families face several problems concurrently. It is likely that among this set the most unambiguous and identifiable problems are solved first. This suggested to Aldous (1971) that the problems which families actually solve are likely to be the unimportant ones. More far-reaching problems may remain undefined or unresolved. This is true for at least two reasons. First, a husband and wife may fixate on different aspects of the problem. A husband, for example, may see the automobile "problem" as uncertainty about getting to work on time or the cost of repairs. His wife, on the other hand, might define the "problem" as the extra burden of monthly payments or her husband's infatuation with cars. Because they do not define the "problem" similarly, it may be dropped and not resolved. A second reason that can delay decisions is the impact which each spouse's solution has on the other spouse, either in the same problem area or in different problem areas. Faced with a limited budget, a new car purchase, for example, precludes new carpeting.

Support for these hypotheses is found in at least two studies. Foote (1974) analyzed data from a three-generation study (Hill, 1970) based on 120 grandparent, 120 parent, and 120 young married families. He found both a high proportion of purchases that were not preceded by plans and a high proportion of planned purchases that were not fulfilled. In fact, in all generations unfulfilled plans and unplanned actions predominated over fulfilled plans and planned actions. The reasons for the discrepancies between plans and actions were numerous and often related to uncontrollable problems and immediate opportunities. This finding is in accord with Weick (1971) and Aldous (1971), who both asserted that families may be more solution oriented than problem oriented. According to Weick, it is the appearance of a solution that really precipitates choice, since family members often have only a vague sense of problems. Families frequently describe disagreements about whether a given purchase was legitimate. They disagree about such things as the timing of a purchase, whether it was *really* necessary, and whether other solutions for satisfying the same need might have existed (Davis, 1972b).

Existing research has tended to focus on "go-ahead" decisions as a means of understanding family decision processes; that is, having made or being about to make a purchase, families are queried about how this came about. Equally important, if not more so, are actions taken to abort or postpone consumer purchases given the interrelatedness of family decisions. Much could be learned about a household's priority patterns and the influence of different family members by recording not only whose purchase suggestions were realized but also whose suggestions were denied or tabled and for what reasons.

Alternative Decision-Making Strategies. Table 1 summarizes various decision-making strategies under the two models of consensus and accommodation. A brief description of each strategy is presented here.[11]

Role Structure. The role-structure strategy serves to lessen or even eliminate the need for discussion by making one person (or sometimes two) responsible for the decision. Frequently, family members come to accept one person as a "specialist" in a particular sphere of activity, thus making legitimate his or her right to decide without interference. Often, this expertise is maintained by developing a specialized jargon, by creating an air of mystery about how to perform the task, or by ridiculing the performance of others when they try to perform the same task.

Budgets. In the budget strategy, which is a second form of bureaucracy, decision responsibility is "controlled" by an impersonal arbitrator. Instead of nightly or morning crises, conflict can be restricted to once-a-week meetings at which time criteria of fairness and equity may receive more attention. Rules also serve to "institutionalize" power or coercion. Parents who believe that children should eat everything on their plates can establish a household rule. Thus, when children object, the mother can respond, "That's the rule—now eat!" If a wife has exceeded the clothing allowance set up by her husband, she may place the blame on the budget itself rather than on her husband for having set up such a small allowance. As Blood (1960, p. 215) concludes, "The process of agreeing on a budget is still liable to plenty of conflict, but, once formulated, a budget tends to divert attention from the hostile antagonist to the operational code."

Problem Solving. When agreement exists about which goals are desirable, problem-solving behavior is likely. "Experts," both within and outside the family, can be relied on to provide "proof" of the merit of one alternative versus others. Family discussion can produce a "better solution" than that originally put forth by any of the members individually. Although there have been few studies of problem-solving effectiveness in families, research on other small groups suggests some factors that may be applicable. Groups, for example, can ask more questions and get more information than any individual could alone. In this case, more alternatives will be generated and more complete information obtained about the likely consequences of each alternative.

An example, perhaps, of a better solution is the "multiple purchase." As a way of resolving conflict or trying to avoid it, two or more brands can be purchased instead of one. Instead of a color TV, two black and white sets can be bought for the same outlay. The family vacation can be divided into two separate two-week segments if members are unable

11. A more detailed description of each strategy is contained in Davis (1972b). Sheth and Cosmas (1975) have also studied four alternative decision strategies in the purchase of automobiles and furniture—problem solving, persuasion, bargaining, and politicking.

TABLE 1
Alternative Decision-Making Strategies

Goals	*Strategy*	*Ways of Implementing*
"Consensus" (Family members agree about goals)	Role structure	"The Specialist"
	Budgets	"The Controller"
	Problem solving	"The Expert" "The Better Solution" "The Multiple Purchase"
"Accommodation" (Family members disagree about goals)	Persuasion	"The Irresponsible Critic" "Feminine Intuition" "Shopping Together" "Coercion" "Coalitions"
	Bargaining	"The Next Purchase" "The Impulse Purchase" "The Procrastinator"

to agree on one site. Blood (1960, pp. 214–15) has observed that "the current trends to a second car, a second television set, and a second telephone result not only in increased profits for the corresponding manufacturers but in decreased tension for family personnel who can now use parallel facilities simultaneously instead of having to compete for control of single channels."

Persuasion Strategies. When family members do not agree about goals, strategies of persuasion and bargaining are likely. The distinction between these two strategies is not a sharp one. Persuasion can be viewed as a way of forcing someone to make a decision that they would not otherwise make. Bargaining, on the other hand, leads to willing agreement since by doing so both parties tend to gain.

Typically, the person who has the authority to make a particular decision also gets the credit or blame for how the decision turns out. Those who are freed from this responsibility can try to seize on certain of the advantages of being dominated. Thus, the "irresponsible critic" can put forth ideas freely without having to worry how realistic they might be. The "nagging wife," for example, can criticize her husband freely. If it turns out that he was right, she has nothing to lose; if he was wrong, she can adopt the self-satisfying stance of "I told you so." In the extreme case, the husband may become so tired of hearing his wife begin the same tirade that he prefers to concede to her regardless of the decision area.

When a wife is dominated by her husband, she may have to resort to a strategy referred to in folklore as "feminine intuition"; that is, she learns to identify the moods in which he is most susceptible to new ideas or persuasion. She may also find types of appeals to which he is especially weak. Television programs in the U.S. are filled with stories of wives "plotting" against their husbands to get a new fur coat, living-room furniture, or the like. The presence of this facility (to the extent that it actually exists) may have some basis in fact. As Turner (1970, p. 189) reasons:

> *Under the long-standing subordination of women to men, learning to detect and interpret the subtle gestures of the opposite sex accurately has been more adaptive for the woman than for the man. Such learning comes partly from individual discovery during the socialization process, partly from the accumulation of a woman's repertoire of folk techniques for understanding and dealing with men, and partly from the selective direction of attention during interaction.*

An interesting persuasion strategy is to take another family member along when shopping for a product. "Shopping together" has the effect of securing a commitment from the other person. Having said Yes, it is more difficult for that person to back out of the decision at a later time.

"Coercion" is the most extreme form of persuasion since it implies unwilling agreement. The use of this strategy within the family is probably common when there are large authority differences among family members and no cultural norms exist against its use.

"Coalitions" can be formed within the family for the purpose of forcing the lone individual or minority to join with the majority. In cohesive groups, such as the family, the success of appeals designed to bring dissenters into line is probably high.

Bargaining Strategies. Unlike the persuasion strategies just mentioned, which represent relatively short-run efforts to win a specific decision, bargaining involves longer-term considerations. Thus, a wife may be willing to lose a given encounter on the grounds that she will "get her way" in a later decision. Given the long-run and diffuse nature of most family relationships, this situation poses difficult problems for researchers interested in understanding the decision process for one specific consumer good at one point in time. Explicit or tacit agreements may exist as a result of a decision made in a quite different area at an earlier time that will affect the outcome of a current choice.

Waiting for the "next purchase" is an obvious approach if one feels that one will lose or "use up" goodwill by forcing a showdown on a contested decision. The husband can say, for example, "O.K., you buy the fur coat but I'm going to take the two-week fishing vacation with the boys."

The timing of a purchase itself can be used as a strategy. An "impulse purchase" is similar to the first move in a game of strategy. A husband can choose to drive home a new car that he has just purchased without any prior discussion with his wife. The wife may view the decision as already having been made. Moreover, having seen the car, she may conclude that she really likes it.

"Procrastinating" is another way of continuing the bargaining process after a choice has been made. If the wife delays making a purchase that has been agreed on, new information may develop or the situation can change such that the original choice can be changed. In this case, she can easily assign the blame to an outside party, thereby concealing her own delaying tactics—e.g., "By the time I got to the travel agent, the tour was completely full," or "The store didn't have any more."

From this discussion of how decisions are made within families, we can see that the approach is much broader than simply determining who is involved in various decisions and tasks. Research should be directed to these alternative decision strategies—to specifying the circumstances under which each will be used in the same family and how their use differs among families.

Consequences of Husband-Wife Involvement and Decision Strategies

In discussing the Ferber (1973b) review paper, Hill and Klein (1973, p. 372) presented Guy Orcutt's comments on the lack of evidence about whether family decision roles make any difference. "I would like to have seen some evidence point up the implications of different role-playing allocations, and different budgeting procedures for the economic behavior and well-being of families."

It remains true that very little effort has been directed to the effects of different family structures, even though this is a critical issue. The usual justification of family research in marketing relates to better targeting of marketing activities. Studies of husband-wife influence have been justified in (1) selecting the proper respondent in consumer research surveys, (2) determining the content of advertising messages, (3) selecting advertising media, (4) guiding product designers to include features that appeal to those who are most influential in the purchase decision, and (5) assisting in the location of retail outlets. Although these reasons are legitimate, they represent only a small part of the justification for studying family-member involvement in consumer decisions.

At least two writers have speculated about the effects of household structure on purchase behavior. Alderson (1957) suggested two concepts that form a typology of households—compatibility of attitudes/preferences and coordination of goal-directed activities. Families can be classified into one of the following four "ideal" types: coordinated and compatible, coordinated and incompatible, uncoordinated and compatible, and uncoordinated and incompatible. Family purchase behavior is hypothesized to differ for each type. To illustrate, the coordinated but incompatible family is likely to be "especially price-conscious, immune to emotional appeal, and hard bargainers in the effort to get their money's worth" (Alderson, 1957, p. 179). In contrast, the uncoordinated but compatible family is hypothesized to be especially susceptible to persuasive efforts such as personal selling.

Scanzoni (1966) hypothesized unique consumption behaviors in families as a function of the aspiration and expectation level of the husband vis-à-vis his wife. If, for example, a husband's aspirations *and* expectations exceeded those of his wife, one would expect him to be the motivating force behind an improved life style. His wife would be more likely to "go along" with his desires for increased consumption to the extent that his income level was high and his education substantially greater than hers. In another pattern, the husband could hope for a higher life style than his wife but actually have lower expectations about what was realistic. Unlike the previous pattern, the wife would probably be the major force behind a higher standard of living for the family and for that specific reason might want to work. According to Scanzoni, this pattern is likely to be present for many working-class families in the United States.

Beyond these speculations are a few empirical studies suggesting that family decision roles do indeed make a difference. Ferber and Lee (1974) found that when husbands were the "family financial officer," a higher proportion of income was saved, more assets were in variable dollar form (i.e., real estate, securities), and automobile purchases were less frequent. Granbois and Summers (1975) reported better estimates of total planned expenditures when interviews were conducted with both spouses together rather than with either the husband or the wife individually.

Considerable research has accumulated showing effective contraceptive use in families characterized by equalitarian roles, high within-family communication, and low extra-familial communication. Rogers (1973) described a family planning effort in Pakistan whose high success was attributed in part to the use of male-female teams as opposed to female workers only.

Finally, the Nowland studies (1964, 1965) found significant differences in purchase behavior depending on whether husbands and wives had the same brand preferences. When brand consensus existed, the preferred brand was usually the brand in the household inventory. When husband and wife did not agree, the wife's preferred brand rather than the husband's was more likely to be purchased.

These studies have just begun to examine the impact of the household on consumer behavior. An important research priority is to extend these tentative findings to many other areas of consumer choice.

Concluding Comments

Three brief summary comments capture the essence of this review.

1. The study of household decision and consumption behavior is not simply another "fashionable" topic for consumer researchers. Rather, the focus on consumers as a group acting collectively suggests a reorientation of many existing theories and methodologies. Research on household decision making will be judged on the extent to which it influences thinking about other areas such as family counseling, information dissemination, and marketing research.
2. Much of the work to date has taken an overly restrictive view of family-member roles. Most of the emphasis has been on who shops and decides within specific product categories. Studies of family decision making have in reality been studies of husband-wife decision making. Little is known about household roles (including children) in information gathering and storage, product use, and post decision evaluation or about family-member roles across product domains. Hill and Klein (1973, p. 373) have suggested that "scanty attention has been paid even to the descriptive questions of how and to what extent feed-back of information from past experience influences family decisions, who evaluates the family experience, who 'stores' the information for future use, and who draws on this information storage when the need arises."
3. A third and final research priority is the need to explore *how* families make decisions rather than simply who is involved. In the final analysis, a theory of household decision making will not emerge by focusing solely on decision outcomes such as who decided or who won. This approach has been described by Sprey (1972) both as "in no way sufficient" and as "highly unsuitable." The

ongoing nature of family relationships, the interrelatedness of their consumer choices, and the financial and time constraints faced by the family define a unique decision environment. The impact of this environment on how households manage consumption and savings is an important question for future research.

References

Alderson, W. *Marketing Behavior and Executive Action: A Functionalist Approach to Marketing Theory.* Homewood, Ill.: Irwin, 1957.

Aldous, J. "A Framework for the Analysis of Family Problem Solving," in J. Aldous, T. Condon, R. Hill, M. Straus, and I. Tallman, eds., *Family Problem Solving: A Symposium on Theoretical, Methodological, and Substantive Concerns.* Hinsdale, Ill.: Dryden Press, 1971, 265–81.

Aronoff, J., and W. D. Crano. "A Re-Examination of the Cross-Cultural Principles of Task Segregation and Sex Role Differentiation in the Family," *American Sociological Review,* 40 (February 1975), 12–20.

Arrow, K. J. "Mathematical Models in the Social Sciences," in D. Lerner and H. D. Lasswell, eds., *The Policy Sciences: Recent Developments in Scope and Method.* Stanford, Calif.: Stanford University Press, 1951, 129–54.

Bales, R. F. *Interaction Process Analysis: A Method for the Study of Small Groups.* Cambridge, Mass.: Addison-Wesley, 1950.

Becker, G. S. "A Theory of Marriage: Part I," *Journal of Political Economy,* 81 (July/August 1973), 813–46.

——. "A Theory of Marriage: Part II," *Journal of Political Economy,* 82 (March/April 1974), Part II, S11–S26.

Beckman, T. N. and W. R. Davidson. *Marketing.* (7th ed.) New York: Ronald Press, 1962.

Bernhardt, K. L. "Husband-Wife Influence in the Purchase Decision Process for Houses." Unpublished doctoral dissertation, University of Michigan, 1974.

Blau, P. M. *Exchange and Power in Social Life.* New York: Wiley, 1964.

Blood, R. O., Jr. "Resolving Family Conflicts," *The Journal of Conflict Resolution,* 4 (June 1960), 209–19.

Blood, R. O., Jr., and D. M. Wolfe. *Husbands and Wives: The Dynamics of Married Living.* Glencoe, Ill.: Free Press, 1960.

Brehl and Callahan Research. *Family Decision Making.* Time Marketing Information Research Report 1428, 1967.

Burgess, E. W. and H. J. Locke. *The Family: From Institution to Companionship.* (2nd ed.) New York: American Book Co., 1960.

Buskirk, R. H. *Principles of Marketing: The Management View.* New York: Holt, Rinehart & Winston, 1961.

Coleman, J. S. "Foundations for a Theory of Collective Decisions," *American Journal of Sociology,* 71 (May 1966), 615–27.

Converse, P. D. and M. Crawford. "Family Buying: Who Does It? Who Influences It?" *Current Economic Comment,* 11 (November 1949), 38–50.

Converse, P. D., H. W. Huegy, and R. V. Mitchell. *Elements of Marketing.* (6th ed.) Englewood Cliffs, N.J.: Prentice-Hall, 1958.

Conway/Milliken Research Corporation. *Report of the First Buyers of Automobiles.* A report prepared for Playboy Market Research, 1969.

Cox, E. P. "Family Purchase Decision Making and the Process of Adjustment," *Journal of Marketing Research,* 12 (May 1975), 189–95.

Cunningham, I. C. M. and R. T. Green. "Purchasing Roles in the U.S. Family, 1955 and 1973," *Journal of Marketing,* 38 (October 1974), 61–64.

Cunningham, R. M. "Brand Loyalty—What, Where, How Much?" *Harvard Business Review,* 34 (January/February 1956), 116–28.

Davis, H. L. "Dimensions of Marital Roles in Consumer Decision Making," *Journal of Marketing Research,* 7 (May 1970), 168–77.

——. "Measurement of Husband-Wife Influence in Consumer Purchase Decisions," *Journal of Marketing Research,* 8 (August 1971), 305–12.

——. "Determinants of Marital Roles in a Consumer Purchase Decision." Working Paper 72-14, European Institute for Advanced Studies in Management, Brussels, April 1972a.

——. "Household Decision Making." Working Paper 72-41, European Institute for Advanced Studies in Management, Brussels, November 1972b.

——. *Consumer Behavior in the Family.* New York: Free Press, in press.

Davis, H. L. and B. P. Rigaux. "Perception of Marital Roles in Decision Processes," *Journal of Consumer Research,* 1 (June 1974), 51–62.

Doyle, P. and P. Hutchinson. "Individual Differences in Family Decision Making," *Journal of the Market Research Society,* 15 (October 1973), 193–206.

Dubey, D. C. and H. M. Choldin. "Communication and Diffusion of the IUCD: A Study in Urban India," *Demography,* 4 (no. 2, 1967), 601–14.

Engel, J. F., D. T. Kollat, and R. D. Blackwell. *Consumer Behavior.* (2nd ed.) New York: Holt, Rinehart & Winston, 1973.

Evans, F. B. "Psychological and Objective Factors in the Prediction of Brand Choice, Ford versus Chevrolet," *The Journal of Business,* 32 (October 1959), 340–69.

Farley, J. U. "A Test of the Loyalty Proneness Hypothesis," *Commentary,* 8 (January 1966), 35–42.

Ferber, R. "Consumer Economics, A Survey," *Journal of Economic Literature,* 11 (December 1973a), 1303–42.

——. "Family Decision Making and Economic Behavior:

A Review," in E. B. Sheldon, ed., *Family Economic Behavior: Problems and Prospects.* Philadelphia: Lippincott, 1973b, 29-61.

Ferber, R. and L. C. Lee. "Husband-Wife Influence in Family Purchasing Behavior," *Journal of Consumer Research,* 1 (June 1974), 43-50.

Ferber, R. and F. Nicosia. "Newly Married Couples and Their Asset Accumulation Decisions," in B. Strumpel, J. N. Morgan, and E. Zahn, eds., *Human Behavior in Economic Affairs: Essays in Honor of George Katona.* San Francisco: Jossey-Bass; Amsterdam: Elsevier, 1972, 161-87.

Foote, N. "Unfulfilled Plans and Unplanned Actions," in S. Ward and P. Wright, eds., *Advances in Consumer Research.* Vol. 1. Proceedings of the 4th Annual Conference of the Association for Consumer Research, 1973. Urbana, Ill.: Association for Consumer Research, 1974, 529-31.

Frank, R. E. "Is Brand Loyalty a Useful Basis for Market Segmentation?" *Journal of Advertising Research,* 7 (June 1967), 27-33.

French, J. R. P. and B. Raven. "The Bases of Social Power," in D. Cartwright, ed., *Studies in Social Power.* Ann Arbor: Research Center for Group Dynamics, Institute for Social Research, University of Michigan, 1959, 150-67.

Granbois, D. H. "A Study of the Family Decision-Making Process in the Purchase of Major Durable Household Goods." Unpublished doctoral dissertation, Indiana University, 1963.

Granbois, D. H. and J. O. Summers. "Primary and Secondary Validity of Consumer Purchase Probabilities," *Journal of Consumer Research,* 1 (March 1975), 31-38.

Granbois, D. H. and R. P. Willett. "Equivalence of Family Role Measures Based on Husband and Wife Data," *Journal of Marriage and the Family,* 32 (February 1970), 68-72.

Gredal, K. "Purchasing Behavior in Households," in M. Kjaer-Hansen, ed., *Readings in Danish Theory of Marketing.* Amsterdam: North-Holland, 1966, 84-100.

Green, R. T. and I. C. M. Cunningham. "Feminine Role Perception and Family Purchasing Decisions," *Journal of Marketing Research,* 12 (August 1975), 325-32.

Haley, Overholser and Associates, Inc. *Purchase Influence: Measures of Husband/Wife Influence on Buying Decisions,* 1975.

Hempel, D. J. "Family Buying Decisions: A Cross-Cultural Perspective," *Journal of Marketing Research,* 11 (August 1974), 295-302.

Hill, R. *Family Development in Three Generations.* Cambridge, Mass.: Schenkman, 1970.

Hill, R. and D. M. Klein. "Toward a Research Agenda and Theoretical Synthesis," in E. B. Sheldon, ed., *Family Economic Behavior: Problems and Prospects.* Philadelphia: Lippincott, 1973, 371-404.

Jacoby, J. and D. B. Kyner. "Brand Loyalty vs. Repeat Buying Behavior," *Journal of Marketing Research,* 10 (February 1973), 1-9.

Jaffe Associates, Inc. *A Pilot Study of the Roles of Husbands and Wives in Purchasing Decisions,* n.d.

Jaffe, L. J. and H. Senft. "The Roles of Husbands and Wives in Purchasing Decisions," in L. Adler and I. Crespi, eds., *Attitude Research at Sea.* Chicago: American Marketing Association, 1966, 95-110.

Kenkel, W. F. "Family Interaction in Decision Making on Spending," in N. N. Foote, ed., *Household Decision-Making.* Consumer Behavior, Vol. IV. New York: New York University Press, 1961, 140-64.

——. "Observational Studies of Husband-Wife Interaction in Family Decision Making," in M. Sussman, ed., *Sourcebook in Marriage and the Family.* (2nd ed.) Boston: Houghton Mifflin, 1963, 144-56.

Lam, P. "Experiences in the Use of Communication Methods in Promoting Family Planning in Hong Kong," in *Report of the Working Group on Communication Aspects of Family Planning Programmes and Selected Papers.* Asian Population Studies Series 3. Bangkok: ECAFE, 1968.

Learner Marketing Research and Development. *New Brand Purchasing Dynamics: An In-Depth Examination of the Critical Incidents and Factors Involved in a New or Different Brand Coming into the Home.* Conducted for *Life* Magazine, December, 1968.

Raymond Loewy/William Snaith, Inc. *Project Home: The Motivations Towards Homes and Housing.* Report prepared for the Project Home Committee, 1967.

Lovell, R. C., R. Meadows, and B. Rampley. "Inter-Household Influence on Housewife Purchases." London: The Thompson Organization, 1968, 7-49.

Male vs. Female Influence in Buying and in Brand Selection. New York: Fawcett Publications, 1948.

Male vs. Female Influence in Buying and in Brand Selection, Vol. II. New York: Fawcett Publications, 1950.

Marshall, H. R. "Differences in Parent and Child Reports of the Child's Experience in the Use of Money," *Journal of Educational Psychology,* 54 (June 1963), 132-37.

Mercado, C. M. "Target Audiences in Family Planning." Paper presented at the IPPF-SEAOR Workshop on Information and Education, Kuala Lumpur, Malaysia, 1971.

Mishler, E. G. and N. E. Waxler. *Interaction in the Family.* New York: Wiley, 1968.

Morgan, J. N. "Some Pilot Studies of Communication and Consensus in the Family," *Public Opinion Quarterly,* 31 (Spring 1968), 113-21.

Mullen, P., R. Reynolds, P. Cignetta, and D. Dornan. "In Favor of Vasectomy—A Survey of Men and Women in Hayward, California." Unpublished working paper, Berkeley, California, n.d.

Munsinger, G. M., J. E. Weber, and R. W. Hansen. "Joint Home Purchasing Decisions by Husbands and Wives," *Journal of Consumer Research,* 1 (March 1975), 60-66.

Nowland and Company, Inc. *Family Participation and Influence in Shopping and Brand Selection: Phase I.* A report prepared for *Life* Magazine, 1964.

——. *Family Participation and Influence in Shopping and Brand Selection: Phase II.* A report prepared for *Life* Magazine, 1965.

Olson, D. H. "The Measurement of Family Power by Self-Report and Behavioral Models," *Journal of Marriage and the Family,* 31 (August 1969), 545–50.

Olson, D. H. and C. Rabunsky. "Validity of Four Measures of Family Power," *Journal of Marriage and the Family,* 34 (May 1972), 224–34.

Palmore, J. "The Chicago Snowball: A Study of the Flow and Diffusion of Family Planning Information," in D. J. Bogue, ed., *Sociological Contributions to Family Planning Research.* Chicago: Community and Family Planning Center, University of Chicago, 1967, 272–363.

Parsons, T. and R. F. Bales. *Family, Socialization and Interaction Process.* Glencoe, Ill.: Free Press, 1955.

Phillips, C. F. and D. J. Duncan. *Marketing: Principles and Methods.* (5th ed.) Homewood, Ill.: Irwin, 1964.

Pillai, K. M. "Study of the Decision Process in Adopting Family Planning Methods," *Bulletin of the Gandhigram Institute of Rural Health and Family Planning,* 6 (1971), 1–55.

Poffenberger, T. *Husband-Wife Communication and Motivational Aspects of Population Control in an Indian Village.* Green Park, New Delhi: Central Family Planning Institute, 1969.

Rogers, E. M. *Communication Strategies for Family Planning.* New York: Free Press, 1973.

Samuelson, P. A. "Social Indifference Curves," *The Quarterly Journal of Economics,* 70 (February 1956), 1–22.

Scanzoni, J. H. "The Conjugal Family and Consumption Behavior." Occasional Paper Series #1. Bryn Mawr, Penn.: McCahan Foundation, 1966.

——. *Opportunity and the Family.* New York: Free Press, 1970.

Scott, R. A. "Husband-Wife Interaction in a Household Purchase Decision," *Southern Journal of Business,* 5 (July 1970), 218–25.

Sharp, H. and P. Mott. "Consumer Decisions in the Metropolitan Family," *Journal of Marketing,* 21 (October 1956), 149–56.

Sheldon, E. B., ed. *Family Economic Behavior: Problems and Prospects.* Philadelphia: Lippincott, 1973.

Sheth, J. N. "A Theory of Family Buying Decisions," in J. N. Sheth, ed., *Models of Buyer Behavior: Conceptual, Quantitative, and Empirical.* New York: Harper & Row, 1974, 17–33.

Sheth, J. N. and S. Cosmas. "Tactics of Conflict Resolution in Family Buying Behavior." Paper presented at the meetings of American Psychological Association, Chicago, September, 1975.

Simon, H. A. "A Behavioral Model of Rational Choice," *The Quarterly Journal of Economics,* 69 (February 1955), 99–118.

Sprey, J. "The Family as a System in Conflict," *Journal of Marriage and the Family,* 31 (November 1969), 699–706.

——. "On the Management of Conflict in Families," *Journal of Marriage and the Family,* 33 (November 1971), 722–31.

——. "Family Power Structure: A Critical Comment," *Journal of Marriage and the Family,* 34 (May 1972), 235–38.

Starch, D. and staff. *Male vs. Female Influence on the Purchase of Selected Products.* A report prepared for *True* Magazine, 1958.

Strodtbeck, F. L. "Husband-Wife Interaction over Revealed Differences," *American Sociological Review,* 16 (August 1951), 468–73.

Szalai, A., ed. *The Use of Time: Daily Activities in Urban and Suburban Populations in Twelve Countries.* The Hague: Mouton, 1972.

Thompson, J. D. and A. Tuden. "Strategies, Structures, and Processes of Organizational Decision," in J. D. Thompson, P. B. Hammond, R. W. Hawkes, B. H. Junker, and A. Truden, eds., *Comparative Studies in Administration.* Pittsburgh: University of Pittsburgh Press, 1959, 195–216.

Travel Research International, Inc. *A Study of the Role of Husband and Wife in Air Travel Decisions.* Conducted for *Sports Illustrated,* September, 1968.

Turk, J. L. and N. W. Bell. "Measuring Power in Families," *Journal of Marriage and the Family,* 34 (May 1972), 215–22.

Turner, R. H. *Family Interaction.* New York: Wiley, 1970.

Weick, K. E. "Group Processes, Family Processes, and Problem Solving," in J. Aldous, T. Condon, R. Hill, M. Straus, and I. Tallman, eds., *Family Problem Solving: A Symposium on Theoretical, Methodological, and Substantive Concerns.* Hinsdale, Ill.: Dryden Press, 1971, 3–32.

Wells, H. L. "Financial Management Practices of Young Families," *Journal of Home Economics,* 51 (June 1959), 439–44.

Wilkening, E. A. and D. E. Morrison. "A Comparison of Husband and Wife Responses Concerning Who Makes Farm and Home Decisions," *Marriage and Family Living,* 25 (August 1963), 349–51.

Wilkes, R. E. "Husband-Wife Influence in Purchase Decisions—A Confirmation and Extension," *Journal of Marketing Research,* 7 (May 1975), 224–27.

Wind, Y. "Brand Choice," in R. Ferber, ed., *A Synthesis of Selected Aspects of Consumer Behavior.* Washington, D.C.: National Science Foundation, 1976.

Wolff, J. L. *What Makes Women Buy: A Guide to Understanding and Influencing the New Woman of Today.* New York: McGraw-Hill, 1958.

Wolgast, E. H. "Do Husbands or Wives Make the Purchasing Decisions?" *Journal of Marketing,* 23 (October 1958), 151–58.

Woodside, A. G. "Effects of Prior Decision-Making, Demographics, and Psychographics on Marital Roles for Purchasing Durables," in M. J. Schlinger, ed., *Advances in Consumer Research.* Vol. 2. Proceedings of the 5th Annual Conference of the Association for Consumer Research, 1974. Chicago: Association for Consumer Research, 1975, 81–91.

Wright, P. L. "The Harassed Decision Maker: Time Pressures, Distractions, and the Use of Evidence," *Journal of Applied Psychology,* 59 (October 1974), 555–61.

Zelditch, M., Jr. "Experimental Family Sociology," in J. Aldous, T. Condon, R. Hill, M. Straus, and I. Tallman, eds., *Family Problem Solving: A Symposium on Theoretical, Methodological, and Substantive Concerns.* Hinsdale, Ill.: Dryden Press, 1971, 55–72.

READING 14

The Information Overload Controversy: An Alternative Viewpoint

Naresh K. Malhotra, Arun K. Jain, and Stephen W. Lagakos

This paper reviews the information overload controversy and presents a methodology for investigating the effects of information load on consumer decision making performance. The proposed framework enables the statistical testing of specific hypotheses and can incorporate several extensions and refinements. The methodology is illustrated by reanalyzing the published data of previous studies; some interesting findings emerge from the analysis. The paper concludes with some public policy and managerial implications of the consumer information overload concept.

Introduction

In recent years the area of consumer information processing has received considerable attention from researchers in marketing. Several studies dealing with various issues in consumer information processing have been reported. Bettman (1974, 1979), Chestnut and Jacoby (1977), Jacoby (1974, 1977), Wilkie (1975, 1978) and Wright (1975) have summarized most of the previous work in this area.

A review of the literature suggests that the results of past research in consumer information processing have not always been clear-cut and precise. Investigations in some areas have given rise to substantial controversy. In particular, considerable disagreement seems to exist regarding the information load paradigm (Malhotra 1982a). Although some researchers have indicated the occurrence of information overload in their experiments (Jacoby et al. 1974a, 1974b), their conclusions and findings have been questioned by others (Russo 1974, Summers 1974, Wilkie 1974).

This paper first reviews the information overload controversy. Next, a methodology using LOGIT framework (Green, Carmone and Wachspress 1977) for examining the information load paradigm is presented. The proposed approach is more flexible than the traditional methodology employed in that it enables the formulation and statistical testing of alternative hypotheses regarding the form of the information load curve and the effect of concomitant variables. The proposed framework is illustrated by reanalyzing the published data of previous studies on information overload. The paper concludes with a discussion of some public policy and managerial implications of the information overload phenomenon.

A Review of Past Research on Information Overload

The information load paradigm is based on the proposition that consumers have finite limits to the amount of information they can assimilate and process during any given unit of time. If these limits are exceeded, overload occurs and consumers become confused and make poorer decisions. Hence, too much information can lead to dysfunctional performance. This concept of information overload derives theoretical support from research in human information processing

Reprinted by permission of the American Marketing Association, from the *Journal of Marketing*, Spring 1982, 27-37.

(Miller 1956, Quastler 1956), statistical prediction (Wherry 1931, 1940), and clinical prediction (Bartlett and Green 1966, Kelly and Fiske 1951). While the basic proposition seems reasonable, the question remains whether the occurrence of information overload in the consumer setting has been empirically demonstrated.

In the recent past, marketing researchers have undertaken several studies to examine the occurrence of information overload. Jacoby et al. (1974a) in their pioneering research systematically varied the amount of information defined in terms of the number of product attributes and brands of laundry detergents at three levels each. The subjects, randomly assigned to one of the nine treatment conditions, were presented with an appropriate number of brands and attributes. They were to provide importance ratings of the product attributes, rate their ideal brand and identify their most preferred brand from among the alternatives in the choice set. The effects of information load were assessed by examining the number of subjects correctly choosing their best brand across the treatment conditions. Best brand was defined as the one coming closest to the subject's ideal brand. In a follow-up experiment, Jacoby et al. (1974b) varied the number of brands and product attributes at four levels each to shed further light on the occurrence of information overload. Scammon (1977) extended the information load paradigm by varying the number of attributes and the format in which information about the experimental stimuli (peanut butter) was provided. Subjects were presented with information about two brands and requested to identify the brand that was more nutritious and preferred for the next purchase. The effects of information load were assessed by examining the number of objectively correct choices (identification of the nutritionally superior brand) and subjectively correct choices (selection of the nutritionally superior brand). All three published studies concluded that the subjects suffered information overload as the amount of information provided was increased. Table 1 presents a brief summary of the published empirical information load studies in marketing.

While commending Jacoby et al. for addressing an important public policy issue, marketing researchers have questioned their operational procedures and rejected their conclusions (Russo 1974, Summers 1974, Wilkie 1974). Three basic reservations have been expressed about their studies.[1] First, it is proposed that the number of brands and the number of information items (attributes) per brand are conceptually as well as psychologically different dimensions. Hence, it is suggested that the total amount of product information should not be defined in terms of the number of brands times the number of items per brand. Next, since the probability of making a correct choice by chance alone is inversely proportional to the number of brands, subjects responding to smaller numbers of brands in the choice set are expected to have a higher probability of correct choice. Therefore, when comparing the effects of the number of alternatives on choice accuracy, the effect of chance factors should be explicitly considered. Finally, the wisdom of using weighted euclidean distances of the brands in the choice set from the ideal brand to measure correct choice was questioned given the problems associated with ideal point measurement. The use of importance weights and variation in the number of attributes over which distances were computed further clouded the accuracy of Jacoby's measures.

However, Jacoby and his associates have generally disagreed with the evaluation of their research procedures and findings (Jacoby 1977, Jacoby et al. 1975). While they accept that their operationalization of total information may not be entirely appropriate, citing studies that report that the number of brands in the choice set affects respondent's ability to make accurate choices, they contend that a definition of total information must take into account the number of brands in the choice set. They acknowledge that chance factors must be controlled when comparing decision quality across the number of brands. To overcome this problem, the researchers suggest that a correlation analysis be used or that the number of brands be kept constant in the experiment. The latter suggestion, however, contradicts their proposition that any operationalization of total information must incorporate the number of brands. Finally, with respect to the appropriateness of the ideal point measure of correct choice, Jacoby (1977) contends that since no single approach for defining decision quality in the consumer context is entirely

1. Additional issues have also been raised. However, these are relatively minor and may be found in the original articles. Here, only the major issues addressed by all three critics have been emphasized.

TABLE 1
An Overview of Published Empirical Work on Information Load in Marketing and a Summary of the Results of Its Reanalysis

	Experimental Design				Original Study				Results of Reanalysis		
					Analytical Approach						
Investigators	*Study*	*Experimental Stimuli*	*Study*	*Experimental Manipulations*	*Study*	*Approach*	*Study*	*Major Findings*	*Study*	*LOGIT Parameters*	*Major Findings*
I. Jacoby Speller and Berning (1975)	1	Instant Rice Sample Size = 192	1, 2	Both the number of brands and the number of attributes per brand were varied at four levels each.	1, 2 1, 2	A. Means and standard deviations for Kendall's coefficient of concordance between the predicted and elicited preference rankings under different treatment conditions. B. Analysis of Variance of the concordance coefficients between the predicted and elicited rankings under different treatment conditions.	1, 2, 3	*All* Jacoby et al. studies conclude that the consumer choice accuracy first increases and later decreases as the "total" amount of information provided is increased.	1.	$\beta_1 = -0.754$ $\beta_2^* = 1.014$ $\beta_3 = -0.487$ $\beta_4 = -0.487$ $\beta_5 = -0.325$ $\beta_6 = 0.759$ $\beta_7^* = 1.124$	1.1 The probability of correct choice increased significantly as the number of (a) attributes increased from 4 to 16 or (b) brands increased from 4 to 8. 1.2 No significant effect on choice accuracy was detected by increase in the number of: (a) attributes from 4 to 8 or 12 or (b) brands from 4 to 12 or 16.
	2	Prepared Dinners Sample Size = 192							2.	$\beta_1 = -1.099$ $\beta_2 = 1.099$ $\beta_3 = -0.000$ $\beta_4 = -0.511$ $\beta_5 = -0.511$ $\beta_6 = 1.435$ $\beta_7^* = 2.708$ $\beta_8 = -0.588$ $\beta_9 = -50.593$ $\beta_{10} = 0.511$ $\beta_{11}^* = -3.833$ $\beta_{12} = -52.539$ $\beta_{13} = -2.224$ $\beta_{14}^* = -3.807$ $\beta_{15}^* = -4.007$ $\beta_{16}^* = -3.496$	2.1 The probability of correct choice does not decline significantly as the number of (a) attributes is increased from 4 to 8, or 12 or (b) brands is increased from 4 to 8, 12, or 16. 2.2 When the information is provided about 4 brands on 16 atrributes (instead of 4), the probability of correct choice improves significantly. However, any concomitant increase in the number of brands at this attribute level leads to a decline in the probability.

II. Jacoby, Speller and Kohn (1974a)	3	Laundry Detergents Sample Size = 153	3	The numbers of brands and attributes were varied at *three* levels each.	3. 3	A. Chi-square analysis of the number of correct choices in each treatment condition. B. Analysis of variance of subjective data under different treatment conditions.			3.	$\beta_1^* = -1.204$ $\beta_2 = -0.181$ $\beta_3 = -0.474$ $\beta_4 = 0.723$ $\beta_5^* = 1.224$	3.1 The probability of correct choice improved significantly as the number of attributes were increased from 2 to 6. 3.2 The number of brands in the choice set does not significantly influence the probability of correct choice.
III. Scammon (1977)	4	Peanut Butter Sample Size = 300		The number of attributes were varied at three levels each while their format was varied at two levels.	4	A. Chi-square analysis of the number of correct choices in each treatment combination. B. Analysis of variance of aided recall accuracy scores.	4.1	Neither the amount nor the format of the information affected subjects' brand preference/intention to buy as judged by subjective criteria.	4.	$\beta_1^* = -1.386$ $\beta_2 = -1.253$ $\beta_3^* = -1.558$ $\beta_4 = -1.253$ $\beta_5 = 2.020$ $\beta_6^* = 2.811$	4.1 Using subjective criteria, subjects made poorer decisions when information about 8 nutrients plus calories was provided in the percentage format than when no information about nutrients was provided. 4.2 Subjects had a tendency to make better decisions when information about 8 nutrients plus calories was provided in the adjective format using subjective criteria than when no information about nutrients was provided.

*Significant at $\alpha = 0.005$.

satisfactory, their operationalization "is as good as any."

Discussion

It is possible to resolve the disagreements with respect to a definition of total information. Total information should not be defined in terms of the product of the number of brands and items per brand. However, there is reasonable evidence (Jacoby et al. 1977, Moreno 1974) to suggest that a definition of total information should not be divorced from a consideration of the number of brands. What is needed is a methodology that would permit an examination, individually as well as jointly, of the effects of the number of brands and the number of items per brand on decision quality. Moreover, the methodology must not force the researcher to adopt a particular definition of total information, yet it must be flexible enough to permit statistical evaluation of different operationalizations of total information.

The analytical framework utilized by previous investigators leaves much to be desired. The chi-square test employed by Jacoby et al. (1974a) and Scammon (1977) is at best a weak test. The two-way chi-square test employed by previous researchers merely examines the independence between two classificatory variables (e.g., number of attributes and number of brands). However, in the information load paradigm the occurrence of information overload is determined by examining the ability of consumers to make correct choices across different treatment conditions. Hence, what needs to be tested is whether the number of correct choices under different treatment conditions are significantly different. If under certain treatment conditions information overload does occur, one would expect the ability of the consumers to make correct choices under those conditions to decrease significantly. This cannot be detected within the conventional chi-square framework employed by the previous investigators.

The information processing strategy adopted by the respondents may be influenced by the particular combination of the number of attributes and the number of brands in the choice set (Jacoby et al. 1976, Payne 1976, Wright 1975). The knowledge of such interactions would provide a richer understanding of the information load phenomenon. The use of analysis of variance (Jacoby et al. 1974a, 1974b; Scammon 1977) on the number of correct choices to examine the effect of different treatment conditions does not permit the estimation of interaction effects. Since there is only one entry per cell, the various interactions between the levels of number of brands and the number of attributes cannot be estimated within the standard ANOVA framework.

The assertion that the determination of best brand, and hence correct choice, is subject to inaccuracies is reasonable. Given that no single measure of choice accuracy is fully satisfactory, it is desirable to adopt different operationalizations of the dependent variable. This could include self-report measures (Weitz and Wright 1979) as well as objective criteria.

Wilkie (1974) has stated that "there is little doubt that the issue of consumer information provision will be one of the major problems confronting marketing researchers and policy makers in this decade" (p. 462). Given the apparent importance of the issue and disagreement with the finding of Jacoby et al. (1974a, 1974b), it would be wise to examine the occurrence of consumer information overload further. With this in mind we next present a methodology for examining information load effects via the LOGIT framework. The proposed framework is then employed to reanalyze the published data of Jacoby et al. (1974a, 1974b) and Scammon (1977). Other applications of this methodology for examining consumer information processing behavior are provided by Malhotra (1982b, 1982c).

A LOGIT Approach to Information Load Paradigm

In the information load paradigm, the dependent variable of interest is the ability of the consumer to make "a correct choice" under different information load conditions. This can be modelled in terms of the probability of making a correct choice. The probability of correct choice can be estimated in several ways (Bishop, Feinberg and Holland 1975; DeSarbo and Hildebrand 1980). However, in view of the binary nature of the dependent variable and the fact that the probability of making a correct choice under each experimental condition (cell) varies between 0 and 1, the linear logistic model (LOGIT) becomes a particularly suited technique for analysis (Green, Carmone and Wachspress 1977).[2] The probability of making a correct choice in each experimental cell could be calculated as a function of the number of brands and the number of attributes per brand on which information is provided. Where information overload does occur, the probability of making correct choices should decrease significantly.

The LOGIT analysis is a flexible approach. In addition to the commonly employed main effects plus interactions and main effects-only models, other models purporting to capture the underlying information load process may also be formulated and statistically tested. For the sake of simplicity, consider the probability of correct choice as a function of only the number of attributes per brand on which information is provided. A general model for the information load paradigm may be represented as:

$$\log_e \left(\frac{P_i}{1-P_i} \right) = \beta_1 + \beta_2 K + \beta_3 Z \qquad (1)$$

where, P_i = the probability of correct choice in the i-th cell (information load condition).

$Z = K$ if $K \geqslant K_0$
0 if $K < K_0$

K = the number of attributes per brand on which information is provided.

K_0 = critical number of attributes specified by the researcher either on the basis of a priori expectations or by looking at the data obtained.

As indicated in Figure 1, the researcher may postulate different forms of information load curve. For example, the log odds of correct choice, when the number of attributes per brand exceed K_0, may:

- first increase and then decrease (e.g., Figure 1-a)
- first decrease and then remain constant (e.g., Figure 1-b)
- increase at different rates (e.g., Figure 1-c)
- increase or decrease at a constant rate (e.g., Figure 1-d)

The hypothesized values of β_2 and β_3 will vary under these conditions as shown in Figure 1 and can be statistically examined. For example, the appropriateness of form 1-a could be investigated by testing the following hypotheses (Cox 1970):

$$\text{H1:} \quad \beta_2 > 0$$

$$\text{H2:} \quad \beta_2 + \beta_3 < 0$$

The model (1) could be generalized to include the number of brands and the combination of the number of brands and attributes in the discrete as well as continuous cases.[3] Using this framework, it is also possible to take into account the effect of chance factors.

Checking for Chance Factors

As critics have rightly pointed out, the probability of making a correct choice based on chance alone decreases as the number of brands in the choice set increases. Thus it seems reasonable to adjust the probability of correct choice for chance factors. There does exist a natural measure for incorporating correction due to chance (Fleiss 1975) as indicated below:

$$\bar{P}_i = \frac{P_{io} - P_{ic}}{1 - P_{ic}} \qquad (2)$$

where, $\bar{P}_i$ = the probability of correct choice in cell i adjusted for chance.

P_{io} = the observed probability of correct choice in cell i.

P_{ic} = the probability of correct choice in cell i by chance alone (1/number of brands).

A chi-square test could be performed to test whether the observed distribution of correct choices (based on P_{io}) is different from what one would expect by chance alone (based on P_{ic}).[4] Furthermore, chi-square analysis could also be conducted to test whether the chance-adjusted distribution of correct choices (based on $\bar{P}_i$) and the observed distribution

2. A second operationalization of performance accuracy consists of a comparison between each subject's actual preference ranking and the ranking predicted from the ideal brand. The response variable may still be treated as binary by comparing actual and predicted choices for all possible brand pairs (Wright 1972). A discussion of the inherent advantages of LOGIT approach for analyzing binary data may be found in Cox (1970).

3. Summers (1974) has pointed out that while examining information load effects, it is desirable to account explicitly for the salience of the attributes on which information is provided and the variability of the attractiveness of the brands. Such extensions could be readily incorporated by introducing additional terms in the model formulation.

4. It may be pointed out that if P_{ic} is greater than P_{io}, the $\bar{P}_i$ should be set equal to 0.

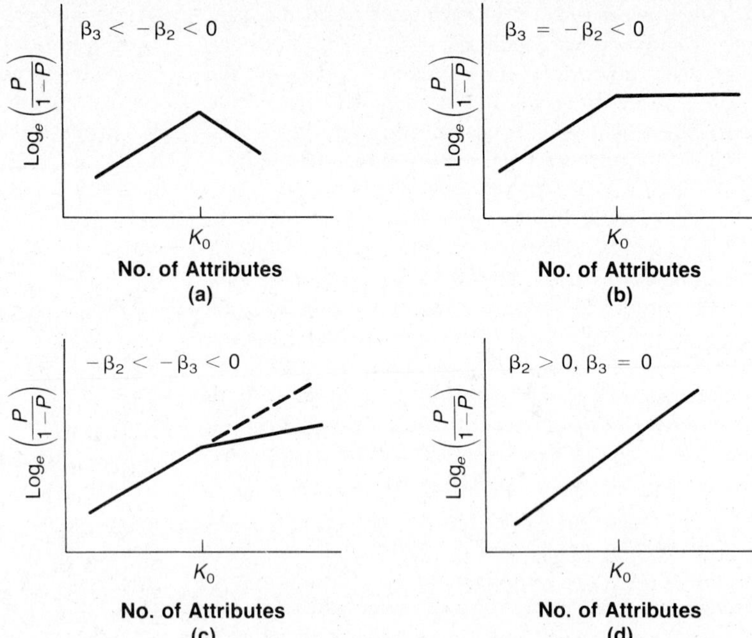

FIGURE 1
Some Possible Forms of Information Load Curve

(based on P_{io}) come from the same population. Where the chance effects are not significant, the $\overline{P}_i$ and P_{io} will be close and the resulting χ^2 statistic not significant. However, the distributions based on P_{io} and P_{ic} will differ significantly (Malhotra 1982a).

A Reanalysis of Published Data from Previous Studies

The proposed methodology was employed to reanalyze the published data of previous investigators. The dependent variable in the reanalysis was the probability that a respondent would make a correct choice under different information load conditions. Given the nature of the published data, the method of determination and definition of correct choice adopted was the same as that used in the original studies. Thus information reported in previous studies (Table 1) on the number of respondents making correct choices under each information load condition, given the total number of respondents in that condition, was used to estimate the probability of correct choice as a function of information load. Both the main effects plus interactions models and the main effects-only models were estimated for all the published data from previous information load studies discussed in Table 1. The estimated parameters were statistically tested to reexamine the hypotheses implied by previous investigators. In the following, results of model estimation and hypotheses testing for each published data set are presented.

Instant Rice Data

A main effects plus interactions model for the probability of correct choice in each cell for the instant rice data may be formulated as:

$$\log_e \left(\frac{P_i}{1 - P_i} \right) = \sum_{i=1}^{16} \beta_i X_i \qquad (3)$$

where:[5] P_i = the probability of correct choice in the i-th cell (information load condition); (i, $i = 1, 2, \ldots, 16$)

$X_1 = 1$

$X_2 = 1$ if the number of brands in the stimuli set is 8

0 otherwise

5. X_1 denotes the constant term similar to that employed in dummy variable regression analysis. In the present formulation, it depicts the presence of four brands each described by four attributes in the experiment.

X_3 = 1 if the number of brands in the stimuli set is 12
0 otherwise
X_4 = 1 if the number of brands in the stimuli set is 16
0 otherwise
X_5 = 1 if the number of attributes per brand is 8
0 otherwise
X_6 = 1 if the number of attributes per brand is 12
0 otherwise
X_7 = 1 if the number of attributes per brand is 16
0 otherwise
X_8 to X_{16} = the interaction terms between the levels of number of brands and number of attributes per brand.[6]
β_1 to β_{16} = the parameters to be estimated.

Alternately, a main effects model may be represented by eliminating X_8 to X_{16} from (3).

Both the main effects plus interactions and main effects-only models were estimated on the instant rice data. The likelihood ratio test revealed that the interaction terms of model (3) were not significant at $\alpha = 0.05$. Thus only the results for the main effects model are presented. A chi-square test of homogeneity (Mendenhall and Schaeffer 1973, pp. 502–508) between the observed and predicted number of people correctly choosing their best brand using the main effects-only model was not significant. This suggests that the observed and predicted distributions came from the same population. The test provides a further indication of the appropriateness of the main effects-only model. In the absence of interactions, different additive models may be indicated. The chi-square test of homogeneity could be used to test the appropriateness of the various models. The results of estimating main effects model are summarized in Table 1.

In terms of the number of brands, the results indicate that the only significant parameter is β_2. This parameter represents the effect of the number of brands on the probability of correct choice when the number of brands in the stimuli set is increased from four to eight. What is more interesting is that the parameter β_2 is positive. Thus in this particular experiment as the number of brands in the choice set increased from four to eight, the probability of making a correct choice increased significantly. Furthermore, while the coefficients β_3 and β_4 are negative, they are not statistically significant at $\alpha = 0.05$. When the number of brands in the choice set is increased from four to twelve or from four to sixteen, although the probability of making a correct choice decreases, the decrease in the probability is not statistically significant. The results for the number of attributes per brand are equally illuminating. We note that the estimated parameters β_6 and β_7 are positive. Furthermore, while β_7 is statistically significant, β_5 is negative and not significantly different from zero. Thus, no definite conclusion can be made regarding the effect of increasing the number of attributes on which information is provided from four to eight (as indicated by β_5) or from four to twelve (as indicated by β_6), because of the lack of statistical significance of the corresponding estimated parameters. However, as the number of attributes on which information is provided is increased from four to sixteen, the probability of making a correct choice (as indicated by β_7) improves significantly. Thus our analysis shows that the subjects in the Jacoby et al. study actually made better decisions when provided with information on sixteen attributes rather than on only four attributes. The effect of chance factors was also investigated using Fleiss' measure (1975) but was not found to be significant.

Prepared Dinners Data

The second data set analyzed in this paper is the one obtained by Jacoby et al. (1974b) on prepared dinners. Since the number of attributes and number of brands varied in this experiment was the same as that for the instant rice experiment, the interactions and main effects-only models for this data set are identical to the models proposed for the instant rice.

Both the interactions (3) and the main effects model were estimated for these data. A likelihood ratio test indicated that the interactions were significant and so only the results of the interactions model are presented in Table 1. Several interesting conclusions can be drawn from the estimated parameters. First, none of the coefficients representing the number of brands are statistically significant. Second, the only significant main effect for the number of attributes is that corresponding to sixteen attributes of

6. For example, X_8 denotes the joint effect of the presence of eight brands with each brand described in terms of eight attributes.

information per brand. This effect, represented by β_7, is positive and therefore indicates that as the number of attributes on which information is provided is increased from four to sixteen, the probability of making correct choices increases. Finally, of the interaction terms, only β_{11}, β_{14}, β_{15} and β_{16} are statistically significant. Moreover, all these coefficients have negative signs indicating a decrease in the probability of correct choice for the corresponding cells (treatment conditions). The significance of β_{14}, β_{15} and β_{16} implies that when consumers were provided with information about sixteen attributes per brand, the probability of correct choice decreased as the number of brands in the choice set were increased from four to eight, four to twelve, and four to sixteen respectively. The significance of the interactions suggests that while providing information on sixteen attributes per brand leads to better choice making, any concomitant increase in the number of brands at this level of information leads to a relative decrease in the probability of making a correct choice. The chance effects, again, were not significant.

Laundry Detergent Data

The data on the laundry detergents experiment obtained by Jacoby et al. (1974a) were reanalyzed by estimating both interactions and the main effects-only models. However, since the likelihood ratio test indicated that the interactions were not significant, only the results of the main effects will be presented. The main effects model for the laundry detergent data may be represented as follows:

$$\log_e \left(\frac{P_i}{1-P_i}\right) = \sum_{i=1}^{5} \beta_i X_i \qquad (4)$$

where, $X_1 = 1$

$X_2 = 1$ if the number of brands in the stimuli set is 8
0 otherwise

$X_3 = 1$ if the number of brands in the stimuli set is 12
0 otherwise

$X_4 = 1$ if the number of items/brand is 4
0 otherwise

$X_5 = 1$ if the number of items/brand is 6
0 otherwise

A chi-square test of homogeneity indicates that the model (4) provides a good fit to the observed data. It can be observed from the results presented in Table 1 that the estimated parameters representing the effect of increasing the number of brands in the choice set, β_2 and β_3, are negative but not statistically significant at $\alpha = 0.05$. Thus our analysis indicates that although the probability of making a correct choice decreases as the number of brands in the choice set is increased from four to eight and four to twelve, the resulting decrease in the probability is not statistically significant. The effects of the increase in the number of attributes per brand on the probability of making correct choice, β_4 and β_5, were found to be positive. It will be observed that β_4 is not statistically significant. As the number of attributes per brand increased from two to four, the probability of making a correct choice increased but the improvement was not statistically significant. However, β_5 is statistically significant at $\alpha = 0.05$. The probability of a consumer making a correct choice increases significantly as the number of attributes per brand increases from two to six. The results show that as the subjects in this experiment were provided with more information per brand, they actually made better decisions. Chance factors were also investigated and were not found to be statistically significant.

Peanut Butter Data

Scammon (1977) used peanut butter brands to examine the information load effects. As in the Jacoby studies (1974a, 1974b), the interactions and main effects-only models were formulated and parameters estimated independently for the subjective standards data.[7] Since the interactions were found to be significant, only the results for the interaction model will be discussed. Such a model may be presented as follows:

$$\log_e \left(\frac{P_i}{1-P_i}\right) = \sum_{i=1}^{6} \beta_i X_i \qquad (5)$$

where, $X_1 = 1$

$X_2 = 1$ if the number of nutrients about which information is provided is 4
0 otherwise

7. An attempt was also made to analyze the objective standards data collected by Scammon using the LOGIT framework. A likelihood ratio test (Mendenhall and Schaeffer 1973) indicated that the interaction terms were significant. However, when a main-effects plus interactions model was estimated, the second derivatives matrix was noninvertible. Consequently the variances could not be estimated and the statistical significance of the model parameters assessed. Hence, the results for objective standards data are not presented.

$X_3 = 1$ if the number of nutrients about which information is provided is 8
0 otherwise
$X_4 = 1$ if the adjective format is used
0 otherwise
$X_5 = X_2 * X_4$
$X_6 = X_3 * X_4$

It will be observed from the results summarized in Table 1 that besides the constant term β_1, only the estimated parameters β_3 and β_6 are statistically significant. Furthermore, β_3 is negative while β_6 is positive. The effect of providing information on eight nutrients plus calories, as compared to the controlled condition of no nutrient information for the percentage format, is represented by β_3. However, the effect of providing information on eight nutrients plus calories as compared to the no-nutrient-information condition under the adjective format is represented by $\beta_3 + \beta_6$. The significance and negative sign of β_3 suggests that the subjects in Scammon's study made poorer decisions when information about eight nutrients plus calories was provided in the percentage format than when no information about nutrients was provided. Furthermore, the sum of $\beta_3 + \beta_6$ is positive. Thus our analysis shows that the subjects had a tendency to make better decisions when provided with information on eight nutrients plus calories in adjective format than when they were not provided with any information about nutrients.

A Comparative Analysis with Previous Findings

The foregoing analysis provides insight into the information load controversy using an alternative analytical framework. Based on reanalysis of the data obtained by Jacoby et al., three broad conclusions can be drawn. First, as the number of attributes on which information was provided to subjects increased, the probability of making correct choice generally improved. It is interesting to note that in all the three experiments of Jacoby et al. (1974a, 1974b) as the number of attributes was increased from the lowest level to the highest, the probability of making correct choices increased significantly. One may reasonably conclude, therefore, that in the Jacoby experiments the provision of more information (in terms of the number of attributes) generally led to improved decision making. This finding is consistent with the observations of Russo (1974) and Wilkie (1974). Second, the effect of increase in the number of brands in the choice set on the probability of making correct choice was not found to be significant. Although the probability of making correct choice declined with an increase in the number of brands, such an effect was not found to be statistically significant. Any claim in these experiments that increasing the number of brands in the choice set led to dysfunctional consequences and hence information overload is untenable. Finally, as found in the prepared dinners data, there may exist significant interactions between the number of brands in the choice set and the number of attributes on which information is provided. This suggests the need to consider explicitly these two variables in the design and analysis of the information load paradigm. Jacoby, Speller and Kohn conclude that consumers "actually make poorer purchase decisions with more information" (1974a). Based on the reanalysis using LOGIT framework the validity of their conclusions is questionable. While their suggestion that "providing substantial amounts of package information can result in poorer purchase decisions" (1974, p. 40) may be a reasonable proposition, it is *not* supported by their reported data.

The reanalysis of Scammon's (1977) data demonstrated the existence of complex interactions between the number of attributes and the type of format. Her chi-square and ANOVA framework could not detect these interaction effects, and her conclusion that "neither the amount nor the format of the information presented to the subjects affected their brand preference/intention-to-buy (p. 152) is *not* supported by our reanalysis.

Some Public Policy and Managerial Implications

Although the findings of previous investigations may be questioned, the concept of consumer information overload has some important implications in terms of the amount of information that should be provided to consumers and the manner in which it should be made available. In the last two decades the products from which consumers must choose have grown enormously in quantity and complexity. Commercial sources are the core of the existing information system, yet there is evidence that consumers are skeptical about the usefulness and truthfulness of this type of information (Day 1976, Jacoby 1974, Newman and Staelin 1972). In an effort to bridge the information gap, public policy makers have recently demonstrated heightened interest in consumer welfare. Programs aimed at providing useful information to consumers in the marketplace have been initiated by many federal, state and local agencies.

Providing consumers with more information is a step in the right direction. The results of our reanalysis suggest that consumers are capable of processing fairly large amounts of information. Yet the capacity of consumers to absorb and process information is not unlimited. It should be recognized that these previous studies were conducted in an artificial environment in which the respondents were motivated to process the information provided due to the demands of the experiment. Research in consumer information processing does suggest that in many situations, the motivation of consumers to acquire and process information is rather low (Bettman 1979, pp. 43–72). If efforts on the part of policy makers and consumer groups to provide consumers with more information are to bear fruit, they should take into account not only the capacity but also the motivation of consumers to process information.

Furthermore, the provision of information should not be independent of the number of choice alternatives facing the consumer and the choice behavior exhibited. The reanalysis of the prepared dinners data set suggests that there may exist, for certain product categories, significant interactions between the number of brands in the choice set and the number of attributes on which information is provided. These aspects need to be emphasized as they are typically ignored by the policy makers (Bettman 1979, p. 294).

The format in which the information is presented can also affect the way in which consumers acquire and process information (Bettman 1979, pp. 219–221; Bettman and Kakkar 1977; Bettman and Zins 1979). As pointed out by several researchers (Russo 1977; Russo, Krieser and Miyashita 1975), one may distinguish between the availability and the processability of information. Our reanalysis of Scammon's study suggests that adjective format, as compared to the numerical format, facilitates the processing of information. If this finding is in fact generalizable, then important public policy implications follow. For example, policy makers could legislate that important information be communicated to the consumers in a verbal format.

The information load paradigm also has important managerial implications. Unlike the policy maker, the marketing manager is more concerned with providing persuasive information that favors his/her brand. This information is communicated through various promotional activities. Such information programs must explicitly recognize the limited capacity and motivation of the target market to process information if the message is to have its intended impact in the market. Even when consumers are capable, the motivation to process the information provided may be low. For example, although a reanalysis of instant rice data indicates that the housewives in the Jacoby et al. (1974b) study were able to process information on 16 attributes, the motivation of housewives to process this much information while actually buying instant rice may be low. Hence, an informational type of advertisement detailing so much product information may have limited impact in the market. Likewise, in deciding on a media mix, the manager needs to be aware that different media vary in the extent to which they facilitate the processing of large amounts of information. Suppose, for example, a marketer believes that his/her brand is, on balance, better than other leading brands if a detailed, rational comparison were made. If so, such information may be more effectively communicated using point-of-sale displays or print advertisements as opposed to broadcast media. The use of point-of-sale displays or print advertisements as in the studies of Jacoby et al. (1974a, 1974b) would allow the consumer greater time to process the information, thereby decreasing the possibility of information overload. Furthermore, the reanalysis of Scammon's (1977) study suggests that such information could be more effectively communicated in a verbal as opposed to a percentage or numerical format. A thorough discussion of public policy and managerial implications of information processing theory in general may be found in Bettman (1979, pp. 293–342) and Wilkie (1975, 1978).

Conclusion

The concept of information overload has important implications both for public policy makers and managers. However, the results of past research in the area have not always produced clear-cut and precise findings. This paper reviews the information load controversy and suggests a methodological framework for examining this paradigm. The methodology proposed and the reanalysis does help resolve some of the problems in investigating the effects of information load on consumers. Our reanalysis of previous studies failed to support the conclusions of their authors that providing more information results in poorer purchase decisions.

The LOGIT framework offers an attractive approach for analyzing the information load paradigm and does not require the researcher to adopt a particular definition of "total information." The methodology is flexible enough to enable the researcher to examine the effects of the number of brands, the number of attributes or other variables of interest on the occurrence of information overload. Moreover, such effects can be examined individually or jointly. Yet the LOGIT framework permits the researcher to model various definitions of "total" information.[8] Furthermore, it is possible to examine complex interaction effects. Knowledge of such effects permitted better interpretation of previous studies. If the researcher desires, additional explanatory variables, such as the salience of information provided, variability of the relative attractiveness of the choice alternatives, and individual variables can be explicitly incorporated in the analysis to develop a richer understanding of information load phenomenon.

References

Bartlett, C. J. and Calvin G. Green (1966), "Clinical Prediction: Does One Sometimes Know Too Much?", *Journal of Counseling Psychology,* 13 (Fall), 267-270.

Bettman, J. R. (1979), *An Information Processing Theory of Consumer Choice,* Reading, MA: Addison-Wesley.

—— (1974), "Decision Net Models of Buyer Information Processing and Choice: Findings, Problems and Prospects," in *Buyer/Consumer Information Processing,* G. D. Hughes and M. L. Ray, eds., Chapel Hill: University of North Carolina Press, pp. 59-74.

—— and P. Kakkar (1977), "Effect of Information Presentation Format on Consumer Information Acquisition Strategies," *Journal of Consumer Research,* 3 (March), 233-240.

—— and Michael A. Zins (1979), "Information Format and Choice Task Effects in Decision Making," *Journal of Consumer Research,* 4 (September), 141-153.

Bishop, Y. M., S. E. Feinberg and P. W. Holland (1975), *Discrete Multivariate Analysis: Theory and Practice,* Cambridge, MA: MIT Press.

Chestnut, R. W. and J. Jacoby (1977), "Consumer Information Processing: Emerging Theory and Findings," in *Consumer and Industrial Buying Behavior,* Arch G. Woodside, J. N. Sheth and P. D. Bennett, eds., New York: Elsevier North-Holland, Inc., 119-134.

Cox, D. R. (1970), *Analysis of Binary Data,* 2nd ed., London: Chapman and Hall.

Day, George S. (1976), "Assessing the Effects of Information Disclosure Requirements," *Journal of Marketing,* 40 (April), 42-52.

DeSarbo, W. S. and D. K. Hildebrand (1980), "A Marketer's Guide to Log Linear Models for Qualitative Data Analysis," *Journal of Marketing,* 44 (Summer), 40-51.

Fleiss, J. L. (1975), "Measuring Agreement Between Two Judges on the Presence or Absence of a Trait," *Biometrics,* 31 (September), 651-59.

Green, P.E., Frank J. Carmone and David P. Wachspress (1977), "On the Analysis of Qualitative Data in Marketing Research," *Journal of Marketing Research,* 14 (February), 52-59.

Jacoby, J. (1977), "Information Load and Decision Quality: Some Contested Issues," *Journal of Marketing Research,* 14 (November), 569-73.

—— (1974), "Consumer Reaction to Information Displays," in *Advertising and the Public Interest,* S. F. Divita, ed., Chicago: American Marketing Association, 101-18.

——, R. W. Chestnut, K. C. Weigel and W. Fisher (1976), "Pre-Purchase Information Acquisition. Description of a Process Methodology, Research Paradigm, and Pilot Investigation," in *Advances in Consumer Research,* Vol. 3, B. B. Anderson, ed., Chicago: Association for Consumer Research, 306-14.

——, D. E. Speller and Carol A. K. Berning (1975), "Constructive Criticism and Programmatic Research: Reply to Russo," *Journal of Consumer Research,* 2 (September), 154-56.

——, —— and C. A. Kohn (1974a), "Brand Choice Behavior as a Function of Information Load," *Journal of Marketing Research,* 11 (February), 63-69.

——, —— and —— (1974b), "Brand Choice Behavior as a Function of Information Load: Replication and Extension," *Journal of Consumer Research,* 1 (June), 33-42.

8. For example, using Jacoby et al.'s (1974a, 1974b) definition of "total" information, the probability of correct choice may be modelled as:

$$\log_e \left(\frac{P_i}{1 - P_i} \right) = \beta_1 + \beta_2 (NB * NA)$$

where NB = number of brands in the choice set and NA = number of attributes per brand on which information is provided. Such a model was estimated for all Jacoby data. The model provided a poor fit to the data collected by them.

——, George J. Szybillo and Jacqueline Busato-Schach (1977), "Information Acquisition Behavior in Brand Choice Situation," *Journal of Consumer Research*, 3 (March), 209-216.

Kelly, E. L. and Donald W. Fiske (1951), *The Prediction of Performance in Clinical Psychology*, Ann Arbor: University of Michigan Press.

Malhotra, Naresh K. (1982a), "Information Load and Consumer Decision Making," *Journal of Consumer Research*, in press.

—— (1982b), "Structural Reliability and Stability of Nonmetric Conjoint Analysis," *Journal of Marketing Research*, in press.

—— (1982c), "Multi-Stage Information Processing Behavior: An Experimental Investigation," *Journal of the Academy of Marketing Science*, in press.

Mendenhall, William and Richard L. Schaeffer (1973), *Mathematical Statistics with Applications*, North Scituate, MA: Duxbury Press.

Miller, George A. (1956), "The Magical Number Seven, Plus or Minus Two: Some Limits On Our Capacity for Processing Information," *Psychological Review*, 63 (March), 81-92.

Moreno, Nelson (1974), "The Effects of Motivation on Consumer Information Processing," unpublished Ph.D. dissertation, Purdue University.

Newman, J. W. and R. Staelin (1972), "Prepurchase Information Seeking for New Cars and Major Household Appliances," *Journal of Marketing Research*, 9 (August), 249-57.

Payne, John W. (1976), "Task Complexity and Contingent Processing in Decision Making: An Information Search and Protocol Analysis," *Organizational Behavior and Human Performance*, 16 (August), 366-87.

Quastler, Henry (1956), "Studies of Human Channel Capacity," in *Information Theory, Proceedings*, C. Cherry, ed., New York: Academic Press, 361-371.

Russo, J. Edward (1977), "The Value of Unit Price of Information," *Journal of Marketing Research*, 14 (May), 193-201.

—— (1974), "More Information Is Better: A Re-evaluation of Jacoby, Speller and Kohn," *Journal of Consumer Research*, 1 (December), 68-72.

——, J. Krieser and S. Miyashita (1975), "An Effective Display of Unit Price Information," *Journal of Marketing*, 39 (April), 11-19.

Scammon, Debra L. (1977), "Information Load and Consumers," *Journal of Consumer Research*, 4 (December), 148-55.

Summers, John O. (1974), "Less Information is Better?", *Journal of Marketing Research*, 11 (November), 467-8.

Weitz, Barton and Peter Wright (1979), "Retrospective Self-Insight on Factors Considered in Product Evaluation," *Journal of Consumer Research*, 6 (December), 280-296.

Wherry, Robert J. (1940), "The Wherry-Doolittle Test Selection Method," in *Occupational Counseling Techniques*, W. H. Stead and L. L. Shartle, eds., New York: American Book Company, 245-252.

—— (1931), "A New Formula for Predicting the Shrinkage of the Coefficient of Multiple Correlations," *Annals of Mathematical Statistics*, 2, 440-51.

Wilkie, William L. (1978), "Consumer Information Processing: Issues for Public Policymakers," in *Consumer Research for Consumer Policy*, M. Denny and R. Lund, eds., Cambridge, MA: MIT Center for Policy Alternatives, 88-117.

—— (1975), "How Consumers Use Product Information: An Assessment of Research in Relation to Public Policy Needs," prepared for the National Science Foundation, Grant No. GI-42037.

—— (1974), "Analysis of Effects of Information Load," *Journal of Marketing Research*, 11 (November), 462-466.

Wright, P. L. (1975), "Consumer Choice Strategies: Simplifying vs. Optimizing," *Journal of Marketing Research*, 12 (February), 60-67.

—— (1972), "Consumer Judgmental Strategies: Beyond the Compensatory Assumption," in *Proceedings, Third Annual Conference*, M. Venkatesan, ed., Chicago: Association for Consumer Research, 316-324.

READING 15

An Appraisal of Low-Involvement Consumer Information Processing

F. Stewart DeBruicker

It is the purpose of this paper to review and extend the currently available conceptual frameworks for studying low-involvement consumer decision processes. It also will deal with the problems of conducting empirical research on low-involvement processes and will review some of the more noteworthy studies on this topic that have recently appeared in the communications literature. These studies are welcome evidence of renewed conceptual and practical interest in the area of how advertising works among audiences that are neither fully attentive to the persuasive message nor particularly involved in the product category or the topic of the message.

The pervasively employed hierarchy of effects model, which posits sequential links between exposure, awareness, interest, trial, and acceptance or rejection of the persuasive message, may in fact be inappropriate for the evaluation of all but a small fraction of actual audience exposure situations. Using an active information processing model, Bauer and Greyser [1968] estimated that a typical consumer was exposed to upwards of 700 marketer-controlled stimuli daily. Of those exposures about 76 generated some level of minimal awareness and about one dozen actually "registered" with the respondent. By these estimates roughly one percent of all marketer-controlled stimuli receive active consideration by consumers in a day, while somewhere between ten and 99 percent of the remaining daily stimuli are processed according to the tenets of a low-involvement information processing model. If this is true then much remains to be learned about the effects of marketer-controlled communications in the vast majority of exposure situations.

This paper addresses five sets of issues pertinent to the study of low-involvement consumer decision making. The first broadens the set of operational definitions of involvement and distinguishes between those characteristics that are useful predispositions to low-involvement information processing and those of the dynamics of processing *per se.* The second discusses low-involvement research conducted on aggregates of consumers and the consequent implications for individual information processing theories. The third identifies mediating individual and situational factors that may determine when low-involvement decision-making processes prevail. The fourth discusses problems of experimental measurement of low-involvement phenomena. The final section specifies the practical consequences of low-involvement consumer decision processing.

Broadening Operational Definitions of Involvement

Krugman [1965, 1968] has termed involvement as a continuum describing the frequency with which a member of an audience makes conscious "'bridging' experiences, connections, or personal references between his or her own life and the stimulus." Krugman indicated that involvement was separate from the notions of attention, interest or excitement, in that the concept of involvement required the making of links between the individual's own knowledge, values and routinized behaviors and the topical con-

Reprinted with permission from *Attitude Research Plays for High Stakes,* John C. Maloney and Bernard Silverman, eds., Chicago: American Marketing Association, 1979, 112–132.

tent of the persuasive measures. Thus, a respondent might be able to demonstrate a near perfect recall of the general theme and specific arguments raised in a persuasive message but still be classified low on involvement if no connections are made between the communication and the individual's life. The static and dynamic implications of Krugman's ideas are worth delineating further.

Low-Involvement Status

Since the definition of involvement relies on the number of connections made between a persuasive message and elements of the respondent's life, there is a clear benefit to the researcher if the number and kind of dimensions that serve as the contact points for those connections can be identified. Understanding the prior cognitive structure or the network of contact points is a problem of defining the status of the individual's prior cognitive structure. The number of contact points might well describe a continuum of latent potential for making connections. This continuum would be a descriptor of the status of an individual's cognitive predisposition for information processing.

Robertson [1976] defined high-commitment information processing in terms of variables of state. High commitment was defined according to the existence of a salient belief system, the existence of perceived product differentiation, and the stipulation that the dimensions of perceived product differentiation be among the more salient dimensions of an individual's belief system. This three-tiered definition of commitment relies heavily upon constructs of predisposition or latent potential for high (or low) commitment processing. This draws attention to the desirability of understanding those individual factors that could precondition the existence and extent of high (or low) commitment information processing. The second and third tiers of Robertson's definition—the existence of product differentiation based on the more salient cognitive dimensions—could be used to define a hierarchical scale of commitment that may be useful in future empirical research.

Low-Involvement Processes

With respect to process Krugman suggested that low-involvement information processing would call for slow changes in cognitive states, which would legitimatize a set of possible behaviors that would have been unlikely except in the event of exposure to low-involvement persuasive messages. Once one or more of the new, possible behaviors had occurred, attitude changes would follow.[1]

Ray and his colleagues [1973] used this processing dynamic hierarchy as the basis for defining the existence of low-involvement phenomena. Unlike the cognitive status ideas of the preceding section, the process definition used by Ray required no explication of prior belief systems. By ex post interpretation of curves of aggregate changes in cognitions, behavioral tendencies and evaluations, Ray and his colleagues found support for the processing dynamic implications of low-involvement theory. The research design had the weakness of not being able to predict *a priori* whether active or low-involvement processing was likely to occur for an individual, but the methodology was commendable. Other implications of Ray's research are discussed later in this paper.

The thrust of these static and dynamic perspectives is that low-involvement processing phenomena need to be examined from both points of view. The phenomena are contingent on variables of *state,* or predisposition to cognitive activity, and on the occurrence of a sequential *process* by which knowledge enables new behaviors which then stimulate new attitudes.

Beyond Information Processing

The concept of low-involvement information processing can be extended to include almost all components of consumer decision processing. While Krugman's initial proposals were offered to rationalize the effects of television advertising exposure, low-involvement concepts can be generalized to other parts of the decision process including involvement with the product class, brands, or brand attributes pertinent to the product class.

To conclude this first section, it has been claimed that the existing definitions of involvement include both descriptions of state, or predispositions to decision processing, and descriptions of the dynamics of decision processing. Authors have used both status and process definitions in identifying low-involvement phenomena, and continued explicit use

1. Whether or not one should expect attitude change as the inevitable consequence of all low-involvement communication is debatable, however. A later section of this paper will pursue the question of the inevitability of attitude change in low-involvement situations.

of these perspectives is recommended. A second conclusion is that the concept of involvement should be extended from that of a binary state of high or low to a more continuous view depending upon the existence of a hierarchy of criteria. The existence of pertinent beliefs, the presence of perceived product differentiation, and the discrimination between products on highly salient dimensions of evaluation are examples of one such hierarchy. Finally, the concept of low-involvement information processing should be extended to apply to other elements of consumer decision processing such as product, brand or attribute involvement.

Individual vs. Aggregate Behavior

The conceptual framework of low-involvement theory is implicitly individual in character, yet the empirical evidence offered in support of low-involvement information processing has dealt with the analysis of aggregated responses. Studies reported by Krugman [1966], Wright [1973], and Ray [1973] all discussed data analyzed at the group level and found some support for the low-involvement model being consistent with the data. The problem with aggregate levels of analysis is that while they assume a certain process of individual information handling, they are unable to bring evidence to light that would support or refute the existence of the assumed underlying individual information processing activity. The need for the analysis of individual differences is an old one throughout consumer decision process research, but the need is not diminished by the number of studies that overlook it.

Krugman's [1972] discussion predicated two very different individual models of information processing, one consistent with the low-involvement view and the other consistent with the active information processing view. However, both models would be consistent with the low-involvement view if random samples of individual responses to communication were to be obtained and analyzed in grouped fashion.

The first model, which Krugman colorfully named the "American rat" process, depended upon many repetitions of a persuasive message and a relatively uninvolved and obstinate respondent. Under this model, changes in cognitions and resultant changes in predisposition to behavior occur gradually and slowly, over protracted time periods. Though the degree of change might be small following an exposure, the process of change was hypothesized as one of slight but steady inevitability.

The other model, which Krugman named the "German rat" process, postulated that only a very small number of exposures were actually responsible for any observed changes in cognition or behavior, and that somewhere between two and four exposures were all that were necessary. This model, therefore, postulated that respondents processed information in the active information processing mode, but did so only for a few exposures and during exposure events that occurred unpredictably within a series of exposures.

Assuming for the moment that both models are true for different individuals, when viewing the cumulative behaviors of respondents who behave purely according to the "German rat" or the "American rat" models, no differences would be detectable at the aggregate level, even though the underlying processes are quite different. Both sets of observations could be judged not inconsistent with group predictions derived only from low-involvement information processing theory. The differences between the two theories, however, are of considerable magnitude in their implications for research and for promotion planning.

The implications for research are familiar ones: While it is certainly acceptable to compare changes in group mean parameters via graphic plots and variance analysis, those group parameters could be derived from a variety of accumulated underlying individual behaviors, only some (or none) of which may be consistent with the hypothesized individual information processing models.

Whether low-involvement information processing is a satisfactory model of *individual* behavior, or whether it is only a model appropriate for describing the *aggregate* behavior of consumer groups is an important question. If the theory proves to be satisfactory only when applied to aggregated observations collected over groups of respondents, then the underlying assumptions about individual information processing must be brought into question. As will be discussed later in this paper, methodological advances will be required in order to develop experimental procedures that yield nonreactive measures of low-involvement individual information processing. There are few data yet reported that bear on this important distinction between group and individual models of information processing.

Mediating Personal and Situational Factors

On the conceptual side, more must be learned about what situational and personal characteristics must prevail in order for the tenets of low-involvement information processing theories to hold. Intervening variables such as perceived product differentiation, the extent of the development of an individual's belief system, and life style characteristics may be important enabling variables with respect to low-involvement information processing.

Involvement as a Personal Descriptor

The state of low involvement, or the predisposition to low-involvement information processing, can be described by the breadth and depth of an individual's beliefs and values about a desired benefit bundle. Consumer use of products and information about products may be assumed to be purposive behavior designed to yield a degree of satisfaction or relief, and the intensity with which a person pursues those satisfactions and reliefs determines whether a state of high- or low-involvement exists for that person at a given time. It is likely that only a few benefit bundles will be intensely important to an individual, and these important benefit bundles will be strongly associated with the individual's chronic personality characteristics. Though the composition of these benefit bundles may change over time, it is expected that they will exhibit a certain amount of stability across situations and within stages of a consumer's life cycle.

The acquisition and maintenance of an individual's desired benefit bundle would constitute a high-involvement set of behaviors, and products and information perceived as relevant to those benefits will receive high-involvement processing by the individual. All other acts of consumption and decision making will be relegated to chronic low-involvement status by the individual. An individual's benefit system may be defined at the product class level, the brand level or the product attribute level, depending upon the intensity of the individual's commitment to the pursuit of a given set of benefits. The greater the commitment the more detailed the individual's knowledge and evaluations of substitute products, brands, and attributes is expected to be. Of course, the opposite case would also be expected; the less important a particular benefit might be to an individual, the less the individual would be expected to know and feel about alternative products, brands or attributes.

This benefit-problem bundle perspective is consistent with the views offered by Haley [1968] and Light [1975], each of whom have suggested that there are relatively few zones a concern that an individual considers salient with respect to a given set of benefits. It further suggests that the most important benefit bundles are those that relate to an individual's fundamental personal values, as articulated by Rokeach [1968] and that lesser benefit bundles represent product or problem-oriented manifestations of these more basic, life-guiding constructs.

Given the relatively minor importance of consumer behavior in the broader spectrum of social and economic behavior, it should probably not be surprising that products and information directed toward consumer needs tend to occupy relatively small fractions of an individual's information processing capacity and to receive low-involvement status in real world information processing situations. This benefit bundle classification notion is independent from the level of perceived product differentiation. It is quite conceivable that individuals who perceive few differences between choice objects remain nonetheless very much involved in the search for benefits promised but not delivered by presently available brands.

Wells [1975] reviewed with favorable conclusions the reliability and validity of psychographic research methods, and these methods are suitable for the study of the existence and importance of individual product class benefit bundles. The ability to measure these personal characteristics has encouraging implications for using survey methods to develop pre-measures of individuals' stated benefit structures which could then be used to assign individuals into various experimental treatments in subsequent information processing studies.

Involvement as a Personal-Situational Interaction

In specifying the conditions under which low-involvement states and processes are most likely to apply, Ray [1973] chose to explain the expected existence of low-involvement information processing in terms of two types of variables: first, the individual's involvement with the topic of a persuasive message, or campaign theme involvement; and second, the degree of the individual's perceived differentiation among the set of alternative choice objects. Ray's Three-Orders model for the prediction of effects of repeated exposure is a valuable contribution to identifying the occasions when low-involvement processing conditions are likely to apply. It is unfortunate, however, that after having specified perceived product differentiation as a key mediating variable, Ray and his colleagues neither manipulated nor controlled perceived product differentiation in their otherwise complete set of experiments.

The Three-Orders model, illustrated in Figure 1, specifies certain combinations of perceived product differentiation and topic involvement that are expected to determine whether information is processed according to the active-processor model, the dissonance reduction model, or the low-involvement model.

The active-processor learning model was specified by the Three-Orders model in those situations in which the individual was highly involved in the topic of the communication and in which the individual perceived relatively large amounts of differentiation between alternative choice objects. Under conditions of high topical involvement and low perceived choice object differentiation, the Three-Orders model predicted that the Dissonance-Attribution attitude change model would apply, wherein behavioral changes were expected to precede changes in evaluations which would then stimulate a search for cognitive data that would verify the already held behavioral and attitudinal positions. Although there may be some minor problems in accepting this view of the role of Dissonance-Attribution theory and Ray could find no empirical support for it, the third implication of the Three-Orders model is more relevant to this paper.

Ray suggested that the low-involvement attitude change hierarchy would apply to those situations in which the respondent held a low level of involvement in the topic or campaign theme, *regardless* of the level of perceived object differentiation. While at first this view seems plausible, on second consideration it offends a sense of symmetry about

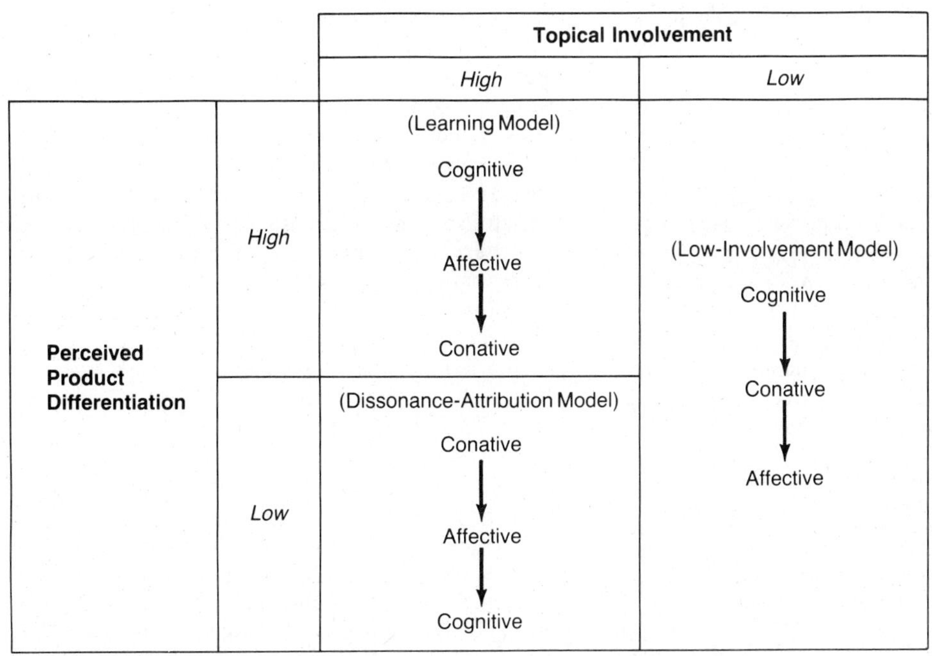

FIGURE 1
Three-Orders Model of Information Processing (Source: Graphic Interpretation of Ray [1973])

TABLE 1
Expected Differential Effects of High and Low Perceived Product Differentiation

Personal Characteristic	*When Perceived Product Differentiation Is High, Individual Tendency Would Be:*	*When Perceived Product Differentiation Is Low, Individual Tendency Would Be:*
Probability of knowledge of a relatively large number of brands	Higher	Lower
Awareness of and ability to verbalize relatively large number of product attributes	Higher	Lower
Information sources used regarding product	More, both personal and impersonal	Fewer, tend not to use impersonal
Likelihood of well developed product specific belief system	Higher	Lower
Willingness to expend energy "rationalizing" apparent inconsistencies among cognitions, evaluations, and behavioral patterns	Higher	Lower
Price sensitivity	Lower	Higher

the important notion of the level of perceived differentiation between choice objects, which according to the Three-Orders model would have no influence on the state or the process of low-involvement communication or decision making.[2]

Among individuals who perceive greater brand differentiation there is no reason on theoretical grounds to dispute the predicted low-involvement processing sequence of cognitive-conative-affective changes. Individuals in this high perceived difference-low topical involvement situation would be expected to experience changes in cognition, behavior and affective evaluation over many repetitions in the sequence suggested by Krugman. Although the rate of change may be relatively slow compared to the active processor model of the learning hierarchy, the certainty of ultimate change in behavior and affect would be rather high for this application of the low-involvement model.

A low-involvement mechanism could be hypothesized for those who perceive little difference among brands that is different from the above model in one important respect. The difference is based on the expected characteristics that distinguish high from low perceived product differentiation individuals as listed in Table 1. These hypothesized differentiating characteristics are the basis for stating a modified low-involvement microtheory for the low perceived differentiation-low involvement cell. The modification is that the expected sequence of response to low-involvement communication when perceived product differentiation is low would begin with eventual changes in cognitive activity followed by slight changes in conative activity and would terminate at that point. There would be no expected change in affective activity in any form, regardless of the length of the time period or the number of exposures.

This modification of the Three-Orders model removes the affective system from the information processing system and suggests only a two-part system made up of cognitive and conative elements. This does not deny the existence of the affective element of information processing, but it does suggest that affective considerations are irrelevant when topical

2. By reporting aggregations of individual mean levels of perception, stated likelihood of redeeming brand coupons, and stated attitudes about brands, Ray was able to identify group mean curves of cognitive-conative-affective change that were consistent with the aggregate predictions of the low-involvement hierarchy. The analysis was vulnerable to the dangers of accepting pooled information as evidence of the implied individual information processing styles, however, and the data must be considered only tentative evidence that individuals actually do process information according to the tenets of low-involvement theory.

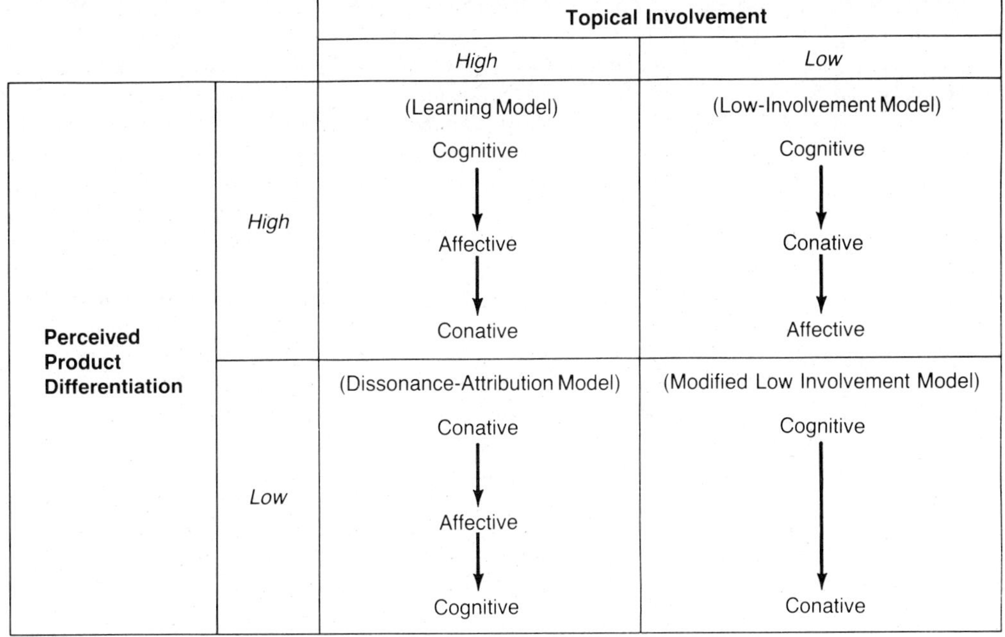

FIGURE 2
A Four-Orders Model of Information Processing

involvement is low and perceived product differentiation is also low. This implies that it would be futile to expect changes in affect to occur in these circumstances and would lead to predictions of *no* change in affect for this cell if experiments were conducted according to the paradigm of high-low topical involvement and high-low product perceived differentiation.

The contrast between the Three-Orders model and the revised form of the Three-Orders model is illustrated in Figure 2. The revised form, dubbed the Four-Orders model because of its obvious debt to the conceptual clarifications of Ray and his colleagues, has several implications. First, it suggests that there are conative and cognitive consequences for all forms of repetitive communication, though the magnitude of those consequences may be small and slow to appear in many situations. Second, it implies that there are expected affective changes in three combinations of perceived product differentiation and communications involvement, but in the fourth situation one would predict no change in affective system, regardless of the number of repetitions to which the individual might be exposed. If true, this would cast doubt on the use of affective measures as useful intermediate responses to communication, at least in low perceived product differentiation-low communications involvement situations. In such situations, measures of cognitive and conative tendencies would be much more relevant indicators of eventual consumer behavior than affective measures.

It further suggests that there is only one element of the Four-Orders model where marketer-controlled communications could be expected to show a direct and relatively sudden link with sales behavior—the traditional learning model of the high involvement-high perceived product differentiation situation. In the remaining three elements of the Four-Orders model, the linkage of media exposure to purchase behavior is neither direct nor sudden, leaving the task of interpreting the relationship between advertising and purchase behavior open to confounding by time and a host of other marketing factors. It also suggests that though the relationship between media exposure and purchase behavior is complicated and indefinitely lagged, media communications are an essential component of the consumer purchase decision process in all four elements of the Four-Orders model.

Measures of Involvement

Krugman [1966] developed an innovative set of measurement methods which were used to measure the number of connections made by respondents when exposed to advertising copy presented via film or print media, under varying pre-exposure instructions about whether post-exposure questions would be directed to the content of advertising copy or the editorial content surrounding the persuasive messages. Respondents were interviewed after exposure, their stated number of connections made between the advertising copy were counted, and the amount of time spent looking at the print advertisements was also recorded. Under instructions to pay attention to the advertising copy, respondents made fewer advertising connections than when instructed to concentrate on the editorial copy, but they tended to spend longer amounts of time examining the ads on a per connection basis as well as on an absolute basis. Since Krugman's manipulation was certainly reactive, it is unlikely that his results could be generalized to most in-home exposure situations. Although he carefully differentiates between involvement and attention, the demand characteristics of his methods still raise doubts as to their validity in other less reactive, more realistic scenarios. In spite of these shortcomings the pooled results are interesting since they suggest that under intense advertising involvement, individuals make fewer but apparently more intensive connections than when they are not so intensely involved.

Wright [1973, 1975], using methods very similar to those of Krugman, conducted information processing experiments involving a manipulation of involvement. It is likely that the indicated high and low levels of content processing involvement were more likely variations within an overall high-involvement exposure situation. In spite of the instructions given the respondents to downplay the more obvious demand characteristics, the novelty of the product category (a soybean derivative meat substitute) would naturally engender higher than normal levels of product involvement, thus improving the likelihood of message involvement. The message itself contained positioning references to natural meat products which would further differentiate the new product and intensify all respondents' involvement in the communication. When these factors are added to the normal demand characteristics of using homemakers in university sponsored research, it is safe to assume that even the so-called low-involvement groups functioned at a level of involvement that would not at all be typical of in-home situations.

The shortcomings of these experimental manipulations of involvement are understandable given the operative research objectives. What is required in future research, however, are improvements in the manipulation of levels of involvement to avoid problems of reactivity. While this paper suggests no definite methods of solving this problem, it is possible that pretesting of respondents to determine their potential for involvement, as discussed in the status versus process section of this paper, would allow predictions to be made as to the direction of experimental changes in cognitions, evaluations and behavioral indicators. If the pre-measures were administered over some significant time interval before the experiment was conducted and if the purposes of the experiment were disguised using procedures similar to those of Ray and his colleagues, many sources of involvement manipulation reactivity might be diminished or eliminated. Clearly, more work needs to be done in this area.

Strategic Implications

An important practical question which cannot be answered until the necessary empirical research has been completed is whether it is to the advantage of the promotion planner to assume that low-involvement processes are important, and therefore plan strategies assuming low-involvement conditions will prevail for the target audience; or should the planner assume that all information processing of practical consequence is by definition active involvement processing and prepare strategies aimed only at active information processors? Assuming that it becomes possible to specify those situations and individual characteristics that typify low-involvement information processing scenarios, what are the strategic consequences of that knowledge? Implications must be sought with respect to issues of desirable reach and frequency of exposure, market segmentation, selection of media, determination of the most effective content of persuasive messages, and identification of those individual characteristics most leveraged to choice behavior under low-involvement decision processing.

A distinct possibility is that low-involvement processes, while perhaps real, are anathemas to promotion strategies *per se* and that all available marketing resources should be devoted to lifting as many possible members of the audience into an active processing state.

Summary and Implications for Future Research

Empirical research claiming to deal with the differences between high- and low-involvement consumer information processing has, for the most part, dealt with differences between high and low levels of acute involvement and has not penetrated the area of genuinely low-involvement phenomena. This has been due to the difficulty of devising nonreactive experimental manipulations of involvement and also to the failure to perceive the concept of involvement as a continuous phenomenon. At this point there are no studies that can claim to have obtained data from individuals that could be termed low involvement in an *a priori* sense. Only the studies reported by Ray and his colleagues [1973] can claim to have observed the process of low-involvement information processing, and their findings are open to the criticism of pooling, and therefore obscuring, the effects of individual differences. Thus there is a scarcity of data that supports the concepts of low-involvement information processing.

There are hopes for improvement in this situation, however. The concept of low involvement can be extended to apply to an entire area of consumer decision making, going beyond the area of information processing after exposure to impersonal media messages. The areas of product, brand or attribute involvement appear to be practical extensions of the traditional views of topic or media involvement. Further, the concept of involvement can be operationalized as a continuum rather than a nominal state. This paper has offered the hierarchical notion that involvement levels increase according to the existence of a strong benefit structure within an individual, the existence of perceived product differentiation, and the existence of perceived product differentiation along one or more relatively salient product benefits. The existence or absence of these three criteria can define four levels of involvement which could be used as an independent measure in future studies of the effects of persuasive messages. They offer advantages over the simple high-low-involvement concept since they accommodate measurement procedures that are conceivably less reactive than those which have been employed to date.

The notions of involvement can be used to measure variables of individual status as well as the dynamic process by which information initiates changes in potential consumer behavior. This suggests that research designs using pre-measures as well as process observations and post-measures are necessary to capture the status and process characteristics implicit in the study of involvement. The broader, continuous concept of involvement opens the field to the use of survey methods typical in psychographic studies as an approach to defining product class involvement at the lower levels. In fact, the entire involvement continuum from benefit structure to differentiation to differentiation on "most salient" benefits are all demonstrably amenable to paper and pencil methods of observation. These observations could be used as pre-measures to classify respondents according to their "state" of involvement.

Individuals so classified could then be invited to participate in information processing field experiments using the commendable methodology developed by Ray and his colleagues, which appears to be well suited to the disguise of the true intent of the study and to the use of a variety of obtrusive and unobtrusive measures of processing activity and post-state reporting. By taking pains to report both individual differences as well as pooled treatment findings, much useful information could be developed about those personal and situational factors that correlate with low-involvement states and low-involvement processing activity. Although this research strategy needs much more consideration than it can receive here, it would be possible to study various product categories and media. In fact, multiproduct studies might well provide suitable disguises for pre- and post-measures.

It would be the goal of such a stream of research to answer the three fundamental questions raised earlier in this paper: Do individuals actually process information as suggested by the low-involvement model; if they do, what are the situational and personal factors that account for the occurrence of low-involvement processing; and what are the implications for promotion decision making, if any? That these questions are important is apparent to any who consider the sheer numbers of messages and the weight of media dollars that undoubtedly fall on unattentive, minimally involved audiences.

References

Bauer, Raymond A. and Stephen A. Greyser (1968), *Advertising in America: The Consumer View,* Boston: Harvard University, Graduate School of Business.

Haley, Russell I. (1968), "Benefit Segmentation: A Decision Oriented Research Tool," *Journal of Marketing,* 32 (July), 30–35.

Krugman, H. E. (1965), "The Impact of Television Advertising: Learning Without Involvement," *Public Opinion Quarterly,* 29 (Fall), 349–56.

—— (1968), "The Learning of Consumer Likes, Preferences and Choices," in *Applications of the Sciences in Marketing Management,* eds., Frank M. Bass, Charles W. King and Edgar A. Pessemier, New York: John Wiley, 207–25.

—— (1966), "The Measurement of Advertising Involvement," *Public Opinion Quarterly,* 30 (Winter), 583–96.

—— (1972), "Why Three Exposures May be Enough," *Journal of Advertising Research,* 21 (December), 11–15.

Light, Larry (1975), "Light Says Problem Research Will Give More Benefits Than Benefit Research," *Marketing News* (September 26), 9.

Ray, Michael (1973), "Marketing Communication and the Hierarchy of Effects," in *Sage Annual Reviews in Communication Research,* eds., F. Gerald Kline and P. Clark, Beverly Hills, CA: Sage Publications.

—— (1975), "Microtheoretical Notions of Behavioral Science and the Problems of Advertising," report no. 75–101, Cambridge, MA: Marketing Science Institute.

Robertson, Thomas S., "Low Commitment Consumer Behavior," *Journal of Advertising Research,* 19 (April), 19–24.

Rokeach, Milton (1968), "The Role of Values in Public Opinion Research," *Public Opinion Quarterly,* 30 (Winter), 547–53.

Wells, William D. (1975), "Psychographics: A Critical Review," *Journal of Marketing Research,* 12 (May), 196.

Wright, Peter (1973), "The Cognitive Processes Mediating the Acceptance of Advertising," *Journal of Marketing Research,* 10 (February), 53–62.

—— (1975), "Factors Affecting Cognitive Resistance to Advertising," *Journal of Consumer Research,* 2 (June) 1–9.

CHAPTER FOUR

Consumer Behavior and Market Segmentation

READING 16

Issues and Advances in Segmentation Research

Yoram Wind

The author reviews the current status and recent advances in segmentation research, covering segmentation problem definition, research design considerations, data collection approaches, data analysis procedures, and data interpretation and implementation. Areas for future research are identified.

Market segmentation long has been considered one of the most fundamental concepts of modern marketing. In the 20 years since the pioneering article by Wendell Smith [97], segmentation has become a dominant concept in marketing literature and practice. Besides being one of the major ways of operationalizing the marketing concept, segmentation provides guidelines for a firm's marketing strategy and resource allocation among markets and products. Faced with heterogeneous markets, a firm following a market segmentation strategy usually can increase the expected profitability (as suggested by the classic price discrimination model, which provides a major theoretical rationale for the segmentation concept [35]).

Realizing the potential benefits of market segmentation requires both management acceptance of the concept and an empirical segmentation study before implementation can begin. The practical importance of segmentation research is reflected in the marketing literature[1] and the actual practice of firms which often undertake segmentation studies and rely, at least to some extent, on the findings in their development and evaluation of marketing strategies.

Examining the current state of the art of segmentation research reveals some discrepancy between academic developments and real-world practice. Academic segmentation research has been one of the most advanced areas of research in marketing. Many of the new analytical techniques proposed in marketing have been applied to and tested in the segmentation area. Real-world segmentation studies, in contrast, have followed one of two prototypical research patterns[2] with little creativity in design or analysis:

1. *An a priori segmentation design* in which management decides on a basis for segmentation such as product purchase, loyalty, customer type, or other factor. The survey results show the segments' estimated size and their demographic, socioeconomic, psychographic, and other relevant characteristics.
2. *A clustering-based segmentation design* in which segments are determined on the basis of a clustering of respondents on a set of "relevant" variables. Benefit, need, and attitude segmentation are examples of this type of approach. As in *a priori* segmentation studies, the size and other characteristics (demographic, socioeconomic, purchase, and the like) of the segments are estimated.

Though segmentation studies have been dominated by these two prototypical designs, several major conceptual and methodological developments have been proposed in the academic literature. The advancement of market segmentation research

Reprinted by permission of the American Marketing Association from the *Journal of Marketing Research*, August 1978, 317–337.

1. See, for example, the selected bibliography on market segmentation recently published by the American Marketing Association [74].

2. The classification of segmentation studies into two categories, the *a priori* and *post hoc*, was suggested by Green [40].

requires, therefore, narrowing the gap between the academically oriented research on segmentation and the real-world application of segmentation research. Segmentation studies should be reevaluated and new designs and analytical approaches considered. Also, the academic work on segmentation should be examined to reflect management's information needs, and to incorporate better the various separate developments in marketing theory (such as the change in the focus of analysis from a single product to an assortment of products [110]) and research (such as the development in overlapping clusters [19] or new measures of attribute importance [48]).

TABLE 1
Some Major Considerations Involved in Segmentation Research Studies

I. *Problem definition*
   A. Managerial requirements
   B. A baseline vs. ongoing segmentation
   C. The segmentation model
      1. Selecting the variables for the model
      2. Traditional *a priori* and clustering-based designs vs. the newer flexible and componential segmentation designs

II. *Research design*
   A. The unit of analysis
   B. Operational definitions
   C. Sample design
   D. Data reliability
   E. Segment stability
   F. Segment homogeneity
   G. Segmentability of the market
   H. Validation
   I. Cost considerations

III. *Data collection*
   A. Primary vs. secondary sources
   B. Conventional vs. newer procedures

IV. *Data analysis*
   A. For determining the segments: classification
   B. For establishing the segments' profiles: discrimination
   C. For simultaneous classification and discrimination

V. *Data interpretation and implementation of results*
   A. Determining the number of segments and selection of target segments
   B. Translating segmentation findings into strategy

Achievement of these objectives requires a critical examination of the current state of the art in segmentation research, assessment of the major issues involved in the design and implementation of segmentation studies, and a perspective on the direction of future work. The purpose of this article is to provide such a review, for both consumer and industrial markets.[3]

Most segmentation studies have been conducted for consumer goods. Yet the concept of segmentation and most of the segmentation research approaches are equally applicable to industrial market situations [80, 106]. Hence, the intention of this review is to discuss the problems and perspectives of segmentation research in *both* consumer and industrial markets. The review, as summarized in Table 1, is organized on the basis of the five major phases of segmentation research—problem definition, research design considerations, data collection approaches, data analysis procedures, and data interpretation and implementation.

Problem Definition

The problem definition stage of segmentation research involves three major considerations: (1) managerial requirements versus the requirements proposed by the normative theory of segmentation, (2) the considerations of conducting a large-scale baseline segmentation study versus a continued series of ongoing segmentation studies, and (3) the specification of the desired segmentation model.

Managerial Requirements

Management acceptance of the market segmentation concept has resulted in the use of segmentation research to answer a wide range of marketing questions about the response of market segments to the firm's marketing strategies (price changes, new product offerings, product changes, advertising themes, promotional efforts, and the like) as well as the selection of target market segments for each of

3. The term "industrial market" refers to all organizational markets [106].

the firm's planned marketing offerings. The typical management questions which trigger and guide many market segmentation studies can be illustrated by the following objectives of several recently conducted concept-testing studies:

> *Which new product coccepts evoke the highest respondent interest, and how do the evaluations of these concepts differ by respondent groups—heavy versus light product users, and users versus nonusers of the company's brand?*
>
> *In terms of target markets for a new product concept, how do interested and disinterested respondents differ by demographic and socioeconomic characteristics, attitudes, and product usage characteristics?*
>
> *Can the market for new product concepts be segmented in terms of the respondents' price sensitivity (or other benefits sought), and what are the concept evaluations, attitudes, product usage, demographic, and other background characteristics of the various price-sensitive segments?*

These and similar questions, which have guided most of the real-world market segmentation studies, have little to do with the type of questions suggested by the normative theory of market segmentation. Normative theory focuses on how information about customer characteristics and their relation to marketing strategy variables *should* be used in the development and evaluation of a marketing strategy. Several models for the allocation of promotional resources to segments in the presence of uncertainty (both about the response to promotion by customers with given characteristics and about the degree to which each advertising medium reaches these customers) have been proposed [35, pp. 186-241] and conceptually can be extended to other marketing strategy variables. Yet the normative segmentation models have rarely, if ever, been implemented. This discrepancy between the prescriptions of the normative theory and the practice of segmentation research can be attributed, at least in part, to the difficulties in operationalizing the segmentation theory. It is this difficulty in determining the needed data on both the response elasticities *and* reachability by media and distribution outlets that calls not only for undertaking the recommendations for further work suggested by Frank et al. [35, p. 249], but also for a critical examination of the nature and value of normative segmentation theory. Understanding management's use of and difficulties in operationalizing segmentation [381], in both profit and nonprofit organizations, is thus a necessary first step toward the reevaluation of the normative theory of market segmentation. The recent work by Tollefson and Lessig [102] and Mahajan and Jain [70], and the new componential segmentation conceptualization suggested by Green and his colleagues [47] therefore represent promising first steps in this direction.

Baseline Versus Ongoing Segmentation Studies

Many segmentation studies have been designed as large, single effort, and expensive "baseline" studies. Such studies are justified in a variety of situations in which management would like to understand the basic structure of the market. Yet this type of study rarely has had subsequent effect on the other studies and strategies of a firm. Not uncommonly, after conducting a baseline study, firms continue to undertake other marketing studies such as concept and product testing with no regard for the concept of segmentation or the findings of the earlier study. This peculiar situation is partly due to habit—the continuation of past practices of analyzing most marketing research studies at the total sample level and not the segment level—and partly due to management disappointment with the relevance and operationalization of the guidelines provided by many segmentation studies.

To benefit fully from segmentation, whether or not baseline studies are conducted, management must employ the concept of segmentation in *all* studies, i.e., analyze the data of *all* studies at the segment level. Furthermore, any monitoring of the firm's product performance (on profitability, market share, or growth, for example) should be undertaken not only at the total market level but at the segment level as well [115].

The Segmentation Model

The segmentation model requires the selection of *a basis for segmentation* (the dependent variable) as well as *descriptors* (the independent variables) of the various segments. The variables used as bases for and descriptors of segments have included *all* variables suggested in the consumer behavior literature. These variables can be divided into two types—*general customer characteristics*, including demographic and socioeconomic characteristics, personality and life style characteristics, and attitudes and behavior toward mass media and distribution outlets, and *situation-specific customer characteristics* such as product usage and purchase patterns, attitudes toward the product and its consumption, benefits sought in a product category, and any responses to specific marketing variables such as new product concepts, advertisements, and the like.

In building an organizational segmentation model, the variables to be included should be not only the characteristics of the relevant organizational decision-making units (DMUs) but also organizational characteristics such as size and SIC. Both sets of variables include "general" *and* "situation-specific" characteristics.[4]

Selection of Variables for the Model. In the selection of variables for the segmentation model, the major considerations are (1) management's specific needs and (2) the current state of the marketing and consumer behavior knowledge about the relevance of various variables as bases for, and descriptors of, market segments.

Management needs are an obvious but somewhat neglected consideration. Conceptually, the bases for segmentation could vary depending on the specific decisions facing management. If, for example, management is concerned with the likely impact of a price increase on its customers, the appropriate basis might be the current customers' price sensitivity. If, however, management is concerned with the loss of customers, the basis for segmentation could be actual or likely switching behavior, which in turn could be coupled with a secondary basis such as the reasons for switching. In contrast to the theory of segmentation that implies that there is a *single best* way of segmenting a market, the range and variety of marketing decisions suggest that any attempt to use a single basis for segmentation (such as psychographic, brand preference, or product usage) for *all* marketing decisions may result in incorrect marketing decisions as well as a waste of resources.

Over the years almost all variables have been used as bases for market segmentation. Although no systematic and exhaustive evaluation of this experience has been undertaken, a consensus seems to have emerged that some variables are "better" than others as a basis for segmentation. Some of the author's "preferred" bases for segmentation for consumer and organizational marketing decisions follow.

- *For general understanding of a market:*
  - —Benefits sought (in industrial markets, the criterion used is purchase decision)
  - —Product purchase and usage patterns
  - —Needs
  - —Brand loyalty and switching pattern
  - —A hybrid of the variables above
- *For positioning studies:*
  - —Product usage
  - —Produce preference
  - —Benefits sought
  - —A hybrid of the variables above
- *For new product concepts (and new product introduction):*
  - —Reaction to new concepts (intention to buy, preference over current brand, etc.)
  - —Benefits sought
- *For pricing decisions:*
  - —Price sensitivity
  - —Deal proneness
  - —Price sensitivity by purchase/usage patterns
- *For advertising decisions:*
  - —Benefits sought
  - —Media usage
  - —Psychographic/life style
  - —A hybrid (of the variables above and/or purchase/usage patterns)
- *For distribution decisions:*
  - —Store loyalty and patronage
  - —Benefits sought in store selection

Common to these variables (and in line with the theory of segmentation which centers on differing elasticities to marketing variables) is the focus on various consumers' (and organizational buyers') responses to marketing stimuli. This emphasis on "situation-specific variables" is consistent with the needs of most marketing managers and current findings [35, pp. 66–89; 53, 73]. The heavy reliance on benefits sought [56] (and, in organizational segmentation studies, on criteria used in the purchase decision) and the product or service purchase pattern reflects not only the author's personal bias but also the

4. For a review of specific variables that have been used in consumer and organizational segmentation studies, see [35].

emphasis of a considerable amount of current segmentation research.

Surprisingly, despite the attention given over the years to *hierarchy of effects* models and more recently to consumers' *information processing* [7, 104], few of the nonpurchase variables, with the exception of benefit, need, and attitude segmentation, have served as a basis for segmentation. Similarly, despite the recent interest in the *entire consumption process* (including usage, maintenance, and disposal [79]), few of the *consumption* (as opposed to *purchase*) variables have been used as a basis for segmentation. Yet, for certain purposes, and especially for public policy decisions, one may want to consider some of these neglected aspects of the consumer decision-making *process* as the dependent variables in a segmentation model [81].

Whereas the selection of a *basis* for segmentation drawn from management needs is straightforward, the selection of variables as *descriptors* of the segments is more complex. This complexity stems from three factors:

1. The enormous number of possible variables. Most of the variables covered in the consumer behavior literature can and have at some time been considered as segment descriptors.
2. The often questionable link between the selected basis for segmentation and the segment descriptors. Segments with varying elasticities to marketing variables may not be identifiable in terms of demographic and other segment descriptors. Conversely, segments defined in terms of demographic and other general customer characteristics tend to be identifiable but may not have varying elasticities to marketing variables. The latter situation restricts management's ability to pursue a segmentation strategy aimed at the given segments (and calls for examination of other possible bases for segmentation). The former situation allows management to follow at least a "self-selection" strategy [35, p. 176].
3. The question of actionability, which relates to management's ability to use information (on the discriminating descriptors) as inputs to the design of the firm's marketing strategy (e.g., product design, copy execution, media scheduling, distribution coverage, etc.).

The second guide to the selection of descriptor variables for the segmentation model is current understanding of the link between the considered variables and actual consumer responses to marketing actions. Surprisingly, despite thousands of academic and commercial studies by marketing and consumer researchers, one can draw very few generalizations as to which variables would have what effect under what conditions. This frustrating state of affairs is primarily due to four factors.

1. Lack of a systematic effort (by both academicians and practitioners) to build a *cumulative* body of substantive findings about consumer behavior.
2. Lack of specific models which link behavior (and other bases for segmentation) to descriptor variables and thus *predict* which descriptor variables should be used.[5]
3. The nonrepresentative nature of most of the academic studies with respect to sample design (e.g., small convenient samples), type of respondents (e.g., students), and tasks (e.g., nonmarketing-related tasks). Even many of the real-world segmentation studies are based on relatively small and nonrepresentative samples.
4. Lack of comparable conceptual and operational definitions of variables across studies.

Because of these limitations all that can be expected from the behavioral sciences and the consumer and organizational buying behavior theories and findings is an initial set of hypotheses on the likely relationship between consumer (and organizational) concepts (variables) and some specific marketing response. Following this approach, one could establish a set of hypotheses such as:

- Consumer likelihood to buy new products increases:
  - the higher the education, income, and occupational status [90].
  - the higher the respondent scores on venturesomeness, cosmopolitanism, social integration, and general self-confidence [82].
  - the lower the perceived risk [90].
- Consumer likelihood to switch brands increases:
  - the larger the number of stores shopped.
  - the less the perceived quality differentiation among the brands.

5. For a notable exception, see Blattberg et al. [10], who built a model of the deal prone household, linked the parameters of the model to household demographic variables, and thus predicted which variables should be used as descriptors.

- Consumer likelihood to choose a low priced brand increases:
  - —the lower the confidence in price as an indication of quality.
  - —the lower the perceived social significance of the brand choice.
- Consumer likelihood to buy private label brands increases:
  - —the higher the education and income of the respondent.
- The likelihood of an organization to buy new products (and have a fast rate of adoption) increases:[6]
  - —the greater the prestige of the organization.
  - —the larger the organization.
  - —the more specialized the organization.
  - —the more financially stable the organization.
  - —the more cosmopolitan the decision makers' orientation.
  - —the greater the risk-taking propensity and the lower the perceived risk.
  - —the younger the decision makers.
  - —the higher the entrepreneurial orientation of the decision makers.
  - —the greater the exposure to supportive mass media communications.
  - —the less formalized the decision process.

These and similar hypotheses can be derived from the current literature on consumer and organizational buying behavior. Such hypotheses can serve as guidelines for the selection of variables in the segmentation model. Subsequent segmentation studies could provide the vehicle for testing these hypotheses.

A relatively neglected area of study has been the examination of the specification of the segmentation models. A notable exception has been regression segmentation models. Examination has suggested that if these models are misspecified by omitted variables or functional forms different from the "true" process, they may be useful descriptors of the true purchase rate (or the group means for similar individuals), although the estimated model coefficient will be biased, except in special circumstances [5]. Beckwith and Sasieni [5] developed misspecification tests for the regression segmentation models. It is desirable to use such tests whenever appropriate and to develop similar ones for other (nonregression) segmentation models.

6. These hypotheses are based on the Rogers and Shoemaker review of the diffusion of innovation literature [92].

Traditional A Priori and Clustering-Based Designs Versus Newer Flexible and Componential Segmentation Models. Four major types of models can be used in an effort to segment a market. They include the traditional *a priori* and *clustering-based* segmentation models, and the new models of flexible [91] and componential segmentation [47], which are based on different sets of assumptions. The selection of a model depends on management's objectives in undertaking a segmentation study.

A priori segmentation models have had as the dependent variable (the basis for segmentation) either product-specific variables (e.g., product usage, loyalty) or general customer characteristics (e.g., demographic factors). The typical research design for an *a priori* segmentation model involves seven stages.

1. Selection of the (*a priori*) basis for segmentation.
2. Selection of a set of segment descriptors (including hypotheses on the possible link between these descriptors and the basis for segmentation).
3. Sample design—mostly stratified and occasionally a quota sample according to the various classes of the dependent variable.
4. Data collection.
5. Formation of the segments based on a sorting of respondents into categories.
6. Establishment of the (conditional) profile of the segments using multiple discriminant analysis, multiple regression analysis, AID, or some other appropriate analytical procedure.
7. Translation of the findings about the segments' estimated size and profile into specific marketing strategies, including the selection of target segments and the design or modification of specific marketing strategy.

Clustering-based segmentation models differ from *a priori* models only with respect to the way the basis for segmentation is selected, i.e., instead of an *a priori* selection of a dependent variable, in the clustering-based approach the number and type of segments are not known in advance and are determined from the clustering of respondents on their similarities on some selected set of variables. Most commonly the variables used in the clustering-based models are needs, attitudes, life style and other psychographic characteristics, or benefits sought. Frequently the clustering procedure is preceded by a factor analysis designed to reduce the original set of variables. Other than the fifth step in the prototypical *a priori* model

—the formation of segments—and occasionally the specific sample design, the rest of the steps in the segmentation research design are the same.

Clustering-based segmentation models occasionally are combined with some *a priori* bases. For example, the sample first can be divided into brand users and nonusers (or heavy and light users, and the like) and then the respondents in each *a priori* segment can be clustered according to some other basis for segmentation such as needs, benefits, or the like. This and similar hybrid approaches such as Peterson's *sequential clustering* [86] (i.e., clustering on demographic characteristics followed by attitudinal clustering within each demographic segment), or Blattberg and Şen's multidimensional approach [11, 12] address the problem of intrasegment heterogeneity. Hybrid approaches are particularly useful in organizational segmentation problems in which the first level of segmentation is based on organizational demographic characteristics (e.g., SIC, size) followed by product usage or criteria used in the purchase decision [114]. Despite their conceptual attractiveness, hybrid approaches do require relatively large sample sizes.

In both the hybrid and "pure" clustering models the researcher is confronted with a series of decisions about the selection of a clustering algorithm and the determination of the number of segments. Some of the major considerations in this area are discussed in a subsequent section.

Flexible Segmentation. In contrast to *a priori* segmentation in which the segments are determined at the outset of the study, the clustering-based segmentation in which the selected segments are based on the results of the clustering analysis, the flexible segmentation model offers a dynamic approach to the segmentation problem. By this approach one can develop and examine a large number of alternative segments, each composed of those consumers or organizations exhibiting a similar pattern of responses to new "test" products (defined as a specific product feature configuration). The flexible segmentation approach is based on the integration of the results of a conjoint analysis study [52, 120] and a computer simulation of consumer choice behavior [84, 117]. Conjoint analysis studies usually consist of three major parts: (1) preference ranking or rating of a set of hypothetical products, each described as different levels on two factors at a time [63, 64] or as different levels on the full set of factors [46, 53] (the data from this task constitute the input to one of the nonmetric or metric conjoint analysis algorithms [16, 50, 67, 68, 95, 100] which produce a vector of utilities—for the various factors and levels—for each respondent); (2) perceptual ranking or rating of the current brands on the same set of attributes used in the preference task; and (3) a set of demographic and other background characteristics.

The simulation uses these three data bases as inputs and requires the active participation of management in designing a set of "new product offerings" (each defined as a unique combination of product features—specific levels on each of the factors included in the conjoint analysis study). Management participation can be on a real time basis in which managers interact directly with the computer simulation. Alternatively, management can specify in advance a number of plausible new product concepts, or react to a number of "best" product combinations.

The consumer choice simulator is based on the assumption that consumers choose the offering (new product or existing brand) with the highest utility.[7] The simulator is designed to establish (1) the consumer's share of choices among the existing brands, which can be validated against current market share data if available, and (2) the consumer's likely switching behavior upon the introduction of any new product. This phase provides a series of brand-switching matrices. Within each matrix management can select any cell or combination of cells as a possible market segment (e.g., those consumers remaining with brand i versus those who switched to new brand j, etc.). Once the desired segments (cell or cell combination) have been selected, the demographic, life style, and other relevant segment characteristics can be deter-

7. Simulators have been developed not only on the basis of such 0,1 choice rules but also on the basis of a probability of choice; i.e., the utility for a given item is calculated as a percentage of the total utility for the brands the respondent considers in his or her feasible set. More sophisticated choice simulators also have been developed and are suggested elsewhere [50]. Experience to date (with five simulators) suggests that the simple simulator described above can reproduce accurately the market share of an existing set of brands. Yet further experimental work is called for to refine the computer's simulations to take into account new features such as consumers' "learning" of factors over time and as a function of the marketing efforts of the firm and its competitors, the description of new item profiles not in terms of deterministic levels for each factor but as a probability distribution over factor levels, etc.

mined by a series of multiple discriminant analyses which can be incorporated in the simulation.

The flexible segmentation approach departs from the traditional *a priori* and clustering-based approaches by offering management the flexibility of "building up" segments (cell or cell combination within any specific brand-switching matrix) based on the consumers' response to alternative product offerings (under various competitive and environmental conditions). In addition, having selected a segment, management has easy (interactive mode) information on the estimated size of the segment and its discriminating characteristics.

Componential Segmentation. The componential segmentation model proposed by Green et al. [47] shifts the emphasis of the segmentation model from the partitioning of a market to a *prediction* of which person type (described by a particular set of demographic and other psychographic attribute levels) will be most responsive to what type of product feature. The componential segmentation model is an ingenious extension of conjoint analysis and orthogonal arrays to cover not only product features but also person features. In componential segmentation the researcher is interested in developing, in addition to parameter values for the product stimuli, parameter values for various respondent characteristics (demographic, product usage, etc.).

In a typical conjoint analysis approach to market segmentation, a matrix of subjects by utilities is developed. This matrix can serve as the input to the determination of the profile of some *a priori* segments (e.g., product users versus nonusers) or alternatively as the input to a clustering program which would result in a number of benefit segments [54]. In componential segmentation, the same design principles which guide the selection of (product) stimuli are applied also to the selection of respondents. For example, in a study for a new health insurance product, four sets of respondent characteristics were identified on the basis of previous experience and management judgment: age (under 50, 50–65, and over 65), sex (male, female), marital status (married, single), and current insurance status (have some health insurance with the given company, have health insurance with another company, and do not have any supplementary health insurance). Given these factors and levels, if a full factorial design were used one would have 36 possible customer profiles (3 × 2 × 2 × 3). Employing an orthogonal array design, one can use only nine combinations. Such a design requires the screening of respondents to select those who meet the nine profile requirements.[8] Each respondent is then interviewed and administered the conjoint analysis task for the evaluation of a set of hypothetical health insurance products (also selected following an orthogonal array design of 18 combinations of five product features each at three levels). Having completed the data collection phase, the researchers would have a 9 × 18 matrix of averaged profile evaluations of the 18 stimuli by the nine groups of respondents. This data matrix then is submitted to the COSEG (*co*mponential *seg*mentation) model [38] which decomposes the matrix into separate parameter values (utilities) for each of the levels of the product feature factors (comprising the stimulus cards) and separate parameter values (saliences) for each of the levels of the four consumer profile characteristics (describing the respondents) which indicate how much each profile characteristic contributes to variation in the evaluative responses.

Given these two sets of parameters, the researcher can make predictions about the relative evaluation of any of the 243 possible product features (3^5) by any of the 36 respondent types. The five product feature utilities and four respondent saliences and the standard deviation of the predictor errors (as estimated for the 9 × 18 matrix) are used with a Monte Carlo simulator to estimate (1) for each respondent segment the frequency of first choices for each of the considered new product combinations and (2) for each new product combination the frequency of first choices across segments.

The COSEG model offers a new conceptualization for market segmentation because it focuses on the building blocks of segments and offers simultaneously an analysis of the market segment for a given product offering and an evaluation of the most desirable product offering (or positioning). The concept and algorithm of componential segmentation can be extended to cover not only two data sets (product feature and respondent characteristics) but three or more data sets by adding, for example, the components of usage situations.

---

8. Care should be given in the survey stage to count carefully the incidence of each profile in the population. This step is essential if one wants to use the componential segmentation model not only for the identification of segments but also for the estimation of the size of each segment.

The model and measurement of componential segmentation apply to both consumer and industrial market situations. In fact, the first commercial application of componential segmentation was conducted by Green and his colleagues for a firm engaged in the marketing of credit cards. This study was conducted with the design of a new credit card and the respondents were retail establishments selected on the basis of four sets of establishment characteristics (type of establishment, size of establishment, the establishment's current favorite card, and the number of credit cards honored by the establishment) [40].

Research Design

Research designs for a segmentation study depend primarily on the segmentation model used and the researcher's creativity and skills. Each of the four segmentation models (*a priori*, clustering-based, flexible, and componential segmentation) requires a unique research design. Because the specific research designs for the four approaches are discussed elsewhere,[9] this section covers some of the more general considerations involved in the design of any segmentation research project (and which to some extent are also relevant for the design of other marketing studies). These considerations include nine major questions.

1. What is the most appropriate unit of analysis (e.g., an individual, a household, a buying center)?
2. How should the variables be defined operationally and what is the most appropriate stimulus execution?
3. What is the most appropriate sample design?
4. How reliable are the data and how should one treat unreliable data?
5. How stable are the segments over time?
6. How homogeneous are the segments?
7. How segmentable is the market?
8. How can the results of a segmentation study be validated?
9. What are the cost considerations in the design of a segmentation study?

9. Research designs for *a priori* and clustering-based segmentation are presented in [35], whereas the research designs for flexible segmentation and componential segmentation are described in [9] and [47], respectively.

The Unit of Analysis

The marketing literature recognizes that most purchase and consumption behavior involves more than a single individual (the social context of, and influence on, purchase and consumption behavior). Yet most of the empirical market segmentation (as well as consumer behavior and marketing) studies ignore this premise and, with few exceptions, center on the individual as the sole unit of analysis.

This discrepancy between the "desired" and actual unit of analysis can be attributed primarily to the conceptual and methodological problems involved in moving from the individual to the multiperson situation. Such a move would require:

1. *Identification of the relevant respondents*—those who should be included in the unit of analysis. In a consumer segmentation study one should determine whether the unit of analysis includes the husband and wife, the mother and children, the husband, the wife, the entire family including both parents and children, etc. Similarly, in an organizational segmentation study one should determine which organizational members should be interviewed—the purchasing agent, the purchasing agent and intended product user, the controller, etc. [113]. The determination of the relevant respondents can either be made in advance or established empirically in the course of the data collection phase by snowball sampling procedures.
2. *Determination of a multiperson dependent variable.* One of the major problems in the analysis of multiperson data is the development of a dependent variable which reflects the decisions of two or more individuals. In this context two cases are trivial: whenever a single measure reflects the results of the preference and decision processes of two or more individuals (as in the case of the actual purchase of a single brand, excluding the case of multibrand purchases, by a household), and whenever the two or more individuals involved are congruent in their preference and choice behavior. There are no statistics on the actual incidence of these two cases. One can safely assume, however, that in many cases there is some degree of incongruency among the members of the buying center.

Analysis of this incongruency can follow two major approaches which differ in the level of analysis. The *aggregate approach* is based on analyzing separately the responses of the husbands and those of the wives and reporting any differences between the two groups (at the total sample or the segment level). This approach can be extended to cover children or any other members of the buying center. Although the easiest for analysis, this approach is conceptually undesirable because it does not solve the problem of intrahousehold (or intraorganizational) incongruency and its effect on the household (or organization) decision process and behavior.

The second approach is based on *individual household analysis*. In this case each *household* serves as the unit of analysis. For the simple husband-wife case, each household is described in terms of two vectors, one for the husband and one for the wife, and households are clustered on the basis of their similarities on the two sets of vectors. This approach was used in two recent studies. In one study among 120 couples in six metropolitan areas, life style attitudinal data were collected from both husbands and wives, and the 120 households were divided into six segments each representing a unique life style-attitudinal profile *and* different pattern of agreement between husband and wife with respect to the given attitudes. The small sample size does not justify delving into the substantive findings, but they suggest that the proposed approach is feasible. The second study on interest areas did not lead, however, to clearcut interpretable results.

The analysis of husband-wife pairs is relatively simple. Applying the same clustering approach to buying centers composed of three or more individuals is somewhat more complex, especially in the case of the household because households differ with respect to the number of children and adults present and the specific individuals involved in any given decision. In these cases a series of cluster analyses can be conducted. The total sample is divided into subsamples, each homogeneous with respect to the number of relevant decision makers (for example, a subsample of husbands and wives with no children, and another subsample of couples with one child, etc.). The data for each subsample are submitted to a separate cluster analysis to obtain a number of segments for each subsample. The resulting clusters are in turn clustered (with respect to some relevant criterion such as amount and type of household purchases) to obtain a set of higher order clusters which comprise segments from various subsamples.

Similar approaches also can be used in considering a segmentation of organizations. In these cases the first subsamples can be determined on the basis of the composition of the buying center, e.g., only purchasing agents, purchasing agent and user, etc.

3. *Accounting for multiperson independent variables.* Whether the dependent variable is a single or multiple measure, reflecting individual or multiperson choice behavior, one can elect to use as explanatory variables the characteristics of a single individual, the characteristics of two or more individuals, or the characteristics of the household (or organization). Whenever the (demographic, psychographic, and other) characteristics of a single individual are included in the analysis, several multivariate statistical techniques (such as multiple regression analysis of AID) can be used to establish the nature and magnitude of the statistical association between the independent variables and the dependent variable.

If more than the characteristics of a single individual are included, one could treat these as another set of independent variables. Following this approach one could, for example, use the same analytical techniques as those used in the single respondent case (e.g., the brand choice of a household will be explained by using the husband's psychographic characteristics *and* his wife's psychographic characteristics). An alternative approach would be to rely on canonical correlation between the husband's and wife's response sets to reveal those items that are most contributory to husband-wife association. (Null cases could be set up by making random pairings of men and women.)

The third case involves the development of "group type" characteristics (such as group cohesiveness, autonomy, intimacy, polarization, stability, flexibility, etc.). This is the least developed area in both household and organizational studies despite some intriguing early developments in the measurement of group dimensions by social psychologists [60]. Once group type characteristics are developed, their analysis is straightforward and similar to the case in which one uses a single set of individual characteristics as the explanatory variable.

Operational Definitions

Having "passed" the managerial relevance and reasonableness considerations, the segmentation researcher should address the question of how to define operationally the dependent and independent variables. Developing operational definitions for selected variables is not a trivial task. Consider, for example, the situation of a clothing manufacturer who plans the introduction of a line with designs portraying musical instruments, notes, and personalities. A suggested basis for market segmentation is "music lovers." But how could the variable be defined? Should it include persons who respond favorably to the statement, "I love music"? Those who go to classical concerts? Or perhaps those who go to rock concerts? Those who play a musical instrument? Or those who listen to an FM classical music station? Furthermore, how should these variables be measured? Should they be rated on some 2, 3, 4, 5, 6, 7, 8, 9, 10, or 11 point scale? Should they be ranked, assigned a constant sum value, or based on some free response data? Or should they be based on recall or on some diary-keeping procedure? It is evident that any of these or other possible definitions might result in different segment sizes and compositions. Such decisions also have a major impact on the nature of the required analytical procedures.

The importance of a careful operational definition of the dependent and independent variables of the segmentation model can hardly be debated. Yet in many segmentation studies little attention is given to an explicit evaluation of alternative operational definitions. Appropriate definitions and the testing of alternative operational definitions are especially crucial in psychographic research [107, 116] and in conjoint-analysis-based segmentation studies. The results of conjoint analysis are limited to the factors and levels included in the design. Omission of an important factor, exaggeration of the levels of any factor, or alternatively too small a difference among the levels of a given factor might lead to erroneous results.

Having defined the variables of interest and the respondent task, the researcher is still confronted with the question of stimuli execution. In benefit segmentation studies, for example, one can consider presenting the benefits (product features) as verbal descriptions, artist's conceptions, color photographs of hypothetical products, or advertisements (or commericals) for the various benefits. A few studies have been conducted in this area, but little is known about the effect of alternative executions on consumer response and more work is needed.

Sample Design

The objective of any segmentation research study is not merely to explain differences among the specific respondents or to segment the sample, but rather to project the results of the study to the relevant universe. The projectability of results requires the use of an appropriate probability sample. Yet the great majority of segmentation studies rely on a quota sample. If quota samples or strict screening for specific respondent profiles (as required by the componential segmentation model) are used, the researcher must select the respondents for the screening interview on the basis of strict probability procedures and must keep accurate records of the screening data.

Another important consideration is the examination of any systematic differences between respondents and nonrespondents. Whereas nonresponse bias is widely recognized, most segmentation (and marketing) studies tend to ignore it. A growing body of evidence suggests that in many situations nonrespondents differ significantly from respondents. For example, a recent segmentation study for a bread product showed that the respondents to a personal interview had considerably higher bread consumption than those respondents who could not be reached in the first attempt and required 4-6 callbacks to recruit.

Because of the increasing cost of data collection ($30–60 per interview is not uncommon for an hour-long personal interview), the need for projectability, and the relatively small universe of many organizational buying firms, greater reliance should be placed, in both consumer and organizational buying segmentation studies, on rigorous telephone screening (which is less expensive) followed by interviews with a relatively small but select sample of respondents, and a small subsample of nonrespondents.

Data Reliability

Despite the importance of assuring that segmentation analysis is conducted on reliable data, little attention is paid to this issue in most segmentation (and marketing) studies, and the data analyzed are assumed to be reliable. Some variables (e.g., demographic characteristics) are more reliable than others (e.g., attitudes and psychographic characteristics). Whenever there is reason to suspect the reliability of some variables, certain safeguards such as test-retest reliability measures should be considered. With respect to attitude data, if test-retest data are collected, the degree of reliability can be considered explicitly in the factoring procedure.

Green [40] proposes a data collection and analysis procedure in which individual item reliability is used in the factoring process itself. Each attitude item is replicated across a group of respondents and the product moment correlation between the test and retest scores constitutes the measure of each item's reliability. The factoring procedure is a modified principal components method in which the entries of the correlation matrix (the usual starting point of the factor analysis) are modified to give greater weight to the more reliable items. In this way the first principal components—those that are usually retained in subsequent rotation—are the most error-free, and the discarded components tend to be those that are more errorful. This approach leads to a more meaningful factor structure because the more reliable items have a greater influence in the delineation of that structure.

This and other procedures to handle unreliable data should be considered in the design of segmentation studies because the implicitly assumed reliability may not in fact exist. Of special interest in this context are the developments in the study of *generalizability* [24]. Traditional reliability measures assume that the design of a measuring procedure has been fixed with the possible exception of the number of items, and that one wants a numerical index of the precision of the device (i.e., reliability coefficient). A generalizability study, in contrast, covers (by appropriate analysis of variance design) all possible causes of discrepancies among observations. To date, the generalizability test has not been applied in segmentation (or other marketing) studies. The concept is intriguing and should be explored in the instrument-development stage of segmentation studies.

Segment Stability

An often neglected aspect of segmentation research is the question of segment stability over situations and time; i.e., given the assignment of individual i to segment j, how likely is it that the individual will remain in the same segment over time and different situations? The answer to this question depends on three sets of factors.

1. The basis for segmentation. In general one might hypothesize that the more specific the basis for segmentation (e.g., price sensitivity for or purchase of a given brand) the less stable the segment. Similarly, the more general the basis for segmentation (benefits sought from the product category or needs) the more stable the segment.
2. The volatility of the marketplace. Changes in the competitive activities and other environmental (political, legal, cultural, economic, etc.) conditions are likely to disturb the stability of the segments, and increase the likelihood of switching among segments.
3. Consumer characteristics. All consumers go through basic life cycle changes; even in the short term (within a life cycle stage), consumers may differ with respect to their likelihood to change and the nature of the change.

The specific variables which operate in each of these three sets of conditions must be identified, and the nature and magnitude of their impact on changes in the stability of various segments (e.g., buyers versus nonbuyers, different benefit segments, etc.) should be assessed.

Most of the current segmentation research efforts are based on cross-sectional data. In these cases the stability question is critical in determining the "aging" of the data, i.e., the length of time—two years? one year? six months?—during which the findings of a segmentation study are likely to hold. To date there are only a few unpublished industry cases in which the same market was segmented two or more times during a period of a few years. In these cases (ranging from frequently purchased food products to insurance policies), surprisingly few changes have been observed in the estimated size and composition of various segments over a relatively short period of time (1-3 years).[10]

Longitudinal data are applicable to an analysis

10. This stability has been observed at the aggregate and *not* individual level. It might, therefore, be similar to the case observed by Bass [3] of stable market shares despite considerable brand switching activities within the market.

of the stability of market segments at the individual level. Yet most of the segmentation researchers using such data have tended to ignore the stability question and instead have tried to develop measures such as brand loyalty, deal proneness, and the like, which reflect the *dynamics* of consumer behavior over a period of time. Whereas the value of such efforts can hardly be debated, it is desirable to use the available longitudinal data to address also the question of segment stability over time and situations. In the few cases in which segment stability was examined (such as [11, 12]), segments based on behavior over time did in fact show stability over three or four years—the length of time for which data were available. Some stability of benefit segments over a two-year period has been found [14]. Similar stability of psychographic segments from two independent samples over a two-year period also was found in an unpublished study by Wells.

Segment Homogeneity

Segmentation studies commonly involve the determination of the segments (based on either *a priori* judgment or a clustering-based approach) followed by the identification of the segment profile on the respondents' other characteristics. The latter stage is usually undertaken by examining the possibility of significant differences between segment means on a set of background variables.

Finding that two or more segments *are* different in terms of their mean profiles does not provide any indication about the possible segments *within* each segment. Members of a "buyer" segment, for example, may buy a given brand for different reasons. They may be very heterogeneous in their needs, demographic characteristics, and information requirements. In principle, almost every segment may, in turn, be decomposable into subsegments. Hence, to achieve intrasegment homogeneity, a very specific multidimensional definition of the basis for segmentation is required.

To fully understand the structure of selected market segments, one must understand the degree of homogeneity of each segment [43] and, in particular, be able to identify the number of subsegments, their relative size, and composition. The most common approach to the identification of subsegments is a hybrid segmentation approach in which the researcher searches for further subsegments among the *a priori* segments by clustering the members of each segment, or alternatively by applying an *a priori* segmentation scheme to each of the segments established by a clustering of respondents. Similarly one can use the sequential segmentation approach suggested by Peterson [86].

More recently, Green and his colleagues [44] suggested the application of Lazarsfeld's latent class analysis [69] and orthogonal array designs to the problem of segment partitioning. Latent structure analysis is concerned with the discovery and measurement of the underlying structure of phenomena (e.g., attitudes), when these underlying variables (attitudes) are only probabilistically related to the responses. In the segmentation context one can envision an aggregate multiway contingency table which displays association among two or more categorical variables (such as high and low product usage and high and low brand loyalty) which is decomposed into two or more subtables (based on some descriptor variables such as age, education, etc.)—the latent classes. The entries of the new subtables do not show association across the original qualitative variables; yet when the cell entries of the subtables are added, the original association reappears.

The operationalization problems associated with latent structure analysis [78] are solved by use of Carroll's CANDECOMP (*can*onical *decomp*osition) model and algorithm [18] to find the size of each latent class and the estimated probabilities of occurrence for each level of each variable for multiway tables involving up to seven variables. The CANDECOMP model and algorithm were applied to a large study on the characteristics of adopters of a new telecommunications service and revealed managerially meaningful subsegments of adopters [44].

The Segmentability of the Market

Segmentation studies are based on the premise that the given market is heterogeneous and can be segmented. Most empirical segmentation studies support this premise. It is not uncommon, however, to find markets in which no significant differences are found among various segments with respect to their demographic or other relevant consumer characteristics such as response elasticities to marketing variables.[11]

11. It is important to note, however, that if segments do not have different characteristics (such as demographic features) but do show differing elasticities to marketing variables, management still can use a self-selection strategy [35].

In these cases it might be of value to be able to assess the degree of segmentability of a market.

A measure of the segmentability of a market recently was proposed in the context of the componential segmentation model [40]. Before application of the COSEG model the researcher can take the respondents' ratings of the set of product stimuli and submit them to a conventional two-way ANOVA. Using Hays' omega square measure [59], the researcher can obtain an index of the importance of the respondents, the stimuli, and the interaction between stimuli and respondents. If the ω^2 for the subjects and the interaction effects (between stimuli and subjects) are small and the ω^2 for stimuli are large, the market does not seem to be amenable to segmentation given the specific set of respondent characteristics and stimuli (product features).

Validation

One of the major discrepancies between the academic and commercial studies of segmentation is with respect to the question of validity. Whereas many academic studies of segmentation do employ some form of validation (primarily cross-validation on a holdout sample), most of the commercially based segmentation studies ignore the question of validity.

The validity of segmentation research is by far the most crucial question facing management. Do the segments discovered in a segmentation study exist in the population? Is the estimated segment size accurate? And how accurate are the estimated segment responses to the firm's marketing actions? Despite the centrality of such questions, only a few validation reports have been published [33, 72] and relatively few firms have made any effort to validate the results of their segmentation studies. Most notable among these efforts is the AT&T validation study of the segments within the residential long distance market. In this and several other unpublished AT&T studies the segmentation results were found to be very predictable of actual market behavior.

In the absence of such external validation, certain validation procedures could be used. The procedure chosen would depend on the specific segmentation model employed. In *a priori* and clustering-based segmentation studies, validation can be undertaken by splitting the sample and predicting segment membership of a holdout sample. In flexible and componential segmentation designs, one can check both the internal validity (e.g., prediction of the evaluation of control stimuli which were ranked or rated by the respondents but were not used in the parameter estimation procedure) and external validity (by comparing the survey's share of choices with the actual share data for each market segment). External validation requires purchase data (e.g., market share) by segment, which are not always available. Similarly, data availability is a problem when one wishes to validate the nonpurchase characteristics of the segments identified in segmentation studies. It is essential, however, for any firm using segmentation research to design and implement follow-up research—either in a test market or the national market—to validate the findings of the segmentation study and the subsequent segmentation strategy.

Cost Considerations

The selection of a segmentation design cannot be done in isolation from cost considerations. Lip service often is given to the concept of cost and value of information. Yet most industry-based segmentation studies are launched with no explicit effort at determining the cost and value of the expected information. Regardless of the politics of setting marketing research budgets, the researcher has a major role in the cost decision because most of the research design considerations and the data collection and analysis procedures have cost implications. One can, for example, assure a higher reliability but it may involve somewhat higher costs. Explicit cost tradeoffs therefore should be made which lead to a selection of research designs based on the intended purpose, the expected information, and the costs involved.

Many design and analysis considerations have only minimal cost implications. In fact, whenever a researcher gives cost considerations as the reason for not using multivariate statistical procedures or for not undertaking some simple cross-validation procedure, one should be suspicious because many of these procedures do not involve higher costs. Furthermore, if a researcher is familiar with and has working knowledge of multivariate statistical techniques, their use in segmentation research can be considerably less expensive both in terms of computer costs and analysts' time.

In most segmentation studies the cost of research design and analysis varies within very narrow ranges. The major variable cost component is data collection. Therefore, major cost savings can be expected from the data collection stage and not from cutting corners at the design and analysis stages.

Compared with the benefits believed to be associated with a segmentation strategy, the cost of segmentation research is often considered trivial. But few efforts have been directed at the assessment of (1) the expected value, in terms of alternative marketing segmentation strategies (versus the base case of no explicit segmentation effort) or (2) the expected cost of implementing different segmentation strategies. More work in this area is required.

Data Collection

The design and evaluation of alternative data collection procedures have received little attention in academically oriented market segmentation literature. Commercial researchers, however, have made significant contributions in this area, although relatively few innovative data collection approaches have been used in segmentation studies.

Primary Versus Secondary Data

Most of the commercially based segmentation studies have used a primary data collection effort and, in particular, cross-sectional surveys. In contrast, the technique-oriented academic segmentation studies tend to use available secondary sources and, in particular, panel data such as the Chicago Tribune and MRCA.

The development and offering of a psychographic data base for the MRCA panel has increased the commercial use of secondary sources in segmentation analysis. Increased usage of this and other secondary data sources (such as TGI or BRI) in segmentation analysis, and their integration with survey data, is desirable because it provides the longitudinal data required for dynamic segmentation analysis.

Other advantages of the greater reliance on secondary data sources are the better samples offered by most national panels, the greater attention (in comparison with the "typical" survey) to quality control of the data collection procedure, and the economic advantages of secondary sources (especially in light of the recent increase in the cost of survey data collection). Of particular interest is the greater accuracy of panel purchase and usage data [118].

Another type of secondary data source of great potential value in segmentation analysis, for many products and services, includes all those data bases which are in some aggregate form rather than based on the individual (or household). For example, census demographic zip code data can offer a rich data base for segmentation analysis of zip codes. They are especially valuable for firms in the direct mail business. Two types of zip code segmentation efforts have been conducted on the basis of selected variables from the REZIDE tapes of the 35,592 U.S. zip codes [22].

1. "Tailor-made" segmentation efforts, on selected variables hypothesized to be related to the response to the specific firm's offering, have been conducted by several firms, resulting in the selection of target zip code areas. Marketing efforts aimed at these segments have led to considerable improvement in response rates.
2. General segmentation of the U.S. based on 71 demographic and socioeconomic census variables was conducted by Computer Cartography, Inc. [23] and offered commercially. These data were factor analyzed and then clustered, resulting in 41 clusters which, in turn, were grouped in 12 major zip clusters. Each residential zip is within one of the 41 clusters (such as "upper class mobile professionals and college students in new towns") and also in one of the 12 major clusters (such as "educated elite suburban white family areas" or "lower-middle to middle blue collar nonmetro areas").

Similarly, the more recent developments of UPC data based on automated checkout data could offer a rich data base for "store area" segmentation analysis, especially when linked to electronic fund transfer payment data.

Conventional and Newer Procedures

Most segmentation studies are based on data collected in personal interviews or mail questionnaires. More recently, with the development of computer-based telephone interviewing, the telephone has become a feasible instrument for segmentation-type data collection. Such telephone interviewing can be very efficient because of response-dependent sequencing of questions, ease of reaching the sample units, and the ability to analyze the results as they come in.

In selecting a data collection method, therefore, one should consider a combination of approaches. The Human Population Laboratory [61] undertook a comparison of three data collection strategies containing personal interviews, telephone interviews, and mail questionnaires in different combinations (order of usage). Rate of return and rate of completeness were high in all three strategies. Similarly, substantive findings were virtually interchangeable and there was little difference in validity. The only difference was the cost per interview, which varied considerably by strategy. Accepting these findings suggests that substantial cost saving could be achieved in segmentation studies without sacrificing quality by designing a cost effective and task efficient mix of data collection procedures. However, other studies have shown differences in the response to, and validity of, various data collection procedures [15, 30, 31]. These differences can be accounted for by several factors. Self-administered questionnaires, for example, were found to be better when the information was available in records or possessed by other members of the respondent family. They were also better with highly educated and high income respondents [104].

The major new developments in data collection procedures include computer-terminal-based data collection procedures, two-way cable TV, and home computers. In addition to computer-based telephone interviews, computer terminals have been used for self-administered personal interviews in central interviewing facilities [80, 119] (such as shopping malls). With the advent of portable terminals, such interviews can be conducted at consumers' homes or industrial buyers' offices. Two-way cable TV has been presented for at least a decade as the panacea for data collection problems. Yet its development and dissemination are still more of a promise than a reality. Home computers are a newer development. The current pricing of microcomputers at less than $600 could have a major impact on their distribution and should not be ignored in the development of new data collection procedures.

Other less frequently used data collection procedures for segmentation are (1) self-recorded protocol data (which, when content analyzed, can be used to identify the respondent's decision process and serve as a basis for segmentation), (2) unobtrusive measures of respondents' shopping, purchase, and usage behavior [105], and (3) projective techniques and other open-ended interviews. The major problem with using these data bases has been the difficulty in the content analysis of the protocols, open-ended responses, and some of the unobtrusive measures. If content analysis is required, care must be given to the development of a dictionary and other procedures commonly used in content analysis [37] and especially the development of interjudge reliability measures [66].

In selecting data collection procedure(s), one should give attention to the respondents' ability to perform the task reliably, the cost in terms of money and time, and the scale properties required for the intended data analysis.

Data Analysis

The market segmentation field has been one of the primary and most prolific testing grounds for data analysis techniques. The diffusion of new data analysis techniques often has started with the publication of an academic article on the applicability of some analytical model and algorithm (usually borrowed from mathematical statistics or mathematical psychology, and less frequently from mathematical economics and sociology). The procedure then is applied to a number of academically oriented marketing studies and finally is picked up by some of the more innovative marketing research firms. The diffusion of MDS and conjoint analysis provides good examples of this pattern.

To know the current state of applications of various data analysis techniques to market segmentation studies, therefore, one must continuously keep up to date with three areas:

1. The analytical techniques currently used in segmentation analysis (with a focus on possible problems associated with their use).
2. The analytical developments suggested in the recent marketing literature.
3. Analytical procedures which have not yet been introduced to the marketing literature and which offer some potential in the segmentation area.

The brief review of these areas is organized according to the three major types of analytical techniques used in segmentation research, namely, techniques for (1) classification of respondents into segments, (2) discrimination among the segments, i.e., the determination of segment profiles, and (3) simultaneous classification and discrimination.

Classification Procedures

Classification procedures for determining membership in market segments vary markedly according to the specific segmentation model used. The procedures most commonly employed in *a priori* approaches are sorting and cross-tabulation. Recently, Blattberg and Sen developed a Bayesian classification procedure [13] which they used successfully. When clustering-based segmentation is used, the most common procedures are clustering, MDS, and AID. Componential and flexible segmentation involve primarily conjoint analysis and computer simulation.

These and similar analytical techniques used for the assignment of consumers to segments are widely used and need no further explanation.[12] The focus of this section, therefore, is on some of the possible pitfalls and unanswered questions involved in the use of these techniques, and some of the recent advances in classification procedures.

Sorting and Cross-Tabulation. The dividing line among *a priori* segments generally is arbitrary. Consider, for example, the commonly used segments of heavy and light brand users. How should the sample be divided? Should it be based on the top and bottom 50% of users or only the top 33% and the bottom 33%? Furthermore, should it be based on a number of items bought, frequency of purchase, total dollar purchased, proportion of purchases devoted to the given brand, etc.? In many segmentation studies, too little attention is given to the conceptual implications of the various operational definitions and the sensitivity of the resulting segments to the definitions used.

A priori sorting of respondents can provide insight as demonstrated in the purchase segments of Blattberg and Sen [12]. It is judgmental and requires careful operational definitions of segment boundaries and the use of interjudge reliability measures among the judges who assign subjects to segments. Another neglected sorting procedure is the complete enumeration of all possible segments by following a set of assignment criteria. This procedure has been used in two cases.

1. The assignment of consumers to *product assortment* segments based on whether each of a set of products was used or not; i.e., if a product category has, for example, eight products, consumers are assigned to one of 256 (2^8) segments. In most product categories in which the product assortment patterns were analyzed, about 5% of the patterns accounted for 90% or so of the total purchases.
2. Benefit segmentation involving a relatively small number of benefits. If there are, for example, only five benefits and each individual can have either a high or low score on each benefit, there are 32 possible segments. Again, in the few cases in which such procedures have been used, a relatively small number of segments accounted for most of the respondents.

Of special interest in this context are the newer procedures for discrete multivariate analysis [8] which are mostly based on *n*-way cross-classification analysis. These procedures allow for nonlinearities and in many cases can be superior to the more conventional multivariate statistical techniques.

Clustering. A large number of clustering models and algorithms are currently available for the grouping of subjects. These techniques (including Q-type factor analysis and its modifications such as the linear typal analysis [26, 83]) differ in their objectives, type of clustering used, and the specific operationalization of the clustering procedures. The objective of clustering techniques as applied to market segmentation should not be limited to finding a typology of the market under study; one can use clustering also for data exploration, data reduction, and hypothesis generation.[13]

Clustering techniques can and have been categorized in a variety of ways. Hartigan [58], for example, suggested a classification based on mode of search into sorting, switching, joining, splitting, adding, and searching.[14] For market segmentation purposes it might be useful to distinguish between two major types of clustering techniques—those which build up clusters (a bottom-up approach) and those which break down a market into clusters (a top-down approach). The *building up* clustering techniques include several of the commonly used joining algorithms, such as the Johnson hierarchical clustering [65], Sneath single linkage algorithm [58], and

12. For a basic review of these data analytical techniques, see [51].

13. Ball [1] has suggested three additional objectives—model fitting, prediction, and hypothesis testing. These objectives have rarely been used in a segmentation context.

14. For other classification systems, see for example [29].

various tree structures. *Breaking down* clustering procedures begin by partitioning subjects into two or more clusters, followed by subsequent partitioning of each of these clusters into subclusters. These techniques include a variety of splitting algorithms which, after an initial partitioning, obtain a new partition by switching objects from one cluster to another. The *K* means and Howard Harris algorithms are examples of this type of breaking down clustering procedure.

In view of the large number of available clustering [58] and pattern recognition [21] techniques, the critical question facing the researcher is which algorithm (and measures of similarity or distance) and type of measures (standardized, weighted, etc.) are most appropriate under what conditions and for what purposes. The current clustering literature does not provide satisfactory answers to these questions, and researchers tend to select an algorithm on the basis of such considerations as familiarity, availability, and cost of operations rather than appropriateness for a specific set of objectives or constraints.

Of special interest in this area are some of the recent developments in *overlapping clustering.* Clustering procedures used in traditional market segmentation studies were based on the premise of exclusivity; i.e., each individual could have been classified in one and only one cluster (segment). Conceptually, there are a number of situations in which a consumer can belong to more than a single segment (especially if one considers multiple brand usage, different usage occasions, multiple benefits sought, etc.). Several models and algorithms are now available for overlapping clustering [19] and can be used whenever it is conceptually desirable.

Multidimensional Scaling. Most multidimensional scaling applications in marketing have been for product positioning [112]. Yet several MDS models and algorithms are suitable for the classification of respondents. Most notable among them is INDSCAL [17, 20] which develops for each respondent a weight on each of the relevant group dimensions. Respondents with similar salience on the perceptual dimensions can thus constitute a segment.

Segments also can be identified on the basis of the commonality of preferences either in a common (total market) perceptual (brand or product feature) space or in spaces unique to each perceptual segment. This grouping of respondents can be undertaken with several alternative models such as MDPREF or PREFMAP [41, 50].

AID and Stepwise Regression. Although both of these techniques commonly are used to establish the profile of a segment (given some dependent variable such as purchase), occasionally the resulting segment descriptors (selected tree structures in AID, or the significant variables in the regression) can be used as a way of classifying the respondents into segments which, in turn, can serve as the basis for segmentation in subsequent analysis. Of particular value in this context is AID [98] which has been used successfully in a large number of commercial segmentation studies.

Newer Approaches. More recently, multidimensional contingency table analysis [39] has been used to segment a market on the basis of the *probability* of being a "loyal" customer. This approach is utilized by Ogilvy and Mather under the name of logistic response analysis [25].

Discrimination Procedures

The analytical techniques used to profile the segments (which were selected *a priori* or identified in the classification stage) do not vary by type of segmentation model employed. To establish the segments' profiles, market segmentation studies still occasionally include cross-tabulations and some univariate statistical technique. More commonly, however, the procedures applied are multiple regression, multiple discriminant analysis, AID, MCA (multiple classification analysis), or some combination of these techniques.

More recently new procedures have been suggested and applied to the problem of identifying segments' profiles. Among these procedures are latent class analysis, logit and multinomial logit, multivariate probit, and nonparametric techniques.

Latent class analysis (as discussed in the section on segment homogeneity) utilizes the CANDECOMP model and algorithm. This approach was applied to the segmentation of the market for a new telecommunication service [44].

The *multinomial logit model* [42] has been applied to the same segmentation problems. It was preceded by an AID analysis (to determine which predictors, categories within predictors, and interactions should be considered). The logit model was applied to obtain parameter estimates for each predictor (or predictor combination) to test alternative models, and to develop probability estimates for the dichotomous criterion variable [42]. The AID/logit approach to segmentation can be extended to cover polytomous variables (and not only dichotomous data) by applying instead of AID the THAID algorithm [75] followed by a multinomial generalization of the logit model.

The *multivariate probit model* has been used recently in a pilot application to the segmentation area using the probability response coefficients (to each of a set of product features) as a basis for segmentation [88].

These and the more conventional discrimination procedures, and in particular AID, THAID, and the AID-like algorithms such as SIMS (*s*urvey *i*mplemented *m*arket *s*egmentation), which is based on a simple cost-profit formulation [71], require relatively large data bases. Whereas this requirement does not create any special difficulty for most consumer market segmentation studies, it does present a major stumbling block for most of the efforts to segment industrial markets. Many industrial market situations involve a relatively small number of customers and require nonparametric statistical procedures and greater reliance on efficient experimental designs. More work on both areas is crucial to progress in industrial market segmentation.

An interesting omission from the segmentation literature is the use of structural equation models (or path analysis) [9, 27]. Conceptually, at least, segmentation models can be constructed as causal diagrams or equivalent sets of linear equations that represent the assumed set of direct and indirect influences among a set of variables. The values of the unknown path coefficients can be estimated to indicate the relative strength of the determinants of the specified dependent variables (in effect a sequence of dependent variables is the recursive model). An excellent example of a segmentation-related problem in which this approach was used is a sociological study on the socioeconomic characteristics of occupational achievement [28].

Simultaneous Classification and Discrimination

Whereas most segmentation studies follow a two-step procedure of first classifying respondents into segments and then establishing their key discriminating characteristics, attempts have been made to develop and apply analytical techniques for the *simultaneous* analysis of classification and discrimination. Canonical correlation analysis has been applied in this context, and more recently the flexible and componential segmentation models.

Canonical correlation has been suggested as a method for segmentation by Frank and Strain [36] who grouped respondents with regard to their cross-classified score categories on each significant canonical variate in the predictor set. However, because canonical correlation measures the shared variation between two sets of variables (by transforming both configurations to some best compromise position), it can be used for segmentation as long as one does not want to relate the predictor set *to* the criterion set. An alternative procedure therefore can be the transformation of the space of predictor variables to best agree with a fixed position occupied by the points in the space of the criterion variables. It can be undertaken by using any number of oblique or orthogonal Procrustes transformations [6, 94].

If the researcher is not concerned with maintaining the distinction of a criterion variable set, canonical-correlation or redundancy analysis [103] (a component method which maximizes Stewart and Love's redundancy index [100]) can be considered as a procedure for simultaneously classifying the respondents and determining the key discriminating profiles of the various segments.

Selection of a Plan of Analysis

The choice of data analysis techniques reflects the researcher's familiarity with, and preference for, various techniques. Several questions should be addressed in selection of a specific analytical plan. They are not unlike the ones facing researchers using any multivariate data analysis technique and include: How should one measure the relative importance of the variables—is R^2, for example, an appropriate measure [48, 76, 108]? Should discrimination among segments be based on individual or group level analysis [2, 4]? How should one identify and measure the effect of any response errors [34]?

Unique to segmentation studies is the need to apply a variety of analytical procedures in tandem. Most segmentation studies involve "complex" designs [35] revolving around several hybrid bases for segmentation [57, 101]. However, because one cannot know in advance which basis for segmentation will lead to the identification of meaningful segments, segmentation studies should be *flexible,* allowing diverse analyses aimed at the identification of relevant segments. This need creates special demands for researchers with knowledge of a large number of analytical procedures, good conceptual understanding of alternative segmentation models, and a high level of research creativity.

Data Interpretation and Implementation of Results

Regardless of how sophisticated the segmentation study, the key to a successful project is the researcher's and user's (management) ability to interpret the results and use them as guidelines for the design, execution, and evaluation of appropriate marketing strategy. The data interpretation stage should be performed *jointly* by the researcher and user, reflecting the researcher's statistical judgment (which differences among segments are statistically significant, etc.) and the manager's product/market knowledge. In this context, two major issues are (1) how to determine the number of segments and select the target segment(s) and (2) how to translate the segmentation findings into marketing strategy.

Determining the Number of Segments and Selection of Target Segments

One of the most complex questions facing researchers who use a cluster-based approach to segmentation is the determination of the number of segments. The two relevant criteria are the statistical measure of cluster (segment) stability and homogeneity, and the managerial consideration of cost of segmentation. The question of segment stability can be assessed by comparing the results of alternative clustering procedures and computing measures of similarities between the different cluster solutions. Estimating the cost of segmentation involves management's subjective judgment.

Whatever segmentation approach is used, it is management that selects the desired *target segments.* The selection of target segments is a complex "art" type of process which should take into account such factors as the segments' expected response to marketing variables, the segments' reachability, the nature of competitive activity within the segment, and management's resources and ability to implement a segmented strategy for the selected segments.

The cost of segmentation, the problems inherent in any effort to reach effectively a large number of segments, and the complexity of managing a large number of segments all encourage the selection of relatively few segments. However, greater segment homogeneity requires a larger number of segments [32]. To balance these two forces, more rigorous analytical models should be developed. Furthermore, the segment selection decision should not be limited to a single product but should encompass the more realistic and complex case of a product line.

A more fundamental question in the selection of target segments faces public policy decision makers. Whereas a profit-oriented firm can decide to concentrate its efforts on a specific target segment(s), the public policy tradition has been to develop a single policy aimed at *all* consumers. As public policy decision makers move toward greater reliance on consumer (and marketing) research as input to their decisions, they face an increasing conflict between the empirical findings (on the heterogeneous nature of the market) and the traditional concept of the "average" or "typical" consumers. If policy formulators could implement a segmented strategy, undertaking public-policy-oriented segmentation research projects would present no difficulty. If public policy decision makers were to insist on a single strategy aimed at an "average" consumer, the concept of segmentation might have to be modified.

Translating Segmentation Findings into Strategy

The most difficult aspect of any segmentation project is the translation of the study results into marketing strategy. No rules can be offered to assure a successful translation and, in fact, little is known (in the published literature) on how this translation occurs.

Informal discussions with and observation of "successful" and "unsuccessful" translations suggest a few generalizable conclusions aside from the obvious ones such as:

1. Involving all the relevant users (e.g., product managers, new product developers, advertising agency personnel, etc.) in the problem definition, research design, and data interpretation stages.
2. Viewing segmentation data as one input to a total

marketing information system and combining them with sales and other relevant data.
3. Using the segmentation data on a continuous basis. The reported study results should be viewed only as the *beginning* of a utilization program.

Difficulties with, and the nature of, the "translation" of segmentation findings into strategy depend on whether the segmentation study is used as input to:

1. Idea and strategy generation or strategy evaluation.
2. Product related decisions (i.e., product positioning, design, and price) or communication and distribution decisions.
3. Decisions about existing products (i.e., no change, product modification, repositioning, or deletion decisions) or new products.

The translation of segmentation findings into new ideas (and strategies) is usually limited only by the creativity of the users. Most segmentation studies, and especially those based on consumers' needs, benefits, life styles, or other psychographic characteristics, offer a rich profile of potential target segments which, in turn, can lead to the generation of a large number of diverse ideas and strategies. Furthermore, if one is concerned, for example, with design of a product or a communication campaign, each idea can be executed in a variety of ways, the success of which depends more on the creativity of the designer than on the segmentation findings.

The translation of segmentation findings is more complex when they are used to *evaluate* (rather than generate) some marketing strategy. In this context, two situations are distinct—consumer reactions to a new strategy (e.g., new concept or new commercial) and consumer satisfaction with the firm's current products and services. In both cases a meaningful evaluation should be done at the market segment level, and in both cases there is a strong tendency to define segments in terms favorable to the corporate decision makers' objectives.

A major difficulty in the translation of segmentation findings into actionable strategy is management's perceived *ability* to implement the strategy. In industrial marketing, one often hears the argument that salesmen cannot handle simultaneously a number of strategies aimed at a number of segments. Furthermore, organizations, whether in consumer or industrial markets, are on the average reluctant to undertake high-risk strategies. Strategies which depart from current strategy or which require new ways of reaching target segments (e.g., direct mail vs. TV, new distribution outlets, etc.) are viewed as high risks. In providing rigorous input to decisions perceived as involving high risks, segmentation findings can have a major impact.

Concluding Remarks

Market segmentation has served as the focal point for many of the major marketing research developments and the marketing activities of most firms. Yet too many segmentation researchers have settled on a fixed way of conducting segmentation studies. This tendency for standardization of procedures is premature and undesirable, Innovative approaches to segmentation have been offered in the past few years, and further work on the new conceptual and methodological aspects of segmentation should be undertaken.

Of particular importance seems to be research on the following areas:

1. New conceptualization of the segmentation problem.
2. Reevaluation and operationalization of the normative theory of segmentation, with emphasis on the question of how to allocate resources among markets and products over *time*.
3. The discovery and implementation of *new variables* for use as bases for segmentation (i.e., new attitudinal and behavioral constructs such as consumption-based personality inventories and variables which focus on *likely change* in attitude and behavioral responses to the marketing variables) of the markets for products, services, and concepts.
4. The development of new research designs and parallel data collection and analysis techniques which place fewer demands on the respondents (i.e., data collection which is simpler for the respondent and data analysis procedures capable of handling missing data and incomplete block designs).
5. The development of simple and flexible analytical approaches to data analysis capable of handling discrete and continuous variables, and selected interaction at a point in time and over time.

6. Evaluation of the conditions under which various data analytical techniques are most appropriate.
7. The accumulation of knowledge on successful bases for segmentation across studies (products, situations, and markets).
8. Undertaking external validation studies to determine the performance of segmentation strategies which were based on findings of segmentation studies.
9. Designing and implementing multitrait, multimethod approaches to segmentation research aimed at both the generation of more generalizable (reliable) and valid data.
10. Integration of segmentation research with the marketing information system of the firm.
11. Exploring alternative approaches to the translation of segmentation findings into marketing strategies.
12. Studies of the organizational design of firms which were successful and unsuccessful in implementing segmentation strategies.

Review of some of the issues and current advances in segmentation research indicate that, despite the great advances in the management of and research practice of segmentation, numerous frontiers still require creative and systematic study. This review and the other articles in this special issue of *JMR* are presented with the hope of stimulating further advances in this important and challenging area.

References

1. Ball, G. H. *Classification Analysis.* Stanford, California: SRI, 1971.
2. Bass, Frank M. "Unexplained Variance in Studies of Consumer Behavior," in John U. Farley and John A. Howard, eds., *Control of "Error" in Market Research Data.* Lexington, Massachusetts: Lexington Books, 1975, 11-36.
3. ——. "Analytical Approaches in the Study of Purchase Behavior and Brand Choice," in Robert Ferber, ed., *Selected Aspects of Consumer Behavior.* Washington, D.C.: National Science Foundation, 1977, 491-514.
4. ——, Douglas J. Tigert, and Ronald T. Lonsdale. "Market Segmentation: Group Versus Individual Behavior," *Journal of Marketing Research,* 5 (August 1968), 264-70.
5. Beckwith, Neil E. and Maurice W. Sasieni. "Criteria for Marketing Segmentation Studies," *Management Science,* 22 (April 1976), 892-908.
6. Berge, J. and M. F. Ten. "Orthgonal Procrustes Rotation for Two or More Matrices," *Psychometrika,* 42 (June 1977).
7. Bettman, James R. *An Information Processing Theory of Consumer Choice.* Reading, Massachusetts: Addison-Welsey, in press.
8. Bishop, Yvonne, Stephen Feinberg, and Paul Holland. *Discrete Multivariate Analysis.* Cambridge, Massachusetts: The MIT Press, 1975.
9. Blalock, H. M., Jr., ed. *Causal Models in the Social Sciences.* Chicago: Aldine-Atherton, 1971.
10. Blattberg, Robert C., Thomas Buesing, Peter Peacock, and Subrata K. Sen. "Identifying the Deal Prone Segment," *Journal of Marketing Research,* 15 (August 1978).
11. —— and Subrata K. Sen. "Market Segmentation Using Models of Multidimensional Purchasing Behavior," *Journal of Marketing,* 38 (October 1974), 17-28.
12. —— and ——. "Market Segments and Stochastic Brand Choice Models," *Journal of Marketing Research,* 13 (February 1976), 34-45.
13. —— and ——. "A Bayesian Technique to Discriminate Between Stochastic Models of Brand Choice," *Management Science,* 21 (February 1975), 682-96.
14. Calantone, Roger J. and Alan Sawyer. "The Stability of Benefit Segments," *Journal of Marketing Research,* 15 (August 1978).
15. Cannell, Charles F. and Floyd J. Fowler, "Comparison of Self-Enumerative Procedure and a Personal Interview: A Validity Study," *Public Opinion Quarterly,* 27 (1963), 250-64.
16. Carroll, J. Douglas. "Categorical Conjoint Measurement," presented at Mathematical Psychology Meeting, Ann Arbor, Michigan, 1969. (Discussed in [49, pp. 339-48].)
17. ——. "Individual Differences and Multidimensional Scaling," in R. N. Shepard, ed., *Multidimensional Scaling: Theory and Applications in Behavioral Sciences,* Vol. I. New York: Seminar Press, 1972.
18. ——. "Application of CANDECOMP to Solving for Parameters of Lazarsfeld's Latent Class Model," presented at the Society of Multivariate Experimental Psychology Meeting, Gleneden Beach, Oregon, November 1975.
19. ——. "Spatial, Nonspatial, and Hybrid Models for Scaling," *Psychometrika,* 41 (December 1976), 439-63.
20. —— and Jih-Jie Chang. "Analysis of Individual Differences in Multidimensional Scaling via an N-Way Generalization of Eckart-Young Decomposition," *Psychometrika,* 35 (September 1970), 61-8.
21. Casey, Richard G. and George Nagy. "Advances in Pattern Recognition," *Scientific American,* 224 (1971), 56-71.
22. Claritas Corporation. *REZIDE: The National Zip Code Encyclopedia.* Washington, D.C.: Claritas Corporation.

23. Computer Cartography, Inc. *Customer Clusters: Development of a Meaningful Socioeconomic Classification System.* Washington, D.C.: Computer Cartography, Inc.
24. Cronback, Lee J. et al. *The Dependability of Behavioral Measurements: Theory of Generalizability for Scores and Profiles.* New York: John Wiley & Sons, Inc., 1972.
25. Cuba, Fred. "Logistic Response Analysis: A Better Way to Slice the Pie," in Y. Wind and M. Greenberg, eds., *Moving A Head With Attitude Research.* Chicago: AMA, 1977, 66-69.
26. Darden, William R. and William D. Perreault, Jr. "Classification for Market Segmentation: An Improved Linear Model for Solving Problems of Arbitrary Origin," *Management Science,* 24 (November 1977), 255-71.
27. Duncan, Otis Dudley. *Introduction to Structural Equation Models.* New York: Academic Press, 1975.
28. ——, D. L. Featherman, and B. Duncan. *Socioeconomic Background and Achievement.* Washington, D.C.: U.S. Office of Education, Bureau of Research, 1968.
29. Everitt, Brian. *Cluster Analysis.* London: Heinemann Educational Books, 1974.
30. Ferber, Robert. "Does a Panel Operation Increase the Reliability of Survey Data: The Case of Consumer Savings," *Journal of the American Statistical Association,* 50 (1955), 210-16.
31. ——. "On the Reliability of Responses Secured in Sample Surveys," *Journal of the American Statistical Association,* 50 (1955), 788-810.
32. Fisher, W. D. "On Grouping for Maximum Homogeneity," *Journal of the American Statistical Association,* 53 (1958), 789-98.
33. Frank, Ronald. "Predicting New Product Segments," *Journal of Advertising Research,* 12 (June 1972), 9-13.
34. —— and William Massy. "Noise Reduction in Segmentation Research," in John U. Farley and John A. Howard, eds., *Control of "Error" in Market Research Data.* Lexington, Massachusetts: Lexington Books, 1975, 145-205.
35. ——, ——, and Yoram Wind. *Market Segmentation.* Englewood Cliffs, New Jersey: Prentice-Hall, Inc., 1972.
36. —— and Charles Strain. "A Segmentation Research Design Using Consumer Panel Data," *Journal of Marketing Research,* 9 (November 1972), 385-90.
37. Gerbner, George et al. *The Analysis of Communication Content.* New York: John Wiley & Sons, Inc., 1969.
38. Gibson, Lawrence D. "Beyond Segmentation or Something is Rotten in Market Segmentation," paper delivered at the Midwest Conference of the AMA, March 1971.
39. Goodman, Leo A. "The Analysis of Multidimensional Contingency Tables: Stepwise Procedures and Direct Estimation Methods for Building Models for Multiple Classifications," *Technometrics,* 13 (1971), 31-62.
40. Green, Paul E. "A New Approach to Market Segmentation," *Business Horizons,* 20 (February 1977), 61-73.
41. —— and Frank J. Carmone. *Multidimensional Scaling and Related Techniques in Marketing Analysis.* Boston: Allyn and Bacon, 1970.
42. —— and ——. "An AID/Logit Approach for Analyzing Large Multiway Contingency Tables," *Journal of Marketing Research,* 15 (February 1978), 132-6.
43. —— and ——. "Segment Congruence Analysis: A Method for Analyzing Association Among Alternative Bases for Market Segmentation," *Journal of Consumer Research,* 3 (March 1977), 217-22.
44. ——, ——, and David P. Wachspress. "Consumer Segmentation via Latent Class Analysis," *Journal of Consumer Research,* 3 (December 1976), 170-4.
45. ——, ——, and ——. "On the Analysis of Qualitative Data in Marketing Research," *Journal of Marketing Research,* 14 (February 1977), 52-59.
46. ——, J. Douglas Carroll, and Frank J. Carmone. "Some New Types of Fractional Factorial Designs for Marketing Experiments," in J. N. Sheth, ed., *Research in Marketing,* Vol. I. Greenwich, Connecticut: JAI Press, 1977.
47. ——, ——, and ——. "Design Considerations in Attitude Measurement," in Y. Wind and M. Greenberg, eds., *Moving A Head With Attitude Research.* Chicago: AMA, 1977, 9-18.
48. ——, ——, and Wayne S. DeSarbo. "A New Measure of Predictor Variable Importance in Multiple Regression," *Journal of Marketing Research,* 15 (August 1978).
49. —— and Vithala Rao. *Applied Multidimensional Scaling: A Comparison of Approaches and Algorithms.* New York: Holt, Rinehart and Winston, 1972.
50. —— and V. Srinivasan. "Conjoint Analysis in Consumer Behavior: Status and Outlook," University of Pennsylvania working paper, 1977.
51. —— and Donald Tull. *Research for Marketing Decisions,* 3rd ed. Englewood Cliffs, New Jersey: Prentice-Hall, Inc., 1975.
52. —— and Yoram Wind. *Multiattribute Decisions in Marketing: A Measurement Approach.* Hinsdale, Illinois: Dryden Press, 1973.
53. —— and ——. "New Way to Measure Consumers' Judgments," *Harvard Business Review,* 53 (1975), 107-17.
54. ——, ——, and Arun K. Jain. "Benefit Bundle Analysis," *Journal of Advertising Research,* 12 (1972), 31-6.
55. ——, ——, and ——. "Analyzing Free Response Data in Marketing Research," *Journal of Marketing Research,* 10 (February 1973), 45.
56. Haley, R. I. "Benefit Segmentation: A Decision-Oriented Research Tool," *Journal of Marketing,* 32 (July 1968).

57. Hanan, M. "Market Segmentation," *American Management Association Bulletin,* 109 (1968).
58. Hartigan, John A. *Clustering Algorithms.* New York: John Wiley & Sons, Inc., 1975.
59. Hays, William L. *Statistics for the Social Sciences,* 2nd edition. New York: Holt, Rinehart and Winston, 1973.
60. Hemphill, John K. and Charles M. Westie. "The Measurement of Group Dimensions," *Journal of Psychology,* 29 (1950), 325–41.
61. Hochstin, Joseph R. "A Critical Comparison of Three Strategies of Collecting Data from Households," *Journal of the American Statistical Association* (September 1967), 976–89.
62. Hulbert, James and Donald R. Lehman. "Assessing the Importance of the Sources of Error in Structured Survey Data," in John U. Farley and John A. Howard, eds., *Control of "Error" in Market Research Data.* Lexington, Massachusetts: Lexington Books, 1975, 81–107.
63. Johnson, Richard M. "Trade-Off Analysis of Consumer Values," *Journal of Marketing Research,* 11 (May 1974), 121–27.
64. ——. "Beyond Conjoint Measurement: A Method of Pairwise Tradeoff Analysis," in B. B. Anderson, ed., *Advances in Consumer Research,* Vol. III. Proceedings of Association for Consumer Research Sixth Annual Conference (1975), 353–8.
65. Johnson, S. C. "Hierarchical Clustering Schemes," *Psychometrika,* 32 (1967), 241–54.
66. Krippendorff, Klaus. "A Coefficient of Agreement for Situations in Which Qualitative Data Are Categorized by Many Judges," University of Pennsylvania, Annenberg School of Communication, 1966, mimeo.
67. Kruskal, Joseph B. "Analysis of Factorial Experiments by Estimating Monotone Transformations of the Data," *Journal of the Royal Statistical Society,* Series B, 27 (1967), 251–63.
68. —— and Frank J. Carmone. "MONANOVA: A FORTRAN IV Program for Monotone Analysis of Variance," *Behavioral Science,* 14 (1969), 165–66.
69. Lazarsfeld, Paul F. and Neil W. Henry. *Latent Structure Analysis.* Boston: Houghton-Mifflin Co., 1968.
70. Mahajan, Vijay and Arun K. Jain. "An Approach to Normative Segmentation," *Journal of Marketing Research,* 15 (August 1978).
71. Martin, Claude R. and Roger L. Wright. "Profit Oriented Data Analysis for Market Segmentation: An Alternative to AID," *Journal of Marketing Research,* 11 (August 1974), 237–42.
72. Massy, William F., Ronald E. Frank, and Thomas Lodahl. *Purchasing Behavior and Personal Attributes.* Philadelphia: University of Pennsylvania Press, 1968.
73. McCann, John M. "Market Segment Response to the Marketing Decision Variables," *Journal of Marketing Research,* 11 (November 1974), 399–412.
74. Michman, Ronald D., Myron Gable, and Walter Gross. *Market Segmentation: A Selected and Annotated Bibliography.* Chicago: AMA, 1977.
75. Morgan, James N. and Robert C. Messenger. *THAID: A Sequential Analysis Program for the Analysis of Nominal Scale Dependent Variables.* Ann Arbor, Michigan: Survey Research Center, 1973.
76. Morrison, Donald G. "Evaluating Market Segmentation Studies: The Properties of R^2," *Management Science,* 19 (July 1973), 1213–21.
77. Myers, John G. "An Interactive Computer Approach to Product Positioning," in Y. Wind and M. Greenberg, eds., *Moving A Head With Attitude Research.* Chicago: AMA, 1977, 157–64.
78. —— and Francesco M. Nicosia. "On the Dimensionality Question in Latent Structure Analysis," in Reed Moyer, ed., *Changing Marketing Systems: Consumer, Corporate and Government Inter-Faces.* Chicago: AMA, 1969.
79. Nicosia, Francesco et al. *Technology and Consumers: Individual and Social Choice.* Berkeley: University of California Report, 1974.
80. —— and Yoram Wind. "Behavioral Models of Organizational Buying Processes," in F. Nicosia and Y. Wind, eds., *Behavioral Models of Market Analysis: Foundations for Marketing Action.* Hinsdale, Illinois: The Dryden Press, 1977, 96–120.
81. —— and ——. "Sociology of Consumption and Trade-Off Models in Consumer Public Policy," in Lunn, ed., *Consumer Research for Public Policy,* in press.
82. Ostland, Lyman E. "Perceived Innovation Attributes as Predictors of Innovation," *Journal of Consumer Research,* 1 (September 1974).
83. Overall, J. E. and C. J. Klett. *Applied Multivariate Analysis.* New York: McGraw-Hill Book Company, 1972, 180–239.
84. Parker, Barnett R. and V. Srinivasan. "A Consumer Preference Approach to the Planning of Rural Primary Health Care Facilities," *Operations Research,* 24 (1976), 991–1025.
85. Pekelman, Dov and Subrata Sen. "Utility Function Estimation in Conjoint Measurement," paper presented at the Fall 1974 Conference of the American Marketing Association, Portland, Oregon.
86. Peterson, Robert A. "Market Structuring by Sequential Cluster Analysis," *Journal of Business Research,* 2 (July 1974), 249–64.
87. ——. "Concept Testing: Some Experimental Evidence," *Mississippi Valley Journal of Business and Economics,* 7 (Spring 1972), 84–88.
88. Rao, Vithala and Frederick W. Winter. "An Application of the Multivariate Probit Model to Market Segmentation and Product Design," *Journal of Marketing Research,* 15 (August 1978).
89. Reynolds, W. H. "More Sense About Market Segmen-

tation," *Harvard Business Review,* 43 (September-October 1965), 107-14.

90. Robertson, Thomas S. *Innovative Behavior and Communication.* New York: Holt, Rinehart and Winston, 1971.
91. Robinson, Patrick J. and Yoram Wind. "Multinational Trade-Off Segmentation," in Y. Wind and M. Greenberg, eds., *Moving A Head With Attitude Research.* Chicago: AMA, 1977, 50-57.
92. Rogers, Everett M. and F. Floyd Shoemaker. *Communication of Innovations.* New York: Free Press, 1971.
93. Samejima, Fumiko. "A General Model for Response Data," *Psychometrika Monograph Supplement,* Monograph 18, Vol. 37 (March 1972).
94. Schönemann, Peter H. "A Generalized Solution of the Orthogonal Procrustes Problem," *Psychometrika,* 31 (March 1966), 1-10.
95. Shocker, Allan and V. Srinivasan. "LINMAP II: Linear Programming Techniques for Multidimensional Analysis of Preferences with Applications to Conjoint Analysis," *Journal of Marketing Research,* 14 (1977), 101-3.
96. Shugan, Steven M. and John R. Hauser. "P.A.R.I.S.: An Interactive Market Research Information System," Northeastern University, Graduate School of Management working paper 602-002, 1977.
97. Smith, Wendell. "Product Differentiation and Market Segmentation as Alternative Marketing Strategies," *Journal of Marketing,* 21 (July 1956), 3-8.
98. Sonquist, John A. *Multivariate Model Building.* Ann Arbor, Michigan: Survey Research Center, 1970.
99. Srinivasan, V. and Allan D. Shocker. "Estimating the Weights for Multiple Attributes in a Composite Criterion Using Pairwise Judgments," *Psychometrika,* 38 (1973), 473-93.
100. Stewart, Douglas and William Love. "A General Canonical Correlation Index," *Psychological Bulletin,* 70 (September 1968), 160-63.
101. Stout, Roy G. et al. "Usage Incidence as a Basis for Segmentation," in Y. Wind and M. Greenberg, eds., *Moving A Head With Attitude Research.* Chicago: AMA, 1977, 45-49.
102. Tollefson, John O. and Parker Lessig. "Aggregation Criteria in Normative Market Segmentation Theory," *Journal of Marketing Research,* 15 (August 1978).
103. Van Den Wollenberg, Arnold. "Redundancy Analysis: An Alternative for Canonical Correlation Analysis," *Psychometrika,* 42 (June 1977).
104. Wallace, D. "A Case for—and Against—Mail Questionnaires," *Public Opinion Quarterly,* 18 (1954), 40-52.
105. Webb, Eugene J. et al. *Unobtrusive Measures: Nonreactive Research in the Social Sciences.* Chicago: Rand McNally, 1966.
106. Webster, Frederick, Jr. and Yoram Wind. *Organizational Buying Behavior.* Englewood Cliffs, New Jersey: Prentice-Hall, Inc., 1972.
107. Wells, William D. "Psychographics: A Critical Review," *Journal of Marketing Research,* 12 (May 1975), 196-211.
108. Wildt, Albert R. "On Evaluating Market Segmentation Studies and the Properties of R^2," *Management Science,* 22 (April 1976), 904-8.
109. Wilkie, William L. *How Consumers Use Product Information.* Washington, D.C.: U.S. Government Printing Office, 1976.
110. Wind, Yoram. "Toward a Change in the Focus of Marketing Analysis: From a Single Brand to an Assortment," *Journal of Marketing,* 41 (October 1977), 12.
111. ——. "A New Procedure for Concept Evaluation," *Journal of Marketing,* 37 (October 1973), 2-11.
112. ——. "The Perception of the Firm's Competitive Position," in F. Nicosia and Y. Wind, eds., *Behavioral Models of Market Analysis: Foundations for Marketing Action.* Hinsdale, Illinois: The Dryden Press, 1977, 163-81.
113. ——. "Organizational Buying Center: A Research Agenda," in Gerald Zaltman and Thomas V. Bonoma, eds., *Organizational Buying Behavior.* Chicago: AMA, in press.
114. —— and Richard N. Cardozo. "Industrial Marketing Segmentation," *Industrial Marketing Management,* 3 (March 1974), 153-65.
115. —— and Henry J. Claycamp. "Planning Product Line Strategy: A Matrix Approach," *Journal of Marketing,* 40 (January 1976), 2-9.
116. —— and Paul E. Green. "Some Conceptual Measurement and Analytical Problems in Life Style Research," in William Wells, ed., *Life Style and Psychographics.* Chicago: AMA, 1974, 97-126.
117. ——, Stuart Jolly, and Arthur O'Connor. "Concept Testing as Input to Strategic Marketing Simulations," in E. Mazze, ed., *Proceedings of the 58th International AMA Conference,* April 1975, 120-24.
118. —— and David Learner. "A Note on the Measurement of Purchase Data: Surveys vs. Purchase Diaries," Wharton School working paper, 1977.
119. —— and John G. Myers. "A Note on the Selection of Attributes for Conjoint Analysis," Wharton School working paper, January 1977.
120. —— and Lawrence K. Spitz, "Analytical Approach to Marketing Decisions in Health Care Organizations," *Operations Research,* 24 (September-October 1976), 973-90.

READING 17

Some Practical Considerations in Market Segmentation

Shirley Young, Leland Ott, and Barbara Feigin

Despite the widespread availability of segmentation techniques and much applied experience, many commercial users appear to be disenchanted with segmentation studies. The authors suggest that one cause is the failure of the marketing researcher to consider the competitive environment sufficiently in designing segmentation studies. They examine the problem in detail, setting forth some instances in which a segmentation approach is not useful and situations in which conventional approaches are not successful through examples from actual case studies.

Over the past 10 to 15 years, segmentation has come of age and most major marketers have conducted several market segmentation studies. Unfortunately, the results of these studies often have been disappointing because the segments derived from the study have not been actionable from a marketing standpoint. A common reason for this lack of applicability is preoccupation with the techniques and method of segmentation such as whether to use generic benefits, problems, lifestyles, psychographics, or preferences and the type of factor or cluster analysis to be performed. In too many instances, marketing researchers have failed to analyze the marketing environment and competitive structure before applying their favorite methodological approach.

In many situations a segmented approach is not even useful as the market should be analyzed in its entirety. In some cases the researcher must modify conventional approaches or develop unique ones that address the pertinent marketing issues. The authors illustrate a few examples of unique approaches based on practical experience in applying segmentation techniques to marketing problems.

Reprinted by permission of the American Marketing Association, *Journal of Marketing Research*, August 1978, 405–412.

When to Segment

In certain instances a segmented marketing strategy is not appropriate. At the outset of a study, the researcher must determine whether a segmented marketing approach is a relevant one for the particular brand or product category being studied. Though no set of guidelines can cover all situations, some of the specific instances in which segmentation is not useful follow.

1. *The market is so small that marketing to a portion of it is not profitable.* For some product categories, the incidence and/or frequency of usage are so low that the market can successfully sustain only one or two brands. Because a brand in such a category must appeal to all segments, decisions on product positioning and marketing strategy must be based on an analysis of the total market.
2. *Heavy users make up such a large proportion of the sales volume that they are the only relevant target.* If volume is skewed so markedly that only a very few consumers account for most of it, marketing efforts must be directed at this group. Conventional attitudinal segmentation is meaningless unless the heavy user group itself is of sufficient size or volume potential to permit a segmented approach.

3. *The brand is the dominant brand in the market.* If an established brand is the dominant one in the market, it draws its appeal from all segments of the market. Under this condition, targeting the product to only one or two segments of the market would not benefit sales.

Because these guidelines are overlapping, they must be examined carefully to determine whether a segmented marketing strategy is possible before large sums of money are wasted on research that does not address the marketing situation.

What to Segment

After determining that the segmentation of the market is the right strategy to pursue, the researcher must decide the basis on which to segment. Too often this decision is made by examining several alternative mathematical or statistical approaches in terms of which one can best reproduce itself. Though there is much scientific argument for such a procedure, it fails to account for the marketing utility of a segmentation approach. Statistical considerations are important only in assessing those alternatives that are relevant from a marketing standpoint.

In the authors' experience segmentation based on benefits desired is usually the most meaningful type to use from a marketing standpoint as it directly facilitates product planning, positioning, and advertising communications. *Though lifestyle, psychographic, or general attitudinal approaches work well statistically, they are* not *always helpful in marketing.*

However, in several important situations a segmentation analysis based on benefits is not relevant for marketing. Three common situations follow.

1. *Traditional price lines have developed so that all marketing activities are based on price levels.* For certain products such as clothing, cosmetics, automobiles, and appliances, traditional price lines have developed to the extent that markets have become segmented into price lines. Because all product offerings and marketing activities are contingent upon the price line offered, marketing considerations dictate that the market be segmented at least initially by price lines. For many product categories, the size of the market for any price line is too low to permit further segmentation.
2. *The benefits desired are determined by the occasion or purpose for which the product is used.* The desires of consumers can vary by the type of occasion for which the product is used. For example, clothes suitable for some occasions would not be suitable for other occasions. For effective marketing, consumer desires must be segmented by usage occasion to determine which products would be most suitable for each occasion. In many complex markets, this type of segmentation is necessary to derive the underlying competitive framework. Conventional segmentation questioning about the product without a specific usage occasion would provide meaningless information.
3. *The style or appearance of the product is the overriding criterion of success.* If fashion appeal is the major consideration in marketing success, the marketer must segment markets on the basis of styling preference in order to market a successful line of styles to each segment. Some examples of style-oriented lines are silverware, small appliances, fashion accessories, apparel, furniture, and automobiles.

In addition to the foregoing examples, other marketing situations dictate a unique approach. For instance, in a study for the National Highway Traffic Administration to develop an advertising program to convince persons to act to prevent a drunk person from driving, respondents had to be segmented on the basis of their willingness to take specific action—e.g., drive a friend home, take keys, stay over for the night.

In the following sections, the authors discuss three studies in which different methods of segmentation were used. The first one is an example of benefit segmentation which illustrates the complicated decisions necessary to ensure that the segmentation study is tailored to the marketing problem. The other two represent instances in which benefit segmentation would not have been appropriate and in which product usage by purpose and styling segmentation approaches were required to address the marketing problem. No example of pricing segmentation is discussed as this approach is rather easy to implement with regular cross-tabular analysis.

Case I. Segmentation on Generic Benefits

The Canadian Government Office of Tourism decided to conduct a marketing segmentation study of the U.S. travel market to obtain a comprehensive picture of Americans who are potential vacation travelers to Canada.[1] Because Canada is a large, diverse country with many different aspects, it truly can be many things to many people. Therefore, a segmentation approach was deemed desirable to ascertain the different groups of potential vacation travelers to Canada and which aspects of Canadian vacations could address their needs and desires. Once the segments had been identified and described, they could be evaluated in terms of the Canadian vacation business potential they offered, and those segments deemed attractive enough to cultivate then could be addressed through advertising and promotion campaigns portraying the advantages for a Canadian vacation of the specific type desired by the target segment(s).

However, because of the complexity of the travel and vacation business, certain conceptual problems and issues had to be resolved in planning and executing the study. Though most segmentation studies will not be as complicated as this one, it demonstrates the process the researcher must follow to resolve three critical issues before designing the questionnaire and fielding the study: (1) who should be interviewed, (2) the frame of reference for questioning, and (3) alternative methods of segmentation.

Who Should Be Interviewed. This critical consideration must be addressed in all studies. Because the purpose of the travel study was to expand the number of Canadian vacations taken by U.S. travelers, it was insufficient to include only those persons who had been to Canada because they accounted for only 5% of the U.S. population. Instead, it was necessary to define relevant prospect groups to obtain new visitors to Canada.

Consideration of the profitability of various types of tourists to Canada dictated a decision to interview only those who had taken a vacation of at least a week's duration in the past, and the vacation decision maker was the specific person to be questioned. Furthermore, the key analytical decision was dictated by the knowledge that the distance people have traveled on past vacations is a strong indicator of how far they would be willing to travel on future vacations. Therefore, the sample was designed to cover only those persons who had traveled the requisite distance for a Canadian vacation—defined in the study as three quarters of the distance to Canada.

Frame of Reference for Questioning. This factor was a particularly difficult problem for this study because most individuals were potential prospects for more than one type of vacation. To question about vacations in general was not relevant as needs and desires would vary by type of vacation. Also, asking about the ideal vacation would likely yield fantasized wishes that would have no relationship to the type of vacation a person would or could take. This problem was overcome by asking the respondent to anchor all responses in terms of the last vacation taken. In this way, responses were based on the reality of a specific vacation experience for which behavioral and attitudinal information were obtained.

Alternative Methods of Market Segmentation. As in most segmentation studies, this was the most critical issue. Because the best way to segment or group U.S. travelers for developing marketing programs was far from obvious, the following alternative methods were investigated.

1. By segmenting consumers on *favorability toward Canada* as a vacation area, U.S. travelers could be grouped on the basis of their attitudes toward Canada. This approach could be most appropriate if Canada were a single entity and if attitudes toward vacationing in Canada were polarized. However, these possibilities did not appear to represent reality.
2. By segmenting on *geographic area,* or proximity to selected areas of Canada, respondents would be assigned by their U.S. locality. This approach would be reasonable as an independent segmentation alternative if travelers' vacation behavior and desires varied dramatically by region in the U.S., but they do not.
3. By segmenting consumers on *desires sought* in their last vacation, respondents could be segmented on what they were seeking in a vacation of the last type taken.

A pilot study consisting of 200 interviews was developed to test the meaningfulness of each approach. The last approach (desires sought in the last vacation) was found to be most meaningful in terms

1. The authors acknowledge Myron Rusk, Marketing Research Manager of the Canadian Travel Office, for granting permission to include this study [13].

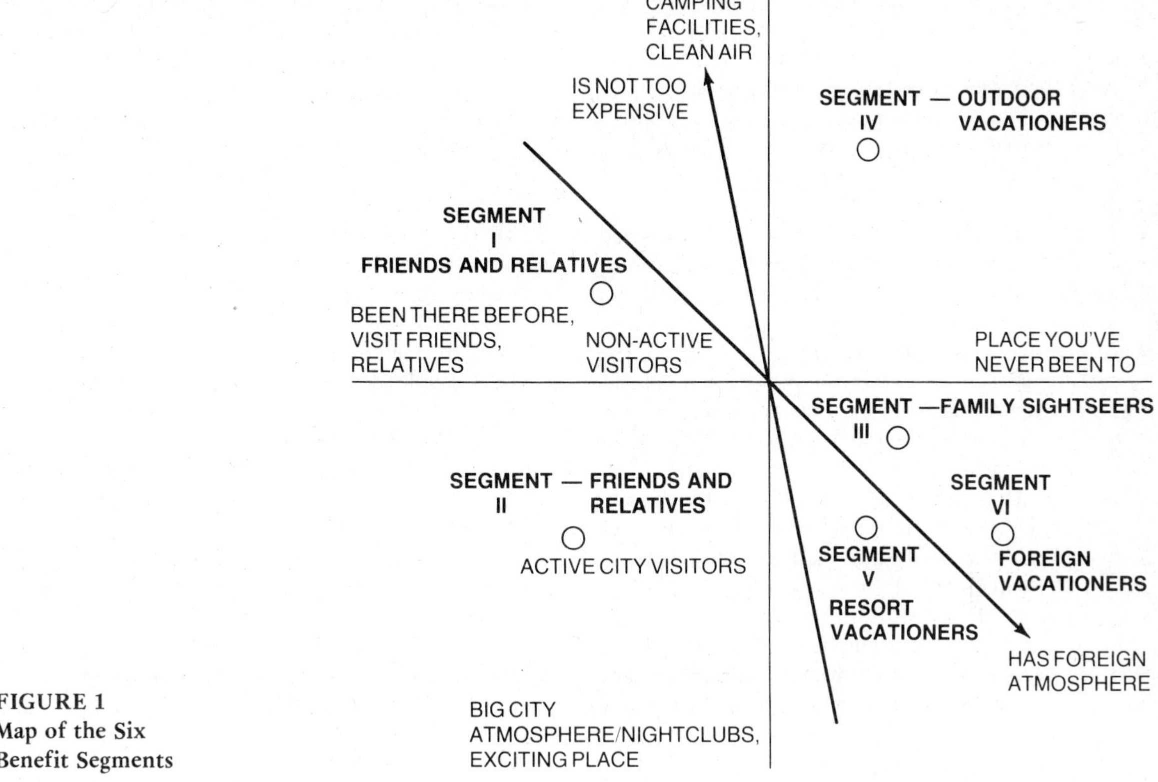

FIGURE 1
Map of the Six Benefit Segments

of marketing and was the approach used in the major study.

Results

The major study consisted of 1,750 interviews with eligible respondents, i.e., those responsible for making a decision about an extended vacation of at least three-fourths the distance to Canada during the last three years. A national probability sample was used with one callback on the household and one on the eligible respondent.

A benefit segmentation was obtained for those desires sought in planning the most recent vacation meeting the eligibility criteria. The technique of segmentation was a *Q*-factor analysis. This approach consists of normalizing the profile of the respondents across all benefits to obtain groups of homogeneous respondents through principal components extraction of eigenvalues and their associated eigenvectors, which subsequently are rotated by the varimax procedure [2–4, 8, 9, 12]. To facilitate the analysis and description of the marketing segments, a perceptual map derived by the multiple discriminant analysis technique is shown in Figure 1 [4, 10, 11].[2] The locations of the six segments are shown in circles; the benefit items shown as vectors indicate those desires sought by each group.

- *Segment I. Friends and relatives–nonactive visitor (29%).* These vacationers seek familiar surround-

2. The discriminant analysis was performed by a stepwise computer program to select those benefit items that can best predict group membership [5]. After the items had been selected, their relationship to the *Q* groups was shown in a two-dimensional space. The procedure was [10, 11]: (1) the eigenvalues and their associated canonical coefficients were computed through the principal components method for those variables that were selected as the best discriminators, (2) each individual then was scored on his first two canonical dimensions and the group means were computed, (3) the canonical scores were correlated with the original items which were plotted as vectors in two-dimensional space to show the relationship of the benefit items to each group.

ings where they can visit friends and relatives. They are not very inclined to participate in any activity.

- *Segment II. Friends and relatives—active city visitor (12%).* These vacationers also seek familiar surroundings where they can visit friends and relatives, but they are more inclined to participate in activities—especially sightseeing, shopping, and cultural and other entertainment.
- *Segment III. Family sightseers (6%).* These vacationers are looking for a new vacation place which would be a treat for the children and an enriching experience.
- *Segment IV. Outdoor vacationer (19%).* These vacationers seek clean air, rest and quiet, and beautiful scenery. Many are campers and availability of recreation facilities is important. Children are also an important factor.
- *Segment V. Resort vacationer (19%).* These vacationers are most interested in water sports (e.g., swimming) and good weather. They prefer a popular place with a big city atmosphere.
- *Segment VI. Foreign vacationer (26%).* These vacationers look for vacations in a place they have never been before with a foreign atmosphere and beautiful scenery. Money is not of major concern but good accommodation and service are. They want an exciting, enriching experience.

Because of their relatively low vacation expenditures, segments I and II offered less attractive business potential than was offered by the other segments. Moreover, Canadian vacations could not provide an opportunity to visit with friends and relatives.

The other segments had vacation needs and desires that could be delivered by various areas of Canada through different types of vacations. For each of these segments, data from the questionnaire were used to determine a profile in terms of behavior, psychographics, travel incentives, and image of a Canadian vacation.

Implementation

Unlike a commercial firm, the Canadian Office of Tourism had special problems in implementing the results of the study. It had to rely on an extensive program to inform the many elements of the travel industry of the study findings through meetings, seminars, and publications. As a result of these efforts, improvements were made in the following areas.

1. *Advertising execution.* The tonality or style of the advertising was made more compatible with the personality traits and lifestyles of the target groups. Creatively, the advertising message stressed the specific benefits sought by each segment, reinforced the positive images of Canada that each group already had, and corrected any undesirable impressions they may have held.
2. *Media considerations.* The study facilitated the selection of vehicles compatible with the life style, demographic features, and personality of target groups. The study was not designed to measure individual media habits, but the results allowed a closer look at the media available and comparison of editorial environment of U.S. consumer magazines with the unique audience profiles and desires for each segment. Television commercials were changed in mood, tempo, and emphasis to attract travelers in the most promising segment.
3. *Merchandising and promotional efforts.* Promotional brochures and specific types of vacation "tours" or packages were developed along the lines suggested by the findings.
4. *Provincial tourist offices.* The results were passed on to the provinces so they could adopt a segmented promotional effort, and to those areas that could deliver the benefits sought by one or more of the target groups.

In addition to providing marketing guidance, the study findings were useful in the planning of new hotels, accommodations, and tourist facilities by the Canadian government and private groups.

Case II. Product Usage Purpose Segmentation

For some product categories, the occasion or purpose of usage dictates the product or brand used. For example, in certain food and beverage categories such as main meal items, snacks, and desserts the benefits desired may differ by the purpose or occasion for which the product is used. Most persons drink various types of beverages, some of which are hot or cold. The person's selection is determined by the time of day, the weather, suitability with meals, and the person's mood. Usage of disposable paper products such as facial tissue, napkins, and towels, varies according to whether the product is to serve functional needs, such as wiping up spills and cleaning, or aesthetic

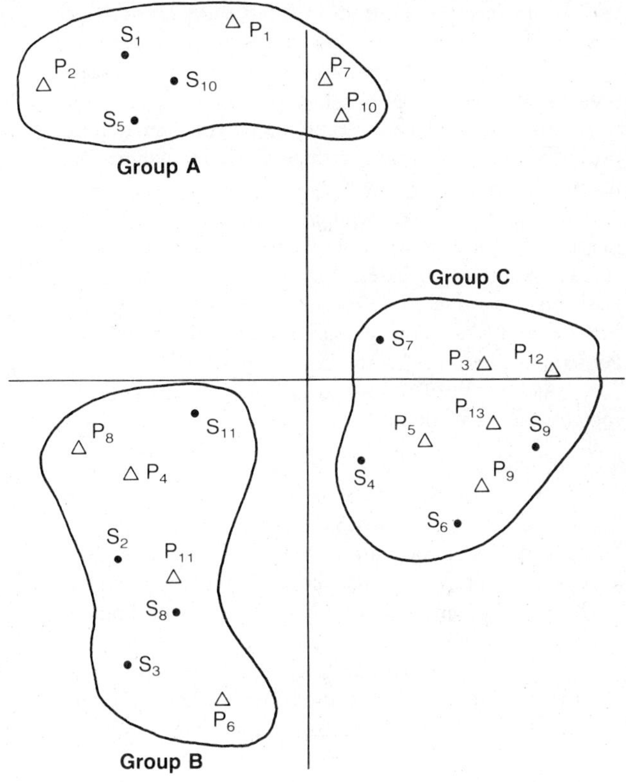

FIGURE 2
Map of Symptoms (S) and Products (P) △

needs, such as looking attractive or decorative. An approach of segmenting on desires in an "ideal" product not anchored to an occasion context would be clearly inappropriate for the marketing of these products.

In the drug area, usage of products and brands is dictated by ailments or symptoms of ailments. An unusual and successful product usage purpose segmentation has been achieved for over-the-counter medicines used in the treatment of various cold symptoms or ailments. In the cold remedy market, numerous products compete with each other for relieving certain specific symptoms such as runny nose, post-nasal drip, fever, aches and pains, sore throat, coughing, etc. Because many of the products offered such as cold tablets, capsules, sprays, cough syrups, analgesics, and throat lozenges address one or more of these symptoms, the cold remedy market must be segmented by those symptoms that occur jointly and those remedies used to treat each group of symptoms.

By listing common symptom clusters and products used to treat them in a joint perceptual space, a researcher can define the appropriate competitive framework. A specific illustration of this type of application is for 13 products and 11 symptoms. The data were obtained by having each respondent indicate the specific remedies used for each symptom suffered the last time he or she had a cold. In Figure 2, the symptoms suffered are mapped in three major groups or segments labeled A, B, and C on two dimensions.[3] On this space the products used to treat

3. The technique used to place symptoms and products in joint space was factor analysis of the products and factor scores of the individual symptoms [4, 7]. For all respondents in the study, each symptom was treated as an observation and the products were treated as variables. For this illustration the input matrix for the factor analysis consisted of 11 rows (symptoms) and 13 columns (products).

As not all persons suffered from all of the symptoms, the incidence of suffering for each symptom was adjusted to 100% to eliminate this bias from the analysis. The products then were factor analyzed by principal components and the first two factors rotated by the varimax procedure [4, 9]. Factor scores were computed for each symptom. The rotated factors loading for the products and the factor scores for the symptoms were plotted to determine those groups of symptoms and products that form competitive clusters.

the symptoms are plotted so that the competitive structure is defined. In this case, there are three distinct competitive groups that must be analyzed separately.

For those product segments offering sufficient potential sales volume, attitudinal and behavioral measures were used to identify needs, dissatisfactions, and problems for each segment to determine (1) the degree of dissatisfaction with the existing products in each segment to assess the need for a new or repositioned product and (2) the specific product qualities or attributes required to overcome the problems consumers are having with existing products.

As a result of the foregoing analysis, the following actions were taken.

1. For existing products, marketing and advertising strategies stressed the benefits in treating specific symptoms. In one instance, recommending use of both an analgesic and a throat remedy was indicated as sore throats usually were accompanied by fever, aches, and pains. This approach would result in more complete treatment than would be possible with the single throat remedy. This approach further associated the remedy with the most commonly used cold product and symptoms group.

   To implement the new strategy, a change in the product was required. New advertising executions, point of sales material, and sales promotional material were needed. Alternative advertising executions were developed and tested to determine the ability to attract attention and collectively communicate the new strategy. The campaign was introduced and has been running for more than four years with positive sales success.
2. Examination of one of the competitive groupings showed a high level of product dissatisfaction as existing products that were efficacious were inconvenient to use. However, the easy-to-use products were not efficacious. This finding indicated a potential for introducing an efficacious product in a convenient form if one could be developed. The implementation of the results required the development of an entirely new product not on the market. Several steps were required. First, research and development of alternative products were carried out to overcome the dissatisfactions obtained from the research. Second, alternative concepts/products were tested to determine whether these dissatisfactions had been overcome. Third, advertising execution, point of display material, and dealer merchandising programs were developed and tested. Finally, the entire marketing program was tested for one year.

As a result of these activities, the new product was successfully introduced nationally. In the study, conventional benefits segments also were developed and reported. However, they were not particularly helpful in the development of better positioning and products because of their inability to define the competitive environment for this product.

Case III. Styling Segmentation

For products in which the style, looks, appearance, or image is the overriding criterion of marketing success, benefit segmentation is *not* appropriate as it can indicate only that styling is important and gives little direction as to what styles are actually preferred. Some examples of categories in which styling problems are critical are silverware, small appliances, fashion accessories, apparel, automobiles, and furniture for which the marketer must decide how many and what styles to offer the consumer in his line.

The problem of line formulation can be approached in two ways.

1. *Pile sorting in terms of similarity.* By this approach, respondents are asked to sort pictures, samples, or actual products into piles of those items they consider similar to each other. The number of piles allowed for sorting usually is left up to the consumer within some minimum or or maximum range. The data are analyzed by determining the frequency with which each pair of items is sorted into the same pile. This matrix of pairwise similarities then can be processed with a multidimensional scaling program such as TORSCA to map clusters of styles into homogeneous segments [6, 14].

   Though this technique is particularly useful for developing a broad overview of the overall styling structure as perceived by respondents, it does not address the critical issue of individual styling preferences. For example, the respondent's preference structure may consist of selecting from different styling groups rather than selecting among those items within a specific styling cluster.

Such selection is particularly common for products for which there is multiple purchasing.

2. *Rating in terms of preference or likelihood of buying.* This method of styling segmentation is more direct as it addresses the respondent's purchasing preference rather than his or her overall perception of a competitive structure.[4] Although the preference ratings can be analyzed by means of *R* and *Q* factor analysis, the *Q* mode is the one required to determine the items that a seller should offer to insure that all major preference segments of the market are covered adequately in a line offering. This analysis is done in the same way as conventional *Q* segmentation except that style ratings are used instead of benefit ratings.

When the *R* mode factor analysis is undertaken, one obtains clusters of style items on preference dimensions. This approach is useful only in a preliminary or pilot stage of research when the number of items must be reduced to a more manageable proportion for subsequent rating by consumers. Even if an *R* analysis is performed, the *Q* segmentation and analysis should be based on the individual items and not the clusters obtained from the *R* analysis.

Table 1 is a simplified illustration taken from a larger study of a *Q* factor analysis for a line of items being considered by a marketer. The data were obtained by asking each respondent to examine the items and rate them according to likelihood of buying on a 6-point scale. The *Q* analysis identified three distinct segments of sufficient size to be relevant for marketing purposes. To determine the styles required in the line to cover adequately each of the basic segments, the percentage who indicated they were "extremely likely to buy" each style was tabulated for each of the segments.

As indicated in Table 1, each segment can be covered adequately by offering only five of the 10 items: for segment A, styles 3 and 4; for segment B, styles 1 and 2; for segment C, style 7.

To determine the total buying likelihood, one can sum each of the five styles for each of the segments. In this illustration, as the total buying likelihood is 98% for segment A, 84% for segment B, and 81% for segment C, the entire market is well covered. From this point, impact on coverage can be evaluated by adding and dropping items in the line. For example, if style number 1 were added as a sixth item, there would be only a slight increase in buying likelihood for all three segments.

TABLE 1
An Example of Styling Segmentation

	Segment		
Style Number	*A* *60%*[a]	*B* *30%*[a]	*C* *10%*[a]
	(% indicating extremely likely to buy)		
3[b]	33	12	13
4[b]	22	2	10
1	16	13	15
9	13	5	8
10[b]	14	25	12
2[b]	16	30	4
8	4	16	5
7[b]	13	15	42
5	9	12	18
6	15	2	9
Total percentage "likely to buy" for each segment[b]	98	84	81

a. Segment size.
b. The total percentage "likelihood to buy" for each segment is obtained by summing the five styles (3, 4, 10, 2, and 7) that would be offered in the line. It can exceed 100% as more than one style could be rated as "extremely likely to buy."

Implementation

The implementation of the results of styling segmentation depends on the nature of the industry and the competitive position of the firm. In this case, the firm was the dominant one and had to compete in all three styling segments. However, a firm's competition might be chosen to permit competition in only one or two of the styling segments.

The following steps were taken in implementing the findings from this study.

4. It is also recognized that rank order preference data can be obtained and mapped through the authors' techniques. It is experience that the scaler ratings are more reliable indicators of purchase intent as ranking does not directly measure buying intent, e.g., a person may not like any of the styles well enough to buy them or he may want to buy several of them.

1. The product line, both in terms of the number of items to offer and the amounts of each to be manufactured, was obtained from the research.
2. Point of purchase displays were rearranged to have maximum impact and to stress those styles indicated by the research.
3. Through an analysis of demographic and psychographic data of the respondents in each styling segment, guidance was provided for developing the appropriate tonality of the advertising and deciding which items to feature.

In a few instances it was possible to differentiate styling groups by media selection. For example, a style preferred by young swingers could be advertised in magazines appropriate to that group, and styles preferred by a group of traditional consumers could be advertised in other appropriate media.

The implementation of the styling segmentation study enabled the manufacturer to reduce his offerings and increase his position in his market. The manufacturer subsequently has undertaken several additional styling segmentation studies to develop product lines as this type of research has become an integral part of his product development and marketing planning procedures.

Conclusions

No single approach can be used to segment all markets as the specific competitive structure and environment determine the appropriate approach. Thus, the marketing researcher must analyze the market carefully to insure that only approaches relevant from a marketing standpoint are considered.

In many situations, markets should not be segmented at all as appeal to all segments is required for marketing success, for example, in the case of (1) product categories with low sales volumes, (2) products for which sales are skewed to a small group of heavy users, and (3) brands dominating a market.

When attitudinal segmentation is the appropriate technique, the successful implementation of a study requires the solution of such issues as (1) whom to interview, (2) the framework of questioning, and (3) the alternative methods of segmentation.

However, many situations requiring segmentation cannot be addressed through conventional approaches. For example:

1. For products for which the usage situation dictates preference, segmentation can be done best by simultaneously mapping usage situations by products used to develop the appropriate competitive framework.
2. For products for which styling is the major factor influencing marketing success, segmentation of styling preferences through *Q* factor analysis provides the guidance necessary for determining the different sets of prospects in the market with different sets of styling preferences, and the line of items required to meet their needs.

These examples represent only a few of the many instances in which conventional segmentation is not applicable. Much more emphasis needs to be placed on classifying competitive environments and those segmentation approaches that are most relevant. This process would be facilitated greatly by wider dissemination of the practical experiences gained from segmentation studies.

References

1. Assael, Henry. "Perceptual Mapping to Reposition Brands," *Journal of Advertising Research,* 11 (February 1971), 39–42.
2. Cattell, R. B. "The Data Box," in R. B. Cattell, ed., *Handbook of Multivariate Experimental Psychology.* Chicago: Rand McNally Company, 1966.
3. ——. "The Meaning and Strategic Use of Factor Analysis," in R. B. Cattell, ed., *Handbook of Experimental Psychology.* Chicago: Rand McNally Company, 1966.
4. Cooley, W. C. and P. R. Lohnes. *Multivariate Procedures in the Behavioral Sciences.* New York: John Wiley & Sons, Inc., 1971.
5. Dixon, W. J. *Biomedical Computer Programs.* Berkeley: University of California Press, 1970.
6. Green, Paul and Frank Carmone. *Multidimensional Scaling and Related Techniques in Marketing Analysis.* Boston: Allyn and Bacon, Inc., 1970
7. ——, Ronald Frank, and Patrick Robinson. "Cluster Analysis in Test Market Selection," *Management Science,* 13 (April 1967), 387–400.
8. —— and Donald Tull. *Research for Marketing Decisions,* third edition. Englewood Cliffs, New Jersey: Prentice-Hall, Inc., 1975.

9. Harman, Harry H. *Modern Factor Analysis.* Chicago: University of Chicago Press, 1967.
10. Johnson, Richard. "Market Segmentation: A Strategic Management Tool," *Journal of Marketing Research,* 8 (February 1971), 13-18.
11. ——. "Multiple Discriminant Analysis," unpublished paper, University of Chicago Workshop on Multivariate Methods in Marketing, 1970.
12. ——. "Q Analysis of Large Samples," *Journal of Marketing Research,* 7 (February 1970), 104-5.
13. Rusk, Myron. *Understanding the U.S. Vacationer: Summary of the Potential Vacation Trip Market for Canada.* Ottawa, Ontario: Marketing Research Office, Canadian Government, July 1974.
14. Young, Forrest. "TORSCA, an IBM Program for Nonmetric Multidimensional Scaling," *Journal of Marketing Research,* 5 (August 1968), 319-21.
15. Young, Shirley. "Pitfalls Down the Primrose Path of Attitude Segmentation," presented to the Fifth Annual Advertising Congress of the American Marketing Association, February 13-18, 1973, Madrid, Spain.
16. ——. "The Why of Travel: Psychographic Research in Action," presented to the Travel Research Association, December 17, 1974.

READING 18

Person-Situation: Segmentation's Missing Link

Peter R. Dickson

Has usage situation been overlooked in market segmentation? A general framework is offered which positions situation and person within situation as theoretically legitimate and potentially useful bases for segmenting demand and targeting marketing strategy.

A recent comprehensive state of the art review of market segmentation concluded that the field has become too fixed in its ways and that new conceptualizations of the segmentation problem should be explored (Wind 1978). One convention that bears examination is the equating of market segmentation with customer segmentation. Markets can also be subdivided by usage situation. Although almost every conceivable person-based characteristic has been used to segment markets over the last two decades, there has been a disturbing lack of consideration of the usage situation as a basis for defining product markets and modelling consumer choice behavior (Leigh and Martin 1981, Shocker and Srinivasan 1979). Market segmentation requires an understanding of the what, when, where, how and why of demand. As demand results from the interaction of a person with his or her environment, a segmentation perspective that includes both the person and the situation is needed to explain demand and target marketing strategy. Person-situation segmentation explicitly segments the market by groups of consumers within usage situations.

Defining markets and demand in terms of people and usage situation is not a new idea. National Analysts introduced their concept of occasion-based segmentation in the mid-1970s.[1] In reporting on the technique McDonald and Goldman (1980) did not deny the existence of stable personal needs that generalize across situations, but they argued that in addition, certain situations can evoke fairly standard consumption roles. The approach has been used to increase consumption among current users by developing new situation usage campaigns (e.g., "orange juice isn't just for breakfast anymore"). The researchers also emphasize the motivational insights provided by their approach. It enabled them to distinguish between the heavy beer drinker who seeks to "escape" and the heavy beer drinker who seeks "social accommodation," the young athlete who drinks beer to quench his/her thirst and the young college party goer. The recognition of situational influence in the consumption of beverages confirms Sandell's (1968) experimental scenario findings. Surprisingly, however, Sandell did not believe that the observed situation-specific beverage preferences resulted from different needs. He claimed that only one single drive existed—thirst.[2] Other research has recorded the influence of usage situations on the choice of snack food, meat and fast food chains (Belk 1974, 1975).

Many other examples of situation segmentation can be found in the design of furniture, appliances, china, bicycles, motorcycles, automobiles and camping equipment. Some lounge suites are designed for

Reprinted by permission of the American Marketing Association, from the *Journal of Marketing,* 46:4 Fall 1982, 56–64.

1. Other proprietary situation-based segmentation research approaches are described by Klein (1982) and Radder (1982).

2. Some other possible goals that people seek in consuming beverages are to relax and reduce shyness, sedate, cool down, warm up, stimulate taste buds, aid digestion, relieve throat irritation, provide nutrition and vitamins, celebrate and impress others.

small apartments, others for beach side holiday homes and yet others for executive suites and lounge bars. Color TVs are designed as feature furniture pieces for family rooms and as robust portables for trailers and bedrooms. Special refrigerators are designed for trailers and basement bars. Expensive china is designed for entertaining guests, while cheap, robust Corelle dinnerware is designed for everyday family use. There are commuting motorcycles, dirt motorcycles, farm motorcycles and highway cruisers. Pick-ups and four-wheel drive station wagons are primarily designed for different usage situations than a VW Rabbit or Rolls Royce. Camping gear is designed to be adaptable, but specialist equipment is designed for use in tropical and/or very cold climates and situations where space and weight are at a premium. The clothing and footwear market has long been person-situation segmented to accommodate not only differing sex and size but also differing weather conditions, physical activities and social role playing (Belk 1979). In practice the product whose unique selling proposition (quality, features, image, packaging or merchandising) is not targeted for particular people in particular usage situations is probably the exception rather than the rule. A manufacturer or retailer's product line can be viewed as a range of products catering to the needs of a diversity of person-situation market segments.

This article discusses conventional market segmentation theory and practice from a person-situation perspective. The analytical, behavioral and demand analysis justifications for the model are first presented. The extent to which usage-situation or person-situation segments conform to Kotler's three criteria for segmentation are then discussed. Having laid this foundation, several of the currently popular segmentation techniques including psychographic and benefit segmentation are reinterpreted from a person-situation perspective. A segmentation framework is offered that integrates several of these techniques. Finally a practical guide to situation-person segmentation is proposed. This introduces the person-situation segmentation matrix, a device designed to improve market opportunity analysis, target market selection and competitive positioning.

Person-Situation Analysis and Theory

An exciting new analytical technique, componential segmentation (Green 1977), can be used to illustrate and quantify the person-situation conceptualization. A two-way ANOVA model partitions the variance of people's ratings of a set of products (objects) into a person effect (P), object effect (O) and their interaction (P × O). A large (P) or (P × O) effect suggests the potential for person-based segmentation. This can be expanded, as noted by Green and DeSarbo (1979), into a three-way model that includes a situation-specific usage effect (S) and its interactions (S × O, P × S, P × S × O).[3] The situation scenario studies of Sandell (1968) and Belk (1975a) provide enough evidence to warrant the inclusion of situation effects within the general componential framework even if inclusion requires more measurement effort. Wind (1978) has advocated probability sampling of individuals to generate valid inferences from person segmentation studies. Similarly, representative usage situations should be sampled properly to assess the viability and stability of situation-based market potential. This is really only a generalization of Brunswick's (1956) situation representativeness concern in experimentation.

If the attitudes and behavior of one group with respect to alternative brands and substitutable products are similar across all usage situations, but are different with respect to the responses of another group across the same situations, then the potential exists for standard person segmentation. In a variance study this potential is indicated by a substantial P or P × O effect. If responses of all people are similar but vary by usage situation (an S or S × O effect), then a potential exists for situation-specific segmentation. A person-situation segmentation opportunity exists when the the differential sensitivity to all or particular products and their characteristics depends on the situation *and* person (a P × S or P × S × O effect).[4] To be at all useful, the differential sensitivity

3. The P, S and P × S effects indicate that attitudes or behavior toward *all* of the objects (brand or products) vary by person, situation and person within situation, respectively. The P × O, S × O and P × S × O effects indicate that attitudes or behaviors toward some of the objects vary by person, situation and person-within-situation. That is, some of the brands or products in the set are influenced by these effects more than others.

4. It is possible to have person and situation segmentation occurring together. This occurs when one has additive P and S effects, where the effects of the situations are the same for the different groups of consumers. This situation is different from person-situation segmentation where different groups have unique reactions to situations. I am indebted to Jim Ginter for this observation.

toward the products that is captured by the P, P X O, P X S, and P X S X O effects must have a particular property. Groups of persons must be identified such that within-group responses are homogeneous and between-group responses are heterogeneous. A segmentation basis that disaggregates all the way down to individual idiosyncratic behavior is useless, practically speaking, unless we are dealing with custom-made products or services.

Person-situation segmentation bases have a theoretical foundation in Lewin's Field Theory (Kassarjian 1973, Lewin, 1936) and modern interactionism (Ekehammer 1974). These perspectives assert that human motivations, intentions and behavior are a function of the interaction between person and situation [$B = f(P \times S)$]. These theories claim that each individual views each physical and social setting somewhat differently. This very subjective view of the world is called our "life-space" and its uniqueness produces the variation in utility functions and consumption behavior that market segmentation attempts to harness. The motivations, attitudes, preferences, attributes utility weights and intentions that we measure are abstractions of this life-space. In this sense they are person-situation characteristics rather than situation-specific or person-specific characteristics.

An interesting feature of the situation-based stream of research in consumer behavior is that, like the contemporary interactionist or environmental psychologists, consumer researchers do not appear to be aware of, or at least interested in, the link between the interactionist analysis of variance studies and Lewin's Field Theory. Belk and others have not conceptually tied observed person-situation interaction effects to Lewin's discussion of the idiosyncratic, psychological situation. On the other hand, Kassarjian's (1973) review of field theory did not quote Sandell's work as an experimental illustration of the interaction between person and situation and the resulting influence of the perceived usage situation on consumer choice behavior.

From a microeconomic perspective, the standard demand curve is an aggregation of a set of demand curves $Q_i = F_i(x_1, x_2, \ldots, x_n)$ where i defines the ith customer and the x's are product characteristics and other marketing variables. These individual demand curves can themselves, however, be conceptualized as aggregations of an individual's usage situation demand curves, perhaps weighted by the situation's frequency of occurrence or importance (see Berkowitz, Ginter and Talarzyk 1977). The person-situation demand function is $Q_{ij} = F_{ij}(x_1, x_2, \ldots, x_n)$ where i defines the ith customer and j defines the jth usage situation.

Aggregate demand can be reconstructed by collapsing across the buyers rather than the situations. This effort produces a set of demand functions $Q_j = F_j(x_1, x_2, \ldots, x_n)$ where j defines the jth situation. If these demand curves require substantially different $(x_1, x_2, \ldots, x_n)$ to maximize demand, then situation segmentation is theoretically viable. Whether such segmentation is sensible depends on profitability and production constraints. Person-situation segmentation is viable when different groups have distinctly different demand schedules for different usage situations. This condition produces demand functions of the form $Q_{ij} = F_{ij}(x_1, x_2, \ldots, x_n)$ where i defines the ith group and j defines the jth usage situation or subset of situations.

A problem with accepting such a segmentation or aggregation of market demand is that people buy products and situations do not. One response is that buyers can be described and categorized just as naturally by the situations they will primarily use the product in as by demographics, personality traits or attitudes. However, the important point is that it is not people or situations that are segmented, but demand curves. These demand curves reflect the needs that arise from consumers' interactions with usage situations.

Segment Measurability, Accessibility, and Substantiality

Kotler (1980) suggests that the usefulness of a particular segmentation approach be assessed in terms of ease of measurement, accessibility and substantiality. The frequency of occurrence of various usage situations can often be established by unobtrusive observation or by recall questions. National Analysts have have found that consumers find it easier to recall their consumption behavior which is tied to a particular situation than behavior not tied to a specific situation (McDonald and Goldman 1980). Just what, in theory, is a "situation" has not been resolved clearly despite debate in the literature (Barker 1975; Belk 1975a, 1975b, 1975c, 1976; Lutz and Kakkar 1975, 1976; Russell and Mehrabian 1976; Wicker 1975). For the purposes of segmentation the most practical approach may be to describe the usage situation in terms of objective characteristics such as temperature or the presence of particular people, or as a stereotypic vignette such as "an August dog-day at the beach." The development of a general situational segmentation taxonomy is likely to be as frustrating as the efforts made by researchers to use general personality scales in segmentation (see Kassarjian 1971). One advantage, however, is that unlike personality, many features of the situation can be directly seen, smelled, heard or touched.

Situation or occasion segments are accessible in two ways. First, consumers can sometimes be reached directly in actual usage situations. The ideal beer for drinking with friends while watching football on TV can be advertised in TV spots during such televised games. The ideal commuting car can be promoted on radio to users travelling to and from work in the morning and early evening. Popcorn and Coke are promoted at baseball games to a market that is not only accessible, but captive. Where usage is tied to geographical location or season, regional media can be used or special catalogs produced (e.g., Sears' regional and seasonal catalogs). The second way to focus distribution and to identify the people who place themselves most often in that usage situation and select the media and channels that concentrate on these people. Featuring the target person and situation in advertising will maximize not only exposure but attention, involvement, learning and recall of the message.

The degree to which situation segments are substantial depends on the frequency of occurrence of the usage situation and the importance of the usage goals or need. Kotler (1980) points out that making special cars for midgets is not likely to be profitable. But special cars are made to carry golfers around golf courses and to carry presidents and governors safely along crowded streets. As with any segmentation basis, a number of usage situations that generate similar needs may have to be combined to become substantial enough to be worth serving. Some products may have to be adaptable enough to be used in multiple situations, although designed primarily for a particular usage setting.

Psychographics and Usage Situation

As well as measuring standard demographics such as age, sex and income, psychographics measures where people live, how they spend their time, how they view themselves and their world and the important things in their surroundings (Plummer 1974). Some researchers also measure media and shopping habits, basic personality measures, values and beliefs, and even the specific benefits sought from products. To some extent psychographics describes enduring individual difference traits; it has been claimed that the power of the approach is that it identifies basic beliefs and attitudes that influence behavior in many situations (Ziff 1971).

A different, complementary (rather than competing) explanation for at least part of the considerable usefulness of psychographics is that it measures the types of usage situations people with different lifestyles are likely to encounter or create (e.g., social events, vacations, sports). The attitudinal questions capture their psychological view of these situations, their likely role playing and consumption needs in such situations (e.g., a young swinger's need for trendy clothes arises because he/she frequents trendy bars or social functions). Reynolds and Darden (1974) describe psychographics as an attempt to "crawl into the skin of the consumers." A more apt phrase might be "seeing into their world or life-space." In fact, psychographic researchers may make the participant-observer mistake of looking at people and reporting personal differences in behavior, rather than looking through their eyes and reporting situational differences in behavior (see Bem and Allen 1974). In contrast to observers, participants more often attribute their behavior to situation effects than to personal characteristics.

Wells and Tigert (1971) describe the use of psychographics to refit a product's previous folksy, homey, small town image to the world of the heaviest users who were, in fact, young swingers. Essentially they were attempting to effect a better matching of the product's image with the target market's typical usage situation. Demby (1968) undertook a psychographic study of the alcoholic beverage market and ended up identifying usage situations (e.g., theater, restaurant, travelling, after sport) and developing an outgoing life campaign around these settings.

In his review Wells (1975) again illustrates the value of psychographics to the advertising copy writer who seeks a good description of the user so that he/she can translate the product, idea or theme into the consumer's world. Of equal value would be a good description of the actual physical and psychological situation within which the product demonstrates a superior performance or its unique selling proposition. Wells describes the heavy user of shotgun shells as a young, lower educated, blue collar male from the rural South. As well as pointing out that it is useful to know where such a person shops and what he reads, Wells emphasizes the usefulness of studying the usage situation and what else such a shotgun user does in that situation (i.e., camps, fishes, boats and plays cards, etc.). This approach provides advertising copy context and also identifies a line of complementary products that are tied to a particular situation or activity (e.g., fishing gear, boats, clothing, camping gear, recreational games). Wells' criticisms of the practical use of defining persons who are users of shotgun shells by abstract personality traits generalizes to the uselessness of defining shotgun usage situations in similarly abstract terms.

Psychographic analysis has been used to cluster the male and female population into general segments. While offering some useful insights, such labeling suffers from the same defects as general personality scales (see Adams 1982). Most readers would very likely identify with half a dozen of the segment profiles described in Wells (1975) because individuals often play different roles in different situations (i.e., for different audiences). Consequently, the use of psychographics without consideration of the situational context can sometimes become a game of shadow boxing rather than target marketing.

Person-Situation Segmentation

Segmentation bases have been divided generally into two types: general customer characteristics such as demographic, socioeconomic and lifestyle measures and so called situation-specific customer characteristics based on measures of customer brand attitudes, brand preferences, benefits sought, product usage and response sensitivity to various elements of the marketing mix. The use of the term *situation-specific* by previous writers to describe attitudinal or behavioral segmentation bases is unfortunate, as their measures were not specific to particular usage situations. Wilkie and Cohen (1977) developed a more sophisticated framework to describe and evaluate segmentation bases. The five levels used were general person descriptors, psychographics, desired values, brand perceptions and purchase behavior.

An integrated person-situation market segmentation framework is presented in Figure 1. The three basic types of segmentation bases are situation, person and person-within-situation. Psychographic segmentation is not explicitly positioned in the framework because it is a mix of person differences, situation factors and the derivative values, attitudes and needs arising from their interaction. The underpinnings of benefit segmentation are usage situations, stable personal characteristics and their interaction. The desired benefits drive the perceived utility or instrumentality of brands or models and the importance weighting of their attributes. The utility structures and situation frequencies are the bases for heavy or light usage, product or brand loyalty and sensitivity to elements of the marketing mix. The framework offers a reductive theory of segmentation in the sense that lower order segmentation bases such as behavior are determined by higher level bases, the highest being situation and/or person characteristics.

Practically speaking, the framework calls for the identification of person-situation combinations that can be aggregated or disaggregated on the basis of their similarity, in terms of the predominant product benefits sought, product and attribute perceptions, and marketplace behavior. This is not a radically new idea. When Haley (1968) introduced benefit segmentation he positioned it as an alternative to segmenting consumers by geographic location, demographic characteristics and volume (light or heavy usage). His method involved clustering or grouping consumers by their ratings of the relative importance of benefits. These ratings were not usage situation-specific. But while his conceptualization and analysis were person-based, he implicitly accepted usage situation's influence on benefits sought. Haley recommended promoting products in appropriate usage "settings." The target segment's usage settings need to be identified and characterized, for example, as "serious environments" or "modern active environment."

In an indirect way Wind (1978) has also acknowledged situational influence by expressing concern over the threat that usage situation poses to segment stability. Calantone and Sawyer (1978) provide some support for this concern. In their longitudinal benefit segmentation study, households were frequently being reclassified into different segments. One explanation of this result was that the weights assigned product feature importance are situation-specific and that the individual's usage situations had changed over time. Shanteau and Ptacek (1978) observed situation-induced changes in the impor-

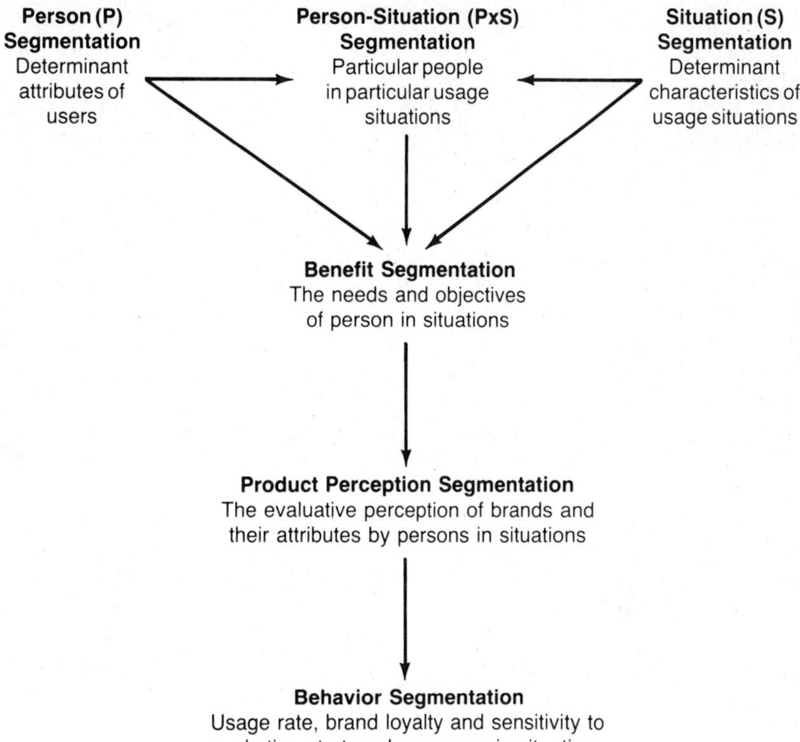

FIGURE 1
Person-Situation Benefit Segmentation

tance weights fitted to attributes of paper towels and batteries (e.g., appearance was a more important paper towel attribute when towels were on display in a social setting). The perceived importance of four of seven attributes of fast food restaurants was also found to be situation-specific in a field study (Miller and Ginter 1979).

Johnson (1971) introduced consumer's product perceptual spaces into market segmentation. He positioned actual objects and people's ideal points in a two dimensional geometric space using multidimensional scaling. The spaces, however, were not situation-specific. As examples he provided mappings of brands of beer and political candidates as perceived by consumers. It would have been interesting to track how sensitive consumers' ideal points were to situation-specific usage settings such as beer after sporting activity, beer with a meal and beer at a party. Hustad, Mayer and Whipple (1975) undertook a usage situation segmentation study of beverages using preference mapping. Their study convincingly illustrated that the consumers' ratings of important beverage attributes and ideal beverages were dependent on use context. Regrettably, they did not examine the situation-specific reactions of different groups of consumers. Even voters' perceptions of and preferences for politicians may change, depending upon whether voters expect the politician to be used in peace time, in a world confrontation crisis (e.g., dealing with the Iranian hostage crisis), in war, in a depression or in good times.

As a simple illustration of how the usage situation can influence utility structures, 40 students were asked to give their pairwise preferences for eight different types of fruit in three different consumption situations. The consumption settings were breakfast, as a snack during the day and a dessert at suppertime. The order of presentation of each of the situation-specific choice inventories was randomized and four different orders of the 28 pairs in the inventory of alternative fruit choices were used.

The students' mean utilities for each fruit in each situation were derived from their pairwise preferences using on orthogonal analysis of variance

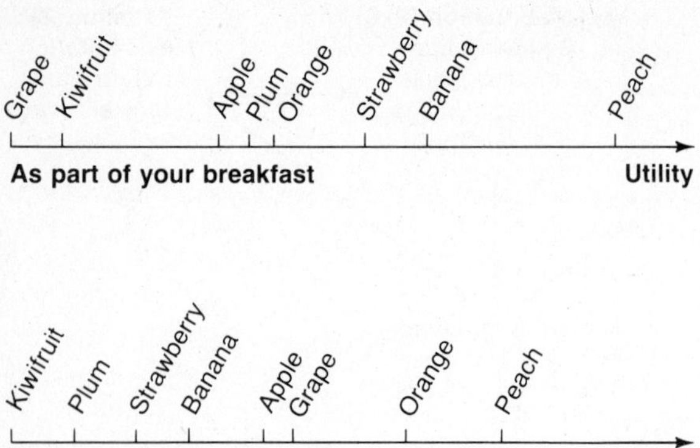

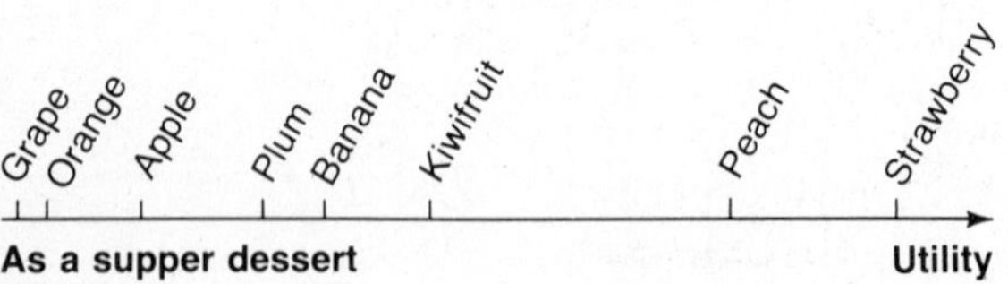

FIGURE 2
Students' Fruit Utility Structures by Three Consumption Situations*

*The three interval scales are not anchored to the same origin. This means that only the relative positions of the fruits can be compared.

scaling program (Bechtel 1976).[5] The results are illustrated in Figure 2. The rank orderings, relative utilities and dispersions vary quite dramatically by situation. Peaches were highly regarded in all three consumption situations but most of the remaining fruits' rankings were quite strongly situation-specific, particularly strawberries, oranges and grapes. If the above results were generalizable to all consumers, then situation segmentation would appear to be a useful basis for marketing some of these fruits. On the other hand, if it were found, as is very likely, that older consumers have very different breakfast, snack and dinner fruit utility structures, then an age-by-situation segmentation basis might be necessary.

5. The three situation utility scales were an excellent fit. They explained 98% of the variation in the pairwise preference scales.

Practical Procedures for Situation-Person Segmentation

The framework is not, in itself, meant to be a how-to-do-it blueprint for practical segmentation. However, an actual segmentation exercise that followed the logic of the framework would very likely proceed through a sequence of steps similar to that presented in Figure 3. It is not suggested that every possible usage situation should be described. Managerial judgment is required to identify the determinant characteristics of usage situations to be used in the major market research undertaken in the second step of the process. The construction of a person-situation segmentation matrix is recommended as a method of visually highlighting the critical differences in the attitudes and behavior of particular groups of consumers in particular usage situations. The person-situation usage combinations that are most attractive because of the uniqueness of their demand function, their submarket size or their lack of competition become foci for product development and marketing strategy.

Table 1 presents a purely illustrative person-situation matrix for suntan lotion. Many more distinct groups of people and situations could be included. Some of the special benefits or features desired in the particular usage situations or sought by the particular groups of users are listed in the row and column margins (some of these are purely speculative). To serve the needs of a particular person-situation submarket, the product should meet the needs listed at the end of the row and the bottom of the column. This demand can result in both person and situation segmentation. Some person-situation cells have unique needs that should be noted in the individual cells (e.g., a winter scented lotion for female skiers). Each cell should also contain an assessment of the size of the market and a list of the company and competitive brands that are designed to meet the specific needs of this market.

A person-situation segmentation matrix could be a very useful aid at the market opportunity analysis, target market selection and competitive positioning stages of the strategic marketing process (see Kotler 1980, p. 81). The placement of the company's current product line and the competition's brands and lines within the matrix will reveal where the company and competitors are positioned relative to market needs, the market relevance of the par-

FIGURE 3
Person-Situation Segmentation Procedure

Step 1	Use observational studies, focus group discussions and secondary data to discover whether different usage situations exist and whether they are determinant, in the sense that they appear to affect the importance of various product characteristics.
Step 2	If step 1 produces promising results, undertake a benefit, product perception and reported market behavior segmentation survey of consumers. Measure benefits and perceptions by usage situation as well as by individual difference characteristics. Assess situation usage frequency by recall estimates or usage situation diaries (Belk 1979).
Step 3	Construct a person-situation segmentation matrix. The rows are the major usage situations and the columns are groups of users identified by a single characteristic or combination of characteristics.
Step 4	Rank the cells in the matrix in terms of their submarket sales volume. The situation-person combination that results in the greatest consumption of the generic product would be ranked first.
Step 5	State the major benefits sought, important product dimensions and unique market behavior for each nonempty cell of the matrix (some person types will never consume the product in certain usage situations).
Step 6	Position your competitors' offerings within the matrix. The person-situation segments they currently serve can be determined by the product feature they promote and other marketing strategy.
Step 7	Position your offering within the matrix on the same criteria.
Step 8	Assess how well your current offering and marketing strategy meet the needs of the submarkets compared to the competition.
Step 9	Identify market opportunities based on submarket size, needs and competitive advantage.

ticular unique selling propositions and campaign themes of the current offering, and possibly submarkets whose needs are not being currently met.

Many marketing executives may decide that all that is required is the first step of the analysis. A series of focus group discussions coupled with basic field observation of product use may provide the experienced manager with new product design ideas and promotional themes centered on particular usage situations. As mentioned earlier, such research may also reveal new complementary product lines. In summary, except for explicit consideration of the usage situation component throughout the analysis, the recommended approach is little different from established practical segmentation procedures.

Conclusion

Market segmentation is one of the most important concepts in the study of marketing. Long established psychological theory, recent experimental research and many case examples provide support for conceptualizing market segmentation in terms of persons, situations and person-situations. This conceptualization is somewhat controversial if only because of the dominance of the individual difference perspective in the market segmentation literature. However, the thrust of this article is that the past focus on the person is outmoded. Even contemporary personality theorists no longer study personal traits but the person within specific situations (Mischel 1977).

There does not appear to be any theoretical reason why usage situation cannot be used as a basis for segmentation. In fact, theory suggests that it should be. Situation segments are often substantial, measurable and accessible. Practically speaking, situation or person-situation analysis is most likely to be useful in product development, packaging design, distribution and the development of promotional contexts, themes, moods and copy. The acceptance of a person-situation segmentation framework should lead more marketing managers explicitly to accept usage situation as a determinant of their marketing strategy. The proposed model is also a useful aid for teachers in explaining segmentation theory and practice. It may even be of some use to public policy makers. A product's safety, the deception in a produce claim and even energy wastage may depend as much on the characteristics of the usage situation as on the characteristics of the consumer.

The use of a framework that links personal traits and usage situation with benefits, preferences, utilities and behavior will produce a much richer description and understanding of target markets. Wind (1978) suggests that different marketing decisions should use different segmentation bases (e.g., a price sensitivity basis for price decisions, media habits for advertising decisions). This suggestion raises a major problem of how to integrate effectively the different components of marketing strategy when each component uses a different segmentation basis. The person-situation framework provides a structure for integrating different bases by reducing them to a common higher order basis. Such an approach should help marketers assess the overall synergistic effect of their marketing strategy.

TABLE 1
Speculative Person-Situation Segmentation Matrix for Suntan Lotion

Persons:	*Young Children*		*Teenagers*		*Adult Women*		*Adult Men*		
Situations	*Fair Skin*	*Dark Skin*	*Fair Skin*	*Dark Skin*	*Fair Skin*	*Dark Skin*	*Fair Skin*	*Dark Skin*	*Situation Benefits/Features*
beach/boat sunbathing	combined insect repellent				summer perfume				a. windburn protection b. formula and container can stand heat c. container floats and is distinctive (not easily lost)
home-poolside sunbathing					combined moisturizer				a. large pump dispenser b. won't stain wood, concrete, or furnishings
sunlamp bathing					combined moisturizer and massage oil				a. designed specifically for type of lamp b. artificial tanning ingredient
snow skiing					winter perfume				a. special protection from special light rays and weather b. antifreeze formula
person benefit/ features	special protection a. protection critical b. non-poisonous		special protection a. fit in jean pocket b. used by opinion leaders		special protection female perfume		special protection male perfume		

References

Adams, Anthony J. (1982), "Lifestyle Research: A Lot of Hype, Very Little Performance," *Marketing News,* 15 (May 16), 5.

Barker, R. G. (1975), "Commentary on Belk, 'Situational Variables and Consumer Behavior,'" *Journal of Consumer Research,* 2 (December), 165.

Betchel, Gordon (1976), *Multidimensional Preference Scaling,* The Hague, Belgium: Mouton.

Belk, Russell W. (1974), "An Explanatory Assessment of Situational Effects in Buyer Behavior," *Journal of Marketing Research,* 11 (May), 156–163.

—— (1975a), "Situational Variables and Consumer Behavior," *Journal of Consumer Research,* 2 (December), 157–164.

—— (1975b), "Situating the Situation: A Reply to Barker and Wicker," *Journal of Consumer Research,* 2 (December), 235–236.

—— (1975c), "The Objective Situation as a Determinant of Consumer Behavior," in *Advances in Consumer Research,* Vol 2, M. J. Schlinger, ed., Association for Consumer Research, 427–437.

—— (1976), "Situational Mediation and Consumer Behavior: A Reply to Russell and Mehrabian," *Journal of Consumer Research,* 3 (December), 175–177.

—— (1979), "A Free Response Approach to Developing Product Specific Consumption Situation Taxonomies," in *Analytical Approaches to Product and Marketing Planning,* Allan D. Shocker, ed., Cambridge, MA: Marketing Science Institute.

Bem, D. J. and A. Allen (1974), "On Predicting Some of the People Some of the Time: The Search for Cross-Situational Consistencies in Behavior," *Psychological Review,* 81 (November), 506–520.

Berkowitz, Eric N., James L. Ginter and W. Wayne Talarzyk (1977), "An Investigation of the Effects of Specific Usage Situations on the Prediction of Consumer Choice Behavior," in *1977 Educators' Proceedings.* B. A. Greenberg and D. N. Bellenger, eds., Chicago: American Marketing Association.

Brunswick, E. (1956), *Perception and the Representative Design of Psychological Experiments,* Berkeley, CA: University of California Press.

Calantone, Roger J. and Alan G. Sawyer (1978), "The Stability of Benefit Segments," *Journal of Marketing Research,* 15 (August), 395–404.

Demby, E. H. (1968), "The Creative Consumer, A Report on Psychographics," Paper presented to the Market Research Station, American Marketing Association Conference (November).

Ekehammer, B. (1974), "Interactionism in Personality from a Historical Perspective," *Psychological Bulletin,* 81 (no. 12), 1026–1048.

Green, Paul E. (1977), "A New Approach to Market Segmentation," *Business Horizons,* 20 (February), 61–73.

—— and Wayne S. DeSarbo (1979), "Componential Segmentation in the Analysis of Consumer Trade-Offs," *Journal of Marketing,* 43 (Fall), 83–91.

Haley, E. I. (1968), "Benefit Segmentation, A Decision-Oriented Research Tool," *Journal of Marketing,* 32 (July), 30–35.

Hustad, Thomas P., Charles S. Mayer and Thomas W. Whipple (1975), "Consideration of Context Difference in Product Evaluation and Market Segmentation," *Journal of the Academy of Marketing Science,* 3 (Winter), 34–47.

Johnson, Richard M. (1971), "Market Segmentation: A Strategic Management Tool," *Journal of Marketing Research,* 8 (February), 13–18.

Kassarjian, H. H. (1971), "Personality and Consumer Behavior: A Review," *Journal of Marketing Research,* 8 (November), 409–419.

—— (1973), "Field Theory in Consumer Behavior," in *Consumer Behavior: Theoretical Sources,* S. Ward and T. S. Robertson, eds., Englewood Cliffs, NJ: Prentice-Hall.

Klein, Robert L. (1982), "CATALYST Measurement, Mapping Method Identifies Competition, Defines Markets," *Marketing News,* 15 (May 14), 3.

Kotler, Philip (1980), *Marketing Management,* Englewood Cliffs, NJ: Prentice-Hall.

Leigh, James H. and Claude R. Martin (1981), "A Review of Situational Influence Paradigms and Research," in *Review of Marketing 1981,* Ben M. Enis and Kenneth J. Roering, eds., Chicago: American Marketing Association.

Lewin, Kurt (1936), *Principles of Topological Psychology,* New York: McGraw-Hill.

Lutz, R. J. and P. Kakkar (1975), "The Psychological Situation as a Determinant of Consumer Behavior," in *Advances in Consumer Research,* Vol. 2, M. J. Schlinger, ed., Association for Consumer Research, 439–53.

—— (1976), "Situational Influence in Interpersonal Persuasion," in *Advances in Consumer Research,* Vol. 3. B. B. Anderson, ed., Association for Consumer Research, 370–378.

McDonald, Susan S. and Alfred E. Goldman (1980), "Strategies of Segmentation Research," in *A Look Back, A Look Ahead,* George B. Hafer, ed., Chicago: American Marketing Association, 30–42.

Miller, Keith E. and James L. Ginter (1979), "An Investigation of Situational Variation on Brand Choice Behavior and Attitude," *Journal of Marketing Research,* 16 (February), 111–123.

Mischel, W. (1977), "On the Future of Personality Measurement," *American Psychologist,* 32 (April), 246–254.

Plummer, Joseph T. (1974), "The Concept and Application of Life Style Segmentation," *Journal of Marketing,* 38 (January), 33–37.

Radder, Jeri M. (1982), "Marketing Diagnostics Analyzes Situations, Reveals How Consumers Select Products," *Marketing News,* 15 (January 22), 11.

Reynolds, Fred and William Darden (1974), "Constructing Life Style and Psychographics," in *Life Style and Psychographics,* William D. Wells, ed., Chicago: American Marketing Association.

Russell, J. A. and A. Mehrabian (1976), "Environmental Variables in Consumer Research," *Journal of Consumer Research,* 3 (June), 62–63.

Sandell, Russell C. (1968), "Effects of Attitudinal and Situational Factors on Reported Choice Behavior," *Journal of Marketing Research,* 5 (August), 405–408.

Shanteau, J. and C. H. Ptacek (1978), "Situational Determinants of Consumer Decision Making," in *Consumer Psychology,* Vol. II, C. Leavitt, ed., Washington, DC: American Psychological Association.

Shocker, Allan D. and V. Srinivasan (1979), "Multiattribute Approaches for Product Concept Evaluation and Generation: A Critical Review," in *Analytical Approaches to Product and Marketing Planning,* Allan D. Shocker, ed., Cambridge, MA: Marketing Science Institute.

Wells, William D. (1975), "Psychographics: A Critical Review," *Journal of Marketing Research,* 12 (May), 196–213.

—— and Douglas J. Tigert (1971), "Activities, Interests and Opinions," *Journal of Advertising Research,* 11 (August), 27–35.

Wicker, A. W. (1975), "Commentary on Belk, 'Situational Variables and Consumer Behavior,'" *Journal of Consumer Research,* 2 (December), 166–167.

Wilkie, William L. and Joel B. Cohen (1977), "A Behavioral Science Look at Market Segmentation Research," in *Moving A Head with Attitude Research,* Yoram Wind, ed., Chicago: American Marketing Association.

Wind, Yoram (1978), "Issues and Advances in Segmentation Research," *Journal of Marketing Research,* 15 (August), 317–338.

Ziff, Ruth (1971), "Psychographics for Market Segmentation," *Journal of Advertising Research,* 11 (April), 3–10.

READING 19

Market Segmentation by Personal Values and Salient Product Attributes

Alfred S. Boote

This article describes an application of an approach to market segmentation that relies on personal values as the key variable in the underlying prediction model. The use of values in conjunction with three more common psychographic variables yielded results that have implications for marketing and advertising strategy.

In June 1975 a national chain (brand A) of medium-priced family restaurants fielded a consumer survey in six major metropolitan areas: Atlanta, Dallas, Boston, Philadelphia, Detroit, San Diego. The company's overall objective was to obtain consumer reactions to both its own restaurants and those of its leading competitor, brand B, in terms of the products and services offered by each and to determine in which ways (if any) each was considered distinctive from the other. Ostensibly, the marketing action affected by the findings from the survey could include product/service modification, additional products/services, advertising themes, etc.

Both male and female respondents were selected by a systematic sampling technique. In order to qualify for the entire interview, a respondent had to be between the ages of 12 and 49, have eaten at brand A and brand B restaurants within the past month, and have a stated preference for either one or the other. A total of 450 persons who were qualified on the foregoing criteria were interviewed in their homes.

The questionnaire consisted mostly of structures questions such as rating scales. The original design included questions that were appropriate for the measurement of variables needed for the segmentation analysis, including a set of 45 value scales. The value items were included in a separate questionnaire, which was given to each respondent at the conclusion of the interview. He/she was asked the complete the form within the following few hours, and the interviewer returned later to pick it up.

Why Market Segmentation?

Segmentation analysis attempts to identify people within the market who are more likely to be influenced by marketing effort, with respect to a particular product or service, than the rest of the market population. In so doing, the analyst must select those criteria that he feels will identify prospective buyers as being more amenable to the appeal of the product/service as reflected in advertising and sales messages.

The marketing objectives of segmentation analysis are

1. to reduce risk in deciding where, when, how, and to whom a new product, service, or brand will be marketed;
2. to increase marketing efficiency by directing effort more specifically toward the designated segment in a manner consistent with that segment's characteristics.

It is, of course, not enough simply to identify groups within the market as being better or worse prospects for a particular product/service. The research should be able to guide marketing decisions concerned with strategy execution (i.e., the means

Reprinted by permission of the Advertising Research Foundation, from the *Journal of Advertising Research*, 21:1 February 1981, 29–35.

of achieving marketing goals). For example, the analysis should be capable of informing the marketer about his product's and brand's positioning in the market with respect to possible substitutes (as perceived by consumers), the ways in which his product or service is distinguished from others by consumers, the saliency of various product attributes to consumers' evaluations of the product and brands within their evoked sets, and the psychological aspects of the consumers that predispose them to buy or not to buy within the product class. This kind of information can provide valuable guidance to marketers in deciding on the strategy and tactics with which to achieve their goals.

The Prediction Model

The segmentation analysis reported here is based on a simple underlying prediction model consisting of four categories of variables: personal values, salient product attributes, brand attitude (or brand preference), and brand choice. Values for this analysis are of the "instrumental" kind—i.e., they are instrumental to the formation of attitudes toward specific products, services, and brands. Values are more general than attitudes in that they guide the choices of modes of behavior of the individual, while attitudes are object specific (e.g., the degree to which a particular object is liked or disliked). Moreover, values are more durable than attitudes because they are acquired over a longer period of the individual's socialization and they are likely to be thoroughly "internalized" by the time the individual reaches adulthood. Thereafter an individual's value structure changes slowly if at all. Thus, personal values offer a sound approach for the segmentation of the market into groups whose common value structures reinforce a predisposition either to buy or not to buy, and thereby underlie attitudes toward specific brands by way of salient product attitudes.

Salient product attributes are defined as those that are both important to the prospective buyer and that are used by the individual to differentiate between brands when deciding on which brand to purchase. Brands perceived as having higher levels of these salient attributes are more likely to achieve high (positive) attitude ratings than those perceived as having lower levels.

Attitude is the individual's affective feeling about the brand—i.e., whether and to what degree he/she likes the brand. Attitude toward a brand predisposes the prospective buyer to react to that brand in a reasonably predictable manner. Thus, the brand most liked by the individual will be the one having highest probability of selection in the market (brand choice). Conversely, the brand least favored will have the lowest probability of selection.

These variables can be combined to form a simple predictive model for the segmentation analysis: values → salient attributes → brand attitudes → brand choice. In other words, values predict the attributes that are salient to individuals. Brand attitudes are predicted by their evaluation on salient attributes, and attitude predicts brand choice. There is much in the marketing literature to support the validity of the stated relations among attributes, attitudes, and brand choice. There is nothing in the way of empirical evidence to support the linkage between personal values and these other three variables. Yet without inclusion of values (or some other underlying dispositional state), the model has relatively little strategic value.

Operationalization of the Variables

Personal Values. The generation and selection of value items for the questionnaire have already been discussed. A typical value item and the scale used by respondents to rate each of the 45 such value items is "extremely important," "very important," "quite important," "slightly important," "not important at all."

Factor analysis was employed to reduce the 45 specific value items to six (for females) and seven (for males) more general values. These general values and the items defining each are:

1. *Food Orientation*
   Eating only the best-quality foods.
   Eating foods with the highest-quality ingredients.
   Having leisurely, relaxed meals.
2. *Rational Orientation*
   Having a familiar routine for getting tasks done.
   Having an orderly way of life.
   Having things tidy and neat.
   Scheduling each week in advance.
   Doing things the best way, even if it takes longer.

3. *Leisure Orientation*
   Being able to relax for a few hours every day.
   Having a lot of leisure time to myself.
4. *Sociability-Novelty*
   Spending a lot of time with friends.
   Being with others most of the time.
   Being with others whether or not I know them.
   Trying new things just for the experience.
   Having possessions that few others have.
5. *Conservative-Insular*
   Living by traditional values.
   Not being different or standing out.
   Having simple meals when I eat out.
   Staying home rather than going out.
6. *Deliberateness*
   Doing things slowly and deliberately.
   Never being rushed.
   Spending a lot of time on household tasks to get them done right.
7. *Individualism*
   Having my own way.
   Doing things my own way.
   Trying to change things I don't like.

Mean scores were computed for each respondent based on the ratings given by that individual to each of the items defining the general value. This mean score represented the level of importance of the general value to the individual, thereby permitting us to array the set of values according to level of importance for each respondent.

Salient Product Attributes. The questionnaire contained 47 phrases describing features of the products and services offered by brands A and B, and the respondents were asked to rate each feature in terms of its importance to him/her in selecting a restaurant of this kind.

Factor analysis of the scale data reduced the 47 features to 10 general product attributes:

1. *Generic Product Characteristics*
   Has good-quality ingredients.
   Gives you big servings.
   Tables properly set up.
   Is kept very clean.
   Has good table service.
2. *Menu Variety*
   Has overall good menu.
   Has a menu providing well-balanced, nourishing meals.
   Has items appropriate for dinner.
   Has items appropriate for a meal.
   Offers a large number of different sandwiches.
3. *Take-Out Service*
   Has good take-out service.
   Has fast service.
   Has take-out food that stays hot.
4. *Menu Appeal*
   Has best menu for men.
   Has best menu for women.
   Has best menu for teens.
   Has best menu for younger adults.
   Has best menu for older adults.
   Has best menu for a family.
5. *Value-Price*
   Has best range of prices.
   Gives you the most value for the money.
   Is least expensive.
   Has best prices for all budgets.
   Frequently gives you special price deals.
6. *Parking-Courtesy (females only)*
   Has courteous personnel.
   Has adequate parking.
7. *Major Entrees*
   Has good steak.
   Has good roast beef.
8. *Comfort (males only)*
   Is a comfortable place to eat.
9. *Lunches and Snacks (males only)*
10. *Accommodations (males only)*

The level of importance of each of these product attributes to each respondent was estimated by computing the mean of the respondent's ratings on each feature defining the particular attribute.

The saliency of each product attribute was determined by multiple regression analyses applied to ratings of brand preference (the dependent variable) on mean ratings of brands on each of the product attributes (independent variables) together with the product attribute's average importance score. The criteria for saliency were that the attribute, on average, was used by respondents to differentiate between the two brands and that the attribute was of importance to respondents. With respect to the former, the regressions were used to estimate the extent of differentiation of an attribute in terms of its ability to reduce the variance associated with the dependent variable. In this sense, the attribute's relative contribution to the coefficient of variation (R^2) was more important in determining saliency than the size of its regression coefficient.

Saliencies of product attributes were determined separately for each of the market segments derived from analysis of the sample data.

Attitude Toward Brand. An appropriate gauge of attitude is the degree to which a brand is liked or disliked. The questionnaire contained no attitude item per se, but an item on brand preference. This item appeared to be an acceptable substitute for the preferred-attitude measurement item. The preference question was posed in the following manner: "You mentioned that you have eaten at both brand B and brand A in the past month. Which of the restaurants do you prefer? Would you say [that you] prefer brand A much more than brand B? prefer brand A a little more than brand B? prefer brand B a little more than brand A? prefer brand B much more than brand A?" (*Note:* Those unable to give a preference were not interviewed.)

Brand Choice. Actual choice of brand in the marketplace was not determined for this project.

Marketing Objective of the Segmentation

Given the constraints imposed on the qualification of respondents for interview (i.e., specifically that respondents had to be customers of both chains and also have a preference for one or the other), a reasonable objective for the segmentation would be to develop a strategy to enable brand A to capture more business from the common pool of customers of medium-priced family restaurants.

Findings

Brand Preference by Major Demographic Characteristics. In general, there were no differences between the proportions of respondents preferring brands A and B, either in the overall sample or within subgroups based on sex, age, or race. The proportion preferring either brand did not vary significantly from 50 percent no matter which demographic categories were used for the analysis. Tables 1, 2, and 3 demonstrate this lack of brand-preference differentiation. The results suggest that neither brand can gain much advantage by segmenting the market on the basis of demographic characteristics.

TABLE 1
Brand Preference by Sex

Sex	*N*	*Prefer Brand A (%)*	*Prefer Brand B (%)*
Male	217	52.1	47.9
Female	225	49.1	50.9
Total sample	442	50.6	49.4

TABLE 2
Brand Preference of Female Respondents by Age and Race

	N	*Prefer Brand A (%)*	*Prefer Brand B (%)*
Age			
12–17	57	46	54
18–24	51	49	51
25–34	60	52	48
35–49	57	49	51
Race			
White	186	49	51
Other	39	49	51

TABLE 3
Brand Preference of Male Respondents by Age and Sex

	N	*Prefer Brand A (%)*	*Prefer Brand B (%)*
Age			
12–17	57	54	46
18–24	61	53	47
25–34	48	52	48
35–49	51	49	51
Race			
White	178	51	49
Other	39	56	44

Segmentation of the Female Subsample on Value Orientations. Since the value structures of males and females frequently vary, it was decided to undertake the segmentation analysis separately for each of these subgroups.

TABLE 4
Segmentation of Female Subsample by Value Orientations

Value-Orientation Segments	*N*	%
Food	65	30.4
Rationality	43	20.1
Leisure	38	17.8
Sociability-novelty	7	3.0
Insularity	1	0.5
Deliberateness	21	9.8
All others (including ties)	39	18.2
	214	99.8

The criterion for assignment of an individual respondent to a particular segment was simply the individual's highest-scoring value orientation. For example, if a respondent scored higher on the food orientation than any of the other value orientations, she was assigned to membership in the food segment. This procedure is a reasonably good approximation of what would have happened had we applied a statistical clustering technique to accomplish the job. The basic weakness of this simple method (compared to statistical analysis) is its inability to cope with ties. However, there were relatively few ties, as shown in Table 4. Thus, it was felt that the simpler approach was adequate for demonstrating the benefits of segmentation analysis.

The top three segments (food, rationality, and leisure) in the table account for about two-thirds of the total sample. Therefore, from a marketing point of view, these three segments constitute the greatest potential for brand A. Subsequent analyses of the female subsample will be restricted to these three segments.

The theoretical justification for using the highest scoring value to identify an individual's segment membership is that in a hierarchy of values, the one that is most important to the individual will tend to dominate in choice-type situations for which several values are applicable. This raises a question concerning the distinctiveness of each segment with respect to its identifying value. For example, do people in the food segment score significantly higher on the food value than people assigned to other segments, and are these people's food scores substantially higher than their scores on other value orientations? Table 5 helps to answer this question. For the interpretation of these numbers, it should be recalled that the means (scores) are based on groups of items rated on an importance scale varying between "extremely important," with a weight of 5, to "not important at all," with a weight of 1.

The italicized scores are those that apply to the values which identify each of the segments, respectively. These means were tested on a pair-wise basis with other means in the same row in which each of the italicized means appears. These simple statistical tests (*T* tests) revealed that each segment is statistically different from the other two with respect to its primary value designation—i.e., the food segment's mean food value score was significantly higher than the food value scores of the rational and leisure segments, and so forth. Moreover, within each segment, the mean score of its primary value is discernibly larger than its mean scores on all other values.

TABLE 5
Value-Importance (Mean) Scores of Major Value Segments (Female Subsample)

	Segments		
Values	*Food Orientation*	*Rational Orientation*	*Leisure Orientation*
Food	*4.129*	3.270	3.273
Rationality	3.214	*3.928*	2.990
Leisure	3.214	2.865	*4.106*
Sociability	2.607	2.519	2.685
Insularity	2.236	2.508	2.273
Deliberateness	2.819	2.608	2.561

TABLE 6
Brand Preference (Female) by Major Value Segments

Value Segments	*N*	*Prefer Brand A (%)*	*Prefer Brand B (%)*
Food orientation	60	42	58
Rational orientation	37	65	35
Leisure orientation	33	45	55

We can conclude, therefore, that the segments are statistically distinct groups whose identities are dominated by their respective highest-scoring (most important) value orientations.

The next step was to analyze brand preference by these three major value segments. Table 6 reveals significant proportions within the segments preferring brand A and brand B. A significantly higher proportion of the food-oriented segment preferred brand B over brand A, while just the reverse was true for the rational segment.

Table 6 provides a striking contrast to Tables 1 and 2, in which there were no differences in proportions of brand preference between brand A and brand B. It is clear that a segmentation based on people's dispositional states (in this case their values) yield far more useful information about the market than does a conventional segmentation based on demographic characteristics.

In this case, brand B enjoys a substantially more favorable position among the important food-oriented segment. From a tactical point of view, brand A must orient its marketing activities toward converting members of this segment from brand B. On the other hand, brand A's greatest strength appears to reside within the rational segment. Its major aim here should be to reinforce its favorable position in this segment without negating or neutralizing its efforts to develop the food-oriented segment.

However, in order to develop an effective advertising campaign to attract these people, it is not enough to know only about their major values. It is critical to have knowledge about the product attributes that are the most salient. It will be recalled that a salient attribute is one that is important to people in the market and one that they use to differentiate among brands in reaching an ultimate choice.

As mentioned earlier, regression analysis was used to determine the extent to which respondents used the various attributes to distinguish between brand A and brand B in reaching their preferences. On the basis of this analysis, the configuration found in Table 7 of value segments and salient product attributes was obtained.

Now the marketing executive should have a clear picture of his major market segments within the female population. They are defined by the food and rationality value orientations with generic-product characteristics, the major entrees, and menu variety as the salient product attributes. Fortified with this knowledge, he can begin to fashion a marketing campaign to attract a larger share of these important fast-food restaurant consumers.

Segmentation of the Male Subsample on Value Orientations. The segmentation analysis of the male subsample was done in the same way in which the female subsample was analyzed. Table 8 shows the basic configuration of segments based on the primary (most important) value orientations of the male respondents. It will be noted that 61 percent of the total subsample is contained within the top

TABLE 7

Value Segments	*Salient Product Attributes*
(I) *Food orientation*	*Product* • Has good-quality ingredients. • Gives you big servings. • Is kept very clean. • Has good food packaging. *Major entree*
(II) *Rational orientation*	*Major entree* *Menu variety* • Has overall good menu. • Has a menu providing well-balanced meals. • Has items appropriate for dinner. • Has items appropriate for a meal. • Offers a large number of different sandwiches.
(III) *Leisure orientation*	*Menu variety*

TABLE 8
Segmentation of the Male Respondents by Value Orientation

Most Important Value Orientation	*N*	%
Individuality	43	19.6
Food	36	16.4
Leisure	28	12.8
Rationality	27	12.3
Sociability	12	5.5
All others	73	33.3
	219	99.9

four segments, and the analysis will be restricted to these major segments.

An important observation is that the male and female value structures are similar. The one major difference is the emergence of individuality in the male subsample. Otherwise, the food, leisure, and rational orientations accrued the largest numbers of respondents, just as they did in the female subsample.

An analysis of the mean value scores within and among the major segments reveals that the segments are statistically distinct groups with respect to their primary value orientations (i.e., the mean primary value score of each segment is significantly higher than any other segment score on the same value). Moreover, each segment's primary value score is substantially higher than its score on any of the other value orientations. Table 9 provides a summary of this information.

As was found for the female subsample, brand preferences of the male segments varied considerably between the two brands. (It will be recalled that there were no differences in brand preferences with age and racial groupings of male respondents.) Several of the actual differences reported in Table 10 are consistent with the findings extracted from the female subsample. In particular, a significantly larger proportion of the food-oriented segment than the rational segment preferred brand B. In fact, the food segment was the only segment that favored brand B, and then by a substantial margin. The segment that is unique to the males, individuality, scored heavily in favor of brand A.

Regression analyses were applied to the brand-attribute ratings in order to isolate those attributes that were, on the average, the ones most used by

TABLE 9
Value Importance (Mean) Scores of Major Value Segments (Male Subsample)

Values	*Individuality*	*Food*	*Leisure*	*Rationality*
Individuality	*4.28*	3.32	2.89	2.59
Food	3.33	*4.36*	3.24	3.22
Leisure	2.95	3.38	*4.29*	2.85
Rationality	3.40	3.48	2.99	*4.08*
Sociability	2.72	2.99	2.65	2.60

TABLE 10
Brand Preference (Male) by Major Value Segments

Value Segment	*N*	*Prefer Brand A (%)*	*Prefer Brand B (%)*
Individuality (1)	43	60.4	39.6
Food (2)	36	33.3	66.7
Leisure (3)	28	60.9	39.1
Rationality (4)	27	74.1	25.9

Note: (1) versus (2) and (4) versus (2), $p < 0.02$; (2) versus (3) and (3) versus (4), $p \leq 0.10$.

TABLE 11

Value Segment	*Salient Product Attributes*
(I) *Individuality*	*Product*
	Defining items same as those shown for the female subsample.
(II) *Food orientation*	*Menu variety*
	Has overall good menu.
	Has a menu providing well-balanced meals.
	Has items appropriate for dinner.
	Has items appropriate for a meal.
	Offers a large number of different sandwiches.
(III) *Leisure orientation*	*Major entree items*
	Product
	Comfort
	Is a comfortable place to eat.
(IV) *Rational orientation*	*Comfort*
	Major entree items.

members of each segment to differentiate between the two brands. The differentiating attributes (yielded by the regressions) that also accrued high mean importance scores were designated as being salient attributes. The distribution of these attributes among the major value segments appears in Table 11.

Conclusions

(1) Brand preference is not differentiated with respect to demographic characteristics of consumers who eat at both restaurant chains and have a stated preference for one or the other.

(2) However, market segments based on value orientations of these fast-food restaurant customers do reveal differences in brand preference. Among both males and females, three of these segments account for two-thirds and two-fifths of all such customers—i.e., food orientation; rational orientation; leisure orientation. In addition, individuality is the most important value orientation to an additional 20 percent of the males.

(3) Among both males and females, brand B has a distinct advantage in the food-oriented segment, while brand A is favored by larger proportions of the rational segment. These two segments together account for about 50 percent of female and 30 percent of male customers. Among males, both the leisure and individuality segments are significantly more likely to prefer brand A than brand B.

(4) Salient attributes (those that are both differentiating and important) are the most effective for predicting brand preference within each segment. These salient attributes for major segments are: *females*—generic-product characteristics, major entree, menu variety; *males*—generic-product characteristics, major entree, menu variety, comfort.

(5) The following are product attributes that are important (to at least one major segment) but not differentiating: *females*—take-out service, parking and courtesy; *males*—none.

(6) The following product attributes are neither differentiating nor particularly important: *females*—menu appeal, value-price; *males*—menu appeal, value-price, accommodations, lunches and snacks.

(7) In general, this research study provides evidence for the validity and utility of market segmentation by people's values as a tool for developing market information not available by means of the conventional analysis of the market by demographic characteristics. The output of this approach informs the marketing executive about the dispositioned states of consumers that predispose them to prefer one brand or the other, and the product attributes that are most salient to them in forming their preferences. This kind of information can be used to build effective advertising campaigns and develop products that incorporate salient product attributes, thereby enhancing the competitive posture of the brand. The end result should be an increase in brand share without a substantial increase in marketing expenditures.

Implications for Marketing/ Advertising Strategy

The foregoing analyses suggest that brand A must take positive action to recruit customers falling into the food-orientation segment. This is a large segment, and a majority of its members currently favor the major competitor. But the advertising campaign devised to accomplish this goal must not neutralize brand A's appeal to males falling into the individuality segment or into the rational and leisure segments, all of which are favorably inclined toward brand A. The appeals used in the advertising copy should incorporate the values of these primary segments and associate these values with the following salient product attributes: generic-product characteristics (i.e., cleanliness, food packaging, nutritious ingredients, etc.), comfort of the accommodations for eating on premises, and the major entree items (i.e., steak and roast beef). In addition, there is a strong indication that the food-orientation segment would be attracted to brand A if the chain were to expand its menu offerings.

CHAPTER FIVE

Consumer Behavior and Product Development

READING 20

Identification of Determinant Attributes: A Comparison of Methods

Mark I. Alpert

Not all product attributes are equally important in determining consumer preferences. This article distinguishes determinant attributes from nondeterminant ones and presents a cross-validation method for testing alternative approaches to identifying these key attributes.

Introduction

Considerable time and money have been devoted to measuring overall consumer attitudes toward companies and products and their particular attributes. However, even when attitudes have been identified, there may be no clear indication of *which* ones determine purchases and preferences.

Image studies [e.g., 5] measure consumer ratings of companies on several attributes and compare these ratings to those of the "ideal" company from which to buy. In these analyses all of these attributes are assumed equally important for a company's success. However, it has been pointed out that some attributes are clearly more important than others in determining purchasing behavior [1, 2, 9, 28.]

Those attributes projected by the product's image which lead to the choice of that product may be called *determinant,* since they determine preference and purchase behavior.[1] For example, consider safety features in cars. Both owners and nonowners of, say, Buicks probably hold comparable opinions about the car's safety, but differ in opinions about handling ability, appearance, and other traits. Thus, it would make more sense to promote the latter attributes rather than safety, which probably strikes most people as being equally present in most cars and, therefore, is not used as a basis of selection.

Objectives

The best way to identify determinant attributes which should be stressed to win customers has been widely debated [6, 8, 11, 17]. There have been few studies of various methods' effectiveness under controlled conditions. This study is an attempt to compare the usefulness of several common methods of identifying determinant attributes. Specifically, the objectives of this study are to:

1. Demonstrate how determinant attributes may be identified for a particular product,
2. Illustrate a means of comparing various methods of identifying these attributes—to indicate how pilot studies for particular products might be carried out,
3. Compare the values of the methods of identification, along with relevant implications for similar marketing research problems (and products).

Methods of Identifying Determinant Attributes

Approaches proposed for identifying determinant attributes might be classified broadly as: (1) direct questioning; (2) indirect questioning, including motivation research and covariate analysis; and (3) obser-

Reprinted by permission of the American Marketing Association, from the *Journal of Marketing Research,* May 1971, 184–191.

1. The notion of determinant attributes implies a correlation between a customer's attitudes toward certain attributes of a product and his overall attitude toward that product. While this correlation cannot establish a causal link between attributes and brand choices, one may expect high preference for the determinant attributes to lead to choice of the brand perceived as having them.

vation and experimentation. Since no one study could encompass a comparison of the myriad variations of these methods, this discussion will be confined to some approaches typifying divergent methods for determinant attribute identification; see also [1, 20].

In direct approaches the respondent is asked to give his reasons for purchase and it is assumed that he knows and will tell which attributes determined his choice. Attributes are then classed as determinant if they are either among the most frequently stated reasons for purchase or have the highest average importance rating in a set of rated attributes, as in [25].

To counter the objection that consumers may not differentiate competing brands in terms of attributes seen as important (e.g., safety in a car), measurements of components other than importance have been developed in order to obtain more than one dimension of attribute ratings [9, 12, 26, 28]. Frequently, *dual questioning* is used; this calls for ratings of various product attributes in terms of: (1) how important each is thought to be in determining choice, and (2) how much difference is perceived among competing products in terms of each attribute. Attributes judged high in combined importance and differences are selected as determinant.

Social psychologists have stressed looking at two dimensions of attitudes towards objects [9, 26], and their work has influenced studies in marketing research [4, 12]. Common to all of these is the idea that overall attitude is a function of beliefs about an object's attributes (i.e., the degree to which it does or does not possess a particular attribute), and the evaluative aspect of these beliefs (i.e., the importance of the attribute to overall satisfaction with the object). With measures of the degree to which products fulfill certain attribute requirements (and of each attribute's influence in determining choice), based on direct questioning of respondents, one could predict overall attitudes toward products relatively easily. Objections that direct measures of the relative influence of attributes wrongly assume that respondents know what gives them most satisfaction and will tell their true feelings [6, 17] can be countered by using indirect methods.

Indirect questioning is any method in which a respondent is not asked *directly* why he bought a product or which attributes influenced his choice. Rather, indirect approaches range from controversial and qualitative (but not necessarily nonquantitative) techniques of motivation research to statistical techniques such as discriminant analysis and multiple regression models. One motivation research technique which can be readily quantified for comparison with a direct questioning counterpart is "third-person" projective questioning. This technique [16, 29] asks respondents to state the importance of various attributes in determining the choices of *most people* for a particular product. The psychological principles underlying this approach are well known and need no further discussion here [11, 16, 17, 29]. In this study, two direct questioning methods will be compared with two similar indirect questioning versions (with "most people" substituted for "you" in appropriate single and dual question forms).

Covariate methods also may be classed as indirect, since they infer determinant attributes from subjects' ratings of products, as related to some measure of behavior toward the products. These approaches typically obtain ratings of various attributes of each brand, along with the information concerning the subjects' overall preferences for each brand, or else which brand each subject normally purchases [3]. Linear discriminant analysis can then be employed to separate respondents into various categories of product usage, based upon the ratings they gave various products in terms of a set of attributes [2, 24]. When the dependent variable (such as overall preference) is continuous, an analogous application of multiple regression analysis enables attributes to be ranked in order of descending contribution to percentage of variation in preference ratings which they helped to explain. Of the methods discussed here, regression and discriminant analysis are the most complex and require the most data, since determinant attributes are inferred from a matrix of attribute ratings for several brands. This study includes a model of "regression coefficient determinance" against simpler methods in identifying determinant attributes.

Another pair of models was included for added comparison of direct and indirect questioning methods. In direct questioning techniques, determinant attributes are often assumed to be objective, rational motives for purchase expressed by subjects. For example, in choosing a pen (the product used in this study) objective attributes might include "comfortable to hold," "freedom from skipping," or "durability." In fact, preliminary direct questioning did

TABLE 1
Attributes Considered as Possible Determinants of Pen Preferences

Variable Number[a]	*Attribute Description*
2	Comfortable to hold
3	Smoothness while writing
4	Writing lifespan
5	Freedom from skipping
6	Attractiveness of pen
7	Convenience in refilling
8	Quality of writing appearance
9	Economy of refills
10	Freedom from smudging
11	Durability
12	Old fashioned–modern
13	Masculine–feminine
14	Nonprestigious–prestigious
15	Formal–informal
16	Would not give as gift–would give as gift
17	Light–heavy
18	Small seller–large seller
19	Careless–perfectionist
20	Sensitive–thick-skinned
21	High social status–low social status
22	Writes a lot–writes very little
23	Tense–relaxed
24	Liberal–conservative
25	Writes signature often–seldom writes signature
26	Creative–noncreative
27	Banker
28	Young socialite
29	Athlete
30	Accountant
31	Taxi driver
32	Top executive
33	Factory worker
34	Physician
35	Sales clerk
36	Housewife
37	Retired person
38	College student

a. Variables 2-11 are objective attributes, 12-28 are subjective, 12-18 describe the product, 19-26 describe the personality of each brand's typical user, 27-38 describe the likelihood of occupational groups' use of each brand.

produce these attributes, numbered 2-11 in Table 1. These were arbitrarily grouped as an objective attributes model for determinant pen traits, for an additional example representation for direct questioning.

Many motivation researchers emphasize attributes which are more subjective in nature [6, 17, 18]. These often vary from product to product, but would include such things as the degree to which a brand is perceived to be "masculine or feminine," "prestigious or nonprestigious," and the types of personality and occupation which might be associated with persons using each product (all components of the brand image). Accordingly, variables 12-38 in Table 1 are designated as subjective attributes, and they are combined in a model to see how much influence they might have on determining brand preferences.

The Comparative Technique

As well as its use in identifying a set of determinant attributes, multiple regression is convenient for judging the predictive validity of a number of potential methods for identifying determinant attributes. If one has a set of attributes regarded as candidates for determinants, along with ratings by subjects about their overall preferences and for individual attributes of each product, it is possible to build multiple regression models of any combination of attributes as predicators of overall preference.[2]

The methodology of this study involves obtaining such a set of ratings and splitting it into two parts, one for parameter estimation and the other for a sample held out for cross-validation. Then, for any method of identifying attributes one can obtain a model which predicts overall preference as a function of ratings given to various brands in terms of attributes selected as determinant by that method. Each model is cross-validated with the sample held out. Next, each model's predicted values of overall preference can be correlated with actual values and the various models intercorrelated (see Table 3).

Cross-validation is necessary for two reasons.

2. Preference, a good predicator of purchase [2], is preferred when nonproduct factors such as shelf-facings, stock-outs, and short-run competitive campaigns are held constant. The identification of brand attributes which determine preference is one important area; other studies can then be initiated to identify other factors that influence purchase besides brand preference [3].

TABLE 2
Selection of Determinant Attributes by Various Methods

	Significance Level of Selection				
Attribute	*Direct Dual Questioning*	*Indirect Dual Questioning*	*Direct Questioning*	*Indirect Questioning*	*Regression Coefficient*
Quality of writing appearance	.0000001	.001	.00005	.0001	.0004
Freedom from smudging	.00003	.00004	.00001	.00003	.9999[a]
Smoothness while writing	.001	.0003	.00001	.00003	.00000001
Comfortable to hold	.02	.02	.0001	.3282	.02
Durability	.02	.62[a]	.0018	.2177[a]	.24[a]
Would not give as a gift—would give as a gift	.04	.34[a]	.8620[a]	.8133[a]	.03[a]
Freedom from skipping	.24[a]	.003	.00001	.00003	.39[a]
Accountant[b]	—	—	—	—	.001
Writes a lot—writes very little[b]	—	—	—	—	.005
Small seller—large seller	.99998[a]	.95[a]	.99999999[a]	.9710[a]	.03
Economy of refills	.999[a]	.97[a]	.9987[a]	.5871[a]	.04

a. Not identified as determinant at the .05 level.
b. Specific attributes of the typical user's personality identified as determinant by regression coefficients model. Neither occupation nor personality of typical user was identified by other methods.

TABLE 3
Correlation Matrix for Cross-Validated Models

Variable	*Overall Preference*	*Model 1*	*Model 2*	*Model 3*	*Model 4*	*Model 5*	*Model 6*	*Model 7*	*Model 8*
Overall preference	1.000	.816	.853	.816	.744	.822	.854	.833	.800
Model 1 All attributes		1.000	.918	.849	.886	.910	.965	.873	.838
Model 2 Direct dual questioning[a]			1.000	.917	.784	.930	.948	.952	.892
Model 3 Indirect dual questioning[a]				1.000	.637	.925	.891	.983	.973
Model 4 Subjective attributes					1.000	.716	.869	.668	.625
Model 5 Objective attributes						1.000	.910	.944	.895
Model 6 Regression coefficient tests[a]							1.000	.902	.862
Model 7 Simple direct questioning[a]								1.000	.956
Model 8 Simple indirect questioning[a]									1.000

a. Method used to select determinant attributes.

First, there is an upward bias in any multiple regression technique (or discriminant analysis) which uses the same data to estimate coefficients and then to measure its predictive validity. Correlated measurement errors can yield a high degree of "boot-strapping" with a probable bias in favor of those methods which choose a large number of attributes. Cross-validating usually causes the measure of predictive validity to "shrink," because of these errors [13]. Second, unless one multiple regression model contains variables which are entirely a subset of another, there is no straightforward technique for comparing their relative abilities to explain variation in the dependent variable. Since different methods often choose sets of attributes which do not meet this restriction, comparing them in terms of multiple r's is impractical. However, cross-validation essentially involves substituting one large independent variable, usually a weighted sum of the held-out sample's independent variables, and the analysis sample's coefficients to obtain a simple r instead of a multiple r. Thus the resulting intercorrelation matrix, as shown in Table 3, can be readily analyzed using a simple t-test for correlated correlation coefficients [19, p. 148].

Research Questions

Given a way to compare various methods but a conflicting body of literature on advantages of these methods, the following comparisons were felt to be most meaningful:

1. *How do direct and indirect questioning methods compare in effectively predicting overall preference?* Relevant comparisons include models generated for simple direct questioning vs. simple indirect questioning, direct dual questioning vs. indirect dual questioning, and, subordinately, the objective attributes model vs. the subjective attributes model. Null hypotheses are that each pair of models produces the same degree of correlation with overall preference (cross-validated).
2. *Is dual questioning superior to simple (single) questioning?* Here direct dual questioning is compared to simple direct questioning and indirect dual questioning to simple indirect questioning. Null hypotheses are that each pair produces equivalent degrees of correlation with overall preference.
3. *How do methods compare with each other?* Each possible pair is tested to see if any clear superiorities or inferiorities emerge.
4. *Which attributes determine overall preference for the test product?* Determinant attributes chosen by each method are indicated, along with relative comparisons of various attributes.

Procedure

A convenience sample of 97 undergraduate business students at California State College at Long Beach was surveyed on attitudes about moderately priced ballpoint and fountain pens. Since comparing methods requires rating competing brands in terms of several attributes, subjects were given four brands of pens to use for a writing exercise in the test room[3] and then asked to rate each in terms of the 37 attributes shown in Table 1. This approach ensures that respondents are reasonably familiar with each brand before rating attributes and giving overall preference.

Three different questionnaires were administered. The first, completed by all subjects, was an attribute rating form in which all four brands were rated, one attribute at a time, after the writing exercise.[4] The second questionnaire had two sections: half of the subjects completed Form A and half Form B. Form A, direct dual questioning, asked "How important is each of these attributes in your own choice of a pen in the one-dollar category?" and "How much difference do you feel there is among these brands, in each of these attributes?" Form B, indirect dual questioning, contained the same two questions, with "most people substituted for "you." To allow use of multiple regression and other parametric statistical techniques, evaluative adjectives were chosen to approximate five-point interval scales. This involved some slight modifications of prescaled adjectives, such as those suggested by Myers and Warner [22].[5] The third questionnaire,

3. Four brands which preliminary study had indicated to be the largest selling one-dollar pens were used. They were also of the modal pen color (black), ink color (blue), and pen point (medium). Their order of use in the writing exercise was randomized.

4. Overall preference ratings were obtained after all other attributes, to lessen the tendency to rationalize specific attribute ratings in terms of overall preference for the brand.

5. Intervals in these two scales were: no importance, slightly important, moderately important, very important, extremely important, and no differences, slight differences, moderate differences, large differences, extreme differences. The attribute rating form called for each brand to be rated on a seven-point scale for 37 attributes plus overall preference. Intervals were: fairly poor, mediocre, all right, fairly good, good, very good, excellent [22].

completed by both groups, asked for data on age, sex, and course load. Post-test comparisons between responses of those who completed Form A and Form B of the second questionnaire revealed no significant demographic differences, implying that differences in responses are due to the direct vs. indirect frame of reference used in questioning.

Fifty usable sets of indirect dual questioning, 42 direct dual questioning, and 82 attribute-rating forms (containing 328 sets of rated brands) were obtained. From this data, models of various methods were constructed and their efficacies compared (see Tables 2-5). Model 1 contains all the subjective and objective attributes used to describe reasons for pen-brand choices. Models 2 and 3 contain attributes selected as determinant by direct and indirect dual questioning respectively. As outlined above, attributes were identified by comparing the combined scores for importance and differences given each attribute with the average combined score for all attributes rated by a particular method. If x represents the importance rating and y the differences rating of a particular attribute by an individual subject, in dual questioning xy indicates the degree of determinancy for the given attribute and subject (since this method uses both importance and differences).

TABLE 4
Rank Order of Models' Predictive Ability

	Cross-Validated Multiple R	R^2
Model 6: Regression coefficients determinance	.854	.729
Model 2: Direct dual questioning	.853	.728
Model 7: Direct questioning (single)	.833	.694
Model 5: Objective attributes	.822	.676
Model 1: All attributes	.816	.666
	tie	
Model 3: Indirect dual questioning	.816	.666
Model 8: Indirect questioning (single)	.800	.640
Model 4: Subjective attributes	.744	.554

If one knew the universe mean xy and its standard deviation, comparing the mean xy for each attribute with this μ_{xy} would allow selection as determinant of those attributes which have means significantly higher than the universe mean. Lacking these parameters, this study followed a heuristic approach assuming the rated attributes to be representative of a population of potentially determinant attributes, μ_{xy} was estimated with the grand mean xy. The standard deviation of the obtained ratings was supposed equal to σ_{xy} since the number of rat-

TABLE 5
Summary Data for Comparisons Between Models

Comparison[a]	T_{data}	*Significance Level*
Model 4 vs. Model 6	−4.068	.0001
Model 2 vs. Model 4	3.217	.001
Model 1 vs. Model 6	−2.724	.007
Model 1 vs. Model 4	2.577	.01
Model 4 vs. Model 7	−2.184	.03
Model 2 vs. Model 8	2.182	.03
Model 6 vs. Model 8	2.005	.048
Model 7 vs. Model 8	1.981	.051
Model 4 vs. Model 5	−1.945	.06
Model 2 vs. Model 3	1.907	.06
Model 1 vs. Model 2	−1.746	.09
Model 3 vs. Model 4	1.666	.10
Model 3 vs. Model 7	−1.642	.11
Model 3 vs. Model 6	−1.584	.12
Model 2 vs. Model 5	1.581	.12
Model 5 vs. Model 6	−1.460	.15
Model 4 vs. Model 8	−1.243	.22
Model 2 vs. Model 7	1.229	.23
Model 3 vs. Model 8	1.174	.25
Model 6 vs. Model 7	.935	.36
Model 5 vs. Model 8	.858	.40
Model 1 vs. Model 7	−.636	.53
Model 5 vs. Model 7	−.597	.55
Model 1 vs. Model 8	.515	.62
Model 3 vs. Model 5	−.277	.78
Model 1 vs. Model 5	−.255	.82
Model 2 vs. Model 6	−.061	.95
Model 1 vs. Model 3	0.000	1.00

a. These tests are not independent of each other because different models may contain some of the same predictor variables.

ings for each of the 19 attributes was about 5% of the universe, and it was felt that none were large enough to seriously bias these estimates of μ_{xy} and σ_{xy}. To the extent that any bias is present, it results in a test which is too conservative because extremely determinant attributes tend to pull the grand mean toward their sample means.[6] Given these parameters, Table 2 gives the probabilities that the obtained mean *xy* ratings for the selected attributes could have exceeded the grand mean by chance sampling variation (a one-tailed *Z*-test). As indicated in Table 2, direct dual questioning chose six attributes as determinant at the .05 level: quality of writing appearance, freedom from smudging, smoothness while writing, comfort in holding, durability, and would not and would give as a gift.

The indirect dual questioning groups' responses identified five attributes (Model 3) indicated in Table 2 as determinant, including four chosen in direct dual questioning. For *single* questioning methods, only mean scores for importance of an attribute were compared with the grand mean score for importance, giving six attributes from direct questioning (Model 7) and a subset of four of these from indirect questioning (Model 8).

Model 6, representing the regression coefficient determinance technique, was obtained slightly differently. Using about two-thirds of the cases, overall preference was regressed on all 37 ratings. Dividing the standardized partial regression coefficients (β) by their standard deviations (s_β), a two-tailed *t*-test [15, p. 339] identified eight attributes as determinant.[7]

To all these attributes were added sets of subjective (Model 4) and objective attributes (Model 5). Cross-validated correlation coefficients (with overall preference) of the eight models (Table 3) were then compared, two by two.

6. Thus this method might be understating the determinance of some attributes (at a stated level of alpha), but attributes might at least be chosen systematically in this manner rather than through mere "eyeballing." At present, no standard technique for choosing "how high is very high" exists.

7. This test was two-tailed because the coefficient which indicates a determinant may be either high or low, whereas in previous tests the ratings had to be significantly high in importance and/or differences. Multicollinearity tends to lessen the stability of the coefficients, but this method is frequently used to identify key attributes [2].

Results

Comparison of Direct and Indirect Questioning

Table 5 shows that simple direct questioning produced a more effective predictive model (Model 7) of overall preference than simple indirect questioning (Model 8). The difference between their cross-validated correlation coefficients is significant at the .05 level (using a two-tailed *t*-test for intercorrelated correlation coefficients). Direct dual questioning (Model 2) surpassed indirect dual questioning (Model 3) at the .06 level. Also, objective attributes (Model 5) were better predictors than subjective attributes (Model 4) at the .06 level. Direct questioning methods were thus superior in identifying determinant attributes, excepting the covariate technique of regression coefficient determinance, which does not involve questions of as comparable a format.

Comparison of Single and Dual Questioning

The comparison of dual and single questioning techniques is not so clear. Direct dual questioning surpassed simple direct questioning, but only at the .23 level, and indirect dual questioning was better than simple indirect questioning at the .24 level. In a Bayesian sense, the decision of whether to use simple or dual questioning would thus depend on cost differences in data collection and the value of improved accuracy given by dual questioning (multiplied by the probability that it is better, about .75).

Comparisons Among All Methods

Tables 4 and 5 compare the various methods modeled and show that no one technique achieved overall superiority. However, simple indirect questioning and subjective attributes models were clearly inferior. Regression coefficient determination appears to be better than most other methods, although it is not more effective than direct dual questioning (alpha = .95). A rank order of methods is given in Table 4, but specific differences must be checked with the comparisons in Table 5.[8]

8. Model 1 (all attributes) was clearly inferior to the regression coefficients determinance model (.007 level) and probably the direct dual questioning model (.09 level), which points out the necessity for cross-validation. Before validation, the r^2 for all attributes exceeds any subset model. Screening the set of attributes can actually increase predictive validity.

Determinant Attributes

Determinant attributes identified by the best methods, regression coefficient determination and direct dual questioning, may be those which determine overall preference. However, the partial regression coefficients model is a poor approximation of the mental process of judging products (since consumers do not logically evaluate attributes ceteris paribus). Ranking by simple raw correlations with overall preference (Table 6) indicates which attributes are most closely associated with overall preference, but differences between rankings should not be taken as significant without first comparing correlation coefficients. The direct dual questioning method gives a simple list of likely determinants of overall preference and has the advantage of not requiring a set of ratings (brand-by-brand) to identify attributes.

Conclusions

Comparing methods of identifying determinant attributes is difficult because there is usually no standard for measuring their relative efficacies. However, this study has demonstrated that cross-validation and regression analysis can be quite useful in demonstrating relative predictive validities of various sets of attributes which alternative methods identify as determinants of buyer preferences. All one needs do is estimate regression models' optimum parameters for each method's chosen attributes and cross-validate the models against a held-out sample of attribute ratings. One may then determine the relationships between predicted values of overall preference and actual values in the second set of data, as well as the interrelationships among predicted values estimated by each model. Comparing obtained measures of predictive ability shows which identification methods are most effective.

In this study direct questioning techniques generally identified determinant attributes more efficiently than indirect methods, with the exception of the regression coefficients determinance technique. However, direct dual questioning may be frequently preferred for straightforward products such as ball-point pens because considerable time and expense may be saved by eliminating the attribute rating. In direct dual questioning subjects need never examine or rate individual brands in terms of

TABLE 6
Relative Value of Simple Raw Correlation Coefficients: All Attributes

Variable Number	*Attribute*	*Simple r*
3	Smoothness while writing	.668
8	Quality of writing appearance	.642
6	Attractiveness of pen	.570
2	Comfortable to hold	.566
11	Durability	.536
7	Convenience in refilling	.519
29	Athlete	.516
38	College student	.506
22	Writes a lot—writes very little	−.502
16	Would not give as gift—would give as gift	.501
10	Freedom from smudging	.491
4	Writing lifespan	.490
12	Oldfashioned—modern	.472
18	Small seller—large seller	.468
30	Accountant	.462
25	Writes signature often—seldom writes signature	−.460
39	Prior experience with brand	.444
34	Physician	.441
55	Freedom from skipping	.416
32	Top executive	.416
35	Sales clerk	.394
27	Banker	.353
14	Nonprestigious—prestigious	.353
28	Young socialite	.340
31	Taxi driver	.311
36	Housewife	.311
33	Factory worker	.284
19	Careless—perfectionist	.210
37	Retired person	.208
21	High social status—low social status	−.203
26	Creative—noncreative	−.163
15	Formal—informal	−.151
13	Masculine—feminine	−.123
9	Economy of refills	.120
24	Liberal-conservative	−.093[a]
17	Light-heavy	−.042[a]
23	Tense-relaxed	−.035[a]
20	Sensitive—thick-skinned	.001[a]

a. Not significantly different from zero at the .05 level. All variables above these are significantly correlated with overall preference.

specific attributes. In addition, dual questioning appears to offer an advantage over simple questioning methods, although the findings are merely suggestive.

Several important limitations inhibit generalizing from the results reported here. Obviously the sample was limited and homogeneous. Further, for products such as one-dollar pens, direct questioning methods may be better than the indirect ones tested here, but for other products involving more subjective buying motives, indirect approaches may be more effective. Other indirect questioning methods might outperform the simple third-person approaches tested here. Probably the regression coefficients method has the best potential to identify subjective *and* objective attributes.

Conclusions must therefore be guarded concerning other products and consumer groups. However, the methodology for *comparing* possible methods for identifying determinant attributes is clearly one which can be used in other cases.

Approaches not compared in this study might eventually prove more valuable for identifying determinant attributes. Multidimensional scaling allows utilization of paired comparisons of products along several attributes, working backwards to those attributes which provide the best explanation of observed comparisons. One might develop a model [10] of selected attributes for a given product and compare its variables with those chosen by alternative methods. Multidimensional scaling's flexibility for nonmetric scaling and the fact that it does not rely on direct questioning may well prove it superior to more traditional approaches.

References

1. Alpert, Mark I. "Identification of Determinant Attributes: A Comparison of Methods," unpublished doctoral dissertation, University of Southern California, 1968.
2. Banks, Seymour. "The Relationship Between Preference and Purchase of Brands," *Journal of Marketing,* 15 (October 1950), 145–57.
3. ——. "Some Correlates of Coffee and Cleanser Brand Shares," *Journal of Advertising Research,* 1 (June 1961), 22–28.
4. Bass, Frank M. and W. Wayne Talarzyk. "A Study of Attitude Theory and Brand Preference," *Proceedings.* Fall Conference, American Marketing Association, 1969, 272–79.
5. Bolger, John F., Jr. "How to Evaluate Your Company Image," *Journal of Marketing,* 24 (October 1959), 7–10.
6. Dichter, Ernest. *The Strategy of Desire.* Garden City: Doubleday, 1960.
7. Evans, Franklin B. "Motivation Research and Advertising Readership," *Journal of Business,* 30 (April 1957), 141–46.
8. ——. "Psychological and Objective Factors in the Prediction of Brand Choice: Ford vs. Chevrolet," *Journal of Business,* 32 (October 1959), 340–69.
9. Fishbein, Martin. "A Behavior Theory Approach to the Relations between Beliefs about an Object and the Attitude Toward the Object," and "Attitude and the Prediction of Behavior," in Martin Fishbein, ed., *Readings in Attitude Theory and Measurement.* New York: John Wiley & Sons, 1967, 389–99, 477–92.
10. Green, Paul E., Frank J. Carmone, and Patrick J. Robinson. *Analysis of Marketing Behavior, Using Nonmetric Scaling and Related Techniques,* Technical Monograph. Marketing Science Institute, 1968.
11. Haire, Mason. "Projective Techniques in Marketing Research," *Journal of Marketing,* 14 (April 1950), 649–52.
12. Hansen, Flemming. "Consumer Choice Behavior: An Experimental Approach," *Journal of Marketing Research,* 6 (November 1969), 436–43.
13. Horst, Paul. "An Overview of the Essentials of Multivariate Analysis Methods," in Raymond B. Cattell, ed., *Handbook of Multivariate Experimental Psychology.* Chicago: Rand McNally, 1966, 129–52.
14. Howard, John A. and Jagdish N. Sheth. *The Theory of Buyer Behavior.* New York: John Wiley & Sons, 1969, 191–228.
15. Johnson, Palmer O. *Statistical Methods in Research.* New York: Prentice-Hall, 1949.
16. Klaus, Bertrand. "Understanding Why They Buy," in Martin M. Grossack, ed., *Understanding Consumer Behavior.* Boston: Christopher, 1964, 71–72.
17. Martineau, Pierre. *Motivation in Advertising.* New York: McGraw-Hill, 1957.
18. Mindak, William A. "Fitting the Semantic Differential to the Marketing Problem," *Journal of Marketing,* 25 (April 1961), 28–33.
19. McNemar, Quinn. *Psychological Statistics.* New York: John Wiley & Sons, 1955.
20. Myers, James H. and Mark I. Alpert. "Determinant Buying Attitudes: Meaning and Measurement," *Journal of Marketing,* 32 (October 1968), 13–20.
21. Myers, James H. and William H. Reynolds. *Consumer Behavior and Marketing Management.* Boston: Houghton-Mifflin, 1967.
22. Myers, James H. and W. Gregory Warner. "Semantic Properties of Selected Evaluation Adjectives," *Journal of Marketing Research,* 5 (November 1968), 409–12.

23. Osgood, Charles E., George J. Suci, and Percy H. Tannenbaum. *The Measurement of Meaning.* Urbana: University of Illinois Press, 1957.
24. Perry, Michael. "Discriminant Analysis of Relations Between Consumers' Attitudes, Behavior, and Intentions," *Journal of Advertising Research*, 9 (June 1969), 34–40.
25. Riter, Charles B. "What Influences Purchases of Color Televisions?" *Journal of Retailing*, 42 (Winter 1966–67), 25–31, 63–64.
26. Rosenberg, Milton J. "Cognitive Structure and Attitudinal Affect," *Journal of Abnormal Psychology*, 53 (November 1956), 367–72.
27. Smith, Gail. "How GM Measures Ad Effectiveness," *Printer's Ink*, 290 (May 14, 1965), 19–29.
28. Twedt, Dik Warren. "How to Plan New Products, Improve Old Ones, and Create Better Advertising," *Journal of Marketing*, 33 (January 1969), 53–57.
29. Weaver, Herbert B. "Evaluating Tourists' Reactions to Hawaii—A Study of Techniques," in Martin M. Grossack, ed., *Understanding Human Behavior.* Boston: Christopher, 1964, 193–220.
30. Westfall, Ralph L., Harper W. Boyd, Jr., and Donald T. Campbell. "The Use of Structural Techniques in Motivation Research," *Journal of Business*, 32 (October 1959), 134–39.

READING 21

Positioning Your Product

David A. Aaker

How should a new brand be positioned? Can a problem brand be revived by a repositioning strategy? Most marketing managers have addressed these and other positioning questions; however, "positioning" means different things to different people. To some, it means the segmentation decision. To others it is an image question. To still others it means selecting which product features to emphasize. Few managers consider all of these alternatives. Further, the positioning decision is often made ad hoc, and is based upon flashes of insight, even though systematic, research-based approaches to the positioning decision are now available. An understanding of these approaches should lead to more sophisticated analysis in which positioning alternatives are more fully identified and evaluated.

A product or organization has many associations which combine to form a total impression. The positioning decision often means selecting those associations which are to be built upon and emphasized and those associations which are to be removed or de-emphasized. The term "position" differs from the older term "image" in that it implies a frame of reference, the reference point usually being the competition. Thus, when the Bank of California positions itself as being small and friendly, it is explicitly, or perhaps implicitly, positioning itself with respect to Bank of America.

The positioning decision is often the crucial strategic decision for a company or brand because the position can be central to customers' perception and choice decisions. Further, since all elements of the marketing program can potentially affect the position, it is usually necessary to use a positioning strategy as a focus for the development of the marketing program. A clear positioning strategy can insure that the elements of the marketing program are consistent and supportive.

What alternative positioning strategies are available? How can positioning strategies be identified and selected? Each of these questions will be addressed in turn.

Positioning Strategies

A first step in understanding the scope of positioning alternatives is to consider some of the ways that a positioning strategy can be conceived and implemented. In the following, six approaches to positioning strategy will be illustrated and discussed: positioning by (1) attribute, (2) price-quality, (3) use or applications, (4) product-user, (5) the product-class, and (6) the competitor.

Positioning by Attribute

Probably the most frequently used positioning strategy is associating a product with an attribute, a product feature, or customer benefit. Consider imported automobiles. Datsun and Toyota have emphasized economy and reliability. Volkswagen has used a "value for the money" association. Volvo has stressed durability, showing commercials of "crash tests" and citing statistics on the long average life of their cars. Fiat, in contrast, has made a distinct effort to position itself as a European car with "European craftsmanship." BMW has emphasized handling and engi-

---

neering efficiency, using the tag line, "the ultimate driving machine" and showing BMWs demonstrating their performance capabilities at a race track.

A new product can upon occasion be positioned with respect to an attribute that competitors have ignored. Paper towels had emphasized absorbency until Viva stressed durability, using demonstrations supporting the claim that Viva "keeps on working."

Sometimes a product will attempt to position itself along two or more attributes simultaneously. In the toothpaste market, Crest became a dominant brand by positioning itself as a cavity fighter, a position supported by a medical group endorsement. However, Aim achieved a 10 percent market share by positioning along two attributes, good taste and cavity prevention. More recently, Aqua-fresh has been introduced by Beecham as a gel paste that offers both cavity-fighting and breath-freshening benefits.

It is always tempting to try to position along several attributes. However, positioning strategies that involve too many attributes can be most difficult to implement. The result can often be a fuzzy, confused image.

Positioning by Price/Quality

The price/quality attribute dimension is so useful and pervasive that it is appropriate to consider it separately. In many product categories, some brands offer more in terms of service, features, or performance and a higher price serves to signal this higher quality to the customer. Conversely, other brands emphasize price and value.

In general merchandise stores, for example, the department stores are at the top end of the price/quality scale. Neiman-Marcus, Bloomingdale's, and Saks Fifth Avenue are near the top, followed by Macy's, Robinson's, Bullock's, Rich's, Filene's, Dayton's, Hudson's, and so on. Stores such as Sears, Montgomery Ward, and J.C. Penney are positioned below the department stores but above the discount stores like K-Mart. Sears' efforts to create a more upbeat fashion image was thought to have hurt their "value" position and caused some share declines.[1] Sears' recent five-year plan details a firm return to a positioning as a family, middle-class store offering top value. Sears is just one company that has faced the very tricky positioning task of retaining the image of low price and upgrading their quality image. There is always the risk that the quality message will blunt the basic "low-price," "value" position.

Positioning with Respect to Use or Application

Another positioning strategy is associating the product with a use or application. Campbell's Soup for many years was positioned for use at lunch time and advertised extensively over noontime radio. The telephone company more recently has associated long distance calling with communicating with loved ones in their "reach out and touch someone" campaign. Industrial products often rely upon application associations.

Products can, of course, have multiple positioning strategies, although increasing the number involves obvious difficulties and risks. Often a positioning-by-use strategy represents a second or third position designed to expand the market. Thus, Gatorade, introduced as a summer beverage for athletes who need to replace body fluids, has attempted to develop a winter positioning strategy as the beverage to drink when the doctor recommends drinking plenty of fluids. Similarly, Quaker Oats has attemped to position a breakfast food product as a natural whole-grain ingredient for recipes. Arm & Hammer baking soda has successfully positioned their product as an odor-destroying agent in refrigerators.

Positioning by the Product User

Another positioning approach is associating a product with a user or a class of users. Thus, many cosmetic companies have used a model or personality, such as Brut's Joe Namath, to position their product. Revlon's Charlie cosmetic line has been positioned by associating it with a specific lifestyle profile. Johnson & Johnson saw market share move from 3 percent to 14 percent when they repositioned their shampoo from a product used for babies to one used by people who wash their hair frequently and therefore need a mild shampoo.

In 1970, Miller High Life was the "champagne of bottled beers," was purchased by the upper class, and had an image of being a woman's beer. Phillip Morris repositioned it as a beer for the heavy beer drinking, blue-collar working man. Miller's Lite beer, introduced in 1975, used convincing beer-drinking personalities to position itself as a beer for the heavy beer drinker who dislikes that filled-up feeling. In contrast, earlier efforts to introduce low-calorie beers positioned with respect to the low-calorie attribute were dismal failures. One even claimed its beer had fewer calories than skim milk, and another featured a trim personality. Miller's positioning strategies are in part why its market share has grown from 3.4 percent in 1970 to 24.5 percent in 1979.[2]

Positioning with Respect to a Product Class

Some critical positioning decisions involve product-class associations. For example, Maxim freeze-dried coffee needed to position itself with respect to regular and instant coffee. Some margarines position themselves with respect to butter. Dried milk makers came out with instant breakfast positioned as a breakfast substitute and a virtually identical product positioned as a dietary meal substitute. The hand soap "Caress" by Lever Brothers positioned itself as a bath oil product rather than a soap.

The soft drink 7-Up was for a long time positioned as a beverage with a "fresh clean taste" that was "thirst-quenching." However, research discovered that most people regarded 7-Up as a mix rather than a soft drink. The successful "un-cola" campaign was then developed to position 7-Up as a soft drink, with a better taste than the "colas."

Positioning with Respect to a Competitor

In most positioning strategies, an explicit or implicit frame of reference is the competition. There are two reasons for making the reference competitor(s) the dominant aspect of the positioning strategy. First, a well established competitor's image can be exploited to help communicate another image referenced to it. In giving directions to an address, for example, it's easier to say, it is next to the Bank of America building than it is to detail streets, distances, and turns. Second, sometimes it's not important how good customers think you are; it is just important that they believe you are better (or as good as) a given competitor.

Perhaps the most famous positioning strategy of this type was the Avis "We're number two, so we try harder" campaign. The strategy was to position Avis with Hertz as a major car rental agency and away from National, which at the time was a close third to Avis.

Positioning explicitly with respect to a competitor can be an excellent way to create a position with respect to an attribute, especially the price/quality attribute pair. Thus, products difficult to evaluate, like liquor products, will often be compared with an established competitor to help the positioning task. For example, Sabroso, a coffee liqueur, positioned itself with the established brand, Kahlua, with respect to quality and also with respect to the type of liqueur.

Positioning with respect to a competitor can be aided by comparative advertising, advertising in which a competitor is explicitly named and compared on one or more attributes. Pontiac has used this approach to position some of their cars as being comparable in gas mileage and price to leading import cars. By comparing Pontiac to a competitor that has a well-defined economy image, like a Volkswagen Rabbit, and using factual information such as EPA gas ratings, the communication task becomes easier.

On Determining the Positioning Strategy

What should be our positioning strategy? The identification and selection of a positioning strategy can draw upon a set of concepts and procedures that have been developed and refined over the last few years. The process of developing a positioning strategy involves six steps:

1. Identify the competitors.
2. Determine how the competitors are perceived and evaluated.
3. Determine the competitors' positions.
4. Analyze the customers.
5. Select the position.
6. Monitor the position.

In each of these steps one can employ marketing research techniques to provide needed information. Sometimes the marketing research approach provides a conceptualization that can be helpful even if the research is not conducted. Each of these steps will be discussed in turn.

Identify the Competitors

This first step is not as simple as it might seem. Tab might define its competitors in a number of ways, including:

a. other diet cola drinks
b. all cola drinks
c. all soft drinks
d. nonalcoholic beverages
e. all beverages

A Triumph convertible might define its market in several ways:

a. two-passenger, low-priced, imported, sports car convertibles
b. two-passenger, low-priced, imported sports cars
c. two-passenger, low- or medium-priced, imported sports cars
d. low- or medium-priced sports cars
e. low- or medium-priced imported cars

In most cases, there will be a primary group of competitors and one or more secondary competitors. Thus, Tab will compete primarily with other diet colas, but other colas and all soft drinks could be important as secondary competitors.

A knowledge of various ways to identify such groupings will be of conceptual as well as practical value. One approach is to determine from product buyers which brands they considered. For example, a sample of Triumph convertible buyers could be asked what other cars they considered and perhaps what other showrooms they actually visited. A Tab buyer could be asked what brand would have been purchased had Tab been out of stock. The resulting analysis will identify the primary and secondary groups of competitive products. Instead of customers, retailers or others knowledgeable about customers could provide the information.

Another approach is the development of associations of products with use situations.[3] Twenty or so respondents might be asked to recall the use contexts for Tab. For each use context, such as an afternoon snack, respondents are then asked to identify all appropriate beverages. For each beverage so identified respondents are then asked to identify appropriate use contexts. This process would continue until a large list of use contexts and beverages resulted. Another respondent group would then be asked to make judgments as to how appropriate each beverage would be for each use situation. Groups of beverages could then be clustered based upon their similarity of appropriate use situations. If Tab was regarded as appropriate with snacks, then it would compete primarily with other beverages regarded as appropriate for snack occasions. The same approach would work with an industrial product such as computers, which might be used in several rather distinct applications.

The concepts of alternatives from which customers choose and appropriateness to a use context can provide a basis for identifying competitors even when market research is not employed. A management team or a group of experts, such as retailers, could employ one or both of these conceptual bases to identify competitive groupings.

Determine How the Competitors Are Perceived and Evaluated

The challenge is to identify those product associations used by buyers as they perceive and evaluate competitors. The product associations will include product attributes, product user groups. and use contexts. Even simple objects such as beer can evoke a host of physical attributes like container, aftertaste, and price, and relevant associations like "appropriate for use while dining at a good restaurant" or "used by working men." The task is to identify a list of product associations, to remove redundancies from the list, and then to select those that are most useful and relevant in describing brand images.

One research-based approach to product association list generation is to ask respondents to identify the two most similar brands from a set of three competing brands and to describe why those two brands are similar and different from the third. As a variant, respondents could be asked which of two brands is preferred and why. The result will be a rather long list of product associations, perhaps over a hundred. The next step is to remove redundancy from the list using logic and judgment or factor analysis. The final step is to identify the most relevant product associations by determining which is correlated highest with overall brand attitudes or by asking respondents to indicate which are the most important to them.

Determine the Competitors' Positions

The next step is to determine how competitors (including our own entry) are positioned with respect to the relevant product associations and with respect to each other. Although such judgments can be made subjectively, research-based approaches are available. Such research is termed multidimensional scaling because its goal is to scale objects on several dimensions (or product associations). Multidimensional scaling can be based upon either product associations data or similarities data.

Product-Association-Based Multidimensional Scaling. The most direct approach is simply to ask a sample of the target segment to scale the various objects on the product association dimensions. For example, the respondent could be asked to express his or her agreement or disagreement on a seven-point scale with statements regarding the Chevette:

"With respect to its class I would consider the Chevette to be:

sporty
roomy
economical
good handling."

Alternatively, perceptions of a brand's users or use contexts could be obtained:

"I would expect the typical Chevette owner to be:

older
wealthy
independent
intelligent."

"The Chevette is most appropriate for:

short neighborhood trips
commuting
cross country sightseeing."

In generating such measures there are several potential problems and considerations (in addition to generating a relevant product association list) of which one should be aware:

1. The validity of the task. Can a respondent actually position cars on a "sporty" dimension? There could be several problems. One, a possible unfamiliarity with one or more of the brands, can be handled by asking the respondent to evaluate only familiar brands. Another is the respondent's ability to understand operationally what "sporty" means or how to evaluate a brand on this dimension.
2. Differences among respondents. Subgroups within the population could hold very different perceptions with respect to one or more of the objects. Such diffused images can have important strategic implications. The task of sharpening a diffused image is much different from the task of changing a very tight, established one.
3. Are the differences between objects significant and meaningful? If the differences are not statistically significant, then the sample size may be too small to make any managerial judgments. At the same time, a small difference of no practical consequence may be statistically significant if the sample size is large enough.
4. Which product associations are not only important but also serve to distinguish objects? Thus, airline safety may be an important attribute, but all airlines may be perceived to be equally safe.

Similarities-Based Multidimensional Scaling. Product-association approaches have several conceptual disadvantages. A complete, valid, and relevant product association list is not easy to generate. Further, an object may be perceived or evaluated as a whole that is not really decomposable in terms of product associations. These disadvantages lead us to the use of non-attribute data—namely, similarity data.

Similarity measures simply reflect the perceived similarity of two objects. For example, respondents may be asked to rate the degree of similarity of assorted object pairs without a product association list which implicitly suggests criteria to be included or excluded. The result, when averaged over all respondents, is a similarity rating for each object pair. A multidimensional scaling program then attempts to locate objects in a two-, three- (or more if necessary) dimensional space termed a perceptual map. The program attempts to construct the perceptual map such that the two objects with the highest similarity are separated by the shortest distance, the object pair with the second highest similarity are separated by the second shortest distance, and so on. A disadvantage of the similarity-based approach is that the interpretation of the dimensions does not have the product associations as a guide.

Analyzing the Customers

A basic understanding of the customer and how the market is segmented will help in selecting a positioning strategy. How is the market segmented? What role does the product class play in the customer's lifestyle? What really motivates the customer? What habits and behavior patterns are relevant?

The segmentation question is, of course, critical. One of the most useful segmentation approaches is benefit segmentation which focuses upon the benefits or, more generally, the product associations that a segment believes to be important. The identity of important product associations can be done directly by asking customers to rate product associations as to their importance or by asking them to make trade-off judgments between product associations[4] or by asking them to conceptualize and profile "ideal brands." An ideal brand would be a combination of all the customers' preferred product associations. Customers are then grouped into segments defined by product associations considered important by customers. Thus, for toothpaste there could be a decay preventative segment, a fresh breath segment, a price segment, and so on. The segment's relative size and commitment to the product association will be of interest.

It is often useful to go beyond product association lists to get a deeper understanding of consumer perceptions. A good illustration is the development of positioning objectives for Betty Crocker by the Needham, Harper & Steers advertising agency.[5] They conducted research involving more than 3,000 women, and found that Betty Crocker was viewed as a company that is:

honest and dependable
friendly and concerned about consumers
a specialist in baked goods

but

out of date, old, and traditional
a manufacturer of "old standby" products
not particularly contemporary or innovative.

The conclusion was that the Betty Crocker image needed to be strengthened and to become more modern and innovative and less old and stodgy.

To improve the Betty Crocker image, it was felt that an understanding was needed of the needs and lifestyle of today's women and how these relate to desserts. Thus, the research study was directed to basic questions about desserts. Why are they served? Who serves them? The answers were illuminating. Dessert users tend to be busy, active mothers who are devoted to their families. The primary reasons for serving dessert tend to be psychological and revolve around the family.

Dessert is a way to show others you care.

Dessert preparation is viewed as an important duty of a good wife and mother.

Desserts are associated with and help to create happy family moments.

Clearly, family bonds, love, and good times are associated with desserts. As a result, the Betty Crocker positioning objective was to associate Betty Crocker uniquely with the positive aspects of today's families and their feelings about dessert. Contemporary, emotionally involving advertising was used to associate Betty Crocker with desserts that contribute to happy family moments.

Making the Positioning Decision

The four steps or exercises just described should be conducted prior to making the actual positioning decision. The exercises can be done subjectively by the involved managers if necessary, although marketing research, if feasible and justifiable, will be more definitive. However, even with that background, it is still not possible to generate a cookbook solution to the positioning questions. However, some guidelines or checkpoints can be offered.

1. Positioning usually implies a segmentation commitment. Positioning usually means that an overt decision is being made to concentrate only on certain segments. Such an approach requires commitment and discipline because it's not easy to turn your back on potential buyers. Yet, the effect of generating a distinct, meaningful position is to focus on the target segments and not be constrained by the reaction of other segments.

   Sometimes the creation of a "diffuse image," an image that will mean different things to different people, is a way to attract a variety of diverse segments. Such an approach is risky and difficult to implement and usually would be used only by a large brand. The implementation could involve projecting a range of advantages while avoiding being identified with any one. Alternatively, there could be a conscious effort to avoid associations which create positions. Pictures of bottles of Coca-Cola with the words "It's the real thing" superimposed on them, or Budweiser's claim that "Bud is the king of beers," illustrate such a strategy.

2. An economic analysis should guide the decision. The success of any positioning strategy basically depends upon two factors: the potential market size × the penetration probability. Unless both of these factors are favorable, success will be unlikely. One implication of this simple structure is that a positioning strategy should attract a sizeable segment. If customers are to be attracted from other brands, those brands should have a worthwhile market share to begin with. If new buyers are to be attracted to the product class, a reasonable assessment should be made of the potential size of that growth area. The penetration probability indicates that there needs to be a competitive weakness to attack or a competitive advantage to exploit to generate a reasonable market penetration probability. Further, the highest payoff will often come from retaining existing customers, so this alternative should also be considered.
3. If the advertising is working, stick with it. An advertiser will often get tired of a positioning strategy and the advertising used to implement it and will consider making a change. However, the personality or image of a brand, like that of a person, evolves over many years, and the value of consistency through time cannot be overestimated. Some of the very successful, big-budget campaigns have run for ten, twenty, or even thirty years.
4. Don't try to be something you are not. It is tempting but naive—and usually fatal—to decide on a positioning strategy that exploits a market need or opportunity but assumes that your product is something it is not. Before positioning a product, it is important to conduct blind taste tests or in-home or in-office use tests to make sure that the product can deliver what it promises and that is compatible with a proposed image.

   Consider Hamburger Helper, successfully introduced in 1970 as an add-to-meat product that would generate a good-tasting, economical, skillet dinner.[6] In the mid-1970s, sales suffered when homemakers switched to more exotic, expensive foods. An effort to react by repositioning Hamburger Helper as a base for casseroles failed because the product, at least in the consumers' mind, could not deliver. Consumers perceived it as an economical, reliable, convenience food and further felt that they did not need help in making casseroles. In a personality test, where women were asked to describe the product as if it were a person, the most prevalent characteristic ascribed to the product was "helpful." The result was a revised campaign to position the product as being "helpful."

Monitoring the Position

A positioning objective, like any marketing objective, should be measurable. To evaluate the positioning and to generate diagnostic information about future positioning strategies, it is necessary to monitor the position over time. A variety of techniques can be employed to make this measurement. Hamburger Helper used a "personality test," for example. However, usually one of the more structured techniques of multidimensional scaling is applied.

A variety of positioning strategies is available to the advertiser. An object can be positioned:

1. by attributes—e.g., Crest is a cavity fighter.
2. by price/quality—e.g., Sears is a "value" store.
3. by competitor—e.g., Avis positions itself with Hertz.
4. by application—e.g., Gatorade is for flu attacks.
5. by product user—e.g., Miller is for the blue-collar, heavy beer drinker.
6. by product class—e.g., Carnation Instant Breakfast is a breakfast food.

The selection of a positioning strategy involves identifying competitors, relevant attributes, competitor positions, and market segments. Research based approaches can help in each of these steps by providing conceptualizations even if the subjective judgments of managers are used to provide the actual input information to the positioning decision.

Endnotes

1. "Sears' New 5-year Plan: To Serve Middle America," *Advertising Age,* December 4, 1978.
2. "A-B, Miller Brews Continue to Barrel Ahead," *Advertising Age,* August 4, 1980: 4.
3. George S. Day, Allan D. Shocker, and Rajendra K. Srivasta, "Customer-Oriented Approaches to Identify Product Markets," *Journal of Marketing,* Fall 1979: 8–19.
4. Paul E. Green and Yoram Wind, "New Ways to Measure Consumers' Judgments," *Harvard Business Review,* July–August 1975: 107–115.
5. Keith Reinhard, "How We Make Advertising" (presented to the Federal Trade Commission, May 11, 1979): 22–25.
6. Reinhard: 29.

READING 22

New Way to Measure Consumers' Judgments

Paul E. Green and Yoram Wind

When developing new products or services—or even when repositioning an existing one—a company must consider two basic problems. First, it must know its market; second, it must understand the nature of the product. It may find both problems hard to solve, especially when the nature of the product under consideration has several disparate qualities, each appealing to a diverse number of consumers with diverse interests. Beyond the fundamental need that the product is to fill often lie several others that the marketing manager would do well to consider. But how does he evaluate those needs? How does he evaluate which of the product's attributes the consumer perceives to be the most important? In order to market the product most effectively, marketing managers must have the means to answer these kinds of questions. In this article the authors demonstrate one research technique that has been used in evaluating consumers' judgments and show how to apply it to a number of complex marketing situations.

Taking a jet plane for a business appointment in Paris? Which of the two flights described below would you choose?

- A B-707 flown by British Airways that will depart within two hours of the time you would like to leave and that is often late in arriving in Paris. The plane will make two intermediate stops, and it is anticipated that it will be 50% full. Flight attendants are "warm and friendly" and you would have a choice of two movies for entertainment.
- A B-747 flown by TWA that will depart within four hours of the time you would like to leave and that is almost never late in arriving in Paris. The flight is nonstop, and it is anticipated that the plane will be 90% full. Flight attendants are "cold and curt" and only magazines are provided for entertainment.

Are you looking for replacement tires for your two-year-old car? Suppose you want radial tires and have the following three options to choose from:

- Goodyear's, with a tread life of 30,000 miles at a price of $40 per tire; the store is a 10-minute drive from your home.
- Firestone's, with a tread life of 50,000 miles at a price of $85 per tire; the store is a 20-minute drive from your home.
- Or Sear's, with a tread life of 40,000 miles at a price of $55 per tire; the store is located about 10 minutes from your home.

How would you rank these alternatives in order of preference?

Both of these problems have a common structure that companies and their marketing managers frequently encounter in trying to figure out what a consumer really wants in a product or service. First, the characteristics of the alternatives that the consumer must choose from fall along more than a single dimension—they are multiattribute. Second, the consumer must make an overall judgment about the relative value of those characteristics, or attributes; in short, he must order them according to some criterion. But doing this requires complex trade-offs, since it is likely that no alternative is clearly better than another on every dimension of interest.

In recent years, researchers have developed a new measurement technique from the fields of mathematical psychology and psychometrics that can aid the marketing manager in sorting out the relative importance of a product's multidimensional attributes.[1] This technique, called conjoint measurement, starts with the consumer's overall or global judgments about a set of complex alternatives. It then performs the rather remarkable job of decomposing his or her original evaluations into separate and compatible utility scales by which the original global judgments (or others involving new combinations of attributes) can be reconstituted.[2]

Being able to separate overall judgments into psychological components in this manner can provide a manager with valuable information about the relative importance of various attributes of a product. It can also provide information about the value of various levels of a single attribute. (For example, if price is the attribute under consideration, conjoint measurement can give the manager a good idea of how sensitive consumers would be to a price change from a level of, say, 85¢ to one of 75¢ or one of 95¢.) Indeed, some models can even estimate the psychological trade-offs consumers make when they evaluate several attributes together.

The advantages of this type of knowledge to the planning of marketing strategy are significant. The knowledge can be useful in modifying current products or services and in designing new ones for selected buying publics.

In this article, we first show how conjoint measurement works from a numerical standpoint. We then discuss its application to a variety of marketing problems, and we demonstrate its use in strategic marketing simulations. The Appendix provides a brief description of how other research tools for measuring consumer judgments work, and how they relate to conjoint measurement.

How Conjoint Measurement Works

In order to see how to apply conjoint measurement, suppose a company were interested in marketing a new spot remover for carpets and upholstery. The technical staff has developed a new product that is designed to handle tough, stubborn spots. Management interest centers on five attributes or factors that it expects will influence consumer preference: an applicator-type package design, brand name, price, a *Good Housekeeping* seal of endorsement, and a money-back guarantee.

Three package designs are under consideration and appear in the upper portion of Exhibit I. There are three brand names under consideration: K2R, Glory, and Bissell. Of the three brand names used in the study, two are competitors' brand names already on the market, whereas one is the company's present brand name choice for its new product. Three alternative prices being considered are \$1.19, \$1.39, and \$1.59. Since there are three alternatives for each of these factors, they are called three-level factors. The *Good Housekeeping* seal and money-back guarantee are two-level factors, since each is either present or not. Consequently, a total of $3 \times 3 \times 3 \times 2 \times 2 = 108$ alternatives would have to be tested if the researcher were to array all possible combinations of the five attributes.

Clearly, the cost of administering a consumer evaluation study of this magnitude—not to mention the respondents' confusion and fatigue—would be prohibitive. As an alternative, however, the researcher can take advantage of a special experimental design, called an *orthogonal array*, in which the test combinations are selected so that the independent contributions of all five factors are balanced.[3] In this way each factor's weight is kept separate and is not confused with those of the other factors.

The lower portion of Exhibit I shows an orthogonal array that involves only 18 of the 108 possible combinations that the company wishes to test in this case. For the test the researcher makes up 18 cards. On each card appears an artist's sketch of the package design, A, B, or C, and verbal details regarding each of the other four factors: brand name, price, *Good Housekeeping* seal (or not), and money-back guarantee (or not). After describing the new product's functions and special features, he shows the respondents each of the 18 cards (see Exhibit I for the master design), and asks them to rank the cards in order of their likelihood of purchase.

The last column of Exhibit I shows one respondent's actual ranking of the 18 cards; rank number 1 denotes her highest evaluated concept. Note particularly that only *ranked* data need be obtained and, furthermore, that only 18 (out of 108) combinations are evaluated.

Package designs

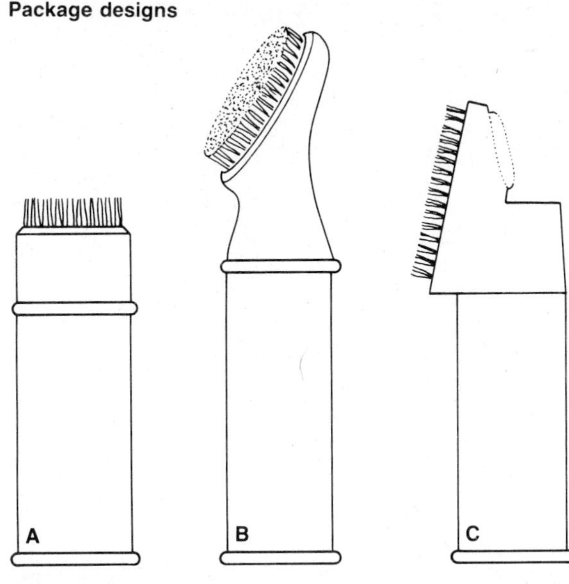

Orthogonal array

Package design	*Brand name*	*Price*	*Good Housekeeping seal?*	*Money-back guarantee?*	*Respondent's evaluation (rank number)*
1 A	K2R	$1.19	No	No	13
2 A	Glory	1.39	No	Yes	11
3 A	Bissell	1.59	Yes	No	17
4 B	K2R	1.39	Yes	Yes	2
5 B	Glory	1.59	No	No	14
6 B	Bissell	1.19	No	No	3
7 C	K2R	1.590	No	Yes	12
8 C	Glory	1.19	Yes	No	7
9 C	Bissell	1.39	No	No	9
10 A	K2R	1.59	Yes	No	18
11 A	Glory	1.19	No	Yes	8
12 A	Bissell	1.39	No	No	15
13 B	K2R	1.19	No	No	4
14 B	Glory	1.39	Yes	No	6
15 B	Bissell	1.59	No	Yes	5
16 C	K2R	1.39	No	No	10
17 C	Glory	1.59	No	No	16
18 C	Bissell	1.19	Yes	Yes	1*

*Highest ranked

EXHIBIT I
Experimental Design for Evaluation of a Carpet Cleaner

Computing the Utilities

Computation of the utility scales of each attribute, which determine how influential each is in the consumers' evaluations, is carried out by various computer programs.[4] The ranked data of a single respondent (or the composite ranks of a group of respondents) are entered in the program. The computer then searches for a set of scale values for each factor in the experimental design. The scale values for each level of each factor are chosen so that when they are added together the *total* utility of each combination will correspond to the original ranks as closely as possible.

Notice that two problems are involved here. First, as mentioned previously, the experimental design of Exhibit I shows only 18 of 108 combinations. Second, only rank-order data are supplied to the algorithms. This means that the data themselves do not determine how much more influential one attribute is than another in the consumers' choices. However, despite these limitations, the algorithms are able to find a *numerical* representation of the utilities, thus providing an indication of each factor's relative importance.

In general, more accurate solutions are obtained as the number of combinations being evaluated increases. Still, in the present case, with only 18 ranking-type judgments, the technique works well. Exhibit II shows the computer results.

As can be observed in Exhibit II, the technique obtains a utility function for each level of each factor. For example, to find the utility for the first combination in Exhibit I, we can read off the utilities of each factor level in the five charts of Exhibit II: U (A) = 0.1; U (K2R) = 0.3; U ($1.19) = 1.0; U (No) = 0.2; U (No) = 0.2. Therefore the total utility is 1.8, the sum of the five separate utilities, for the first combination. Note that this combination was ranked only thirteenth by the respondent in Exhibit I.

On the other hand, the utility combination 18 is 3.1 (0.6 + 0.5 + 1.0 + 0.3 + 0.7), which is the respondent's highest evaluation of all 18 combinations listed.

However, as can be easily seen from Exhibit II, if combination 18 is modified to include package Design B (in place of C), its utility is even higher. As a matter of fact, it then represents the highest possible utility, even though this specific combination did not appear among the original 18.

Importance of Attributes

By focusing attention on only the package design, the company's marketing researchers can see from Exhibit II that Design B displays highest utility. Moreover, all utility scales are expressed in a com-

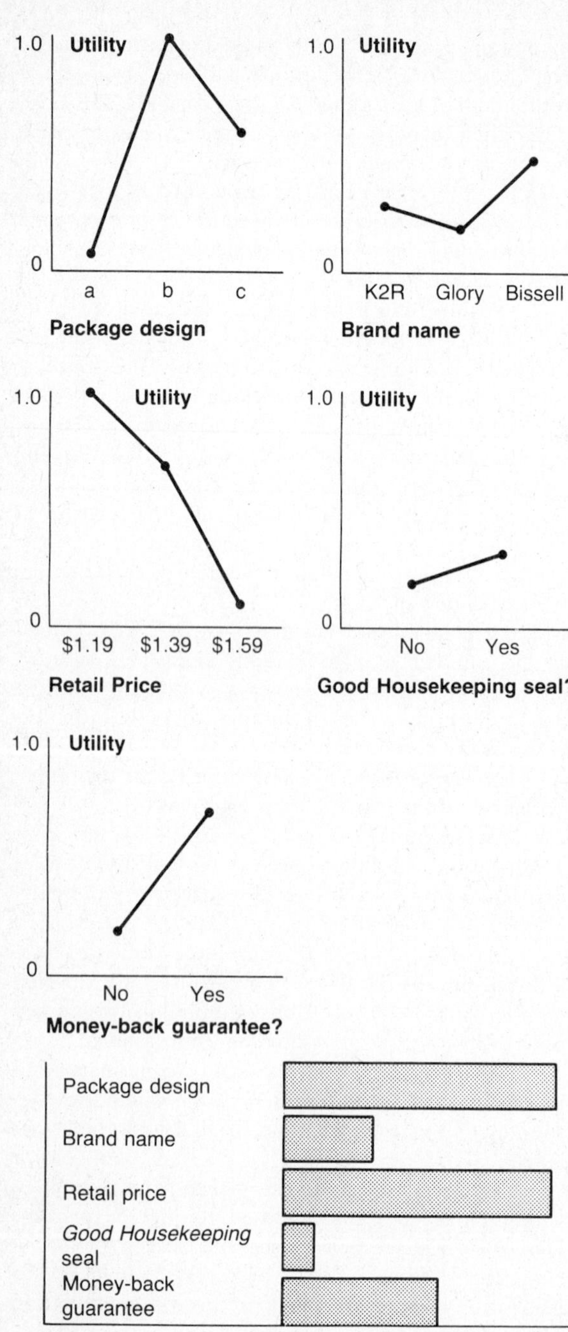

EXHIBIT II
Results of Computer Analysis of Experimental Data of Exhibit I

mon unit (although their zero points are arbitrary). This means that we can compare utility ranges from factor to factor so as to get some idea of their relative importance.

In the case of the spot remover, as shown in Exhibit II, the utility ranges are:

- Package design (1.0 − 0.1 = 0.9)
- Brand name (0.5 − 0.2 = 0.3)
- Price (1.0 − 0.1 = 0.9)
- *Good Housekeeping* seal (0.3 − 0.2 = 0.1)
- Money-back guarantee (0.7 − 0.2 = 0.5)

How important is each attribute in relation to the others? The lower portion of Exhibit II shows the relative size of the utility ranges expressed in histogram form. As noted, package design and price are the most important factors, and together they account for about two thirds of the total range in utility.

It should be mentioned that the relative importance of a factor depends on the levels that are included in the design. For example, had price ranged from $1.19 to a high of $1.89, its relative importance could easily exceed that for package design. Still, as a crude indication of what factors to concentrate on, factor importance calculations provide a useful by-product of the main analysis regardless of such limitations.

Managerial Implications

From a marketing management point of view the critical question is how these results can be used in the design of a product/marketing strategy for the spot remover. Examination of Exhibit II suggests a number of points for discussion:

- Excluding brand name, the most desirable offering would be the one based on package Design B with a money-back guarantee, a *Good Housekeeping* seal, and a retail price of $1.19.
- The utility of a product with a price of $1.39 would be 0.3 less than one with a price of $1.19. A money-back guarantee which involves an increment of 0.5 in utility would more than offset the effect of the higher price.
- The use of a *Good Housekeeping* seal of approval is associated with a minor increase in utility. Hence including it in the company's product will add little to the attractiveness of the spot remover's overall offering.

- The utility of the three brand names provides the company with a quantitative measure of the value of its own brand name as well as the brand names of its competitors.

Other questions can be answered as well by comparing various composites made up from the utilities shown in Exhibit II.

The Air Carrier Study

What about the two Paris flights you had to choose between? In that study, the sponsor was primarily interested in how air travelers evaluated the B-707 versus the B-747 in transatlantic travel, and whether relative value differed by length of flight and type of traveler—business versus vacation travelers. In this study all the respondents had flown across the Atlantic at least once during the preceding 12 months.

Exhibit III shows one of the findings of the study for air travelers (business and vacation) flying to Paris. Without delving into details it is quite apparent that the utility difference between the B-707 and the B-747 is very small. Rather, the main factors are departure time, punctuality of arrival, number of stops, and the attitudes of flight attendants.

The importance of type of aircraft did increase slightly with length of flight and for business-oriented travelers versus vacationers. Still, its importance to overall utility was never greater than 10%. It became abundantly clear that extensive replacement of older aircraft like the B-707 would not result in major shifts in consumer demand. On the contrary, money might better be spent on improving the scheduling aspects of flights and the attitudes and demeanor of flight personnel.

The air carrier study involved the preparation of some 27 different flight profiles (only two of which appear at the beginning of the article). Respondents simply rated each flight description in terms of its desirability on a seven-point scale. Only the order properties of the ratings were used in the computer run that resulted in the utility scales appearing in Exhibit III.

The Replacement Tire Study

The conjoint measurement exercise in the replacement tire study was part of a larger study designed to pretest several television commercials for the sponsor's brand of steel-belted radial tires. The sponsor was particularly interested in the utility

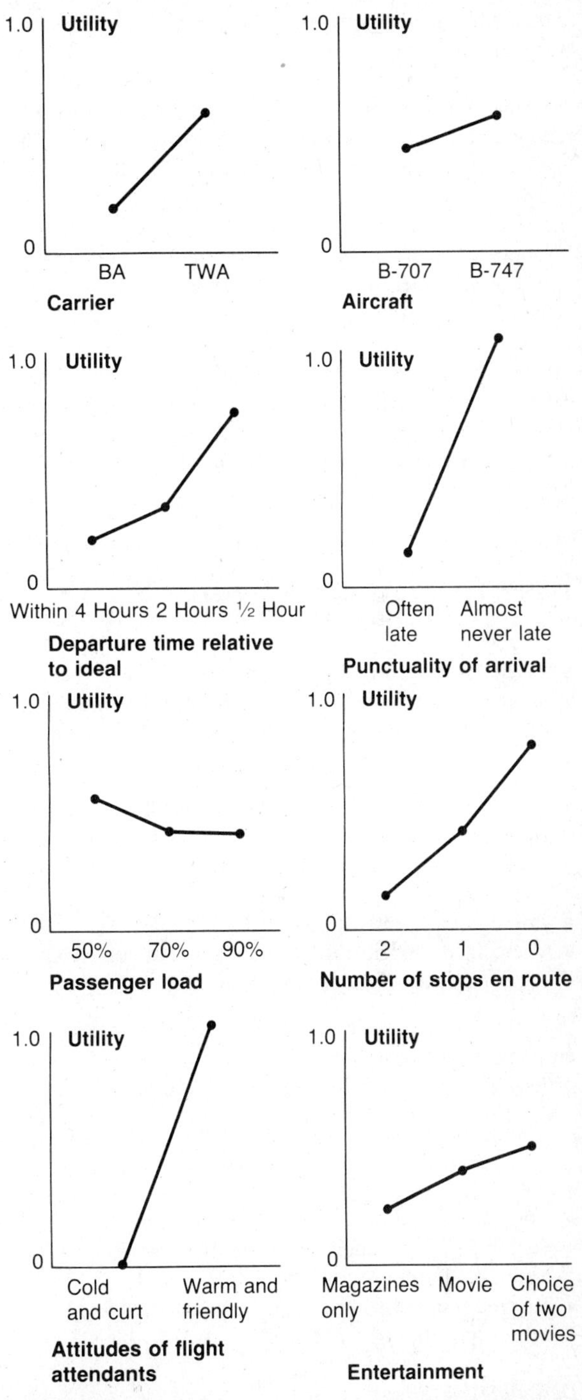

EXHIBIT III
Utility Functions for Air Travelers to Paris

functions of respondents who expressed interest in each of the test commercials.

The respondents considered tread mileage and price as quite important to their choice of tires. On the other hand, brand name did not play an important role (at least for the five brands included in the study). Not surprisingly, the most popular test commercial stressed tread mileage and good value for the money, characteristics of high appeal to this group. What was surprising was that this group represented 70% of the total sample.

This particular study involved the preparation of 25 profiles. Again, the researchers sorted cards into seven ordered categories. The 25 profiles, also constructed according to an orthogonal array, represented only one twenty-fifth of the 625 possible combinations.

Potential Uses of Conjoint Measurement

The three preceding studies only scratch the surface of marketing problems in which conjoint measurement procedures can be used. For example, consumer evaluations can be obtained on:

- New product formulations involving changes in the physical or chemical characteristics of the product
- Package design, brand name, and promotional copy combinations
- Pricing and brand alternatives
- Verbalized descriptions of new products or services
- Alternative service designs

Moreover, while the three preceding examples emphasized preference or likelihood-of-purchase orderings, any explicit judgmental criterion can be used. For example, alternatives might be ordered by any of these criteria:

- Best value for the money
- Convenience of use
- Suitability for a specified type of consumer or for a specified end use
- Ruggedness, distinctiveness, conservativeness, and other "psychological images"

Designing Bar Soaps

In one recent study researchers related the psychological imagery of physical characteristics of actual bars of soap to end-use appropriateness; this study was conducted for the laboratory and marketing personnel of a diversified soap manufacturer.

While the designing of a bar of soap—by varying weight, size, shape, color, fragrance type and intensity, surface feel, and so on—may seem like a mundane exercise, the fact remains that a cleverly positioned bar soap (for example, Irish Spring) can rapidly become a multimillion-dollar enterprise. Still, the extent of knowledge about the importance of such imagery is woefully meager. The researchers formulated actual bars of soap in which color, type of fragrance, and intensity of fragrance were constructed according to a design in which all possible combinations of the experimental factors appeared. All the other characteristics of the soap were held constant.

Respondents examined the soaps and assigned each bar to the end use that they felt best matched its characteristics—moisturizing facial soap, deep-cleaning soap for oily skin, woman's deodorant soap, or man's deodorant soap. The data were then analyzed by conjoint measurement techniques, leading to a set of psychophysical functions for each of the characteristics.

The study showed that type of fragrance was the most important physical variable contributing to end-use appropriateness. Rather surprisingly, the type of fragrance (medicinal) and color (blue) that appeared best suited for a man's deodorant soap were also found to be best for the deep-cleaning soap, even though deep-cleaning soap had been previously classed for marketing purposes as a facial soap. On the other hand, fragrance intensity played a relatively minor role as a consumer cue for distinguishing among different end uses.

In brief, this study illustrated the feasibility of translating changes in various physical variables into changes in psychological variables. Eventually, more detailed knowledge of these psychological transformations could enable a laboratory technician to synthesize color, fragrance, shape, and so forth to obtain soaps that conjure up almost any desired imagery. Moreover, in other product classes—beers, coffees, soft drinks—it appears possible to develop a psychophysics of taste in which such elusive verbal descriptions as "full-bodied" and "robust" are given operational meaning in terms of variations in physical or chemical characteristics.

Verbalized Descriptions of New Concepts

In many product classes, such as automobiles, houses, office machines, and computers, the possible design factors are myriad and expensive to vary physically for evaluation by the buying public. In cases such as these, the researcher usually resorts to verbalized descriptions of the principal factors of interest.

To illustrate, one study conducted among car owners by Rogers National Research, Inc. employed the format shown in Exhibit IV. In this case the researchers were interested in the effects of gas mileage, price, country of manufacture, maximum speed, roominess, and length on consumer preferences for new automobiles. Consumers evaluated factor levels on a two-at-a-time basis, as illustrated in Exhibit IV. Market Facts, Inc. employs a similar data collection procedure.[5]

In the Rogers study it was found that consumer evaluations of attributes were highly associated with the type of car currently owned and the type of car desired in the future. Not surprisingly, gas mileage and country of manufacture were highly important factors in respondent evaluations of car profiles. Somewhat surprising, however, was the fact that even large-car owners (and those contemplating the purchase of a large car) were more concerned with gas economy than owners of that type of car had been historically. Thus, while they fully expected to get fewer miles per gallon than they would in compact cars, they felt quite strongly that the car should be economical compared to others in its size class.

Organizations as Consumers

Nor is conjoint measurement's potential limited to consumer applications. Evaluations of supply alternatives by an organizational buyer are similar to benefits sought by the consumer. Thus, one can argue, these evaluations are among the most important inputs to industrial marketing strategy.

As an illustration, the management of a clinical laboratory was concerned with the problem of how to increase its share of laboratory test business. It had a study conducted to assess how physicians subjectively value various characteristics of a clinical laboratory in deciding where to send their tests.

Each physician in the study received 16 profiles of hypothetical laboratory services, each showing a different set of characteristics, such as reliability of test results, pick-up and delivery procedures, convenience of location, price range of services, billing procedures, and turnaround time. Utility functions were developed for each of these factors. On the basis of these results the management of the laboratory decided to change its promotion by emphasizing a number of convenience factors in addition to its previous focus on test reliability.

Marketing Strategy Simulations

We have described a variety of applications of conjoint measurement, and still others, some in conjunction with the other techniques outlined in the Appendix, could be mentioned.[6] What has not yet been discussed, and is more important, is the role that utility measurement can play in the design of strategic marketing simulators. This type of application is one of the principal uses of conjoint measurement.

As a case in point, a large-scale study of consumer evaluations of airline services was conducted in which consumer utilities were developed for some 25 different service factors such as on-ground services, in-flight services, decor of cabins and seats, scheduling, routing, and price. Moreover, each utility function was developed on a route (city-pair) and purpose-of-trip basis.

As might be expected, the utility function for each of the various types of airline service differed according to the length and purpose of the flight. However, in addition to obtaining consumers' evaluations of service profiles, the researchers also obtained information concerning their *perceptions* of each airline (that is, for the ones they were familiar with) on each of the service factors for which the consumers were given a choice.

These two major pieces of information provided the principal basis for developing a simulation of airline services over all major traffic routes. The purpose of the simulation was to estimate the effect on market share that a change in the service configuration of the sponsor's services would have, route by route, if competitors did not follow suit. Later, the sponsor used the simulator to examine the effect of assumed retaliatory actions by its competitors. It also was able to use it to see what might happen to market share if the utility functions themselves were to change.

Each new service configuration was evaluated against the base-period configuration. In addition, the simulator showed which competing airlines would lose business and which ones would gain business under various changes in perceived service levels. Thus, in addition to single, ad hoc studies, conjoint

What is more important to you? There are times when we have to give up one thing to get something else. And, since different people have different desires and priorities, the automotive industry wants to know what things are most important to you. We have a scale that will make it possible for you to tell us your preference in certain circumstances—for example, gas mileage vs. speed. Please read the example below which explains how the scale works—and then tell us the order of your preference by writing in the numbers from 1 to 9 for each of the six questions that follow the example.

Example:
Warranty vs. price of the car

Procedure:

Simply write the number 1 in the combination that represents your first choice. In one of the remaining blank squares, write the number 2 for your second choice. Then write the number 3 for your third choice, and so on, from 1 to 9.

Years of warranty

Price of car	3	2	1
$3,000	1		
$3,200			
$3,400			

Step 1 (Explanation)

You would rather pay the least ($3,000) and get the most (3 years). Your first choice (1) is in the box as shown.

Years of warranty

Price of car	3	2	1
$3,000	1	2	
$3,200			
$3,400			

Step 2

Your second choice is that you would rather pay $3,200 and have a 3-year warranty than pay $3,000 and get a 2-year warranty.

Years of warranty

Price of car	3	2	1
$3,000	1	3	
$3,200	2		
$3,400			

Step 3

Your third choice is that you would rather pay $3,000 and have a 2-year warranty than pay $3,400 and get a 3-year warranty.

Years of warranty

Price of car	3	2	1
$3,000	1	3	6
$3,200	2	5	8
$3,400	4	7	9

Sample

This shows a sample order of preference for all possible combinations. Of course, your preferences could be different.

For each of the six questions below, please write in the numbers from 1 to 9 to show your order of preference for your next new car.

Miles per gallon

Price of car	22	18	14
$3,000			
$3,200			
$3,400			

Miles per gallon

Maximum speed	22	18	14
80 mph			
70 mph			
60 mph			

Miles per gallon

Length	22	18	14
12 feet			
14 feet			
16 feet			

Miles per gallon

Roominess	22	18	14
6 passenger			
5 passenger			
4 passenger			

Miles per gallon

Made in	22	18	14
Germany			
U.S.			
Japan			

Price of car

Made in	3,000	3,200	3,400
Germany			
U.S.			
Japan			

EXHIBIT IV
A Two-At-A-Time Factor Evaluation Procedure

measurement can be used in the ongoing monitoring (via simulation) of consumer imagery and evaluations over time.

Prospects and Limitations

Like any new set of techniques, conjoint measurement's potential is difficult to evaluate at the present stage of development and application. Relatively few companies have experimented with the approach so far. Capability for doing the research is still concentrated in a relatively few consulting firms and companies.

Conjoint measurement faces the same kinds of limitations that confront any type of survey, or laboratory-like, technique. First, while some successes have been reported in using conjoint measurement to predict actual sales and market share, the number of applications is still too small to establish a convincing track record at the present time.

Second, some products or services may involve utility functions and decision rules that are not adequately captured by the models of conjoint measurement. While the current emphasis on additive models (absence of interactions) can be shifted to more complex, interactive models, the number of combinations required to estimate the interactions rapidly mounts. Still, little is known about how good an approximation the simpler models are to the more elaborate ones.

Third, the essence of some products and services may just not be well captured by a decomposition approach that assumes that the researcher can describe an alternative in terms of its component parts. Television personalities, hit records, movies, or even styling aspects of cars may not lend themselves to this type of reductionist approach.

While the limitations of conjoint measurement are not inconsequential, early experience suggests some interesting prospects for measuring consumer tradeoffs among various product or service characteristics. Perhaps what is most interesting about the technique is its flexibility in coping with a wide variety of management's understanding of consumers' problems that ultimately hinge on evaluations of complex alternatives that a choice among products presents them with.

Appendix: Other Techniques for Quantifying Consumers' Judgments

Conjoint measurement is the latest in an increasing family of techniques that psychometricians and others in the behavioral and statistical sciences have developed to measure persons' perceptions and preferences. Conjoint measurement can often be profitably used with one or more of the following:

Factor Analysis. Factor analysis in marketing research has been around since the 1940s. However, like all the techniques to be (briefly) described here, factor analysis did not reach any degree of sophistication or practicality until the advent of the computer made the extensive computations easy to carry out. A typical input to factor analysis consists of respondents' subjective ratings of brands or services on each of a set of attributes *provided by the researcher.* For example, a sample of computer systems personnel were asked to rate various computer manufacturers' equipment and services on each of the 15 attributes shown in Table I.

The objective of factor analysis is to examine the commonality across the various rating scales and find a geometric representation, or picture, of the objects (computers), as well as the attributes used in the rating task. As noted in Table I, International Business Machines (IBM) was ranked highest on virtually all attributes while Xerox (XDS), a comparatively new entrant at the time of the study, National Cash Register (NCR), and Control Data Corporation (CDC) were not perceived as highly as the others with regard to the various attributes of interest to computer users.

The tight grouping of the attribute vectors also suggests a strong "halo" effect in favor of IBM. Only in the case of price flexibility does IBM receive less than the highest rating, and even here it is rated a close second. Thus as Table I shows, factor analysis enables the researcher to develop a picture of both the things being rated (the manufacturers) and the attributes along which the ratings take place.

Perceptual Mapping. A somewhat more recent technique—also abetted by the availability of the computer—is perceptual mapping. Perceptual mapping techniques take consumer judgments of *overall* similarity or preference and find literally a picture in which objects that are judged to be similar psychologically plot near each other in geometric space (see Table II). However, in perceptual mapping the respondent is free to choose *his own* frame of reference rather than to respond to explicitly stated attributes.

The perceptual map of the 11 automobiles shown was developed from consumers' judgments about the relative similarity of the 55 distinct pairs of cars that can be made up from the 11 cars listed. The dimension labels of *luxurious* and *sporty* do *not* come from the technique but rather from further analysis of the map, once it is obtained from the computer. Ideal points I and J are shown for two illustrative respondents and are fitted into the perceptual map from the respondents' preference judgments. Car points near a respondent's ideal point are preferred to those farther away. Thus respondent I

TABLE I
Factor Analysis of Average Respondent Ratings of Eight Computer Manufacturers' Images on Each of 15 Attributes

Note: The closer an image is to the head end of the arrows the more it is credited with possessing the attribute associated with each vector. To compare companies along any one vector simply mark a position on the arrow by dropping a line *perpendicular to the arrow* from each company position.

Axis 2
XDS
NCR
CDC
Burroughs
Honeywell
UNIVAC
Axis 1
RCA
IBM
Innovativeness
Performance/cost
Virtual memory
Price flexibility

Reliability
Software extensiveness
Education/training
Technical backup
Sales presentations
Systems personnel acceptance

Programming language
Ease of changeover
Service after sale
Time sharing
Overall preference

TABLE II
Perceptual Mapping of Respondents' Judgments of the Relative Similarity of 11 Cars and Two Respondents' Preference Orderings

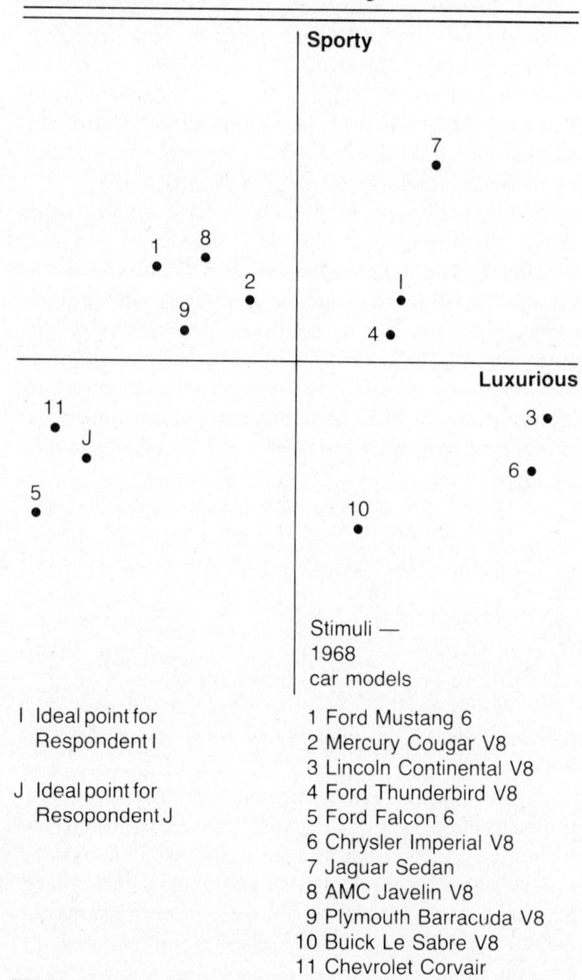

most likes Ford Thunderbird, while respondent J most likes Chevrolet Corvair. In practice, data for several hundred respondents might be used to find regions of high density for ideal points.

Cluster Analysis. Still another way to portray consumers' judgments is in terms of a hierarchical tree structure in which the more similar a set of objects is perceived to be, the more quickly the objects group together as one moves from left to right in the tree diagram. Thus the words *body* and *fullness* are perceived to be the two most closely associated of all of the descriptions appearing in Table III that characterize hair. Note further that smaller clusters become embedded in larger ones until the last cluster on the right includes all 19 phases. The words in this example were based on respondents' free associations to a set of 8 stimulus words. The researchers assumed that the more a stimulus evoked another word, the more similar they were.

TABLE III
Hierarchical Cluster Analysis of 19 Phrases Evoked in a Free Association Task Involving Women's Hair Shampoos

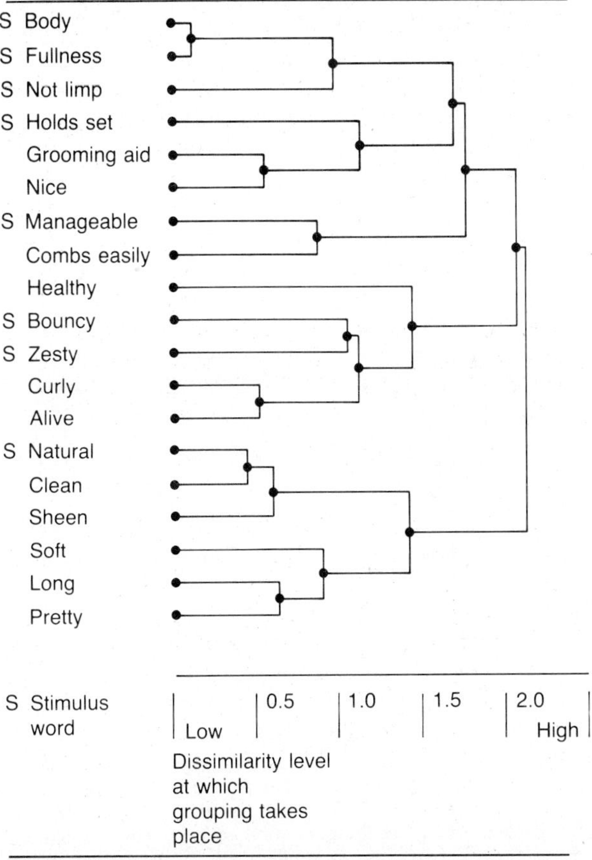

Relationship to Conjoint Measurement. These three methods are best noted for their complementarities—both with each other and with conjoint measurement. Factor analysis and perceptual mapping can be used to measure consumers' perceptions of various products or services, while conjoint measurement can be used to quantify how consumers trade off some of one attribute to get more of another. Cluster analysis can be used in a variety of ways, either as a comparison technique for portraying the similarities of various objects or as a basis for grouping people with common perceptions or preferences. In short, all these techniques can—and frequently are—applied in the *same* study. As such, their combined use can heighten different aspects of the same general types of input data.

Endnotes

1. R. Duncan Luce and John W. Tukey, "Simultaneous Conjoint Measurement: A New Type of Fundamental Measurement," *Journal of Mathematical Psychology,* February 1964, p. 1.
2. The first marketing-oriented paper on conjoint measurement was by Paul E. Green and Vithala R. Rao, "Conjoint Measurement for Quantifying Judgmental Data," *Journal of Marketing Research,* August 1971, p. 355.
3. A nontechnical discussion of this special class of designs appears in Paul E. Green, "On the Design of Experiments Involving Multiattribute Alternatives," *Journal of Consumer Research,* September 1974, p. 61.
4. As an illustration, see Joseph B. Kruskal, "Analysis of Factorial Experiments by Estimating Monotone Transformations of the Data," *Journal of the Royal Statistical Society,* Series B, March 1965, p. 251.
5. Richard M. Johnson, "Trade-Off Analysis of Consumer Values," *Journal of Marketing Research,* May 1974, p. 121.
6. Paul E. Green and Yoram Wind, *Multiattribute Decisions in Marketing: A Measurement Approach* (Hinsdale, Ill.: Dryden Press, 1973).

READING 23

Customer-Oriented Approaches to Identifying Product-Markets

George S. Day, Allan D. Shocker, and Rajendra K. Srivastava

The need to identify the boundaries of increasingly complex product-markets has spawned a number of analytical methods based on customer behavior or judgments. The various methods are compared and contrasted according to whether they are consistent with a conceptual definition of a product-market, and their ability to yield diagnostic insights.

The problems of identifying competitive product-markets pervade all levels of marketing decisions. Such strategic issues as the basic definition of the business, the assessment of opportunities presented by gaps in the market or threats posed by competitive actions, and major resource allocation decisions are strongly influenced by the breadth or narrowness of the competitive arena. Share of market is a crucial tactical tool for evaluating performance and guiding territorial advertising, sales force, and other budget allocations. The quickening pace of antitrust prosecution is a further source of demands for better definitions of relevant market boundaries that will yield a clearer understanding of the competitive consequences of acquisitions.

This paper is primarily concerned with the needs of marketing planners for strategic analyses of competitive product-markets.[1] Their needs presently are served by approaches to defining product-markets which emphasize similarity of production processes, function, or raw materials used. Seldom do these approaches give a satisfactory picture of either the threats or the opportunities facing a business. In response, there has been considerable activity directed toward defining product-markets from the customers' perspective. Our objectives are first, to examine the merits of a customer perspective in the context of a defensible definition of a product-market, and second, to evaluate progress toward providing this perspective. The paper's structure corresponds to these objectives. The first two sections are concerned with the nature of the strategic problem, and the development of a customer-oriented definition of a product-market. This definition is used in the third section to help evaluate a variety of methods for identifying product-market boundaries. In this discussion, a sharp distinction is drawn between methods which rely on purchase or usage behavior and those which use customer judgments.

Sources of Demand For Better Insights

Ultimately all product-market boundaries are arbitrary. They exist because of recurring needs to comprehend market structures and impose some order on complex market environments. But this situation could not be otherwise. One reason is the wide variety of decision contexts which dictate different definitions of boundaries.

Market and product class definitions appropriate for tactical decisions tend to be narrow, reflecting

Reprinted by permission of the American Marketing Association, from the *Journal of Marketing,* 43:4 Fall 1979, 8–19.

1. Many of the same issues are encountered during efforts to define the relevant product-market for antitrust purposes. Here the question is whether a company so dominates a market that effective competition is precluded, or that a past or prospective merger has lessened competition. The conceptual approach to this question is very similar to the one developed in this paper (Day, Massy, and Shocker 1978). However, because of the adversarial nature of the proceedings and the existence of prior hypotheses of separation to be tested, the treatment of "relevant market" issues is otherwise quite different.

the short-run concerns of sales and product managers who regard a market as "a chunk of demand to be filled with the resources at my command." These resources are usually constrained by products in the present product line. A longer-run view, reflecting strategic planning concerns, invariably will reveal a larger product-market to account for (1) presently unserved but potential markets; (2) changes in technology, price relationships, and supply which broaden the array of potential substitute products; and (3) the time required by present and prospective buyers to react to these changes.

Of necessity, a single market definition is a compromise between the long-run and the short-run views. All too often, the resulting compromise is not consistent with customer's views of the competitive alternatives to be considered for a particular usage situation or application. One consequence of these problems is the development of different definitions for different purposes. Thus, for some strategic planning purposes. General Electric treats hair dryers, hair setters, and electric brushes as part of distinct markets while for other purposes they are part of a "personal appliance" business since they tend to compete with one another in a "gift market." General Foods has taken an even broader approach in a reorganization of its process-oriented divisional structure into strategic business units. Each SBU now concentrates on marketing families of products made by different processing technologies but consumed by the same market segments (Hanon 1974). Thus, all desserts are in the same division whether they are frozen, powdered, or ready-to-eat.

A further reason for the inevitable arbitrariness of product-market boundaries is the frequent absence of natural discontinuities which can be readily identified—and accepted—without argument. Moran (1973) states the problem bluntly:

> *In our complex service society, there are no more product classes—not in any meaningful sense, only as a figment of file clerk imagination . . . To some degree, in some circumstances, almost anything can be a partial substitute for almost anything else. A (fifteen-cent) stamp substitutes to some extent for an airline ticket.*

When a high degree of ambiguity or compromise is present in the identification of the product-market, a number of problems are created. Some will stem from inadequate and delayed understanding of emerging threats in the competitive environment. These threats may come from foreign competition, product substitution trends, shifts in price sensitivity, or changed technological possibility. Thus fiberglass and aluminum parts have displaced steel in many automotive applications due in some measure to increasing willingness to pay higher prices to obtain lower weight and consequent gas economy. Conversely, opportunities may be overlooked when the definition is drawn too narrowly for tactical purposes and the nature and size of the potential market are understated. Finally, whenever market share is used to evaluate the performance of managers or to determine resource allocations (Day 1977), there is a tendency for managers to manipulate the market boundaries to show an increasing or at least static share.

A Customer-Oriented Concept of a Competitive Product-Market

Market definitions have, in the past, focused on either the *product* (as with the following definition, ". . . products may be closely related in the sense that they are regarded as substitutes by consumers." Needham 1969, which assumes homogeneity of consumer behavior), or on the *buyers* (". . . individuals who in the past have purchased a given class of products." Sissors 1966). Neither approach is very helpful for clarifying the concept, or evaluating alternative approaches for identifying product-market boundaries.

A more productive approach can be derived from the following premises:

- People seek the benefits that products provide rather than the products per se. Specific products or brands represent the available combinations of benefits and costs.
- Consumers consider the available alternatives from the vantage point of the usage contexts with which they have experience or the specific applications they are considering (Belk 1975; Lutz and Kakkar 1976; Stout et al. 1977). It is the usage requirement which dictates the benefits being sought.[2]

2. This premise was directly tested, and supported, in a study of the variation of judged importance of various fast food restaurant attributes across eating occasions (Miller and Ginter 1979). This study and others also have found that some needs, and benefits sought, are reasonably stable across situations. Thus it is usually productive to segment a market on the basis of both people and occasions (Goldman and McDonald 1979).

From these two premises, we can define a product-market as the *set of products* judged to be substitutes, within those usage situations in which similar patterns of benefits are sought, and the *customers* for whom such usages are relevant.

This definition is *demand* or customer-oriented in that customer needs and requirements have primacy. The alternative is to take a *supply* perspective and define products by such operational criteria as similarity of manufacturing processes, raw materials, physical appearance, or function. These criteria are the basis of the Standard Industrial Classification (SIC) system—and have generally wide acceptance because they appear easy to implement. They lead to seemingly stable and clear-cut definitions, and importantly, involve factors largely controllable by the firm; implying that the definition is somehow controllable as well. They are also helpful in identifying potential competitors, because of similarities in manufacturing and distribution systems. Demand-oriented criteria, on the other hand, are less familiar and consequently appear more difficult to implement (as a consequence of the variety of methods available and the inevitable problems of empirical measurement, sampling errors, and aggregation over individual customer differences). Moreover, such definitions may be less stable over time because of changing needs and tastes. Finally, the organization must initiate a research program to collect and analyze relevant data and monitor change rather than relying on government or other external sources to make the information available. The consequence is most often a decision to use supply-oriented measures despite their questionable applicability in many circumstances (Needham 1969).

Hierarchies of Products. The notion of a unique product category is an oversimplification in the face of the arbitrary nature of the boundaries. Substitutability is a measure of degree. Thus it is better to think in terms of the levels in a hierarchy of products within a generic product class representing all possible ways of satisfying a fundamental consumer need or want. Lunn (1972) makes the following useful distinctions between:

- Totally different *product types* or subclasses which exist to satisfy significantly different patterns of needs beyond the fundamental or generic. For example, both hot and cold cereals serve the same need for breakfast nutrition, but otherwise are different. Over the long run, product types may behave like substitutes.
- Different *product variants* are available within the same overall type, e.g., natural, nutritional, presweetened, and regular cereals. There is a high probability that some short-run substitution takes place among subsets of these variants (between natural and nutritional, for example). If there is too much substitution, then alternatives within the subset do not deserve to be distinguished.
- Different *brands* are produced within the same specific product variant. Although these brands may be subtly differentiated on many bases (color, package type, shape, texture, etc.), they are nonetheless usually direct and immediate substitutes.

There may be many or few levels in such a hierarchy, depending on the breadth and complexity of the genuine need and the variety of alternatives available to satisfy it. Thus, this typology is simply a starting point for thinking about the analytical issues.

Submarkets and Strategic Segments. The product-market definition proposed above implies submarkets composed of customers with common uses or applications of the product. These are segments according to the traditional definition of groups that have similar purchase or usage behavior or reactions to marketing efforts (Frank, Massy, and Wind 1973). For our purposes, it is more useful to consider these as submarkets within *strategic market segments.* While each of these submarkets may serve as the focus of a positioning decision, the differences between them may not present significant strategic barriers for competitors to overcome. Such barriers may be based on factors such as differences in geography, order quantities, requirements for technical assistance and service support, price sensitivity, or perceived importance of quality and reliability. The test of strategic relevance is whether the segments defined by these or other characteristics must be served by substantially different marketing mixes. The boundaries could then be manifested by discontinuities in price structures, growth rates, share patterns, and distribution channels when going from one segment to another.

Analytical Methods for Customer-Oriented Product-Market Definitions

Customer-oriented methods for identifying product-markets can be classified by whether they rely upon behavioral or judgmental data. Purchase behavior provides the best indication of what people actually do, or have done, but not necessarily what they might do under changed circumstances. As such, its value is greater as a guide to tactical planning. Judgmental data, in the form of perceptions or preferences, may give better insights into future patterns of competition and the reasons for present patterns. Consequently, it may better serve as the basis for strategic planning. In this section we will evaluate seven different analytical approaches within the two basic classes as follows:

Purchase or Usage Behavior	*Customer Judgments*
A1. Cross-elasticity of demand	B1. Decision sequence analysis
A2. Similarities in behavior	B2. Perceptual mapping
A3. Brand switching	B3. Technology substitution analysis
	B4. Customer judgments of substitutability

Within the broad category of customer judgments of substitutability (B4), five related approaches, using free associations, the "dollar metric," direct grouping of products, products-by-uses analysis and substitution-in-use analysis will be examined.

Analysis of Purchase or Usage Behavior

A1. Cross-Elasticity of Demand is considered by most economists to be the standard against which other approaches should be compared (Scherer 1970). Despite the impressive logic of the cross-elasticity measure, it is widely criticized and infrequently used:

- The conceptual definition of this measure presumes that there is no response by one firm to the price change of another (Needham 1969). This condition is seldom satisfied in practice.
- It is a static measure, and "breaks down in the face of a market characterized by changing product composition" (Cocks and Virts 1975). This is so because a priori it is not known what all the potential substitutes or complements may be. Over time new entrants or departures from a market may affect the cross-elasticity between any two alternatives.
- Finally, "in markets where price changes have been infrequent, or all prices change together, or where factors other than prices have also changed, there is simply not enough information contained in the data to permit valid statistical estimation of the elasticities," (Vernon 1972).

These problems may be overcome with either an experimental study, which can introduce problems of measure validity, or extensive monitoring of the factors affecting demand and use of econometric methods to control, where possible, for the effects of such factors. Not surprisingly, such studies are expensive and rather infrequently undertaken. Generally, empirical cross-elasticity studies have focued on only two goods (typically product-types as opposed to variants or brands). It is also worth noting that if simultaneous estimation of all cross-elasticities were to be attempted, some a priori determination of the limits to a product-market would be needed in order to include price change and other market data for all potential competitive brands. The estimation of any specific cross-elasticity should be sensitive to such product-market definition.

A2. Similarities in Customer Usage Behavior. This approach was successfully used in a study of the ethical pharmaceutical market (Cocks and Virts 1975). The basic question was the extent to which products made up of different chemicals, but with similar therapeutic effects, could be significant substitutes. The key to answering this question was the availability of a unique set of data on physician behavior. Each of the 3,000 physicians in a panel recorded: (1) patient characteristics, (2) the diagnosis, (3) the therapeutic measures—drugs—used to treat the patient, (4) the desired action of the drugs being used, and (5) characteristics of the reporting physician.

The first step in the analysis was to estimate the percentage usage of each drug in the treatment of patients diagnosed as having the same ailment. When a drug was found to be the only one used for a certain disease, and seldom or never used in the treatment of any other diagnosis, it was assumed to represent a distinct class. Generally, it was found that several drugs were used in several diagnosis categories.

The next step was to see if drugs which were used together had similar desired actions. Some drugs, such as analgesics, are frequently used along with other drugs, without being substitutes (strictly speaking, they also are not complements). Finally, drugs were classed as substitutes—and hence in the same product class—if 10% or more of the total usage of each drug was in the treatment of a specific diagnosis.

While it was not claimed that every drug in the resulting product-market competed for all uses of every other drug in that market, the data revealed a substantial amount of substitutability. The key to understanding the patterns of competition in this market was knowledge of the usage situation. As yet, few consumer panels have incorporated similar data with the usual measures of purchase behavior. The potential to conduct similar analyses suggests that usage data could be valuable when available for categories which are purchased for multiple uses.

A3. Brand Switching measures are usually interpreted as conditional probabilities, i.e., the probability of purchasing brand A, given that brand B was purchased on the last occasion. Such measures are typically estimated from panel data where the purchases of any given respondent are represented by a sequence of indefinite length. The probabilities are computed from counts of the frequency with which each condition arises in the data (e.g., purchases of brand A are preceded by different brands in the sequence). The premise is that respondents are more likely to switch between close substitutes than distant ones and that brand switching proportions provide a measure of the probability of substitution.

As with cross-elasticity, the brand switching measure is usable only after a set of competitive products has first been established. Since estimation of brand-switching rates is based upon a sequence of purchases, there must be some logical basis to determine which brands to include in such a sequence. Similarity of usage patterns, as discussed above, is one promising basis.

Brand switching rates as measures of degree of substitutability are flawed in several respects. (1) Applicability is typically limited to product categories having high repeat purchase rates to ensure that a sufficiently long sequence of purchases is available over a short time period for reliable estimates of switching probabilities. (2) The customer choice process, which determines switching, must be presumed stable throughout the sequence of purchases. If a long time series is used to provide reliable estimates, this assumption may be questionable. (3) Panel data, upon which switching probabilities are based, often obscure individual switching behavior since data are typically reported by only one member of a family who completes a diary of purchases. Apparent switching can result from different members of the family making consistent but different brand choices at differing points in time. A similar distortion is created by an individual who regularly purchases different brands for different usage occasions. (4) Analyses of panel data are further complicated by multiple brand purchases at the same time (does purchase of A precede B or vice versa in determining the sequence?), by lack of uniformity in package sizes across brands (since package size affects frequency of purchase), and by different sized packages of the same brand (is purchase of a large size equivalent to some sequence of purchases of smaller sizes?).

The *Hendry model* (Butler and Butler 1970, 1971) uses brand switching data directly to determine the market structure. Although details have been slow to appear in the literature (Kalwani and Morrison 1977; Rubison and Bass 1978) there has been a good deal of utilization of the empirical regularities uncovered by the model for marketing planning purposes.

This model does not rely solely on behavioral data, as it can also incorporate retrospective reports of switching or purchase intentions data from surveys. In essence, the model seeks an underlying structure of brand switching maximally "consistent" with the input data. It posits a hierarchical ordering in consumer decision making: consumers are presumed to form categories within the product class (e.g., cold or hot, presweetened or regular, Kelloggs, General Mills, or Post cereals), select those classes in which they are interested, and then consider for purchase only the alternatives within the chosen class (e.g., brands within a particular type of product *or* product types within a brand name). Analysis is carried out at each submarket level. Customers may purchase brands within more than one submarket, but within any submarket all customers are considered potential purchasers of all brands. Each customer is assumed, at equilibrium, to have stable purchase probabilities.

To determine which ordering or structuring of the market best characterizes customer views, a heuristic procedure is employed. Initially, judgment is used to hypothesize a limited number of plausible partitionings of a market, i.e., *alternative* submarket definitions. For each hypothesized definition, the Hendry framework is used to predict various switching probabilities among the products/brands within each submarket and between submarkets (switching *between* submarkets should be much less than *within* any one submarket). The predictions can then be compared with the actual data. That hypothesized partitioning (market structure) yielding switching patterns in closest correspondence with actual data is selected as the appropriate definition for the structure of the market.

A procedure elaborating hierarchical partitioning concepts similar to those of Hendry, but with the ability to incorporate usage occasion has recently been discussed by Urban and Hauser (1979). As in the Hendry model, a hierarchical tree structure is specified. More switching should occur within than between branches. Individual probability estimates are derived by measuring preferences among products with a consumer interview and statistically matching these preferences to observed or reported purchase behavior using the conditional logit model (McFadden 1970). The derived trees are tested by comparing predicted with actual choices in a simulated buying situation which occurs at the end of the consumer interview.

The Hendry procedure has a substantial subjective component, depending upon the criterion used to generate the hypothetical market structure definitions to be evaluated. (The alternative to a good criterion is the testing of potentially large numbers of definitions.) It is also quite arbitrary, possessing elements of the chicken-egg controversy: the prior specification of "the market" is quite critical to the empirical determination of "market shares" for each brand but these in turn are necessary to calibrate the Hendry model (i.e., estimate its parameters). Thus the "correct" definition of the market will depend upon how well predictions of the model correspond to the actual data. The model ought to always do reasonably well in predicting switching patterns in the same market environment from which share data were taken. In other words, to use the model for purposes of selecting the superior market definition, one must presume the model valid. But to test its validity, one must already possess a valid definition of the market. Thus the Hendry model may provide a reasonable approach to market definition only if either the model itself can be independently validated or if independent criteria exist for validating the market definition it suggests.

The Hendry model presumes all customers have stable probabilities of purchasing every brand within a partition (submarket). This assumes preferences, market shares, attitudes, and all other factors of significance are stable and that learning is negligible. Such assumptions may suggest applicability of the Hendry framework only in mature product categories, where such conditions may reasonably hold. Moreover, confirmation of any a priori partitioning of a market rests solely upon analysis of the aggregate switching probabilities as these become the measures of substitutability. Since analysis is carried out on an aggregate level, individual or segment differences are largely ignored. The premise that any given brand may have a varying set of competitors depending upon intended usage and brand familiarity is assumed away by such aggregation.

Summary. Behavioral measures suffer from an endemic weakness because they are influenced by what "is" or "was" rather than what "might be." Actual switching is affected by current market factors such as the set of existing brands, their availability, current pricing structures, promotional message and expenditures, existing legislation and social mores, etc. An imported beer could be substitutable for a local brand insofar as usage is concerned, but price differences may discourage actual substitution. Similarly, a private label brand may be substitutable for a nationally distributed one, but unless the customer shops the stores in which the private label is sold, they cannot make the substitution. If data are developed over long periods of time or from a diverse set of people in differing circumstances, sufficient variability may have taken place in the determinants of demand to reveal such potential substitutability. Otherwise, if some kind of behavioral measure is desired, laboratory manipulation may be necessary.

Analyses Based Upon Customer Judgments

Customers often have considerable knowledge of existing brands through personal or friends' experiences and exposure to promotion. Their perceptions may not always correspond to what manufacturers may believe about their own or competitive products. They may have purchase and consumption objectives which influence their consideration of alternatives and choices among them. They may create new uses for existing products. If such perceptual and decision making processes prove relatively stable, they may be useful for predicting which products and brands will be regarded as potential or actual substitutes and why.

B1. Decision Sequence Analysis utilizes protocols of consumer decision making, which indicate the sequence in which various criteria are employed to reach a final choice (Bettman 1971; Haines 1974). The usual procedure asks individuals to verbalize what is going through their mind as they make purchase decisions in the course of a shopping trip. This verbal record is called a protocol as distinguished from retrospective questioning of subjects about their decisions. With such data, a model of the way the subject makes decisions can be developed. These models specify the *attributes* of the choice objects or situations that are considered and the *sequence* and *method* of combination of these attributes or cues. Generally, the attributes or cues are arrayed in a hierarchical structure called a decision tree. The order in which they are examined is modeled by the path structure of the tree. The branches are based merely on whether or not the level of the attribute is satisfactory or a certain condition is present ("is the price too high?" "is the store out of my favorite brand?").

Analysis of protocols is at the individual level. This has the advantage of enabling individual differences in knowledge and beliefs about alternative products and choice criteria to be recognized. Individuals may, in principle, be grouped into segments on the basis of similar decision procedures. Measures of the extent of competition between brands can be obtained from protocols of different segments by noting which alternatives are even considered and when they are eliminated from further consideration by criteria used at each stage of the decision process (alternatives eliminated at later stages should be more competitive than those eliminated earlier).

Applications of decision sequence analysis have focused on choices at the brand level. Yet the real benefits of this approach would seem to be better insights into the hierarchy of product types and variants within a generic product class. Thus in understanding patterns of competition in the vegetable market, it is important to know whether buyers first decide on the type of vegetable (corn, beans, peas, etc.) or the form (fresh, frozen, or canned). Proposals for a similar kind of study have been made by economists in connection with the concept of a "utility tree" (Strotz 1957) and are similar in intent to the Hendry procedure.

There are numerous empirical problems to be considered in any effort to collect protocols of choice hierarchies. The typical representations of decision sequences appear quite complex and pose serious difficulties for aggregation of the individual models into any small number of segments. Aggregation requires some definition of "similarity" in order to group different decision structures. Further, since it is generally expensive to develop protocols, a representative sample of customers may be unrealizable. Customers are not used to reporting their decision processes so explicitly. A trained interviewer is needed to coax information which is specific enough to be meaningful (e.g., what is too high a price or a satisfactory level of preference?) and yet not unduly bias the process. Since customer decision making for some product categories may take place over prolonged periods of time it may be necessary for the length of the interviewing to be similarly extended or to rely on respondent's recall of certain events. Finally, since protocol data are collected in the context of the purchase situation, factors associated with that situation may assume greater importance than factors of intended usage. This could place misleading emphasis on in-store factors as determinants of competition.

B2. Perceptual Mapping includes a large family of techniques used to create a geometric representation of customer's perceptions of the qualities possessed by products/brands comprising a previously defined product-market (Green 1975). Brands are represented by locations (points or, possibly, regions) in the space. The dimensions of this space distinguish the competitive alternatives and represent benefits or costs perceived important to the purchase. Thus any product/brand might be located in such a space according to a set of coordinates which represent the extent to which the product is believed to possess each benefit or cost attribute. Relative "distances" between product alternatives may be loosely interpreted as measures of perceived substitutability of each alternative for any other.

There are several different techniques which can be used to create perceptual configurations of product-markets (e.g., direct scaling, factor analysis, multiple discriminant analysis, multidimensional scaling). Analysis may be based upon measures of perceived overall similarity/dissimilarity, perceived appropriateness to common usage situations, and correlations between attribute levels for pairs of products. Unfortunately such diversity of criteria and method can lead to somewhat different perceptual maps and possibly different product-market definitions. Much empirical research is still needed to compare the alternatives and assess which product definitions are more valid for particular purposes (Shocker and Srinivasan 1979).

When perceptual maps can be represented in two or three dimensions without destroying the data, there is a great improvement in the understanding of the competitive structure. Further, to the extent that substitutability in such a representation corresponds in some straightforward way to interproduct distance, analytic techniques such as cluster analysis (or simply looking for "open spaces" in the map) could prove useful in identifying product-market boundaries. The eventual decision must necessarily by judgmental, with the geometric representation simply facilitating that judgment. Customers or segments may also be represented in such a space by the location of their "most preferred" combinations of attribute levels—termed their ideal point.

The major advantage offered by perceptual mapping methods is versatility. Maps can be created for each major usage situation. When care is taken to control for customer knowledge of available product/brand alternatives, perceptual homogeneity may be sufficient to permit the modeling of preference and choice for different user segments within a common perceptual representation (Pessemier 1977). Moreover, perceptual maps can be created for different levels of product competition to explore competitive relations at the level of product types, variants, or brands. For example, Jain and Etgar (1975) have used multidimensional scaling to provide a geometric representation of the beverage market which incorporates all these different levels in the same configuration. These analyses become cumbersome when it is not possible to assume perceptual homogeneity. (Day, Deutscher, and Ryans 1976). Then it is necessary to cluster the respondents into homogeneous "points-of-view" groups, based on the commonality in their perceptions, and conduct a separate analysis for each group. Alternatively, one can assume that respondents use the same perceptual dimensions, but differ with respect to the weights they attach to the various dimensions.

In principle, new product concepts can be positioned in the space, or existing brands repositioned or deleted, and the effects on the individual or segment choice behavior predicted. Unfortunately, the relation between interproduct distances in the perceptual space and substitutability is not rigorously established. Stefflre (1972) has argued that a perceptual space contains only labeled regions and hence that gaps may simply represent discontinuities. The question is not whether such discontinuities in fact exist, but rather whether a preference model based upon distances from ideal-points to products remains a reasonable predictor of individual or segment behavior. If so, the decision framework of a common perceptual space coupled with models of individual/segment decision making can be used to assess the relative substitutability of different brands for each segment. These measures can then be aggregated over segments to estimate patterns of competition for the broader market.

B3. Technology Substitution Analysis adapts the idea of preference related to distance in a multiattribute space to the problem of forecasting the substitution of one material, process, or product for another—aluminum for copper in electrical applications and polyvinyl for glass in liquor bottles, for example. Each successful substitution tends to follow an S-shaped or "logistic" curve representing a slow start as initial problems and resistance to change have to be overcome, followed by more rapid progress as acceptance is gained and applications can be publicized, and finally a slowing in the pace of substitution as saturation is reached.

A simple approach to forecasting the course and speed of the substitution process is to project a function having the appropriate logistics curve, using historical data to determine its parameters (Lenz and Lanford 1972). This curve-fitting method overlooks many potential influences on the process, such as: the age, condition, and rate of obsolescence of the capital equipment used in the old technology; the price elasticity of demand; and the "utility-in-use" or relative performance advantage. Recent efforts to model substitution rates have focused on relative "utility" as the basis for improvements in forecasting ability (Stern, Ayres, and Shapanko 1975). The procedure for assessing "utility-in-use" involves: first, identifying the relevant attributes and performance characteristics of each of the competing products or technologies, followed by ratings by experts of the extent to which each alternative possesses each attribute and the perceived importance of each attribute in each end-use market. Finally, an overall utility for each product in each usage situation is obtained by multiplying the attribute possession score by the importance ratings, summing the resulting products, and adjusting for differences in unit price. While criticism can be made of the model structure and the seeming reliance on measurable physical properties to specify the attributes, the value of the basic approach should not be discounted. The outcome is a highly useful quantitive measure of utility which can be used to estimate substitutability among competing products or technologies in specific usage situations.

B4. Customer Judgments of Substitutability may be obtained in a variety of ways. The simplest is to ask a sample of customers to indicate the degree of substitutability between possible pairs of brands on a rating scale such as: none, low, some, or substantial substitutability. Beyond this familiar approach, several methods of utilizing customer judgments have recently been developed which provide far greater diagnostic insights into patterns of competition.

1. The Free Response Approach (Green, Wind, and Jain 1973). Respondents are presented with various brands and asked to free-associate the names of similar or substitute brands. Two kinds of data are obtained. One is the *frequency* of mention of one brand as a substitute for another, which could be used as a measure of similarity of the two brands in order to establish a perceptual space. Secondly, the *order of mention* of substitute brands can be treated as rank-order data (Wind 1977). These data represent an aggregate judgment across situations, and leave it to the respondent to decide how similar two brands must be before they become substitutes.

A useful variant of the free-response question asks respondents what they would do if they were unable to buy their preferred brand. One advantage of this question is that it can realistically be tailored to specific situations. For example, one study asked scotch drinkers what they would do if scotch were not available in a variety of situations, such as a large cocktail party in the early evening. Evidently, there were some situations where white wine was the preferred alternative.

2. The Dollar Metric Approach (Pessemier et al. 1970/71). Respondents first are presented with all possible pairs of brands, each of the brands being marked with their regular prices. In each case, the respondent selects the brand he/she would buy in a forced choice purchase. They are then asked the price to which the preferred brand must rise before they would switch their original preference. Strength of preference is measured in terms of this price increment. Such data must be further "processed" to compute aggregated preference measures.

This procedure is somewhat analogous to a laboratory measurement of cross-elasticity of demand. The set of potentially competitive brands must be again identified in advance. The procedure is reasonably easy to administer and analyze: although the simplicity may be eroded if considerations of intended usage, brand familiarity, and market segmentation are incorporated. It appears that respondents are able to reveal their preferences for different alternatives in the forced-choice situation. Whether they can relate validly how they arrived at the preference—by estimating the minimum price change that would cause a switch—remains an open question (Huber and James 1977).

3. Direct Grouping into Product Categories. Bourgeois, Haines, and Sommers (1979) have taken broadly related sets of brands and asked samples of customers to: (1) divide the set into as many groups as they consider meaningful, (2) explain the criteria used for each grouping, and (3) judge the similarity of the brands within each group. A measure of the similarity of brands is created by summing across customers to find the frequency with which pairs of brands are assigned to the same group. These data are analyzed by nonmetric, multidimensional scaling programs to obtain interval-scaled measures of brand similarity (according to their proximity in a reduced space). These are input to a cluster analysis routine to obtain groupings of brands regarded as "customer product types." Products are assigned to one type only. An application of this procedure to the generic "personal care" market yielded intuitively appealing groups of brands. However the data were reported to be quite "noisy," which is not surprising in view of the wide latitude given the respondents. Potentially, respondents could differ both in the frame of reference for the task (the intended application or usage) and the criterion for grouping. Some, for example, might emphasize physical similarity while others might elect appropriateness-in-use or similarity of price as the criterion.

4. *Products-By-Uses Analysis.* In the procedure developed by Stefflre (1979; Myers and Tauber 1977), a sample of customers is given a list of target products or brands and asked to conjecture as many uses for them as possible. They are then asked to suggest additional products or brands appropriate to these same uses and additional uses appropriate to these new products. This sequence of free response questions generates large lists of products/brands and potential uses. An independent sample is then asked to judge the appropriateness of each product for each use. In one study of proprietary medicines, for example, respondents were asked to judge the acceptability of each of 52 medicines for 52 conditions of use ranging from "when you have a stuffy nose" to "when the children have a fever."

Two assumptions underlie analyses of the products-by-uses matrix: (1) the set of products constitutes a representative sample of the benefits sought by customers and (2) two usage situations are similar if similar benefits are desired in both situations. If these assumptions are valid, then grouping usage situations according to similarity of products judged appropriate should be equivalent to grouping them explicitly by the benefits desired. The net result is a somewhat circular procedure:

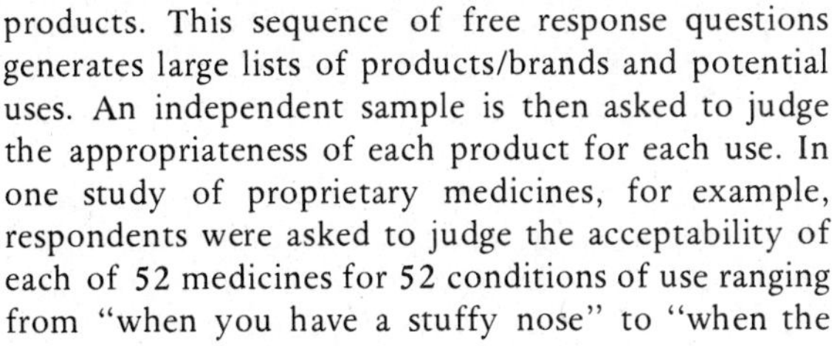

SIMILAR USAGE SITUATIONS		COMPETITIVE PRODUCTS
= those in which similar product alternatives are judged appropriate	⇄	= those judged appropriate in similar usage situations

The merits of the Stefflre (1972, 1979) procedure are first, that the introduction of specific situations gives respondents frames of reference for their judgments of substitutability or appropriateness and second, that the criteria can be modified to reflect greater concern with *potential* competition (respondents are asked which existing products or descriptions of concepts would be appropriate to specified uses) or with *actual* competition (which products they would consider for purchase in the situation). This ability to use descriptions of concepts greatly extends the flexibility of the approach to provide data relevant to actual or proposed changes in the product-market. A further advantage, shared with the direct grouping approach, is an ability to cope with large numbers of alternatives if necessary, without a requirement for large numbers of respondents because of a high degree of homogeneity in perceptual judgments.

These advantages are seemingly offset by the evident impracticability of the demands on respondents to complete a matrix with as many as 2,500 cells. For many purposes, however, it is not necessary that each respondent complete the entire matrix. A related problem is the lack of a sound basis for deciding how many situations and at what level of specificity, to include in the matrix.

5. *Substitution-In-Use Analysis.* This extends the Stefflre procedure in two directions (Srivastava, Shocker, and Day 1977). First, a separate analysis step is introduced to ensure that the set of usage situations is parsimonious and representative. If the latter condition is not met, it is likely there will be too many of one "type" of situation, with consequent distortion in the grouping of products. Secondly, the measure of appropriateness-in-use is modified to measure the degree of suitability. This is feasible as the number of situations the respondents are given is significantly smaller than in the Stefflre procedure. The result is a three-stage procedure:

1. The *exploratory* stage uses free response plus repertory grid and focused group methods to elicit usage situations associated with a generic need.
2. A *typology* of usage situations is then developed from a principal components analysis of the products-by-uses matrix (after a check for perceptual homogeneity). Both uses and products can be plotted in the reduced space described by the first two or three principal components. A typology of uses may be derived from factorial combinations of different levels of the independent dimensions of this space.
3. A new sample is employed to obtain a measure of the suitability or appropriateness of each brand or product for each of the usage situations in the typology. Each alternative can be rated

separately, or all alternatives can be ranked, within each situation.

There are several ways to analyze the resulting matrix. Insights into a firm's competitive position within distinct situational submarkets can be obtained from a principal components analysis similar to stage 2 of the procedure described above. Experience with breath fresheners and banking services (Srivastava and Shocker 1979) indicates that ideas for new products or product positions can come from the identification of inadequately served usage situations. A useful test of the effectiveness of a company's positioning efforts is the extent of variability of customer perceptions of the appropriateness of a specific brand for a distinct usage submarket. The analysis can also help assess the possibility of cannibalization. If two or more products or brands of a single manufacturer are seen as appropriate for the same usage submarket, then efforts to promote one may be at the expense of a loss in sales of the other.

The data can also be analyzed with categorical conjoint or similar procedures, as long as the factorial combinations of usage situations are properly balanced. Here the focus would be on both the patterns of competition within a usage situation and the elements of the situation which have the greatest influence on these patterns. Wind (1977) used this approach to study the relative positions of finance companies. Automobile dealers were given 16 different financing situations and asked to assign each to one of five possible financing alternatives. The situations represented combinations of six different factors including customer's credit rating, familiarity with customer, amount to finance, and length of term. The estimated utility functions suggested the degree of appropriateness of each source of financing for each level of the six factors. It was found, for example, that the client (a finance company associated with an automobile dealer) faced quite different competition depending on the amount to be financed.

Many of the advantages of the substitution-in-use approach derive from the consistency of the approach with the conceptual definition of a product-market. Despite these potential advantages, the procedure produces only a relative measure of substitutability. Managerial judgment must still decide the level of judged appropriateness that permits each product/brand to be considered as part of a situational submarket.

Summary and Conclusions

The questions of how to identify product-market boundaries cannot be separated from the ways results are to be used. Strategic or long-run definitions of market structure inevitably hold more significance even though they are mainly obtainable from customer judgments rather than behavior. Very narrowly defined boundaries appear adequate for short-run, tactical decisions in most product categories. The value of a valid and strategically relevant product-market definition lies in "stretching" the company's perceptions appropriately far enough so that significant threats and opportunities are not missed, but not so far as to dissipate information gathering and analysis efforts on "long shots." This is a difficult balance to achieve given the myriad of present and potential competitors faced by most companies.

The principal conclusions from the analysis of the nature of boundaries and the various empirical methods for identifying competitive product-markets are:

- boundaries are seldom clear-cut—ultimately, all boundaries are arbitrary,
- the suitability of different empirical methods is strongly influenced by the character of the market environment,
- on balance, those empirical methods which explicitly recognize the variety of usage situations have widest applicability and yield maximum insights. The concept of usage situation appears to be the most prevalent common denominator of market environments which can be used as the basis for empirical methods,
- most methods, particularly those based upon behavioral measures are static and have difficulty coping with changes in preferences or additions and deletions of choice alternatives in the market,
- regardless of method, the most persistent problem is the lack of defensible criteria for recognizing boundaries.

These conclusions add up to a situation where the state of knowledge has not kept abreast of either the present need to understand, or the changing technological, social, and economic factors which are constantly reshaping market environments. To redress this situation, there is a clear need for a strategically oriented program of research in a variety of market situations. Research in each market should be characterized by the use of multiple techniques to seek confirmation through cross validation and longitudinal approaches in which judgmental methods are followed by behavioral methods which can validate inferences. As we have noted, different methods have different strengths and weaknesses, and more needs to be learned about the sensitivity of results to the shortcomings of each method. Also there will inevitably be points of contradiction and consistency in the insights gained from boundaries established by different methods. The process of resolution should be most revealing, both in terms of understanding a firm's competitive position and suggesting strategy alternatives.

References

Belk, Russell (1975), "Situational Variables and Consumer Behavior," *Journal of Consumer Research,* 2 (December), 157-164.

Bettman, James R. (1971), "The Structure of Consumer Choice Processes," *Journal of Marketing Research,* 8 (November), 465-471.

Bourgeois, Jacques D., George H. Haines, and Montrose S. Sommers (1979), "Defining an Industry," paper presented to the TIMS/ORSA Special Interest Conference on Market Measurement and Analysis, Stanford, CA, March 26.

Butler, Ben Jr. and David H. Butler (1970 and 1971), "Hendrodynamics: Fundamental Laws of Consumer Dynamics," Hendry Corp., Croton-on-Hudson, NY, Chapter 1 (1970) and Chapter 2 (1971).

Cocks, Douglas L. and John R. Virts (1975), "Market Definition and Concentration in the Ethical Pharmaceutical Industry," Internal publication of Eli Lilly and Co., Indianapolis.

Day, George S. (1977), "Diagnosing The Product Portfolio," *Journal of Marketing,* 41 (April), 29-38.

——, Terry Deutscher, and Adrian Ryans (1976), "Data Quality, Level of Aggregation and Nonmetric Multidimensional Scaling Solutions," *Journal of Marketing Research,* 13 (February), 92-97.

——, William F. Massy, and Allan D. Shocker (1978), "The Public Policy Context of The Relevant Market Question," in *Public Policy Issues in Marketing,* John F. Cady, ed., Cambridge, MA: Marketing Science Institute, 51-67.

Frank, Ronald, William F. Massy, and Yoram Wind (1973), *Market Segmentation,* Englewood Cliffs, NJ: Prentice-Hall, Inc.

Goldman, Alfred and Susan S. McDonald (1979), "Occasion Segmentation," paper presented to American Marketing Association Attitude Research Conference, Hilton Head, S.C., Feb. 25-28.

Green, Paul E. (1975), "Marketing Applications of MDS: Assessment and Outlook," *Journal of Marketing,* 39 (January), 24-31.

——, Yoram Wind, and Arun K. Jain (1973), "Analyzing Free Response Data in Marketing Research," *Journal of Marketing Research,* 10 (February), 45-52.

Haines, George H. (1974), "Process Models of Consumer Decision-Making." in *Buyer/Consumer Information Processing,* G. D. Hughes and M. L. Ray, eds., Chapel Hill, NC: University of North Carolina Press.

Hanon, Mack (1974), "Reorganize Your Company Around Its Markets," *Harvard Business Review,* 79 (November-December), 63-74.

Huber, Joel and Bill James (1977), "The Monetary Worth of Physical Attributes: A Dollarmetric Approach," in *Moving A Head with Attitude Research,* Yoram Wind and Marshall Greenberg, eds., Chicago: American Marketing Association.

Jain, Arun K. and Michael Etgar (1975), "How to Improve Antitrust Policies with Marketing Research Tools," in *1975 Combined Proceedings of the American Marketing Association,* Edward M. Mazze, ed., Chicago: American Marketing Association, 72-75.

Kalwani, Manohar U. and Donald G. Morrison (1977), "A Parsimonious Description of the Hendry System," *Management Science,* 23 (January), 476-477.

Lenz, Ralph C. Jr. and H. W. Lanford (1972), "The Substitution Phenomena," *Business Horizons,* 15 (February), 63-68.

Lunn, Tony (1972), "Segmenting and Constructing Markets," in *Consumer Market Research Handbook,* R. M. Worcester, ed. Maidenhead, Berkshire: McGraw-Hill.

Lutz, Richard J. and Pradeep Kakkar (1976), "Situational Influence in Interpersonal Persuasion," in *Advances in Consumer Research,* Vol. III, Beverlee R. Anderson, Atlanta: Association for Consumer Research, 370-378.

McFadden, Daniel (1970), "Conditional Logit Analysis of Qualitative Choice Behavior" in *Frontiers in Econometrics,* P. Zarembka, ed., New York: Academic Press, 105-142.

Miller, Kenneth E. and James L. Ginter (1979), "An Investigation of Situational Variation in Brand Choice Behavior and Attitude," *Journal of Marketing Research,* 16 (February), 111-123.

Moran, William R. (1973), "Why New Products Fail," *Journal of Advertising Research,* 13 (April), 5-13.

Myers, James H. and Edward Tauber (1977), *Market Structure Analysis*, Chicago: American Marketing Association.

Needham, Douglas (1969), *Economic Analysis and Industrial Structure*, New York: Holt, Rinehart, and Winston, Chapter 2.

Pessemier, Edgar A. (1977), *Product Management: Strategy and Organization*, Santa Barbara, CA: Wiley/Hamilton, 203–254.

——, Philip Burger, Richard Teach, and Douglas Tigert (1970/1971), "Using Laboratory Brand Preference Scales to Predict Consumer Brand Purchases," *Management Science*, 17 (February), 371–385.

Rubison, Joel R. and Frank M. Bass (1978). "A Note on 'A Parsimonious Description of the Hendry System,'" paper 658, West Lafayette, IN: Krannert School, Purdue, March.

Scherer, Frederic (1970), *Industrial Market Structure and Economic Performance*, Chicago: Rand McNally.

Shocker, Allan D. and V. Srinivasan (1979), "MultiAttribute Applications for Product Concept Evaluation and Generation: A Critical Review," *Journal of Marketing Research*, 16 (May), 159–180.

Sissors, Jack Z. (1966), "What is a Market?" *Journal of Marketing*, 30 (July), 17–21.

Srivastava, Rajendra and Allan D. Shocker (1979), "The Validity/Reliability of a Method for Developing Product-Specific Usage Situational Taxonomies," working paper, Pittsburgh: University of Pittsburgh, Graduate School of Business (September).

——, ——, and George S. Day (1978), "An Exploratory Study of Situational Effects on Product Market Definition," in *Advances in Consumer Research*, Vol. V, H. Keith Hunt, ed., Ann Arbor: Association for Consumer Research, 32–38.

Stefflre, Volney (1972), "Some Applications of Multidimensional Scaling to Social Science Problems," in *Multidimensional Scaling: Theory and Applications in the Behavioral Sciences*, Vol. III, A. K. Romney, R. N. Shepard, and S. B. Nerlove, eds., New York: Seminar Press.

—— (1979), "New Products: Organizational and Technical Problems and Opportunities," in *Analytic Approaches to Product and Marketing Planning*, A. D. Shocker, ed., Cambridge, MA: Marketing Science Institute, April Report 79-104, 415–480.

Stern, M. O., R. V. Ayres, and A. Shapanko (1975), "A Model for Forecasting the Substitution of One Technology for Another," *Technological Forecasting and Social Change*, 7 (February), 57–79.

Stout, Roy G., Raymond H. S. Suh, Marshall G. Greenberg, and Joel S. Dubow (1977), "Usage Incidents as a Basis for Segmentation," in *Moving A Head with Attitude Research*, Yoram Wind and Marshall Greenberg, eds., Chicago: American Marketing Association.

Strotz, Robert H. (1957), "The Empirical Implications of a Utility Tree," *Econometrica*, 25 (April), 269–280.

——, and John R. Hauser (1979), "Market Definition" in *Design and Marketing of New Products and Services*, Cambridge, MA: MIT, Sloan School of Management, Ch. 5.

Vernon, John (1972), *Market Structure and Industrial Performance*, Boston: Allyn and Bacon.

Wind, Yoram (1977), "The Perception of a Firm's Competitive Position," in *Behavioral Models for Market Analysis*, F. M. Nicosia and Y. Wind, eds., New York: The Dryden Press, 163–181.

CHAPTER SIX

Consumer Behavior and Pricing Policy

READING 24

An Experiment in Brand Choice

P. Charlton and A. S. C. Ehrenberg

The experiment shows how effects of marketing action on the consumer can be investigated by use of small ad hoc consumer panels and door-to-door selling. The effects of price differentials, a promotion, advertising, an out-of-stock condition, the introduction of a new product, and certain weak forms of brand differentiation are examined. The experiment also confirms earlier findings that buyer behavior under semi-artificial conditions resembles that in real life.

Introduction

The study of consumer dynamics—how people change their purchasing habits—is facilitated greatly by experiments in which marketing factors are deliberately varied. The cost of such experimentation in the marketplace is usually prohibitive (both in real terms and in terms of risk to existing sales), but experiments under artificial conditions are more practicable.

One such experiment, reported herein, is a followup and extension of an earlier similar study [7]. Once a large series of such experiments has led to a consistent body of new knowledge and understanding under experimental conditions, practical relevance can be established in a relatively small number of validation checks and prototype applications under real life marketplace conditions.

The experimental procedure used consisted of offering a panel of consumers the opportunity to buy certain artificial "brands" of a product week after week. In the earlier experiment this procedure was explored and the growth of normal brand loyalty, the effects of brand "names" on brand choice, and the effects of a short price promotion were reported.

The new experiment tested the earlier findings for repeatability, checked on certain suggestions and unsolved problems that had arisen, assessed the price promotion at two different stages of brand loyalty (by use of a split-run design), and extended the scope of the study by introducing a second product field, a price differential, a form of brand advertising, a new brand, an out-of-stock condition, and attitudinal questions.

Experimental Design

The experiment was conducted in the UK by means of doorstep selling during 25 weeks. A quota sample of 180 housewives, of whom 158 successfully completed the experiment, were given the opportunity each week to buy one pack from a small number of brands in each of two product fields—detergent, as in the previous experiment, and leaf tea. The brands available were artificial, the detergent being sold at 8 pence in blank "large size" packs coded with the letters C, J, M, and V, and the tea being sold in blank ¼ lb. packs coded 4, 5, and 6. The tea codes also represented the prices, in UK new pence, at which the housewives could buy the three brands (about half the normal UK market prices then). The brands did not differ in product formulation, but this was not made known explicitly to the housewives taking part.

As in the previous experiment, housewives were recruited deliberately from among heavy users of detergents. They were not obliged to buy every week but were encouraged to do so and, on average, each week more than 90% of those contacted did buy. They were not constrained from buying detergent or

Reprinted by permission of the American Marketing Association, from the *Journal of Marketing Research,* 13:2 May 1976, 152–160.

tea from sources outside the experiment. A fuller account of the experimental procedure is given in [7].

At the start of such an experiment buyer behavior is very dynamic, with the housewives experimenting and switching between the unfamiliar brands. A few weeks at least are required before their behavior approaches stationarity. The subsequent marketing inputs to the present experiment (with the same random split-half design throughout) were:

- *A promotion*—2p off the price (8p) of the Brand J detergent (split-run in weeks 7–9 as in the first experiment, and in weeks 13–15 when brand loyalty had developed further).
- *Advertising*—slogans attached to the 4p and 6p teas (split-run in weeks 10–12 and in weeks 16–18).
- *Out-of-stock condition*—Brand M detergent made unavailable (split-run in week 21 and for twice the period in weeks 22–23).
- *New brand*—tea bags introduced (total panel in weeks 19–21 and then withdrawn).

The housewives were asked to express their attitudes toward the different brands of the experiment, once fairly early (at weeks 5 and 6) and again at the end, when they also were asked to give their opinion of the experiment itself. (Most housewives thought there were differences between the experimental brands—82% in the case of detergent and 94% in the case of tea. About 40% thought the purpose of the experiment was to assess the differences between brands and 20% thought it was to help launch a new brand. When asked how loyal they thought they were to their normal brands of washing powder and tea, about 80% of housewives said they were "loyal" to their normal brand.)

Brand Loyalty

The previous experiment [7] and other studies [e.g., 10, 13] had shown that housewives exhibited considerable brand switching (search behavior) under the initial impact of the unfamiliar brands. As the experiments proceeded, however, more normal buyer behavior developed. The same general pattern was found in the present experiment.

First Few Weeks

The initial weeks of the experiment were characterized by much switching among the brands, most housewives adopting a deliberate search procedure of trying each brand in turn.

For detergents the first 6 weeks of the experiment repeated the earlier study and, except in one respect, the results produced were much the same. For example, in the first experiment 73% of housewives had tried all 4 brands of detergent by the time of their sixth purchase and in the present experiment the figure was about the same at 70%. As a consequence high penetration levels quickly were achieved, 83% after 4 weeks for the average brand in the first experiment and 79% in the present one. The only basis for brand choice was whatever the housewives themselves read into the brand names C, J, M, and V. Yet this coding alone was sufficient to create clear brand preferences. In the first experiment most housewives' initial purchase was of Brand M (42%) and only a few (6%) choice Brand V. (Brand V quickly caught up subsequently, in the general process of the search procedure). In the present experiment the results were in the same direction, M again being most preferred at the first purchase (32%) and V least (18%), but the differential was not as large; the difference between the two experiments was statistically highly significant (a χ^2 value of more than 9 with 3 degrees of freedom). The only known difference in procedure between the two experiments was the presence of the extra product field, tea. Perhaps faced with *two* sets of artificial brands, the housewives felt that less significance (i.e., hidden meaning) lay behind the code letters C, J, M, and V. (This hypothesis can be tested readily in a later experiment when samples of detergent and tea are again available; only a split-run involving a single purchase is required.)

For tea the brand choice facing the housewives at initial purchase involved a price differential, which provided a more "rational" basis for choice. The first few purchases of tea showed the same signs of deliberate search behavior among the housewives as were found in the case of detergent. Again about 70% of housewives had tried all the brands of tea by their sixth purchase, which is a high percentage even with only *three* brands to choose from.

The favorite first choice was the middle-priced 5p tea (56%), which seems reasonable. With three unknown brands, buying the most expensive may have been thought of as rash, whereas the association of price with perceived quality might have acted against the cheapest brand. An alternative interpretation could be that, faced with a choice between three consecutive numbers, 4, 5, and 6, most people choose the middle one. However, in McConnell's experiment with a price differential [10–12], three artificial brands of beer were labeled L, M, and P, L being the *middle-priced* brand. The fact that it received the most initial purchases would argue in favor of the more "rational" explanation of the housewives' initial preference for Brand 5.

Growth of Brand Loyalty

The high level of brand switching observed in the first few weeks did not last. After the period of search, buyer behavior began to settle down as illustrated by the 3-week penetration levels and average buying frequency levels. These useful forms of analysis are discussed elsewhere [3]. The average figures summarized in Table 1 reflect those for the individual brands (the comparable results from the earlier study are documented more fully in [7]).

The pattern for each brand in the first half of the experiment was a downward trend of penetration and an upward trend of the average buying frequency. From this is seen the development of brand loyalty. Initially most housewives bought *each* brand in a 3-week period (penetrations of more than 50%), but few bought any one brand more than once (low average buying frequency). As the experiment progressed some housewives developed preferences for certain brands and bought those brands more often than others. The total number of people buying any one brand in a 3-week period fell, and the average buying frequency per buyer (a measure of repeat buying) rose. The figures then steadied in the second half of the experiment.

Stationary Buyer Behavior

The higher level of repeat buying was not the prerogative of any one brand, there being little difference between the brands in terms of average buying frequency. Instead, what differentiated Brand M from Brand V, for example, or the 5p tea from the 6p tea, was that in each case the more successful of the two brands had more buyers. This feature of buyer behavior is found in the real-life marketplace [6].

In the first experiment under such semilaboratory conditions most other patterns of buyer behavior also were similar to those observed in real life, e.g., the numbers of housewives buying 0, 1, 2, etc. packs in a given time period, the way penetration and average buying frequency increased with increasing length of time period, and repeat buying and brand duplication behavior. The method used was to compare the experimental data with the NBD and certain multi-brand buying models which are known to summarize the corresponding patterns generally observed for data from large national consumer panels [6]. Analyses of data from other artificial buying situations have given similar results [3, 4], and the present experiment confirms these findings.

In the earlier experiment only the repeat buying behavior differed somewhat from that described by the NBD model. For each of the four brands of detergent the number of housewives repeat buying, i.e., buying in two consecutive 3-week periods, was 20% higher than the theoretical NBD level. The same is true of 3-week repeat buying in the present experiment for both detergent and tea. However, as noted earlier [7], it is a feature of the theory that even under stationary real-life conditions the theoretical model often underpredicts the level of repeat buying

TABLE 1
Three-Week Penetrations and Average Buying Frequencies for the Average Brand in Each Product Field

	3-Week Periods (Week Numbers)							
Product Field	*1–3*	*4–6*	*7–9*	*10–12*	*13–15*	*16–18*	*19–21*	*22–24*
Detergent								
Penetration	63	53	51[a]	47	42[a]	43	44	49[b]
Av. buying freq.	1.1	1.3	1.3	1.4	1.5	1.5	1.5	1.5
Tea								
Penetration	76	55	50	50	44	47	21[c]	40
Av. buying freq.	1.2	1.5	1.8	1.7	1.7	1.9	1.8	2.1

a. Promotion of Brand J detergent.
b. Brand M detergent out of stock.
c. Tea bags available during weeks 19–21 only.

in time periods as short as 3 weeks (due to a breakdown of the underlying Poisson assumption for *very* short time periods—see [6]). The design of the first experiment, however, precluded the examination of stationary repeat buying in time periods longer than 3 weeks.

In the present experiment, despite the intrusion of various pieces of marketing activity in 3-weekly cycles, it was possible to select two adjacent 6-week periods in which the sales of three detergent brands, J, M, and V, each approximated stationarity (i.e., to within ±10% or less). The results of the repeat buying analyses are shown in Table 2. Clearly in the longer time period, with a nearly stationary situation, the level of repeat buying of detergent in the experiment was close to that predicted by the NBD model.

For tea it was also possible to find nearly stationary 6-week periods for the 4p and 6p teas (different periods in each case and only in one half of the panel) and the observed and theoretical NBD results were again in close agreement. Hence the relatively high 3-week repeat buying level is seen to be due to the short time period involved.

The results reported in this section confirm and extend the major findings of the earlier experiment. In particular, they show that "brand loyalty" can develop for totally unfamiliar brands in the presence of very weak brand stimuli—for detergents, just the brand codes C, J, M, and V. Further, the kind of buyer behavior these artificial circumstances generate is like normal real-life buyer behavior.

TABLE 2
Brand Penetrations and Percentage of Repeat Buyers in Two Adjacent 6-Week Periods (Observed and Theoretical Results)

	Penetration		*Percentage Repeat Buying*	
Detergent Brand	*Weeks 12–17*	*Weeks 18–23*	*O*	*T*
J	67	68	79	77
M	66	61	74	73
V	60	58	71	69
Average	64	62	75	73

Market Stimuli

The various market stimuli presented to the housewives were of an exploratory nature, to determine what could be achieved within a limited framework under semilaboratory conditions. For example, could an effective advertising campaign be mounted? What would be the effect of introducing a new brand or an out-of-stock situation at a stage when brand loyalty had developed? And would any effects generalize to other experiments?

A Promotion

The price promotion of Brand J detergent lasted for 3 weeks at two different times—for one half of the housewives during weeks 7–9 as in the first study, and for the other half during weeks 13–15.

Compared with average 3-week figures of about 40% buying 1.4 times, Brand J achieved a 95% penetration and an average buying frequency of 2.5 in weeks 7–9. These levels replicated the weeks 7–9 results in the *first* experiment (87% buying 2.4 times). The effect was much greater than would be observed in real life. Possibly brand loyalty had hardly developed at this stage. But the promotion during weeks 13–15, when something like brand loyalty had developed, was also very effective, even though the impact was in fact smaller, with 71% of housewives buying J. Other possible reasons for these dramatic results are that the price cut was relatively large (2p off the usual price of 8p), that the offer received 100% exposure, or that the artificiality of the experiment created a form of "hot housing." This can be tested in subsequent work by determining whether other possibly less attractive forms of promotion still produce unexpectedly large results.

Several more detailed results are noteworthy. First, analysis of several real-life promotions has shown that although extra sales may be attracted, those to repeat buyers (people buying both before and during the promotion) may be relatively unaffected [e.g., 6, pp. 107–15; 8]. This effect was found also in the *later* promotion (in the weeks 7–9 promotion virtually everyone was affected anyway).

In the first experiment there was a slight but possibly statistically significant suggestion that brand loyalty was stronger for the promoted Brand J than for the other brands of detergent *after the promotion* (an above-average purchase frequency).

Checking on this effect in the present experiment produced no evidence to confirm that it occurred; that it did not must be the effective conclusion for *both* experiments.

More generally, repeat buying analyses of the periods immediately before and just after the promotion gave results similar to those of analyses of the same two time periods for the half of the panel where no promotion intervened. The promotion therefore seems to have had no disturbing effect beyond its actual duration, as has been observed also in some real-life cases [e.g., 6]. This phenomenon is a technical advantage when operating within the limited time span of such an experiment, but if more widely confirmed it is of course of major importance for practical marketing management.

A suggestion in the present data is that the weeks 7–9 promotion seemed to accelerate the overall development of brand loyalty in its half of the panel, in terms of the general trend toward lower penetration levels and higher average frequencies of purchase. This effect needs confirmation, but a promotion near the beginning of such an experiment therefore might be used to bring about normal buying behavior more quickly. Such a result also would have much more general implications for new-brand introductions.

The interaction between the promoted and unpromoted brands before, during, and after the promotion is summarized in Table 3. During the promotion the three unpromoted brands lost penetration, and hence sales, heavily and by approximately equal amounts, but recovered quickly afterward. The lost sales were almost entirely the result of a fall in penetration, i.e., the number of people buying. The average frequency with which the remaining buyers bought the unpromoted brands was largely unchanged by the promotion, so that these remaining buyers were not exceptionally heavy (i.e., loyal) buyers of the unpromoted brands. Clearly, these findings aid the understanding of how promotions work.

TABLE 3
Brand J and Average of Other Detergents in 3-Week Periods Before, During, and After Promotion

	Penetration			*Av. Buying Frequency*		
	Before	*During*	*After*	*Before*	*During*	*After*
Early promotion						
Brand J	44	95	42	1.2	2.5	1.4
Av. other brands	55	10	43	1.3	1.4	1.5
Later promotion						
Brand J	51	71	38	1.3	2.2	1.4
Av. other brands	51	36	48	1.4	1.3	1.5

Advertising

In the case of the promotion of Brand J detergent a dramatic effect was expected and achieved. The corresponding marketing factor for tea was advertising and here the question was whether a detectable effect would be produced at all in the study context.

The following slogans were associated with the 4p and 6p teas for 3 weeks:

4p tea: "an improved blend at the same price"
6p tea: "the tea with the smaller leaf for faster brewing"

in the form of display cards shown to the housewives at the time of purchase, in weeks 10–12 for one half of the panel, and in weeks 16–18 for the other half.

In each case penetration increased during the campaigns, as set out in Table 4; the effects were mostly small, but overall statistically significant, especially in the context of generally decreasing penetrations at about weeks 10–12 (Table 1). But the average 3-weekly *buying frequencies* remained at about 1.7 or 1.8 purchases per buyer and showed no significant systematic difference between the advertised and nonadvertised brands.

The increase in penetration was large only for the 4p tea during weeks 16–18. Why the effect should

TABLE 4
Advertising: 3-Week Penetrations Before, During, and After Campaigns

	3-Week Penetrations					
Tea Brand	*Before*	*Weeks 10–12*	*After*	*Before*	*Weeks 16–18*	*After*[a]
4p	49	52	44	40	60	(27)
6p	45	50	39	33	40	(17)
5p	64	54	52	53	44	(31)

a. Tea bags were available during the 3-week period.

be strongest for the cheaper tea, and later in the experiment rather than earlier (unlike the promotional effect), cannot yet be explained, nor can it even be tested rigorously for statistical significance. It may not be a repeatable result, but its size makes it worth examining in more detail.

The buyers of a brand during the campaign can be divided into two groups—"repeat buyers" who also had bought the brand in the period before, i.e., weeks 13–15, and so-called "new" buyers, who had not. Comparison with the other half of the panel (who were not at that time exposed to the advertising) indicates how many buyers in each category were extra "new" buyers attracted by the campaign, and how many were extra repeat buyers. (The use of the otherwise more powerful theoretical repeat buying norms is difficult for such short periods, as was noted.) This comparison showed that the level of "repeat buying" of the advertised brands was virtually unaffected, the extra buyers attracted for both the 4p and 6p teas mainly being of the "new" buyers category, i.e., housewives who had not bought the brands in question in the 3 weeks before the campaign, and who therefore would at best be relatively infrequent buyers. (Analyses over still longer periods were precluded by the experimental design.) The 4p tea, with the largest number of extra buyers, attracted three times as many such "new" buyers when advertised as when not. These extra buyers of the 4p and 6p brands naturally came from the 5p brand. This brand lost buyers (Table 4), and the indications are that it did so by failing to retain its "normal" number of repeat buyers.

The present experiment was not designed to assess the longer term effect of the advertising slogans. But in the one case where a large effect was noted, for the 4p tea, the brand suffered less than the other brands from the introduction of tea bags that followed immediately after the campaign. However, one should not read too much into one observation (a formal test of significance is not possible). A more clear-cut finding is that when the tea bags were withdrawn, the sales of the 4p tea returned to the same level as before the advertising campaign. If there *was* a real aftereffect (i.e., one which generalizes to other such cases) it would not have lasted very long!

Out-of-Stock Condition

Toward the end of the experiment Brand M detergent was withdrawn from sale for 1 or 2 weeks. The housewives were told that this brand was temporarily out of stock.

Most housewives did not seem to have any problem in substituting other purchases for Brand M. Those who did not buy detergents at all then were light buyers of the product field in general who probably would not have bought anyway. The total sales of detergents did not fall significantly during Brand M's absence and the other brands gained sales, 50% for Brand J and 30% for the other two brands. Why Brand J benefited most from Brand M being out of stock is difficult to pin down at this stage, but it may have been a consequence in some way of J's earlier promotion. Although this promotion had no aftereffects in terms of explicit buyer behavior, perhaps it gave J an added identity that enabled it, more than the other brands, to exploit the absence of Brand M. Or the advantage may have been the effect of housewives' more extensive *experience* of J. The same kind of speculation was mooted in the case of the 4p tea proving most resistant to the impact of tea bags after the advertising campaign. The possibilities can be tested by further experiments of this kind.

The most important result to emerge from the temporary withdrawal of Brand M concerned its subsequent sales. These sales did not seem to be affected at all. When M became available again, its sales were at once at the same level as before it went out of stock. The sales of the other brands also reverted to the same levels as before the out-of-stock condition. This result would be significant if it could be shown to generalize. Marketing management invests considerable resources to avoid going out of stock, without knowing what the real cost of such a situation is. If it can be shown, as this experiment suggests, that the cost in terms of the consumer generally is confined to the period when the brand is actually out of stock, the value of keeping a brand continually in stock could be assessed better.

A New Brand

During weeks 19–21 the housewives were given the opportunity to buy tea bags as an alternative to the three brands of leaf tea. The introduction of the tea bags proved very successful. Tea bags achieved a 70% penetration level during the 3 weeks they were available, and about 40% of housewives bought nothing else. Consequently the three brands of *leaf* tea suffered considerable losses in sales. Sales of the 4p and 6p teas were 60% below their level before the arrival of tea bags; the 5p tea, the brand leader, showed a 40% loss.

These losses in sales were reflected in a reduction in the number of buyers each brand attracted. The average frequency with which they bought was largely unaffected. (The same effect was noted for detergents C, M, and V while Brand J was being promoted.) The housewives who continued to buy a brand despite strong competition therefore were not as a group exceptionally heavy buyers of that brand.

After the tea bags ceased to be available, sales of the three brands of leaf tea returned to their previous levels. Individual buyer behavior also showed no aftereffects; repeat buying between the 6 weeks immediately before the introduction of tea bags and the 3 weeks after their withdrawal (and before the experiment finished) compared closely with the NBD expectations of what would have happened under normal stationary conditions, i.e., without any "blips" in sales.

Lack of Aftereffects

None of the four marketing stimuli introduced during the experiment produced significant aftereffects. This finding is of considerable interest. First, it makes it possible to draw simple conclusions from experiments of this type where several stimuli are applied in a limited time span. Second, it has a direct bearing on the assessment of learning models in the realm of consumer behavior [e.g., 12, 14]; in the present experiment linear learning models would not explain the immediate recoveries after each marketing stimulus ceased (e.g., of Brand M after the out-of-stock situation). Third, and most significant, if the lack of aftereffects can be generalized and extended to the marketplace, there are practical implications for marketing management in the areas of promotion, advertising, distribution, and new brand competition.

Consumer Attitudes

The foregoing analysis has been solely in terms of what brands housewives bought. This section concerns what they said about the various brands when their attitudes were assessed.

The method chosen to measure attitudes had been used commercially for several years and was easy to administer [9]. For each product field the interviewer had a list of seven pairs of statements, relating to the positive or negative aspect of a product attribute, such as "lather" for detergents.

> "It makes a better lather than most powders do."
> "It doesn't make as good a lather as some powders do."

After each statement had been read out by the interviewer the housewife was asked to name any of the brands in the experiment for which she thought the statement was true. The same attitude questionnaire was administered twice during the experiment, early in week 5 or 6 when the initial period of search behavior was coming to an end and the housewives had had a chance to try all brands, and again in week 25 after they had made their final purchase.

Three aspects of the results can be reported, the difference between brands (brand image), the relationship between attitudes and brand usage, and the changes in attitude and usage that occurred during the course of the experiment.

Brand Image

An established attitude measurement technique generally produces a known kind of results [e.g., 1, 2]. For example, it is known that, for many different attribute statements in many different product fields, the larger a brand is in terms of usership, the more positive attitudinal responses it generally attracts. In addition, there are occasional large deviations, usually relating to any real physical differences between brands, e.g., in color, texture, perfume, price, etc.

In line with these general findings, the 5p brand of tea, which attracted the highest usership level, also attracted the most positive responses for all attributes except one. The exception was "strength," for which the *highest priced* (6p) tea received the highest positive attitude response. Although this was the brand with the lowest usership level, it was in fact more highly regarded than the 4p tea on all attributes. This special association between attitude and price was strongest for those attribute statements relating to quality, to flavor, and to strength itself.

For detergents there were no significant differences between the brands in terms of the attitude responses. This finding conforms with the real-life results as there were also no differences in ultimate usership levels or in product formulation.

Attitudes and "Loyal" Users

The foregoing discussion of the attitude responses has considered only whether or not a housewife had bought a brand at all. Now more detailed aspects of buyer behavior are taken into account.

Mutually exclusive groups of "loyal" users of a brand of tea have been defined as those buying a brand four or more times in a certain 6-week period that was free of marketing activity. (Use of a stronger criterion, e.g., five purchases or more, or 100% loyalty, would have given too few people; even so the base numbers are still small.) Table 5 shows the level of positive attitude response given by these "loyal" users of a brand of tea for that brand and other brands, averaged across all attributes other than "strength." For example, of the housewives who were "loyal" to the 4p tea, 77% named it in response to the average positive attribute statement, but only 41% of them named the 5p tea and 37% the 6p tea. This pattern recurs for the other two brands, the high diagonal figures in the table being statistically highly significant. (The loyal buyers of the 6p tea gave relatively few responses to the two other—cheaper—brands, but the statistical significance of this added factor cannot be assessed.)

The pattern of response for the attribute "strength" was somewhat different. The influence of price was evident. Only 30% of the loyal users of the 4p tea thought that brand "made a strong tea" in comparison with the average of 77% in Table 5 for the other attributes; perhaps these loyal buyers of the 4p tea wanted a weak tea and were led by the price differential into believing that this was what they were getting. At the other end of the price scale, *none* of the loyal users of the 6p tea thought either of the other two brands was a strong tea.

TABLE 5
Brand Loyalty and Level of Positive Attribute Response for Tea (Average Attribute at Week 25)

Loyal Users of		*% Giving Positive Response for* 4p	5p	6p
4p	32	77	41	37
5p	41	32	78	49
6p	23	22	26	82

For detergents, the absence of a sufficient number of heavy buyers makes a similar analysis unprofitable. But the relationship between attitudes and behavior can be turned around. Those housewives who gave a positive attitudinal response to a brand bought it more often during the 25 weeks (7 times on average) than those who gave a negative response (5 times on average). The difference was perhaps not dramatically large, but it was fairly consistent from brand to brand and from attribute to attribute.

For tea the corresponding analysis shows an even more marked association between attitude and behavior. On average housewives giving a brand a negative response bought it only half as often as those giving a positive response—averages of 5 and 10 purchases, respectively.

Attitude Change

Finally, the attitudinal responses given at week 5 or 6 and those given at week 25 can be distinguished. On aggregate there were only slight differences. Changes occurring for tea reflected an increasing influence of price, but they were small, and were significant only in that they were consistent across the attributes. More generally, a small net increase of a percentage point or two in the incidence of responses, positive or negative, occurred the second time the questions were asked. However, at the level of the individual housewife there was more change; about 50% changed their minds for the average brand and attribute. Most of the changes involved housewives moving into or out of the "no response" category. Nevertheless, some housewives' responses involved a complete reversal in their expressed attitude toward a brand on a specific attribute.

It seems to be widely assumed that repeated administration of an attitude questionnaire cannot measure attitude change. The first questionnaire is thought to interfere with the second; housewives may remember their responses and just repeat them; or perhaps they "forget" and any differences measured are due to "error." In the present study there was certainly no overwhelming consistency between the two responses. But to assess whether any of the changes were *real*, it is now shown that a change in response tended to correspond with a change in behavior.

The period of the experiment was divided into two halves. Table 6 shows how much the sales of each brand changed between the two halves for those people whose attitude responses showed a positive

TABLE 6
Attitude Change and Behavioral Change

	Percentage Increase in Sales	
	Positive Attitude Shift	*Negative Attitude Shift*
Detergents		
Brand C	15	−22
Brand J	32	−16
Brand M	7	−25
Brand V	30	−36
Average	21	−25
Tea		
4p	0	−24
5p	17	−32
6p	0	−61
Average	6	−39

shift and for those whose responses showed a negative shift, averaged across each of the attitudinal measures.

The housewives who increased their opinion of a brand generally bought that brand more often in the second half than in the first (4 positive, 2 zero, and 0 negative results). Those whose opinion declined generally bought less in the second half than in the first (7 out of 7 negative results). The differences in some cases were small but they were consistent not only on average but also for most individual attitudes. More work of this type is needed, but it seems that the attitude changes measured in this experiment reflected something real. It is not possible, however, to tell which changed first, attitudes or behavior, as the experiment was not designed for that purpose.

Conclusions

This study is the second of two similar experiments on consumer dynamics. It confirms and extends the earlier findings.

The evaluation of experimental buyer behavior under *stationary* conditions turned out to be simple because there is a generalized body of knowledge which summarizes stationary behavior in real life and the same patterns were found to recur under the experimental conditions. But for the *dynamic* situation, of course, there is no such body of real-life knowledge. Indeed, these experiments were directed toward producing some generalizable results under dynamic market conditions. Two things are required if this is to be achieved. First, many experiments must be conducted to determine whether results generalize even within the experimental context. Second, once a reliable and coherent body of experimental results has been built up, their validity must be tested in the marketplace.

This later stage of translation to real life probably will not always be a direct or easy one, e.g., for the detergent promotion, which appeared to be much too "successful." The experimental situation may act as a "hothouse" for certain market stimuli. But the experimentation can be used to assist tactical decisions, e.g., not so much for assessing absolute levels or for deciding whether promotions are generally more effective than advertising, but for comparing two or more relatively similar promotional devices and determining which works "better" [c.f. 5], and in particular also for learning *how* they work.

The main purpose of the experimentation is in fact to increase *understanding* of consumer dynamics. The technique can be used to generate experimentally based hypotheses or theories about buyer behavior. One such hypothesis is the limitation to the short term of the effects of the marketing stimuli used here. This limitation would be important if it extends to real life.

The results of the two experiments reported must be augmented by many more. What about different kinds of promotion? Different (and more "realistic") forms of advertising? What if the promotion had been tried in the presence of a price differential and the advertising not? And in addition to attempting to simulate direct marketing action, one can introduce artificial variations designed to elucidate consumer choice behavior as such—for example, the nature of price factors could be clarified by the simple device of assessing consumer choice of the 6p tea when the 4, 5, and 6p prices are increased evenly to 5, 6, and 7p or when only the two top prices are changed, say to 4, 6, and 8p. And so on.

At the present stage of investigation, each experiment opens up many new questions, as well as answering several old ones. But one fact which clearly has emerged is that experiments conducted within the semilaboratory framework discussed herein are an effective means of investigating consumer behavior.

References

1. Bird, M. and A. S. C. Ehrenberg. "Consumer Attitudes and Brand Usage," *Journal of Market Research Society,* 12 (October 1970), 233–47.
2. Chakrapani, T. K. and A. S. C. Ehrenberg. "The Pattern of Consumer Attitudes." Aapor-Wapor Conference, Lake George, New York, 1974.
3. Charlton, P. and A. S. C. Ehrenberg. "McConnell's Experimental Brand Choice Data," *Journal of Marketing Research,* 10 (August 1973), 302–7.
4. —— and B. Pymont. "Buyer Behaviour Under Mini-Test Conditions," *Journal of Market Research Society,* 14 (July 1972), 171–83.
5. —— and ——. "The Evaluation of Marketing Alternatives," *Journal of Market Research Society,* 17 (April 1975), 90–103.
6. Ehrenberg, A. S. C. *Repeat-Buying: Theory and Applications.* Amsterdam: North Holland. New York: American Elsevier, 1972.
7. —— and P. Charlton. "An Analysis of Simulated Brand-Choice," *Journal of Advertising Research,* 13 (February 1973), 21–33.
8. —— and G. J. Goodhardt. "The Evaluation of a Consumer Deal," *Admap,* 5 (September 1969), 388–93.
9. Joyce, T. "Techniques of Brand Image Measurement," in *New Developments in Research.* London: Market Research Society, 1963, 45–63. Also in A. S. C. Ehrenberg and G. F. Pyatt, eds., *Consumer Behaviour.* London and Baltimore: Penguin Books, 1970.
10. McConnell, J. Douglas. "The Development of Brand Loyalty: An Experimental Study," *Journal of Marketing Research,* 5 (February 1968), 13–19.
11. ——. "The Price-Quality Relationship in an Experimental Setting," *Journal of Marketing Research,* 5 (August 1968), 300–3.
12. ——. "Repeat Purchase Estimation and the Linear Learning Model," *Journal of Marketing Research,* 5 (August 1968), 304–6.
13. Tucker, W. T. "The Development of Brand Loyalty," *Journal of Marketing Research,* 1 (August 1964), 32–5.
14. Wierenga, K. *An Investigation of Brand Choice Processes.* Rotterdam: Rotterdam University Press, 1974.

A Theoretical and Empirical Evaluation of Price Deals for Consumer Nondurables

Robert C. Blattberg, Gary D. Eppen, and Joshua Lieberman

Food retailers regularly offer products for less than normal market price in special sales or deals. This paper briefly examines several common explanations for this phenomenon and finds the analyses to be less than complete. It then presents an explanation for dealing of storable products based on the idea of transferring inventory carrying costs from the retailer to the consumer. An inventory control model is described in which both consumers and the retailer act so as to minimize their own costs. Results derived from this model are then presented. Data relevant to both the consumer and the retailer model are presented and analyzed. The conclusion is that the data are consistent with the predictions of the models. Finally, the strategic implications of the model for manufacturers and retailers are discussed.

Over the last half century, retailers, on a regular basis, have offered consumers periodic short term price cuts called deals.[1] Deals are one of the major forms of price competition used by retailers. A natural question is, "Why do retailers prefer to offer substantial price reductions for a short period of time, and then raise the price to its normal level rather than permanently reduce price by less than the deal price?"

There are a number of alternative explanations though almost no published research exists on this topic. The most common explanation is that retailers deal to attract customers from other stores. We note that any given retailer would gain customers if he/she deals and his/her competitors do not retaliate also by dealing. However, it is very likely that other retailers also will respond by offering deals. A possible result is that all the retailers in the market offer deals but none of the retailers has increased profits. Unless there were other economic benefits to dealing, it would be unprofitable to the retailer.

The following analogy illustrates the point. Three gasoline dealers on the same corner engage in a price war. Dealer one reduces prices and gains customers. Quickly his/her competitors respond by reducing prices and their market shares return to their previous levels. The result is that the reduced prices do not increase volume enough so that total profits for the three stations are reduced below the pre-price war levels. It is almost always the case that after some relatively short period, the stations raise the price to pre-price war levels.

Food retailers price numerous items, and therefore, their environment is more complex than for a single-price retailer such as a gas dealer. The question remains, however, "If retailers can imitate one another, why do they continue to offer deals?" Eventually there should be an incentive to eliminate deals

Reprinted by permission of the American Marketing Association, from the *Journal of Marketing,* 45 Winter 1981, 116–129.

1. Dealing will be defined as a short-term, usually a week or shorter, price cut to the consumer. After the deal is over, the price reverts back to its old level.

and simply charge lower prices. Other forms of promotion such as trading stamps, games and give-aways last a relatively short period of time,[2] yet dealing has persisted for 50 years. Another explanation for the persistence of dealing seems to be required.

Many researchers and store managers believe that retailers deal to attract customers. The previous discussion shows that dealing may lead to a zero-sum game. It is, of course, possible that retailers reach a nonoptimal equilibrium in which each retailer cannot stop dealing because each retailer is worse off if he/she stops dealing and no one else does. Cases such as gas wars imply that these nonoptimal equilibria do not occur often. However, this proposition is very difficult to test with existing data sources. This article will propose an alternative explanation that future research may be able to contrast to the store traffic argument.

An alternative explanation of the cause of dealing is that manufacturers offer trade deals which require price reductions by the retailers. The manufacturers offer trade deals for two reasons: to increase market share, and to get nontriers of their products to learn about their form of attributes at a lower risk level (reduced price).

The first explanation is similar to the one just discussed for the retailer. Suppose the industry cannot increase category volume by dealing. Then if one firm offers a deal and its competitors follow, the overall price is reduced and profits are reduced. Thus, only if price reductions increase category volume enough to increase category profits, will dealing be economically viable. In most product categories it is unlikely that this will happen. Therefore, manufacturers will eventually stop offering trade deals. However, this has not happened.

The second explanation, offering consumers a reduced price to try their brand, will be analyzed in more detail in later sections of the paper discussing model implications and empirical results. It will be shown to be inconsistent with the empirical results.

2. An example of retail promotions that are started and halted are games that retailers frequently offer to customers. These promotions initially attract customers to the first retailer who introduces the game. Quickly, other retailers adopt similar games and the profits due to the game for the first retailer are driven to zero. Soon all retailers drop the games and the market returns to its initial position. Games do not persist because they do not offer a sustained economic benefit to the retailer.

The explanation studied in this paper is that dealing occurs because retailers have higher inventory holding costs than some consumers. The retailer is motivated to take a reduction in sales revenue if the consumer will hold some of the inventory. The consumer is willing to carry some inventory in return for a reduction in price. A deal is the condition needed to complete this exchange, since consumers cannot be persuaded to hold inventory by a constant price.

The inventory holding costs under consideration have two main components: the value of the capital tied up in inventory and the value of the space committed to holding the inventory. It seems clear that the second term is much greater for the retailer. Shelf space is a major concern for food retailers. Products and suppliers vie vigorously for shelf space. On the other hand, for a number of consumers the cost of some additional storage space is extremely low. Another dozen boxes of tissue in the bathroom closet or an additional case of pickles in the fruit cellar is of almost no concern. These costs alone seem sufficient to conclude that the opportunity for a mutually profitable exchange exists.

The idea that consumers buy and hold inventory when deals occur has appeared elsewhere in the literature. Frank and Massy (1967) used distributed lag models to measure the effect of past purchasing on a brand's sales and market share. Kunreuther (1973) and Blattberg et al. (1978) developed models of the household in which they traded off holding costs, transaction costs, and deal discounts to decide the quantity to buy each period. However, none of these papers tested an explicit inventory model. In addition, the retailer, i.e., the supply side of the model, was not considered. The purpose of this paper is to extend the holding cost theory to include the interaction between the consumer (demand) and retailer (supply), and thus be able to determine the magnitude and frequency of deals and the quantity sold on deal.

This paper is in the spirit of economic models in which the consumer and the firm (retailer) maximize their own objective function. This model is used to understand how deals work and to derive testable implications. Data are then used to test these implications.

Understanding and explaining dealing is complex. Economic reasoning was used to raise questions about several of the explanations of dealing commonly given. More detailed empirical tests are needed before any of these explanations can be accepted or rejected. In all likelihood, different explanations exist for the existence of dealing in different circumstances. The purpose of this paper is to offer an explanation as to why retailers deal in certain cases. It is shown that this explanation is consistent with consumer purchase data.

Section 2 of this article describes the model's structure, while Section 3 gives the testable implications. Section 4 tests these implications, and Section 5 gives a summary and our conclusions.

The Model's Structure

This section of the paper will outline two models, one for the consumer and one for the retailer. Each optimizes his/her own welfare in response to an action by the other. The equilibrium result is a dealing policy for the retailer. The retailer's model has implications regarding the quantity sold on deal and the frequency and magnitude of deals; the consumer model has implications regarding the quantity bought on deal and the time between purchases.

Before outlining the model, it is useful to list certain assumptions that will be used throughout this section. (Other assumptions that will be made are described in the appropriate section of the paper). The first two are not restrictive but simplify the mathematics: time is a continuous variable, and all quantities sold and purchased are perfectly divisible.[3] The next four assumptions are more restrictive but are made to make the mathematics more tractable, so that a closed-form solution can be found for the optimal dealing price. These assumptions are: there is a single store in the market; deals are offered on a single brand only; the regular (nondeal) price of the deal brand, P, is fixed; and no trade allowances are offered to the retailer.

These assumptions do not perfectly mirror the real world. The first two assumptions are perhaps the worst offenders in this respect. However, they permit the construction of a relatively simple model that captures the essence of the inventory holding argument, yields analytically tractable results, and leads to conclusions that are empirically confirmed.

The assumption that the regular (nondeal) price is fixed, is not very restrictive because the relative prices in a category do not change substantially over short periods of time. The consumer's and store's behavior would not change dramatically if normal price fluctuations were included in the model.

The assumption of no trade allowances is consistent with the purpose of this paper. The goal is to demonstrate both with models and data analysis that deals by retailers are a reasonable economic activity with no additional outside motivation. It is not necessary or useful to include manufacturers in the model to establish this point. Other environments involving the three-way interaction between manufacturers, retailers, and consumers might also provide motivation for retailer dealing. This research does not claim to exclude all other reasons for dealing, but simply to establish the inventory explanation as a viable alternative. Other explanations and the associated research are left to other papers at another time.

The rest of this section includes an overview of the model, the consumer model, the retailer model, and testable implications.

An Overview of the Model

The model begins with the consumer. The consumer is assumed to respond to deals by "forward" buying additional items and holding inventory. The consumer decides his/her inventory level by trading off holding costs against the reduced price of the item. (See Blattberg et al. 1978 or Kunreuther 1973 for a discussion of this assumption.)

The model assumes that not all consumers have the same holding costs. For simplicity, there are two types of consumers: low-holding-cost consumers and high-holding-cost consumers.[4] Aggregation is done by weighting the two groups in the market by their relative size.

The retailer's objective is to maximize his/her profits. His/her main trade-off is that by dealing he/she can reduce his/her inventory but lose revenue from the reduced deal price. The retailer controls the quantity bought on deal since the amount consumers will buy depends on the size of the deal. Figure 1 gives an overview of the model and shows that the

3. Perfectly divisible means any amount of the product can be purchased.

4. Splitting the market into two groups rather than having more segments or a distribution across the population to represent holding costs should have no effect on the results. The degree of response to deals will vary by segment but the general behavior should be similar.

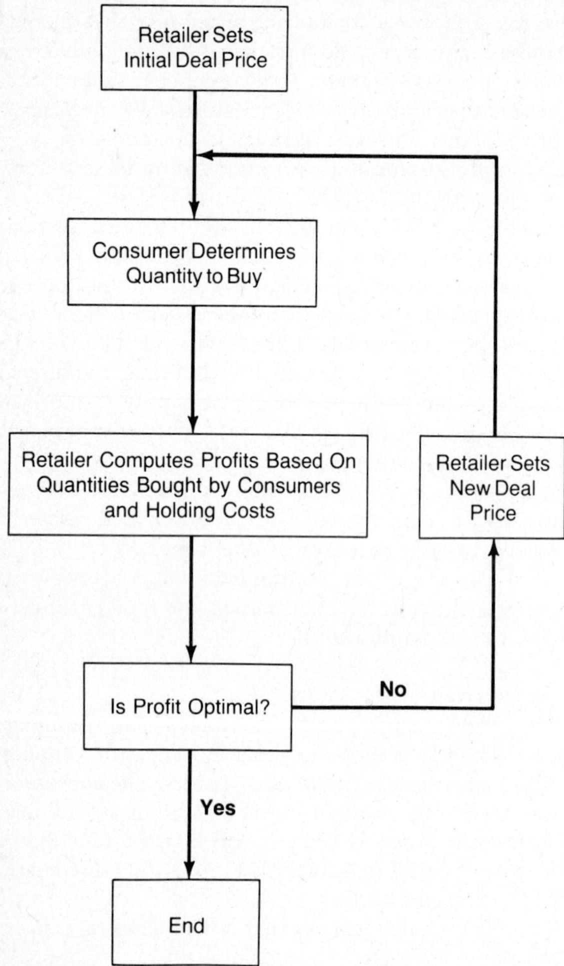

FIGURE 1
Overview of Model

retailer fixes his/her deal price as a function of the consumer's response to deals and his/her own cost of holding inventories.

Consumer Model

The consumer's objective function is to minimize his/her total costs subject to the constraint that he/she satisfy his/her demand at any point in time. It will be assumed that each consumer conducts regular shopping trips to the store, and on each trip he/she buys a bundle of items which may or may not include the deal brand. Each consumer, i, consumes the product category at a fixed rate per unit of time, c_i, and has a fixed holding cost per unit of time, h_i, for the product category. (Note that h_i is the cost of holding one unit (e.g., a box or a can) of the product for one period of time. Thus, the holding cost for the same product (aluminum foil) will vary with the size of the box purchased.) In responding to deals the consumer never makes a special trip to the store, thus buying deal items during his/her regular trips, and responds to deals by changing purchase timing but not consumption of the product category.[5]

Based on these assumptions, the following model has been developed. In buying ahead on deal, the individual consumer, i, incurs a holding cost, h_i, on the quantity, q_i, which he/she stockpiles on deal but also gains a price reduction, D, for each unit bought on deal. The consumer wishes to minimize the total cost function, $TC(q_i)$, when he/she buys on deal subject to the constraint that he/she consumes c_i units per period and all consumption demand is satisfied. This leads to:

$$TC(q_i) = \int_0^{q_i/c_i} h_i(q_i - c_i t)dt - Dq_i$$

$$= \frac{h_i q_i^2}{2c_i} - Dq_i. \tag{1}$$

The time period of analysis is q_i/c_i which is the time required to consume q_i units. Equation (1) indicates that the cost of buying q_i units for the household is proportional to the holding costs (h_i) and the square of the quantity bought (q_i). It is inversely proportional to the consumption rate (c_i). As the deal (D) increases, costs also decrease.

From equation (1) one can determine the optimal quantity (q_i) to buy on deal. This yields

$$q_i^* = \frac{Dc_i}{h_i} \tag{2}$$

and the optimal purchase period is

$$t^* = \frac{D}{h_i} \tag{3}$$

5. For products such as soft drinks and nonstaple items, it is likely that dealing will increase the consumption rate. Therefore, c_i becomes a function of price, $c_i(p)$. The household will still forward buy, but the quantity bought will depend upon the effect of the deal on consumption as well as on the holding costs. The general results should not change, though it would be difficult to separate the two effects. The products studied in the empirical section are products whose consumption rates will not be greatly affected by dealing.

Equation (2) shows that the optimal quantity to be bought increases as the deal magnitude (D) and consumption rate (c_i) increase, and it decreases as holding costs (h_i) increase. Equation (3) shows that the optimal purchase period increases as the deal magnitude (D) increases. The optimal purchase period decreases as the holding cost (h_i) increases.

To aggregate across consumers, it is assumed that all consumers have the same consumption rate, c.[6] Regarding holding costs, there are two segments in the market, one with a low per-unit holding cost, h_L, and the other with a high per-unit holding cost, h_H. Let there be N consumers in the market. α is a number lying between 0 and 1 so that there are αN consumers with low holding costs and $(1-\alpha)N$ consumers with high holding costs. It will be assumed that only consumers with low holding costs buy ahead on deal. The consumers with high holding costs just buy enough to meet their consumption per period.

From these assumptions, the aggregate quantity bought *on deal* is

$$Q_D = (\alpha N)q^* = \alpha Nc\frac{D}{h_L} \tag{4}$$

Note that in (4) the term Nc is the accumulated rate of demand. Thus, if a deal occurs and another one is not offered for t* or more weeks, the total amount bought on sale is

$$\alpha Q\frac{D}{h_L} \text{ or } \alpha Qt^*, \tag{5}$$

where Q is the cumulative rate of demand. In this derivation, it is assumed that the consumers with high holding costs do not buy any items on deal. In developing the model, it is assumed that the sale is instantaneous; i.e., that all items sold on deal are removed from the inventory instantaneously. It would be a simple matter to include some of the demand of high holding cost consumers in the quantity bought. However, it would add nothing new to the model except for some additional notation, and thus, this option was rejected. By the same token, other patterns for the demand of low holding cost during the deal could be assumed. These assumptions produce a model that is similar to the EOQ model, and thus, seemed worth exploring.

One generalization, however, is included in the model. At least in the early parts of the development, it is assumed that α is a function of D and $\alpha(D)$ is introduced as a nondecreasing function of D that represents the proportion of consumers who buy on deal.

The Retailer Model

To model the retailer, certain assumptions will also be made. The unit cost to the retailer, m, is fixed. He/she incurs a fixed set-up cost per order, K, and a fixed holding cost per unit, h_R. The retailer must satisfy all demand. Deliveries and sales are instantaneous. There is only one deal per inventory cycle, and deals are offered with a fixed time interval between them, k. Lastly, the same offer is made on each deal.

The purpose of dealing for the retailer is to be able to shift inventories to consumers, hence reducing his/her holding costs. The cost to the retailer is reduced profits per unit sold because the deal reduces his/her revenue on each unit sold at the deal price. The retailer will choose an inventory and dealing policy to maximize profits.

The optimal inventory policy will not be derived in this paper. Interested readers are referred to Lieberman (1978) and Eppen and Lieberman (1980). The main results with enough discussion to make them understandable follow.

It is shown that deals are offered at the beginning of the inventory cycle and that if $h_R > 2h_L$, the optimal value of the discount, D*, is

$$D^* = kh_L$$

where k is the length of the inventory cycle. The retailer's cost as a function of the inventory cycle is

$$TC(k) = K + D\alpha(D)kQ + \frac{h_R Q}{2}[k^2 - \alpha(D)k^2] \tag{5}$$

It is interesting to note that if $\alpha(D) \to 0$ as $D \to 0$, then TC(k) approaches the standard EOQ model as $D \to 0$. The objective is to minimize the cost per unit time (TC(k)/k). Using (5) and the fact that $D^* = kh_L$ yields

$$\frac{TC(k)}{k} = \frac{K}{k} + Kh_L\alpha(kh_L)kQ + \frac{h_R Q}{2}[k^2 - \alpha(kh_L)k^2] \tag{6}$$

6. This assumption avoids integrating $TC(q_i)$ with respect to c which would greatly complicate the mathematics. The results would change, but the direction of the model's implications should not because each household will still forward buy. Only the quantity bought per household will vary.

To proceed, one must assume a functional form for $\alpha(D)$. The results in this paper consider the case where $\alpha(D) = \alpha$. This is an abstraction of the notion that the proportion of deal buyers is not sensitive to the level of the discount. It also yields closed form expressions that can be conveniently compared to the EOQ model (see Eppen and Lieberman 1980). The next most simple assumption, $\alpha(D) = \alpha D$, yields a cubic during minimization, and thus, immediately turns one to a numerical investigation.

The retailer's inventory holding is shown in Figure 2. It shows that at the time of the deal, the retailer sells αkQ units on deal. Then the nondeal consumers buy at the rate of c units per unit of time.

The optimal deal magnitude can be shown to be

$$D^* = \left[\frac{Kh_L}{Q\left(\alpha + (1-\alpha)\dfrac{h_R}{2h_L}\right)}\right]^{1/2} \qquad (7)$$

The optimal reorder period is

$$k^* = \frac{D^*}{h_L} \qquad (8)$$

and the minimum cost per unit of time is

$$TC_D^* = 2QKh_L\left[2 + (1-\alpha)\frac{h_R}{h_L}\right]^{1/2}$$

Equation (7) shows that the deal magnitude increases with the set-up cost (K), and decreases with the quantity bought by consumers (Q) and the retailer's holding cost (h_R). If a product is purchased frequently, then the deal magnitude is less. The optimal reorder time is proportional to the deal magnitude. The minimum cost per unit of time increases with the cumulative demand rate (Q), the set-up cost (K), and the retailer's holding cost (h_R).

Discussion

The model just described shows that the consumer and retailer decisions are interrelated. The consumer determines the optimal quantity to buy on deal given the optimal deal magnitude. The retailer sets an optimal deal magnitude given the quantity consumers buy on deal. The retailer increases his/her profits by dealing because he/she reduces the inventory carrying cost. A necessary condition for dealing to be profitable is that certain consumers have a holding cost for the product category that is less than one-half that of the retailer.

Implications from the Model

In the previous section a jointly optimal retailer-consumer dealing model was developed. The dealing and inventory policies as derived from the model result in a set of implications that will be used to test

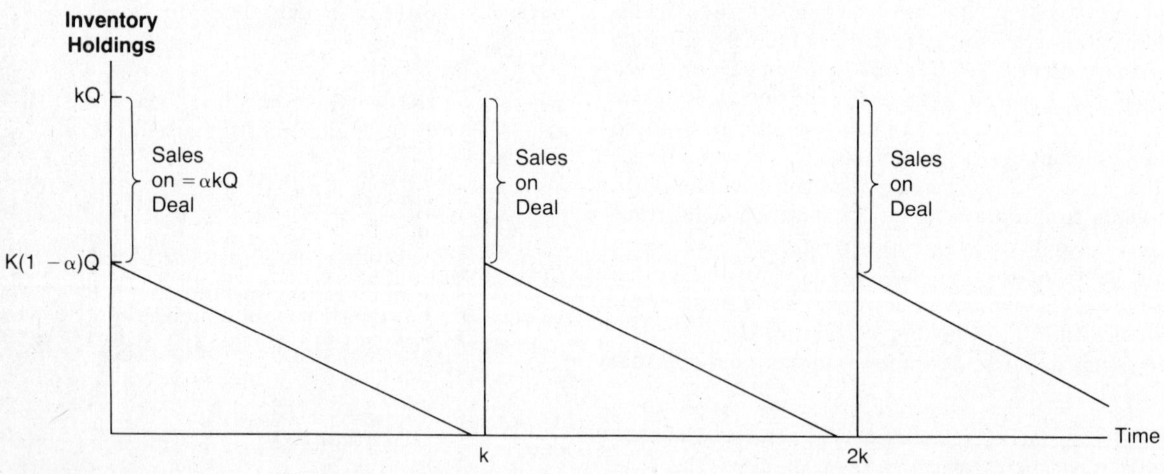

FIGURE 2
The Dealing-Inventory Policy

the model with consumer panel data. The purpose of this section is to determine and discuss these implications.

Optimal Deal Magnitude, Dealing Frequency, and Quantity Bought on Deal

There are three parameters that will be used in deriving the testable implications of the model: optimal deal magnitude, D^*; optimal dealing frequency, F^*; and optimal quantity bought, q^{**}.[7] Equation (7) gives the optimal deal magnitude:

$$D^* = \left[\frac{Kh_L}{Q\left(\alpha + (1-\alpha)\frac{h_R}{2h_L}\right)}\right]^{1/2} \tag{7}$$

The dealing frequency is the number of deals offered during any given time interval, T. From the previous section, the jointly optimal time between deals is $t^{**} = D^*/h_L$. The optimal dealing frequency, therefore, is the reciprocal of t^{**} times T, or

$$F^* = T\frac{1}{t^{**}} = T\frac{h_L}{D^*}. \tag{9}$$

Substituting (7) for D^* gives

$$F^* = T\left[\frac{Q(2\alpha h_L + (1-\alpha)h_R)}{2K}\right]^{1/2}. \tag{10}$$

To compute the optimal quantity bought on deal, the quantity bought by the low-holding-cost consumers is $q^* = Dc/h_L$. Replacing D by D^* gives the jointly optimal quantity to be bought on deal for each consumer responding to deals,

$$q^{**} = \frac{D^*c}{h_L} = c\left[\frac{2K}{Q(2\alpha h_L + (1-\alpha)h_R}\right]^{1/2}. \tag{11}$$

As can be seen from equations (7), (10), and (11), the dealing strategy parameters are strongly interrelated because F^* is inversely related and q^{**} is directly related to D^*. Therefore, factors influencing D^* also affect F^* and q^{**}. Thus, the effects of D^*, F^*, and q^{**} should be treated as interdependent when studying the implications of changing a given parameter. This approach is taken throughout the remainder of this section.

7. ** denotes jointly optimal for the retailer and consumer.

Implications

The equations derived in the previous section make it possible to trace the effects of the various parameters on the optimal dealing policy of the retailer. Consider K, the ordering cost. As K increases, the retailer is motivated to order less often and thus to offer deals often (F^* decreases). Then in order to persuade the consumer to buy enough on deal to carry him/her over to the next deal, the retailer must make a larger price reduction (D^* increases). This implies that the consumer will purchase more when the sale occurs (q^{**} increases).

As Q increases, it is clear from (7) and (10) that D^* increases and F^* decreases. Thus, a popular product, one with a large consumption rate, should be dealt often but with a small discount. Since $Q = Nc$ and these two parameters have opposite effects on q^{**} [equation (11)], it is impossible to specify the effect that an increase in Q would have on q^{**}.

To see the effect of h_L, the consumer's holding cost, on the retailer's decisions, it is convenient to hold the ratio h_R/h_L constant. Let $\lambda = h_R/h_L$. Rewriting (7), (10), and (11) in terms of λ yields

$$D^* = \left\{\frac{Kh_L}{Q[\alpha + (1-\alpha)\lambda/2]}\right\}^{1/2}, \tag{12}$$

$$F^* = T\left[\frac{Q[2\alpha + (1-\alpha)\lambda]\,h_L}{2K}\right]^{1/2}, \tag{13}$$

$$q^{**} = c\left[\frac{2K}{Q[2\alpha + (1-\alpha)\lambda]\,h_L}\right]^{1/2}. \tag{14}$$

These three equations show that D^* and F^* increase when h_L increases, whereas q^{**} decreases. As h_L increases, the consumer is less anxious to hold inventory. The retailer responds to this reluctance by making the deals more attractive (increasing D^*), and by enabling the consumer to carry inventory over a shorter interval (by increasing F^*). Since F^* increases, the consumer will buy less on deal at each sale, i.e., q^{**} decreases.

These three equations show the following. The deal magnitude increases when holding cost to the consumer (h_L) increases and the set-up cost (K) increases. As the rate of demand (Q) increases, more deals will occur, F^* increases, but the deal magnitude decreases.

The frequency of deals increases with higher

holding costs (h_L) and rate of demand (Q) and decreases as the set-up cost increases.

Inventory vs. Information Explanation

The implications just derived for the retailer and consumer models can be contrasted to the following explanation. Manufacturers offer trade deals to force retailers to reduce price. For the manufacturers, the purpose of the reduced price is to increase trial among nonusers of their brands. Once new consumers have tried the brand, some percentage will repurchase. Thus, dealing is a mechanism for reducing the consumer's cost of experimenting with a brand they rarely use.

The above explanation fits consumer and manufacturers' behavior for a new product introduced into the market. The consumer is seeking information and the manufacturer is trying to reduce the cost of trial. Manufacturers offer free samples, coupons, and smaller trial sizes. This explanation has also been given for the cause of dealing for existing brands.

The implications for the information explanation just given are different than for the holding cost explanation. First, the manufacturer should offer deals on smaller sizes to reduce the risk of trial to the consumer. For new products, manufacturers often introduce a "trial" size which is substantially smaller than the regular sizes. Second, consumers would not stockpile if they are sampling "new" brands. Instead they would try only one unit of the product and would not change their purchase timing. Third, brands which have lower consumption rates relative to other brands in the category (lower share brands) would have greater dealing activity because fewer consumers use these brands.[8]

The implications of the two theories are contrasted in Figure 3. In the empirical section, data are used to compare the two theories.

FIGURE 3
Explanation

Holding Cost	*Trial*
Sizes with higher consumption rate will be dealt	Small sizes will be dealt
Consumers will stockpile dealt brand	Consumers will purchase only the unit on deal
High market share brands will be dealt more frequently	Low market share brands will be dealt more

It should be noted that trade dealing activity occurred in all the categories studied. The model given in Section 3 does not incorporate trade dealing. Some of the results may be due to the retailer receiving trade deals. However, if this sector of the model were included, one could assume the manufacturer was responding to the retailer. How this would change the result is unknown.

Empirical Findings

To test the model's implications, consumer panel data for four product categories will be used. The data do not give all the information (e.g., holding costs) that is needed to test the model's implications. However, these data do offer some evidence about the theory.

Description of the Data

The consumer panel data are from the *Chicago Tribune* panel over the period 1958–1966. The advantage of this panel is that the data are from one city, and it is possible to identify deals much more accurately.

The purchase data contain number of units purchased, price paid, brand bought, size bought, store, and deal code. The key problem faced in using the deal code produced by the consumer is that it is not accurately recorded. This appears to be true across most panels. Therefore, a separate procedure was developed for coding deal purchases.

Private labels were not included in the study because it was impossible to compare them because of potential differences in quality across time. To keep the analysis consistent, only national brands were used. Casual observation of the data indicated that private labels were dealt and heavily stockpiled.

The Deal Code

For each store the price for a given brand and size combination was listed by day. It is possible to identify changes in the price of an item because most chains and voluntary chains have the same price for an item (size/brand combination) across stores. A statistical procedure was developed to identify the

8. Ehrenberg (1972) shows that brand penetration is highly correlated with market share.

regular price in a given period. Once the regular price was determined, the deal price was found by defining the differential between the regular price and the reported price paid. If this differential exceeded a predetermined limit, the transaction was coded as a deal transaction.

While the procedure just described may result in some errors in coding deal purchases, it appears to be far more accurate than the consumer's recorded deal code. By looking at actual transaction data, one can quickly identify when a deal is occurring because of the heavy purchasing matching a price cut. Quite frequently consumers did not record these purchases as deals. Thus, any simple visual analysis of the transaction data shows the improved accuracy of the revised deal code.

Not all of the data were analyzed because certain stores did not deal certain items. This poses a problem because if A&P buyers have different consumption rates than Jewel buyers, and A&P does not deal, this may bias the results. Voluntary chains were not used in the analysis because the data are accumulated, and there is too much variability in dealing practice (price, amount of discount) within the voluntary chains.

Empirical Results

Stockpiling. To see if consumers were stockpiling, two analyses were done: number of units bought on deal, and average interval between purchases. If consumers stockpile, this is evidence that the inventory theory is influencing the purchasing strategy. The most direct way to measure stockpiling is to see if more units are bought on deal purchases than for nondeal purchases. However, for certain categories consumers rarely buy more than one unit because the rate of consumption is low. They may still stockpile by buying earlier than they would if no deal were offered. Thus, both measures are necessary in analyzing deal purchases.

The results in Table 1 show that consumers do stockpile on deal. In eight of nine cases, the quantity bought on deal is higher than for nondeal purchases.[9] Waxed paper and facial tissues show much greater quantities stockpiled. If consumers are stockpiling by buying earlier than they normally would if a deal occurs, then one would expect that the time before the next purchase would be greater after buying on deal than it would be if they did not buy on deal. To measure this effect, one must first put all purchases in standard units.[10] Next, the number of standard units bought is divided into the number of days in the interval following the purchase resulting in the number of days between purchase for a standard unit. This number is calculated for intervals following either a deal purchase or a nondeal purchase in which the next purchase is a nondeal purchase.[11]

The inventory theory implies that the number of units bought per day will be less after a deal purchase than a nondeal purchase. To show this, suppose household 1 buys one unit on deal at time t_0. At the time of their purchase they had one unit in stock and they normally consume two units per month. They do not buy until they run out unless a deal occurs. Assuming no deals occur until after the next purchase, they will next buy one month after time t_0. If no deal occurred, they would have waited to purchase for two weeks, purchase one unit and repurchase again two weeks later. Thus, the interval to next purchase is longer after their deal purchase (one month) than after their nondeal purchase (two weeks). Stockpiling is occurring but not through more units per purchase occasion but through a higher on-hand inventory. A measure of this is the number of days between purchases.

The results are given in Table 2. They support the inventory dealing theory. For all four product categories the difference is quite large, and, no doubt, highly significant statistically. If one divides the difference by the interval following nondeal purchases, one sees that the time between purchases increases after a deal purchase between 23% and 36%, depending upon the category. It is apparent that there is stockpiling occurring even for categories (aluminum

9. A simple sign test reveals this is highly significant. The p-value is .02. Some of the differences are small (e.g., .02). These are categories in which purchase timing is usually affected.

10. The standard units are: aluminum foil-25 ft. roll, waxed paper-100 ft. roll, liquid detergent-22 oz. size, facial tissue-400 tissue box.

11. Since the objective is to see whether dealing changes the purchase interval, one wants to hold fixed one end of the interval, i.e., the last purchase is nondeal. The prior purchase is then on deal or not. These two cases can then be compared. Adding deal to deal purchases does not allow us to hold fixed one end of the interval to make the comparisons required. It was therefore omitted from the analysis.

foil and liquid detergent) which had small quantity stockpiling.

Deal Magnitude and Deal Frequency. The first of these implications is the effect of consumption rate, c, and number of buyers, N, on the optimal values of deal magnitude and dealing frequency as set by the retailer. Since Nc = Q this implication will be analyzed in terms of Q, or the sales level of the retailer. The prediction is that within given product/size/chain combinations, brands with higher sales levels (higher values of Q) will be offered on deal more frequently and for lower deal magnitudes than brands with lower sales levels. These effects are directly observable from equations (7) and (10). The implication is analyzed at the brand level because this holds the holding cost of the product constant. Performing the analysis for given chains keeps constant chain variables (e.g., set-up cost, which may vary from chain to chain).

To account for possible dealing effects on sales (Q), weekly sales of each brand studied were regressed against their weekly prices to obtain an estimate of normal sales after adjusting for dealing effects. Substituting the normal (nondeal) price of the brand for the independent variable in the resulting regression equations and solving the equations gives normal (deal controlled) weekly sales for each brand. The normal weekly sales were then multiplied by the number of weeks included in the recorded history of each brand

TABLE 1
Consumers' Responses to Deals Through Stockpiling

Product Category	*Package Size*	*Mean Number of Units Bought per Deal Transaction*	*Number of Deal Transactions*	*Mean Number of Units Bought per Nondeal Transaction*	*Number of Nondeal Transactions*	*Difference*	*P-value*[g]
Aluminum foil[a]	25.0 ft.	1.21 (0.035)[e]	160	1.04 (0.01)	441	+0.17	less than .001
	37.5 ft.	1.01 (0.005)	102	1.03 (0.03)	97	−0.02	.07
	75.0 ft.	1.03 (0.015)	60	1.00 (0.00)	230	+0.03	.05
Facial tissue[b]	400 ts.	1.99 (0.03)	733	1.24 (0.01)	2,510	+0.75	less than .0001
Liquid detergent[c]	12 oz.	1.03 (0.006)	250	1.02 (0.005)	1,061	+0.01	.20
	22 oz.	1.03 (0.005)	602	1.01 (0.003)	891	+0.02	.001
	32 oz.	1.08 (0.0296)	165	1.02 (0.009)	572	+0.06	.05
Waxed paper[d]	100 ft.	1.68 (0.043)	69	1.25 (0.016)	789	+0.43	less than .0001
	125 ft.	1.29 (0.024)	106	1.02 (0.004)	1,409	+0.27	less than .0001

a. Reynolds and Alcoa in Jewel.
b. Kleenex and Scotties in A & P, National, Jewel, Kroger, and Walgreens.
c. Ivory, Joy, and Lux (and 22 oz. Gentle Fels) in A & P, National, and Jewel.
d. Rapinwax, Freshrap (100 ft.) and Cut Rite (125 ft.) in A & P, National, and Jewel.
e. Number in parentheses is standard error.
f. Some transactions were eliminated when it was uncertain whether they were deal or nondeal purchases.
g. P-value is the significance level for which the null hypothesis is rejected.

TABLE 2
The Effect of Deals on Post-Deal Purchase Timing

Product Category	*Mean Time Interval (in Days) between Deal and Nondeal Purchases*	*Number of Intervals*	*Mean Time Interval (in Days) between Deal and Nondeal Purchases*	*Number of Intervals*	*Difference (in Days)*	*P-value*[b]
Aluminum foil	95.65 (5.55)[a]	374	71.65 (0.575)	1,198	24.00	less than .0001
Facial tissue	63.61 (2.4)	935	47.6 (1.2)	3,543	15.98	less than .0001
Liquid detergent	66.18 (3.39)	745	53.72 (1.58)	2,524	12.36	.0005
Waxed paper	135.88 (8.88)	255	100.25 (3.625)	1,005	35.63	.0002

a. ( ) indicates standard error.
b. P-value is the significance level for which the null hypothesis is rejected.

which resulted in normal (adjusting for deals) sales volumes. Brands are then compared in terms of their normal sales. Section 3 showed that it is expected that brands with higher normal sales will have a higher dealing frequency and be offered at a lower mean deal magnitude than brands with lower normal sales.

These predictions are tested only in terms of their directions, not magnitudes. Using Table 3 as an example, it is expected that for the 25 ft. aluminum foil in Jewel food chain, Reynolds (normal sales = 395) will be offered on deal at a higher frequency than Alcoa (normal sales = 143). The results show that these predictions are confirmed. A summary of the results for the aluminum foil category is given by Table 4.

To save space the detailed results for the other product categories are not presented here. However, summary results for all product categories are reported in Table 5. These results seem to support the

TABLE 3
The Effects of Normal Sales on Deal Magnitude and Dealing Frequency in the Aluminum Foil Product Category

Package Size	*Chain*	*Brand*	*Normal Purchasing Rate (in units)*	*Mean Deal Magnitude (in cents)*	*Dealing Frequency*
25.00 ft.	National	Reynolds	96	4.50	2
		Alcoa	78	6.00	1
		Kaiser	31	7.20	5
	Jewel	Reynolds	395	6.12	17
		Alcoa	143	9.08	6
		Kaiser	18	—	0
37.50 ft.	Jewel	Reynolds	177	15.63	19
		Alcoa	30	17.00	3

TABLE 4
Summary of Predictions for Aluminum Foil

Dealing Parameters	*Deal Magnitude*[c]	*Dealing Frequency*
Number of predictions	5	7
Number of correct predictions	5[a]	5[b]
Percentage of correct predictions	100.0	71.4

a. 25.00 ft. (Reynolds, Kaiser) and (Reynolds, Alcoa) in National and Jewel and (Reynolds, Alcoa) in Jewel; 37.50 ft. (Reynolds, Alcoa) in Jewel.
b. 25.00 ft. (Reynolds, Alcoa) in National and Jewel, (Reynolds, Alcoa) and (Alcoa, Kaiser) in Jewel; 37.50 ft. (Reynolds, Alcoa) in Jewel.
c. Fewer deal magnitude predictions exist because no deals occurred for Kaiser at Jewel. Thus, the deal magnitude is unknown.

inventory dealing model. The null model would imply correct prediction 50% of the time.[12]

The second implication concerns the effect of joint (to consumer and retailer) per unit holding cost on the parameters of deal magnitude and dealing frequency. This implication is tested at the package size level. By varying the package-size of an item (within given product/chain combinations), its holding cost varies. However, by varying the package-size variable the sales variables may change as well, which will have its own effects on both dealing parameters. Since it is impossible to hold sales constant, the analysis will

12. A statistical test is very difficult to apply because predictions are not independent. Therefore, a standard binomial test of $p = .5$ cannot be used.

TABLE 5
Summary of Predictions for Brand Dealing Parameters: All Product Categories

Dealing Parameters	*Deal Magnitude*	*Dealing Frequency*
Number of predictions	46	49
Number of correct predictions	29	31
Percentage of correct predictions	59.2	63.3

TABLE 6
Summary of Predictions for Dealing Parameters at the Package-Size Level

Theory	*Inventory*	
Dealing Parameters	*Deal Magnitude*	*Dealing Frequency*
Number of predictions	3	12
Number of correct predictions	3	8
Percentage of correct predictions	100.0	66.7

focus on the combined effect of per-unit holding cost and sales on the two dealing parameters. This, however, requires some care since sales (Q) and holding cost (h_L) affect the deal magnitude (D^*) and the dealing frequency (F^*) differently. Consider equations (12) and (13). It is clear that we can determine the behavior of D^* and F^* in four cases. These cases are described in Table 7, where + stands for an increase and — stands for a decrease in the variable in question.

Predictions about the behavior of dealing parameters are generated from data by rank ordering different package-sizes (within given product/chain combinations) by size and normal sales. The data are summarized in Table 8. The relationships in Table 7 are then used to make as many predictions as possible. Consider, for example, facial tissues at A&P. Since both h_L and Q are greater for the 400-tissue size, Table 7 suggests that it should be dealt more often, and that no prediction can be made regarding D^*. The prediction is correct. All of the results on facial tissue and waxed paper can be interpreted this way.

TABLE 7
The Effect of Q and h_L on D^* and F^*

Q	h_L	D^*	F^*
+	—	—	
—	+	+	
+	+		+
—	—		—

The situation with liquid detergent is somewhat more complicated. Again, consider the A&P data. The model suggests that the 32 oz. size should be dealt more often than the 12 oz. size. This prediction is incorrect. It is not possible to make a prediction about the relative frequency of deals for the 32 oz. and the 22 oz. sizes. However, the prediction that the 22 oz. size will be dealt more often than the 12 oz. size is correct.

It is also possible to use the data on liquid detergent to make predictions about deal magnitude. For example, compare the 32 oz. size to the 22 oz. size at A&P. Note that h_L is greater and Q is smaller. Table 7 predicts that the discount on the 32 oz. size will be greater, and the prediction is correct. Table 6 summarizes the results of the fifteen possible predictions.

Inventory vs. Information Explanation

Earlier, we stated several contrasting implications for the information and the inventory explanations. Using the data shown, the contrasting implications can be evaluated. The information explanation would imply that consumers would not stockpile products whereas the inventory explanation assumes consumers do stockpile products; the data given above show that consumers do stockpile all four products analyzed.

TABLE 8
The Combined Effect of Holding Cost and Normal Sales on Deal Magnitude and Dealing Frequency at the Package-Size Level

				Standardized Normal Purchasing Rate			
Product Category	*Chain*	*Package Size*	*Unit Holding Cost: Rank Ordering*	*Rank Ordering*	*Units (in thousands)*	*Dealing Frequency*	*Mean Deal Magnitude (in cents)*
Facial tissue[a]	A & P	200 ts.	2	2	15.4	0	
		400 ts.	1	1	126.0	9	
	National	200 ts.	2	2	77.6	0	
		400 ts.	1	1	420.0	23	
	Jewel	200 ts.	2	2	51.0	1	
		400 ts.	1	1	325.6	18	
Liquid detergent[b]	A & P	12 oz.	3	3	3.68	12	
		22 oz.	2	1	5.72	33	8.74
		32 oz.	1	2	5.25	8	13.43
	National	12 oz.	3	3	5.20	27	
		22 oz.	2	1	9.46	51	8.12
		32 oz.	1	2	8.58	17	12.05
	Jewel	12 oz.	3	3	7.2	27	
		22 oz.	2	1	18.85	67	8.06
		32 oz.	1	2	10.34	27	10.49
Waxed paper[c]	A & P	100 ft.	2	2	21.7	1	
		125 ft.	1	1	63.75	10	
	National	100 ft.	2	2	48.6	4	
		125 ft.	1	1	50.5	10	
	Jewel	100 ft.	2	2	39.2	11	
		125 ft.	1	1	70.75	11	

a. Including the brands of Kleenex and Scotties.
b. Including the brands of Ivory, Joy and Lux (and Gentle Fels for the 22 oz. package size category).
c. Including the brands of Freshrap and Rapinwax for the 100 ft. size and Cut Rite for the 125 ft. size category.

Next, the information explanation implies that lower volume items would be dealt more frequently, whereas the inventory explanation implies that higher volume items would be dealt more frequently. The results given above show that higher volume items deal more frequently. Again, the results favor the inventory explanation.

Finally the information explanation implies that smaller sizes should be dealt more frequently than larger sizes. The inventory explanation implies higher volume sizes would be dealt more frequently. In Table 1 for liquid detergent, it is shown that the smaller size (12 oz.) is dealt far less frequently than the 22 oz. which has slightly higher volume. Thus, volume, not size, appears to be a more important determinant of which item to deal.

The data presented appear to favor the inventory explanation in all three analyses. A more rigorous comparison is needed before one can reject the information explanation, but on the basis of the data presented in this study, it is less likely that dealing occurs as a form of information (for existing products) than as a form of shifting holding costs. It is also possible that a certain proportion of dealing is done to induce trial and the remainder related to transferring holding costs to low holding cost consumers.

Strategy Implications for Manufacturers and Retailers

The implications from the consumer and retailer model can be used to help design dealing strategies for both manufacturers and retailers.

Manufacturer's Dealing Strategy

The model and the empirical results suggest that consumer stockpiling is an important reaction to dealing for established, storable products. This fact has serious implications for the manufacturer who wishes to attract new customers to his/her product. Much of the cost of a retailer deal may not be at all related to new trials. A manufacturer thus may wish to devote increased attention to other devices such as home delivered samples and demonstrations in stores in attempting to attract new customers.

However, the manufacturer can use stockpiling behavior to his/her advantage. Trade deals can be timed to match production runs so that retailers and consumers stockpile the product, thus carrying inventory the manufacturer would otherwise be forced to carry. For products with high set-up costs and infrequent production runs, dealing can be an efficient mechanism for transferring inventory.

It is important to note the effect of the function $\alpha(D)$, the proportion of consumers who buy on deal, on the effectiveness of dealing. In equation (5) note that if $\alpha(D)$ is small, the retailers' costs are essentially the same as in the no deal case. Thus, the trade will have little effect. In these situations manufacturers should consider reducing trade dealing activity and attempting to offer retailers higher margins through lower case prices.

For products with low consumption rates, trade deals are very unlikely to be passed on to the consumer. Again, equation (4) shows that Q_D depends upon c. Retailers will take small ads in the Saturday paper ("obituary" ads) and reduce price on Monday–Wednesday (weak shopping days) to comply with the agreement. The manufacturer may be more successful using other forms of promotions or directly advertising to the consumer.

For sizes with low consumption rates, the retailer is unlikely to deal the product even with a trade deal. To increase the purchase of low volume sizes, manufacturers can consider alternative actions like special consumer promotions, tie in promotions with stronger sizes, and special consumer advertising.

Retailer's Dealing Strategy

The models discussed in this paper can be used by retailers to develop a more effective dealing strategy. An approach followed by Eppen and Lieberman (1980) is to derive and compare expressions for the cost per unit time with and without dealing. This approach leads to two main conclusions: (a) High-volume items, those with a large value of Q, yield greater profits to the retailer if he/she deals. We have already seen that for such products the optimal dealing policy involves frequent deals with relatively small discounts. (b) Items with widely different holding costs between the retailer and a segment of consumers are advantageous for the retailer to deal. This suggests that bulky items like paper products are good candidates for dealing.

Another strategy implication of the theory is dealing locally. This follows from the model because dealing is efficient when the proportion of low holding cost consumers is high. This may not be uniform over an SMSA. Obviously there are efficiencies in buying newspaper ads throughout an SMSA. However, through the use of flyers and store specials, retailers can also develop local deals which may be successful in one area but not another. Factors which influence the selections of items to deal are similar to those just discussed for the total market. However, consumption rates of products and storage costs may vary by region. For areas where households have freezers, retailers should deal items for the freezer. For areas with larger homes, bulkier products should be dealt. From scanning data it becomes possible for the retailer to analyze sales data by item by store so that more effective dealing can be done.

Within brands of a category it is rarely profitable for the retailer to deal low share items. Unless a strong performance contract exists, the retailer should run these items during low volume days such as Monday, Tuesday, and Wednesday so that he/she can perform on the trade deal requirements.

Conclusions

This paper began with the assumptions that the consumer purchases in order to minimize total cost (purchase cost and holding cost) and that the retailer sets price to maximize his profits. Based on these assumptions and other assumptions made throughout, the optimal deal price, frequency of dealing and quantity bought on deal were derived. Testable implications were then generated and using panel data, they were tested empirically. The empirical results showed that the inventory explanation for dealing is consistent with the data.

A major benefit of the view that consumers respond to deals by inventorying is that it leads to certain implications for the measurement of the consumer's response to deals. Instead of assuming that dealing increases sales through brand-switching, the inventory theory explanation implies sales increase because consumers stockpile. This results in a trough in sales after a deal. Unless the dealing response model accounts for this trough, the effect of a deal will be greatly overstated.

This article offers a different explanation than the one most commonly held that dealing is used to attract customers to the store. Both explanations can be true and the cause of dealing. Theoretical and empirical work needs to be done comparing the inventory theory, proposed here, with other explanations for dealing. It is hoped that further work is developed to study these issues.

References

Blattberg, Robert C., Thomas Buesing, Peter Peacock, and Subrata Sen (1978), "Identifying the Deal Prone Segment," *Journal of Marketing Research,* 15 (August), 369–377.

Ehrenberg, A. S. C. (1972), *Repeat Buying,* Amsterdam, Netherlands: North-Holland Publishing Company.

Eppen, Gary and Yehoshua Lieberman (1980), "Why Do Retailers Deal? An Inventory Explanation," working paper.

Frank, Ronald E. and William F. Massy (1967), "Effects of Short-Term Promotional Strategy in Selected Market Segments," in *Promotional Decisions Using Mathematical Models,* Patrick J. Robinson, ed., Boston: Allyn & Bacon, 147–225.

Kunreuther, Howard (1973), "Why the Poor May Pay More for Food: Theoretical and Empirical Evidence," *Journal of Business,* 46 (July), 368–383.

Lieberman, Joshua (1978), "A Theory of Price Deals in Supermarkets," Ph.D. dissertation, University of Chicago.

Wagner, Harvey M. and Thomson M. Whitin (1958), "Dynamic Version of the Economic Lot Size Model," *Management Science,* 5, No. 1 (October), 89–96.

READING 26

Repeat Rates of Deal Purchases

Robert W. Shoemaker and F. Robert Shoaf

Kuehn (1962) has demonstrated a strong and consistent association between a consumer's purchase history and his probability of making a repeat purchase. This suggested a number of interpretations on how consumers choose brands (Frank, 1962; Howard, 1963; Kuehn, 1962; Massy et al., 1970) and provided a basis for testing stochastic models of consumer brand choice (Massy et al., 1970).

In this paper, we extend Kuehn's original work by including deal effects. The questions we examine are:

1. Is the association between past brand choice and repeat-purchase probabilities significantly related to whether past purchases were made at deal (sale) or regular prices?
2. If associations between deal purchasing and repeat-purchase probabilities are noted, are the associations consistent between different brands and product classes?
3. Are differences in repeat-purchase probabilities related to the percentage of the product purchased at deal prices?

In Kuehn's original analysis, a consumer's past four purchases were summarized as a pattern of Ss or Os to indicate a purchase of Snow Crop (S) or other (O) brands of frozen orange juice. For example, SSOO indicated two Snow Crop purchases followed by two purchases of another brand. The probability of repurchasing Snow Crop on the fifth purchase of the sequence was positively correlated to both the number and recency of past Snow Crop purchases.

Kuehn found that given the purchase sequence OSSS, the probability of a repeat purchase of Snow Crop on the fifth purchase occasion was .690, while for OSSO the repeat probability was .414. Similar procedures for studying purchase-sequence data have been used by Carman (1966) for toothpaste and Massy et al. (1970) for coffee. In these prior studies, however, purchases were not analyzed as to whether they were on a consumer-perceived price deal or at the regular price.

Certain relationships between deal purchasing and repeat-purchase probabilities have been analyzed by Lawrence (1969). He studied diary panel data on toothpaste purchases and analyzed all sequences of nine consecutive purchases that satisfied the following conditions:

1. the first five purchases were all of the same brand;
2. the sixth purchase was a switch to a different brand.

He concluded that nondeal switchers were significantly more likely to continue buying the switch brand than were deal-pack switchers. Lawrence's findings are of direct interest to our investigation. But his findings apply to only a rather special situation—namely, purchasing subsequent to five consecutive purchases of a certain brand. The objective of the current study is to examine the association between deal purchases and repurchase probabilities in a broader context.

Method

The three objectives stated above were evaluated using data from several permanent diary panels. These panel records showed the sequence of brand choices

Reprinted by permission of the Advertising Research Foundation, Inc., from the *Journal of Advertising Research*, 17:2 April 1977, 47–53.

TABLE 1
Description of Product Classes and Panels

Product Class	*Panel Size*	*Period Studied (Months)*	*Average Transactions per Household per Month*	*Percent of Buying Households Purchasing Three or More Times*		*Number of Three Purchase Sequences*
				Households	*Volume*	
Laundry cleaning (L)	2,362	8	.99	80.0	96.4	5,146
Baking mix (M)	6,000	18	.11	36.9	70.0	2,290
Beverage 1 (B1)	4,200	9	.37	59.1	88.9	2,435
Beverage 2 (B2)	4,200	9	.66	68.7	94.5	4,513
Paper product (P)	6,000	12	.99	84.1	97.6	7,389
Average	4,552	11.2	.62	65.8	89.6	4,354

over time, including whether the purchases were recognized as being on deal to the consumer. The products studied included: laundry cleaning products (L); a class of baking mix (M); beverage class 1 (B1); beverage class 2 (B2); a class of disposable paper products (P). Each of the diary panels was relatively large. The panel sizes ranged from 2,400 to 6,000 households with a panel's average size being 4,552. Further descriptive information for the products studied is shown in Table 1.

To meet the current study objectives, the research procedures used by Kuehn and others were modified as follows:

1. the recording of purchases as deal or nondeal in addition to brand;
2. the analysis of 30 individual brands rather than one brand;
3. the analysis of five separate product classes rather than one product class;
4. the use of shorter but more detailed purchase histories;
5. the use of nonoverlapping purchase sequences;
6. the exclusion of sequences involving purchase of two different brands on the same day.

These six modifications are explained below.

1. Recording of Deal and Nondeal Purchases. Past-purchase sequences were coded both in terms of the brands purchased and whether the brands were purchased at the regular or at a deal price. The consumer's diary record was the criterion for determining a deal price versus a regular price.

2. Analysis of More than One Brand. Many past empirical analyses have focused on a particular brand such as Snow Crop orange juice, Crest toothpaste, or a household's favorite brand of coffee. In the current analysis, the six leading brands in each of five separate product classes were studied. This greatly expanded sample of brands provides a basis for evaluating the effects of market share and consistencies within product classes.

3. Analysis of Five Product Classes. Five product classes were studied. This provides a basis for comparing purchase patterns between food and nonfood products. It also allows for examining frequently purchased products versus infrequently purchased products.

4. Length and Detail of Purchase History. Any number of purchases in a sequence could be used as a history. However, as the length of the sequence is increased the number of classifications or past histories increases, resulting in a reduction in sample size per category. This problem is further confounded when purchases are classified as deal or nondeal purchases since there are more classifications. For example, if four past purchases were examined and each purchase was classified as deal or nondeal, 256 subgroups would be required, resulting in many cells with sample sizes too small for meaningful comparisons.

In the present study, histories of two past purchases were selected as representing the most useful balance between length of history and adequate sample size within each classification. Each past purchase was classified as the subject brand or other brand and as deal or nondeal. This produced four states for each past purchase. With a history of length two, there are 16 possible classifications.

5. Overlapping versus Nonoverlapping Sequences. Kuehn developed his findings from a relatively small consumer diary panel. However, he was able to generate a large number of observations by overlapping sequences from a single household. For example, a series of seven orange-juice purchases by one household was considered as three overlapping sequences of five purchases—e.g., 1 to 5, 2 to 6, 3 to 7. The precise effect of treating these sequences as being independent observations in a statistical analysis is not clear, as noted by Blattberg and Sen (1973) and Massy et al. (1970).

In an effort to reduce the possibility of dependence between successive purchases, no overlapping sequences were used in the present study. For example, a household history of six purchases provided only two sequences versus the four that could have been obtained had they been overlapped.

6. Exclusion of Sequences Involving Purchase of Two Brands on the Same Day. In a small number of cases, some households purchased two different brands on the same day. In this case it is impossible, and perhaps meaningless, to determine which brand was selected first. It appears that some researchers have assumed that the order of data as received represents the correct chronological order. However, since panel data are frequently sorted by brand for purposes of editing, this appears to be a poor assumption. Therefore, in those situations where two or more purchases were recorded on the same day, the sequence was excluded. In any event, the effect of inclusion or exclusion is small since these situations appeared in less than 1 percent of the sequences.

Data Analysis. A separate analysis was made for each of the six leading brands in each of five product classes for a total of 30 analyses. The brands in each class were selected by processing a sample of the data and identifying the six brands with the largest market shares. The market shares for each of the 30 brands are shown in Table 2. On the average, the leading brand in each class had a share of 25.8 percent; the second, a share of 14.6 percent; the third a share of 10.2 percent; down to 2.6 percent for the sixth brand. The percent of sales on deal ranged from 10.4 percent for class M up to 43.0 percent for class B1.

In the analysis for each of the 30 brands, the

TABLE 2
Market Shares by Brand and Product Class

	Product Class					
Brand	*L*	*M*	*B1*	*B2*	*P*	*Average*
1	28.3%	39.3%	18.3%	23.3%	19.9%	25.8%
2	6.9	15.7	17.5	14.8	18.4	14.6
3	5.7	6.2	14.7	6.4	17.9	10.2
4	5.4	3.9	9.5	6.2	4.8	6.0
5	5.4	2.5	9.5	5.7	3.9	5.4
6	5.0	1.5	4.5	1.0	1.0	2.6
7[a]	43.5	30.9	26.1	42.6	34.0	35.4
Total	100.0	100.0	100.0	100.0	100.0	100.0
Percent of purchases on deal	38.0	10.4	43.0	38.8	31.2	

a. Brand 7 = other brands.

TABLE 3
Association between Past Two Brand Choices and Repeat Probability

	Repeat-Purchase Probability			
Past Two Purchases	*Kuehn*[a]	*Carman*[b]	*Massy et al.*[c]	*Present Study*[d]
11	.736	.513	.847	.759
01	.446	.453	.622	.355
10	.347	.433	.557	.278
00	.065	.172	.414	.035

a. Figures are derived from Kuehn (1962).
b. Data apply only to "nonloyal" purchasers (see Carman, 1966).
c. Data refer to a buyer's "favorite brand" (see Massy et al., 1970).
d. Stated figures are the average of 30 brands in five product classes.

subject brand was coded as brand 1; "all other" brands in that product class were coded as 0. The sequences of three purchases were then classified into 16 groups on the basis of the first two purchases. The percentage of sequences ending in brand 1 is the estimate of the repeat-purchase probability given a particular purchase history.

Study Objective and Predictions. Table 3 is the springboard from which the hypotheses are derived. For illustration, data from the studies of Kuehn and Massy et al. are compared with those of 30 brands examined in the first phase of the present study. These repeat-purchase probabilities are conditional on the last two brand purchases. For example, the probability of repurchasing Snow Crop, given SS, is .736; the probability of repurchasing Crest, given CC, is .513; the probability of repurchasing one of the 30 subject brands in the present study, given 11, averages .759. The pattern of decreasing probability from a 11 to a 00 situation is similar in all four studies.

The major question being considered in this study is whether conditional probabilities are significantly altered when deal purchases are distinguished from nondeal purchases—i.e., is the probability of repurchasing a given brand (Snow Crop, Crest, or any of the 30 brands in this study) dependent on whether the two past purchases were made at deal or regular prices?

For purposes of discussion, the following notation is adopted. A prime sign (′) is used to indicate a deal purchase—e.g., 1′ denotes a deal purchase of brand 1, and 0 denotes a regular-price purchase of all other brands. An underscore indicates that the purchase was either a deal or regular-price purchase—e.g., $\underline{1}$ means the purchase was brand 1, either at regular or deal price. The notation $P(\underline{1}\ 10')$ indicates the probability of purchasing brand 1 subsequent to the history 10′—i.e., a purchase of brand 1 at its regular price followed by a switch to another brand on deal.

Predicted Results. It was predicted that if two purchase histories were similar except for deal purchases, the repurchase probability of the nondeal brand would be higher than the repurchase probability of the deal brand. For example, it was predicted that:

$$P(\underline{1}|10') > P(\underline{1}|10)$$

where $P(\underline{1}|10')$ indicates the probability of repurchasing brand 1 given the chronological purchase history 10′—i.e., brand 1 followed by a deal purchase of some

TABLE 4
Predicted Relationships between Conditional Purchase Probability (Past Sequences Identified by Brand and Deal)

Brand Sequence	*Predicted Relationships*[a]
11	$P(\underline{1}\|11) > P(\underline{1}\|1'1) > P(1\|11') > P(1\|1'1')$
01	$P(\underline{1}\|0'1) > P(\underline{1}\|01) > P(1\|0'1') > P(1\|01')$
10	$P(\underline{1}\|10') > P(\underline{1}\|10) > P(1\|1'0') > P(1\|1'0)$
00	$P(\underline{1}\|0'0') > P(\underline{1}\|00') > P(1\|0'0) > P(1\|00)$

a. $P(1|01')$ indicates the probability of purchasing brand 1, whether at regular or deal price, subsequent to having purchased another brand, 0, followed by a purchase of brand 1 at a deal price. That is, the chronological pattern was 0 1′$\underline{1}$ for the three purchases.

other brand. The other relationships predicted prior to the empirical analysis are summarized in Table 4.

Basis for Prediction. It was anticipated that the availability of deal savings would convince some buyers to purchase brands that would not have been purchased had the brand not been on deal. Consequently, a nondeal purchase was considered indicative of nonprice appeal for a premium-priced brand. A deal purchase was regarded as ambiguous. It could indicate either a switch for deal savings or a purchase of the household's favorite brand that just happened to be on deal when purchased.

As can be noted in Table 4, a total of 12 relationships were predicted.

Findings

The repeat-purchase probabilities for one brand, L-1, are shown in Table 5. Several factors are evident.

First, the repeat-purchase probabilities are significantly different depending on whether past purchases were made at the regular or deal price. For example, if both past purchases were brand L-1 and not on deal, the probability of making a repeat purchase is .823 versus .575 if both were L-1 on deal.

Second, each of the predicted associations held true for this brand despite the relatively small sample sizes for certain sequences. However, while the relationships held, several of the differences in repurchase rates were not statistically significant—at least not for this one brand.

A similar analysis was made for each of the 30 brands. The weighted average for all 30 brands is shown in Table 6.

Again, there are large and statistically significant differences in the repeat rates, depending on whether previous purchases were made at deal or regular prices. For example, if both past purchases

TABLE 5
Association between Repeat-Purchase Probabilities and Past-Purchase Sequences Classified by Brand and Deal (Illustrated for Brand L-1)

Past-Purchase Sequence[a]	*Probability of Repurchasing Brand 1*	*Reduction in Probability*[b]	*Sample Size*	*Standard Error of Estimate*
11	.823	—	590	.016
1′1	.651	.172[c]	74	.055
11′	.648	.003	89	.051
1′1′	.575	.073[c]	99	.050
0′1	.528	.047	106	.049
01	.517	.011	172	.038
0′1′	.400	.117[c]	95	.050
01′	.295	.105[c]	61	.059
10′	.515	−.220[c]	99	.050
10	.387	.128[c]	165	.038
1′0′	.259	.128[c]	108	.042
1′0	.246	.013	69	.052
0′0′	.115	.131[c]	668	.013
00′	.091	.024[c]	435	.014
0′0	.082	.009	402	.014
00	.073	.009	1,281	.007
Total			4,513	

a. 1 indicates a purchase of the subject brand (L-1). A prime sign (′) indicates that the purchase was on deal.
b. This column indicates the reduction in probability from the preceding sequence.
c. The difference in repeat-purchase probability is significant at the .16 level or less based on a one-tailed test.

were the subject brand at regular price, the repeat probability is .806 versus .635 if both were made on deal.

Eleven of the 12 predicted associations held for the average of the 30 brands. Seven of these predicted differences were statistically different from zero at the .16 level. Four other differences had the predicted sign but were not large enough to be statistically significant. The sole exception was not large enough to be statistically significant (.042 versus .043).

It is interesting to note that P(1|01) is significantly greater than P(1|10) for both brand L-1 and the average of 30 brands. However, as can be noted in Tables 5 and 6, P(1|10′) is significantly greater than P(1|01′). That is, information on whether the purchase was made at regular or deal prices can alter the association between brand-purchase sequence and repeat-purchase probabilities.

The repeat probability, given 10′, is .515 and greater than the repeat probability for 0′1′ (.400) and much greater than for 01′ (.295). If one neglects deals, the probability of repurchasing is greater following 01 than for 10. However, knowledge of whether the purchases were made on deal can reverse this relationship.

Derived Conditional Probabilities. The data from Tables 5 and 6 can be used to derive a number of other conditional probabilities:

1. probability of repurchase conditional on the last two brands only, deals not considered;
2. probability of repurchase conditional on the last purchase only, brand and deal considered;
3. probability of repurchase conditional on the last brand purchase only, deal not considered;
4. probability of repurchase, given no past-purchase information.

TABLE 6
Weighted Average of Repeat Rates for 30 Brands

Past-Purchase Sequence[a]	*Probability of Repurchasing Brand 1*	*Reduction in Probability*[b]	*Sample Size*	*Standard Error of Estimate*
11	.806	—	5,337	.005
1′1	.708	.098[c]	681	.018
11′	.691	.017	695	.018
1′1′	.635	.056[c]	1,345	.013
0′1	.427	.208[c]	804	.017
01	.412	.015	2,196	.010
0′1′	.296	.116[c]	1,675	.011
01′	.271	.025[c]	998	.014
10′	.338	−.067[c]	837	.016
10	.277	.061[c]	2,204	.020
1′0′	.270	.007	1,724	.010
1′0	.243	.027[c]	970	.014
0′0′	.042	.201[c]	22,574	.002
00′	.043	−.001	12,782	.002
0′0	.042	.001	12,377	.002
00	.029	.013[c]	63,439	.001
Total			130,638	

a. 1 indicates a purchase of the subject brand. A prime sign (′) indicates that the purchase was on deal.
b. This column indicates the reduction in probability from the preceding sequence.
c. The difference in repeat-purchase probability is significant at the .16 level or less based on a one-tailed test.

These four types of repurchase probabilities are shown in Table 7 for brand L-1 and the weighted average of 30 brands. As can be noted, the probability of repurchasing a brand is significantly greater if the most recent purchase was made at the regular price (.669) versus a deal price (.446). It is also of interest to note that P(1|11) is greater than P(1|1) for both L-1 and the average of 30 brands.

Repurchase Rates and Market Share. An analysis of the 16 repeat rates for the 30 brands showed that repeat rates tend to be lower for brands with smaller market shares. To provide a measure of this effect, the difference in repeat rates between the largest and fourth largest brand was computed as shown in Table 8. Brand 4 was selected because the sample size for brands 5 and 6 was generally too small for meaningful comparisons. The results show that 63 of the 77 valid comparisons resulted in a larger repeat rate for brand 1 than for brand 4. Most of the 14 exceptions occurred for the sequences and product classes with small samples and thus are probably due to sampling error.

Repurchase Rates and Product Class. A second analysis was made to determine if repeat rates varied systematically by product class. This was done by computing the weighted average of repurchase rates for each product class and comparing each product class with the overall weighted average for all five product classes. The results are shown in Table 9.

If one considers only the histories ending in 1 or 1′, the results are striking. The average repeat rates for product classes L and P are almost always lower than the overall average while classes M, B1, and B2 are almost always higher. The exact cause of this difference is not known. However, classes L and P are nonfood products while M, B1, and B2 are food products. These data suggest that con-

TABLE 7
Repeat Purchase Rates Shown for Special Purchase Histories of Brand L-1 and the Weighted Average of 30 Brands

Past-Purchase Sequence	*Probability of Repurchase*	
	For Brand L-1	*For Average of 30 Brands*
Conditional on last two purchases only, deal not considered		
$\underline{1}\ \underline{1}$	.760	.759
$\underline{0}\ \underline{1}$	.463	.355
$\underline{1}\ \underline{0}$	.362	.278
$\underline{0}\ \underline{0}$	.087	.035
Conditional on last purchase only, brand and deal considered[a]		
$\underline{1}$	.720	.669
$\underline{1}'$	.496	.446
$\underline{0}'$	.149	.059
$\underline{0}$	.108	.041
Conditional on last brand purchase only, deal not considered		
$\underline{1}$	.659	.592
$\underline{0}$	.125	.050
Probability of purchasing, given no past-purchase information		
Anything	.277	.104

a. A prime sign (′) indicates a deal purchase. An underscore indicates either a deal or nondeal purchase.

sumer preferences or loyalties are stronger for food products.

Conclusions

There are distinct and predictable associations between past deal purchases and repeat-purchase probabilities. If two purchase histories are the same except for deals, there is a higher probability of purchasing the subject brand if it had not been purchased on deal or if the other brands had been purchased at deal prices.

These associations tend to hold for the six leading brands in each of five product classes. Repeat probabilities are higher for food than for nonfood products and for brands with larger market shares.

TABLE 8
Differences in Repeat Rate of Largest Market-Share Brand Minus Fourth Largest Brand

	Product Classes					
	L	*M*	*B1*	*B2*	*P*	
Market share for Brand 1	28.3	39.3	18.3	23.3	19.9	
Market share for Brand 4	5.2	3.9	9.5	6.2	4.8	
Past-Purchase Sequence	*Brand 1 Minus Brand 4 Probability*					
11	.120	.079	−.077	.035	.133	
1′1	.049	.159	.018	—	.355	
11′	−.015	.191	.028	.172	.175	
1′1′	.128	.165	−.106	−.295	.458	
0′1	.395	−.047	.500	.264	.426	
01	.290	.042	.061	−.093	.118	
0′1′	.044	−.375	−.115	.287	.343	
10′	.083	.000	−.029	.065	.042	
10	.292	.075	.113	−.017	.043	
1′0′	.137	−.100	−.001	.274	.158	
1′0	.108	.237	.135	−.739	.278	
0′0′	.059	.132	.063	.113	.137	
00′	.058	.138	.061	.083	.082	
0′0	.050	.141	.037	.100	.090	
00	.053	.139	.037	.040	.051	
Summary						*Total*
Brand 1 exceeds Brand 4	15	11	10	11	16	= 63
Brand 4 exceeds Brand 1	1	3	6	4	0	= 14

TABLE 9
Difference in Repeat-Purchase Probabilities (Product Class Average Minus Average for Five Product Classes)

Past Purchases	*Product Class*				
	L	*M*	*B1*	*B2*	*P*
11	−.013	.013	.013	.037	−.029
1′1	−.018	.051	.033	.056	−.058
11′	−.069	.117	.057	.086	−.094
1′1′	−.098	−.016	.121	.049	−.098
0′1	−.001	.131	.009	.008	−.026
01	.008	.046	.095	.047	−.058
0′1′	−.016	.246	.046	−.016	−.069
01′	−.041	.045	.082	.004	−.010
10′	.029	.001	.047	.040	−.049
10	.025	.035	.017	.034	−.039
1′0′	.105	−.020	.017	−.012	−.056
1′0	.063	−.046	.116	−.028	−.052
0′0′	−.007	−.013	−.001	−.019	.018
00′	−.003	−.004	.004	−.012	.012
0′0	−.008	−.006	−.002	−.008	.014
00	−.004	.003	−.002	−.010	.009

References

Blattberg, Robert C., and Subrata K. Sen. An Evaluation of the Application of Minimum Chi-Square Procedures to Stochastic Models of Brand Choice. *Journal of Marketing Research*, Vol. 49, November 1973, pp. 421–427.

Carman, James M. Brand Switching and Linear Learning Models. *Journal of Advertising Research*, Vol. 6, June 1966, pp. 23–31.

Frank, Ronald E. Brand Choice as a Probability Process. *Journal of Business*, Vol. 35, January 1962, pp. 43–56.

Howard, Ronald A. Stochastic Process Models of Consumer Behavior. *Journal of Advertising Research*, Vol. 3. September 1963, pp. 35–42.

Kuehn, Alfred A. Consumer Brand Choice as a Learning Process. *Journal of Advertising Research*, Vol. 2, December 1962, pp. 10–17.

Lawrence, Raymond J. Patterns of Buyer Behavior: Time for a New Approach? *Journal of Marketing Research*, Vol. 6, May 1969, pp. 137–144.

Massy, William F., David B. Montgomery, and Donald G. Morrison. *Stochastic Models of Buying Behavior.* Cambridge, Mass.: M.I.T. Press, 1970.

READING 27

Consumer Response to In-Store Price Information Environments

Valarie A. Zeithaml

A laboratory experiment evaluated the impact of eight in-store information environments on consumer processing of price information. Results reveal that the format of information provision significantly affected subjects' cognitive, affective, and behavioral responses. Findings suggest that both item marking and a list of unit prices facilitate processing of grocery-store prices.

The primary purpose of the study reported here was to evaluate the impact of different in-store information environments on consumer processing of price information. This purpose embodied two dimensions. First, the research investigated the relationship between the traditional method of displaying raw prices, called "item marking," and consumers' ability to recall and use price information. Second, it compared four methods of shelf pricing to determine which method or methods, if any, best facilitated consumer information processing.

The traditional method of pricing grocery items, "item marking," consists of stamping the raw price on each individual product. This practice was instituted primarily to provide supermarket checkers with accurate prices to charge customers. Electronic scanning checkout systems, which now operate in over 5,000 supermarkets in the United States, make item marking unnecessary. With the new scanning systems, price information is coded into the store's computer and read at the register from the item's UPC symbol. Supermarkets with scanners can eliminate the traditional price stamps and replace them with shelf pricing, thereby realizing significant cost savings.

Consumer advocates and public-policy makers in many states oppose the practice of removing raw prices from individual items on the grounds that it will harm consumers. Specifically, consumer advocates contend that item-price removal will reduce shoppers' awareness of prices, will make price comparisons between similar product categories (e.g., between canned green beans and frozen green beans) more difficult, and will force consumers to invest more time in shopping. Supporters of item-price removal refute these criticisms by claiming that consumers will be able to operate as effectively and efficiently with shelf pricing, that price comparisons will be facilitated because consumers will make greater use of unit-price information, and that shopping time will be reduced because consumers will no longer need to handle individual items to find prices.

Neither critics nor supporters of price removal have sufficient facts on which to base their claims. The single study conducted to differentiate between the two pricing systems showed that item marking marginally improved consumer price awareness, but that overall awareness was high in both groups (Allen, Harrell, and Hutt 1976). Fueled by these inconclusive results, however, consumer activists in seven states have pressed for and attained mandatory price-marking legislation. Other groups have spoken in favor of pricing legislation in both houses of Congress.

Reprinted with permission from the *Journal of Consumer Research,* 8:4 March 1982, 357–369.

The research reported here was designed to provide experimental data concerning the effects of item-price removal and the information environments that would prevail if item-price removal were implemented. The study examined a broad range of effects by partitioning responses into cognitive, affective, and behavioral stages. Rather than concentrating only on the end result of the process (i.e., purchase choice), or emphasizing only initial processing stages, the study provided a comprehensive examination by obtaining multiple measures throughout the hierarchy of effects. The approach is consistent with recent public policy-related experiments regarding advertising messages (Houston and Rothschild 1980; Wright 1979) and offers both public-policy makers and marketers improved data on which to base decisions about information provision.

Research Orientation

A major research issue in information processing concerns the choice of dependent measures that most appropriately capture the effects of information. Some researchers (e.g., McGuire 1976) contend that the ultimate criterion must involve behavior (i.e., purchase choice). They claim that perceptual measures, such as comprehension and recall, can provide results that either disappear or are reversed in later processing stages and are only tenuously related to the ultimate goal of behavior change. For this reason, they discourage emphasis on measuring the effects of early stages of processing. Alternatively, other researchers (Bettman 1975; Wilkie 1975) contend that behavior change is not always the goal. Some public-policy programs, for example, are designed to aid consumers in perceiving and processing information. In these cases, recall, knowledge, and awareness variables become more critical than behavior or attitudinal variables. Bettman (1975) summarizes the controversy surrounding the selection of appropriate criterion measures by dichotomizing the intent of information environments into (1) "processing" normative and (2) "policy" normative. If the intent is "processing" normative, a program is designed to help consumers perceive and process information without a commitment to how (or even if) consumers use such information. On the other hand, a "policy" normative intent requires that the objective of the information program involve changing the consumer's behavior. According to Bettman (1975) and others (Hutton, McNeill, and Wilkie 1978), the intent of information provision dictates the choice of dependent variables. If the program is policy normative, measures should involve attitudes, intentions, and behavior (e.g., brand choice or purchase). If the program is processing normative, the appropriate dependent measures are recall, awareness, and knowledge.

Recently, researchers have emphasized the need to include dependent measures of the entire hierarchy of effects, i.e., cognitions, attitudes, and behaviors, within the scope of evaluation (Houston and Rothschild 1980). The rationale for this approach is that both processing and policy normative orientations are likely to be present to some degree in any information-provision program. Both orientations would be present in any program concerning grocery store prices. Therefore, all levels of the hierarchy of effects are considered in the present study.

A conceptual model that depicts the steps in the processing of price information, thereby offering a framework for investigating effects at multiple levels, is illustrated in Figure A1 (Jacoby and Olson 1977). This model divides consumer reactions to price into stages corresponding to cognition (encoding of objective (O) price and storage of psychological (P) price), affect (attitude toward P-price), and behavior (responses such as purchase). The links between this conceptual schema and the research reported here are shown in Figure A.

The stimulus or input in the general conceptual schema could be any form of price information. In the experiment reported here, stimuli include three forms of price information:

1. shelf prices only (i.e., the absence of item marks on individual products);
2. shelf prices plus item marking; and
3. unit prices displayed in a structured list form.

In the general conceptual schema, the organism receives the input in a form isomorphic to the external stimulus (acquisition of O-price), but may change the information in the process of encoding it. As an example, the external stimulus may be 79 cents, yet the individual may assign it a meaning of "inexpensive" when encoding it. This interpretation of the external price stimulus by the organism results in the psychological price (P-price). This stage of the schema has received little attention by researchers (Jacoby and Olson 1977; Olson 1978, 1980) perhaps due to the difficulty of operationalizing and measuring encoding. In the research reported here, encoding is operationalized and measured because it may critically affect subsequent stages of processing. Encoding is viewed as a mediating variable, rather than as a dependent variable, because (1) encoding style may be affected more by individual differences in consumers than by types of information, and (2) measures of subsequent stages of processing (such as recall or purchase behavior) are of more direct interest to marketers and public-policy makers.

The levels-of-processing framework (Craik and Lockhart 1972) provided the conceptual base for encoding constructs measured in this study. In contrast to the traditional structural model of memory (Atkinson and Shiffrin 1968) that postulates multiple and distinct repositories for information (e.g., sensory, short-term, and long-term memory stores), this model hypothesizes a single memory, an overall processing capacity, and the ability to engage in different levels of processing (Bettman 1979b). According to the model, individuals encode stimuli at a variety of

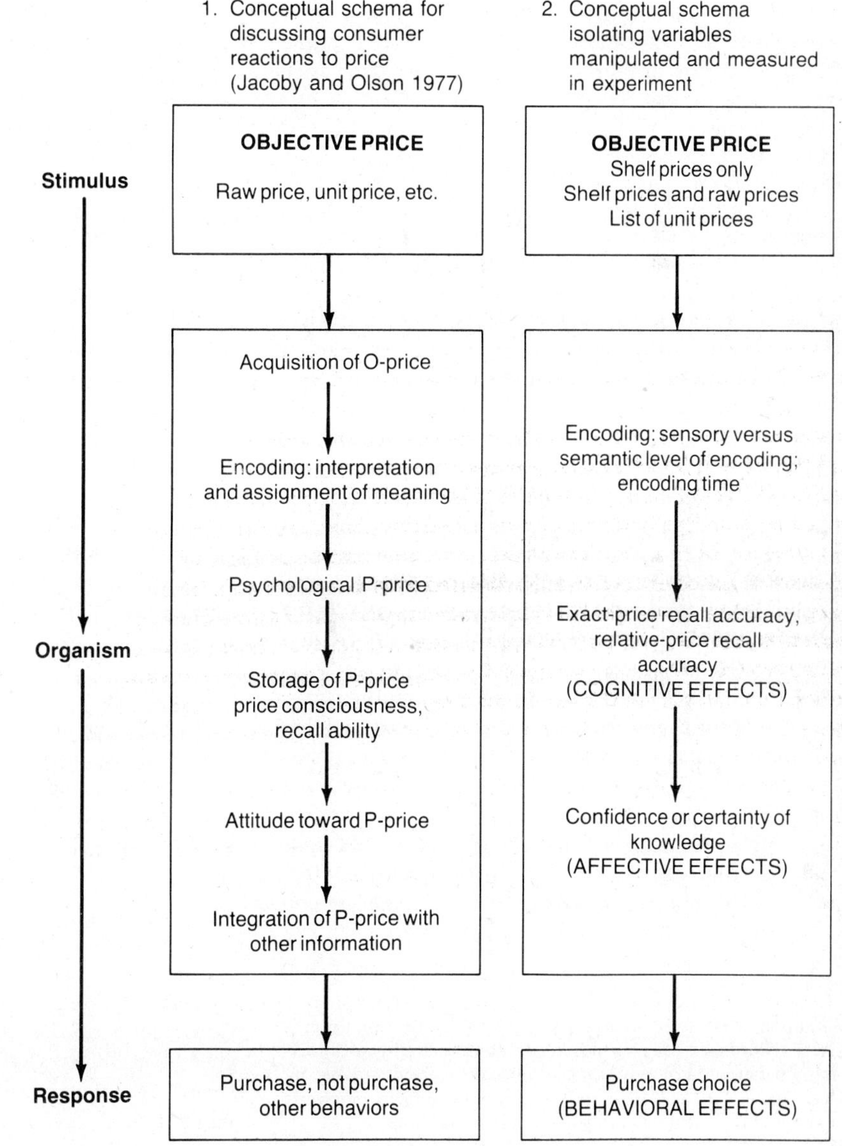

FIGURE A
Conceptual Models of Consumer Processing of Price Information

levels, which can range from "shallow" sensory analysis to "deep" semantic or cognitive analysis. The durability of information in memory appears to be a function of the depth of analysis, with deeper levels associated with more elaborate, longer lasting, and stronger memory traces (Craik and Lockhart 1972). The levels-of-processing framework is more parsimonious, less cumbersome, and more consistent with recent data than older, mechanistic notions about memory stores. (See Bettman 1979a, b; Olson 1978, 1980 for a complete comparison of the models of memory.)

The remaining processing steps in the general conceptual model parallel variables measured in the study. "Storage of P-price" is operationalized as price recall (cognition); "attitude toward P-price" is defined in terms of certainty of price knowledge (affect); and "purchase" is measured in terms of unit prices paid for products.

Cognitive Effects

A subject's familiarity with information influences subsequent processing. Information that is familiar tends to be processed more readily than unfamiliar information because it is compatible with existing cognitive structures (Craik and Lockhart 1972). Because item marking is familiar to consumers, and the absence of item marking is not,[1] it is hypothesized that:

H1: Item marking will decrease errors in recall of the exact prices of products.

An experiment conducted to compare stores with and without item marking (Allen, Harrell, and Hutt 1976) lends support to this hypothesis. A significant reduction in price awareness (i.e., the ability to find and recall prices) was found in stores without item marking.

A consistent finding regarding unit pricing is that it enables consumers to make better price comparisons (Friedman 1966, 1972; Gatewood and Perloff 1973; Houston 1972). Since unit pricing is printed only on shelf tags in grocery stores, consumers who rely solely on item marks for price information may not use unit prices in selecting products. Thus, item marking may actually interfere with the processing and use of unit-pricing information. Consequently, it is hypothesized that:

H2: Item marking will increase errors in recall of the relative prices of products.

Organization of stimuli in the information environment may influence subsequent processing. The format or structure of stimuli affects processing, largely because subjects tend to deal with information in the form in which it is presented. Slovic (1972) labeled this tendency "concreteness":

> *Concreteness represents the general notion that a judge or decision maker tends to use only the information that is explicitly displayed in the stimulus object and will use it only in the form in which it is displayed. Information that has to be stored in memory, inferred from the explicit display, or transformed tends to be discounted or ignored (Slovic 1972, p. 12).*

The tendency toward "concreteness" has been verified empirically. Bettman and Kakkar (1977), van Raaij (1976), and Svenson (1974) found in separate studies that subjects processed information in exactly the manner it was provided and did not reorganize or transform the stimuli into other processing configurations. In another experiment, Johnson and Russo (1978) revealed congruence between memory structures and input organization. Finally, results reported by Russo, Kreiser, and Miyashita (1975) and Russo (1977) verified that consumers used comparative price information to a greater extent when it was provided in an organized list of unit prices. Based upon these findings, it is hypothesized that:

H3: A structured list of unit prices will decrease errors in recall of the prices of products.

The type of shelf tag used to present prices may affect subsequent recall of those prices. Factors such as size of printing, presence of colors that emphasize unit pricing, and size of the tag itself influence the legibility of a shelf tag. For this reason, it is predicted that:

H4: There will be a negative relationship between legibility of shelf tags and errors in price recall.

Affective Effects

Consumer attitudes can be operationalized as the degree of certainty that consumers feel regarding their knowledge of prices in an information environment. While this does not represent a direct affective re-

1. At the time this research was conducted, no major grocery chains had removed item marks. In most states, item marks were voluntarily maintained due to consumer and consumerist resistance; in seven states item marks were mandated by legislation. Further, all grocery stores in the city in which the experiment was conducted provided item marking.

sponse toward the price information itself, it is an implicit attitude reflecting consumers' feelings about their ability to comprehend different types of price information. Because consumers are familiar with item marking, the following hypothesis is proposed:

H5: Item marking will increase certainty associated with the recall of exact prices of products.

With a structured list of unit prices (Russo, Kreiser, and Miyashita 1975; Russo 1977), part of the processing of price information is accomplished for the consumer. Instead of calculating and comparing unit prices of products in their heads, consumers can consult a printed source listing products from least expensive to most expensive. Because the information processing task is predicted to be easier with the list, it is hypothesized that:

H6: A structured list of unit prices will increase certainty associated with the recall of relative prices of products.

Behavioral Effects

If consumers employ more familiar forms of information, i.e., item marking, to the exclusion of less familiar forms, they may never use shelf pricing (and therefore unit pricing) when item marking is present. Previous studies (Friedman 1966, 1972; Houston 1972) have shown that consumers experience difficulty in determining the most economical purchases without unit pricing. Even though consumers can avail themselves of unit-pricing information when item marking is present, it is predicted that they will do so to a lesser extent, and consequently:

H7: Item marking will increase the unit prices paid for products.

Russo et al. (1975) and Russo (1977) demonstrated experimentally that consumer expenditures decreased between 1.4 and three percent when an organized list of unit prices was displayed on grocery shelves. Consistent with these findings, it is hypothesized that:

H8: A list of unit prices will decrease the unit prices paid for products.

Methodology

A laboratory setting that simulated the actual conditions of exposure facing consumers when they process price information was selected as the environment in which to examine consumer responses to price stimuli. The laboratory environment offered the well-documented advantage of greater internal validity, because levels of independent variables were controlled and extraneous variables were minimized. In addition, the laboratory setting provided an efficient means to evaluate the entire scope and nature of stimuli used for presenting price information.

The Sample

The frame for this study was Columbus, Ohio, females who were at least 18 years old. While other individuals (e.g., men or younger women) could also have served as respondents, the frame was limited to include only primary household grocery shoppers (Yankelovich, Skelly, and White 1979), thereby focusing on those individuals who most frequently use price information. The data were collected in April of 1980. Subjects were selected systematically on an every-nth-name basis from a computerized mailing list of female heads of households, compiled by a market research firm from a list of single family dwelling units in Columbus. Women selected were telephoned and screened to determine whether they qualified. Among the respondents contacted, 64 percent qualified, although follow-up calls were often required to reach them. Of the qualified individuals contacted, 53 percent agreed to participate in the study.[2]

Respondents were recruited by telephone ap-

2. Little information was available with which to determine differences between those who agreed to participate and those who did not. Reasons offered for nonparticipation most frequently involved scheduling problems and lack of transportation. Demographic characteristics of the sample were comparable to those of the population of Columbus. The median school years completed by respondents in the sample was 12.5; the median school years completed by females 25 years or older in Columbus was 12. Although the median family income reported by sample respondents was approximately $3,000 higher than that of the population, the difference may be explained by nonresponse (nine percent), by inflation (1970 Census figures were used), and by the possibility that some respondents overreported income. The distribution of respondents by income groups was comparable to that of the population. Distribution of household size and age of sample respondents approximated population distributions in Columbus, except in the 20–24 age category. Because of university students, this age category is larger than any other in Columbus. By design, the sample did not reflect this concentration, because college students did not live in single-family dwellings and were not typical of primary household shoppers.

proximately three weeks before the experiment. They were promised product samples and a monetary incentive for participating in a study concerning shopping habits of Columbus women. After agreeing to participate in the experiment, subjects were assigned randomly to eight experimental cells. They were telephoned again the week prior to the experiment to confirm their appointments.

Laboratory Environment

A 24-foot grocery aisle was simulated and equipped with 90 different brands and sizes of products in 12 categories (Table 1). During half of the experiment, products were displayed without their item prices. During the other half of the experiment, items were price stamped with a standard ink price marker. Slots in the shelves under products held tags that contained both item prices and unit prices.

Procedures

Subjects entered the laboratory individually and were greeted by an interviewer, who briefed the subject, gave her a scenario disguising the nature of the experiment (by claiming that it was designed to compare shopping habits of women in different cities in the United States), and presented her with a shopping list itemizing 12 product categories. The interviewer instructed the subject to "shop" for the listed items, to stay within a budget of ten dollars, and to select one brand and size from each category. The ten-dollar budget, which was designed to encourage a realistic approach to the shopping task, was sufficient to purchase the largest sizes of all twelve products.

Each subject performed the shopping task individually. Immediately after the interviewer sent her into the experimental room, a stopwatch was started. As the subject exited the room after the "shopping trip," her total shopping time was recorded. Another interviewer greeted her, took her shopping cart and money, and sent her into one of three subject booths to complete a questionnaire, after which she was debriefed by the experimenter. Included in the debriefing session were questions probing the purpose of the experiment,[3] questions soliciting comments on procedure, and questions concerning differences between the laboratory setting and actual grocery stores. As recommended by Tybout and Zaltman (1974), the experimenter then revealed the true purpose of the experiment, explained the reason for the disguise, and apologized for the deception. Respondents appeared to be satisfied with the explanation, frequently offering comments and suggestions for improving grocery-store pricing. Finally, the subject was asked to remain silent concerning her participation in the experiment.

TABLE 1
ANOVA Results for Unit Price Paid
(All Shelf Tag Levels)

	F-statistics		
Product	*Item Marking*	*Shelf-Tag Level*	*IM × STL*
AVERAGE	9.63[b]	40.67[a]	9.55[a]
Canned green beans	3.38	9.40[a]	4.65[b]
Canned peas	4.85[c]	12.58[a]	3.90[b]
Canned fruit cocktail	<1.00	15.90[a]	3.39[c]
Canned tuna	110.96[a]	5.39[b]	16.49[a]
Peanut butter	6.16[c]	26.11[a]	12.11[a]
Syrup	2.83	9.62[a]	<1.00
Furniture polish	6.29[c]	58.91[a]	3.32[c]
Deodorant soap	50.54[a]	156.73[a]	76.23[a]
Paper towels	5.02[c]	4.50[b]	30.11[a]
Liquid dish detergent	5.43[c]	73.68[a]	23.05[a]
Ketchup	11.31[b]	1.77	13.10[a]
Salad dressing	<1.00	12.57[a]	5.29[b]

a. $p \leq 0.001$.
b. $p \leq 0.01$.
c. $p \leq 0.05$.
NOTE: Unit prices of eleven products (all experimental products except paper towels) were combined to form this average.

Research Design

A four (shelf-pricing formats) by two (item marking and no-item marking) between-subjects factorial design was employed in the laboratory experiment.

Operationalization of Independent Variables

Two experimental factors, each with several levels, were manipulated. The first factor, level of shelf-pricing legibility, involved four different shelf-pricing formats arranged on an hypothesized continuum of

3. This question was also asked before subjects completed the questionnaire to investigate the success of the experimental disguise. Only one subject (who was replaced) guessed that the experiment concerned price information.

legibility. The second factor, level of item marking, was operationalized as the presence or absence of raw prices on individual items.[4]

Shelf-Pricing Formats. The selection of shelf-pricing formats was based on two criteria: (1) their ability to typify formats currently used by retailers, and (2) their ability to demonstrate an hypothesized level of legibility. The first criterion was satisfied by analyzing and categorizing nearly 100 sample shelf tags assembled in an industry survey (Zeithaml 1980). Past research studies and industry experience led to the selection of tags to fulfill the second criterion.

Categorization of the industry tags revealed three major format clusters, each one produced by a different mechanical process. The first cluster, prepared by computer, consisted of tags that were printed in small numerals the size of standard computer-printout characters. Because the small numeral size and light printing make these tags difficult to read from a distance, a tag from this cluster was selected to represent level one, the least legible format. The second cluster contained tags prepared by Printronix equipment, an improved computer-printing method offering larger, bolder numerals. The third cluster contained tags prepared by phototypography, an expensive process whereby type is set by machine to provide a clear, distinct print. The final shelf format employed the same tag as that used in level three, but added a structured list of unit prices (Russo 1977) to the shelves. Russo, Kreiser, and Miyashita (1975) and Russo (1977) found that a list of unit prices presents information in a more processible form than standard shelf tags alone. The combination of shelf tag and list was used, rather than the list alone, because it seems inconceivable that the list would ever stand alone (due to legal restrictions), and because this procedure replicates Russo's information environment.

4. A series of questions was used to check on the effectiveness of the experimental manipulations. The first question asked subjects to identify the location of price information in their treatments and was designed to check on the item-marking manipulation. Most (94 percent) of the subjects responded with the accurate location. In the shelf-tag manipulation check, subjects were shown a display containing all four shelf tags. They were asked to choose the tag used in their treatment (93 percent chose the correct tag) and to evaluate the set of tags in terms of legibility. Answers confirmed that the four shelf tags were ordered along a continuum from least to most legible.

Dependent Variables

Measures of Cognitive Effects. Subjects were asked to recall both the exact and the relative prices of products. Two forms of price recall were chosen as dependent measures because two types of price information (exact prices and relative prices) are helpful in consumer decision making. Exact-price information allows consumers to stay within a budget limit at the grocery store and to follow trends (especially increases) in product prices, while relative-price information tells the consumer which products are most economical.

Recall of exact prices was operationalized as *exact-price recall error,* the percentage of error made by a respondent in remembering exact prices of products. To control for involvement, subjects were required to recall exact prices only for the 12 products they selected in the experimental task. Recalled prices were compared to actual prices, and the percentage of recall error was calculated for each product by the following formula:

$$\%\ \text{Error} = \frac{\text{Recalled Price} - \text{Correct Price}}{\text{Correct Price}}$$

The summary measure of this variable was the average percentage of error for the 12 products selected by each respondent.

The other recall measure, called *price-comparison error,* involved respondent errors in ranking categories of products by their prices. Errors in ranks were tabulated by counting the absolute difference in rank units between the correct rank and the subject's recalled rank. Thirteen sets of rankings were required, one set for each of eleven product categories and two sets for the twelfth product category, which contained two dissimilar package sizes. The summary measure for this variable was the total number of rank errors over all sets.

Subjects were asked to rank products by price before they were asked to recall exact prices in order to avoid testing effects.

Measures of Affect. Feelings generated by price stimuli were measured by questions concerning the impact of the different stimuli on respondent perceptions of their own price knowledge. Seven-point certainty scales (ranging from very uncertain to very certain) followed each of the memory tasks. Specifically, one certainty scale was displayed at the bottom of each of two pages containing ranking problems.

It queried, "How certain are you that the rankings above are correct?" Similarly, one scale was displayed next to each of 12 spaces in which consumers recorded the exact prices of products. It queried, "How certain are you that the price you remember is the price you paid?" The dependent variable called *certainty of price comparison* was formed by summing the two certainty scales associated with the ranking problems. *Certainty of exact-price recall* was formed by summing the 12 individual certainty scores.

Measures of Behavioral Effects. Russo et al. (1975) calculated the average price paid per unit in a product category prior to posting a structured list of unit prices and compared it to the price paid after the information had been presented, thereby quantifying the "value of unit-price information." A measure similar to the one developed by Russo was employed in this study to examine the behavioral effects of the price-information environments. The *price paid per unit* for each consumer purchase was calculated by dividing the item price of the selected product by its weight. The price paid per unit (e.g., price per ounce per square foot) was computed for each product selected by a subject. Finally, an average unit price paid for the eleven products measured in ounces was calculated. For each subject, a total of 13 unit prices (12 individual-product unit prices and one average unit price) measured the behavioral effects of the price information environments.

Mediating Variables

Individual differences among subjects were anticipated to account for some variation in their processing of price information. To factor out these individual differences, several mediating variables were operationalized and measured.

Demographic Variables. Standard demographic questions regarding age, income, education, household size, and marital status were included at the end of the questionnaire. Empirical evidence (Day 1976; Engledow 1972) suggests differential use of information as a function of these characteristics.

Encoding Time. Encoding time was operationalized as the total number of seconds the subject spent in the test area. While subjects may have engaged in behaviors other than the encoding of price information (e.g., looking at nutritional information or reading package directions), the measure provided a way to factor out extreme variations in the amount of time spent in the test area. The variation could have been controlled by imposing a time limit on respondents, but such a constraint was thought to be atypical of actual shopping trips and may have interfered with the measurement of other variables.

Levels of Encoding. Consumers appear to have two main categories of interest in grocery prices, which correspond to different depths of encoding. The first, interest in the exact price of products, involves encoding prices in the form in which they are presented (e.g., 79 cents) and is roughly representative of a sensory level of processing (Craik and Tulving 1975; Olson 1978). The second type, interest in relative prices, involves encoding relative prices of products (e.g., Product A is cheaper than Product B), and represents a more semantic level of processing (Craik and Tulving 1975; Olson 1978).

Rather than specifying a priori that subjects use one of these two types of encoding, this study allowed subjects to employ their own characteristic encoding methods. Then, following the memory performance test, subjects responded to a series of questions designed to indicate the degree to which the two processing levels, sensory and semantic, had been used to encode the prices.

Subjects indicated on five-point scales (ranging from disagree to agree) the extent to which statements described their own typical shopping behaviors. Three statements were used to measure encoding at the sensory level ("I notice the prices of products I buy in the grocery store"; "I notice price changes"; "I remember the prices of products I buy in the grocery store"), and a scale formed by summing the responses to these statements constituted the overall measure called *degree of sensory encoding.* Three statements were used to measure encoding at the semantic level ("I buy the lowest-priced product in a product category"; "I make price comparisons between different forms of a product (canned versus frozen green beans, for example)"; "I use unit pricing to compare the prices of products"), and a scale formed by summing the responses to these statements constituted the overall measure called *degree of semantic encoding.* As measured by these scales, the greater the agreement with these questions, the greater the extent of encoding at that level.

Because there were no studies in the literature

that measured encoding of prices, scales were developed for this purpose. Following a review of the literature concerning prices and encoding (Craik and Lockhart 1972; Gabor and Granger 1964; Olson 1978), a focus-group interview with consumers, and a pretest, the sensory and semantic encoding scales were constructed. Coefficient α was calculated on these scales in a pretest and in the experiment reported here. The value of coefficient α for *degree of sensory encoding* was 0.85 in the pretest and 0.81 in the study reported here. The coefficient α value for *degree of semantic encoding* was 0.54 in the pretest and 0.42 in the study reported here.

Brand Loyalty. If a consumer tends to be loyal to particular brands of products, she may not notice or consider prices in her purchase choices. It is possible, then, that the degree of brand loyalty a consumer exhibits will mediate the effectiveness of price information. To measure this potential intervening variable, two statements were included: (1) "I prefer to buy my favorite brand of a product regardless of its price," and (2) "I buy name brand items." Subjects indicated on five-point scales (ranging from disagree to agree) the extent to which these statements described their own typical shopping behaviors. A scale formed by summing these two responses represented the measure called *brand loyalty.* The coefficient α value for this scale was 0.72, indicating relatively high internal consistency.

Results

Cognitive Effects

Analysis of variance was used to examine the effects of item marking on exact-price recall error. Before applying the ANOVA model, a preliminary analysis was conducted to determine whether mediating variables should be included as covariates.

First, the intervening variables of encoding time, degree of sensory encoding, degree of semantic encoding, and brand loyalty were examined to determine their relationship to exact-price error. Encoding time did not appear to significantly affect subjects' price-recall error (Pearson product-moment correlation coefficient = 0.038; $p \leqslant 0.6304$). Likewise, brand loyalty did not demonstrate a significant relationship (Spearman's Rho = 0.08; $p \leqslant 0.2323$). However, degree of sensory encoding was significantly correlated with exact-price recall error (Spearman's Rho = 0.24; $p \leqslant 0.0002$) and, therefore, was introduced as a covariate.

Following an examination of demographic variable frequencies and percentages by cell, and their relationships with exact-price recall error, age was isolated as the only concomitant demographic variable (Spearman's Rho = 0.22; $p \leqslant 0.01$). The positive correlation between age and exact-price recall error indicates that error increased with the age of the respondents.

The combined model controlling for both age and degree of sensory encoding is shown in Table 2. In this model, the item marking effect had an F-value of 5.17 and was significant at $p \leqslant 0.0244$. Therefore, Hypothesis 1 is supported. The overall adjusted group mean for item marking was 17.53 percent error in exact-price recall. Without item marking, the adjusted group mean was 21.27 percent error.

The two-way ANOVA model for price-comparison errors (Table 2B) incorporated age as the single covariate, as no other demographic and no encoding variables were significant. As was the case with exact-price recall error, older respondents made more errors in recall than younger respondents (Spearman's Rho between age and price-comparison errors = 0.30; $p \leqslant 0.0001$). The mean number of price-comparison

TABLE 2
ANOVA Results for Cognitive Effects

Source	*MS*	*F*
A. Analysis of variance of exact-price recall error, controlling for effects of age, and degree of sensory encoding		
Item marking (A)	541.15	5.17[b]
Shelf-tag level (B)	67.74	0.65
A X B	181.38	1.73
Age	516.56	4.93[b]
Degree of sensory encoding	475.53	4.54[b]
B. Analysis of variance of price-comparison error, controlling for effects of age		
Item marking (A)	270.18	0.67
Shelf-tag level (B)	848.86	2.12
A X B	489.70	1.22
Age	3,470.42	8.67[a]

a. Significant at 0.01 level.
b. Significant at 0.05 level.

errors in the two treatments, item marking versus nonitem marking, were 53.56 and 56.20, respectively. Contrary to Hypothesis 2, fewer price-comparison errors occurred in the item marking condition than in the nonitem marking condition. However, the difference between the two treatments was not significant ($p \leqslant 0.4127$) and may be attributable to random error.[5]

A reduced ANOVA model, using only shelf-tag levels three (shelf tag three with no list of unit prices) and four (shelf tag three with a list of unit prices) was employed to analyze Hypothesis 3. Although the mean without the list was larger (59.82) than with the list (55.16), this difference was not significant ($F = 1.29; p \leqslant 0.2599$).

When controlling for age, the effect of shelf-tag level on price-comparison errors (Hypothesis 4) was significant only at a relatively high alpha risk of 0.0986 ($F = 2.12$). The treatment means were not ordered in the manner suggested by the hypothesis; mean errors were lowest in shelf-level two (48.67), followed by level four (54.00), level one (58.18), and level three (58.64), respectively.

Affective Effects

The median test revealed a significant difference ($X^2 = 9.02; p \leqslant 0.03$) in the direction predicted in Hypothesis 5 between the item-marking and nonitem-marking conditions with regard to the degree of certainty experienced by the respondents.

The results of a median test comparing certainty scores in shelf-tag levels three and four (without and with a list of unit prices, respectively), indicated a significant difference in the direction predicted in Hypothesis 6 between the treatments ($X^2 = 4.07; p \leqslant 0.05$).

Behavioral Effects

As shown in Table 1, analysis of variance for the average unit price paid (the summary measure averaging the unit prices paid for the eleven products measured in ounces) reveals a significant effect of item marking ($F = 9.63; p \leqslant 0.0023$) and a significant interaction effect of item marking with shelf-tag level ($F = 9.55; p \leqslant 0.0001$). The overall mean without item marking was 6.89 and the overall mean with item marking was 6.72. While there was a statistically significant difference between the unit prices paid with and without item marking, the difference was not in the direction hypothesized. Rather than increasing the average unit price paid for products, item marking actually appeared to decrease the average unit price paid. Thus, Hypothesis 7 is rejected.

Examination of the means for unit prices paid within each product category revealed inconsistent effects of item marking: in five cases, unit prices paid were lower with item marking; in seven cases, unit prices paid were lower without item marking. In eight of the 12 cases, the differences were significant. In eleven of the 12 cases, interaction effects were also significant.

A reduced ANOVA model, isolating shelf-levels three and four, was employed to test the effect of posting a list of unit prices on the resultant unit prices paid for products. The unit prices paid for each of 12 individual products were calculated, and a summary measure of the unit price paid was formed by averaging the prices for the eleven items measured in ounces. Since preliminary analysis revealed no significant concomitant variables, the model contained no covariates.

As shown in Table 3, the average unit price paid shows significant effects associated with the list of unit prices ($F = 67.13; p \leqslant 0.001$), confirming Hypothesis 8. The average unit price paid without the list of unit prices was 7.28 cents per ounce; the average unit price paid with the list of unit prices was 6.59 cents.

At the individual-product level of analysis, a significant effect of the list was disclosed in ten of the 12 product categories (seven at $p \leqslant 0.0001$, two at $p \leqslant 0.01$, and one at $p \leqslant 0.05$). In six of these product categories, interaction effects of the list with item marking were also revealed. Figure B plots the results of four representative cases and illustrates the single consistent finding: the list of unit prices significantly reduced the unit price paid. The interaction effect

5. Some retailers claim that the consumer's level of price information may be lower with item marking than without it, because item marking may preclude the use of shelf tags. Since shelf tags contain additional price information (in the form of unit prices), the consumer who uses shelf tags may be more informed than one who depends on item marks. Consistent with this notion was the finding that respondents in the cells that contained item marking reported significantly lower exposure to shelf-pricing information than respondents in cells not containing item marking. The percentages of subjects who reported using shelf-price information averaged 75 percent in the item-marking cells and averaged only 58.75 percent in the nonitem-marking cells. The difference in use of shelf pricing was significant at $p \leqslant 0.03$ ($X^2 = 4.76$, 1 DF).

TABLE 3
ANOVA Results for Unit Price Paid (Shelf Tag Levels Three and Four Only)

	F-statistics		
Product	*Item Marking*	*Shelf-Tag Level*	*IM × STL*
AVERAGE	38.15[a]	67.13[a]	<1.00
Canned green beans	4.4[c]	30.99[b]	14.75[a]
Canned peas	14.39[b]	24.17[c]	<1.00
Canned fruit cocktail	2.55	29.73[a]	2.55
Canned tuna	148.7[a]	1.24	4.58[c]
Peanut butter	3.22	19.40[a]	<1.00
Syrup	<1.00	18.80[a]	<1.00
Furniture polish	1.82	91.92[a]	10.27[b]
Deodorant soap	665.81[a]	873.84[a]	99.66[a]
Paper towels	13.66[b]	14.71[b]	66.78[a]
Liquid dish detergent	16.51[a]	86.72[a]	6.00[c]
Ketchup	15.13[b]	<1.00	6.72[c]
Salad dressing	4.45[c]	19.67[a]	10.36[b]

a. $p \leq 0.001$.
b. $p \leq 0.01$.
c. $p \leq 0.05$.
NOTE: Unit prices of eleven products (all experimental products except paper towels) were combined to form this average.

with item marking shows mixed results. In two cases, item marking appeared to depress the effect of the list of unit prices; in two others, it appeared to increase the effect.

Discussion

The Effects of Item Marking

The effects of item marking on four dependent variables were investigated. Hypothesized relationships between item marking and exact-price recall error, and between item marking and certainty of exact-price recall, were confirmed. A significant relationship between item marking and price-comparison errors was not found. Finally, a significant relationship between item marking and unit price paid was revealed, but this relationship was not in the direction specified by the hypothesis.

The findings at the cognitive level, which illustrate the advantages of item marking on price recall, corroborate the single previous study on the subject (Allen, Harrell, and Hutt 1976). This reduced ability to recall prices in the absence of item marks may account for respondents feeling more uncertain about their price knowledge when item marking was absent than when item marking was present.

Item marking did not increase price-comparison error. Retailers' claims that item marking would result in decreased use of shelf tags was demonstrated to be true, as measured by subjects' self-reports of their use of price information. However, when recall was measured, i.e., price comparison errors, there was not an increase in errors due to item marking. Therefore, the predicted negative consequences of the item-marking information environment did not materialize.

Finally, item marking demonstrated somewhat ambiguous results in terms of its effect on the unit prices paid for products. Although the average unit price paid was significantly lower with item marking (contrary to the hypothesis), the effects appeared to depend on which shelf level accompanied the item-marking treatment. In levels one and two, item marking did increase (as predicted) the unit price paid; however, in shelf-levels three and four, item marking was associated with a decrease in unit price paid. One possible explanation for this result is the inferiority of the shelf tags used in levels one and two. Item marking, although a weak substitute for unit pricing on shelf tags, may have been helpful to some degree in providing relative price information.

Two variables appeared to mediate the effects of item marking on exact-price recall. First, respondents' intentions to notice and remember exact prices (called *degree of sensory encoding* in this research) were strongly related to their ability to subsequently recall exact prices. The research also showed that recall of price information was strongly related to the age of the respondent. Research regarding reasons for this finding may be valuable, as several causes might be proposed. For example, older respondents' memory skills may not be as sharp, their mathematical ability and education may not be equal to that of younger respondents, or they may simply be more resistant to change, thereby ignoring new types of price information. In the past, researchers have emphasized education and income to a greater degree when exploring the effects of information. This study suggested that the age variable may deserve increased attention.

In summary, item marking appears to increase the certainty of price recall and to decrease both

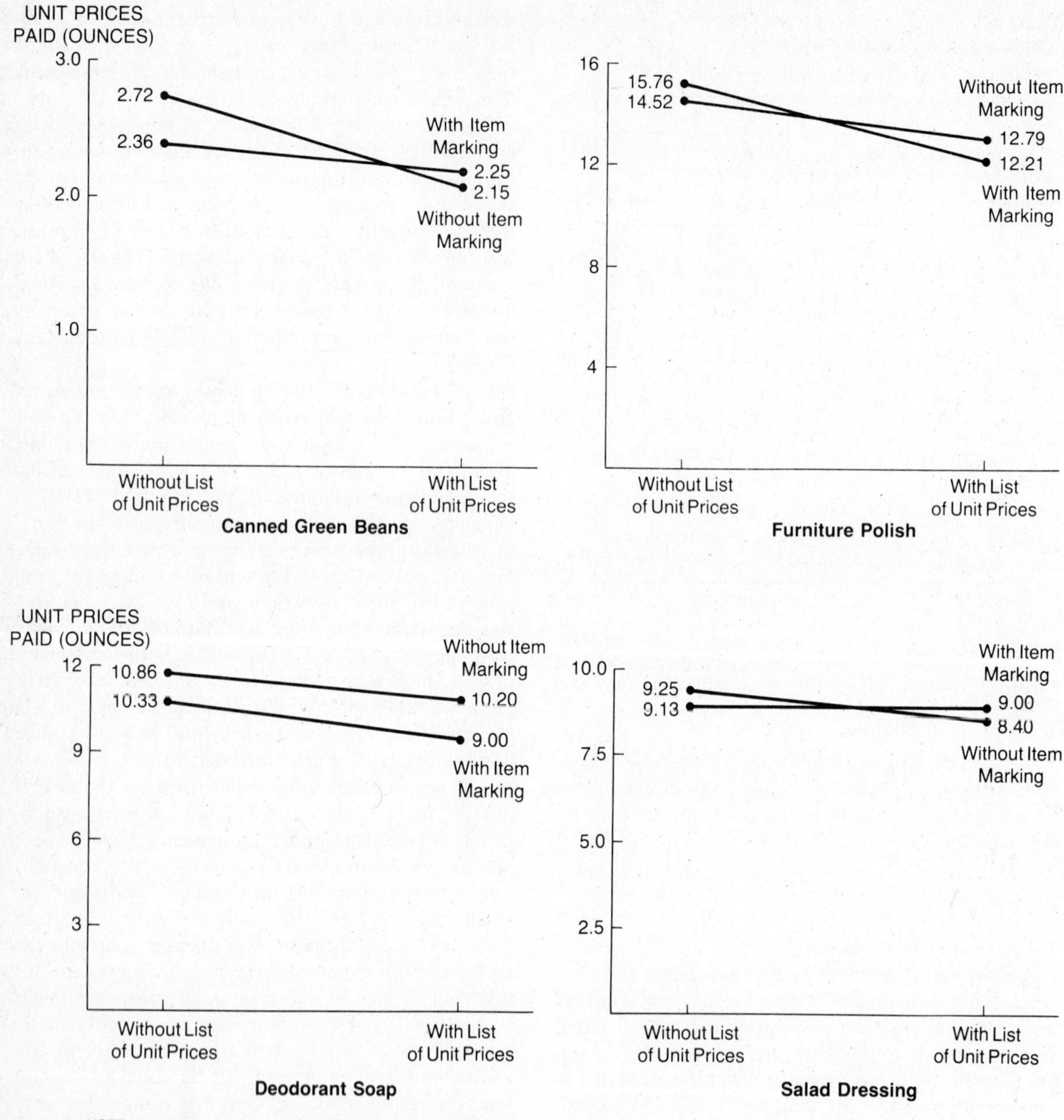

NOTE: All interaction effects are significant at the p ≤ .05 level.

FIGURE B
Graphic Presentation of Unit Price Paid in Selected Product Categories

errors in exact-price recall and unit prices paid for products. It does not appear to affect price-comparison errors. The age of the respondent and her intention to remember exact prices appear to mediate the effects of item marking on exact-price recall.

The Effects of Shelf-Pricing Level

Hypotheses focused on two aspects of shelf-pricing level: (1) the differential effects of the three representative current shelf-tag formats; and (2) the differential effects of a novel format, a list of unit prices (Russo et al. 1975; Russo 1977). The hypothesis concerning the former was not supported strongly, whereas the hypothesis concerning the latter showed mixed effects throughout the hierarchy.

Although there did appear to be some differences in price-comparison errors due to level of shelf format, the differences were not highly significant. Shelf-level two resulted in the fewest price-comparison errors, indicating that it may be more effective in conveying relative price information than the other levels. Alternatively, the differences may have resulted from irregularities in the data. Specifically, examination of the residuals for the ANOVA model of price-comparison error revealed that the cell with the lowest price-comparison errors also exhibited a much smaller variance than any other cell. Unfortunately, the reason for this lower variance could not be identified by examining any of the measured variables, i.e., neither intervening nor demographic variables were responsible for the reduced variance. Therefore, the difference may be attributed to the shelf format, chance, or some other unmeasured differences in the cell respondents, such as better memory skills or higher intelligence. A revised ANOVA model, adjusting for the heteroscedasticity, revealed no significant effect of shelf-tag level.

A number of alternative explanations regarding the relatively weak effect of shelf-tag level are possible. By their own admission, some respondents did not use shelf-tag information in the experiment. Whether due to the novelty of the information (none of the tags were like those used in Columbus supermarkets) or because subjects were in an experimental rather than a real shopping situation, the shelf-price information may not have been assimilated.

The effects of the novel format, the list of unit prices, were significant at the affective and behavioral levels, but not at the cognitive level. Respondents provided with the unit-price list reported feeling more certain about their recall of relative prices, and actually made more economical purchases, but they did not demonstrate better recall of relative prices than those respondents without the list. There are several possible explanations for these findings. One likely explanation is that subjects may have read and used the list (which would account for their increased certainty and decreased unit price paid) without assimilating the information in internal memory. Respondents may have used external memory (Bettman 1979a) when making their relative-price decisions, relying heavily on shelf tags and the list. Having identified and selected the appropriately priced item, they may not have integrated and stored the product prices in internal memory, especially since they may not have perceived these experimental prices as useful to them in their future shopping.

The presence of behavioral effects due to the list of unit prices supports Russo's (Russo et al. 1975; Russo 1977) findings concerning the beneficial effects of a structured list. Russo's data were obtained for a six-week period, during which time shoppers could familiarize themselves with the list. The data for this study were obtained after a brief introductory exposure to the information. It is notable that the results in this study are stronger than the results of Russo's studies. Whereas Russo found a 1.4 to three percent decrease in unit prices paid due to the list, the percentage decreases due to the list ranged from two to 18.5 percent, and averaged 8.7 percent in this study. It could be argued that some of this decrease is attributable to demand characteristics, i.e., subjects noticing the list may have felt that the appropriate behavior was to buy lower-priced items. However, questions probing for this response revealed only one subject (who was consequently eliminated and replaced) reacting to the list in this manner. An alternative explanation is that a stronger effect should be expected in a laboratory as compared to a field setting.

Implications and Directions for Future Research

The study reported here confirms the potential of using laboratory experiments as "impact-prediction studies" (Houston and Rothschild 1980) for public policy-related issues. However, in order to be certain that the findings of the study represent outcomes that would occur in the actual information setting, future research should be conducted.

First, field experiments should be designed to validate the effects found in the laboratory, where respondents are exposed to information under ideal, purified conditions. There were no other shoppers to talk to them, no distractions, and no time constraints. Further, an actual grocery store contains many more products and forms of information (e.g., nutritional labeling, sale and discount tags) that could interfere with the effects of information.

Second, longitudinal studies examining new forms of information would be valuable to assure that effects found in studies such as the one reported here were not due to initial reactions (e.g., resistance to change) that would disappear over time.

Third, future studies should evaluate the effects of proposed information environments on special subgroups of the population, in addition to the general population (Bettman 1975; Houston and Rothschild 1980). Target audiences such as men, the poor, and working women could be isolated for study to determine if the information effects differ in these subgroups.

Fourth, attention should be devoted to developing better measures of the encoding constructs, which may mediate the effectiveness of information. Further development on the reliability and validity of the constructs could offer researchers useful measures to account for individual differences in the use of information.

The methodology employed here is not limited to studies of pricing, but could be used to evaluate the effects of other information environments (e.g., nutritional information, safety guidelines, warning messages).

Summary and Conclusions

To reduce operating costs, managers of grocery stores with electronic scanners may desire to remove price marks from products. This study suggests that the price-removal practice may have two immediate negative consequences. First, consumers will notice the absence of item marks and will feel less certain about their knowledge of prices. If price knowledge is important to them, and self-reports from this study suggest that it is, then consumers may be dissatisfied with the retail store and may even change store loyalties. Second, feelings of uncertainty without item marks are appropriate, at least in the short-run, since respondents made higher percentages of error and spent more money on purchases when prices were not stamped on the items. On the other hand, a list of unit prices appears to be readily decipherable and immediately useful to subjects who represent the frequent grocery shopper.

References

Allen, John W., Harrell, Gilbert D., and Hutt, Michael D. (1976), *Price Awareness Study*. Washington, DC: Food Marketing Institute.

Atkinson, Richard C., and Shiffrin, Richard M. (1968), "Human Memory: A Proposed System and Its Central Processes," in *The Psychology of Learning and Motivation: Advances in Research & Theory, Vol. 2*, eds. Kenneth W. Spence and J. T. Spence, New York: Academic Press, pp. 89–195.

Bettman, James R. (1979a), *An Information Processing Theory of Consumer Choice*. Reading, MA: Addison-Wesley.

——— (1979b), "Memory Factors in Consumer Choice: A Review," *Journal of Marketing*, 43, 37–53.

——— (1975), "Issues in Designing Consumer Information Environments," *Journal of Consumer Research*, 2, 169–77.

———, and Kakkar, Pradeep (1977), "Effects of Information Presentation Format on Consumer Information Strategies," *Journal of Consumer Research*, 3, 223–40.

Craik, Fergus I.M., and Lockhart, Robert S. (1972), "Levels of Processing: A Framework for Memory Research," *Journal of Verbal Learning & Verbal Behavior*, 11, 671–84.

———, and Tulving, Endel (1975), "Depth of Processing and the Retention of Words in Episodic Memory," *Journal of Experimental Psychology: General*, 104, 268–94.

Day, George S. (1976), "Assessing the Effects of Information Disclosure Requirements," *Journal of Marketing*, 40, 42–62.

Engledow, Jack (1972), "The Consumer Reports Subscriber: Portrait of an Intense Consumer," *Indiana Business Review*, 47, 32–40.

Friedman, Monroe P. (1966), "Consumer Confusion in the Selection of Supermarket Products," *Journal of Applied Psychology*, 50, 529–34.

——— (1972), "Consumer Price Comparisons of Retail Products: The Role of Packaging and Pricing Practices and the Implications for Consumer Legislation," *Journal of Applied Psychology*, 56, 439–46.

Gabor, André, and Granger, Clive W. (1964), "Price Sensitivity of the Consumer," *Journal of Advertising Research*, 4, 40–44.

Gatewood, Robert D., and Perloff, Robert (1973), "An Experimental Investigation of Three Methods of Providing Weight and Price Information to Consumers," *Journal of Applied Psychology*, 57, 81–85.

Houston, Michael J. (1972), "The Effects of Unit-Pricing on Choices of Brand and Size in Economic Shopping," *Journal of Marketing*, 36, 51–69.

——, and Rothschild, Michael L. (1980), "Policy-Related Experiments on Information Provision: A Normative Model and Explication," *Journal of Marketing Research*, 17, 432–49.

Hutton, R. Bruce, McNeill, Dennis L., and Wilkie, William (1978), "Some Issues in Designing Consumer Information Studies in Public Policy," in *Advances in Consumer Research*, Vol. 5, ed. H. Keith Hunt, pp. 131–140.

Jacoby, Jacob, and Olson, Jerry C. (1977), "Consumer Response to Price: An Attitudinal Information Processing Perspective," in *Moving Ahead in Attitude Research*, eds. Yoram Wind and Marshall Greenberg, Chicago: American Marketing Association.

Johnson, Eric, and Russo, J. Edward (1978), "The Organization of Product Information in Memory Identified by Recall Times," in *Advances in Consumer Research*, Vol. 5, ed. H. Keith Hunt, Chicago: Association for Consumer Research, pp. 79–86.

McGuire, William J. (1976), "Some Internal Psychological Factors Influencing Consumer Choice," *Journal of Consumer Research*, 2, 302–19.

Olson, Jerry C. (1980), "Implications of an Information Processing Approach to Pricing Research," in *Theoretical Developments in Marketing*, eds. Charles W. Lamb, Jr. and Patrick M. Dunne, Chicago: American Marketing Association, pp. 13–16.

—— (1978), "Theories of Information Encoding and Storage: Implications for Consumer Research," in *The Effect of Information on Consumer and Market Behavior*, ed. Andrew Mitchell, Chicago: American Marketing Association, pp. 49–59.

van Raaij, W. Fred (1976), "Direct Monitoring of Consumer Information Processing by Eye Movement Recorder," unpublished results, Tilburg University, The Netherlands.

Russo, J. Edward (1977), "The Value of Unit Price Information," *Journal of Marketing Research*, 14, 193–202.

——, Kreiser, Gene, and Miyashita, Sally (1975), "An Effective Display of Unit Price Information," *Journal of Marketing*, 39, 11–19.

Slovic, Paul (1972), "From Shakespeare to Simon: Speculations—and Some Evidence—About Mom's Ability to Process Information," *Oregon Research Institute Research Monograph*, Eugene, OR.

Svenson, Ola (1974), "Coded Think-Aloud Protocols Obtained When Making a Choice to Purchase One of Seven Hypothetically Offered Houses: Some Examples," unpublished results, Psychology Department, University of Stockholm.

Tybout, Alice H., and Zaltman, Gerald (1974), "Ethics in Marketing Research: Their Practical Relevance," *Journal of Marketing Research*, 11, 357–68.

Wilkie, William L. (1975), *Assessment of Consumer Information Processing Research in Relation to Public Policy Needs.* Washington, DC: United States Government Printing Office.

Wright, Peter (1979), "Concrete Action Plans in TV Messages to Increase Reading of Drug Warnings," *Journal of Consumer Research*, 6, 256–69.

Yankelovich, Skelly, and White (1979), *Supermarket Trends—1979 Update.* Washington, DC: Food Marketing Institute.

Zeithaml, Valarie A. (1980), "Consumer Response to Grocery Store Price Information," unpublished doctoral dissertation, Marketing Department, University of Maryland.

CHAPTER SEVEN

Consumer Behavior and Communications Programs

READING 28

Perception and Advertising

Irwin A. Horowitz and Russell S. Kaye

Perception is a process by which meaning is attached to sensory input. It is a function of both the stimulus attributes of the environment and the personal cognitive world of the observer. Within this "world" reside the attitudes, needs, and past experiences of the observer. These factors may contribute to an expectation of future sensory input, a selective facilitation or gating of certain inputs, or a spurious interpretation or distortion of some such input. This paper will restrict perception to visual phenomena.

Several classical studies (Bruner and Goodman, 1947; Jones and Bruner, 1954; Hastorf and Cantril, 1954; Postman, 1948; Atkinson and Walker, 1956) illustrate the importance of the individual's cognitive set, personality, and need-value systems in the perceptual process. These studies emphasized that perception is selective and organized. Bruner (1957) explained that perception is an act of categorization. Perceptual readiness or accessibility, and thus the likelihood of a given percept, depend upon the perceiver's past experience, the learned probability of a particular input, and the observer's needs. The system tunes the perceptual process to those elements of the environment important to the observer.

The advertising industry was quick to realize the importance of perception to consumer behavior, in that the consumer's attitudes, needs, and values may influence his purchasing decisions. Until the turn of the century, consumer behavior was a simple matter of satisfying one's survival needs. Man the consumer was economically and functionally oriented, guided by the question "Do I need this?" Price, quality, and durability were the primary considerations. But as the economy prospered, the consumer found more money in his pockets and more products and brands on the shelves of the marketplace. The practical attributes of the product lessened in importance as the consumer placed a symbolic meaning on the product (Levy, 1954).

The advertiser became aware of the fact that he was promoting not only a product, but also a symbol of the consumer's self-concept and his striving for social recognition. How an individual consumer perceives a product depends on how well it agrees with his personal cognitive world. Krech, Crutchfield, and Ballachey (1962) and Bruner (1958) stated that a consumer's perception of a particular product depends upon personal factors and the physical attributes of the product.

The physical attributes refer to the nature of the product, its package design, and its advertisement. The choice of model, the use of various colors in packaging, the position of the advertisement on a page, among other things, affect the consumer's perception. A more detailed consideration follows.

Personality and Cognitive Factors

Personal factors, such as needs, values, and motives, serve to modify the message communicated by the packaging or the advertisement. The product as a symbol may serve to reinforce the consumer's self-concept or allow him to identify himself with some reference group. Walters (1970) considers the marketing implications of this symbolization, in first stating that the product does not exist in a vacuum, but that it exists in various symbolic forms in the cognitive

Reprinted by permission of the Advertising Research Foundation, Inc., from the *Journal of Advertising Research*, 15:3 June 1975, 15–21.

worlds of the consumers. An advertiser must be aware of the possible symbolization that a product may acquire, of the form of symbolization most probable in a market segment, and of the methods used to promote the product as a particular symbol. Allison and Uhl (1964) stated that a usual explanation for a good or bad market emphasizes the physical attributes of the product itself. Their study suggested personal factors as a possible supplementary or alternative explanation. The study involved having beer drinkers rate major brands of labeled and unlabeled beer. The brands were rated on overall goodness and on specific characteristics, such as taste and smoothness. Results showed that the participants' favored brands received the highest ratings on the labeled test, but in the unlabeled (blind comparison) test, the drinkers generally could not discern any taste differences. It was concluded that the evaluation of a brand depended more upon the label and its associations than upon the product itself. This study emphasized the importance of brand images in influencing a purchasing decision.

Grubb and Grathwohl (1967) stated that much of the early work in the effect of personality on the consumer's perception did not develop any theoretical relationships between this effect and the product's image. An organized coherent investigatory strategy was clearly lacking in this area. There was a need for a conceptual framework that would allow interrelationships and hypothesis generation. They also proposed the development of an approach that would relate the psychological concept of self-concept to the symbolic value of the product. The concept of self has more specific operational referents than does personality, hopefully leading to a facilitation of measurement.

Self-Theory

Carl Rogers is mostly responsible for the development of self-theory. The self becomes differentiated from the phenomenal world, the totality of experience, through learning and maturation. It consists of those values, attitudes, emotions, and strivings that an individual recognizes as his own, as part of the "I" and "me." The development of the self is influenced by an interaction with others' values and strivings. Within this phenomenal field, the self acts as an organized whole as it attempts to satisfy its needs. There is one primary need: the need to actualize, maintain, and enhance the self. The self strives for consistency and congruence between itself as perceived and the actual experiences of the individual. Behaviors emitted by the individual are those that are consistent with the concept of the self, consistent with the value-belief system that an individual assumes represents himself (Rogers, 1951; Hall and Lindzey, 1957).

The self-theory approach to consumer behavior emphasizes the striving for consistency and the interaction between the self-image and its significant references. Since products have images, as determined and perceived by the consumer, it would be predicted that the consumer would consider only those that are acceptable to or consistent with the self-image. Dolich (1969) investigated the congruent relationship between self-images and product brands. Using the semantic differential to measure consumers' evaluations of these two variables, the results showed that preferred brands were evaluated as significantly more congruent with self-images than the nonpreferred brands. The favored brands were consistent with the self-concept, and thus tended to maintain and enhance the individual's conception of himself.

Hamm and Cundiff (1969) studied the relationship between product images and real-self and ideal-self images. A measure of the degree of satisfaction of the need for self-actualization was developed. Subjects were housewives from similar familial circumstances. Each was asked to sort 50 product names on a sorting board into categories ranging from "most like" to "most unlike" (Q-sort technique). Instructions for sorting involved a self-sort in which product names were ranked 1 to 50 according to "how much you think they describe you," and an ideal-sort in which they were ranked according to "what you want to be." A discrepancy score was computed between the rankings of each product name on the two sorts. This score was assumed to reflect the degree of need for actualization satisfaction, in that the higher the satisfaction, the closer the real self would be to the ideal self. Certain products, such as house, car, and dress were most often ranked as most like the consumer's self. TV dinners, fur coats, hormone creams, and health foods were ranked usually as least like the self (both real and ideal). Therefore, as Hamm and Cundiff (1969) noted, the marketing implication involves associating lowly ranked products with higher ranked products, such as advertising TV dinners with an emphasis on the time freed for cleaning in the house. Cigarettes were ranked as least like the ideal self, which suggests that the marketing strategy should not emphasize the product as descriptive of an ideal housewife, but rather should emphasize the inherent nature of the cigarettes themselves. DeLozier (1971) contributed to the mounting data relating the self-image to the product image. When presented with a set of fictitious brands of shampoos and perfumes, consumers chose those products whose names they rated (semantic differential) as most descriptive of their self-concept. The author suggested that new brands should be developed using semantic differential descriptions of self-concepts, and that advertising campaigns should reduce psychological distance between the self and the product image, by using themes and slogans that are also descriptive of the self-image of the intended consumer.

Cognitive Dissonance

As stated in self-theory, an individual strives for consistency among his beliefs, opinions, values, and actions (his "cognitions"). Festinger (1957) advanced the theory of cognitive dissonance to explain the consequences of a situation where an individual finds that one cognition does not follow logically from a related cognition. Such a situation involves "dissonance," which is an aversive motivational state that demands reduction. An example of a dissonant state involves the cigarette smoker, whose behavior is at odds with his knowledge of the dangers of smoking. The amount of dissonance experienced is a function of the degree of volition involved in the action, the number and/or importance of cognitions consonant with the behavior, and the number and/or importance of cognitions dissonant with that behavior. Volition is important in that if a person is forced to perform a behavior that is against (at dissonance with) his value-belief system, he will allow himself to disavow any responsibility for the action or consider his action as being adequately justified because of the coercion. There are several outlets for the reduction of dissonance: (1) an elimination of the dissonant element, possibly involving an attitude change (switching brands, for instance); (2) a denial of the responsibility for the behavior, depending on the degree of volition involved; (3) a distortion of dissonant information (selective perception); (4) a minimizing of the importance of the dissonant cognition ("I didn't do well, but it was only because I really wasn't interested"); and (5) a selective involvement with new information (Festinger, 1957; Sherwood, 1969; Kassarjian and Cohen, 1965).

As with self-theory, cognitive dissonance theory has been applied to the consumer's perception of himself and of the product that he consumes. When a consumer makes a choice between two equally attractive products, one finds that the purchased product, post-decisionally, is revalued more favorably, while the rejected product is devalued (Brehm, 1962). Reduction of dissonance may occur as a result, therefore, of a change of attitude in buying the other brand the next time around, of increasing the importance of the brand's advantages, of a change in the product's perceived image, or of a selective exposure to advertisements reassuring the consumer of his wise purchasing decision (Kassarjian and Cohen, 1965).

Several studies will serve as representatives of the research in post-decisional dissonance. Mittelstaedt (1969) studied the role of dissonance in establishing brand loyalty. He found that when a consumer commits himself to a purchasing choice, some degree of dissonance is inevitable. If the product proves satisfactory, then the dissonance is reduced and the probability of a repurchase is increased. The attitudes toward the purchased product and the rejected products should become antipodal, in that the number and importance of the consonant cognitions should increase over the number and importance of the dissonant cognitions.

The findings of LoSciuto and Perloff (1967) suggest that since the consumer is sensitive or attuned to self-reinforcing information, the advertiser should ensure that it is available. The type of presentation of such information must be considered carefully. Letters, for example, seem to be more affective than telephone calls (Hunt, 1970), despite the current campaign by Bell System to suggest that phone calls are effective means of obtaining sales. Consumers may associate telephone calls with sales gimmicks, while letters may suggest and imply greater concern, effort, and sincerity on the part of the merchant.

Several investigators have questioned the applicability of cognitive dissonance to advertising and consumer behavior (Oshikawa, 1968; 1969). It may be, however, that the difficulties in employing cognitive dissonance theory within the realm of consumer behavior may be less a function of the inherent limitations of the theory, than the attempt to apply the theory to a whole spectrum of different product purchases. A critical determinant of whether or not dissonance is elicited by some decision-making behavior is the individual's perception of the degree of volition involved in the behavior. If an individual was compelled, for whatever reason, to engage in a behavior or buy a product, dissonance will not ensue. If, however, the individual perceives that his choice was made freely between a number of equally attractive alternatives, then dissonance will likely occur.

It seems reasonable to suggest, therefore, that cognitive dissonance theory as an exploratory model for consumer behavior is most clearly applicable to those products or items which might be termed discretionary, or "luxury," items. Those products that the consumer deems essential, such as basic food products, functional clothing items, or perhaps even an automobile utilized for basic transport, would not be candidates for a cognitive dissonance explanation of consumer behavior. The reasons for the purchasing of those products are compelling. A consumer may ask only that these products serve their basic function. Within limits, relative quality and attractiveness might not be critical factors.

Cognitive dissonance theory may be a viable explanatory model in those situations where a consumer spends some of his discretionary income on a product. When a consumer purchases more than a basic suit of clothes or an automobile that costs more than basic transport and requires greater expenditure for its maintenance, then the consumer, psychologically, is required to defend his purchase. It is precisely in this area of purchases of "luxury" products that the consumer has a greater degree of freedom of choice.

Oshikawa's contention (1968, 1969) that cognitive dissonance theory has been valuable in brand loyalty studies seems to be quite accurate. We would, however, suggest that its applicability may be specifically limited to nonessential luxury, or discretionary, purchases. As indicated above, the purchase of these items requires resolution of dissonance. Once the consumer has defended his choice publicly, he is in terms of cognitive dissonance committed to that product. This kind of psychological commitment would be critical for ensuring brand loyalty.

Hunt's technique of mailing reassuring literature after a purchase (1970), therefore, has a sound psychological base. Reassuring literature allows the consumer to resolve the dissonance aroused by his purchase in a positive way. After all, it is possible that the purchase of a particular product could engender so much dissonance that the only way to resolve it would be either to return the item or vow never to make a repurchase. The reassuring letter relieves the purchaser's anxiety, resulting in a positive image for the store and the product, which in turn, may establish or maintain brand loyalty.

Physical Attributes

Beyond the personal factors that influence perception of a particular product, the physical attributes of the product itself play an important role. No one would doubt that there is an interaction between personality factors and the physical attributes of the product, in that the image the product assumes is a function not only of the consumer's own biases, but also of the ability of the attributes of the product to facilitate or inhibit the operation of a bias. The attributes to be discussed refer only to the packaging design and magazine advertisements. This discussion will concentrate solely on intrinsic factors which refer to the physical and emotional tone characteristics of the package or the advertisement. Such factors as color, the use of sex, the choice of the model, and the positioning of the model contribute to the perceptual interpretation and attention-getting properties of these product attributes.

Color is the characteristic wavelength or wavelengths that are reflected by a surface. Color can create physiological reactions. Walking into a room painted vivid red will increase the pulse rate, while a green room will have the inverse effect. More importantly, color can create psychological reactions, in that a particular color may be associated with a certain idea or emotion. Blue can imply a celestial calmness. Color may imply degrees of quality or the existence of special product features. Yellow implies cheapness, while lush, dark colors imply wealth and importance. Poisons are generally contained in black and yellow cans. Toothpastes, on the other hand, are usually found in white tubes that imply cleanliness and sparkle (Griffin and Sacharow, 1972).

Smith (1953) found that photographs of faces that were friendly and pleasant were perceived as being physically closer than those depicting unfriendly and unpleasant faces. Smith (1970) extended this research to the effect of sexual illustrations on consumer perception. He studied the effect of pasting a picture of a sexually attractive woman into a magazine advertisement for a particular brand of car. Sixty adults were asked to rate a car according to how it appeared in a magazine advertisement. Sixty other adults were asked to rate the same car, but with the addition of a sexually attractive woman. The car was found to be rated higher on such features as "more appealing," "more youthful," and "better design" when the woman was added. But features such as "safe-unsafe" did not receiver higher ratings. This study suggests that the consumer's perception of a product can be manipulated by the choice of model and the subsequent appeal to his emotions.

The pictorial subject matter of an advertisement must initially attract the intended consumer, and then communicate its message effectively. Another variable in this process is the extent to which the visual display deviates from the consumer's expectations. The television program "Candid Camera" enjoyed success by developing ploys that provided a transient disruption of people's basic beliefs about physical and social reality. Vignettes concerning automobiles that apparently levitated or the like abound in the "Candid Camera" approach.

Rokeach (1968) has suggested a similar approach to advertising, exemplified by an advertisement that appeared in *The New Yorker* magazine (1963). "How to Keep Water Off a Duck's Back" visually displayed a duck wearing a tailored London Fog raincoat. As Rokeach noted, this advertisement presents visually a juxtaposition of an inconsequential belief about a brand of rainwear with a very primitive, basic belief about the essential nature of a duck. Ducks just do not wear raincoats. Our primitive belief, manifested in our expectation, about the nature of ducks and their essential nakedness is disrupted, creating great visual impact and attraction. However, the authors have not been able to ascertain whether more raincoats were sold as a result of this advertisement.

Techniques and Findings

Before considering the positioning of the model, it is fruitful to first explore a technique that has been used to study all of the preceding factors and that has led to the discovery of still another, namely, the effect of the degree of pupil dilation of the model.

Pupillography. Davson (1972) has reviewed the reflexes of the pupil of the eye, and by far the most interesting is the psycho-sensory. This phenomenon is an indicator of ongoing mental activity and has been studied in relation to the interest value of visual stimulation.

Hess and Polt (1960) presented a series of slides to adult males and females which included a picture of a baby, a mother and a baby, a partially nude male, a partially nude female, and a landscape. The dependent measure was the percent change in mean pupil area between the test stimulus (a picture) and the control slide (a blank, uniformly lighted field). Light-dark contrasts on the picture slides were reduced or blurred to prevent a light reflex. As predicted, male subjects' pupil sizes were significantly larger than those of the female subjects when both sexes viewed the partially nude female. On the other hand, female subjects' pupil sizes were significantly larger when viewing the baby, the mother and baby, and the partially nude male. The results reflected the differential interests of the two sexes.

Hess (1964) extended this research to other aspects of mental activity reflected by the pupil size. It was found that the pupil responded to differences in tastes, even when the taster could not articulate the differences. This is important for research into product evaluations. One reported experiment has special significance for advertising research. Male subjects were asked to indicate their preference between two photographs of a young woman. The pictures were identical, except that in one the pupils were dilated. Subjects invariably chose the photograph with the dilated pupils, though none could state the difference between the two pictures. The woman with the larger pupils may have suggested an interest in the observer. This suggests that an important facet of the model is the degree of dilation of the pupils, in that a dilated condition may attract more attention and interest to the advertisement.

Halpern (1967) applied the pupil response to a before and after experiment in which subjects were exposed to new information between observations of a product. When subjects were exposed to positive information, their pupil sizes increased significantly on the second observation relative to the first observation. Other groups received either negative or neutral information, and consequently displayed a significant decrease in pupil size or no significant change, respectively. This study relates to the studies in dissonance, where it was found that the introduction of consonant (positive) information allows a consumer's choice to become more favorable (possibly more interesting) to him, supporting and enhancing the self-image.

Direction of Gaze. Another aspect of visual behavior relevant to advertising is the direction of gaze, or what is called conjugate lateral eye movement. King (1972) states that most people can be classified as predominately left-lookers or right-lookers. Looking to the right while thinking indicates a dominance of the left hemisphere of the brain, whereas looking left reflects a right hemispheric dominance.

It has been suggested that man's more poetic or imaginative behavior may stem from the right hemisphere. Right hemispheric dominance reflects the general notion that left-lookers may be characterized as more emotional, artistic, suggestible (more amenable to hypnosis) and less verbally facile than right-lookers. Tasks of synthesis and spatial perception are generally assigned to the right hemisphere (Nebes, 1974).

Left hemispheric dominance, or right-lookers, indicates a priority of verbal, analytical and sequential behaviors. Therefore, right-lookers would be considered more rational, precise, and logical than left-lookers.

The immediate importance of direction of gaze is revealed by King's (1972) study which found that observers prefer photographs of models depicting a gaze direction (either left- or right-lookers) that coincided with their own left or right tendencies. None of the subjects could articulate the reason for his choice. These results suggest that the initial attracting power of a product or its advertisement would be enhanced by depicting a model with the same directional tendency as that of the intended consumer.

Beyond this, it seems reasonable to suggest that advertisements placed on the left side of a page be visually complex, emotional in appeal, and contain few, if any, verbal cues. In general, the right hemisphere seems better at grasping the total picture of a scene. Furthermore, as Pines (1973) noted, social class and racial differences are related to right or left hemisphere dominance. Children from poor black neighborhoods generally learn to use their right hemisphere more than their left (Pines, 1973). While they score worse than whites on verbal tasks, these black children perform better than whites on visual tasks, such as pattern recognition. One might suspect, therefore, that a lower-class black audience or a comparable white audience would contain a predominance of left-lookers and thus the general guidelines presented above might fruitfully be observed. Concomitantly, it would be expected that right-lookers would react more favorably to a logical, nonvisual, highly verbal advertisement. The more favorable the reaction, the more effective is the communication of the message. One would expect that the current advertisements defending the policy of major oil companies would be likely to appeal primarily to right-lookers, since these advertisements follow the above guidelines. Advertisements stressing the scientific aspects of a particular brand would be better placed on the right side than the left side of the page.

Summary

Perception has been shown to be an important determinant of consumer behavior. The consumer's perception is mediated as much by the consumer's own cognitive facets as by the product itself. The purchasing decision is influenced by the perceived image of the product as determined by the consumer's present state of mind and by the advertiser's manipulation of the product attributes to create the desired image, an image that will suit the intended consumer.

References

Allison, R. I. and K. P. Uhl. Influence of Beer Brand Identification on Taste Perception. *Journal of Marketing Research,* Vol. 1, 1964, pp. 36–39.

Atkinson, J. W. and E. L. Walker. The Affiliation Motive and Perceptual Sensitivity to Faces. *Journal of Abnormal and Social Psychology,* Vol. 53, 1956, pp. 38–44.

Baker, Stephen. *Visual Persuasion.* New York: McGraw-Hill, 1961.

Brehm, J. W. and H. R. Cohen. *Explorations in Cognitive Dissonance.* New York: Wiley, 1962.

Bruner, J. S. On Perceptual Readiness. *Psychological Review,* Vol. 64, 1957, pp. 123–37.

Bruner, J. S. Social Psychology and Perception. In Kassarjian and Robertson (Ed.). *Perspectives in Consumer Behavior.* Glenview, IL: Scott, Foresman and Company, 1968.

Bruner, J. S. and C. C. Goodman. Value and Need as Organizing Factors in Perception. *Journal of Abnormal and Social Psychology,* Vol. 42, 1947, pp. 33–44.

Davson, Hugh. *The Physiology of the Eye.* New York: Academic Press, 1972.

DeLozier, M. W. A Longitudinal Study of the Relationship Between Self Image and Brand Image. *Dissertation Abstracts International,* 1971, 4775–A.

Dolich, E. W. Congruence Relationships Between Self Images and Product Brands. *Journal of Marketing Research,* Vol. 6, 1969, pp. 80–83.

Festinger, L. *A Theory of Cognitive Dissonance.* Stanford: Stanford University Press, 1957.

Griffin, R. C. and S. Sacharow. *Principles of Package Development.* Westport, CT: The Avi Publishing Company, 1972.

Grubb, E. L. and H. L. Grathwohl. Consumer Self-Concept, Symbolism, and Marketing Behavior: A Theoretical Approach. *Journal of Marketing,* Vol. 31, 1967, pp. 22–26.

Grubb, E. L. and G. Hupp. Perception of Self, Generalized Stereotypes, and Brand Selection. *Journal of Marketing Research,* Vol, 5, 1968, pp. 58–61.

Hall. C. S. and G. Lindzey. *Theories of Personality.* London: John Wiley & Son, 1957.

Halpern, S. Application of Pupil Response to Before and After Experiments. *Journal of Marketing Research,* Vol. 4, 1967, pp. 332–22.

Hamm and Cundiff. Self-Actualization and Product Perception. *Journal of Marketing Research,* Vol. 6, 1969, pp. 470–73.

Hastorf, A. and H. Cantril. They Saw a Game: A Case Study. *Journal of Abnormal and Social Psychology,* Vol. 49, 1954, pp. 129–34.

Hess, E. H. Attitude and Pupil Size. *Scientific American,* Vol. 212, 1965, pp. 46–54.

Hess, E. H. and J. M. Polt. Pupil Size as Related to Interest Value of Visual Stimuli. *Science,* Vol. 132, 1960, pp. 349–50.

Hunt, L. Post-Transaction Communications and Dissonance Reduction. *Journal of Marketing,* Vol. 34, 1970, pp. 46–49.

Jones, E. E. and J. S. Bruner. Expectancy in Apparent Visual Movement. *British Journal of Psychology,* Vol. 45, 1954, pp. 157–65.

Kassarjian, H. H. Personality and Consumer Behavior: A Review. *Journal of Marketing Research,* Vol. 8, 1971, pp. 409–12.

Kassarjian, H. H. and J. B. Cohen. Cognitive Dissonance and Consumer Behavior. *California Management Review,* Vol. 8, 1965, pp. 55–64.

King. A. S. Pupil Size, Eye Direction, and Message Appeal. *Journal of Marketing,* Vol. 36, 1972, pp. 55–60.

Krech, D., R. S. Crutchfield, and E. L. Ballachy. *Individual in Society.* New York: McGraw-Hill, 1962.

Levy, S. J. Symbols for Sale. *Harvard Business Review,* Vol. 37, 1959, pp. 117–24.

LoSciuto, L. A. and R. Perloff. Influence of Product Preference on Dissonance Reduction. *Journal of Marketing Research,* Vol. 4, 1967, pp. 286–90.

Mittelstaedt, E. A Dissonance Approach to Repeat Purchasing Behavior. *Journal of Marketing Research,* Vol. 6, 1969, pp. 144–47.

Nebes, R. D. Hemispheric Specialization in Commisurotomized Man. *Psychological Bulletin,* Vol. 81, 1974, pp. 1–14.

Oshikawa, A. The Theory of Cognitive Dissonance and Experimental Research. *Journal of Marketing Research,* Vol. 5, 1968, pp. 429–31.

Oshikawa, A. Can Cognitive Dissonance Theory Explain Consumer Behavior? *Journal of Marketing,* Vol. 33, 1969, pp. 44–49.

Pines, M. *The Brainchangers: Scientists and the New Mind Controls.* New York: Harcourt, Brace and Jovanovich, 1973.

Postman, L., J. S. Bruner, and E. McGinnies. Personal Values as Selective Factors in Perception. *Journal of Abnormal and Social Psychology,* Vol. 43, 1948, pp. 142–54.

Rogers, C. *Client-Centered Therapy: Its Current Practice, Implications, and Theory.* Boston: Houghton Mifflin, 1951.

Rokeach, M. *Beliefs, Attitudes and Values.* San Francisco: Jossey-Bass, 1968.

Smith, George Horsley. Size-Distance Judgments of Human Faces. *Journal of General Psychology,* Vol. 49, 1953, pp. 45–64.

Smith, George Horsley. Unpublished experiment, reported by Donovan Bess, *San Francisco Chronicle,* 1970.

Walters, C. A. and G. W. Paul. *Consumer Behavior: An Integrated Framework.* New York: R. D. Irwin, Inc., 1970.

READING 29

Subliminal Advertising: What You See Is What You Get

Timothy E. Moore

This paper provides an evaluation of the evidence and arguments advanced in support of the effectiveness of various and subliminal advertising techniques. Such practices are purported to influence consumer behavior by subconsciously altering preferences or attitudes toward consumer products. While there is some marginal evidence that subliminal stimuli may influence affective reactions, the marketing relevance of this finding remains to be documented. The notion that subliminal directives can influence motives or actions is contradicted by a large body of research evidence and is incompatible with theoretical conceptions of perception and motivation.

In September 1957 some unwitting theatre audiences in New Jersey were invited to "drink Coca-Cola" and "eat popcorn" in briefly presented messages that were superimposed on the movie in progress. Exposure times were so short that viewers were unaware of any message. The marketing firm responsible reported a dramatic increase in coke and popcorn sales, although they provided no documentation of these alleged effects. Public reaction was, nevertheless, immediate and widespread:

> ". . . *the most alarming and outrageous discovery since Mr. Gatling invented his gun.*" (Nation, *1957, p. 206)*

> "*. . . take this invention and everything connected with it and attach it to the center of the next nuclear explosive scheduled for testing.*" *(Cousins 1957, p. 20)*

Opponents were indignant that unforgivable psychological manipulations would be visited upon innocent and unknowing consumers. Minds had been "broken and entered" according to the *New Yorker* (1957, p. 33). There was much talk of *Brave New World* and *1984.* But even while laws were being drafted prohibiting the use of subliminal advertising on television, Hollywood was incorporating the idea into two new movies, and a Seattle radio station started broadcasting 'subaudible' messages such as "TV's a bore."

In May 1978 police investigators in an unnamed midwestern city attempted to apprehend a murderer by interspersing subliminal messages among frames of TV news film describing the murder (*New York Times* 1978, p. c22). Later that year some department stores in Toronto began broadcasting subliminal auditory messages whose intent was to deter shoplifters. The "sinister implications" of such practices worried the *Globe and Mail.* Could unscrupulous prime ministers deliver political propaganda subliminally? (*Globe and Mail* 1978, p. 6). In British Columbia the following year, a Ministry of Human Resources policy manual on child abuse was denied inclusion in a government-commissioned publication because the manual's cover contained "sickening and obscene" sexual imagery imbedded in an apparently innocuous photograph of an adult's hand clasping a child's.

Reports of various forms of subliminal manipulation are fairly common. Evidently the practice is

Reprinted by permission of the American Marketing Association, from the *Journal of Marketing,* 46:2 Spring 1982, 38–47.

still with us, although a few twists have been added since 1957. Given its covert nature and the ethical considerations involved, the prevalence of subliminal advertising is very likely underestimated by reliance upon published reports. At any rate, such techniques are believed to be widespread by a great many people who can hardly by faulted for vigorously protesting against their use. John Q. Public has his hands full trying to cope with forms of exploitation of which he is fully aware. Should he also be worried that Madison Avenue is sneaking directives into his subconscious through the back door? Such a possibility has pervasive ramifications (Brown 1960). The potential importance of the topic has not escaped those in marketing (Hawkins 1970, Kelly 1979, Saegert 1979); however, all lament the dearth of empirical research.

There are at least three identifiable means of subliminal stimulation for which strong behavioral effects have been claimed. The first of these involves very briefly presented visual stimuli. Presentation is usually by means of a tachistoscope, a device for carefully controlling the exposure duration of a visual stimulus. Directives or instructions are flashed so quickly that the viewer is unaware of their presence. Such stimulation purportedly registers subconsciously and allegedly affects subsequent behavior. This method of stimulus presentation has been used frequently by investigators interested in subliminal perception, although their purposes have usually been quite different. As a result, a body of research literature exists that bears on the claims being made for some kinds of subliminal advertising. Some examples from this literature will be described and some studies analyzed in detail. It should be emphasized that stimulation below the level of conscious awareness *can* be shown to have measurable effects upon some aspects of behavior. The point at issue is whether these effects are sufficient to warrant the conclusion that goal-directed behavior can be manipulated by such stimulation.

Another means by which behavior control is attempted is through the use of accelerated speech in low volume auditory messages. Here too, the claim is that while the message may be unintelligible and unnoticed at a conscious level, it is nevertheless processed subconsciously and imparts direction to the receiver's behavior.

The third procedure consists of embedding or hiding sexual imagery (or sometimes words) in pictorial advertisements. These are concealed in such a way that they are not available to conscious perusal. They have, however, a subconscious effect or so it is argued.

The effects attributed to these procedures may consist of either (1) general, nonspecific, affective consequences that are assumed to have some positive but unspecified persuasive influence, or (2) a highly specific, direct impact upon some particular motive or behavior. In what follows, the evidence and arguments put forth in defense of the effectiveness of these procedures will be reviewed and critiqued.

Subliminal Perception

Measurable responses of one kind or another can sometimes be shown to be contingent upon stimulation that the perceiver is unaware of. Pierce and Jastrow (1884) demonstrated that subjects could make reliable discriminations among stimuli differing in weight, even though they reported that the stimuli were *not* discriminably different. In this classic study, subjects indicated the degree of confidence in their judgments concerning very slight differences in pressure applied to the subjects' fingers. In those instances where no confidence at all in perceived variation of pressure was reported, subjects were nevertheless obliged to say which of the two pressures was greater. Their judgments were correct 60% of the time.

The Threshold Concept

Today, the notion that people can respond to stimuli without being able to report on their existence is accepted and well documented (Bevan 1964a, 1964b; Dixon 1971; Erdelyi 1974). Taken literally, subliminal means "below threshold." However, there exists no absolute cut-off point for stimulus intensity below which stimulation is imperceptible and above which it is always detected. When stimuli of varying intensities are presented over several trials, the minimum signal strength that is always detected is much higher than the one that is almost never detected. If some absolute threshold existed, then there ought to be a determinable stimulus intensity above which the receiver always responds and below which there is no response. Instead, a particular stimulus is sometimes detected and sometimes goes unnoticed. As a result, an individual's perceptual threshold is usually defined as that stimulus value that is correctly detected 50% of the time. The threshold, or limen, is, therefore, a statistical abstraction.

For a given individual, this threshold may vary from day to day or from minute to minute. Moreover, thresholds differ rather widely between individuals. Many studies of subliminal perception are flawed because the investigators assumed that some specific exposure duration or stimulus intensity automatically guaranteed that the stimulus would be sufficiently below threshold that its presence would be undetected for all the experimental subjects on all the trials. Often this assumption is unwarranted. Stimuli below the statistical limen (which itself fluctuates) may be noticed as much as 49% of the time. As a result, studies that make little or no effort to determine a threshold for individual subjects are at a risk because stimuli are presented that are effectively *supra*liminal for some subjects on some trials. The results may thus be due to the effects of weak (but not subliminal) stimulation.

Obviously the notion of a perceptual limen is of limited usefulness. For present purposes we may use the term subliminal perception to refer to the following situations (Dixon 1971, p. 12):

a. The subject responds to stimulation the energy or duration of which falls below that at which he *ever* reported awareness of the stimulus in some previous threshold determination.
b. he responds to a stimulus of which he pleads total unawareness.
c. he reports that he is being stimulated but denies any awareness of what the stimulus was.

In these instances the subject cannot recognize the stimulus. "These situations define subliminal perception, and are to be distinguished from those where the individual, though unaware of the stimulus response contingency, is either not necessarily unaware of the stimulus, or, alternatively, could be *made aware* of the stimulus if his attention were drawn to it" (Dixon 1971, p. 13). People are often unaware of stimulation or of the processes mediating the effects of a stimulus on a response (Nisbett and Wilson 1977). This is a separate issue from subliminal stimulation, wherein the subject *cannot* identify the stimulus.

Some Illustrations of Subliminal Perception

There is ample evidence that weak stimuli that are not reportable *can* be demonstrated to influence behavior. For example, a number of studies by Bevan and his associates (Bevan 1964b) have shown that subliminal stimuli can alter judgments of perceived intensity of supraliminal stimuli when the former are interpolated into the presentation series. In one of these studies subjects were asked to judge the intensity of weak electric shocks delivered to their wrists. Between trials subliminal levels of shock were also administered. Careful control procedures ensured that these stimuli were not detected. The effect of these interpolated stimuli was to elevate the judged intensities of the detectable shocks. A control group that received no subliminal stimulation routinely estimated their shocks to be less intense than the experimental group. A similar effect was found for judgments of the perceived loudness of tones. Apparently the subliminal stimuli trigger physiological activity that affects the perception of similar supraliminal stimuli.

Signal detection research provides another example. In a signal detection task, weak stimuli are presented; some are detectable, some are not. If subjects are asked to provide confidence ratings of their judgments about the presence or absence of a signal, their ratings are highly correlated with the stimulus intensity. This is true even for signals that were reportedly not detected (Green and Swets 1966, Swets 1961).

Perceptual defense literature provides yet another sort of illustration. Many studies have shown that taboo or emotionally loaded words have higher recognition thresholds than do neutral words. That is, it takes a longer exposure duration for *whore* to be identified than for *shore.* At first this may appear illogical. How can something taboo be defended against unless it is first recognized as being taboo? The paradox is resolved if it is assumed that "perception" is by no means a discrete experiential event that is automatically determined by some particular stimulus pattern. Rather, perception is treated as a multiprocess chain of events that begins with stimulus input and terminates (subjectively) with conscious recognition of an object or event. However, not all input is subjected to the same sequence of mental processing. Stimuli are selectively filtered, transformed and attended to according to a variety of factors that are independent of the particular input. These include memory, expectations, attention, affect and other variables. Perception then, as we conventionally use the term, represents ". . . the conscious terminus of a sequence of nonconscious prior processes" (Erdelyi 1974). Conscious recognition need not be and often is not the end point for many sorts of input. Some stimuli may initiate mental activity of one sort or another without being available to conscious reflection or report. This is what is typically meant by the term subliminal perception. In the case of taboo items, some kind of defensive selectivity operates to bias the processing of emotionally charged input—such selectivity having its impact *prior* to a conscious recognition of the input.

Recently Zajonc (1980) has reviewed evidence from several studies showing that under some circumstances, unattended stimuli can be processed to a degree that is sufficient to elicit a subsequent affective reaction (i.e., like/dislike) *without* their being recognized as having been previously encountered. "Affective reactions can occur without extensive perceptual cognitive encoding. Reliable affective discriminations (like/dislike ratings) can be made in the total absence of recognition memory (old-new judgments)" (Zajonc 1980, p. 151). While unattended stimuli are not necessarily subliminal, one study purports to show that affect can be influenced by stimuli that *are* truly subliminal (Kunst-Wilson and Zajonc 1980). That some behavioral processes may be influenced by stimuli whose presence is not consciously noticeable by the receiver is not at issue here. The preceding examples testify to the validity of subliminal perception as a phenomenon. The important question is whether the subliminal effects obtained justify the claims made for subliminal advertising. This question is critical because what must be posited in order to support such a proposition is not merely *an* effect, but specific, (relatively) powerful and enduring effects on the buying preferences of the public.

Subliminal Advertising

Could subliminally presented stimuli have a marketing application? Can advertising effectiveness be enhanced through subliminal stimulation? Before reviewing the few laboratory studies that have addressed this question directly, it will be useful to consider what sorts of subliminal influences would be necessary in order to obtain some marketing relevance. At a minimum, we might hypothesize that a subliminal stimulus produces (or increases) some positive affective reaction to that stimulus. Whether or not such an affective response, if obtained, could have any relevant motivating influence is another question. It is probably safe to assume that positive affect would not do any harm and could conceivably influence a product's attractiveness. A much stronger prediction for subliminal effects would be one that hypothesizes some direct behavioral consequence (i.e., purchasing). Since the former prediction does not *necessarily* entail any interesting marketing implications, and the latter prediction clearly does, these hypotheses will be referred to as weak and strong claims respectively.

Practical Difficulties

Regardless of which claim is under investigation, there are some profound if not insurmountable operational constraints associated with presenting subliminal stimuli in a typical marketing context. One problem has to do with individual differences in threshold. There is no particular stimulus intensity or duration that can guarantee subliminality for all viewers. In order to preclude detection by those with relatively low thresholds, the stimulus would have to be so weak that it would not reach viewers with higher thresholds at all. Lack of control over position and distance from the screen would further complicate matters. Finally, without elaborate precautions, supraliminal material (i.e., the film or commercial in progress) would almost certainly wash out any potential effects of a subliminal stimulus. In order to duplicate the results of laboratory studies that have shown subliminal effects, it is crucial to duplicate the conditions under which the effects were obtained. From a practical standpoint, this is virtually impossible. Nevertheless, it could be argued that if 1% of 10 million viewers are influenced by a subliminal ad that completely misses the other 99%, the subsequent behavior of that 1% might make the exercise cost effective.

Does the relevant research indicate that some positive affect could become associated with a particular product through the use of subliminally presented stimuli? The evidence is not strong. The Kunst-Wilson and Zajonc (1980) study referred to earlier used irregular, randomly constructed octagons as stimuli. The stimuli themselves were first presented at one-millisecond durations and filtered so that recognition was at chance level. Subjects were instructed to pay close attention to the screen, even if nothing was distinguishable. The same stimuli were subsequently presented for one-second intervals, paired with new stimuli. Subjects' recognition of old versus new stimuli was reported to be at chance; however, the old stimuli were judged to be preferable to the new ones 60% of the time. The effect was subtle but statistically reliable ($p < .01$, 2-tail).

It is tempting to speculate that repeated subliminal exposures could bring about an increasingly stronger affective reaction, with the stimuli themselves remaining unrecognized. A study by Shevrin and Fritzler (1968) does not support such a notion. These authors demonstrated a differential effect of two different subliminal stimuli upon evoked potentials (EEG) and free word associations in the absence of a conscious discrimination between the stimuli. The effect was a fleeting one, however: "the subliminal verbal effects appeared only in the first .001-second condition, suggesting that, beyond a certain point, multiple exposures of stimuli work against subliminal influences" (Shevrin and Fritzler 1968, p. 298). Two points about the Kunst-Wilson and Zajonc study are worth emphasizing.

First, the stimuli themselves, consisting of (relatively) meaningless geometric shapes, were subjected to subliminal exposure levels; this exposure seems to have had a subsequent effect upon preference. Second, the experimental subjects were actively attending to the stimuli throughout the subliminal viewing condition; during this time, no other stimulation was present that could distract attention or mask the subliminal stimuli.

Could this procedure be utilized in an advertising context? It is possible that a display's attractiveness could be subliminally enhanced by having that same display exposed for subliminal durations prior to its supraliminal presentation. Whether the magnitude of the resultant effect could have any practical importance is not known. Moreover, it is not obvious how the subliminal exposure could be accomplished. Superimposing the subliminal display on top of supraliminal material is not a good bet:

> *". . . Ongoing supraliminal stimulation to which attention may be directed almost certainly will swamp any effect by a simultaneous stimulus below the awareness threshold . . . at a peripheral level, lateral inhibition and contour suppressing mechanisms could well block any neural transmission from the weaker of two stimulus arrays . . . a similar effect of restricted channel capacity would almost certainly operate centrally as well. The potential effects of one stimulus may be completely negated by the presence of another" (Dixon 1971, p. 175–76).*

Splicing or somehow integrating the subliminal stimulus into ongoing supraliminal material (even if technologically possible) is not too promising either, because unless a sufficient blank interval is included before and after the insert, supraliminal material will mask the subliminal stimulus (Kahneman 1968). If such intervals are provided, the viewer will most probably be aware of an interruption, even though the stimulus itself may not be detectable. At least 100 milliseconds of "clean" background on either side of the target stimulus would be necessary to preclude a masking effect. As a result, subjects could infer the presence of a stimulus. If complete unobtrusiveness is a priority, the stimulus and surrounding interval would have to be carefully located at naturally occurring breaks or cut points. Even then, completely disguising the fact of stimulation may not be possible.

Evidence Involving the Weak Claim

In addition to Kunst-Wilson and Zajonc (1980), two other studies report subliminal effects relevant to the weak claim. Byrne (1959) flashed the word "beef" for successive five millisecond intervals during a sixteen-minute movie. Experimental and control subjects did not differ in their verbal references to beef, as measured by word association tests. Nor did experimental subjects report a higher preference for beef sandwiches, when given a list of five alternatives. Experimental subjects did, however, rate themselves as hungrier than control subjects. This difference held up when ratings were co-varied with hours of food deprivation. Byrne offered no explanation for this finding. It is not obvious why the word "beef" should induce hunger particularly when it failed to influence semantic associates. Moreover, the method of presentation involved superimposing the stimulus on the movie. For reasons outlined earlier, such a procedure is likely to interfere with rather than enhance any potential subliminal effects.

In a similar study, Hawkins (1970) flashed the word "coke" for 2.7 millisecond-intervals during the presentation of other supraliminal material. Subjective thirst ratings were higher for the "coke" group than for a control group that received a subliminal nonsense syllable. Hawkins concludes that "a simple subliminal stimulus can serve to arouse a basic drive such as thirst." (p. 324). As Saegert (1979) has pointed out, "Hawkin's results may simply be a Type I error, especially in view of the fact that other tries have been made" (p. 55). The fact that Hawkins performed five independent 1-tail statistical tests where one analysis would have sufficed lends support to Saegert's position. There are methodological shortcomings in both of these studies. Even if the results are taken at face value, their relevance to advertising is minimal.

Evidence Involving the Strong Claim

The strong claim for subliminal advertising posits specific behavioral consequences as a result of a subliminal directive. A study by Zuckerman (1960) requiring student nurses to write stories describing the contents of a series of pictures that were projected onto a screen in front of them is pertinent to this issue. Unknown to the subjects, the instructions "write more" and "don't write" were tachistoscopically superimposed on the pictures at successive points during the presentations. A control group was treated in a similar fashion but received blank slides in place of those containing the subliminal directives.

The study was composed of three successive conditions: (1) baseline, during which no subliminal messages were presented, (2) "write more," during which subjects in the experimental group received a "write more" instruction for .02 seconds, concurrently with the picture they were asked to describe, and (3) "don't write," during which the experimental subjects received a "don't write" directive, again superimposed for .02 seconds on the picture being projected. During each condition, pictures were presented for 10 trials each. After each trial, subjects wrote a description of what they had seen. Zuckerman found that nurses in the experimental group wrote more during condition 2 ("write more") than they had during baseline. Furthermore, he noted a slight drop in output between condition 3 ("don't write") and condition 2, and interpreted this as evidence that the subliminal instructions were effective.

Unfortunately, there is a strong possibility that these results were due to a methodological artifact which psychologists call a "ceiling effect." This occurs when performance reaches an asymptote and cannot be further improved upon. The slight drop that Zuckerman observed may not have been a real decrease in performance but rather, a levelling off. This interpretation is supported by a comparison of the performances of experimental and control subjects. For some reason the students in the experimental group were enthusiastic writers. They wrote much more during baseline than did the controls. They wrote still more during condition 2 ("write more"), and the controls increased their output as well. By condition 3 the experimental subjects may have reached asymptote. They were all "written out," and a slight drop was observed in the number of words written.

Because of time constraints (and possibly writer's cramp), experimental subjects may already have been writing as much as could reasonably be expected by the end of condition 2. The slight drop during condition 3 may be due to statistical artifact. When variability is possible in only one direction (in this case down), a slight decrease in performance is predictable. Controls were still increasing their output during condition 3 and by the end, their output had barely surpassed that of the experimental subjects' performance during baseline. When differences between groups are large prior to any experimental manipulation, it is risky to attribute some subsequently observed differences to that manipulation. In this study, the preexisting difference between experimental and control subjects was as great or greater than any other subsequently observed difference between or within groups. Zuckerman has little to say by way of explaining the finding, but submits that "the subject's operant behavior is supposedly brought under control by suggestive cues of which he is not aware" (p. 404). This is not an explanation but rather a description of the outcome couched in operant terminology.

Dixon (1971), commenting on Zuckerman's results, speculates that "it may be impossible to resist instructions which are not consciously experienced" (p. 177). Again, this is more an assertion than an explanation, but it does reflect an apparently prevalent (although not articulated) notion that instructions, directives and/or slogans are intrinsically compelling. When the instruction is delivered supraliminally the receiver can counter-argue or derogate the source, thereby diminishing the stimulus' influence. However, if the instruction is presented subliminally, the recipient is unaware of its presence and is consequently unable to counter-argue.

Several researchers have investigated and described some of the cognitive processes that may mediate acceptance of advertising claims (Harris et al. 1979, Wright 1973). Wright analyzed the responses of 160 women who were exposed to a target ad embedded in other surrounding material, and subsequently queried about their reactions to the arguments contained in the advertising message. Counterarguing by the receiver was identified as an important processing strategy. Neither the reliability nor validity of this finding is being disputed. However, it would be a mistake to assume that "resistive cognitions" are an inevitable consequence of advertising. Such a position is reminiscent of a behavioristic view of people as passive receivers of inputs to which they respond in automatic and stereotyped ways.

Perhaps the single most important lesson to be learned from cognitive psychology in the last decade is that the meaning of a stimulus does not reside in the stimulus itself. Meaning is constructed by the receiver in active, complex and often specialized ways. With respect to advertising the selectivity of attention and the active control over subsequent processing of the input means that stimulation is not a sufficient condition for any response at all, let alone some particular response. We are constantly subjected to a barrage of external and internal stimuli, of which only a fraction acquire phenomenal representation. Some neural activity is no doubt provoked by stimuli that are not consciously processed. But to attribute to a subliminal stimulus a strong influence, which it cannot be shown to have when supraliminal, is not justified by any theoretical rationale. For this reason it is appropriate to insist on especially clear well-replicated empirical evidence before accepting such a proposition. To the author's knowledge, Zuckerman's (1960) finding has *not* been replicated, and the study itself is vulnerable to an important methodological criticism.

There is an additional problem with procedures that attempt subliminal persuasion through the use of written directives. In order for a subliminal message to exert a behavioral effect (the "strong" claim), the full and precise meaning of the message would have to be extracted from it. Dixon (1971) has reviewed many subliminal perception studies showing that when words are used as stimuli, "the stimulus tends to elicit responses from the same sphere of meaning" (p. 102). Since competitors' products may well be contained in this sphere, it would be essential that the full meaning of the stimulus words be identified. An effusion of mere semantic associates would be insufficient. There are no published studies that demonstrate that people educe the full meaning of a subliminal word stimulus, and there are at least two studies casting some doubt on the possibility (Heilbrun 1980, Severance and Dyer 1973). For this reason, it is difficult to construe a subliminal directive as an argument that cannot be consciously resisted.

Summary

Before turning to other methods that attempt subliminal persuasion, it will be useful to summarize the evidence reviewed. Research supporting the null hypothesis is much less likely to find its way into print than that which demonstrates some potential influence. The paucity of evidence may simply be a reflection of its lack of availability. On the basis of what little data are available, one could tentatively conclude that subliminal presentation of a stimulus may produce a positive affective response to that stimulus (Kunst-Wilson and Zajonc 1980). This positive affective response was obtained with subjects who were attending only to the subliminal stimuli. Whether this finding could be utilized successfully in a marketing context remains to be seen. Apart from the question of the magnitude of the effect, not to mention its validity (Birnbaum 1981, Mellers 1981), there are some practical difficulties associated with achieving a real-world application.

The evidence that subliminal directives can exert any control over behavior is much less compelling (Zuckerman 1960), although there has been ample opportunity for replication. Moreover, this strong claim for subliminal influence is not accompanied by a coherent explanatory rationale. Previous reviews of the strong claim have reached similar conclusions. One of the first rigorous scrutinies of this issue was described by McConnell et al. (1958), no doubt precipitated by the furor generated by the popcorn ad in New Jersey. These authors were sceptical that any but the simplest forms of behavior could be affected by stimulation below the level of conscious awareness. Bevan (1964a) concluded that the "influences of subliminal stimulation upon preference and choice, if they occur at all, are highly subtle, and the possibility that they could constitute an effective means of controlling consumer behavior or political opinion is highly unlikely" (p. 91). Equally strong misgivings were expressed by Goldiamond (1966) and Anastasi (1964). Empirical documentation has remained elusive: "all things considered . . . secret attempts to manipulate people's minds have yielded results as subliminal as the stimuli used" (McConnell 1977, p. 231).

Subaudible Messages

The eye is capable of receiving far more information in a short period of time than is the ear. Thus most studies of subliminal perception have involved visual stimulation because the investigator can attempt to determine what particular features of a display are responsible for various sorts of neural activity that may occur below the level of conscious awareness. In contrast, studies addressing auditory reception have been concerned primarily with signal detection–determining the presence versus absence of a weak signal. Because auditory information is, perforce, temporally extended, it is particularly vulnerable to loss through lack of attention or auditory masking.

This probably accounts for the total absence of published studies investigating possible effects of subaudible messages. While the eye is sensitive primarily to spatial information, the ear is basically a processor of temporal information, especially in the case of speech perception. The difference is an important one. A great deal of information can be presented simultaneously in a visual display. An auditory stimulus is more extended in time; information arrives in consecutive bits. A speech stimulus may be thought of as a sound pattern whose acoustic features fluctuate over time. Consequently, there is no procedure for creating tachistoscopic-like auditory stimuli. Controlling the exposure duration of a visual stimulus does not change the stimulus itself; it merely limits the time available for processing it.

If speech is compressed or telescoped in time, the signal itself is altered. While the speech stream can be subjected to a surprising amount of mutilation without intelligibility being affected (Licklider and Miller 1951), there is a limit to the amount of distortion that can be tolerated without a loss in comprehension. Information is transmitted at the rate of about 150 words per minute in normal speech. Studies have shown (Foulke and Sticht 1969) that comprehension declines fairly rapidly at rates beyond 300 words per minute. There are two reasons for this. The first involves signal degradation. When playback speed is increased, component frequencies and pitch are both altered. The intelligibility of the signal consequently suffers. Secondly, channel capacity is taxed when a critical word rate is reached. Speech comprehension requires the continuous registration, encoding and storage of informaion. These operations take time. When the word rate is too fast, not all the input can be processed as it is received. The result is that some speech information is lost. Reducing the volume of accelerated speech will only compound these difficulties. Mass media accounts of subaudible messages report presentation rates of greater than 2,300 words per minute (*Toronto Star* 1978, p. c1; *Washington Post* 1979, p. c4; *Time* 1979, p. 63). The message is simply repeated 8 or 9,000 times an hour. Because of the fast rate, what may once have been a message is rendered an unintelligible scratching sound. That such stimuli could have any influence on behavior (except to annoy) is a claim totally lacking empirical support. Since the stimulus has no apparent meaning, presenting it at a supposedly subaudible level does not thereby confer any added significance.

The accelerated nature of subaudible messages is perhaps a tangential issue. Could such messages have an influence if the presentation rate were normal, but the volume at a subthreshold level? Relevant evidence mitigates against such a notion. Weak auditory stimuli are very susceptible to auditory masking. Moreover, there is some experimental evidence that attentional focus can effectively prevent weak auditory stimuli from receiving any processing at all (Broadbent 1958, Eriksen and Johnson 1964, Peterson and Kroener 1964). Studies in dichotic listening reveal that very little of the content of an unattended message is processed when attention is focused on another concurrent message (Kahneman 1973, Moray 1969, Treisman and Geffen (1967). Moreover the unattended stimuli used in these investigations are by no means subliminal in strength.

Speech sounds are different in principle from other auditory inputs (Liberman et al. 1967). Because of speech's temporal dimension, a certain minimal amount of attention may be essential for comprehension. This would make subliminal presentation of auditory messages not just difficult but impossible. In fact, it is difficult to conceive of a means by which speech could be rendered subliminal according to the conventional definition outlined earlier (see Dixon 1971, 1981). Neither accelerating the message nor reducing its volume seems to provide appropriate analogs to the methods used in the visual modality.

At any rate, the procedures tried to date do not appear promising.

Whether or not subliminal effects could be obtained from auditory messages under more carefully controlled conditions remains to be seen. At the present time there is no evidence that such influence is possible, let alone any practical application. It should also be emphasized that a change in modality does not provide a defense against some of the objections raised earlier regarding the subliminal effects of visual stimuli. The assumption that behavior can be automatically triggered by the presentation of some particular stimulus is as unwarranted for auditory messages as it is for visual ones.

Embedded Stimuli

A different kind of procedure for achieving subliminal effects has been described by Key (1973, 1976, 1980). In these books the author alleges that various erotic images or words have been surreptitiously concealed in magazine, newspaper and television advertisements. High-speed photography and airbrushing are among the techniques whereby subtle appeals to subconscious sex drives are hidden. Their use is ubiquitous. Ritz crackers have the word *sex* baked into them; a Gilbey's Gin ad is full of microscope erotica. None of these are visible to the naked eye. In fact, it apparently requires weeks of analysis for many of them to be discovered, and sometimes they are embedded upside down.

According to Key, ". . . humans can be assumed to have at least two sensory input systems, one encoding data at the conscious level and a second operating at a level below conscious awareness" (Key 1973). A concealed word or symbol, ". . . usually invisible to consciousness appears instantly perceivable at the unconscious level" (Key 1976). He goes on to claim that visual or auditory stimulation whose speed and/or intensity are beyond the range for normal sensory reception can nevertheless be transmitted directly into the unconscious, whence subsequent behavior is manipulated. Precisely how these implanted cues affect a given product's desirability is not too clear, but Key assures us that they are very effective. The Ritz crackers, in fact, are reported to taste better because they have the word *sex* stamped onto them. Key provides no documentation for the effects that he attributes to embedded stimuli. For this reason, his assertions should be regarded as hypotheses awaiting empirical investigation. Key also describes some psychological mechanisms through which embedded stimuli purportedly operate. These latter claims involving perception, memory and the subconscious have probably rendered his speculations quite unpalatable to research psychologists. Man's sensory apparatus has been studied extensively for many years. There is no evidence for more than one class of sensory input systems, as Key claims, nor is there evidence of unconscious perception of stimuli that fall outside the functional range of our receptor organs. Key appears to invent whatever features of perception and memory would be necessary to achieve the results imputed to embedded stimuli. The notion of a separate super-powerful sensory system serving the subconscious (exclusively) cannot be accommodated by any theory of perception, past or present. It is not surprising that Key's books have not been favorably reviewed by the scientific community (Schulman 1981). They are mentioned here because while they contain the least scientific substance, these books are probably largely responsible for the promulgation of a belief in the power of subliminal manipulation.

Whether or not erotic imagery has been deliberately planted is not relevant to a consideration of the imagery's alleged effects. A diligent search for a phallic symbol will probably be successful. How its presence and relationship to an advertised product might be interpreted is another matter, but the consequence is by no means predictable. The amount of information available from a purposeful scrutiny of a display is limited only by the viewer's imagination. Holding advertisers responsible for one's erotic musings is analogous to accusing Rorschach of insinuating particular themes into the inkblots. A cursory glance yields far less information than a careful inspection. Under typical circumstances, the ad's most salient characteristics will receive the lion's share of perceptual activity (Hochberg 1978), if they receive any attention at all. Completely ignoring a stimulus is an option that people frequently exercise. If you do not actively search for hidden extras, what you see is what you get, and there is nothing subliminal about such perusal. The fine print near the bottom of an ad is likely to be far more important than any concealed genitalia could be.

While Key appears to have misjudged the efficacy of embedded stimuli, it would be a mistake to dismiss out of hand all of his remarks concerning the latent effects of advertising. Ads may influence us in some ways which have nothing to do with consumer behavior per se. For example, ads help to transmit various cultural stereotypes. If women are consistently portrayed in insignificant or demeaning roles, the viewer may develop an attitude towards them that is ultimately prejudicial and harmful to women as a group. Moreover, these attitudes are not consciously formed. The rich literature on observational learning investigates how such learning taks place (Comstock et al. 1978). While the acquisition of such attitudes may occur subconsciously, there is nothing subliminal about the presentation of the role models. On the contrary, they are distressingly conspicuous. This kind of implicit learning can have important and pervasive consequences (Poe 1976; Rush 1980; Walstedt, Geis and Brown 1980).

Conclusion

A century of psychological research substantiates the general principle that more intense stimuli have a greater influence on people's behavior than weaker ones. While subliminal perception is a bona fide phenomenon, the effects obtained are subtle and obtaining them typically requires a carefully structured context. Subliminal stimuli are usually so weak that the recipient is not just unaware of the stimulus but is also oblivious to the fact that he/she is being stimulated. As a result, the potential effects of subliminal stimuli are easily nullified by other ongoing stimulation in the same sensory channel or by attention being focused on another modality. These factors pose serious difficulties for any possible marketing application.

A second major problem pertains to the psychological mechanism through which a subliminal stimulus could in principle influence behavior. The proposition is appropriate only if one characterizes a person as a static organism who processes stimulus input passively and responds in automatic predictable ways. In fact, psychological research has generated a large body of evidence that such a characterization would be false. There is substantial evidence for the importance of centralized control and mediating processes and good reason to believe that humans have highly mobile selective attention. The sheer volume of constant sensory stimulation implicates a constructive, synthetic model of focal attention and perception rather than a purely receptive one. As Broadbent (1973) said, ". . . the brain is made of unreliable components, so that it is very unlikely that any particular impulses in any particular nerve cells will occur predictably and consistently whenever a particular stimulus strikes our senses. In addition, we are being bombarded all the time by a very large quantity of information; and in relation to this large quantity of information we are all, like Winnie the Pooh, "bears of very little brain" (p. 31).

Empirical support for subliminal influences of a pragmatic nature is neither plentiful, nor compelling. On the basis of research evidence accumulated to date, the most one could hope for, in terms of marketing application, would be a potential positive affective response to a subliminal stimulus. Whether such an effect could actually be obtained in a realistic viewing situation, and whether the magnitude of the effect would make the exercise worthwhile is still an empirical question. There is no empirical documentation for stronger subliminal effects, such as inducing particular behaviors or changing motivation. Moreover, such a notion is contradicted by a substantial amount of research and is incompatible with experimentally based conceptions of information processing, learning, and motivation.

None of this is to deny the existence of motives of which one may be unaware, nor to deny that subliminal stimulation can be used to investigate differences between unconscious and conscious processes (Carr and Bacharach 1976, McCauley et al. 1980, Shevrin and Dickman 1980). The point is simply that subliminal directives have not been shown to have the power ascribed to them by advocates of subliminal advertising. In general, the literature on subliminal perception shows that the most clearly documented effects are obtained only in highly contrived and artificial situations. These effects, when present, are brief and of small magnitude. The result is perhaps best construed as an epiphenomenon—a subtle and fleeting by-product of the complexities of human cognitive activity. These processes have no apparent relevance to the goals of advertising.

References

Anastasi, A. (1964), "Subliminal Perception," in *Fields of Applied Psychology*, A. Anastasi, New York: McGraw-Hill.

Bevan, W. (1964a), "Subliminal Stimulation: A Pervasive Problem for Psychology," *Psychological Bulletin*, 61 (no. 2), 89–99.

—— (1964b), "Contemporary Problems in Adaptation Level Theory," *Psychological Bulletin*, 61 (no. 3), 161–187.

Birnbaum, M. (1981), "Thinking and Feeling: A Skeptical Review," *American Psychologist*, 36 (no. 1), 99–101.

Broadbent, D. E. (1958), *Perception and Communication*, New York: Pergamon.

—— (1973), *In Defence of Empirical Psychology*, London: Camelot Press.

Brown, K. C. (1960), "Hemlock For the Critic: A Problem in Evaluation," *Journal of Aesthetics and Art Criticism*, 18 (no. 3), 316–19.

Byrne, D. (1959), "The Effect of a Subliminal Food Stimulus on Verbal Responses," *Journal of Applied Psychology*, 43 (no. 4), 249–251.

Carr, T. and V. Bacharach (1976), "Perceptual Tuning and Conscious Attention," *Cognition*, 4 (no. 3), 281–302.

Comstock, G., S. Chaffer, N. Katzman, M. McCombe and D. Roberts (1978), *Television and Human Behavior*, New York: Columbia University Press.

Cousins, N. (1957), "Smudging the Subconscious," *Saturday Review*, 40 (October 5).

Dixon, N. F. (1971), *Subliminal Perception: The Nature of a Controversy*, London: McGraw-Hill.

—— (1981), *Preconscious Processing*. London: Wiley.

Erdelyi, M. H. (1974), "A New Look at the New Look: Perceptual Defense and Vigilance," *Psychological Review*, 81 (no. 1), 1–25.

Eriksen, C. W. and H. J. Johnson (1964), "Storage and Decay Characteristics of Nonattended Auditory Stimuli," *Journal of Experimental Psychology*, 68 (no. 1), 28–36.

Foulke, E. and I. G. Sticht (1960), "Review of Research on the Intelligibility and Comprehension of Accelerated Speech," *Psychological Bulletin*, 72 (no. 1), 50–62.

Globe & Mail (1978) (October 13), 5.

Goldiamond, I. (1966), "Statement on Subliminal Advertising," in *Control of Human Behavior*, Volume 1, R. Ulrich, T. Stachnik and J. Mabry, eds., Glenview, IL: Scott Foresman.

Green, D. M. and J. A. Swets (1966), *Signal Detection Theory and Psychophysics*, New York: Wiley.

Harris, R. J., T. M. Dubitsky and S. Thompson (1979), "Learning to Identify Deceptive Truth in Advertising," in *Current Issues and Research in Advertising*, J. H. Leigh and C. R. Martin, eds., Ann Arbor: U. of Michigan Graduate School of Business Administration, Division of Research.

Hawkins, D. (1970), "The Effects of Subliminal Stimulation on Drive Level and Brand Preference," *Journal of Marketing Research*, 8 (August), 322–26.

Heilbrun, K. S. (1980), "Silverman's Subliminal Psychodynamic Activation: A Failure to Replicate," *Journal of Abnormal Psychology*, 89 (no. 4), 560–566.

Hochberg, J. (1978), *Perception*, 2nd ed., Englewood Cliffs, NJ: Prentice-Hall.

Kahneman, D. (1968), "Method, Findings and Theory in Studies of Visual Masking," *Psychological Bulletin*, 70 (no. 6), 404–425.

—— (1973), *Attention and Effort*, Englewood Cliffs, NJ: Prentice-Hall.

Kelly, J. S. (1979), "Subliminal Embeds in Print Advertising: A Challenge to Advertising Ethics," *Journal of Advertising*, 8 (no. 3), 20–24.

Key, W. B. (1973), *Subliminal Seduction*, Englewood Cliffs, NJ: Signet.

—— (1976), *Media Sexploitation*, Englewood Cliffs, NJ: Prentice-Hall.

—— (1980), *The Clamplate Orgy*, Englewood Cliffs, NJ: Prentice-Hall.

Kunst-Wilson, W. and R. Zajonc (1980), "Affective Discrimination of Stimuli That Cannot Be Recognized," *Science*, 207 (no. 1), 557–558.

Liberman, A. M., F. S. Cooper, D. P. Shankweiler and M. Studdert-Kennedy (1967), "Perception of the Speech Code," *Psychological Review*, 74 (no. 6), 431–461.

Licklider, J. and G. Miller (1951), "The Perception of Speech," in S. Stevens, ed., *Handbook of Experimental Psychology*, New York: Wiley.

McCauley, C., C. Parmelee, R. Sperber and T. Carr (1980), "Early Extraction of Meaning From Pictures and Its Relation to Conscious Identification," *Journal of Experimental Psychology: Human Perception and Performance*, 6 (no. 2), 265–76.

McConnell, J. V. (1977), *Understanding Human Behavior*, 2nd ed., New York: Holt, Rinehart & Winston.

——, R. Cutter and E. McNeil (1958), "Subliminal Stimulation: An Overview," *American Psychologist*, 13 (no. 3), 229–42.

Mellers, B. (1981), "Feeling More Than Thinking," *American Psychologist*, 36 (no. 7), 802–803.

Moray, N. (1960), *Attention: Selective Processes in Vision and Hearing*, London: Hutchinson Ltd.

Nation (1957), "Diddling the Subconscious: Subliminal Advertising," 185 (October 5), 206.

New York Times (1978) (May 18), c22.

New Yorker (1957), 33 (September 21), 33.

Nisbett, R. E. and T. O. Wilson (1972), "Telling More Than We Can Know: Verbal Reports on Mental Processes," *Psychological Review*, 84 (no. 3), 231–59.

Peterson, L. R. and S. Kroener (1964), "Dichotic Stimulation and Retention," *Journal of Experimental Psychology*, 68 (no. 2), 125–130.

Pierce, C. S. and J. Jastrow (1844), "On Small Differences of Sensation," *Memoirs of the National Academy of Sciences,* 3, 73-84.

Poe, A. (1976), "Active Women in Ads," *Journal of Communication,* 26 (no. 4), 185-92.

Rush, F. (1980), "Child Pornography," in *Take Back the Night: Women on Pornography,* L. Lederer, ed., New York: Morrow.

Saegert, J. (1979), "Another Look at Subliminal Perception," *Journal of Advertising Research,* 19 (no. 1), 55-57.

Schulman, M. (1981), "The Great Conspiracy," *Journal of Communications,* 31 (no. 2), 209.

Severance, L. J. and F. N. Dyer (1973), "Failure of Subliminal Word Presentations to Generate Interference to Color-naming," *Journal of Experimental Psychology,* 101 (no. 1), 186-89.

Shevrin, H. and S. Dickman (1980), "The Psychological Unconscious: A Necessary Assumption for All Psychological Theory?" *American Psychologist,* 35, 421-34.

—— and D. Fritzler (1968), "Visual Evoked Response Correlates of Unconscious Mental Processes," *Science,* 161 (no. 19), 295-298.

Swets, J. A. (1961), "Is There a Sensory Threshold?" *Science,* 134 (no. 3473), 168-177.

Time (1979), 114 (September 10), 63.

Toronto Star (1978) (October 23), c1.

Treisman, A. M. and G. Geffen (1967), "Selective Attention: Perception or Response? *Quarterly Journal of Experimental Psychology,* 19 (no. 1), 1-17.

Walstedt, J. J., F. Geis and V. Brown (1980), "Influence of Television Commercials on Women's Self-Confidence and Independent Judgment," *Journal of Personality and Social Psychology,* 38 (no. 2), 203-210.

Washington Post (1979), (May 27), c4.

Wright, R. (1973), "The Cognitive Processes Mediating Acceptance of Advertising," *Journal of Marketing Research,* 10 (February), 53-62.

Zajonc, R. B. (1980), "Feeling and Thinking: Preferences Need No Inferences," *American Psychologist,* 35 (no. 2), 151-175.

Zuckerman, M. (1960), "The Effects of Subliminal and Supraliminal Suggestions on Verbal Productivity," *Journal of Abnormal and Social Personality,* 60 (no. 3), 404-11.

READING 30

Fear: The Potential of an Appeal Neglected by Marketing

Michael L. Ray and William L. Wilkie

Considerable social psychology and communications research show that intelligent use of fear messages can have favorable effects on attitude change and action. Yet the unique persuasive possibilities offered by the fear appeal have been neglected by marketing. This is in sharp contrast to the creative pursuit of positive advertising appeals. This article presents a marketing-oriented discussion and summary of research on the fear appeal.

Marketing's neglect of the fear appeal is a prime example of the field's failure to take full advantage of communication research findings. While a large number of behavioral studies on fear have been published, marketing ignores their hints for segmentation, communication goal setting, message construction, and product differentiation. Instead of looking at these detailed results, marketing seems content to ask the simple question, "Is fear effective or not?," and to reach the premature conclusion that fear is not effective as an appeal.

There is now enough evidence from research and from practical applications to indicate that fear should no longer be eliminated from consideration as a marketing and advertising appeal. This paper is an attempt to present some of these research results on fear; it suggests how they might be used to make marketing decisions.

Reprinted by permission of the American Marketing Association, from the *Journal of Marketing,* 34:1 January 1970, 54-62.

Past Marketing Treatment of Fear

A search of the marketing literature reveals either that fear appeals are not mentioned, or that they are guardedly rejected for marketing and advertising application on the basis of Janis and Feshbach's 1953 research on fear appeals and dental hygiene.[1] Their findings indicated that a strong fear appeal was less effective than moderate or mild fear appeals in producing reported adherence to recommended dental hygiene practices. This negative finding—the more the fear the less the effect—is the only research result on fear reported by Cox.[2] In Crane's text the Janis and Feshbach study is outlined under the headline "'Scare Appeal' on Teeth Boomerangs."[3] Myers and Reynolds list as "Principle S-2" the notion that "strong appeals to fear, by arousing too much tension in the audience, are less effective in persuasion than minimal appeals."[4] Engel, Kollat and Blackwell, while citing a wide range of fear studies in their one-page treatment of the area, decide only that "Further research is needed."[5]

The fact is that further research has been done. Over 90 studies have been reported in *Psychological Abstracts* since the Janis and Feshbach research. Further, quite a few of these studies have actually found that high fear was more effective than low or no fear. This is the reverse of what Janis and Feshbach found and the reverse of what marketing has seemingly been assuming over the last 15 or 16 years.

But the key point from these studies is not that high fear, low fear, or no fear was successful. The key point is that these studies provide information which could help marketers make advertising decisions. Fear research has been conducted with many types of people and should provide hints for segmentation. The findings should help marketers set communication goals, because several levels of effect—from interest and awareness to attitude and action—have been studied. And a number of different message approaches have been tried. These findings should be of particular interest to advertising copy and media people.

While marketing as a whole tended to ignore fear research, the American Cancer Society and other anti-cigarette forces used these indications on fear when their advertising campaign was stepped up in 1967, 1968, and 1969. In 1968—for the first time since 1964 when the Surgeon General's report on smoking was issued—there was a drop in per capita and total cigarette consumption.[6]

As in all advertising situations, it is difficult to determine causality in the case of anti-cigarette advertising and the drop in smoking. In the first place the nature of the fear appeals that were used is not unambiguous. Some fear appeals dealt with the pestiferous nature of smoking, some with the ridiculous addiction of smokers, some with the effect of parental smoking on children and the family, some with the strength of the evidence against smoking, and some with well-known spokesmen (William Talman, Tony Curtis) who argued against the practice.[7]

The drop in smoking could be due to any of the above appeals or to increased and more efficient advertising media spending. It could also be due to increasing environmental support. While it is obvious that the switch to strong fear appeals cannot be given total credit for the drop in smoking, it is now abundantly clear that marketing can no longer ignore fear appeals.

The General Evidence on Fear

The picture emerging from the more recent research on fear is that neither extremely strong nor very weak fear appeals are maximally effective.[8] It seems that appeals at a somewhat moderate level of fear are best. A simple explanation for this might be that if an appeal is too weak it just does not attract enough attention. If it is too strong, on the other hand, it may lead people to avoid the message or ignore the message's recommendations as being inadequate to the task of eliminating the feared event.

A more thorough explanation is presented in Figure 1. Here there are two types of effects hypothesized to occur as fear increases. First, there are the facilitating effects that are most often overlooked in marketing. If fear can heighten drive, there is the possibility of greater attention and interest in the product and message than if no drive were aroused. This aspect of fear appeals should be especially attractive in the context of the need in marketing for distinctive approaches. A sufficiently strong fear might lead to acceptance of the message recommendation by first inducing interest in the ad and then prompting a search for solution to the problem presented.

But fear also brings the important characteristic of inhibition into the picture. The lower curve in Figure 1 representing inhibiting effects shows the possible results of "irrational" behavior caused by high fear. If fear levels are too high, there is the possibility of defensive avoidance of the ad, denial of the threat, selective exposure or distortion of the ad's meaning, or a view of the recommendations as being inadequate to deal with so important a fear. Marketing, in it examination of fear, has unwittingly put all its emphasis on these inhibiting effects of fear.

The dashed line in Figure 1 shows the resulting total effects curve resulting from both facilitating and inhibiting effects. This curve represents the higher effectiveness for moderate fear appeals mentioned earlier.

If this curvilinear or nonmonotonic explanation is true, however, why did Janis and Feshbach find the most minimal fear level to be most effective? Why do other researchers find maximal fear levels to be most effective? And, more important for marketers, how can this curvilinear explanation be used to plan advertising?

In order to answer these questions, it is helpful to examine the differences between two studies which obtained opposite results on fear. The Janis and Feshbach study and another piece of research by Insko, Arkoff, and Insko[9] serve as good examples for this purpose.

In the Janis and Feshbach research four

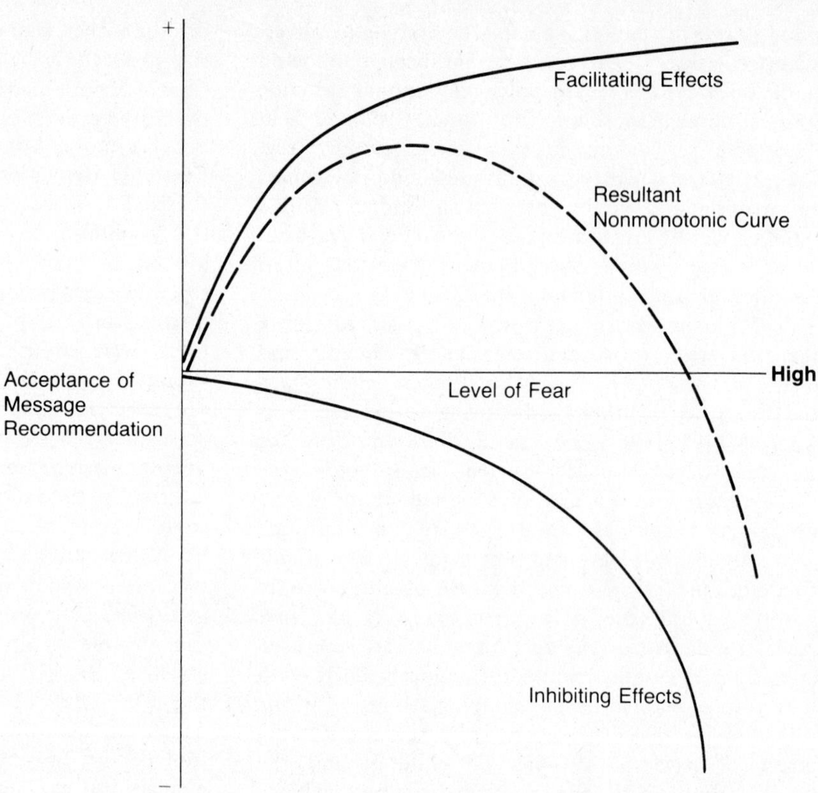

FIGURE 1
Facilitating and Inhibiting Effects Leading to Nonmonotonic Curve

groups of 50 Connecticut high school students were each exposed to one of the following 15-minute lecture-slide presentations on the consequences of improper dental hygiene:

- *Strong Appeal:* The message contained 71 references to unfavorable consequences presented in a threatening, personalized, "this-can-happen-to-you" manner.
- *Moderate Appeal:* The message contained 49 references to unfavorable consequences presented in a more factual and less personal way than the strong message.
- *Mild Appeal:* The message contained 18 references to unfavorable consequences, again presented factually and impersonally. The scare material of the other messages was replaced with relatively neutral material having to do with the growth and formation of the teeth.
- *Control:* The message was on a topic (the human eye) irrelevant to the dental hygiene lectures received by the other groups.

Insko, Arkoff and Insko studied the reactions of 144 seventh-grade students in Honolulu. Half of the group saw each of the following messages on smoking and lung cancer.

- *High Fear:* The message consisted of full color slides of cancerous body parts described in an "it-could-happen-to-you" manner. The link between smoking and lung cancer was made explicit and suggestions to avoid smoking were made.
- *Low Fear:* The message mentioned the smoking-lung cancer link, and there were black and white photomicrographs of diseased tissue which were discussed dispassionately. This message also recommended that the students avoid smoking.

In both studies there was the appropriate reaction to fear. In other words, people become more nervous in response to the stronger fear messages. But beyond this, the results of the two studies seem quite contradictory. The Janis and Feshbach research indicated that the stronger the fear appeal the less the reported adherence to the messages' recommendations on dental hygiene. Insko et al., on the other hand, found that the high fear message was more effective than the low in decreasing the seventh graders' stated intentions to smoke in the future.

Figures 2 and 3 demonstrate the usefulness of the curvilinear explanation in dealing with the seemingly contradictory results of the two studies. In Figure 2 the emphasis is on the degree of fear in the messages. All of Janis and Feshbach's messages are positioned on the high end of the curve. This seems reasonable since even their mild appeal contained as many as 18 references to the unfavorable consequences of improper dental hygiene. The Insko et al. messages are placed on the low end of the fear continuum, because, although the messages contained references to smoking and lung cancer, these references could not be extremely threatening to seventh graders who did not smoke and who probably considered themselves to be far from a disease state. This positioning of the messages in the two studies is entirely consistent with the results: The high fear message being most effective in Insko et al., the mild fear message in Janis and Feshbach.

The explanatory approach taken in Figure 3 is really more useful for marketing, however, because it treats different consumer segments and topics (product categories) with different curves. With such a treatment marketers can realistically consider the fear appeal response functions within various segment-product category groupings. In the case of the research discussed here, the high schooler-dental hygiene grouping is seen as lower on the fear continuum (responding better to lower levels of fear) than the seventh-grader smoking and cancer grouping. Thus, Figure 3 demonstrates, even if the fear levels of the messages in the studies were equivalent, the groups would respond differently because they have different fear response functions.

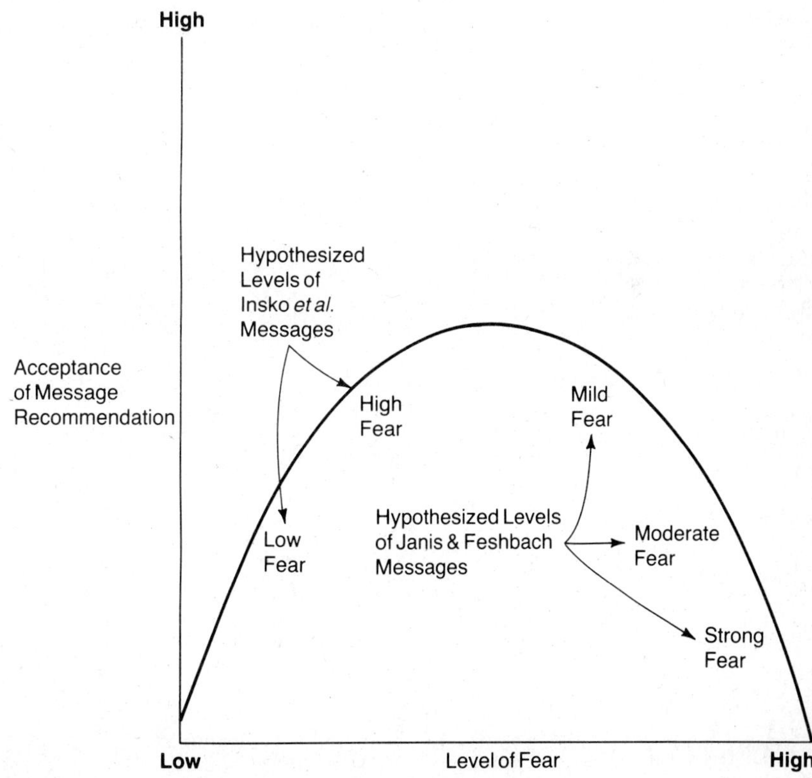

FIGURE 2
Nonmonotonic Reconciliation of Janis and Feshbach and Insko et al. Findings

It is interesting to note that Insko and his associates were attempting to find a segment and topic for which there was such a response function. Their hypothesis was that for seventh graders, the topic of smoking would not be as threatening (i.e., would not produce as many inhibiting effects), because the messages would not be dealing with a present, personal behavior of the seventh graders. One might speculate that if the Insko group had constructed additional, stronger fear messages which underlined dangers of lung cancer *to seventh graders,* they may have tapped the part of the response function in which extremely high fear is hypothesized to be less effective.

Segmentation Hints from Fear Research

Figure 3 actually could be considered as a model of how marketing's concept of segmentation might utilize fear research. The basic idea is simple. If the marketer is dealing with a segment that has a response curve like that of Insko's subjects, it should be possible to effectively use a relatively strong fear appeal in advertising, in product positioning, etc. A segment with a response function like that hypothesized for the Janis and Feshbach group, however, would be less responsive to fear, and it might be better to use low fear or some other kind of appeal.

This segmentation approach to fear appeals is quite viable, because the fear research findings on segment response functions include all three of the basic segmenting approaches used in marketing: socioeconomic, personality, and usage.

Personality was probably the first segment characteristic studied in fear appeal research. In a paper published in 1954, Janis and Feshbach[10] analyzed their 1953 study, separating the sample into high and low anxiety groups with the use of test scores and teacher ratings. The low anxiety group

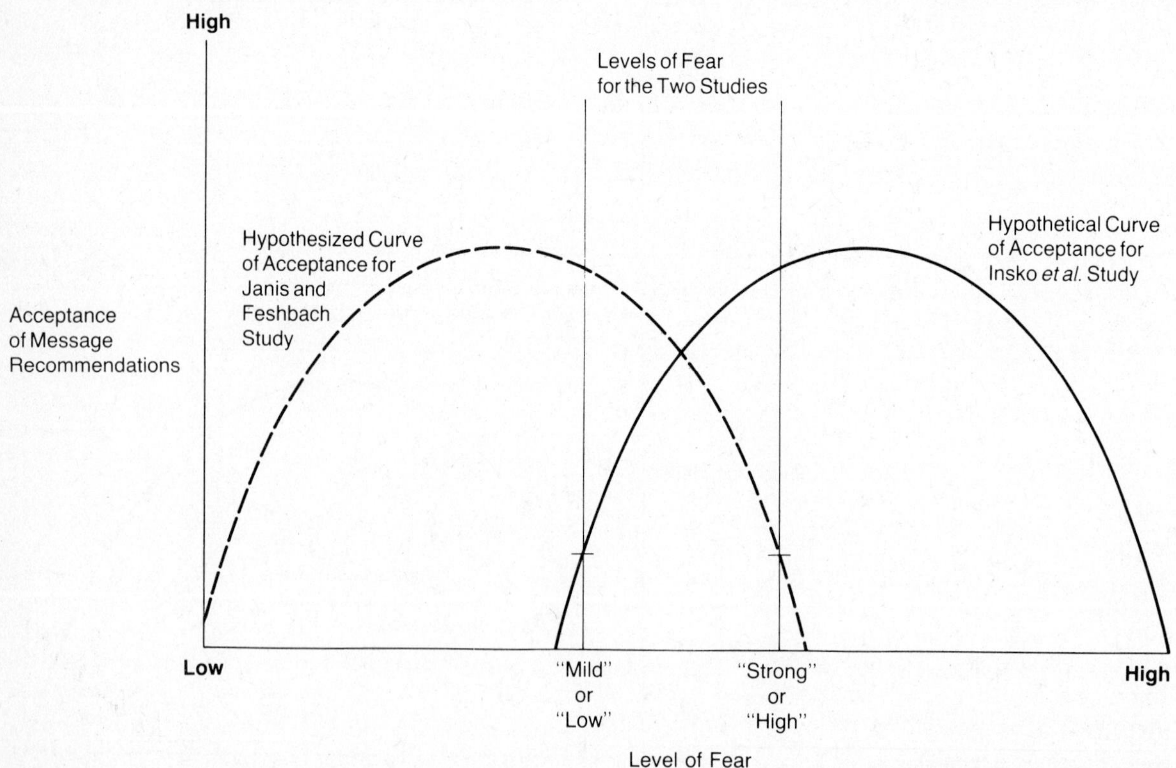

FIGURE 3
Nonmonotonic Reconciliation of Fear Findings with Curves for Two Kinds of Audiences and Topics

was more heavily influenced by the strong fear message than was the high anxiety group. For the minimal fear message the reverse pattern was true; i.e., the high anxiety group was affected more by the message than was the low anxiety group. The same sort of finding—positive effect of fear in low anxiety groups and negative in high anxiety—occurred in a study by Niles on smoking.[11] Niles' anxiety measure was the subjects' perceived vulnerability to lung cancer.

Related personality results are reported in a study by Goldstein[12] dealing with copers (those who characteristically make active efforts to deal with impulses and dangers) and avoiders (those who deny dangers). Copers did not react differently to high and low fear messages. Avoiders, however, were less receptive to recommendations under high than under low fear. Leventhal[13] has conducted a series of studies utilizing the personality variable of self-esteem. His general finding is that the higher a person's self-esteem, the higher is his optimal level of fear. Most of this research was done with communications recommending tetanus innoculation.

"Usage" (or topic relevance) was probably the second segmenting variable studied in the fear area. The general finding is that the greater the relevance of the topic for the audience, the lower the optimal level of fear appeal. For instance Insko et al. found a positive relation between fear and acceptance of anti-smoking messages when respondents were not smokers. Berkowitz and Cottingham found that greater automobile usage was associated with diminished effectiveness of a strong fear message advocating the use of seat belts. Leventhal and Watts found the same sort of negative relationship between usage of cigarettes and acceptance of strong fear messages on smoking.[14]

Few fear studies have been conducted using the common socioeconomic segmenting descriptions. In most cases the fear experiments utilize fairly small samples with all respondents coming from one socioeconomic class. Two studies, by Haefner and by Singer, seem to suggest that fear appeals are more effective with lower than with high socioeconomic classes, but the results are confused by source effects (such as deference to authority).[15]

In general, then, fear research mirrors marketing findings in that the segmenting characteristics which have discriminated best have been those most closely related to the product or topic. High fear appeals have worked best with people who are low in anxiety and high in self-esteem, who exhibit coping behavior, who normally find the topic or category of low relevance, and who normally see themselves as having low vulnerability to the threat in the fear message.

An interesting conclusion for marketing is that fear motivation should be most effective for those who have not seen themselves as part of the market for the recommended product or brand. Thus, it might be surmised that strong Cancer Society appeals would be more effective for younger than older smokers, since younger smokers are less likely to see themselves as vulnerable to the cancer threat. If the anti-cigarette forces can further segment the market to find low anxiety, high self-esteem copers among the smokers, they will have segments for which extremely strong fear messages should be effective if presented well.

In a similar way, insurance companies might find that fear appeals work best with groups who typically do not see themselves as needing insurance, even though they have already been exposed to insurance ads dealing with security, benefits, etc. Mouthwash advertisers might find that fear appeals would work best with those who have not really considered the bad breath problem. Dietetic foods might be sold with fear appeals to those on the verge of gaining weight who have not yet considered weight gain a problem. Safety features in cars might best be sold with fear to those infrequent drivers who have not considered the dangers of short trips in the city.

The list of possible applications is virtually endless. The general implication, however, can be stated in a brief way. Fear motivation seems to be more effective in opening new segments rather than selling old ones.

Fear and the Several Levels of Communication Effect

Despite the fact that they are stimulating, the ideas on segmentation presented above leave many questions about the use of fear appeals in marketing. For instance, fear appeals are more effective for some groups in the laboratory, but are they not likely to be avoided in a more realistic exposure situation? How does the high arousal caused by fear affect learning? What about behavior; does fear really get people to act on recommendations?

All of these are questions about levels of effect.

Most of the discussion of fear to this point has dealt with reported acceptance of recommendations. But in order to use fear in specific situations in marketing, it is necessary to have some idea of its effect on several levels—exposure, learning, action—as well as acceptance.

Fear's Effect on Message Exposure

Although direct fear research evidence on exposure is sparse,[16] considerable evidence can be gleaned from the broader research area of selective exposure to all types of messages. A number of studies in the selective exposure literature deal with the differential interest people have in being exposed to positive and negative arguments on a series of topics.[17] In general, people seem to prefer positive arguments, but persons who have had a history of exposure to only positive arguments express greater interest in exposure to the negative.

Thus the segmentation decision discussed in the preceding sections is intimately related to exposure potential. Exposure for single fear messages is more likely for individuals who have already been exposed to positive messages and for those whose anxiety and arousal on the topic, product, or brand is initially low. In most marketing conditions, it would seem that fear appeals would be particularly effective with those segments which would not normally search for information in the product category. In such situations the more intrusive broadcast media might be used to overcome the problem. Or ad implementation will have to be handled in such a way as to quickly inform the reader of the problem.

Fear's Effect on Learning

Given that the novelty of the fear appeal can induce exposure to a communication, the real question remains of whether or not this initial arousal can be converted to continuing attention and resultant learning. Janis, in an excellent review covering research from physiological psychology through fear messages to disaster situations, concludes that there is little effect on cognitive efficiency within the range of fear levels used in most attitude change studies.[18] While there is a loss in efficiency (e.g., distraction, errors, poor retention) for *extreme* fear situations, there does not seem to be any negative effect on attention and learning for fear levels up to this threshold. And some research shows an increase in attention accompanying an increase in fear within this relevant range.[19]

There are, however, distinct problems in directly adopting these findings for marketing. The research has tended to measure quantity rather than quality of learning. It has always been done in settings which strongly discouraged "leaving the field," and thus has implicitly encouraged attention, comprehension, and learning. Respondents have no options like switching TV channels, going to the kitchen to get a drink, or engaging in a short conversation (possible "inhibitors" in a marketing setting). On the other hand, the novelty and distinctiveness of the fear appeal versus the common expectations generated by most advertisements has not been tested either. This characteristic, plus the hypothesis that marketing objectives would not lead to the use of an extremely high level of fear anyway, indicates that the question of attention and learning with fear in marketing should be kept open for examination in each individual problem situation.

Fear's Effect on Action

The real focus of marketing communications is on eliciting some form of desired behavior, and considerable fear research on action has been conducted. Respondents have been induced to get tetanus inoculations, improve dental practices, see their doctor, receive a free toothbrush or dental hygiene booklet, stop smoking, sign petitions, and take chest X-rays.[20] Specific results on action response range from Janis and Feshbach's research, in which there was less adherence to recommended dental practices two weeks after strong fear messages, to a study of emotional role playing by Mann and Janis[21] in which a single one-hour fear session was shown to be effective in decreasing smoking over an 18-month period.

General findings parallel marketing communication knowledge in the action or behavior area. Recommended behavior is more likely to occur if consumers have been adequately exposed to messages, if the environment is supportive of the message recommendation, if the action is not too difficult to undertake, and if there is little time delay between message recommendation and action.

Thus, the problems of eliciting action with fear messages are not greatly different from the problems of eliciting action with messages utilizing other types of appeals. As such, however, fear appeals must be used carefully in order to promote behavior. A study by Leventhal and Watts on smoking and lung cancer illustrates this point.[22]

At first glance it seems that Leventhal and Watts' results represent an example of low attitude-behavior correlation. The paper and pencil acceptance of recommendations correlated positively with respondent fear, while the frequency of the recommended behavior of actually getting a chest X-ray showed a highly significant decrease going from the low to the high fear condition.

There were further results, however, that made the study more interesting. The study was done at the New York State Fair, and many of the respondents in the high fear condition said they wanted to go to their doctors to get an X-ray rather than take one at the Fair. This seemed reasonable to Leventhal and Watts, since respondents in the high fear condition might have thought something could really have been wrong with them. So the researchers sent a questionnaire to participants five months after the original interviews. Few new X-rays were reported, but those in the high fear groups reported significantly more success in stopping smoking than did the lower fear groups. Leventhal and Watts explain these results on the basis that the act by individuals to stop smoking was an effective way to deal with the fear raised in the strong fear messages. Getting X-rays or seeing a doctor, on the other hand, might merely increase the chance of fear. Further analysis of their data produced support for this interpretation.

If Leventhal and Watts were marketing men attempting to sell chest X-rays, they might have considered their strong fear message a failure, even though it was most effective in getting people to stop smoking. In this case, it may have been better to emphasize the effectiveness of the X-ray in detecting and preventing disease rather than to strongly emphasize the threat of cancer. Or it may be that the message could have been more specific as to how to secure the X-rays.

These kinds of questions can be asked every time fear appeals are attempted in marketing. Fear research provides many of the answers. For instance, in the Leventhal and Watts study there are data on segmentation characteristics, eligibility for X-rays, perceived threat, and degree to which recommendations were seen as efficacious. In other fear studies there are findings about the order of fear evocation and recommendations within a message (probably better to put the fear first), the object of the threat (better to threaten someone close to the prospect rather than the prospect himself), source credibility (quite important when fear is used), and the physical size of the message (important when the audience is likely to have low self-esteem). It is up to marketing to use findings like these and to add to them with results in the marketing area.[23]

Summary and Conclusions

The purpose of this paper has *not* been to thoroughly review the behavioral literature on fear or to argue strongly for the use of fear appeals in a wide variety of marketing situations. Rather the purpose has been to systematically sample the research evidence on fear, and show how it can be used to determine when and how fear appeals might be used in marketing.

A large number of studies have been done on the question of fear appeals and, surprisingly, marketing's emphasis has been on only one of these, a study reported by Janis and Feshbach about 16 years ago.[24]

Behavioral research on fear indicates that fear produces some effects which are facilitating and some which are inhibiting to audience acceptance of recommendations. These facilitating and inhibiting effects underlie a curvilinear explanation for the diverse results on fear.

Marketing's technique of segmentation can be used to find groups for which relatively high fear appeals are effective. In general, these seem to be people who do not see the product category in question as highly relevant to them, thus offering the possibility that fear appeals should be especially considered for opening new segments. In addition to this usage or interest characteristic, segments with high fear potential are those characterized by low anxiety, high self-esteem, and the tendency to attempt to cope with problems rather than avoiding them.

While marketing has typically emphasized the potential inhibiting effects of fear motivation, the recent research indicates that fear can have facilitating effects. In situations where consumers have heard all the positive arguments on a category, it is likely that negative fear appeals will generate interest. There is also evidence that fear can facilitate learning and action on recommendations, although the problems of eliciting action from fear communication are just as severe as with communications utilizing other types of appeals. The fear research provides a number of hints for message construction which may lead to consumer action.

The greatest problem with the application of fear in marketing is the same problem that occurs for the use of any kind of appeal or motivation. It can only be applied in specific situations, and no amount of previous research can indicate the effect of fear in a new situation. Behavioral research can answer many questions; on segmentation, on levels of effect, and on message construction. By applying the results of fear reported here and in more thorough reviews, the marketer should be able to determine whether fear can be applied in his situation, and what some of the most likely results of this application will be. But it is also likely that he will have to make assumptions or conduct further research in the following areas:

1. *Level of fear*—The curvilinear model of fear mentioned in this paper has not often been fully tested within a single study. This is likely to happen in a marketing study, especially since marketing is very likely to utilize the very low levels of fear.
2. *Source credibility*—Most of the studies reported here deal with situations in which the source is unspecified or of high credibility (e.g., the medical profession, the Cancer Society). Even then the audiences often questioned strong fear appeals. But in marketing the basic source will be the brand or company, and ways of overcoming the obvious bias of such a source will have to be developed.
3. *Consideration of other types of fear*—Most of the behavioral research on fear deals with physiological fear. In marketing it will be necessary to do some research to determine if findings hold for other kinds of fears such as social fears.
4. *Repetitive effects*—Use of fear in marketing will undoubtedly raise questions about repetitive use in competitive conditions. Behavioral research has been done in these areas, but other, more realistic work can be done in marketing. Some research is under way at Stanford on the repetitive use of fear.

In addition to these questions the issue of ethics should naturally be considered. The basic question here is whether the fear necessary for effective marketing communications may have deleterious consequences for those high anxiety persons who happen to be in the message audience. Considering the nonmonotonic notion and relevant communication research, however, it seems likely that the level of fear that is effective in marketing would not be high enough to be even remotely unethical. It must be remembered that the primary advantage of the fear appeal for marketing lies in its novelty. Because of this, destructively high levels of fear should not be necessary for effective marketing communication.

Fear is only one of several areas in communication research that has been neglected and handled in a rather unsophisticated way by marketing. Hopefully, this paper has illustrated how the findings from such research might be used in conjunction with various marketing techniques. Careful analysis is necessary to utilize behavioral findings. However, it should provide numerous dividends in the form of rewards to marketing and knowledge in the behavioral area itself.

Endnotes

1. Janis and S. Feshbach, "Effects of Fear-Arousing Communications," *Journal of Abnormal and Social Psychology*, Vol. 48 (January, 1953), pp. 78–92.
2. D. F. Cox, "Clues for Advertising Strategists: I," *Harvard Business Review*, Vol. 39 (September-October, 1961), pp. 160–164.
3. E. Crane, *Marketing Communications: A Behavioral Approach to Men, Messages and Media* (New York: John Wiley and Sons, Inc., 1965), pp. 137–138.
4. J. H. Myers and W. H. Reynolds, *Consumer Behavior and Marketing Management* (Boston: Houghton Mifflin Co., 1967), p. 280.
5. J. F. Engel, D. T. Kollat, and R. D. Blackwell, *Consumer Behavior* (New York: Holt, Rinehart and Winston, Inc., 1968), p. 203.
6. R. Kessler, "Kicking the Habit. Cigaret Foes Suggest a Long-Term Decline in Smoking Has Started," *Wall Street Journal* (March 27, 1969), pp. 1 and 19.
7. Same reference as footnote 6.
8. A number of excellent reviews of the fear literature have recently appeared. For instance, see K. L. Higbee, "Fifteen Years of Fear Arousal: Research on Threat Appeals, 1953–1968," *Psychological Bulletin*, Vol. 72 (in press, 1969); I. L. Janis, "When Fear is Healthy," *Psychology Today*, Vol. 1 (April, 1968), p. 46 ff.; or W. F. McGuire, "Attitudes and Opinions," *Annual Review of Psychology*, Vol. 17 (1966), pp. 484–485. Janis and

McGuire are most responsible for the nonmonotonic (moderate fear best) reconciliation of fear findings presented here. See also W. J. McGuire, "Personality and Susceptibility to Social Influence," in *Handbook of Personality Theory and Research,* E. F. Borgatta and W. W. Lambert, eds. (Chicago, Illinois: Rand McNally, 1968).

9. C. A. Insko, A. Arkoff and V. M. Insko, "Effects of High and Low Fear-Arousing Communications upon Opinions Toward Smoking," *Journal of Experimental Social Psychology,* Vol. 1 (August, 1965), pp. 256–266.
10. I. L. Janis and S. Feshbach, "Personality Differences Associated with Responsiveness to Fear-Arousing Communications," *Journal of Personality,* Vol. 23 (December, 1954), pp. 154–166.
11. P. Niles, "The Relationship of Susceptibility and Anxiety to Acceptance of Fear-Arousing Communications," unpublished doctoral dissertation, Yale University, 1964.
12. M. Goldstein, "Relationship Between Coping and Avoiding Behavior and Response to Fear-Arousing Propaganda," *Journal of Abnormal and Social Psychology,* Vol. 58 (March 1959), pp. 247–252.
13. H. Leventhal, "Fear—For Your Health," *Psychology Today,* Vol. 1 (September, 1967), pp. 54–58.
14. L. Berkowitz and D. R. Cottingham, "The Interest Value and Relevance of Fear Arousing Communications," *Journal of Abnormal and Social Psychology,* Vol. 60 (January, 1960), pp. 37–43; H. Leventhal and J. C. Watts, "Sources of Resistance to Fear Arousing Communications on Smoking and Lung Cancer," *Journal of Personality,* Vol. 34 (June, 1966), pp. 155–175.
15. D. Haefner, "Use of Fear Arousal in Dental Health Education," unpublished paper cited in McGuire, same reference as footnote 8 (1966); R. P. Singer, "The Effects of Fear-Arousing Communications on Attitude Change and Behavior," unpublished doctoral dissertation, University of Connecticut, 1965.
16. See, for example: C. F. Cannell and J. C. MacDonald, "The Impact of Health News on Attitudes and Behavior," *Journalism Quarterly,* Vol. 33 (Summer, 1956), pp. 315–323; J. C. Nunnally and H. M. Broben, "Variables Governing the Willingness to Receive Communications on Mental Health," *Journal of Personality,* Vol. 27 (March, 1959), pp. 38–46; P. R. Robbins, "Self-Reports of Reactions to Fear-Arousing Information," *Psychological Reports,* Vol. 11 (December, 1962), pp. 761–764.
17. J. L. Freedman and D. O. Sears, "Selective Exposure," *Advances in Experimental Social Psychology,* Vol. 2 (1966), pp. 58–97.
18. I. L. Janis, "Effects of Fear Arousal on Attitude Change: Recent Developments in Theory and Experimental Research," *Advances in Experimental Social Psychology,* Vol. 3 (1967), pp. 167–225.
19. See, for example, Janis and Feshbach, same reference as footnote 1; Berkowitz and Cottingham, same reference as footnote 14.
20. For a review of most of these studies see same reference as footnote 18.
21. L. Mann and I. L. Janis, "A Follow-Up Study on the Long-Term Effects of Emotional Role Playing," *Journal of Personality and Social Psychology,* Vol. 8 (April, 1968), pp. 339–342.
22. Same reference as footnote 14.
23. H. Leventhal and R. P. Singer, "Affect Arousal and Positioning of Recommendations in Persuasive Communications," *Journal of Personality and Social Psychology,* Vol. 4 (February, 1966), pp. 137–146; F. A. Powell, "The Effects of Anxiety-Arousing Messages When Related to Personal, Familial and Impersonal Referents," *Speech Monographs,* Vol. 32 (June, 1965), pp. 102–106; M. A. Hewgill and G. R. Miller, "Source Credibility and Response to Fear-Arousing Communication," *Speech Monographs,* Vol. 32 (June 1965), pp. 95–101; same reference as footnote 13.
24. Same reference as footnote 1.

An Experimental Investigation of Comparative Advertising: Impact of Message Appeal, Information Load, and Utility of Product Class

Stephen Goodwin and Michael Etgar

A three (message appeal: supportive, brand X, and comparative) by two (product class utility: social and functional) by three (information load: low, medium, and high) factorial experimental design (with covariates) was used to explore communications effectiveness of the three modes of advertising appeals. ANOVA results show that the comparative mode appears to be superior only for the affective responses to the ad itself. The brand X mode of message appeal generally is superior to other modes for cognitive, affective, and conative responses toward the promoted brand. However, the differences are only partially significant at $p < .05$*. In no case is the supportive mode superior. Some weak evidence of information overload is also uncovered. Several personality variables did not have significant effects on the relative effectiveness of the different appeals. Lack of substantial interaction effects among the three factors indicates that advertisers can determine message appeal, amount of information provided, and type of products to be promoted independently of each other.*

Because it involves direct comparisons between a promoted brand and one or more of its competitors on specific dimensions/attributes, comparative advertising has been lauded by the Federal Trade Commission and some advertising practitioners as beneficial to consumers. The FTC has strongly encouraged advertisers to name competing brands in commercials as a method of providing consumers with more factual information (Ulanoff 1975).

Advertisers, however, are primarily interested in the effectiveness of comparative advertising in terms of conveying information to an audience, making consumers aware of the promoted product, persuading consumers to like it, and eventually convincing the target market(s) to make a repeat purchase. Currently, there is substantial disagreement among practitioners about the communication effectiveness of comparative advertising vis-à-vis other forms of message appeals. Some practitioners forward evidence for its success and others claim the opposite (Kershaw and Tennenbaum 1976; Rockey 1976).

Recently, the effectiveness of comparative advertising has been the focus of several empirical studies (Golden 1976; Levine 1976; McDougall 1976, Prasad 1976; Pride, Lamb, and Pletcher 1977; Wilson 1976). Although these studies have explored several important aspects of comparative advertising, a substantial number of problems of importance to advertising managers have not been researched (Etgar and Goodwin 1977a). A review of these studies reported elsewhere (Etgar and Goodwin 1977b) suggests the need to examine the issue of communicative effectiveness of comparative advertising while considering

Reprinted by permission of the American Marketing Association, from the *Journal of Marketing Research*, 17:2 May 1980, 187–202.

a somewhat broader framework of analysis. The authors present the results of a study of comparative advertising effectiveness exploring several additional dimensions not previously discussed or addressed in research in this area.

Issues in Comparative Advertising

Amount of Attribute Information

The nature of comparative advertising implies that a substantial part of the ad is devoted to actual comparative evaluation of the promoted and the compared brands on one or more attributes. An important question for an advertising manager therefore is whether there are differential effects due to presentation of different amounts of attribute information and, if so, what they are.

Research on consumer information processing (Bettman 1975) suggests that "information overload" may often take place (Jacoby, Speller, and Kohn 1974), i.e., too much information may reduce subjects' attention and comprehension and be disfunctional. In that case, consumer evaluation of ads and brands advertised follows some kind of an inverted U-shaped function of the number of attributes presented in the ad. A comparative ad that presents comparisons on many dimensions may reduce consumer interest in and comprehension of the ad, an ad that considers only one or a few attributes may not be effective enough, and one that uses some intermediate level of number of attributes may be most effective.

Product Typology

The diversity of the products used in previous studies of comparative advertising effectiveness raises the issue of generalization of results from a particular product/brand to a somewhat broader group. Specifically, it is important to know whether comparative advertising effectiveness differs across product groups and is sensitive to differences in product attributes. Unfortunately, the substantial diversity in design and methodology among studies precludes such comparisons.

One appealing approach is to focus attention on the "measurability" problem. A large number of products are traditionally bought primarily for their measurable, physical attributes. Consequently, advertisers promote specific brands by emphasizing their measurable attributes and the capacity of these brands to perform specific measurable tasks and to provide measurable benefits. A large number of products, however, are bought not because of their task-related capacities but because of the psychological or social benefits they promise. Such benefits are elusive and difficult to compare; advertisers often may be restricted by governmental regulation and threat of litigation.

The relative effectiveness of a comparative advertising message vis-à-vis a regular supportive mode promoting one brand only may therefore depend on whether the advertised product provides primarily functional, utilitarian, and easy-to-compare benefits or more elusive social/psychological ones.

Nature of Comparisons

Though explicit naming of compared brands is a relatively new phenomenon in advertising, marketers have often used the so-called "brand X approach" whereby the promoted brand is compared with unnamed brand(s) such as the "leading brand(s) in the market." In evaluating the effectiveness of comparative advertising, researchers therefore should consider two alternative message modes, a supportive ad (wherein only the promoted brand is described) and a brand X ad, and should compare the performance of the comparative mode with that of the other two.

It should be remembered, however, that the brand X communication may in fact be perceived by the consumer as a comparative ad, particularly if the consumer is very familiar with the product class either through usage experience or general knowledge.

Control for Exogenous Variables

The specific characteristics of comparative advertisements suggest that such ads differ from traditional supportive ads in their emphasis on the information provided. Consequently, the effectiveness of comparative advertising may be substantially affected by the capacity and tendencies of the target audience to process this information. A review of the audience characteristics usually used for market segmentation (Engel, Fiorillo, and Cayley 1972; Frank, Massy, and Wind 1972) suggests several potential factors that may be of importance here.

Knowledge of the Product Class/Brands. To derive evaluation conclusions from a message presented by a comparative communication, the consumer will draw upon knowledge already held about the promoted and compared brands. It is reasonable to assume that lack of such knowledge will have some impact on the evaluation process; at the extreme, evaluation of the comparison claims may be meaningless to a particular viewer who is unknowledgeable about the product class and/or brands promoted and compared.

Therefore, it could be important for the advertising researcher to establish in pretests the nature of evaluation functions between consumers who hold different degrees of prior knowledge. A useful surrogate for product knowledge, perhaps, is usage rate which details the extent of the consumer's buying or use of various brands from the pertinent product class(es).

Brand Loyalty. Consumers who exhibit substantial brand loyalty to the compared brand(s) in comparative advertisements may be more likely to resent the comparative claim(s) and to disbelieve them, perhaps in response to cognitive dissonance.

Personality Traits. Widespread and indiscriminate use of general personality inventories for explaining consumer behavior is criticized by most marketing researchers today (Kassarjian 1971). However, traits that pertain to the consumer's information processing ability and motivation are of some interest.

For example, the Mehrabian-Russel Arousal-Seeking Tendency scale (Mehrabian and Russel 1974) measures the general tendency or proneness for curiosity-seeking/variety-seeking behavior. Some writers (Wilkie and Farris 1975) have pointed out that comparative ads are likely to be perceived as more novel than "ordinary" supportive message appeals; if so, one could expect to find that consumers high in arousal-seeking tendency would evaluate comparative ads more positively than consumers less prone to seek curiosity.

Another personality factor of possible importance here is the consumer's characteristic mode of resolving cognitive uncertainty. Kelman and Cohler's (1967) test for cognitive style identifies two major types: *clarifiers* (people who react "positively" to uncertainty by seeking clarification, additional information, etc.) and *simplifiers* (people who simplify their environments by keeping out obtrusive cognitions and tend to avoid uncertainty, Cox 1967).

Golden (1976), Levine (1976), Prasad (1976), and Wilson (1976) considered the problems of brand loyalty and usage in their studies. None, however, considered both of these factors jointly, nor attempted to control the possible effects of personality variables.

Manipulation Checks

In experimental designs, subjects are expected to react to different conditions (stimuli) in which they are positioned. An important factor affecting internal validity of experiments is the assurance of the validity of the measures used to represent the various dimensions and the ability of the subjects to differentiate among the different levels presented to them.

The effectiveness of a comparison between two or more brands on a specific attribute dimension in terms of consumer evaluative response may depend on the targeted audience. If the discussed characteristics provide important benefits to the consumer, the comparison may be interesting as well as informative, and likely to make a positive net impact. Consumers who are only marginally interested in the brand attribute(s) discussed may not be influenced at all. Consequently, pretesting the salience of brand attributes should be a basic initial step in any comparative communication design. The authors therefore decided to include in their study several manipulation checks designed to assess the validity of the measures used and pretests on the attribute importance space explored.

The study differs from previous work in the area along the following dimensions.

1. It is an attempt to explore simultaneously the relative effectiveness of comparative advertising vis-à-vis supportive and brand X ads.
2. It compares the effectiveness of using supportive, brand X, and comparative advertising for products which provide functional and tangible vis-à-vis social/psychological nontangible benefits.
3. It incorporates different levels of attribute information, all dimensions having been discovered through pretests to be salient to the subjects used in the study.
4. Control is provided for the potential effects of four personality variables and of usage and brand loyalty variables.
5. It measures communicative effectiveness of comparative ads in terms of both ad- and brand-related measures.

6. It includes manipulation checks to ensure the validity of the independent variables used in the experiment.

Research Method

Subjects

Data for the study were obtained in two phases from 180 student subjects in business administration classes in a northeastern state university in the U.S. in spring 1977. The use of student subjects as a convenience sample requires the researchers to be especially careful in their research design (Etgar and Goodwin 1977b). A problem occurs if students are used in studies of advertised products primarily used and/or purchased by consumers in advanced life-cycle stages. Yet the student sample may be entirely acceptable and consistent with improved external validity if the product classes advertised are salient to them.

Design

A 2 X 3 X 3 factorial between-subjects design, with 10 subjects in each cell, was operationalized. It consisted of two types of products (functionally and socially oriented), three levels of number of attributes (two, five, and seven), and three levels of message appeals (supportive, brand X, and comparative). The experimental manipulations are depicted in Figure 1.

Phase One. In the first phase of the study, subjects were administered a preliminary questionnaire that was primarily intended to collect data for the manipulation checks as well as about several personality and usage variables.

Phase Two. One month after the first questionnaire was administered, the subjects took part in the experimental treatments. Each subject was given one ad and a booklet designed to measure reactions to the ad along two vectors of product-oriented and ad-

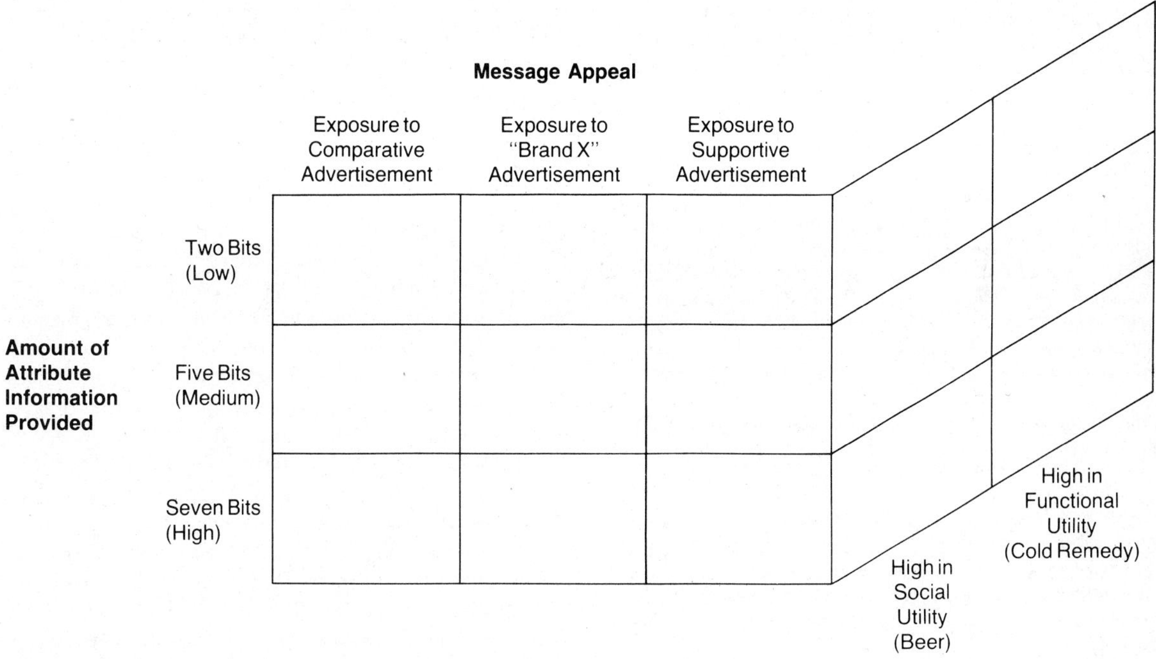

FIGURE 1
Research Design

Our new quality brew was awarded first place in a recent *Philadelphia Inquirer* beer-tasting test. In a "blind review" of the 100 beer-drinking panel members surveyed (50 females and 50 males), the majority favored Crick Premium Beer's full-bodied, smooth taste over a group of leading-seller American and Canadian beers.* And Crick Premium provides great drinking pleasure, but *without the premium price*.

Great Taste! Great Price!
Graduate to Crick Premium Beer
The Next Step in Beer Drinking Pleasure
Go With A Winner!

*Crick Premium beer is brewed from pure spring water, choice hops, and aged a minimum of three full weeks.

For more details on the consumer test, write to:
Crick Premium Beer
Philadelphia Inquirer Beer Test
Box 2222
Philadelphia, Pennsylvania 19185

Graduate to Crick Premium Beer . . .

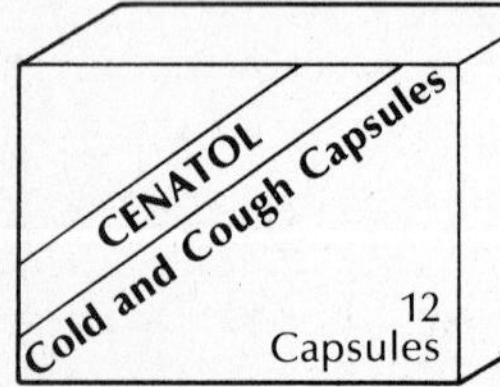

- Relieves stuffy nose
- Controls cough
- Reduces chest congestion
- Alleviates arthritic pain

CENATOL is a new, powerful yet completely safe non-prescription drug. In a recent impartial test run by the *Philadelphia Inquirer*, CENATOL was found to be more effective than Tylenol, Bayer Aspirin and Excedrin, providing quicker relief (12 minutes on average), better value per dosage, and longer relief (over eight hours) while exhibiting no negative side effects. CENATOL also includes more components that reduce inflammation, alleviate nose congestion and ease inhalation. Finally, out of 50 physicians acquainted with CENATOL on a trial basis for over six months, the majority were found to recommend CENATOL to their patients who complained of colds, headaches and arthritic symptoms.*

For Greater Relief Turn To CENATOL!
Fast Relief! Great Value!

*CENATOL is available in a variety of flavors including Orange, Strawberry, Lemon, Cherry, and Mint as well as the regular non-fruit flavor. 1000 adult panel members participated in the consumer test over a four week period in Winter 1977. For details about the consumer test and physicians' testimonials, write to:

CENATOL
Box 2222
Philadelphia, PA 19185

FIGURE 2
Examples of Crick and Cenatol Ads

oriented variables. The respondents were asked to review the ad for several minutes and then respond to the questions in the accompanying booklet. The ad presented a promotional message for a new (imaginary) brand. The students were told that the stimulus was a prototype for an ad for the particular brand and that they were participating in a study conducted on behalf of an advertising agency which was designed to indicate people's responses to the particular prototype. Figure 2 portrays two of the mock print ads used in the study, one for the new brand of beer (Crick) and one for the new brand of cold/headache remedy (Cenatol).

Several steps were taken to minimize bias. First, the substantial time lag between administration of the pretest and experimental material was expected to counteract error due to history (Campbell and Stanley 1963). Second, the experimental material was administered by a different person and was presented as part of a separate study on the evaluation of print advertising prototypes. Subjects were not informed of the fact that they were actually participating in a study about alternative advertising message modes. Finally, the experimental treatments were distributed randomly and subjects were seated far enough apart to preclude their seeing the stimulus material presented to their peers.

Manipulation Checks and Pretests

Product Type. To ensure that product classes selected were differentiated by the subjects as functionally or socially/psychologically utilitarian, the preliminary questionnaire presented five products with which students can be expected to be familiar and requested they be rated on a seven-point Likert-type scale in terms of their usage anchored at "usage is primarily functional" (rated 7) and "usage is primarily social" (rated 1). The average ratings for all five products are presented in Table 1.

A means test revealed that beer and cold/headache remedies had respectively the highest and the lowest mean ratings and that the differences between the two were significant at $p < .05$. The results suggest that subjects view beer as a product primarily used to satisfy social needs whereas cold/headache remedies are used primarily because of their functional, utilitarian characteristics. Consequently, these two products were selected for the analysis.

TABLE 1
Average Utility Perceptions of Five Product Classes[a]

	X	$\hat{\sigma}$
Beer	4.3	2.00
Tennis Balls	5.5	2.35
Deodorant	5.7	1.80
Felt-tip Pens	6.1	1.60
Cold/Headache Remedies	6.6	1.30

a. Utility scales were Likert-type, anchored by 1 (the product is primarily purchased because of its effect on how others view me—social utility) and 7 (the product is primarily purchased because of its performance—functional utility).

Identity of Compared Brands. In the preliminary survey, subjects were also requested to list for each of the five product classes the names of the brands that he/she bought. A frequency listing ranked all brands according to their popularity in the sample (i.e., number of people who bought them). The top three beer and cold/headache remedies were used for the experimental design and their names were used as the compared brands. The specific brands thus selected were Miller, Labatts, and Genesee (for beer) and Bayer, Tylenol, and Bufferin (for cold/headache remedies).

Selection of Attributes. The initial questionnaire was also used to identify the salient product dimensions which subjects consider important when selecting brands from the analyzed product classes. This information was solicited by requesting subjects to list, for each of the five product classes in any order, the most important product characteristics that they use to compare brands. The open-ended reports were content analyzed to arrive at one list for each product class, and frequency counts for each attribute/dimension were computed. The top two, five, and seven attributes for each product class were incorporated in the actual experimental print ads. Table 2 identifies the attributes used for both product classes.

TABLE 2
The Seven Most Important Attributes for the Studied Product Classes: Beer and Cold/Headache Remedies[a]

Beer	*Cold/Headache Remedies*
Smooth taste	Quickness of relief
Alcohol content	Lack of negative side effects
Aroma	Reduces inflammation and congestion
Bitterness	Recommended by doctors
Calorie count	Price
Price	Dosage frequency
Availability in a variety of containers	Availability of a variety of flavors

a. Attributes are not listed in any order of importance.

Number of Attributes Selected. A manipulation check tested whether subjects perceived the three levels of product attributes selected both as distinct and as monotonically increasing amounts of information. Two different groups of 24 respondents each were drawn from the same population as the experimental subjects and were administered a supportive ad either for the new beer brand (one group) or for the new brand of cold remedy (the other group). Both groups were partitioned into three subsets; each subset received an ad which discussed either two, five, or seven attributes. Subjects were requested to read over the ad, and to rate it in terms of amount of information provided on an 11-point Likert-type scale with endpoints "very little information" (anchored by 11) and "very much information" (anchored by 1). The ratings were averaged for each group, for each product class, and mean differences were tested by the Scheffé test (1959). Though the mean differences are only marginally significant, the fact that all are in the expected direction for both product classes suggests that the attribute information chosen was perceived by subjects in a manner consistent with the experimenters' expectations.

TABLE 3
Manipulation Check Data on Subjects' Perceptions of Amount of Information Provided[a]

Ad for New Beer Brand			*Ad for New Cold/Headache Remedy Brand*		
Number of Attributes			*Number of Attributes*		
2	5	7	2	5	7
5.2	6.2	7.65	5.4	6.6	7.55

a. Averaged response to an 11-point Likert-type scale with endpoints 1 (ad provides very little information) and 11 (ad provides a lot of information).

Dependent Variables

Table 4 is a list of the dependent variables measured. The format is based on the framework of the hierarchy of effects model (Lavidge and Steiner, 1961) and includes variables measuring subjects' awareness, knowledge, liking, and intention. Six of the variables are product/brand-related and nine are ad-related.

TABLE 4
The Dependent Variables[a]

		Response Domain (Linked to the Hierarchy-of-Effects Model)
Product-Related Criterion Measures		
(D.1)	Extent of knowledge enhancement about product class	Cognitive
(D.2)	Promoted brand is a better buy than other leading brands	Cognitive
(D.3)	Perceived risk for buying promoted brand	Cognitive
(D.4)	Promoted brand has higher quality than other leading brands	Affective
(D.5)	Overall affect toward promoted brand	Affective
(D.6)	Intent to buy promoted brand	Conative
Ad-Related Criterion Measures		
(D.7)	Understandability of the ad	Cognitive
(D.8)	Impersonality of the ad	Cognitive
(D.9)	Extent to which the ad does not provide useful information	Cognitive
(D.10)	Irrelevance of the ad to consumer needs	Cognitive
(D.11)	Unbelievability of the ad	Cognitive
(D.12)	Perceived offensiveness of the ad	Affective
(D.13)	Attractiveness of the ad	Affective
(D.14)	Interestingness of the ad	Affective
(D.15)	Likeability of the ad	Affective

a. All measures were tapped by using 11-point Likert-type scales, except for the perceived risk measure which was modeled as in Peter and Tarpey [19].

Covariates

When a researcher does not collect predispositional measures that presumably relate to informational processing of advertising stimuli, error variance may be unnecessarily large, resulting in nonsignificant differences. Two approaches might profitably be taken to reduce error variation (or to adjust for extraneous sources of error). First, the researcher might design experiments that include important predispositional variables (e.g., treatment-by-levels designs, also referred to as randomized block designs; see Lindquist 1956 or Winer 1971) as one (or more) of the factors. Alternatively, the researcher might consider using such predispositional variables as covariates, which allow statistical adjustment for any contaminating influences. The latter approach was used in the authors' study. Table 5 identified the covariates measured.

Analysis and Results

Before analysis of the experimental data, a pretest was carried out. The purpose of this pretest was

TABLE 5
The Covariates

		Measured By
C.1	Dogmatism	Rokeach Dogmatism Scale, Form E [23]
C.2	Tolerance for uncertainty	Cox Scale [3]
C.3	Cognitive clarity	Kelman and Cohler Scale [11]
C.4	Arousal-seeking tendency	Mehrabian and Russel Scale [18]
C.5	Total consumption of product class per year	Annual purchase of beer/cold remedies [in standardized units]
C.6	Brand loyalty	Percent of total consumption devoted to the three compared-to-brands for beer/cold remedies

TABLE 6
Intercorrelations Between Product-Related Measures and Ad-Related Measures

	D.1	*D.2*	*D.3*	*D.4*	*D.5*	*D.6*
Product-Related Dependent Variables[a]						
D.1		.207	.023	.226	.303	.095
D.2			−.164	.540	.307	.156
D.3				−.126	−.243	−.260
D.4					.350	.225
D.5						.529

	D.7	*D.8*	*D.9*	*D.10*	*D.11*	*D.12*	*D.13*	*D.14*	*D.15*
Ad-Related Dependent Variables[b]									
D.7		−.089	−.193	−.246	−.089	−.242	.236	.186	.396
D.8			.186	.171	.321	.199	−.206	−.303	−.388
D.9				.493	.374	.213	−.079	−.156	−.452
D.10					.436	.303	−.051	−.141	−.381
D.11						.188	−.173	−.167	−.371
D.12							−.041	−.016	−.272
D.13								.545	.406
D.14									.524

a, b. See Table 4 for the definitions of each dependent variable.

to determine whether a MANOVA or an ANOVA analytical framework should be used. The use of MANOVA is recommended particularly when individual response measures are intercorrelated and therefore should be analyzed jointly (Wind and Denny 1974). Consequently, the use of multiple analysis of variance should be carefully considered for evaluating advertising effectivenesss studies that involve hierarchy of effects components, as those are often considered to be highly related (Lavidge and Steiner 1961). For that purpose, an intercorrelation matrix was developed for each set of criterion measures (i.e., product/brand- and ad-related). The two correlation matrices (Table 6) show that although the directionality of the correlations in all cases conforms to that expected, the revealed correlations are generally of very low magnitude and many are insignificant, implying that the various response dimensions generally tend to be independent of each other. Accordingly, a univariate analysis of variance framework is appropriate and was selected for the study.

After the establishment of the analytical mode to be used in the study, a second pretest was carried out to determine the covariates to be included in the analysis. For that purpose, correlations between each criterion measure and each proposed covariate were analyzed. Whenever a significant correlation was discovered, the covariate(s) was included in the analysis of variance. The inclusion of the covariate(s) did not appreciably influence the results in any instance; though the error mean squares were reduced, none of the relationships uncovered without the use of covariates were changed (in magnitude or direction) with covariate inclusion. Accordingly, the following discussion focuses on the analysis of variance without covariate inclusion. The univariate marginal response means and respective standard deviations are reported in Table 7.

Product-Related Measures

The results of the univariate ANOVAs are presented in Table 8 which lists for each of the six response measures the calculated *F*-ratios for all interaction and main effects. The results are further summarized in Table 9.

Three major conclusions can be drawn from the two tables. First, for all six product/brand-related criterion measures, the brand X treatment is at least marginally superior. However, there appears to be no difference between the comparative and supportive modes. Second, there is some (though weak) evidence of information overload. In the one signifi-

TABLE 7
Marginal Means and Standard Deviations[a]

	Independent Variables							
							Product Class	
Dependent Variables	*Message Appeal*			*Attribute Information*			*High Social Utility (Beer)*	*High Functional Utility (Cold Remedy)*
	Supportive	*Brand X*	*Comparative*	*Low (2 bits)*	*Medium (5 bits)*	*High (7 bits)*		
I. Product-Related[b]								
D.1	2.78	2.85	2.37	2.45	2.78	2.67	2.87	2.40
	(1.97)	(1.78)	(1.48)	(1.58)	(1.63)	(2.01)	(1.99)	(1.50)
D.2	4.95	5.13	4.85	4.75	5.28	4.90	5.49	4.47
	(2.02)	(2.53)	(2.32)	(2.23)	(2.17)	(2.52)	(2.53)	(2.06)
D.3	139.02	113.12	114.22	130.67	127.18	108.50	105.21	139.02
	(80.19)	(98.84)	(99.59)	(126.91)	(80.27)	(71.44)	(91.17)	(94.57)
D.4	4.22	4.48	3.95	3.66	4.62	4.27	4.12	4.13
	(2.26)	(2.45)	(1.95)	(2.24)	(2.15)	(2.27)	(2.26)	(2.17)
D.5	3.52	4.50	3.83	3.68	3.93	4.23	3.98	3.92
	(2.31)	(2.34)	(2.17)	(2.05)	(2.42)	(2.45)	(2.19)	(2.34)
D.6	2.68	3.15	2.78	3.05	2.92	2.65	3.13	2.61
	(2.49)	(2.53)	(1.97)	(2.26)	(2.43)	(2.31)	(2.62)	(2.03)
II. Ad-Related[b]								
D.7	8.43	8.67	8.98	9.98	8.18	8.88	8.37	8.82
	(2.09)	(3.00)	(1.94)	(2.13)	(2.70)	(2.20)	(2.64)	(2.04)
D.8	7.78	6.58	7.22	7.28	7.27	7.03	6.93	7.46
	(1.78)	(2.78)	(2.14)	(2.04)	(2.21)	(2.21)	(2.46)	(2.02)
D.9	5.52	5.40	6.00	5.72	5.38	4.98	5.70	5.58
	(2.46)	(3.03)	(3.24)	(2.53)	(2.96)	(3.17)	(3.10)	(2.72)
D.10	5.23	4.86	4.88	4.72	5.08	5.18	5.73	4.26
	(2.38)	(2.70)	(2.47)	(2.29)	(2.60)	(2.66)	(2.89)	(2.25)
D.11	6.02	5.97	6.18	5.92	6.17	6.08	5.96	6.16
	(2.45)	(2.65)	(2.73)	(2.27)	(2.83)	(2.74)	(2.89)	(2.33)
D.12	3.60	3.53	4.17	3.83	3.70	3.63	3.73	3.80
	(2.11)	(2.53)	(2.35)	(2.30)	(2.27)	(2.33)	(2.53)	(2.07)
D.13	4.52	4.25	4.98	4.65	4.28	4.82	4.33	4.36
	(2.01)	(2.71)	(2.35)	(2.51)	(2.42)	(2.13)	(2.41)	(2.30)
D.14	4.42	4.50	5.07	4.88	4.45	4.65	4.79	4.53
	(2.05)	(2.72)	(2.14)	(2.11)	(2.45)	(2.38)	(2.36)	(2.27)
D.15	5.73	5.93	6.10	6.35	5.77	5.65	5.80	6.04
	(1.74)	(2.88)	(1.94)	(1.96)	(2.29)	(2.23)	(2.16)	(2.16)

a. Numbers in parentheses reflect standard deviations.
b. Refer to Table 4 for definitions of the criterion measures.

TABLE 8
Summary of Univariate Analysis of Variance: Product-Related Criterions

	F Statistics for Experimental Factors						
Dependent Variables[a]	*Message Appeal (MA)*	*Attribute Information (AI)*	*Product Class (PC)*	*MA X AI*	*MA X PC*	*AI X PC*	*MA X AI X PC*
D.1	.94	.50	2.83[c]	1.82	3.27[b]	1.36	.33
D.2	.15	.90	6.93[b]	1.49	1.76	.13	.78
D.3	1.21	.80	4.78[b]	.45	1.93	.32	.83
D.4	.62	3.37[b]	1.26	1.56	1.71	.16	.81
D.5	2.80[c]	.85	.02	1.29	2.13	1.02	.44
D.6	.75	.33	2.69[c]	.89	1.52	.61	.31

a. Refer to Table 4 for criterion variable definitions.
b. $p < .05$
c. $p < .10$

cant main effect of the attribute information variable, the intermediate number of attributes is superior to other treatments with low or high levels of attributes.

Third, respondents' perceptions are generally more favorable for product classes providing social/psychological benefits than for those providing functional/performance benefits. Finally, product class and number of attributes do not affect the impact of the different types of appeals (almost no interaction effects).

Ad-Related Measures

Table 10 shows ANOVA results for the ad-related criterion measures and the *F*-ratios and significance levels for all interactions and main effects. Table 9 summarizes the major results.

The data in these two tables indicate three cases in which message appeal effect was significant either directly or in interactions. Mean comparison shows the brand X appeal to be superior to the other two modes of appeal, generating better ad perceptions (though the differences are not all significant).

The relative size and directions of the marginal means for each level of the three experimental factors for each of the ad-related criterion measures were also examined. However, as only a few of the main effects are statistically significant, inferences to be drawn are speculative.

Examination of the cognitive response variables (D.7–D.11) for the message appeal factor reveals that the *brand X* mode is superior to the others in all but one instance. That is, mean values for that group of treatments show better cognitive response. The affective response variables (D.12–D.15), however, indicate that here the *comparative mode* is superior to the other modes of appeal in all but one instance D.12).

These findings suggest that if cognitive response dimensions are of primary concern to the advertiser, those dimensions are likely to be improved by use of a *brand X* message appeal. If affective response dimensions are of utmost concern to the advertiser, such responses generally should be improved by the use of a comparative message appeal. These suggestions refer only to ad-related responses, and are speculative because most of the mean differences are not statistically significant.

For the other two experimental factors (amount of attribute information and product class), no consistent patterns are in evidence. It is interesting to note, however, that for the attribute information factor, in *no case* does the intermediate level of information provide the most positive impact. This outcome is in marked contrast to the findings about the product-related criterion measures.

Implications

Because of the research design, the results have general implications extending beyond the specific study. In particular, use of control variables (product type

TABLE 9
Overall Summary of Results

Predictor Variables	*Criterion Variables*	*Implications*
I. *Product related measures*		
a. *Interactions*		
1. Second order: none		
2. First order: Message Appeal X Product Class	Extent of knowledge enhanced	Message Appeal differs only for the functional/utilitarian product class: BX > C[a], BX > S.
none of the other interactions is significant.		
b. *Message Appeal*		
1. only one effect is significant[c]	Affect towards the brand	BX > S[a], BX > C[b]
2. Brand X is superior though not significantly over comparative and supportive appeals in terms of all other product/brand communications.		
3. There are no consistent differences between supportive and comparative ads.		
II. *Ad-Related Measures*		
a. *Interactions*		
1. Second order: none		
2. Message Appeal X Product Class	Personality of the ad	Beer product class BX > S[b], C > S[b]. Cold/headache remedies: BX > C[a], BX > S[a]
3. Message Appeal X Amount of Attribute Information	Relevance of the ad to consumer needs	At high attribute level: BX > C, S[b] At other levels: no significant differences
4. Product Class X Amount Attribute Information	Offensiveness	Beer: ad is found more offensive when the number of attributes is increased, opposite for cold/headache remedies.
b. *Product Class*		
1. One significant main effect[c]	Relevance to consumer needs	cold/headache remedy more effective than the beer ad.
c. *Attribute Information*		
1. only one significant main effect[c]	Quality assessment	Medium level (5 attributes) has a greater impact (positive) than low or high levels of attributes. (Evidence of information overload)

TABLE 9 (continued)
Overall Summary of Results

Predictor Variables	*Criterion Variables*	*Implications*
d. *Product Class*		
1. Significant effect[c]	Extent of knowledge enhancement	Respondent's perceptions significantly more favorable for social/psychological products class than for those providing funtional/performance benefits
2. Significant effect[c]	Better buy	
3. Significant effect[c]	Lower risk	
e. *Message Appeal*		
1. One significant main effect[c]	Personality of the ad	BX > S[a], BX > C[b]

BX—brand X appeal; C—comparative appeal; S—supportive appeal.

a. the difference between means is significant at $p < .05$.
b. the difference between means is not significant at $p < .05$.
c. at $p < .05$.

and amount of information), salience and discriminating checks, and of product/brand- and ad-related criterion measures increases the validity and applicability to a broad range of product types and advertising appeals.

Overall, the study shows comparative advertising to be less effective than expected. Comparative advertising was only marginally advantageous in improving consumers' feelings toward the ad presented, and it did not improve respondents' attitudes toward the promoted brand itself. As advertisers are eventually more interested in the latter than in the former, comparative advertising did not perform well. The study also indicates some evidence that advertisements using the brand X mode of message appeal may be more effective in generating positive feelings toward the promoted brand and in enhancing ad-related cognitions than other advertising modes. Supportive message appeals did not emerge as superior in any case. The reasons for the possible rela-

TABLE 10
Summary of Univariate Analysis of Variance: Ad-Related Criterions

	F Statistics for Experimental Factors						
Dependent Variables[a]	*Message Appeal (MA)*	*Attribute Information (AI)*	*Product Class (PC)*	*MA × AI*	*MA × PC*	*AI × PC*	*MA × AI × PC*
D.7	1.89	1.41	1.09	.35	.13	.34	.62
D.8	4.15[b]	.36	1.33	1.85	2.70[c]	.27	.45
D.9	.70	.35	.07	.64	.09	.64	.75
D.10	.34	.49	13.83[b]	2.05[c]	.01	.05	1.38
D.11	.10	.14	.23	1.81	.06	.55	.82
D.12	.68	.49	.01	.68	.24	2.28[c]	.21
D.13	1.44	.73	1.51	1.88	1.92	.35	.31
D.14	1.37	.51	.52	.34	.06	.02	.66
D.15	.42	1.70	.54	1.82	.03	1.18	.73

a. Refer to Table 4 for criterion variable definitions.
b. $p < .05$
c. $p < .10$

tive superiority of the brand X mode are not clear. Tentatively, one may suggest that because the comparative ads used in the study attempted to attack directly the leading brands in the pertinent markets and extolled the relative virtues of unknown brands, these ads were disbelieved as a result of the inherent strength of belief in the currently leading brands. When subjects are requested to believe that a new and unknown brand is better than the leading brands they know, they may resist or disbelieve that message. In contrast, the brand X message appeal was more effective in creating positive attitudes toward the new brands, because it provided anchor points for comparison with the new brands without straining consumer beliefs about the leading brands.

It was surprising to find that, altogether, individual usage and psychological differences do not substantially affect differences among subjects' reactions to different modes of advertising. The use of covariates that provided control for these factors did not affect in any way the results of the ANOVA.

The impact of differences in the type of product promoted and the amount of information included in the ad on the relative effectiveness of the different message appeals is also relatively low. Of the 12 possible interaction effects for product-related criteria, only one turned out to be significant at $p < .10$; for the 18 possible interactions for the ad-related criteria, only two were found to be significant at $p < .10$. These results suggest that both factors may influence only marginally the relative effectiveness of the various message appeal types. Advertising managers may therefore in effect make decisions about message appeal modes to be selected, amount of information to be provided in the ad, and type of products to be promoted independently of each other.

A major shortcoming of this study is the use of one-time exposure to ads. Because comparative ads are relatively new and complex, consumers may need several exposures before they become accustomed to this type of message appeal and start utilizing the pertinent information. Therefore, studies involving repeated exposures and over-time measures are recommended as a next stage of research in this area (Sawyer 1973). The inferences drawn from this study are also limited to convenience goods which differ with respect to social and functional utility. Future research should consider shopping/specialty goods as well.

References

Bettman, J. A. (1975), "Issues in Designing Consumer Information Environments," *Journal of Consumer Research*, 2 (December), 169-77.

Campbell, D. T. and J. C. Stanley (1963), *Experimental and Quasi-Experimental Designs for Research.* Chicago: Rand McNally.

Cox, D., ed. (1967), *Risk-Handling and Information-Handling in Consumer Behavior.* Cambridge: Harvard University Press.

Engel, J. F., H. F. Fiorillo, and M. A. Cayley (1972), *Market Segmentation: Concepts and Applications.* New York: Holt, Rinehart and Winston.

Etgar, M. and S. A. Goodwin (1977a), "Comparative Advertising: Issues and Problems," in *Advances in Consumer Research*, 5, K. Hunt, ed., Association for Consumer Research.

—— and —— (1977b), "Empirical Research on Comparative Advertising: A Review of the Evidence." Buffalo, New York: School of Management, State University of New York at Buffalo (September).

Frank, R., W. Massy, and Y. Wind (1972), *Market Segmentation.* Englewood Cliffs, New Jersey: Prentice-Hall, Inc.

Golden, Linda (1976), "Consumer Reactions to Comparative Advertising," in *Advances in Consumer Research*, 3, B. B. Anderson, ed., Association for Consumer Research, 63-67.

Jacoby, Jacob, D. E. Speller, and C. A. Kohn (1974), "Brand Choice Behavior as a Function of Information Load," *Journal of Marketing Research*, 11 (February), 63-69.

Kassarjian, H. H. (1971), "Personality and Consumer Behavior: A Review," *Journal of Marketing Research*, 8 (November), 409-18.

Kelman, H. and R. Cohler (1967), "Test for Cognitive Style," in *Risk Handling and Information Handling in Consumer Behavior.* Cambridge: Harvard University Press.

Kershaw, A. G. and S. I. Tannenbaum (1976), "For and Against Comparative Advertising," *Advertising Age* (July 5), 25-28.

Lavidge, R. J. and G. A. Steiner (1961), "A Model for Predictive Measurements of Advertising Effectiveness," *Journal of Marketing*, 25 (October), 59-62.

Levine, P. (1976), "Commercials That Name Competing Brands," *Journal of Advertising Research*, 16 (December), 7-14.

Lindquist, E. F. (1956), *Design and Analysis of Experiments.* Boston: Houghton-Mifflin.

Mazis, Michael (1976), "A Theoretical and Empirical Examination of Comparative Advertising," working paper, University of Florida.

McDougall, Gordon (1976), "Comparative Advertising: An Empirical Investigation of Its Role in Consumer Information," Working Paper No. 167, School of Business Administration, The University of Western Ontario (December).

Mehrabian, A. and J. A. Russel (1974), *An Approach to Environmental Psychology.* Cambridge: MIT Press.

Peter, J. and L. Tarpey (1975), "A Comparative Analysis of Three Consumer Decision Strategies," *Journal of Consumer Research,* 2 (June), 29–37.

Prasad, V. K. (1976), "Communications Effectiveness of Cognitive Advertising: A Laboratory Analysis," *Journal of Marketing Research,* 13 (May), 128–37.

Pride, W. M., C. W. Lamb, and B. A. Pletcher (1977), "Are Comparative Advertisements More Informative for Owners of the Mentioned Competing Brands Than for Non-Owners?" in *Contemporary Marketing Thought,* B. A. Greenberg and D. N. Bellenger, eds. Chicago: American Marketing Association, 298–301.

Rockey, E. A. (1976), *Comparative Advertising: Fair or Unfair, Effective or Ineffective?* New York: ANA Television Workshop, February 24.

Rokeach, M. (1960), *The Open and Closed Mind.* New York: Basic Books.

Sawyer, A. G. (1973), "The Effects of Repetition on Reputational and Supportive Advertising Appeals," *Journal of Marketing Research,* 10 (February), 23–33.

Scheffé, H. (1959), *The Analysis of Variance.* New York: John Wiley & Sons, Inc.

Ulanoff, Stanley M. (1975), *Comparative Advertising: A Historical Perspective.* Cambridge: Marketing Science Institute.

Wilkie, W. L. and P. W. Farris (1975), "Comparison Advertising: Problems and Potential," *Journal of Marketing,* 39 (October), 7–15.

Wilson, R. Dale (1976), "An Empirical Evaluation of Comparative Advertising Messages: Subjects' Responses on Perceptual Dimensions," in *Advances in Consumer Research,* 3, B. B. Anderson, ed., Association for Consumer Research, 53–57.

Wind, Y. and J. Denny (1974), "Multivariate Analysis of Variance in Research on the Effectiveness of TV Commercials," *Journal of Marketing Research,* 11 (May), 136–42.

Winer, B. J. 1971, *Statistical Principles in Experimental Design,* 2nd ed. New York: McGraw-Hill Book Company.

READING 32

Consumer Initial Processing in a Difficult Media Environment

Peter H. Webb

Research on the effects of television advertising has focused on source, message, and audience characteristics, but much less on the situational aspects of the message environment. This article shows how the structure of the environment in which a commercial is embedded affects an individual viewer's attention to and comprehension of the commercial.

The study of information processing can be divided into research pertaining to the acquisition of information necessary to make choices, and research pertaining to how the information, once acquired, is used to make choices (here designated as "central processing"). The acquisition of information can be further subdivided into that pertaining to the active search for information and that pertaining to cognitive and perceptual processes at the time the information is acquired.

The former is exemplified in the macromodels of consumer behavior (Engel, Kollat, and Blackwell 1968; Howard and Sheth 1969; Nicosia 1966), and in the research on decision nets by Bettman (1974) and others. The latter research, labeled "initial processing" research by Ray (1974), focuses on those processes that occur during and just after exposure to information, up to and including short-term memory.[1] Further processing of information committed to long-term memory would fall under the heading of central processing.[2]

Thus, a temporal distinction can be seen between information search, initial processing, and central processing. The research described herein is in initial processing. Specifically, it centers on short-term effects of television advertising, with emphasis on environmental characteristics of the television medium.

A Model of Environmental Effects

Research on the response of consumers to television advertising has concentrated heavily on characteristics of the message itself and of the message audience, but much less on the situational aspects of the message environment. However, recent alarm at the rapidly escalating costs of TV time is causing advertisers to take a hard look at the effectiveness of TV advertising relative to that of less expensive media. One result of this examination is a growing concern that the environment in which a commercial is aired may be just as important in determining response to the commercial as message or audience characteristics.

The Figure presents a descriptive initial-processing model of the effects of environment on response

Reprinted by permission from the *Journal of Consumer Research*, 6:3 December 1979, 225–236.

1. Examples of such research include Ray and Sawyer (1971), the effects of repetition on advertising response; Silk and Vavra (1974), the impact of affective qualities of advertising; Wright (1974), cognitive response measures of reactions to advertising; Rothschild (1978), involvement and political advertising; and Russo (1978), eye movements as a measure of advertising response.

2. Notable examples of such research include David (1970) and Ferber and Lee (1974), family decision making; Jacoby (1974), information overload; Robertson and Rossiter (1974) and Ward (1974), consumer socialization; and Wright (1978), consumer decision simplifying mechanisms.

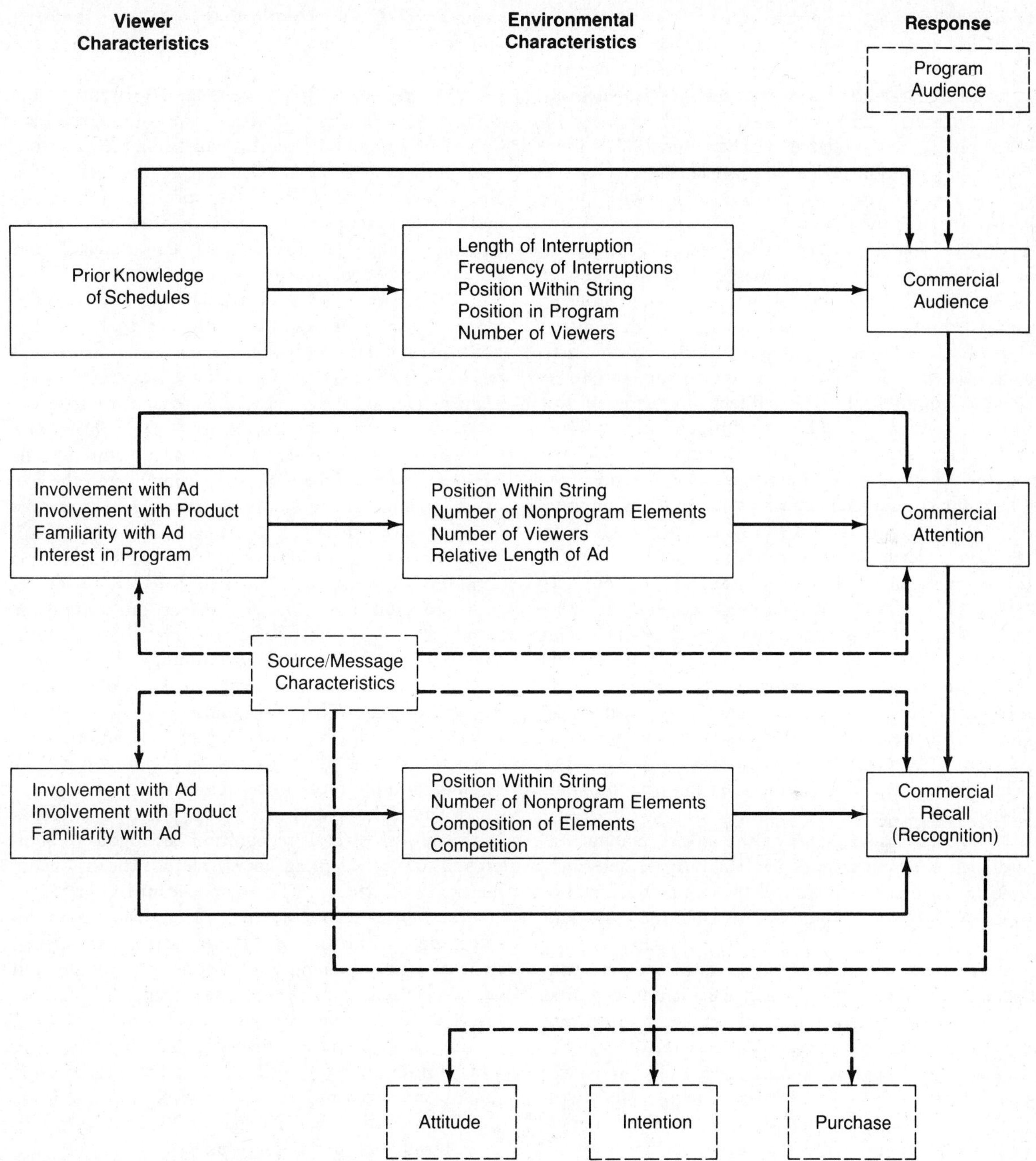

FIGURE
Effects of Environment on Response to Television Advertising

to TV advertising. It identifies a variety of environmental characteristics that may influence response to individual commercials. The major independent variables are characteristics of the commercial environment, although, in many instances, the effects of environment are mediated by characteristics of individual viewers. Source and message characteristics are included to indicate their relationships with those variables explicitly modeled.

The model is a three-stage recursive one with hierarchical dependent variables, similar in structure to McGuire's (1969) model of information processing and the N. W. Ayer model of new product introductions (Claycamp and Liddy 1969). At the first stage, the presence of a viewer in the audience for a specific commercial is dependent on being in the program audience,[3] and is also influenced by several characteristics of the commercial environment. These include the length of the interruption or break in which the commercial appears, the frequency of commercial interruptions in the program, the position of the commercial within the "string" of elements in the commercial break, the position of the commercial break within or between programs, and the number of other viewers in the immediate audience. The probability of being in the commercial audience is also influenced by the viewer's prior knowledge of how commercials are scheduled in the particular environment, e.g., greater knowledge of commercial scheduling permits more flexibility in leaving the commercial audience without leaving the program audience.

At the second stage of the model, commercial audience becomes an independent variable determining the degree of attention to the commercial in conjunction with a second set of environmental and viewer characteristics (as well as exogenous source and message characteristics). Additional environmental characteristics at this stage include the total number of nonprogram elements in the interruption, and the length of the commercial relative to the length of surrounding commercials. Relevant viewer characteristics include the level of involvement with the product category and with the specific commercial (not necessarily the same), familiarity with the commercial (how often it has been seen before), and level of interest in the program containing the commercial.

At the third stage, commercial attention becomes an independent variable determining the likelihood of commercial recall/recognition along with a third set of environmental and viewer characteristics. New environmental characteristics at this stage include the "composition" of the elements within the interruption (not all are necessarily commercials), and the nearness of competitive commercials.

The listed environmental characteristics affecting each level of response reflect actual and hypothesized relationships from present and related research. It should be noted that a variable may affect a given stage of the process, independent of its effect at another level. Thus, for example, the position of a commercial within a string of adjacent commercials has been shown to have a strong influence on the size of the commercial audience (Burke 1972). However, given presence in the commercial audience, position has a second, independent effect on attention to this commercial. Similarly, given a specific level of attention, position has a further effect on subsequent recall or recognition of the commercial. In fact, in some instances the same environmental or viewer characteristic may affect different levels of response in opposite ways. Thus, for example, the more familiar a viewer is with a particular commercial, the less attention s/he is likely to pay to it, but the greater the likelihood of recall or recognition.

The highest level of effect explicitly considered in this model is recall/recognition (analogous to comprehension or learning in characterizations of the hierarchy of effects). This is not meant to imply that environmental characteristics of television have no effect on still higher order responses to advertising, such as attitude change, intentions to purchase, and actual purchase. Such responses typically do not result from a single exposure to a TV ad, and thus, are not part of initial processing. As Ray (1974, p. 145) points out: "Over the long term (i.e., through repetition) initial processing can affect basic attitude structures, but it has its main effects in terms of short-term communication responses."

This conclusion is supported in the work of Krugman (1965). His low involvement theory of TV advertising suggests that individual TV messages will have little or no effect on higher order levels of response—that only through repetition will there be

3. If the commercial is in a between-programs spot, the relevant program may be the last program, the next program, or both. In rare instances, e.g., channel switching, presence in the commercial audience is not absolutely dependent on being in some program audience.

a gradual shift in cognitive structure, which will affect attitudes only after actual purchase, if at all. Thus, commercial audience, commercial attention, and recall/recognition of commercials are the most appropriate dependent measures of the effects of environment on the responses to individual TV commercials.

Research on Commercial Environment: Past and Present

As noted earlier, published research on the effects of commercial environment is sparse. Advertisers concerned with environment have concentrated attention on the various elements of television fare that are not program material. The term "clutter" has been coined to describe the overall set of such elements. Clutter is the result of too much "nonprogram material which includes commercials, billboards, promotional announcements, credits, public service announcements, and promos for the same program" (American Association of Advertising Agencies 1972, p. 1). Although debate about clutter among advertising practitioners has been steadily increasing in the past five years, the publication of data to support contentions that clutter is a problem has been rare.

In fact, the only major published study specifically designed to test the effects of clutter was conducted by Burke Marketing Research, Inc., using extensive field data gathered from 1965 to 1971 (Burke 1972). Using standard day-after recall techniques, this study measured the size of commercial audiences and recall of commercials as a function of position in "strings" of from five to eight consecutive commercials. Two major findings emerged. First, a curvilinear relationship was found between the placement of a commercial in a string of commercials and the size of the audience for that commercial. Commercials "interior" to the string (e.g., second, third, or fourth in a string of five commercials) suffered as much as a ten percent reduction in audience size relative to those "exterior" to the string (first or fifth).[4] The explanation was that when a commercial interruption occurs people gradually drift into other activities, and later rejoin the audience in anticipation of the program resuming or a new program starting.

The study also found that for those people in the commercial audience, recall rates were unaffected by position in the string. Thus, recall rates were lower for interior positions, but only to the extent that the audience for commercials in these positions was smaller.

Several weaknesses exist in this study, the most serious of which casts doubt on the second finding—that recall is invariant to position if audience size differences are removed. Data for each position in the string are presented without regard to the length of the string. Thus, a commercial occurring in the fifth position is external in a string of five commercials, but internal in longer strings. In justifying this, the report says:

> *We do not consider length of chain to be a factor in a study about clutter. The reason is simply this—when a commercial is telecast, the viewer has no idea what will follow: it could be an isolated commercial, the first of two, or the first of ten. Unless he works at the television station, he just doesn't know (Burke 1972, p. 10).*

Results of the Webb study (1978) indicate emphatically that this statement is false. Many TV viewers have a very good conception of when and how many commercials to expect for varying types of programming and time of day. In fact, Burke's assumption is contradicted by their own findings with respect to commercial audience size. If viewers have no idea what will follow a given commercial, there is no reason to expect a curvilinear relationship between position and audience size.

Other shortcomings in the Burke study include failure to separate effects of specific commercials from effects of position, failure to account for a major decrease in average commercial length over the seven-year period during which data were gathered, and reliance on respondents' recollections of their whereabouts during specific intervals of time as short as 30 seconds, some 24 hours later. Despite these shortcomings, the Burke study still represents the only published field study of any merit in this area.

The effects of environment on television commercials can be highly complex. As shown in the

4. Extension of this study, including data gathered through 1974, showed a weakening of audience size estimates for the last two positions in strings of seven or eight consecutive commercials (Schneider 1976).

Figure, the environment is characterized by a large number of potentially relevant variables, with no clear indication of the relative magnitudes of main effects or interactions. Problems of this type are particularly suited for preliminary investigation in a laboratory setting. The laboratory offers a degree of control necessary to assess the relative importance of each variable, and to determine in what situations variables interact with each other to produce second-order or even third-order effects. Results of laboratory experiments can then be validated in the field, using a much more efficient design.

The remainder of this article reports on the first of several laboratory studies conducted to assess the impact of environment on response to television commercials. The selection of variables for inclusion in these studies from the many possibilities indicated in the Figure was guided by past field research (most notably the Burke study) and several notions from the behavioral sciences. The description of the study is followed by a discussion of implications of the findings for management, public policy, and further study of environmental influences on commercial effectiveness.

The Study

Subjects were brought to a central location to view closed-circuit television programs. They were told that they were participating in a study of humor and violence on television.[5] Participants saw two program segments (each approximately ten minutes in length) taped at an earlier date: one from a prime time situation comedy, the other from a prime time crime drama series. Each segment included 30 seconds of lead-in from the beginning of the show, and was edited in such a way that it could stand by itself as a complete story.

Placed between the two program segments was a simulated station break that contained various elements of clutter comprising the experimental treatments. Thus, the videotaped elements employed in this study were edited and combined in such a way as to realistically represent the transition from one television program to another. Subjects saw either zero, four, or eight commercials, credits for the first program, and a station identification. All commercials were 30 seconds in length.

The two tapes representing low clutter conditions contained four commercials in two groups of two each, separated by the program credits and station identification. The tapes differed in that in this string of six consecutive nonprogram elements, commercials occupying external positions on one tape (first and sixth) were rotated to internal positions on the other (second and fifth). The two tapes representing high clutter conditions contained eight commercials (including two public service announcements) in two groups of four each, again separated by the program credits and station identification. As before, in this string of ten consecutive nonprogram elements, commercials occupying external positions on one tape (first, second, ninth, and tenth) were rotated to internal positions on the other (third, fourth, seventh, and eighth).

The specific variables under consideration were, therefore, the number of commercials (referred to as the level of clutter) and position. The experimental design was a 2 $\times$ 2 factorial with two levels of clutter and two message sequences. In addition to the factored variables, the presence of four test commercials in all conditions and four additional commercials in the two high clutter conditions allowed examination of the interactions between the factored variables and message characteristics of the test commercials.

The particular characteristic selected for systematic variation was involvement. According to Krugman (1965, p. 584), involvement is defined as:

> *The number of connections, conscious bridging experiences or personal references per minute that the viewer makes between the content of the persuasive stimulus and the content of his or her own life. This may vary from none to many.*

Using a separate group of 59 respondents (recruited from those in married-student housing at Stanford University), a large number of commercials was screened for their level of involvement using procedures developed by Krugman (1966), with modifications suggested by Wright (1974) and Webb (1978). The highest and lowest involvement

5. The description of the study given to subjects was adapted from that used by Ray, Ward, and Lesser (1973) in a project designed to improve pretesting of anti-drug abuse public service announcements. Ease of subject recruitment due to interest in the project, success in reducing undue attention to commercials, and the adaptability of this cover story to the study of clutter were the reasons for its selection here.

EXHIBIT
Research Design

Program Sequences	
Low Clutter	*High Clutter*
Program introduction (humor)	Program introduction (humor)
Program segment (humor)	Program segment (humor)
Two consecutive 30-second messages	Four consecutive 30-second messages
Program credits (humor)	Program credits (humor)
Station break	Station break
Two consecutive 30-second messages	Four consecutive 30-second messages
Program introduction (violence)	Program introduction (violence)
Program segment (violence)	Program segment (violence)

Nonprogram Segments										
Clutter	*Experimental Conditions*									
Low			A_1	a_2	c	bk	A_2	a_1		
			a_2	A_1	c	bk	a_1	A_2		
High	A_1	a_2	A_3	a_3	c	bk	A_4	a_4	A_2	a_1
	A_3	a_3	A_1	a_2	c	bk	A_2	a_1	A_4	a_4

Note: A = high-involvement advertisement; a = low-involvement advertisement; c = program credits; bk = station break.

commercials were then selected for inclusion in the study. The Exhibit presents a diagram of the full research design.

A total of 113 women and 41 men, aged 18 to 55, from predominantly middle-income families in the South San Francisco area were recruited by a professional agency to view the programs. Each of the four tapes was viewed by eight groups of five subjects (six of the 32 groups were missing one subject). Subjects viewed the tapes in a room set up to look like a living room. They were instructed to act as they would watching TV at home, including talking with each other if they wished, getting coffee and cookies (placed at the back of the room), or browsing through magazines placed on a coffee table in front of the TV monitor.[6]

6. Although 40 subjects were assigned to each condition, they viewed the tapes in groups of five. Pretesting revealed strong interdependence of observational patterns within groups. If one person stopped watching the program, it was often to talk with another person. In fact, because this interaction occurs in normal home viewing situations, it was explicitly encouraged in this study. Hence, analysis of attention and recall data must be done using the group as the unit of analysis, reducing the replication factor from 40 to 8.

Dependent Measures

During the sessions, three observers watched the subjects through a one-way mirror. Measurements of the subjects' levels of attention to the TV monitor were taken every 60 seconds during the program segments, and every ten seconds during the commercials. Using a three-point scale, attention was measured as no attention, partial attention, or full attention. Scale points were coded 1, 2, and 3, respectively, and averaged for an individual across all readings taken for a given program or nonprogram segment to arrive at an overall attention score for that segment.[7]

Following the presentations, subjects filled out a questionnaire that included a series of questions about the programs (designed to be consistent with the cover story, and to eliminate short-term memory traces), recall of commercial messages, attitudes toward test products, television, and television commercials, purchase intentions for advertised products, and perceptions of clutter levels.

7. This measure was adapted from studies of children's television viewing habits (Ward and Wackman 1974; Wartella and Ettema 1974).

Hypotheses

The hypotheses refer to the test commercials aired during the simulated station break in each manipulation. Within the station break, the position of a commercial refers to its placement relative to all other nonprogram elements, including the program credits and station identification occurring in the middle of the break in all five conditions. A commercial occupying an external position is one at or near the end of the first program segment, or the beginning of the second program segment (first or last position in the nonprogram element strings in low clutter; first two or last two positions in the nonprogram element strings in high clutter). Therefore, a commercial occupying an internal position has one or more commercials (two or more in high clutter) preceding and following it.

H1: Attention to a given commercial will be greater when the commercial occupies an external position than when it occupies an internal position.

This is essentially what Burke found with respect to audience size. Although audience size, in the sense of physical presence, was constant in this study, subjects had every opportunity to leave the commercial (or program) audience mentally by talking with one another, getting refreshments, reading a magazine, or simply not paying attention.

H2: For any given commercial, attention will be greater in the low clutter than in the high clutter conditions.

This follows from Hypothesis 1, in that as clutter increases, the number of internal positions in strings of commercials increases relative to the number of external positions.

H3: Differences in attention, due to different positions and different levels of clutter, will be less for high-involvement than for low-involvement commercials.

Krugman's (1965) theory suggests that a low-involvement message affects a viewer through constant repetition in situations of lowered perceptual defenses. This requires surpassing a minimum or threshold level of perception. In low clutter and/or in external positions in commercial strings, this threshold is likely to be relatively low, allowing a reasonable probability of perception of a commercial regardless of how involving it is. However, as the number of commercials increases, this threshold is likely to increase, especially for positions internal to strings. In such situations, high-involvement commercials may still stand out, but low-involvement commercials will be lost.

H4: Recall of a given commercial will be higher when the commercial occupies an external position than when it occupies an internal position.

There are two reasons for this hypothesis. First, attention is likely to be lower for commercials internal to strings (Hypothesis 1). Second, even if attention was constant, research has shown that information presented serially, such as a string of commercials, is learned differentially as a function of position in the list. As far back as the turn of the century, Ebbinghaus (1902) found that to learn nonsense syllables from a list required fewer exposures if the syllables were near the beginning or end of the list than if they were in the middle. The most frequent explanation for this finding is that interference of one stimulus with another inhabits learning of either stimulus, and that stimuli in the middle of a list are subject to more interference than those at the beginning or end.[8]

This hypothesis is counter to the findings of the Burke study, which showed no relationship between recall and position for constant audience size. However, the two results may not be inconsistent. In the Burke study, those in the commercial audience were presumably in it voluntarily, whereas in the current study this was not the case. As a result, attention levels to all commercials may have been higher in the Burke study (attention was not measured) than anticipated in the current study. This could have suppressed recall differences due to attention differences, although it is unlikely to have had any bearing on differences due to serial positioning.

H5: For any given commercial, average recall will be higher in low clutter than in high clutter conditions.

As with Hypothesis 4, part of the reason for this hypothesis rests on lower attention to commercials in high clutter (Hypothesis 2). In addition, the

8. Ebbinghaus's findings were replicated by Strong (1912), using advertisements rather than nonsense syllables as stimuli.

work of Jacoby, Speller, and Kohn (1974) on information overload tends to support this hypothesis. For example, in experiments requiring subjects to process information for varying numbers of brands, Jacoby, et al. found that as the number of brands increases, the amount of time spent processing information about each brand increases, but by less than a constant proportion.[9]

H6: Differences in recall cue to different positions and different levels of clutter will be less for high-involvement than for low-involvement commercials.

This hypothesis is analogous to, and follows directly from, Hypothesis 3. To the extent that an interaction is observed between involvement and position or clutter level, for attention of the viewer, this same interaction should carry over to recall, as something less well attended to is less likely to be remembered at a later time.

Results

Attention

The effects of commercial position and clutter level on attention are presented in Table 1 for the four commercials that appeared in both high and low clutter manipulations. The commercials showed significant differences in attention levels, with Sominex the most attended to (mean = 2.51), Heartland the least (mean = 2.15), and the others in between ($F = 2.98$, 3 and 112 df, $p < 0.03$).[10]

Hypotheses one and two received weak support. Attention levels were slightly higher for commercials occupying external positions in strings (mean = 2.32) than for those occupying internal positions (mean = 2.27), although the difference was not significant. Also attention levels were lower for high clutter (mean = 2.22) than for low clutter (mean = 2.37), although, again, the difference was not large ($F = 1.97$, 1 and 112 df, $p < 0.16$).

TABLE 1
Mean Attention Levels of Test Commercials in High and Low Clutter Conditions, by Position in String[a]

	Low Clutter		*High Clutter*	
Commercial	*External*	*Internal*	*External*	*Internal*
Sominex	2.42	2.56	2.62	2.44
United California Bank	2.66	2.04	2.24	2.17
Master Charge	2.34	2.30	2.19	2.16
Heartland	2.02	2.61	2.09	1.87

a. Scale: 1.00 = no attention; 3.00 = full attention.

Table 1 also shows no consistent support for the predicted interactions between the level of involvement of the commercials and their positions in strings or the level of clutter (Hypothesis 3). Prior testing showed that Sominex and Master Charge were high-involvement commercials, whereas United California Bank and Heartland were low-involvement commercials (indeed, they were selected for this reason). Despite the weak main effects of clutter level and position, it can be seen that Sominex and Master Charge are relatively less affected by clutter level and position than United California Bank. This supports the hypothesis. However, Heartland performs significantly better in the internal position under low clutter, and averages higher attention scores in high clutter than in low clutter. This runs counter to the hypothesis.

Table 2 presents attention data for the four test commercials included in just the high clutter conditions. As with the other test commercials, there is a significant difference in attention among these four commercials ($F = 2.72$, 3 and 56 df, $p < 0.05$). This main effect is due entirely to the public service announcement for anti-drug abuse—clearly, the most provocative commercial of any in the study (mean attention = 2.69). There is also a main effect due to position, with commercials occurring in the second half of strings of four showing lower attention levels

9. However, an important distinction exists between processing information for the purpose of committing it to memory (initial processing) and processing information for the purpose of choosing among alternatives (central processing). In light of contradictory findings regarding these two tasks (Bettman 1975), it is not clear that the Jacoby experiments, which focus mainly on central processing, are directly applicable to problems of initial processing, such as are being considered here.

10. Significance tests are based on the group, rather than on the individual, as the unit of analysis, due to the intragroup interactions discussed earlier. The tests are, therefore, conservative.

TABLE 2
Mean Attention by Position for High-Clutter Commercials[a]

Commercial	Position External	Position Internal
Florists' Transworld Delivery (FTD)	2.59	2.09
Brotherhood Public Service Announcement	2.37	2.12
Anti-Drug Abuse Public Service Announcement	2.65	2.73
Klean n' Shine	2.27	2.31

a. Scale: 1.00 = no attention; 3.00 = full attention.

TABLE 3
Mean Percentage Recall Scores of Test Commercials in High and Low Clutter Conditions, By Position in String

	Low Clutter		*High Clutter*	
Commercial	*External*	*Internal*	*External*	*Internal*
Sominex	66%	63%	83%	47%
United California Bank	70	43	47	33
Master Charge	40	48	41	48
Heartland	28	50	20	39

(mean = 2.31) than in the first half (mean = 2.47). This again supports the hypothesized effect of position (Hypothesis 1), although the effect is not statistically significant.

The hypothesized interaction between involvement and position does not hold for these advertisements. The two commercials suffering most in internal positions are FTD (Florists' Transworld Delivery), a high-involvement commercial, and the Brotherhood Public Service announcement, a low-involvement commercial. Klean n' Shine, the other low-involvement commercial, did not show any drop in attention when aired in internal positions.

Recall

The basic measure of recall employed in this study was unaided recall of commercial messages. Subjects were asked to "play back" anything they could remember from each commercial in any order they wished. The instructions included a sample protocol to be used as a guideline (Webb 1978). Space was provided on the questionnaire for recall of 13 commercials, although eight was the maximum number aired in any manipulation. Subjects were not told how many commercials they had seen. They were encouraged to take the time to list all the commercials they could remember, but were also told not to worry if they could not remember all that they had seen.

From these protocols, three distinct measures of recall were derived: simple recall, first recall, and brand name recall. Only one of these—simple recall—is reported here. This was a dichotomous measure, classifying a protocol as a recall if it mentioned any identifiable part of the commercial. This could be the brand name, the setting, the characters, the soundtrack, or any combination.[11]

The effects of commercial position and clutter level on recall are presented in Table 3 for the four commercials appearing in both high and low clutter. Again, at the group level, the commercials showed significant differences independent of clutter level and position ($F = 7.27$, 3 and 112 df, $p < 0.001$). The relative recall rates exhibit the same rank order pattern as did attention levels (Table 1), with Sominex receiving the highest average recall score (65 percent) and Heartland the lowest (34 percent).

As with attention, the main effects on recall of both position and clutter are in the predicted directions (Hypotheses 4 and 5), but neither is statistically significant. External positions averaged 49 percent recall compared with 46 percent in internal positions. Low clutter averaged 51 percent recall compared with 45 percent in high clutter.

Table 4 shows recall by clutter level for high- and low-involvement commercials. It can be seen that despite the weak main effect due to clutter there is an interaction between involvement and clutter level, as predicted (Hypothesis 6). The high-involvement commercials are unaffected by clutter level whereas the low-involvement commercials show

11. First recall (i.e., the first protocol listed by a subject on the questionnaire), a measure shown empirically to be a better predictor of brand choice than simple recall (Axelrod 1968), showed similar and, in some cases, stronger effects of independent variables, but added little to interpretations. Brand name recall paralleled simple recall to such a degree as to add nothing to the analysis.

TABLE 4
Percent Recall by Clutter Level for High- and Low-Involvement Commercials

Commercial	*Clutter Level* *Low*	*High*	*Percent Decrease for High Clutter*
High Involvement			
Sominex	64%	65%	−1
Master Charge	44	44	0
Low Involvement			
United California Bank	56	40	29
Heartland	39	30	23

20 to 30 percent decreases in recall in the high clutter conditions.

However, the predicted interaction between involvement and position (Hypothesis 6) is not supported. As with attention, recall rates of Sominex and Master Charge (high involvement) are relatively less affected by position than United California Bank (low involvement). However, Heartland, the other low-involvement commercial, shows higher recall rates in internal positions for both high and low clutter conditions. This is not surprising in the low clutter condition where attention was significantly higher for the internal position. However, there is no apparent reason for the reversal of this effect in high clutter.

Table 5, which presents recall data for the four commercials included in only the high clutter conditions, shows significant main effects attributable to the commercials ($F = 5.58$, 3 and 56 df, $p < 0.002$) and to position ($F = 7.12$, 1 and 56 df, $p < 0.01$).

TABLE 5
Percent Recall by Position for High Clutter Commercials

Commercial	*Position* *External*	*Internal*
Florists' Transworld Delivery (FTD)	66%	28%
Brotherhood Public Service Announcement	34	8
Anti-Drug Abuse Public Service Announcement	68	44
Klean n' Shine	39	59

These effects are similar to those for attention (see Table 2). The highest recall rate is for the anti-drug abuse public service announcement (56 percent), and the lowest for the Brotherhood public service announcement (21 percent).

The position main effect is supportive of Hypothesis 4. The lower recall rates for second half positions occur for all commercials except the Klean n' Shine commercial, which shows a higher recall rate for its second half position than for its first half position. There is no readily apparent reason for this reversal.

Other Measures

In addition to attention and recall, several other measures were included in the posttest questionnaire. Attitude and purchase intention measures for products represented by test commercials were placed following the recall section of the questionnaire (each respondent filled out just one of these measures to avoid biasing interactions between the two closely related measures). Relative to competitive products, these measures showed minor effects consistent with hypothesized results, but none was statistically significant. The lack of significant effects of position and clutter level on "higher order" response measures of attitudes and intentions is not surprising. Such effects have rarely been found in laboratory studies that feature a single exposure to advertisements (Ray 1973).

Two secondary measures of response included on the posttest questionnaire also yielded results consistent with hypothesized effects. Thoughts that came to mind while viewing specific commercials [referred to as "cognitive responses" by Greenwald (1968), Roberts and Maccoby (1973), and Wright (1973), and in this study generated after each commercial recall] were more frequently negative when the clutter level was high. This suggests the possibility of negative carry-over effects from adverse environmental factors to advertised products. Such effects have often been observed with respect to characteristics of commercial messages themselves (Silk and Vavra 1974; Strong 1925).

Finally, subjects' estimates of the amount of time devoted to commercials consistently exceeded actual amounts (by an average of 33 percent in the four commercial conditions and 42 percent in the eight commercial conditions). One possible explanation for this is that strings of commercials represent complex stimuli relative to programs, and complex stimuli have longer perceived time durations than simple stimuli (Ornstein 1968). Another reason might be that commercials are often annoying to viewers, and annoying stimuli seem to take more time than pleasant or neutral stimuli.

Discussion

The results presented are far from strongly supportive of hypothesized effects. In most instances, the results are in the predicted directions, but few results are statistically significant, and there are several exceptions even in directionality.

In such situations, a postmortem should be conducted addressing three major issues—theory, procedure, and measurement—any or all of which might be responsible for unanticipated results. In this case, it appears that the theory is sound, and except for the insensitivity of the attention measure to subtle nonvisual variations in attention, measurement techniques are adequate.

This leaves procedure. It was anticipated that the nonprogram material presented during the break between program segments would be regarded as a single string of six or ten nonprogram elements depending on the manipulation. As such, attention was expected to follow a U-shaped curve (Hypothesis 1), dropping off toward the center of the string and gradually increasing thereafter. This would have been consistent with past results (Burke 1972). But, this was not the case. In fact, the credits element for the first program showed consistently higher attention scores than most of the commercials preceding or following it.

Although unanticipated, the reasons for these results seem readily apparent. The U-shaped curve observed in the Burke study of clutter, and hypothesized for this study, is based on well-formed viewer expectations of television scheduling. When a program concludes, viewers expect one or more commercials, a station identification, and other nonprogram elements, such as credits and promotions. This allows them to leave the audience physically and/or mentally, without fear of missing the beginning of the next program. Uncertainty as to the exact length of time between programs would then explain any gradual buildup in attention towards the end of the string. This would result in the second half of the U-shaped attention curve.

The instructions given in the present study, prior to airing the presentations, effectively eliminated these expectations. Subjects were told: "What you will be watching are some parts of recent television shows. They were taped as they were shown, and then put together." Thus participants had no idea what elements to expect, or in what order.

This suggests that instead of a curvilinear relationship between position and attention, a monotonic relationship is more likely, with higher attention scores at the beginning of strings, declining scores in the middle, but no "recovery" at the end. Table 6 recasts the position data to reflect this alternative hypothesis. Instead of comparing internal with external positions, the first position in the string is compared with later positions. Since, as noted, the 30 seconds of credits and five-second station identification embedded in the commercial strings consistently "snapped viewers back to attention," commercials are considered to be in two separate strings in this Table, either prior to or subsequent to the credits and station break. Thus, "first position" is either the very first commercial, or the first commercial immediately following the station identification.

Analyzed in this manner, a new pattern emerges in the data. The main effect due to position (Hypothesis 1) is now significant ($F = 4.86$, 1 and 120 *df*, $p < 0.03$). The mean level of attention to com-

TABLE 6
Mean Attention by Position for High- and Low-Involvement Commercials[a]

Commercial	*Position* *First*	*Other*	*Percent Decrease for Positions Other Than First*
High Involvement			
Sominex	2.52	2.50	1
Master Charge	2.23	2.27	−2
Low Involvement			
United California Bank	2.66	2.15	19
Heartland	2.61	1.99	24

a. Scale: 1.00 = no attention; 3.00 = full attention.

mercials in first position is 2.44 compared with 2.19 in other positions. In addition, the commercial by position interaction is also mildly significant ($F = 2.35$, 3 and 120 df, $p < 0.07$). From the last column in Table 6, it is readily apparent that the low-involvement commercials suffer major decreases in attention in positions other than first position, whereas the high-involvement commercials do not (Hypothesis 3).

Table 7 presents similar data for recall. Again the main effect due to position (Hypothesis 4) is significant ($F = 13.72$, 1 and 120 df, $p < 0.001$). The mean percentage recall of commercials in first position is 60 percent compared with just 40 percent in all other positions. Although the commercial-by-position interaction is not significant (due to the fact that all commercials suffer recall decreases in positions other than first), it can be seen from the last column in Table 7 that the low-involvement commercials do show greater decrements in positions other than first position than the high-involvement commercials (Hypothesis 6).

Thus, although the original hypotheses concerning effects of commercial positions were not strongly supported, reanalysis of the data in light of the apparent artifact introduced in the instructions lends support to the contention that it was the procedure rather than the theory that produced the unanticipated results.

One other potential procedural problem deserves mention. Although the high-clutter conditions contained twice as many commercials as the low-clutter conditions (67 percent more nonprogram elements if credits and the station identification are included), there are many "real world" comparisons in which this ratio might be three to one, four to one, or even higher.[12] While it was anticipated that a more disparate manipulation of clutter would cause an intolerable level of suspicion on the part of the subjects concerning the true nature of the study, it might also be speculated that wider variance in the clutter-treatment conditions would produce more significant results.

TABLE 7
Percent Recall by Position for High- and Low-Involvement Commercials

Commercial	*Position* *First*	*Other*	*Percent Decrease for Positions Other Than First*
High Involvement			
Sominex	74%	55%	27
Master Charge	48	41	15
Low Involvement			
United California Bank	70	41	41
Heartland	50	29	42

Limitations

Although subjects were recruited from the population of interest—the television-viewing public—the sample was necessarily a convenience sample. The typical subject was female, 25 to 35 years old, with a high school education, married, with two children, and an annual family income of $10,000 to $15,000. In addition, the typical subject reported viewing an average of 14.5 hours of television per week. While these characteristics are reasonably representative of the entire population, homogeneity of the sample suggests that sampling variation is understated. One major concern was the predominance of women (72 percent). However, analysis revealed no major difference in responses to the posttest questionnaire due to sex.

Although there is no way of knowing how results might differ for a different sample, generalization of the findings to the entire viewing public should be guarded. The artificiality of the setting for this study suggests the possibility of demand artifacts, which might also threaten both internal and external validity. Wherever possible, steps were taken to reduce the incidence of demand bias. This included the absence of any pretest, careful arrangement of posttest questions to minimize interactions, and the use of a carefully pretested cover story.

In addition, elaborate procedures were undertaken to make the viewing situation as close to a home environment as possible. Subjects viewed the

12. A commercial within a program might be adjacent to a single other commercial or to no commercials at all, whereas the same commercial purchased as a between-program spot might be surrounded by as many as ten or twelve nonprogram elements (see, for example, Spengler 1978).

presentations in small groups, as typically occurs in the home. Although they were viewing predominantly with strangers, 63 percent of the subjects already knew at least one other person in their session. In addition, groups gathered in a waiting room before each session and, in many instances, took this time to get acquainted. By means of explicit instructions, every effort was made to make subjects comfortable, relaxed, and unconcerned about any subsequent effects upon them due to their participation. Discussions with participants in pretest sessions indicated the success of these procedures.

Implications

This study has implications for advertising management and for public policy. For individual advertisers, perhaps the two most important results are the differences in commercial effectiveness due to different positions in strings of commercials, and the effects of involvement on response to commercials. The study supports the superiority of early positions in commercial strings, especially the first position.

Time costs are determined by program ratings, which are based directly on estimates of the number of households viewing the program. The more commercial time available (currently as high as 16 minutes per hour in nonprime time), the longer individual strings of commercials tend to be. To the extent that response measures show significant decreases in effectiveness after the first position, this means that a higher percentage of unfavorable positions exists in long strings of commercials. Buying time in high clutter environments, therefore, increases the likelihood of receiving a poor position.

The second major implication of this research for advertising managers is the differential effect of involvement on commercial response in different clutter situations. Low-involvement commercials suffer much larger decrements in response to high clutter or poor position in strings than high-involvement commercials. Although it has been suggested that most television advertising is low involvement (Krugman 1965), involvement is a relative concept. Thus, certain commercials may be described as uninvolving compared with other types of persuasive communications, but moderately or even highly involving relative to other commercials.

The research also has important implications for policy makers. In the regulatory arena, the Code Authority of the National Association of Broadcasters is charged with the responsibility "to maintain a continuing review of all programming and advertising material presented over television, especially that of subscribers to the Television Code of NAB"[13] (*The Television Code* 1978, p. 32). Each year the Code Authority conducts hearings to determine what changes in programming practices should be required of member stations and recommended to the industry as a whole. In 1978, in response to recommendations to reduce allowable nonprogram material, the Code Authority reviewed research pertaining to actual increases in nonprogram material, and the likely effects of such increases (including the results of this and two additional research projects).

These findings helped strengthen arguments that increases in nonprogram material do have a deleterious effect on individual message effectiveness. In response to these arguments, the Code Authority recommended new restrictions on nonprogramming material, effective January 1, 1979. Although there is considerable disagreement over the likely impact of the new measures, research efforts, such as described herein, should prove valuable in further efforts to reduce negative environmental effects.

Future Research

This study represents only the beginning of research to assess the effects of environmental factors on response to television advertising. As the Figure indicates, many of the environmental and related viewer characteristics hypothesized to have important influences on response have not yet been considered. In two subsequent studies (Webb and Ray 1979), several additional variables have been researched. These include length and frequency of commercial interruptions, position of commercial in program (versus in strings), total number and composition of nonprogram elements, relative length of commercials, competition, and viewers' prior knowledge of commercial schedules. Combined with the results reported here, a more accurate picture will emerge of the overall

13. On November 1, 1978, the Code Authority had 468 subscribers, or 67 percent of the total U.S. television stations (information obtained by telephone from the Code Authority).

effects of environmental variables on viewer response to television commercials.

It is anticipated that this research will contribute to the overall knowledge of commercial effectiveness in two important ways. First, the effects of source and message variables can be better understood when considered within particular environments. For example, the nearly universal change-over from 60-second commercials to 30-second commercials was precipitated by research showing that the 30-second commercial is almost as effective as its 60-second counterpart at half the price.[14] Unfortunately, such research ignores the effects of change it creates in the commercial environment. Thus in a string of four 60-second commercials, changing any one to a 30-second commercial will likely result in less than a 50 per cent decrement on any measure of response, but changing the entire string to eight 30-second commercials may well diminish the effectiveness of an individual message by 50 percent or more.

Second, the effects of environment on initial processing can be used to better understand how advertising affects higher order measures of response, such as attitudes, purchase intentions, and behavior. For example, even the most sophisticated field research techniques used to assess the responses of viewers to a specific message or to an ongoing campaign cannot pick up the impact of nearby competing messages, already known to have important effects on attitudes. Although this could be considered a random occurrence in a research design, it is unlikely to be random unless time purchases for the test commercial are random, which is rarely, if ever, the case.

References

American Association of Advertising Agencies (1972), "Television Clutter," unpublished paper presented at the American Association of Advertising Agencies' Board of Directors Meeting. New York, NY.

Axelrod, Joel K. (1968), "Attitude Measures That Predict Purchase," *Journal of Advertising Research*, 8, 3-17.

Bettman, James R. (1974), "Decision Net Models of Buyer Information Processing and Choice: Findings, Problems, and Prospects," in *Consumer Information Processing*, eds. G. David Hughes and Michael L. Ray, Chapel Hill, NC: University of North Carolina Press.

14. By 1971, Burke (1972) reported that just eight percent of all commercials were 60 seconds long.

—— (1975), "Issues in Designing Consumer Information Environments," *Journal of Consumer Research*, 2, 169-77.

Burke Marketing Research, Inc. (1972), "Viewer Attitudes Toward Commercial Clutter on Television and Media Buying Implications," paper presented at the 18th Advertising Research Foundation Conference, New York, NY.

Claycamp, Henry J., and Liddy, Lucian E. (1969), "Prediction of New Product Performance: An Analytical Approach," *Journal of Marketing Research*, 6, 414-20.

David, Harry L. (1970), "Dimensions of Marital Roles in Consumer Decision Making," *Journal of Marketing Research*, 7, 168-77.

Ebbinghaus, Hermann (1902), *Grundzuge der Psychologie*, Leipzig, Germany: Veit and Co.

Engel, James F., Kollat, David T., and Blackwell, Roger D. (1968), *Consumer Behavior*, Hinsdale, IL: Dryden Press.

Ferber, Robert, and Lee, Lucy Chao (1974), "Husband-Wife Influence in Family Purchasing Behavior," *Journal of Consumer Research*, 1, 43-50.

Greenwald, Anthony G. (1968), "Cognitive Learning, Cognitive Response to Persuasion, and Attitude Change," in *Psychological Foundations of Attitudes*, eds. A. G. Greenwald, T. C. Brock, and T. M. Ostrom, New York: Academic Press, Inc., pp. 147-70.

Howard, John A., and Sheth, Jagdish N. (1969), *The Theory of Buyer Behavior*, New York: John Wiley & Sons.

Jacoby, Jacob (1974), "Consumer Reaction to Information Displays: Packaging and Advertising," in *Advertising and the Public Interest*, ed. S. F. Divita, Chicago: American Marketing Association.

——, Speller, Donald E., and Kohn, Carol A. (1974), "Brand Choice Behavior as a Function of Information Load: Replication and Extension," *Journal of Consumer Research*, 1, 33-42.

Krugman, Herbert E. (1965), "The Impact of Television Advertising: Learning Without Involvement," *Public Opinion Quarterly*, 29, 349-56.

—— (1966), "The Measuring of Advertising Involvement," *Public Opinion Quarterly*, 30, 583-96.

McGuire, William J. (1969), "An Information-Processing Model of Advertising Effectiveness," unpublished paper presented at the Behavior and Management Science in Marketing Symposium, University of Chicago, Chicago.

Nicosia, Francesco M. (1966), *Consumer Decision Processes: Marketing and Advertising Implications*, Englewood Cliffs, NJ: Prentice-Hall, Inc.

Ornstein, Robert E. (1968), "On the Experience of Duration," unpublished Ph.D. dissertation, Department of Psychology, Stanford University.

Ray, Michael L. (1973), "Marketing Communication and the Hierarchy-of-Effects," Research Paper No. 180, Graduate School of Business, Stanford University.

—— (1974), "Consumer Initial Processing: Definitions,

Issues and Applications," in *Consumer Information Processing,* eds. G. David Hughes and Michael L. Ray. Chapel Hill, NC: University of North Carolina Press, pp. 145–56.

——, and Sawyer, Alan G. (1971), "Behavioral Measurement for Marketing Models: Estimating the Effects of Advertising Repetition for Media Planning," *Management Science,* 18, Part II, 73–89.

——, Ward, Scott, and Lesser, Gerald (1973), *Experimentation to Improve Pretesting of Drug Abuse Education and Information Campaigns,* Washington, D.C.: National Institute of Mental Health.

Roberts, Donald F., and Maccoby, Nathan (1973), "Cognitive Processes in Persuasion," in *New Models for Mass Communication Research: Sage Annuals in Communication Research, Vol. 2,* eds. F. Gerald Kline and Peter Clarke, Beverly Hills, CA: Sage Publishing Co., pp. 269–307.

Robertson, Thomas S., and Rossiter, John R. (1974), "Children and Commercial Persuasion: An Attribution Theory Analysis," *Journal of Consumer Research,* 1, 13–28.

Rothschild, Michael L. (1978), "Political Advertising: A Neglected Policy Issue in Marketing," *Journal of Marketing Research,* 15, 58–71.

Russo, J. Edward (1978), "Eye Fixations Can Save the World: A Critical Evaluation and a Comparison Between Eye Fixations and Other Information Processing Methodologies," in *Advances in Consumer Research, Vol. 5,* ed. H. Keith Hunt, Chicago: Association for Consumer Research, pp. 561–70.

Schneider, Robert A. (1976), "Television–From Exposure to Effect," unpublished paper presented at the European Society of Opinion Marketing and Research Seminar, Budapest, Hungary.

Silk, Alvin J., and Vavra, Terry G. (1974), "The Influence of Advertising's Affective Qualities on Consumer Response," in *Consumer Information Processing,* eds. G. David Hughes and Michael L. Ray, Chapel Hill, NC: University of North Carolina Press, pp. 157–86.

Spengler, Peter J. (1978), "TV Clutter . . . Enough Already?" paper presented to Association of National Advertisers TV Workshop, New York, NY.

Strong, Edward K. (1912), "The Effect of Length of Series Upon Recognition," *Psychology Review,* 19, 44–7.

The Television Code (1978), Washington, D.C.: National Association of Broadcasters.

Ward, Scott (1974), "Consumer Socialization," *Journal of Consumer Research,* 1, 1–14.

——, and Wackman, Daniel B. (1974), "Children's Information Processing of Television Advertising," in *New Models for Communication Research,* eds. G. Kline and P. Clarke, Beverly Hills, CA: Sage Publishing Co., pp. 81–119.

Wartella, Ellen, and Ettema, James S. (1974), "A Cognitive Developmental Study of Children's Attention to Television Commercials," *Communication Research,* 1, 69–88.

Webb, Peter H. (1978), "Consumer Information Acquisition in a Difficult Media Environment: The Case of Television Clutter," unpublished Ph.D. dissertation, Graduate School of Business, Stanford University.

——, and Ray, Michael L. (1979), "Effects of TV Clutter," *Journal of Advertising Research,* 19, 7–12.

Wright, Peter L. (1973), "The Simplifying Consumer: Perspectives on Information Processing Strategies," unpublished paper presented at American Marketing Association Doctoral Consortium, East Lansing, MI.

—— (1974), "On the Direct Monitoring of Cognitive Response to Advertising," in *Consumer Information Processing,* eds. G. David Hughes and Michael L. Ray. Chapel Hill, NC: University of North Carolina Press, pp. 220–48.

CHAPTER EIGHT

Managing Consumer Research

READING 33

Designing Research for Application

Bobby J. Calder, Lynn W. Phillips, and Alice M. Tybout

Two distinct types of generalizability are identified in consumer research. One entails the application of specific effects, whereas the other entails the application of general scientific theory. Effects application and theory application rest on different philosophical assumptions, and have different methodological implications. A failure to respect these differences has led to much confusion, regarding issues such as the appropriateness of student subjects and laboratory settings.

There is always the expectation in conducting research that the findings ultimately will be useful in addressing situations beyond the one studied. Yet, there exists a concern that much of consumer research, and behavioral research in general, is not generalizable. It frequently is argued that research procedures, particularly the use of student subjects and laboratory settings, necessarily limit the application of findings. Underlying this contention is a failure to recognize that generalizability is not a single issue. Two distinct types of application may be identified in consumer research. The purpose of this paper is to examine the two types of application, and to specify their implications for research design.

The first type of generalizability, which we term *effects application,* maps observed data directly into events beyond the research setting. That is, the specific effects obtained are expected to mirror findings that would be observed if data were collected for other populations and settings in the real world.[1] The second type, which we term *theory application,* uses only scientific theory to explain events beyond the research setting. Effects observed in the research are employed to assess the status of theory. But, it is the theoretical explanation that is expected to be generalizable and not the particular effects obtained.

The paper beings by elaborating the distinction between the goals of effects application and theory application. Then, the ramifications of this distinction are discussed by addressing the following questions:

- What specific research procedures are appropriate when each type of application is intended?
- What are the resulting implications of these differences in research procedures for methodological controversies in the literature regarding the use of student subjects and laboratory settings?
- What philosophical assumptions underlie each type of application, and what then should be done to improve our ability to make each type?

In examining these issues, it is shown that the two types of application lead to different priorities when designing studies. It is argued that the failure to distinguish between the research designs optimum for each type has led to inappropriate conclusions regarding the impact of student subjects and laboratory settings on generalizability. Finally, it is observed that, despite the need for both effects application and theory application in consumer research, each rests on assumptions and can be improved by consideration of the validity of these assumptions.

Reprinted by permission from the *Journal of Consumer Research,* 8:2 September 1981, 197–207.

1. The term "real world" is employed in reference to all situations not constructed for, or altered by, the conduct of research. It is not meant to imply that research settings do not have their own reality.

Distinguishing Research Goals

Effects application and theory application have common elements as well as distinguishing features. Research seeking either type of generalizability necessarily involves some framework or reasoning that might be loosely referred to as "theory." And in both instances, research entails observations of some "effects" related to the theoretical framework. The distinction lies in whether the researcher's primary goal is to apply the specific effects observed or to apply a more general theoretical understanding. In this section, we examine the goals and procedures for achieving each type of generalization.

Effects application is based on a desire for knowledge about the events and relationships in a particular real-world situation. The primary goal of this type of research (hereafter referred to as "effects research") is to obtain findings that can be applied directly to the situation of interest. A theoretical framework may be used to identify and measure effects.[2] But it is the effects themselves that are generalized rather than being linked by inference to theoretical constructs and the hypothesized theoretical network then used to deduce patterns of outcomes.

Application of effects calls for correspondence procedures. It is necessary to assess effects in a research setting that corresponds to a real-world situation. Complete correspondence is difficult to achieve, however. The mere fact of data collection usually distinguishes the research setting from its real-world counterpart. And, because interest rarely is limited to present situations, temporal differences often exist as well. These differences, and others, between the research setting and the real world are inevitable. Effects application, nonetheless, is characterized by the premise that there is *sufficient* correspondence to expect the effects observed to be repeated in the real world.

In contrast, theory application is based on a desire for scientific knowledge about events and relationships that occur in a variety of real-world situations. The primary goal of such research (hereafter referred to as "theory research") is to identify scientific theories that provide a general understanding of the real world. Theory applications call for falsification test procedures. These procedures are used to test a theory by creating a context and measuring effects within that context that have the potential to disprove or refute the theory. The research context and effects are not of interest in their own right. Their significance lies in the information that they provide about the theory's adequacy. Theories that repeatedly survive rigorous falsification attempts are accepted as scientific explanation (subject to further more stringent testing), and are candidates for application.[3] Scientific theories typically are universal and, therefore, can explain any real-world situation within their domain.

The actual application of theory entails using the scientific explanation to design a program or intervention predicted to have some effect in the real world. In a marketing context, the intervention may take the form of a product, price, communication strategy, etc. It is crucial to note that, whatever the strategy, the process of translating from theory to intervention is necessarily a creative one. Theories neither specify how their abstract constructs can be embodied in real-world interventions nor identify the level(s) that uncontrolled theoretical variables will assume in a particular application. Moreover, theories are always incomplete—they deal with a subset of variables that exist in the real world. Consequently, the design process must rely on some assumptions about the operation of both theoretical and nontheoretical variables.

Because intervention design is creative, basing

2. The theoretical framework underlying effects research can be either scientific (i.e., a general theory that has survived rigorous testing) or intuitive (i.e., a theory generated to address a particular situation, which may be consistent with informal observations, but which has not undergone any rigorous testing). This is in contrast to theory research, which is restricted to the examination of general scientific theories. Although we subscribe to the view that scientific theory has advantages over intuitive theory even in effects research, this is obviously a debatable issue. Moreover, because this issue is only tangentially related to ones surrounding the conduct and application of effects research, we leave its discussion to some other forum.

3. It should be noted that the view of theory testing outlined here is a falsificationist one (Popper 1959; 1963). Theories are not proven. They are accepted pending further research. Although many issues surround the falsificationist perspective (Kuhn 1970; Lakatos 1970), they are largely peripheral to the concerns of this paper. The important point is that theory tests must attempt to expose theories to refutation by observed data, and must be conservative in accepting theories that escape refutation.

EXHIBIT 1
Summary of Two Approaches to Applicability

	Effects Application	*Theory Application*
Research goal	To obtain findings that can be generalized directly to a real-world situation of interest.	To obtain scientific theory that can be generalized through the design of theory-based interventions that are viable in the real world.
Research procedure	Generalizing effects requires procedures to ensure that the research setting accurately reflects the real world. These are termed *correspondence procedures.*	Generalizing theory requires two stages of *falsification procedures.* First, *theory falsification procedures* are used to ensure that the abstract theoretical explanation is rendered fully testable. Theories that survive rigorous attempts at falsification are accepted and accorded scientific status. Accepted theory is used as a framework for designing an intervention. Then, *intervention falsification procedures* are used to test the intervention under conditions that could cause it to fail in the real world. Only interventions surviving these tests are implemented.

an intervention on theory that has survived rigorous falsification attempts is not sufficient to ensure that the intervention will yield the theoretically predicted outcome. Separate falsification procedures are required to test a theory and a theory-based intervention. Perhaps an example can best illustrate this. Theories of aerodynamics explain the processes underlying flight. It is not possible, however, to design an airplane solely from aerodynamic theory. Any number of stress studies and the like are necessary to calibrate the theory to conditions in a particular real-world situation. These studies, which we term efforts at intervention falsification, systematically subject the intervention to conditions that might cause it to fail in a particular situation. If the intervention does not perform as predicted by the theory, then its weaknesses are exposed. As in theory testing, failures are more informative than successes. But, the failure of an intervention need not imply inadequacies in the theory. Indeed, failure of the theoretical explanation can be implied only when theory falsification procedures are employed.[4] Theory falsification procedures are, thus, the foundation of any effort to apply theory.

4. This is not to say that intervention-falsification procedures might not sometimes suggest theory-falsification procedures. Nor does it mean that in some cases the two procedures might not be identical.

If it succeeds, confidence that the intervention is viable increases. As a result, the intervention may be used in the real world. In contrast to effects application, however, *no attempt is made to generalize any particular outcomes observed in testing the theory or the intervention.* It is only the theoretical relationship that the intervention is presumed to represent that is applied beyond the research setting.

The goals of research leading to effects application and to theory application are summarized in Exhibit 1. As we have indicated, different research procedures are necessary to achieve each of these goals. We now examine these research procedures in greater detail.

Comparison of Correspondence and Falsification Procedures

Effects application relies on research methods not only different from, but also largely incompatible with, the methods leading to theory application. The former requires correspondence procedures to ensure that all features of the real world are represented in the research setting. The latter requires falsification procedures to ensure, first, that the abstract scientific explanation is rendered fully testable, and, second, that the concrete theory-based intervention is viable under conditions present in the real world.

EXHIBIT 2
Comparison of Research Procedures Optimal for Correspondence, Theory Falsification, and Intervention Falsification

Methodological Issues	*Correspondence Procedures*	*Falsification Procedures*	
		Theory	*Intervention*
Selection of respondents	Use a sample statistically representative of the real-world population.	Use a sample homogeneous on nontheoretical variables.	Use a sample that encompasses individual differences that might influence performance of the intervention.
Operationalization of key variables	Operationalize variables in the research to parallel those in the real world.	Ensure that empirical operationalization of theoretical constructs cannot be construed in terms of other constructs.	Operationalize variables to reflect the manner in which an intervention is to be implemented in the real world.
Selection of a research setting	Choose a research setting statistically representative of the environmental variation present in the real world.	Choose a setting that allows operationalization of theoretical constructs and is free of extraneous sources of variation.	Choose a setting encompassing environmental heterogeneity that might influence the performance of the intervention.
Selection of a research design	Use a design that preserves the correspondence between the research environment, and provides the type of information required for decision making (e.g., descriptive, correlational, causal).	Use a design that affords the strongest possible inferences about the relationships between theoretical constructs.	Use a design that affords the strongest possible test of the intervention subject to constraints imposed by the need to represent real-world variation.

In this section, research procedures leading to effects application and those leading to theory application are compared with respect to selecting respondents, operationalizing variables, choosing research settings, and selecting research designs. This entails contrasting correspondence, theory falsification, and intervention falsification procedures. Primary consideration is given to the comparison of correspondence and *theory* falsification procedures because they are maximally different, and their differences are particularly relevant to methodological controversies in the literature. Theory falsification procedures also are emphasized because they lie at the heart of any theory application. Discussion of the distinguishing features of intervention falsification procedures is deferred until the end of the section. (See Exhibit 2 for a comparison of all three procedures.)

Selecting Respondents

When effects application is the goal, correspondence procedures require that research participants match individuals in the real world setting of interest. Ideally, this is accomplished by carefully defining the relevant population for the effects of interest, and then employing in the investigation a strictly representative sample of individuals from this target population.[5] This procedure is necessary if any generalization from the sample to the population is to be statistically valid. But, because strict statistical sampling often is not feasible, other procedures may be invoked to enhance the representativeness of indi-

5. Although for ease in exposition we use the term "individuals" to refer to respondents, the issues discussed apply equally well when the units of analysis are groups.

viduals in the research. For example, it may be possible to replicate the study with different subgroups of the target population. Alternatively, one might purposively sample individuals who vary on important dimensions that characterize members of the target population. Some degree of representativeness could even be achieved by sampling only the most prevalent type of individual in the target population (Cook and Campbell 1975).

The underlying theoretical framework may be useful in determining important dimensions for any nonrepresentative sample. When alternatives to statistical sampling are employed, however, the application of the results must rest on belief that the sample(s) accurately reflects the population and not on any statistical principle. Thus, confidence in generalizing is severely weakened when statistical sampling is not used.

The criteria are quite different when theory application is the goal. The theory falsification procedures, which underlie this type of generalization, require only that research participants be selected to provide a rigorous test of the theory at issue. Because most scientific theories are universal in scope, any respondent group can provide a test of the theory's predictions (Kruglanski 1973; Webster and Kervin 1971).[6] The ideal theory falsification procedure, however, is to employ maximally homogeneous respondents.[7] This entails sampling from groups of individuals that are similar on dimensions likely to influence the variables of theoretical interest. (For example, for some theories, students or housewives with similar profiles on relevant dimensions may qualify as homogeneous respondents.)

Homogeneous respondents are desired for two reasons. First, they permit more exact theoretical predictions than may be possible with a heterogeneous group. For instance, by employing a homogeneous student sample it might be possible to predict that purchases of a particular product known to be used by students would decrease with advertising exposure. In contrast, if a more heterogeneous sample were selected it might be possible only to predict a decline in some broad category of products. The greater variability in behavior associated with a heterogeneous group makes precise predictions more difficult. This makes failure of the theory harder to detect. Thus, heterogeneous respondents may weaken the theory test.

Homogeneous respondents also are preferred because they decrease the chance of making a false conclusion about whether there is covariation between the variables under study. When respondents are heterogeneous with respect to characteristics that affect their responses, the error variance is increased and the sensitivity of statistical tests in identifying the significant relationships declines. Thus, heterogeneous respondents constitute a threat to statistical conclusion validity (Cook and Campbell 1975). They increase the chance of making a Type II error and concluding that a theory was disconfirmed when, in fact, the theoretical relationship existed but was obscured by variability in the data attributable to nontheoretical constructs. By selecting maximally homogeneous samples, or by conducting full or partial replications of the research for each level or "block" of a respondent characteristic believed to inflate error variance, these random sources of error can be controlled, and the likelihood of making a Type II error decreased (Cook and Campbell 1975; Winer 1971). As a result, the researcher can be more confident that any negative results reflect failure of the theoretical explanation.

It should be noted that nothing in the theory falsification procedure rules out statistical sampling from a relevant population. But a representative sample is not required because *statistical* generalization of the findings is *not* the goal. It is the theory that is applied beyond the research setting. The research sample need only allow a test of the theory. And, any sample within the theory's domain (e.g., any relevant sample), not just a representative one, can provide such a test.

In summary, effects application requires correspondence between the research sample and the population of interest. This is best achieved through

6. Although any respondent group can be used to test a universal theory, characteristics of the particular group chosen affect, or are affected by, the operationalizations of theory variables. Operationalizations that are relevant for the subject population (Ferber 1977) should be employed to avoid the possibility that Type II errors will weaken the theory test.

7. An exception to this preference for homogeneity occurs when an individual difference variable that cannot be manipulated by the researcher (e.g., extroversion) is of theoretical interest. Here, testing the theory requires that variability be achieved by sampling individuals who differ on the dimension of interest. This exception is consistent with providing the strongest possible test of the theory.

statistical sampling. Only such sampling justifies statistical generalization of the research findings. In contrast, theory application requires a research sample that permits falsification of the theory. Although any sample in the theory's domain can potentially falsify the theory, homogeneous samples are preferred because they typically provide a stronger test of the theory. Only the theory is applied and its applicability is determined by its scientific status, not by statistical sampling principles.

Operationalizing Independent and Dependent Variables

Whether the goal is effects application or theory application, valid operationalizations of the independent and dependent variables are necessary. The two types of application differ, however, in the nature of the variables they strive to capture and, thus, in their criteria and procedures for achieving this objective. When the goal is theory application, theory falsification procedures require that the operationalization of constructs (i.e., the independent and dependent variables) render the theory testable. This involves making certain that there is a high degree of correspondence between the empirical operationalizations and the abstract concepts they intend to represent, and that the empirical indicators used to represent the theory's constructs cannot be construed in terms of other constructs. This is necessary to ensure that any failure to disconfirm the theory is not due to the use of empirical operationalizations not measuring the theoretical constructs and, thus, not testing the relationship of interest. This mislabeling of operationalizations in the theory-relevant terms is referred to as a threat to the construct validity of research results (Cook and Campbell 1975).[8]

Attaining construct validity in theory research requires rigorous definition of the theoretical constructs so that empirical measures can be tailored to them. Further, because single exemplars of any construct always contain measurement components that are irrelevant to the theoretical construct of interest, validity is enhanced by employing multiple operationalizations of each construct (Campbell and Fiske 1959; Cook and Campbell 1975). Multiple exemplars of each construct should demonstrably share common variance attributable to the target construct, and should differ from each other in unique ways (Campbell and Fiske 1959). Such "multiple operationalism" allows one to test whether a theoretical relationship holds even though measurement error is present in each operationalization (Bagozzi 1979).

When the goal is effects application, the operationalization of variables is determined by the need for correspondence. Indices of the independent and dependent variables in the research setting are chosen to parallel events in the real world. They are not tailored to abstract theoretical constructs that these variables may be presumed to represent.

Similarity between the operationalizations of variables and their real-world counterparts is maximized by using naturally occurring events in the target setting as independent variables, and naturally occurring behaviors in the target setting as dependent variables (Tunnell 1977; Webb, Campbell, Schwartz, and Sechrest 1966). Events and behaviors are considered to be "natural" if they occur in the real world. This does not necessarily imply that such events will be uncontrolled by the researcher. Price, advertising strategy, etc., are determined by decision makers; thus, their systematic variation for research purposes would not compromise naturalness, provided that their variations reflected any real-world constraints (e.g., any practical constraints preventing disentangling related components of a marketing program in the real world). On occasion, however, the researcher may be concerned with effects on variables for which no naturally occurring measures are available, e.g., attitudes. Then, measures must be designed to assess these variables, while still preserving the correspondence between the research setting and the real world. Generally, this is achieved by making these measures as unobtrusive as possible. Regardless of the variables being examined, measurement error is a concern. Therefore, multiple measures of variables also are desirable in research leading to effects application.

The objectives when operationalizing variables for theory research are largely incompatible with the objectives when operationalizing variables for effects research. As just noted, the correspondence needed for effects application is achieved best by employing naturally occurring events and behaviors as variables, whenever possible. However, naturally occurring events and behaviors generally are inappropriate variables in research testing theory. They do not permit the researcher much latitude in tailoring operationalizations to theoretical constructs. Moreover, naturally

---

8. For a more comprehensive discussion of construct validity, see Bagozzi (1979, Chap. 5).

occurring events often serve as indicators of a complex package of several theoretically distinct constructs. Rarely can they be taken as indicators of a single unidimensional construct. Theory falsification procedures aim to untangle these packages into several distinct variables that can be labeled in theoretical terms. Correspondence procedures aim to preserve these packages as single variables to reflect events in the real world more accurately. Thus, these two types of construct validity typically cannot be pursued simultaneously.

Choosing a Research Setting

The goals of effects application and theory application also imply different criteria in choosing a research setting. The correspondence procedures associated with effects application lead to maximizing the similarity between the research setting and the real-world situation of interest (Ellsworth 1977; Tunnell 1977). This real-world situation usually is heterogeneous on a number of background factors. For example, it may include variation in the time of day, the season, the complexity of the products involved, or the characteristics of salespersons who deliver influence attempts. To enhance transfer of the research findings to the real world, the research setting must reflect the heterogeneity of the background factors. Ideally, a random sampling of background factors present in the real world would be employed (Brunswik 1956). From a statistical perspective, only this method of treating the heterogeneity in such factors allows generalizing the results from the research to the real world.

Often it is infeasible, if not impossible, to represent systematically all the variation in the real-world setting within a single study. In such circumstances, the researcher may try to identify the background factors most likely to impact the effects of interest. The underlying theoretical framework may be used for this purpose. Then, these factors may be represented in several ways. The study may be replicated in settings representing different levels of these background factors. Alternatively, variation on significant factors may be built into a single study without randomly sampling such factors. Or, some degree of representativeness might be achieved by including only the most frequent or typical setting factor(s) found in the real world (Cook and Campbell 1975). When these approaches are employed, however, generalization of the effects must rest on judgment that all important background factors have been properly represented, and not on a statistical principle.

Regardless of which procedure for treating setting heterogeneity is followed, representativeness is best achieved through field research. Field research refers to "any setting which respondents do not perceive to have been set up for the primary purpose of conducting research" (Cook and Campbell 1975, p. 224). The idea is to conduct the research in the real world with as little intrusion as possible. When effects research must be conducted in nonfield (i.e., laboratory) contexts, efforts should be made to incorporate the critical background factors from the real-world setting into the laboratory setting (Sawyer, Worthing, and Sendak 1979).

The theory falsification procedures associated with theory application lead to selection of an entirely different research setting. To test a theory, its constructs must be tied to a particular set of observables in a specific circumstance. It is not important, however, that these events be representative of some set of events that occur in another setting. Rather, the particular events at issue in the research setting are only important as operationalizations of the theory. What is required is that a theory's operationalization in the test setting allow it to be falsified. Typically, this involves choosing a research setting relatively free of extraneous sources of variation, e.g., free of variation on variables not of theoretical interest, and free of variation in treatment implementation. Extraneous variation can produce spurious effects on the dependent variable, and, at a minimum, inflates error variance (Cook and Campbell 1975). To the extent that theoretically irrelevant factors are at work, significant relationships between the phenomena under study may be obscured and the risk of Type II error may be increased. Insulated test settings minimize such irrelevancies.

Most often, the best procedure for reducing the number of random irrelevancies is to employ a controlled laboratory setting. In contrast to field settings, laboratory settings facilitate the use of standardized procedures and treatment implementation, and allow the researcher to control rigorously the stimuli impinging upon respondents. Moreover, laboratory settings possess other inherent advantages, relative to field settings, in conducting the strongest possible test of a theory. Homogeneous respondents are obtained more easily in the laboratory, because the investigator typically has greater control over who participates in a study. Similarly, the laboratory provides greater latitude for tailoring empirical operationalizations to the constructs they are meant to represent, because operationalizations in the laboratory are only limited by the ingenuity of the investigator, and not by naturally occurring variation and real-world constraints. And, the laboratory possesses greater potential for achieving multiple operationalizations of independent and dependent variables, because the expense associated with exposing individuals to a number of independent variables and administering a number of dependent variable responses typically is lower for the laboratory than for the field. Thus, laboratory settings generally are better geared to achieving high degrees of statistical conclusion validity and theoretical construct validity.

The advantages of the laboratory in terms of increasing statistical power and enhancing construct validity are not without limit. Tests of certain theoretical hypotheses may lead to the field if they involve variables not easily examined in laboratory settings. Thus, the advantages of insulated settings may sometimes have to be given up in order to achieve adequate empirical realizations of a theory's constructs. Nevertheless, such limits to the utility of employing laboratory settings in theory tests do not contradict our thesis. They simply reaffirm the general rule that settings yielding the strongest test of the theory should be employed when the goal is theory application. In many cases, this will be the laboratory.

Selecting a Research Design

The choice of a research setting either determines or is determined by the research design to be used. For example, laboratory research is usually associated with "true" experimental designs wherein respondents are randomly assigned to treatments (Campbell and Stanley 1966; Cook and Campbell 1975). When the goal is theory application, and theory testing is being conducted, true experimental designs are preferred because they allow the strongest test. Unlike other designs, such as the survey method or the case study, true experiments permit the investigator to minimize the possibility that third variables cause any observed relation between the independent and dependent variables. This is necessary to ensure that any failure to disconfirm the theory linking the variables is not due to the spurious impact of irrelevant third variables. Moreover, true experiments allow the investigator to establish that the independent variable precedes the dependent variable in time, thus ruling out the possibility that the dependent variable initiates changes in the independent variable, rather than vice versa. The capacity for establishing temporal antecedence and for ruling out third variable rival explanations enables true experiments to eliminate most plausible threats to internal validity, i.e., threats to the conclusion that a demonstrated statistical relationship between the independent and dependent variables implies causality (Cook and Campbell 1975). This is a critical aspect of theory falsification procedures because most theories are stated in a causal framework. True experiments, by ranking higher than other research designs on internal validity, allow the strongest test of causality.[9]

The general preference for true experimental procedures does not mean that all research testing theory will employ such designs. On occasion, the independent variable(s) of interest is not subject to manipulation by the researcher, and conditions prevent random assignment of respondents to different treatments. When this occurs, correlational or quasi-experimental designs must be employed. In certain cases, these designs permit causal inferences (Bagozzi 1979; Cook and Campbell 1975), and even when they do not, they are often of sufficient probing value to be worth employing. However, research designs of less efficiency than true experiments should be used only when true experiments are not feasible (Campbell and Stanley 1966). This is in keeping with the criterion that the research design chosen be the one that offers the strongest test of the theory.

When the goal is effects application, the need for correspondence necessitates different research design priorities. The design depends on the nature of the event structure of interest and the particular information needed regarding that structure. If it is important to establish the causal sequence of the events in the real world, then true experiments are preferred whenever possible. Yet, true experiments

9. The major threats to internal validity that remain in laboratory experiments are participants uncovering the hypothesis and responding to it rather than to the independent variables alone, or participants responding to demand characteristics, i.e., to inadvertent cues given by the experimenter regarding the appropriate behavior. Procedures such as carefully constructed cover stories, between subjects' designs, and "blind" experimenters can be used to reduce the plausibility of these threats; see Rosenthal and Rosnow (1966) for a discussion of these procedures.

may not be feasible to examine certain variables. And, true experiments may seriously compromise the naturalness of the research setting. In these circumstances, or when causal statements regarding the event structure are not required as a basis for decision making, research seeking effects application should opt for correlational or quasi-experimental designs. Such designs are far less intrusive and, hence, enhance correspondence between the research setting and the real-world situation.

Summary

Effects application and theory application differ sharply in the research procedures upon which they depend. When effects application is the goal, correspondence procedures are required to ensure that the findings are generalizable to some real-world situation of interest. These procedures allow *nothing* to be done that might cause an important mismatch between the research and the real-world situation. Ideally, this goal is achieved by employing a representative sample of respondents, using natural events and behaviors as variables in a field context, and selecting a research design that preserves the natural setting (see Exhibit 2). To the extent that similarity between the research and the real world is achieved, the empirical outcomes observed may be applied in the real world.

When theory application is the goal, falsification procedures are required to assess the scientific status of the theory. These procedures allow *anything* to be done that will ensure a rigorous test of the theory. Such a test is provided when internal, construct, and statistical-conclusion validity are maximized. As summarized in Exhibit 2, this entails selecting homogeneous respondent samples, tailoring multiple empirical operationalizations to the abstract theoretical concepts that they are meant to represent, and conducting true experiments in laboratory or other settings that are relatively free of extraneous sources of variation. If research provides a strong test of the theory, and if the theory escapes refutation, then the theory is accepted as a scientific explanation of real-world events.

Theory application is done through the design of a theory-based intervention. But, before such an intervention is implemented in the real world, intervention falsification procedures are required to test its performance. Like theory falsification procedures, intervention falsification procedures seek the most rigorous test possible. But, in contrast to a theory test, a rigorous intervention test is not provided by minimizing variation on nontheoretical factors. Instead, such a test is obtained by exposing the intervention to real-world variability that might cause it to fail. Thus, internal, construct, and statistical-conclusion validity are pursued within limits created by the need to reflect important dimensions of the real world. As summarized in Exhibit 2, this entails selecting research respondents and choosing a research setting that are heterogeneous on variables likely to affect intervention outcomes, operationalizing variables to reflect the manner in which the intervention would be implemented in the real world, and employing the most rigorous research design possible given the need to capture aspects of real-world variability. Only interventions that yield outcomes predicted by the theory in such a test situation are applied in the real world.

Although superficially similar, intervention falsification procedures and correspondence procedures are distinct. Correspondence procedures demand that the research provide an *accurate representation* of the real-world situation of interest. This is necessary because the goal is to apply the particular effects observed in the research to the real world. Intervention falsification procedures only require that the research subject the intervention to *levels of variability* that it might encounter in the real world. The research need not mirror the real world because it is the theoretical relationship represented by the intervention, and not the particular effects observed in the research, that is applied.

The Methodological Literature

Much confusion in the methodological literature has resulted from a lack of realization that different procedures are optimal for achieving the two types of generalizability. This confusion is particularly evident in criticism of laboratory studies with student respondents. It is instructive to review this criticism with the research procedures underlying effects application and theory application in mind.

Objections to laboratory studies have traditionally centered on the "artificiality" of the findings obtained (Aronson and Carlsmith 1968; Opp 1970; Webster and Kervin 1979). But in recent years these objections have manifested themselves in two specific lines of criticism (Kruglanski 1975). One has been the concern that because much research employs student, volunteer, and other convenience samples, it cannot be generalized to broader population groups. In consumer research, this concern has prompted a number of investigations attempting to determine whether students' responses to marketing stimuli are representative of the responses made by individuals comprising some larger target population, such as housewives, businessmen, etc. (Albert 1967; Cunningham, Anderson, and Murphy 1974; Enis, Cox, and Stafford 1972; Khera and Benson 1970; Park and Lessig 1977; Sheth 1970; Shuptrine 1975). Moreover, it has led to the appeal for use of more relevant and more representative subject samples in laboratory research (Ferber 1977; McNemar 1946; Rosenthal and Rosnow 1969b; Schultz 1969; Shuptrine 1975). Relevance refers to the need for samples or target populations appropriate to the topic under investigation (Ferber 1977). Representativeness refers to how accurately the sample reflects characteristics of the target population.

A second major line of criticism has been the argument that, because the laboratory is characterized by unique features not found in the real world, laboratory studies necessarily yield nongeneralizable results. The unique features most commonly referred to include the unrealistic character of the interaction between the experimenter and the subject (Orne 1962; Reicken 1962; Silverman 1968; Sawyer 1975; Venkatesan 1967), and the unrealistic contextual features that make up the laboratory background (Banks 1965; Cox and Enis 1969; Green 1966; Uhl 1966). For example, it is often contended that studies of persuasion in laboratory settings differ from real-world persuasion situations in terms of such contextual factors as audience involvement, attention, noise, exposure time, motivation, and opportunity to make cognitive responses (Gardner 1970; Greenberg 1967; Ray 1977) and, thus, are limited in their relevance to the real world. This argument has been the impetus for suggestions that true experiments be conducted in field settings whenever possible (Banks 1965; Caffyn 1964; Cartwright and Zander 1968, p. 36; McGuire 1969; Ross and Smith 1968; Tunnell 1977; Uhl 1966), and that when laboratory settings are employed, research procedures be altered to take into account the real-world dimensions of the phenomenon under investigation (Fromkin and Streufert 1975; Ray 1977).

When effects application is the goal, the above concerns are well-founded. Correspondence between the subjects and the setting used in the research and those in the real world is a necessary condition for effects application. To the extent that the use of student or other convenience samples and laboratory settings undermines this correspondence, applicability of the effects observed is limited. Thus, procedures that enhance the match between the research environment and the real world, such as the use of relevant representative samples and field settings, are appropriate when effects application is desired.

Yet, when the goal is theory application, the call for research subjects and settings representative of the real world is inappropriate. The foundation of theory application is rigorous theory testing. It is a mistake to assume that the people and events in a theory test must reflect people and events in some real-world situation. Rather, the test circumstance simply must provide the strongest test of the theory possible. Features of the test are only constrained by the requirement that they not undermine the degree to which any demonstrated construct relationship can be generalized to other settings not ruled out by the theory. Any sample is relevant if it permits operationalization within the domain of the theory. Homogeneous convenience samples may thus be employed in theory research. In fact, homogeneous samples are preferred because their use enables more precise predictions and enhances statistical-conclusion validity, thereby increasing the rigor of the theory test.

Similarly, laboratory settings generally are desirable in theory testing research. The controlled environment of the laboratory typically allows the researcher to employ true experimental designs, to tailor variables to abstract theoretical constructs, and to minimize extraneous sources of variation. These features lead to high internal, construct, and statistical-conclusion validity, thereby providing a strong theory test.

The only damaging criticisms of the laboratory setting are those that specify why its unrealistic features might operate as plausible threats to internal, construct, or statistical-conclusion validity. For example, if the artificiality of the laboratory facilitates participants in guessing the experimental hypothesis, then internal validity may be threatened and the theory test weakened. If valid arguments can be made to this effect, generalizability of the observed construct relationship is impaired. Otherwise, the use of insulated environments, standardized procedures, and other "unrealistic" features may constitute perfectly acceptable theory-testing procedures.

Recommendations for alternatives to the controlled laboratory setting, such as the suggestions that true experiments be conducted in field settings or that real-world features be introduced into the laboratory, are detrimental to achieving a rigorous theory test. Conducting true experiments in field settings is likely to reduce internal validity because there are numerous obstacles to forming and maintaining randomly constituted groups in the field (Cook and Campbell 1975). Construct validity also may be lower because tailoring operationalizations to abstract constructs may be difficult in the field. In addition, statistical-conclusion validity is likely to suffer because the field affords less opportunity for using standardized procedures and controlling stimuli.

Likewise, attempts to incorporate real-world features into the laboratory may undermine construct and statistical-conclusion validity. These features can represent plausible sources of distortion regarding the theoretical labeling of the independent variables, as well as uncontrolled sources of error variance in dependent variable responses (Aronson and Carlsmith 1968; Cook and Campbell 1975; Webster and Kervin 1971). Thus, because these strategies could potentially decrease the internal, construct, and statistical-conclusion validity of research results, they should be avoided in theory-testing research whenever possible. Their implementation could compromise the severity of the theory test.

The conclusion is not that variation in people and events found in the real world is irrelevant to theory application, however. On the contrary, it simply assumes a different role than in effects application. In theory application, accepted theory is used to design an intervention. This intervention, then, must be shown to perform successfully in the face of variability that it is likely to encounter in the real world. To test the performance of an intervention, it may be implemented in an uncontrolled environment such as a field setting, or it may be exposed to extreme levels of important variables in a controlled (laboratory) environment. But, as we observed earlier, the test environment need not be *representative* of any particular real-world situation (as is the case when effects application is sought); it only must expose the intervention to stress that could cause it to fail. Repeated failure of interventions based on a particular theory may suggest the need for a better explanation. However, testing procedures for any new theory remain controlled. The applicability of an explanation is never improved by weakening its test.

Philosophies Underlying the Two Types of Applicability

Clarification of the procedural implications of the two types of applicability does much to resolve the confusion in the methodological literature. The distinction between effects application and theory application is more than a procedural one, however. Also at stake are two basic philosophies of how to go about application. Discussion rarely gets beyond the vague perception of research pursuing effects application as "intuitively practical" and research pursuing theory application as "academically respectable." Not surprisingly, many studies end up trying to embrace both, with little appreciation that they represent different philosophies. Accordingly, it is appropriate to end the present discussion with an explicit statement of the philosophical rationale underlying each approach to application.

Traditionally, the application of effects has rested philosophically on the principle of induction. The notion that observed effects will be repeated in the real world, given the use of correspondence procedures, is an inductive argument. The observation that something has happened is said to imply that it (or something similar) will happen again.

It must be pointed out, however, that, although intuitively plausible, induction turns out, on close examination, to be an extremely hollow form of argument. Induction actually has no basis in logic. With any logical argument, true premises should yield true conclusions. Yet even though the sun has come up every day so far, whether or not it comes up tomorrow is not a matter of logical necessity. True premises may yield a false conclusion. Induction is not a logical argument.

The intuitive appeal of an inductive argument is such that many researchers are willing to subscribe to it as a matter of experience, if not logic. After all, the sun appears to come up every day. Even the appeal from experience, however, is suspect. It amounts to using induction to justify itself. Because induction has seemed to work before, it will work in the future. The circularity of such reasoning is devastating in the case of effects application. The researcher has only a few observations on which to base conclusions. Conclusions about the real world must really be based on an uncritical faith in induction rather than any experience with observations.

It might seem that the problem of induction could be escaped by resorting to probabilistic conclusions. Given observed effects, the occurrence of a real-world event is not proven, but it is made more highly probable. Under any standard concept of probability, however, this turns out to be not very helpful. In principle, the researcher could observe an effect an infinite number of times. The number of observations actually available is obviously finite. Thus, the probability of any effect must be zero if the number of possible observations of the effect is infinite. Probabilities are not meaningful in the context of infinite possibility.

Our conclusion must be that effects application rests on very soft grounds. While this approach appears to be the epitome of rigorous application, it is mostly a matter of blind faith. Induction itself cannot support going from observed effects to conclusions about the real world.

Effects application might better be viewed as reasoning by analogy. There is no logical principle involved. Rather, outcomes observed in the research are related to outcomes of the real world. If the research conditions seem to be analogous to events in the real world, then the analogy is completed by concluding that observed effects will hold in the real world. Reasoning by analogy depends, not on logic, but on the researcher's insight. Although correspondence procedures may provide some basis for analogy, this process is ultimately qualitative in nature.[10] This argument cannot be pursued here; however, it is our opinion that effects application could be improved by the increased use of qualitative methods (Calder 1977).

In contrast to effects application, theory application rests on the logical principle that it is possible for observed effects to contradict a theory, thereby falsifying it. Theories are tested in situations where they can possibly fail. Only those that survive these tests, then, are accepted and are candidates for application.

The logical principle of falsification requires that theory testing be bound to formal methodological procedures. These procedures are designed to expose the theory to refutation, and should follow directly from the theoretical explanation itself. It is only where theory fully dictates observation that observation can contradict theory. Thus, qualitative methods are not essential in testing theory.

The falsification procedures employed to test theory are not sufficient to ensure successful theory application, however. Accepted theories can provide only a framework for designing interventions. These interventions also must be tested before they are applied in the real world. Again the logic of falsification is invoked. Research procedures are designed to expose the intervention to refutation. These procedures should follow directly from the underlying theory *and* the real-world circumstances that the intervention will face. If the intervention performs as predicted by the theory, it may be implemented. If, however, the intervention does not lead to expected outcomes, it must be modified. Careful assessment of theoretical and nontheoretical variables as part of the testing process may provide insight for this redesign.

Application of theory often stops short of efforts to falsify interventions. It is mistakenly assumed that accepted theories will yield usable interventions without further work. But, whereas such theories do provide efficient frameworks for design, testing the intervention designed is still necessary. Theory application in consumer research would be greatly improved by recognition of the need for, and role of, intervention falsification procedures.[11]

Conclusion

Consumer researchers pursue two distinct types of generalizability. One involves the application of specific effects observed in a research setting. The other involves the application of a general scientific theory. Although both types of generalization are tenable, it is important to determine which will be the primary goal prior to designing a study. Effects applica-

10. See Wright and Kriewall (1980) for an empirical demonstration of the need for effects research to capture individuals' "state-of-mind" in the real-world setting of interest.

11. O'Shaughnessy and Ryan's (1979) discussion of the distinction between science and technology in some ways parallels and complements our discussion of the difference between theory testing and intervention design and testing.

tion and theory application are based on different philosophical assumptions and, therefore, require different research procedures.

Effects application rests on the presumption of correspondence between the research and some real-world situation of interest. If these two situations are analogous, then the outcomes observed in one can be expected to occur in the other. When effects application is the goal, the research subjects, setting, and variables examined must be representative of their real-world counterparts. Any procedures likely to impair the match between the research and the real world, such as convenience samples and laboratory settings, should be avoided. Because objective correspondence is impossible to achieve fully, and can never ensure equivalent *experience*, qualitative insight may assist the researcher in judging whether or not the research experience matches that of the real world.

Theory application rests on the acceptance of the scientific explanation itself. This acceptance is determined by the logical principle of falsification. Theories that survive rigorous efforts at disproof are accepted. The only requirement for research testing theory is that it provide the strongest test possible. Because homogeneous samples and laboratory settings often lead to a stronger test of the theory than heterogeneous samples and field settings, they may be preferred in this type of research. But, theory tests alone are not sufficient for theory application. Accepted theories must be calibrated to the real world through the design and testing of interventions.

In sum, the research procedures optimal for effects application and theory application are incompatible. This does not mean that there cannot be synergy between research pursuing each type of applicability. It does mean that research procedures can only be evaluated with reference to the type of generalizability being pursued. To do otherwise only leads to needless criticism and poor communication within the discipline.

References

Albert, Bernard (1967), "Non-Businessmen as Surrogates for Businessmen in Behavioral Experiments," *Journal of Business*, 40, 203-7.

Aronson, Elliot, and Carlsmith, J. Merrill (1968), "Experimentation in Social Psychology," in *Handbook of Social Psychology, Vol. 2*, eds. Gardner Lindzey and Elliot Aronson, Reading, MA: Addison-Wesley Publishing Co.

Bagozzi, Richard (1979), *Causal Models in Marketing*, New York: John Wiley & Sons.

Banks, Seymour (1965), *Experimentation in Marketing*, New York: McGraw-Hill Book Co.

Brunswik, Egon (1956), *Perception and the Representative Design of Psychological Experiments*, 2nd edn., Berkeley: University of California Press.

Caffyn, J. M. (1964), "Psychological Laboratory Techniques in Copy Research," *Journal of Advertising Research*, 4, 45-50.

Calder, Bobby J. (1977), "Focus Groups and the Nature of Qualitative Marketing Research," *Journal of Marketing Research*, 14, 353-64.

Campbell, Donald, and Fiske, Donald (1959), "Convergent and Discriminant Validation by the Multitrait-Multimethod Matrix," *Psychological Bulletin*, 56, 81-105.

——, and Stanley, John (1966), *Experimental and Quasi-experimental Designs for Research*, Chicago: Rand McNally & Co.

Cartwright, Dorwin, and Zander, Alvin (1968), *Group Dynamics*, New York: Harper & Row.

Cook, Thomas, and Campbell, Donald (1975), "The Design and Conduct of Experiments and Quasi-experiments in Field Settings," in *Handbook of Industrial and Organizational Research*, ed. Martin Dunnette, Chicago: Rand McNally & Co.

Cox, Keith, and Enis, Ben (1969), *Experimentation for Marketing Decisions*, Scranton, PA: International Textbook Co.

Cunningham, William, Anderson, W. Thomas Jr., and Murphy, John (1974), "Are Students Real People?" *Journal of Business*, 48, 399-409.

Ellsworth, Phoebe (1977), "From Abstract Ideas to Concrete Instances: Some Guidelines for Choosing Natural Research Settings," *American Psychologist*, 32, 604-15.

Enis, Ben, Cox, Keith, and Stafford, James (1972), "Students as Subjects in Consumer Behavior Experiments," *Journal of Marketing Research*, 9, 72-74.

Ferber, Robert (1977), "Research by Convenience," *Journal of Consumer Research*, 4, 57-58.

Fromkin, Howard, and Streufert, Siegfried (1975), "Laboratory Experimentation," in *Handbook of Industrial and Organizational Psychology*, ed. Marvin Dunnette, Chicago: Rand McNally & Co., pp. 415-63.

Gardner, David (1970), "The Distraction Hypothesis in Marketing," *Journal of Advertising Research*, 10, 25-30.

Green, Paul (1966), "The Role of Experimental Research in Marketing: Its Potentials and Limitations," in *Science, Technology, and Marketing*, ed. Raymond Haas, Chicago: American Marketing Association, pp. 483-94.

Greenberg, Allan (1967), "Is Communications Research Really Worthwhile?" *Journal of Marketing*, 31, 48-50.

Khera, Inder, and Benson, James (1970), "Are Students Really Poor Substitutes for Businessmen in Behavioral Research?" *Journal of Marketing Research,* 7, 529–32.

Kruglanski, Arie (1973), "Much Ado About the 'Volunteer Artifacts,'" *Journal of Personality and Social Psychology,* 28, 348–54.

—— (1975), "The Two Meanings of External Invalidity," *Human Relations,* 28, 653–59.

Kuhn, Thomas (1970), *The Structure of Scientific Revolutions,* Chicago: University of Chicago Press.

Lakatos, Imre (1970), "Falsification and the Methodology of Science Research Programs," in *Criticism and the Growth of Knowledge,* eds. Imre Lakatos and Alan Musgrave, London: Cambridge University Press.

McGuire, William (1969), "Theory-oriented Research in Natural Settings: The Best of Both Worlds for Social Psychology," in *Interdisciplinary Relationships in the Social Sciences,* eds. M. Sherif and C. Sherif, Chicago: Aldine Publishing.

McNemar, Quinn (1946), "Opinion-Attitude Methodology," *Psychological Bulletin,* 43, 289–374.

Opp, Karl-Dieter (1970), "The Experimental Method in the Social Sciences: Some Problems and Proposals for its More Effective Use," *Quality and Quantity,* 34, 39–54.

Orne, Martin (1962), "On the Social Psychology of the Psychological Experiment with Particular Reference to Demand Characteristics and Other Implications," *American Psychologist,* 17, 776–83.

O'Shaughnessy, John, and Ryan, Mile (1979), "Marketing, Science and Technology," in *Conceptual and Theoretical Developments in Marketing,* eds. O. C. Ferrell, Stephen Brown, and Charles Lamb, Chicago: American Marketing Association.

Park, C. Whan, and Lessig, V. Parker (1977), "Students and Housewives: Differences in Susceptibility to Reference Group Influence," *Journal of Consumer Research,* 4, 102–10.

Popper, Karl R. (1959), *The Logic of Scientific Discovery,* New York: Harper Torchbooks.

—— (1963), *Conjectures and Refutations,* New York: Harper Torchbooks.

Ray, Michael (1977), "When Does Consumer Information Processing Actually Have Anything to Do with Consumer Information Processing?" in *Advances in Consumer Research, Vol. 4,* ed. William Perreault, Jr., Atlanta: Association for Consumer Research.

Riecken, Henry (1962), "A Program for Research on Experiments in Social Psychology," in *Decisions, Values, and Groups, Vol. 2,* ed. Norman Washburn, New York: Pergamon Press, pp. 25–41.

Rosenthal, Robert, and Rosnow, Ralph (1969a), *Artifact in Behavioral Research,* New York: Academic Press.

——, and Rosnow, Ralph (1969b), "The Volunteer Subject," in *Artifact in Behavioral Research,* eds. Robert Rosenthal and Ralph Rosnow, New York: Academic Press, pp. 61–112.

Ross, J., and Smith, P. (1968), "Orthodox Experimental Designs," in *Methodology in Social Research,* ed. Hubert Blalock and Ann Blalock, San Francisco: McGraw-Hill Book Co.

Sawyer, Alan (1975), "Demand Artifacts in Laboratory Experiments in Consumer Research," *Journal of Consumer Research,* 1, 20–30.

——, Worthing, Parker, and Sendak, Paul (1979), "The Role of Laboratory Experiments to Test Marketing Strategies," *Journal of Marketing,* 43, 60–7.

Schultz, Duane (1969), "The Human Subject in Psychological Research," *Psychological Bulletin,* 72, 214–28.

Sheth, Jagdish (1970), "Are There Differences in Dissonance Reduction Behavior Between Students and Housewives?" *Journal of Marketing Research,* 7, 243–45.

Shuptrine, F. Kelly (1975), "On the Validity of Using Students as Subjects in Consumer Behavior Investigations," *Journal of Business,* 48, 383–90.

Silverman, Irwin (1968), "Role-Related Behavior of Subjects in Laboratory Studies of Attitude Change," *Journal of Personality and Social Psychology,* 8, 343–48.

Tunnell, Gilbert (1977), "Three Dimensions of Naturalness: An Expanded Definition of Field Research," *Psychological Bulletin,* 84, 426–77.

Uhl, Kenneth (1966), "Field Experimentation: Some Problems, Pitfalls, and Perspectives," in *Science, Technology, and Marketing,* ed. Raymond Haas, Chicago: American Marketing Association, pp. 561–72.

Venkatesen, M. (1967), "Laboratory Experiments in Marketing: The Experimenter Effect," *Journal of Marketing Research,* 4, 142–47.

Webb, Eugene, Campbell, Donald, Schwartz, Richard, and Sechrest, Lee (1966), *Unobtrusive Measures: Nonreactive Research in the Social Sciences,* Chicago: Rand McNally & Co.

Webster, Murray, and Kervin, John (1971), "Artificiality in Experimental Sociology," *Canadian Review of Sociology and Anthropology,* 8, 263–72.

Winer, B. J. (1971), *Statistical Principles in Experimental Design,* New York: McGraw-Hill Book Co.

Wright, Peter, and Kriewall, Mary Ann (1980), "State-of-Mind Effects on the Accuracy with which Utility Functions Predict Marketplace Choice," *Journal of Marketing Research,* 17, 277–94.

READING 34

Making Marketing Research Accountable

Jeffrey Gandz and Thomas W. Whipple

Analysis of the potential payoffs from a proposed research project, during a time of tight budgetary constraints, proved helpful in obtaining the required funds and improved the quality of the research itself.

Introduction

Marketing research managers who regularly participate in the development of research projects, present them to management for approval, and make recommendations based on the results are faced with new constraints today. The depressed economy of the 1970's has caused many companies to reexamine their policies on marketing research expenditures. The trimming of excess items from budgets, tighter financial controls, hiring restrictions, and the inflated cost of additional staff all contribute to a reappraisal and general "belt-tightening." The need to justify expenditures in terms of their impact on the "bottom line" has moved from good business practice to an imperative. The "selling" of proposed projects to management, many of whom have a limited appreciation for marketing research, has become more difficult and therefore requires better planning and presentation skills.

Company managements must be assured that every dollar spent on research is seeking to maximize the degree of actionable information it produces. In particular, marketers should attempt to explore more thoroughly the possible outcomes of research before engaging in it and to determine the value of the added information. Then, money spent on research can be viewed as a sound investment, not as a necessary expense.

The authors describe an approach for planning and conducting research designed to show the profit consequences of alternative business strategies. The example used illustrates how the impact of hypothetical price/market share relationships on brand profit can be investigated to determine whether it is necessary to conduct consumer research for empirical identification and modeling of the relationship.

Project Development

The development, evaluation, and execution of the authors' approach to research are presented in sequence with the project. Although the procedure was designed for a specific project, it is generalizable for a wide range of research problems. Such a disciplined approach should improve research efficiency and effectiveness. The stages in the procedure are described in the context of a research project conducted in 1975 for a brand of fast food product, "Meaty." The illustration, financial data, and research results are diguised to prevent competitive disadvantages.

Background

Meaty is an instant food product manufactured under license by a co-packer and sold to the food trade through specialized food brokers. The costs involved in this co-packing mode of manufacture, coupled with the high commissions paid to the brokers, resulted in extremely poor profit margins. Despite achieving excellent market penetration, reaching a 20% share after three years, the brand had been con-

Reprinted by permission of the American Marketing Association, from the *Journal of Marketing Research,* 14:2 May 1977, 202–208.

sistently unprofitable. Its unprofitability had not concerned management in the early years because Meaty was viewed as a springboard for penetration of the food market by the company. By the end of the fourth year, however, it became clear that additional unprofitable years would not be acceptable.

Problem Definition

The gross profit margin had to be increased from the present 20% to at least 35% to make the brand profitable. In addition, the increase had to be achieved with minimal share loss to make the volume of profit worth the investment required to achieve it.

The following four factors were identified as contributors to the brand's losses:

1. A very high cost of goods, resulting from the use of a co-packer for manufacturing rather than a company-owned facility.
2. A pricing level on Meaty which was set 5–10% higher than the prices of competitive brands. The price premium was justified on the basis of superior packaging format for Meaty. However, it was believed that brands in this market were extremely price elastic and that any unilateral upward movement in price would result in substantial share loss.
3. Current high levels of advertising and trade promotion support could not be reduced because such activity was required to remain competitive. Trade support, in terms of distribution, pricing, and merchandising of the brand at store level, was dependent on high advertising and promotional activity.
4. Sales brokers would have to be used for the foreseeable future because the company's own salesforce had neither the training nor the slack capacity to take on the Meaty line.

Alternative Solutions

Three proposals for increasing the profit margin were considered. The problems due to high cost of goods could be alleviated by maintaining market share and either moving to "in-house" manufacture or raising selling prices. Alternatively, the company could raise prices and accept a reduction in market share, which eventually would lead to a "milking" of the business to the point where Meaty would be discontinued. Other solutions, such as selling the brand to a food company, were ruled out by corporate policies.

A manufacturing facility could be built for an amortized cost of $175,000 per year for 10 years. In-house manufacturing would reduce the variable cost of Meaty from $3.55 per case to $2.75. Given current share levels and market growth trends, this alternative may lead to the brand at least breaking even in operating profit terms. Any reduction in volume, however, could result in substantial underutilized investment in fixed overhead. Cost reduction through in-house manufacture, though it could lead to the brand "breaking even," may not result in a profit-contributing brand. Instead, marketing costs would be incurred for a brand that is not contributing to profitability.

Selling prices could be raised, but what would the impact be on market share and sales volume? Because the economics of in-house manufacture would vary with unit volume, any significant volume loss could severely compromise the lowered cost of goods obtained by the investment in manufacturing facilities.

Project Evaluation

The best combination of price and manufacturing mode depends on the degree of elasticity of consumer loyalty to the brand and the speed with which competitors would respond to a price increase by Meaty. Historical precedent indicated that competitive response probably would be slow, if it happened at all. Thus, the main research problem was to predict the probable consumer response to an increased selling price.

The empirical question was to determine the relationship between the share of market held by Meaty and its price in relation to its major competitors, other factors being equal. If such items as trade discount margins are held constant and retailers are assumed to maintain a steady markup based on their purchasing price, then the shelf price differential is related to manufacturer's net list price as a constant proportion. If market size and trend are taken into account, the net list price can be related to profit. The exact calculations depend on the company's accounting system.

If the relationship between market share and price could be established, then it would be possible to calculate brand profit under different conditions of manufacturing costs, market sizes, and expendi-

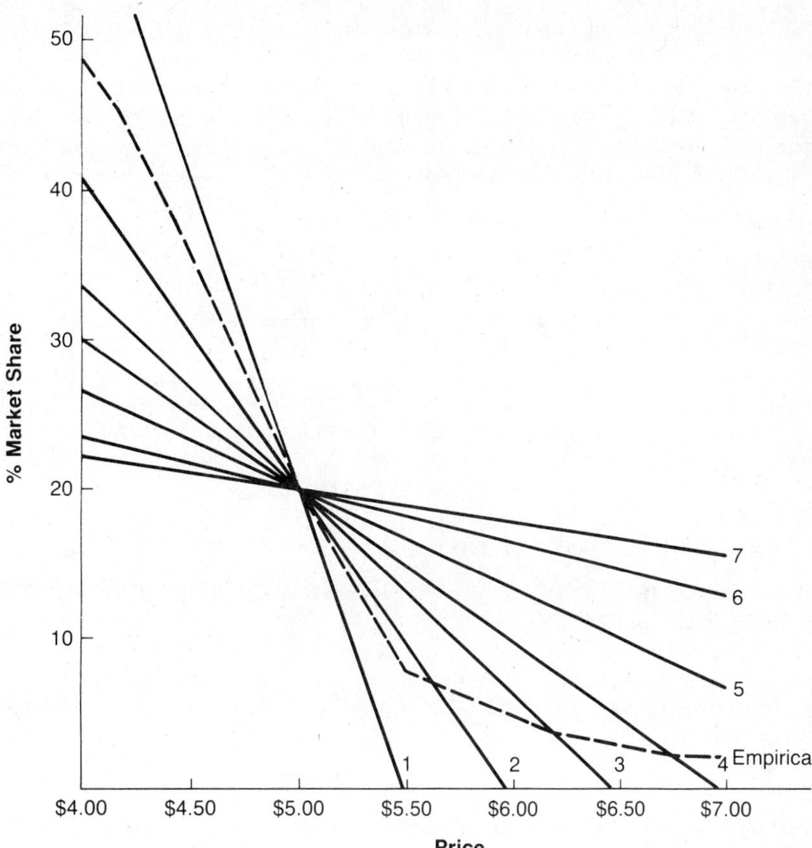

FIGURE 1
Hypothetical and Empirical Relationships Between Price and Market Share

tures. The combination of pricing and manufacturing mode that optimized profit could be selected and recommended.

Evaluation of Alternative Solutions

The determination of empirical price/market share relationships is often time-consuming and expensive. In addition, the results need to be qualified because of the extremely artificial conditions under which testing usually is done. To determine (1) whether such research was warranted, (2) what types of action should result from the research if it was undertaken, and (3) what specific questions the research should seek to answer, the marketing research manager decided to investigate the impact of different hypothetical price/market share relationships on brand profit.

Seven linear functions, representing possible relationships between the price of Meaty and its market share, were drawn as in Figure 1. Function 1 represents the most price elastic relationship whereas function 7 represents the most brand loyal or inelastic relationship. The decision to use linear functions, despite an *a priori* assumption of nonlinearity, was made consciously. The marketing research manager knew he would face enough difficulty without having to explain complex curvilinear function to senior management.

Because a large number of possible price/market share relationships needed to be investigated and analyzed, a simple BASIC program was written to calculate market share from each of the seven hypothetical functions. Different expenditures resulted in a profit and loss statement at each price/market share level. A typical computer run, including both input instructions and summary output information, is shown in Table 1.

More than 100 computer runs were conducted to investigate the various elements of the pricing decision. Manufacturing costs, commission structures, market sizes, and advertising and promotion expenditures were varied and the impact of price on profit was determined [7]. The actual relationship between price and market share remained unknown.

The results enabled comparisons to be made under the assumptions of different scenarios. For example, what would be the difference in profit if price were established at $5.50 per case and co-packing were used rather than manufacturing in a company-owned plant? If function 6 represented the price/market share relationship the results would

TABLE 1
Typical Computer Run

```
GET BRDSIM
RUN
BRDSIM
DO YOU WANT TO CHANGE VALUES FOR M,L,C,O,A,Z,K, (Y/N)?Y
ENTER VALUES FOR M,L,C,O,A,Z,K?1800,0,2.75,175,100,50,20
ENTER PRICE RANGE–START,STOP,STEP?4.80,5.20,.10
CURVE NUMBER TO START?1
SUMMARY CHART ONLY (Y/N)?Y
```

PRICING ANALYSIS WITH VARIABLE SHARE

MARKET SIZE (M CASES)	=	1800
VAR.COG (PER CASE)	=	2.75
FIXED OVERHEAD ($M)	=	175
ADVERTISING ($M)	=	100
CONS. PROM. ($M)	=	50
TRADE DISCOUNT (%)	=	9.0
VOL. REBATE (%)	=	1.0
BROKER COMM. (%)	=	4.5
FREIGHT (CASE)	=	.25
MARKETING RESEARCH ($M)	=	20
CASH DISCOUNT (%)	=	0.9

		Curve Number						
	Price	1	2	3	4	5	6	7
GROSS SALES		2540.2	2177.3	2056.3	2004.5	1935.4	1979.3	1954.1
MKT. SHARE	4.80	29.4	25.2	23.8	23.2	22.4	21.7	21.5
OP/G PROFIT		216.4	136.2	109.4	99.0	82.7	70.1	54.8
GROSS SALES		2222.6	2037.4	1975.5	1949.2	1913.9	1994.9	1872.5
MKT. SHARE	4.90	25.2	23.1	22.4	22.1	21.7	21.4	21.2
OP/G PROFIT		174.6	131.3	116.8	110.6	102.4	95.6	92.7
GROSS SALES		1890.0	1890.0	1890.0	1990.0	1890.0	1990.0	1990.0
MKT. SHARE	5.00	21.0	21.0	21.0	21.0	21.0	21.0	21.0
OP/G PROFIT		119.9	119.9	119.9	119.9	119.9	119.9	119.9
GROSS SALES		1542.2	1735.0	1799.3	1926.8	1863.5	1993.8	1906.7
MKT. SHARE	5.10	16.8	18.9	19.6	19.9	20.3	20.6	20.8
OP/G PROFIT		52.5	102.2	118.8	125.9	135.4	143.2	146.5
GROSS SALES		1179.3	1572.5	1703.5	1759.7	1834.6	1996.3	1922.5
MKT. SHARE	5.20	12.6	16.8	18.2	19.8	19.6	20.3	20.5
OP/G PROFIT		27.7	78.1	113.4	129.5	148.6	165.3	172.3

TABLE 2
Operating Profit (Loss) at Different Price Levels ($000)

	Curve 1		*Curve 3*		*Curve 6*	
Price	*Co-packer*	*In-house*	*Co-packer*	*In-house*	*Co-packer*	*In-house*
$4.00	($642)	$91	($432)	($103)	($355)	($174)
$4.50	(165)	265	(167)	62	(167)	(13)
5.00	(8)	120	(8)	120	(8)	120
5.50	(170)[a]	(345)[b]	45	72	124	225
6.00	(170)	(345)	(9)	(83)	227	302
6.50	(170)	(345)	(170)	(345)	303	350
7.00	(170)	(345)	(170)	(345)	350	370

a. Maximum possible loss at 0 sales = $170,000 for advertising, promotion, and research.
b. Maximum possible loss at 0 sales = $170,000 + $175,000 for fixed plant assets.

be a $124,000 profit for the co-packing mode but a $225,000 profit for in-house manufacture. However, if function 1 represented the real relationship, a loss of $345,000 would be realized with in-house manufacture compared with a loss of $170,000 if a co-packer were used. Tables 2 and 3, which show the "co-packer versus in-house" decision for curves 1, 3, and 6, illustrate the type of analysis performed.

In addition to the construction of scenarios, this form of investigation facilitated a systematic determination of the dimensions and boundaries of the pricing and manufacturing decisions. Because of the ability to effect "instant" financial evaluations, the decision parameters were investigated carefully to allow alternative strategies to be mapped out and considered. Table 4 summarizes the relative profit potential from building a manufacturing facility.

Research Questions

The price/market share analyses suggested two unanswered questions which required empirical research:

1. What market share would Meaty be expected to achieve at different relevant price levels?
2. How much is the "unique" packaging of Meaty worth to the brand in terms of added consumer loyalty?

TABLE 3
Profitable Price Ranges

	Curve 1		*Curve 3*		*Curve 6*	
Profit Criteria	*Co-packer*	*In-house*	*Co-packer*	*In-house*	*Co-packer*	*In-house*
Profit ⩾ 0:						
From	—	$4.00	$5.10	$4.30	$5.40	$5.10
To	—	5.10	5.90	5.70	7.00+	7.00+
Profit ⩾ 100M:						
From	—	4.00	—	4.80	5.40	5.00
To	—	5.00	—	5.30	7.00+	7.00+
Profit ⩾ 15%:						
From	—	—	—	—	6.30	5.90
To	—	—	—	—	7.00+	7.00+
Maximum	5.00	4.50	5.50	5.00	7.00	7.00
profit	(8)[a]	265	45	120	350	370

a. Profit (loss) at profit-maximizing price in $000.

TABLE 4
Advantage (Disadvantage) of Building Manufacturing Facility

	Curve Number						
Price	*1*	*2*	*3*	*4*	*5*	*6*	*7*
$4.00	733[a]	430	329	286	228	181	151
4.50	430	279	229	207	178	154	144
5.00	128	128	128	128	128	128	128
5.50	(175)	(24)	27	48	99	101	111
6.00	(175)	(175)	(74)	(30)	27	75	94
6.50	(175)	(175)	(175)	(111)	(24)	47	77
7.00	(175)	(175)	(175)	(175)	(74)	20	62

a. Difference between in-house and co-packer profit or loss in $000.

Financial Evaluation of Research

The estimated cost of empirically determining the relationship between price and market share was $30,000. This figure could be amortized over several brands to result in a cost for Meaty of $18,000. The consequences of a wrong decision, based on faulty assumptions about the price/market share relationship, depend on the amount of price increase and the mode of manufacture. Table 4 shows that the opportunity cost of a wrong decision would reach $733,000. Further investigation into the the uncertain "costs" of a wrong decision was deemed unwarranted at this stage because the downside risk probably could be reduced substantially by a research expenditure of only $18,000.

Project Execution

The major objective of the research was to identify and model the relationship between the price differential of Meaty and its major competitor (which had 50% share of market) and the market share held by Meaty. Originally, the empirical research plan called for a field experiment on the effect of alternate prices, in different markets, on market share. However, it became evident, after discussions with persons in the retail trade, that control over price differentials could not be exercised with enough precision or maintained for a sufficient period of time to determine the share elasticity. Consequently, a consumer survey technique was used to obtain the pricing and market share data.

After a lengthy consideration of alternative survey vehicles, the data collection method chosen was a hierarchical rank-order choice procedure. This procedure is a variation of the trade-off technique described in [5] and later applied in [6]. An overview of several applications of conjoint measurement methods is contained in [4].

A clustered random sample of 195 female heads of household, who had used the product category within the previous month, was selected from a large metropolitan area.[1] After answering qualifying questions, the survey respondent was put into a hypothetical shopping situation where she was shown photographs of the two brands side by side. Each photograph was accompanied by a price label indicating parity pricing at 40 cents. The respondent was asked to indicate which brand she would buy at the indicated price. Hierarchical brand-price preferences were obtained by increasing the price of the brand chosen by 5 cents after each response and asking the respondent to choose again. This sequential hierarchical choice procedure was continued until the price range of 40 to 70 cents was exhausted or until the respondent indicated that she would not buy any of the brands and would seek a substitute or discontinue usage of the product.[2]

The estimated brand share for Meaty was calculated by summing the first choices for Meaty, at escalating price differentials between Meaty and its major competitor, across all respondents. Because of the extreme fragmentation of the 30% of the market not held by the two leading brands, it was assumed that the minor brands would be priced at the same level as Meaty's major competitor, the market leader. The brand share data, therefore, were adjusted by deflating Meaty's share by 30% to reflect this assumption.

Research Findings

The choice procedure allowed brand choices to be made at a number of absolute price levels. Choice was found to be a function of price difference and

1. The research was conducted by Market Facts of Canada, Limited.

2. The decision to investigate an extended price range was influenced by the extremely rapid inflation in food prices during 1975. Market share predictions based on the extreme price levels were viewed with skepticism, while providing full opportunity for the curve to flatten.

was unaffected by absolute level within the price range explored.

After the adjustment for the total number of brands in the market, the derived relationship between price and market share for Meaty is typified by the data in Table 5. The results indicate low brand loyalty resulting from a high degree of price sensitivity. The empirically derived relationship is most similar to the hypothetical relationship depicted by function 2 in Figure 1.

Because marketing applications of conjoint measurement techniques are relatively new, there are few reports of the validation of conjoint measurement predictions by use of actual behavior [1] and other analysis techniques [2, 3]. However, these studies provided sufficient evidence to conclude that the empirically derived market-share curves accurrately reflect actual market behavior. Concerted effort to reduce "game playing" and to assure that the first-choice procedure was perceived as realistic increased the face validity of the task and the resulting data.

The response to one of the questions asked during the interview shed light on the reason for the high degree of price sensitivity evidenced. When asked how much of a premium they would pay for the unique packaging of Meaty, assuming it could be purchased in conventional packaging, most respondents indicated "no price premium" (see Table 6).

The final stage of the research was to replace the hypothetical linear price/market share relationships with the data from the consumer study. The

TABLE 5
Market Share and Operating Profit of Meaty When Competitive Brands Are Held at a 45¢ Retail Shelf Price

Shelf Price	*Equivalent Net Case List Price*	*Market Share (%)*	*Operating Profit (Loss)*[a]	
			Co-packer	*In-house*
40¢	$4.00	49	(537)	(6)
45	4.50	35	(166)	163
50	5.00	20	(15)	98
55	5.50	8	(47)	(107)
60	6.00	5	(55)	(158)
65	6.50	3	(78)	(210)
70	7.00	2	(94)	(240)

a. $000.

TABLE 6
Preference for Unique Over Conventional Packaging

Price Differential	*Percentage (N = 145)*
No premium price	55.9
At a 5¢ premium	31.6
At a 10¢ premium	12.8
At a 15¢ premium	7.5

survey results were input with the assumption that the slope of the curve between each price point was linear. This assumption, in effect, resulted in the price range of $4.00 to $7.00 per case being divided into six separate linear functions which approximated the relationship over the full price range.

The major findings are presented in the last two columns of Table 5 and are portrayed best by the plots of the profit/price relationship for the two manufacturing alternatives, co-packer or in-house (Fig. 2). The co-packer alternative is not profitable at any price, producing a minimum loss of $6,100 at $5.20 per case. In contrast, in-house manufacturing is profitable over the price range of $4.00 to $5.30. Maximum profits of $169,000 are achieved at a case price of $4.60.

Recommendation

In view of the findings, the best course of action was to invest in a manufacturing facility and to price at the present level of $5.00 per case. The decision not to lower the price to the $4.60 optimum level indicated by the research was based on the problems which might ensue if the major competitors reduced their prices in response. The potential risk of reducing Meaty profits of $98,000, with a 20% market share and a case price of $5.00, was investigated by use of a version of the computer program. The results showed that if all prices in the market dropped so that Meaty was priced at $4.60, still 11% higher than competition, its share still would be 20%. However, Meaty profits would fall to only $6,000. Because management believed that competition was more likely than not to lower prices correspondingly following Meaty's lead, the current $5.00 per case price level should be maintained. The upside benefit of obtaining optimal profits of $169,000 was not great enough to overcome the downside risk of reducing profits from $98,000 to only $6,000.

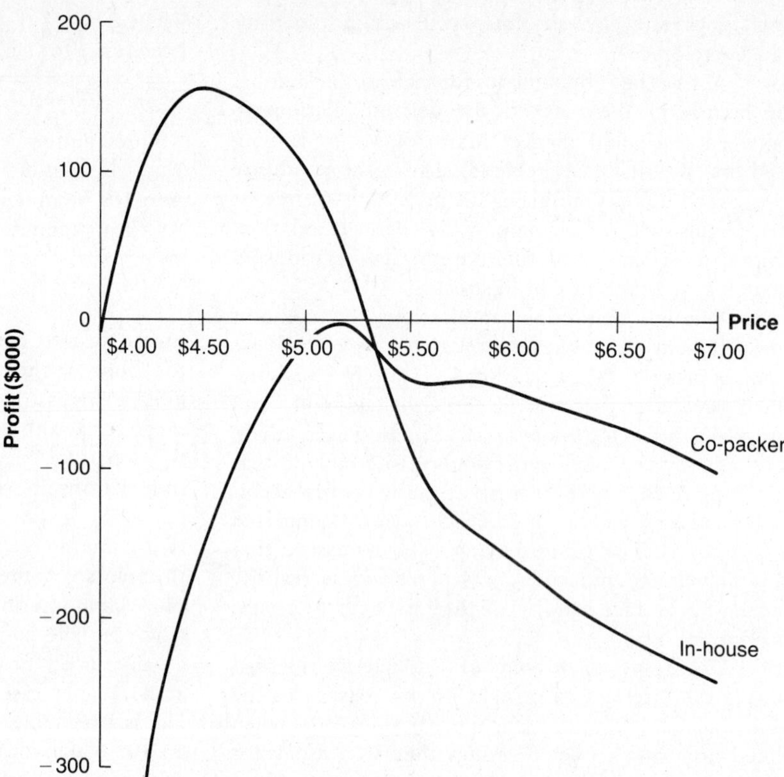

FIGURE 2
Profit/Price Relationship from Empirical Research

Conclusion

Not all research projects can be defined as clearly as the one described, nor is it possible to predict the range of possible outcomes for all types of research. Yet, as effectiveness and efficiency are increasingly considered virtues in themselves in the conduct of goal-directed business activity, marketing research should be oriented in a similar fashion.

The tools and techniques of the analysis and quantification of decision outcomes are no longer solely in the domain of management scientists. Most marketing research managers today have received the training necessary to do the analysis described here. What often is lacking is the insistence, on the part of senior managements, that requests for funds for such activities as marketing research be fully supported by analyses that clearly identify the purposes of the research, explore the range of outcomes, and establish outcome-dependent strategies with estimated financial implications.

As the priorities of and constraints on senior managements change because of economic and other environmental shifts, marketing research managers must be prepared to accept the additional responsibility. Thus better, more effective and efficient research will be done. In some cases, proposed research will not be undertaken; in others, problems may be identified before commitment is made to unalterable fieldwork. The aim is to maximize the *actionable* output of research activities.

References

1. Fiedler, John A. "Condominium Design and Pricing: A Case Study in Consumer Trade-Off Analysis," *Proceedings,* Third Annual Conference of Association of Consumer Research, 1972, 279–93.

2. Green, Paul E. and Michael T. Devita. "A Complementary Model of Consumer Utility for Item Collections," *Journal of Consumer Research*, 1 (December 1974), 56–67.
3. —— and Yoram Wind. *Multiattribute Decisions in Marketing: A Measurement Approach.* Hinsdale, Illinois: The Dryden Press, 1973.
4. —— and —— "New Ways to Measure Consumers' Judgments," *Harvard Business Review*, (July–August 1975), 107–17.
5. Johnson, Richard M. "Trade-Off Analysis of Consumer Values," *Journal of Marketing Research*, 11 (May 1974), 121–27.
6. Jones, D. Frank. "A Survey Technique to Measure Demand Under Various Pricing Strategies," *Journal of Marketing*, 39 (July 1975), 75–77.
7. Kotler, Philip. *Marketing Management: Analysis, Planning and Control*, Third Edition, Englewood Cliffs, New Jersey: Prentice-Hall, Inc., 1976, 158–80.

READING 35

Four Subtle Sins in Marketing Research

John A. Martilla and Davis W. Carvey

Today's marketing manager finds himself faced with a growing accumulation of research data that he must read, interpret, and translate into policies and programs. This information is provided by a variety of sources, including the firm's own marketing intelligence group, independent marketing research and consulting firms, advertising agencies, trade associations, and a wide range of research studies reported in the professional literature. The usefulness of this information is often diminished because of poor communication between researchers and managers.

At least two factors contribute to this situation. First, there is the problem of semantics. Terms such as *significant, correlation, variance,* and *random* have statistical meanings that vary from their vernacular usage. A second factor is carelessness. Data seldom, if ever, speak for themselves; they have to be interpreted.

The purpose of this article is to present a clear, basic treatment of four common sources of misunderstanding in conducting and interpreting marketing research studies:

1. Using interval scale statistics for ordinal scale data
2. Equating statistical significance and practical importance
3. Interpreting confidence intervals as measures of total research error
4. Employing false criteria for causality

Presumably less serious than the capital sins of gluttony, lust, and covetousness, these subtle sins may occasionally be expensive and in all cases reflect poorly on their perpetrators.

Reprinted by permission of the American Marketing Association from the *Journal of Marketing,* January 1975, 8–15.

Sin 1: Using Interval Scale Statistics for Ordinal Scale Data

In measuring attitudes, opinions, and intentions to purchase, rating scales are frequently used in marketing. The data obtained are then assigned numerical values for purposes of summarization and comparison. Once these numerical values are assigned, however, the distinction between ordinal and interval scales becomes confused.

Ordinal scales are best characterized by rank order data that only permit comparisons of greater than, less than, or equal to (e.g., rank number two is greater than rank number three and less than rank number one). Given these types of data, no inference can be made that the distances between consecutive numbers are equal. The implications of ordinal data can still be effectively explored using relatively simple statistics such as the mode, median, and percentiles. More sophisticated measures are also applicable, including Spearman's rank order correlation, Kendall's tau, Kendall's Q, and Goodman and Kruskal's tau.

On the other hand, *interval* scales not only have the same basic characteristics as ordinal scales, but they also have the property of equal intervals; that is, the distance between item one and item two is equal to the distance between item three and item four. The property of equal intervals is crucial to many of the commonly used statistics, including the mean, standard deviation, and product-moment correlations, as well as the t, F, and Z tests.

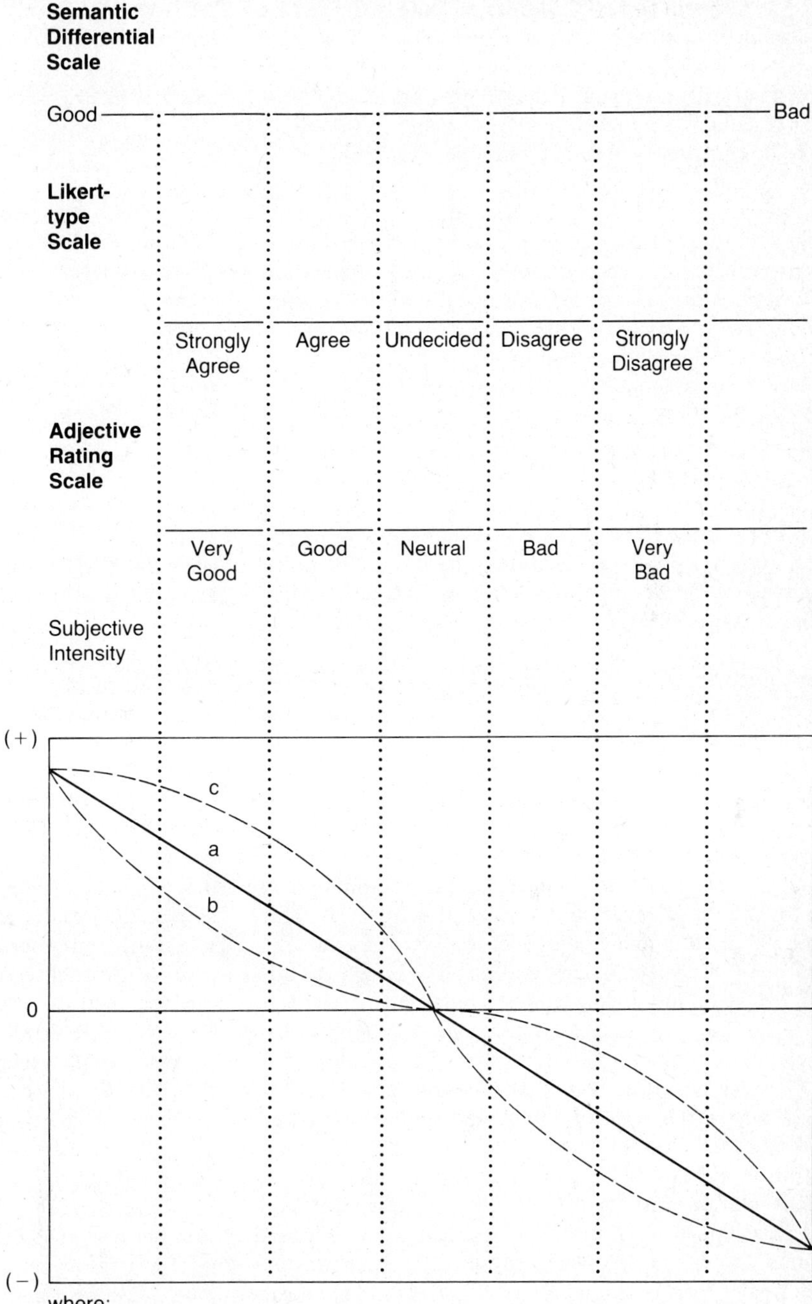

where:
a indicates an equal interval scale
b and c indicate nonequal interval scales

FIGURE 1
Possible Relationships Between Scale Values and Subjective Intensities

A frequent temptation is to take attitude and opinion rating data that may have only ordinal scale properties and apply interval scale statistics and tests of significance to them. Figure 1 presents examples of three common rating scales: the semantic differential, the Likert-type scale, and the adjective rating scale. A common method of analysis is to assign numerical values to each point on the scale, implicitly assuming that these numbers represent subjectively equal intervals, and then to compute mean values and standard deviations for each scale. This equal interval assumption is depicted by the straight line relationship "a" illustrated in the lower half of Figure 1.

The assumption of equal intervals for rating scales should be questioned on both logical and empirical grounds. Logically, there is no assurance that the respondent will be able to judge equal units or that the units of one respondent will match those of another. In fact, it can be argued that the psychological distance between positions one and two on an attitude scale is probably greater than between positions two and three. Brown and Beik report that there is "some evidence that respondents tend to avoid extremes on any judgment scale, and sometimes they avoid a neutral or zero center position, thus forming a skewed or possibly a bimodal distribution."[1] This possibility is illustrated by curve "b" in Figure 1.

Other empirical research on adjective rating scales casts further doubt as to whether the intervals are in fact subjectively equal for the respondent. A pilot study by Myers and Warner presented 50 commonly used scaling adjectives to four respondent groups.[2] Each respondent was asked to assign the adjectives to a modified 21-point Thurstone differential scale. The results showed that the apparent polar adjectives frequently did not form interval scales.

For example, among housewives, "very good" was nearer the scale midpoint and showed a greater amount of variation than "very bad," as illustrated from Myers and Warner's data shown in Table 1 here. This relationship suggests that the subjective distance between positions 1 and 2 is less than between positions 2 and 3 (1.1 vs. 4.5) and, similarly, that the distance between positions 4 and 5 is less than between positions 3 and 4 (0.7 vs. 5.9). Presented in graphical form, the relationship would approximate curve "c" in Figure 1.

Marketing and other researchers frequently succumb to the temptation to use interval scale statistics for ordinal scale data in the belief that their scale is only mildly curvilinear, hoping to realize the greater efficiency of parametric over distribution-free statistics. In summarizing the research concerning the degree of risk involved, Stevens reports that the results are mixed. Certain statistics such as the t test are affected rather dramatically when the assumption of linearity (equal intervals) is violated; in other instances, the distortion is slight relative to the flexibility afforded by the use of parametric tests.[3]

TABLE 1
Subjective Distances between Common Scaling Adjectives

	Position				
	1	*2*	*3*	*4*	*5*
Adjective	Very good	Good	Neutral	Bad	Very bad
Mean scale value (Housewives)	15.4	14.3	9.8	3.9	3.2
Standard deviation	2.8	2.1	1.5	2.2	2.1

Source: James H. Myers and Gregory Warner, "Semantic Properties of Selected Evaluation Adjectives," *Journal of Marketing Research,* Vol. 5 (November 1968), p. 411.

What alternatives, then, are open to the marketing researcher? The conservative position would be to use ordinal scale statistics for ordinal scale data. In many instances this presents no difficulty. For example, the results of semantic differential scales are frequently summarized in terms of a comparative profile.[4] In such cases, it is a simple matter to use the median, instead of the mean, as the "average" value for each scale. Similarly, the median is an appropriate statistic for adjective and Likert-type scales as well. In determining whether differences between two sample medians are greater than might be attributed to sampling error, tests of statistical significance may still be performed.[5]

On the other hand, in instances where the researcher wishes to combine the responses from several different rating scale questions into a single score, he may have few alternatives to assuming an interval scale. However, when this is done to permit the use of parametric tests of statistical significance, the results should be viewed with critical skepticism inasmuch as a basic assumption of these tests probably has been violated. In such cases, examining the magnitude of the difference between the scores may be more appropriate.

Sin 2: Equating Statistical Significance and Practical Importance

One of the most commonly encountered statements in marketing research is of the type which says that the difference in weekly sales between brands A and B is statistically significant at the .05 level. Given this information, it is tempting to assume that a meaningful and substantive difference is present. While this *may* be a correct interpretation, more likely it is not.

Statistical significance refers to the probability that some apparent difference between sample means or proportions may be attributable to sampling error rather than to a true, underlying difference in the populations. To say that the difference between two sample means is statistically significant at the .05 level indicates that one would expect to observe such results no more than 5% of the time if the two groups were in fact equal. Conversely, the researcher is 95% confident that the two group means are not *precisely* equal. Once the research design and statistical tests have been determined, statistical significance depends on at least three factors:

1. The magnitude of the difference between the two means
2. The sample size
3. The dispersion (standard deviation) of the two groups

An example may serve to illustrate the effects of these three variables on the level of statistical significance.

Table 2 presents hypothetical average weekly sales figures for two brands, A and B, in a common product category. In the first comparison the difference between 87 and 85 units per week is not statistically significant at the .05 level. However, when the difference is increased by one unit per week (88 vs. 87), as in the second comparison, the results become statistically significant at the .05 level. This conforms to our intuitive concept of significance—larger differences between means should result in higher levels of statistical significance. And they do, but so do larger sample sizes and smaller standard deviations, thus complicating the practical inferences that may be drawn from significance levels.

Comparison 3 shows that when the original difference between A and B of two units is maintained, but the sample size is increased for even one brand, a previously insignificant difference now becomes significant. In fact, with a large enough sample size any difference, no matter how small, will turn out to be statistically significant. Similarly, when observations are closely grouped around the mean, small differences between the means will appear to be statistically significant. This is illustrated in Comparison 4, where the standard deviation for Brand B is reduced from twelve to six.

The same temptation to equate statistical and practical significance is also encountered with so-called "tests of independence," such as chi-square. In its simplest form (a 2 X 2 contingency table), the chi-square test attempts to answer whether one variable is related to, or dependent upon, a second variable. In the hypothetical example in Table 3, the question is asked whether average weekly supermarket sales of Brand B are independent of the region of the country

TABLE 2
Hypothetical Average Weekly Unit Sales Comparisons for Two Brands

Analysis	*Brand A*	*Comparison 1* *Brand B*	*Comparison 2* *Brand B*	*Comparison 3* *Brand B*	*Comparison 4* *Brand B*
Mean	85	87	88	87	87
Sample size	100	100	100	1000	100
Standard deviation	8	12	12	12	6
Computed Z value		1.38	2.08	2.26	2.00
Level of statistical significance[a]		N.S.	.05	.05	.05

a. Computations are made using a two-tailed Z test, with a value of 1.96 required for statistical significance at the .05 level. N.S. indicates not statistically significant at the .05 level.

TABLE 3
Two Hypothetical Studies of Weekly Sales by Geographical Region for Brand B

	Study I *N = 100 supermarkets*		*Study II* *N = 200 supermarkets*	
Average Weekly Supermarket Sales	*Eastern Region*	*Western Region*	*Eastern Region*	*Western Region*
Less than 87 units	29	21	58	42
87 units or more	21	29	42	58
Total	50	50	100	100
	$\chi^2 = 2.56$[a]		$\chi^2 = 5.12$[b]	

a. Not statistically significant at the .05 level.
b. Statistically significant at the .05 level.

in which the supermarket is located. In Study I of Table 3, with a sample size of 100 supermarkets, the difference between East and West is not statistically significant at the .05 level. This leads one to question whether a true relationship exists. However, as depicted in Study II of the same table, when the sample size is increased to 200 the computed chi-square value becomes statistically significant. Hence, stronger evidence of a relationship between weekly sales of Brand B and geographical region is presumed to exist. Further, it should be noted that in both studies the relative proportions are identical: 42% of the supermarkets in the East and 58% of the supermarkets in the West reported average weekly sales in excess of 87 units per week. While in the first instance the difference may have appeared trivial, in the second it turned out to be statistically significant because the chi-square value had increased from 2.55 to 5.12. More generally, when the proportions in the cells remain unchanged, the chi-square value varies directly with the number of observations. For example, when the sample size is doubled, the chi-square value is doubled as well.[6]

These examples illustrate an important point in interpreting marketing research studies: a difference may be significant in a statistical sense, yet trivial in a practical or substantive sense. Statistical significance refers only to the probability that the observed differences cannot be attributed to sampling error. It is a measure of whether *any* difference exists, not a measure of the magnitude of the difference. Only the manager can interpret whether the results have any practical importance.

Sin 3: Interpreting Confidence Intervals as Measures of Total Research Error

Marketing managers continually must rely on statistical data that are subject to potential error. Such data frequently include some estimate of the magnitude of this error, generally stated in terms of confidence intervals. Given this information, it is up to the marketing manager to weigh the risks involved and assess the extent to which the data should influence subsequent decisions. For example, suppose that the marketing manager is presented with a survey report indicating that his firm's brand share is estimated to be 20% with a 95% confidence interval of ±4%. The question becomes, then, how should he interpret these data? If he assumes he can be 95% certain that his true market share is somewhere between 16% and 24%, he almost certainly will be wrong. He will have fallen victim to what Brown calls the "confidence trick" in greatly overestimating the accuracy of his research data.[7]

This problem arises directly from the fact that classical confidence intervals take into account only one source of error (i.e., random error), which is incurred as a result of taking a sample rather than a census. A multitude of other possible types of error are ignored, including those that may result from a nonrepresentative sample, nonrespondents, and inaccurate responses. In fact, the magnitude of these nonrandom errors may well exceed the error attributable to random sampling. Yet, for the busy executive reading marketing survey results, these other errors are seldom considered. Even if they are recognized, it is not readily apparent how they may be statistically combined with the familiar, albeit overly optimistic, confidence interval.

Brown has proposed a personal probability method of credence analysis termed "Error Ratio Decomposition," which permits the researcher to break down the target variable (here, share of market —SOM) into components and then to assess the magnitude of error to which each component may be subject.[8] The assumption underlying this approach is that the individual error components may be more readily and accurately assessed than the aggregate figure.

An abbreviated marketing research illustration of error ratio decomposition is presented in Table 4. The initial market survey results suggest a market share of 20% and a 95% confidence interval of 16%

TABLE 4
Assessing the Accuracy of a Market Survey Using Error Ratio Decomposition

Problem

To determine the share of market (SOM) for Brand B

Research Approach

Using a mail questionnaire, randomly sample 300 of the 25,000 U.S. supermarkets

Survey Results

Usable responses:	200 questionnaires—67% returned
Average SOM reported:	20%
95% confidence interval:	16%–24%

Credence Decomposition	*Expected Error Ratio*	*95% Credible Interval*
Random Error Estimate: taken from survey Expected error ratio = (.20/.20) = 1.0 Credible interval = (.16/.20) to (.24/.20) = 0.8–1.2	1.0	0.8–1.2
Reporting Error Estimate: researcher's judgment Belief that participating stores would underreport true SOM by 20%. Considerable uncertainty about estimate with a credible interval of between 40% and 200% of the reported SOM value. Expected error ratio = [.20 + .2(.20)]/.20 = 1.2	1.2	0.4–2.0
Nonresponse Error Estimate: researcher's judgment Belief that supermarkets not responding had lower sales of Brand B, which would revise reported SOM downward by 10%, with a credible interval of between 80% and 100% of the average SOM reported. Expected error ratio = [.20 − .1(.20)]/.20 = .09	0.9	0.8–1.0

Revised Estimate SOM

Target Variable	=	Reported Percentage	X	Random Error	X	Reporting Error	X	Nonresponse Error
21.6%	=	20%	X	1.0	X	1.2	X	0.9

95% Credible Interval

$$21.6\% \times \sqrt{\left[\frac{1.2-0.8}{(1.2+0.8)/2}\right]^2+\left[\frac{2.0-0.4}{(2.0+0.4)/2}\right]^2+\left[\frac{1.0-0.8}{(1.0+0.8)/2}\right]^2} = \text{about } 30\%$$

Interval Edges: 11%–41%[a]

a. The actual edges of the credible interval are chosen to make them "geometrically" symmetrical around the expected value: Upper Boundary/Expected Value = Expected Value/Lower Boundary.

Source: This example is adapted from Rex V. Brown, "Just How Credible Are Your Market Estimates?" *Journal of Marketing*, Vol. 33 (July 1969), pp. 46–50.

to 24%. These results may be used directly in the first step of error ratio decomposition as an estimate of the target value (SOM) and the magnitude of random error associated with that estimate. In addition to random error, the researcher believes that further error may have been incurred as the result of inaccurate reporting by supermarkets participating in the survey and bias due to nonrespondents. In each case the researcher makes two estimates. The first is a point estimate of the target value if the particular form of error were eliminated. In the case of reporting error, the researcher believed the target value (SOM) would have been about 20% greater if this source of error had not been present. This value is expressed as a fraction of the survey value (24%/20%), resulting in an expected error ratio of 1.2. The second type of estimate required by the researcher is that of a 95% credible interval, which may be thought of as a judgmental equivalent of the confidence interval used in classical statistics. In the case of nonresponse error, the researcher felt 95% certain that if all 300 supermarkets had participated in the survey the reported SOM for Brand B would have been within the range of 80% to 100% of the reported SOM value. This model assumes that each error component is independent of all other error components and the value of the target variable (SOM).

Based on these survey and judgment inputs, the estimated SOM for Brand B changes from 20% to 21.6% and the 95% interval increases from a range of 8 percentage points (16%–24%) to 30 percentage points (11%–41%). This hypothetical example suggests that considering only sampling error, as provided by classical confidence intervals, may have two results: (1) the point estimate of the target variable (here SOM) may be biased, and (2) the estimate of total research error is likely to be greatly understated. Since reporting error and nonresponse error are generally present in marketing studies in addition to random error, it seems reasonable that their magnitude should also be estimated and reported.

The optimum time for a marketing manager to consider total research error is when it is most controllable, and that point is prior to conducting the study. Mayer has shown how error ratio analysis can be performed to evaluate several alternative research approaches.[9] This sequence accomplishes both the selection of the most accurate research design and the estimation of the total error in the results obtained from that design.

Sin 4: Employing False Criteria for Causality

This sin is generally encountered in two subtle forms: failing to adequately consider the accepted criteria for establishing causality, and being overly restrictive in denying causal relationships.

There are at least three widely accepted scientific criteria for inferring causality: association, sequence of events, and nonspurious relation.[10] While causality is never proved, only inferred, the more criteria of causal evidence that are satisfied, the greater the confidence one has in his inference. Conversely, to establish noncausality, one has only to demonstrate that a single criterion has been violated.

An association must exist between attitudes and buying behavior for the former to be a cause of the latter. There are two characteristics of this association that will strengthen the conclusion that a causal relationship exists. The first is the *magnitude,* or strength, of the association. For example, if consumers with favorable attitudes are four times as likely to buy Brand A as those with unfavorable attitudes, the researcher would have more confidence that a causal relationship exists than if the ratio were two to one. A second characteristic of association to be considered is *consistency.* If this relationship persisted in different geographic regions, among both males and females, and for different ethnic and racial groups, the plausibility of a causal relationship would be greater than if the association were observed under a more restricted set of conditions.[11]

A second criterion for a causal relationship is that the causal factor (i.e., the independent variable) must occur or change prior to the dependent variable. In other words, for attitudes to be a cause of buying behavior, they must occur before the purchase is made. In marketing research the sequence of events criterion is most convincingly established in experimental studies or longitudinal analyses of panel data.

However, even if the criteria of association and sequence of events are satisfied, the relationship may be spurious rather than causal. The criterion of nonspuriousness may well create the greatest confusion in establishing causality because of the possibility of a developmental sequence. Two short examples may clarify this distinction.

Attendance at college football games may be highly correlated with, and regularly precede, purchases of automobile antifreeze; yet the relationship is unlikely to be causal. Both events can be explained by a third variable, the season of the year. This, however, does not eliminate the possibility of a causal relationship. It should further be determined that the third variable "is not an intrinsic part of the developmental sequence which produced the apparent explanation."[12] Since it does not seem plausible that the season of the year leads one to attend football games, which in turn results in the purchase of antifreeze, one would reject the possibility of a developmental sequence and conclude that the relationship is spurious. [See Figure 2(a).] The apparent relationship here between attendance at football games and the purchase of antifreeze can reasonably be considered spurious. In less transparent situations, control procedures may be necessary to enable one to make this assessment.

In the same context, the situation frequently arises in marketing where a psychological variable is suggested as intervening between two events. For example, a favorable rating of "brand x" appearing in *Consumer Reports* might change the salience of the brand's attributes, which in turn might stimulate purchase of the brand. In this instance the identification of a third, intervening variable (the shift in salience) actually strengthens the inference of a causal relationship between the favorable rating and increased sales. A developmental sequence of intrinsically related events appears to be present. [See Figure 2(b).]

Researchers may also err at the other extreme and be overly zealous in rejecting the existence of causal relationships. They employ the false criterion of assuming that if the relationship between two variables is not perfect, it is not causal. This false criterion may take several forms—ranging from the argument that for attitude to be a cause of sales it must be a "necessary and sufficient" condition for sales, to the slightly less demanding condition that favorable attitudes must be at least "characteristic" of people who buy the brand. Hirschi and Selvin correctly point out that it is the strength of the relationship that matters, that is, the difference in the proportion of purchasers and nonpurchasers having favorable attitudes.[13] Further, these authors note, perfect association between two variables implies single causation. Such a situation is virtually unknown in marketing. If the reality of multiple causation is accepted, the marketer must expect to find less-than-perfect associations in the relationships being investigated.

For the marketing manager the issue of causality can be resolved in a Bayesian fashion asking, first, how much causal information do I now have and, second, how much is additional causal information worth to me? In answering the first question, the manager must avoid being either insufficiently rigorous or overly demanding in applying the criteria of causality. In resolving the second, he may conclude in many instances that an investigation of how consumers behave and the identification of behavioral correlates—such as demographics, psychographics, and perceptions—constitute a better expenditure of limited research funds than the more scientifically precise study of causality.

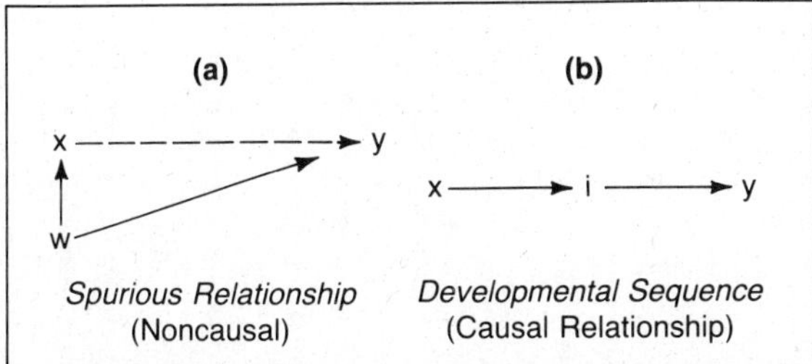

FIGURE 2
Spurious Relationships vs. Developmental Sequences

Summary

Even experienced and competent practitioners and users of marketing research information may on occasion fall victim to one or more of the troublesome problems outlined in the preceding discussion. Recalling the "logic traps" behind these subtle sins in research may help the marketer avoid personal or professional embarrassment.

1. Commonly used rating scales in marketing frequently have only ordinal scale properties which restrict the range of appropriate statistical measures. When interval scale statistics are used, measures of statistical significance should be interpreted with caution.
2. Statistical significance says very little about practical importance. With a large enough sample size, even the smallest difference between two groups can turn out to be statistically significant.

3. Confidence intervals in classical statistics reflect only the magnitude of sampling error. Errors resulting from incorrect reporting and nonresponse may be of equal or greater importance. The technique of error ratio decomposition is a useful approach for arriving at a measure of total research error as well as for revising survey estimates of the target variable.
4. In making inferences of causality, three criteria are commonly accepted: association, sequence of events, and absence of other possible causes. Careful judgment is required to avoid the extremes of being too lenient or too demanding in inferring causal relationships.

Endnotes

1. Lyndon O. Brown and Leland L. Beik, *Marketing Research and Analysis,* 4th ed. (New York: The Ronald Press Co., 1969), p. 278.
2. James H. Myers and Gregory Warner, "Semantic Properties of Selected Evaluation Adjectives," *Journal of Marketing Research,* Vol. 5 (November 1968), pp. 409–412.
3. S. S. Stevens, "Measurement, Statistics, and the Schemapiric View," *Science,* Vol. 161 (August 1968), pp. 849–856.
4. William A. Mindak, "Fitting the Semantic Differential to the Marketing Problem," *Journal of Marketing,* Vol. 25 (April 1961), pp. 28–33.
5. Robert Ferber, *Market Research* (New York: McGraw-Hill Book Co., 1949), p. 122.
6. Hubert M. Blalock, *Social Statistics* (New York: McGraw-Hill Book Co., 1960), pp. 225–227.
7. Rex V. Brown, *The Credibility of Estimates: A New Tool for Executives and Researchers* (Boston, Mass.: Harvard Business School, Div. of Research, 1969); Rex V. Brown, "Evaluation of Total Survey Error," *Journal of Marketing Research,* Vol. 4 (May 1967), pp. 117–127; and Rex V. Brown, "Just How Credible Are Your Market Estimates?" *Journal of Marketing,* Vol. 33 (July 1969), pp. 46–50.
8. See Brown, "Just How Credible Are Your Market Estimates?" same reference as footnote 7.
9. Charles S. Mayer, "Assessing the Accuracy of Marketing Research," *Journal of Marketing Research,* Vol. 7 (August 1970), pp. 285–291.
10. Herbert H. Hyman, *Survey Design and Analysis* (Glencoe, Ill.: The Free Press, 1955), pp. 178–274; and Paul E. Green and Donald S. Tull, *Research for Marketing Decisions,* 2d ed. (Englewood Cliffs, N.J.: Prentice-Hall, 1970), p. 23.
11. Sanford Labovitz and Robert Hagedorn, *Introduction to Social Research* (New York: McGraw-Hill Book Co., 1971), pp. 3–11.
12. See Hyman, same reference as footnote 10, p. 256.
13. Travis Hirschi and Hanan C. Selvin, "False Criteria of Causality in Delinquency Research," *Social Problems,* Vol. 13 (Winter 1966), pp. 254–268.

READING 36

Decision Support Systems for Marketing Managers

John D. C. Little

In the past 10 years, a new technology has emerged for assisting and improving marketing decision making. We define a marketing decision support system as a coordinated collection of data, models, analytic tools, and computing power by which an organization gathers information from the environment and turns it into a basis for action. Where such systems have taken root, they have grown and become increasingly productive for their organizations.

The combination of large potential payoffs, highly motivated professional staffs, evolving OR/MS techniques, and rising computer power is making an impact on marketing management. A problem-solving technology is emerging that consists of people, knowledge, software, and hardware successfully wired into the management process. Following Gorry and Scott Morton (1971), we shall call the set of facilitating tools a decision support system or, more specifically a *Marketing Decision Support System* (MDSS). Intellectual contributions to MDSS have come from many disciplines: OR/MS, marketing research, computer science, behavioral science, and statistics, to name a few. We view the results collectively as an advance in management science or, more specifically marketing science. Our purpose is to define and illustrate the concept of an MDSS and show its effects on marketing practice.

Reprinted by permission of the American Marketing Association, from the *Journal of Marketing*, 43:3 Summer 1979, 9–26.

What Is It? A Black Box View

A manager takes action with respect to an environment in order to achieve the objectives of his organization. To do this he must perceive and interpret the market, even if imperfectly. Then he must think up strategies, analyze them, and converge on one to put into practice. This process is conducted through a complicated system of people, paper, and machines. We call the inanimate part of this an MDSS. Figure 1, modified from Montgomery and Urban (1969), shows the MDSS and its components and traces their roles in interpreting and analyzing the environment.

Data Bank. A stream of information comes into the organization from the world at large in many ways: from members of the organization; from talking to people; from reading the *Wall Street Journal;* from purchasing market research; and especially from distilling the multitude of individual transactions of the business–orders, shipments, purchases, records of internal action, and much more. The data are stored in varied forms: on paper, in people's heads, and, most relevant for our present purposes, in large chunks on machine readable media. The amount of data handled by a large company is staggering. Business runs on numbers. Sales alone have vast detail, and might, for example, be broken out by time period, market area, brand, package size, salesperson, and customer. How did people get along before computers? (Quite well, thank you, but they missed many profit opportunities open to us now.)

Less obvious than the flood of data washing over companies is the information they do *not* have.

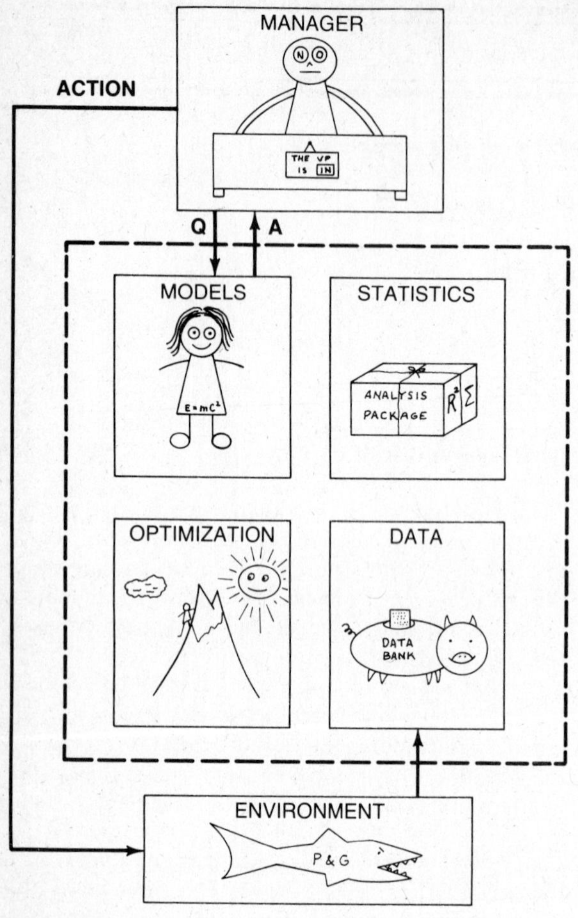

FIGURE 1
A Manager Uses a Marketing Decision Support System (MDSS) to Learn About the Business Environment and Take Action with Respect to It.

Often they may have it in principle, but not in practice. For example, I recently asked a large and successful company for the following data, which they could not supply: product category sales by month and major market area, competitive advertising, and even more surprising, the company's own promotional spending by market area. At another company, I once sought advertising expenditures by month, but they could only be provided in terms of when the bills were paid, not when the advertising was run. This was not too helpful for marketing analysis. Certain data are simply not gathered, others are aggregated and the original detail lost or prohibitively costly to recover. Competitive data usually comes from syndicated services as hard copy which is inadequate for any, but the most aggregate analysis.

Clearly, a basic task of any MDSS is to capture major marketing variables such as sales, advertising, promotion, and price in reasonable detail and truly accessible form. Remarkably few companies do an adequate job today. The issue is cost and therefore value, since data for data's sake is a worthless luxury. It takes skillful analysis and effective coupling with management to provide the benefits that justify the cost, but the payback can be large.

Models. Whenever a manager (or anybody else) looks at data, he or she has a preconceived idea of how the world works and therefore of what is interesting and worthwhile in the data. We shall call such ideas *models.* Even a person who is browsing through tables has a set of constructs in mind that signal when a particular number is important and worth further consideration. Thus, a manager or management scientist uses theories to determine what aggregations or manipulations are meaningful for the decision at hand. The data user may want to confirm or disprove a hypothesis, guide an action, or learn the magnitude of a past number so as to judge the reasonableness of a current one. Manipulation of the numbers may cause an old theory to be discarded and a new one created to conform better to the facts.

Some models remain in people's heads, but the ones of most interest here are those that find explicit mathematical and computational representation. These aid planning, decision making, and many less publicized supporting tasks required for understanding and analyzing the market.

Statistics. We shall call the process of relating models to data *statistics.* The most important statistical operation is addition. This makes big important numbers out of small, trivial ones. Many sophisticated techniques also are available for model and hypothesis testing and they often prove useful. However, it is not widely realized, except by those with their hands on the data, that the most frequent operations are basic ones like segregating numbers into groups, aggregating them, taking ratios, making comparisons, picking out exceptional cases, plotting, tabulating summaries, etc. These manipulations are required by such standard managerial models as proforma profit and loss statements, budgeting, and forecasting, to say nothing of more complicated models for new product tracking, marketing-mix planning, and the like.

Optimization. A manager constantly seeks to improve the performance of his organization. Abstractly this is optimization. The most frequent operations are deceptively simple: calculating two numbers and seeing which is larger, ranking a set of numbers, or sorting a set of alternatives into categories of effectiveness. In addition, there are many cases where formal OR/MS optimization methods such as linear programming and its extensions offer substantial payoffs.

Q/A. Finally, the manager and his or her staff must communicate with the system. Insofar as the required skills, talent, and information are distributed throughout the organization, communication involves the standard processes of meetings, studies, and reports. As the systems become formal and automated, some of the communication takes place through interactive time-shared computing. Individual tools are stored as computer programs. With the right software, data and files pass easily between analyses, and a management scientist or other person can perform a wide scope of analysis smoothly, quickly, and efficiently.

To summarize, a marketing decision support system is a coordinated collection of data, systems, tools, and techniques with supporting software and hardware by which an organization gathers and interprets relevant information from business and environment and turns it into a basis for marketing action.

The Critics

We have described the concept, but what about the practice? Management science has its critics. Let's see what C. Jackson Grayson Jr. (1973) says in the *Harvard Business Review.* Grayson, a Harvard DBA, author of a book applying decision analysis to oil drilling decisions, former dean of a business school, and currently head of a productivity institute, writes:

> *Management Science has grown so remote from and unmindful of the conditions of "live" management that it has abdicated its usability.*

We would like to dismiss this as an isolated complaint, not likely to be repeated. But wait, let's see what John D.C. Little (1970), professor of Operations Research and Management at M.I.T., says in *Management Science:*

> *The big problem with management science models is that managers practically never use them.*

This situation must be serious! On close examination, however, Grayson's article and mine are quite different in content and tone. Grayson reports that in the most important administrative role of his career (Chairman of the U.S. Price Commission), he found no use for his management science training. He goes on to describe managers generally as confused and dissatisfied with management science activities in their organizations and admonishes management scientists and managers to build bridges to each other. One can hardly advocate that they should not, but this proposal seems patronizing at best and indicates an ignorance of a great deal of useful work that has gone on.

My own paper, written three years earlier, sought to draw on a variety of practical experiences to describe "how-to-do-it" in building useful models. By 1970 much had been learned, sometimes by painful trial and error, about doing OR/MS successfully in business and government. Regrettably, good applications often lie concealed because little incentive exists for their revelation and, worse yet, strong forces favor secrecy. Fortunately, studies are beginning to appear more regularly. (See for example, the prize paper issues of *Interfaces,* Nigam, 1975, 1976, 1977.)

OR/MS practitioners and marketing researchers have continued to learn what works and what does not. This paper tries to report some of this.

How an MDSS Works. A True Story.

The Marketing Manager, the Management Scientist and the MBA

Once upon a time (1973), an MBA student took a summer job with a large food manufacturer. He reported to a management scientist in the principal division of the company. The MBA was assigned to put key marketing information, basically store audit data, on a time-shared computer. The goal was an easy-to-use retrieval system, essentially the DATA box of Figure 1.

O.K. He did this.

By the end of the summer, word of the system had reached the marketing manager of the major product of the division who asked for a demonstration and so the three met. The MBA and the management scientist showed the marketing manager how simple, English-like commands could retrieve data items: sales, share, price, distribution level, etc., each by brand, package size, and month.

The marketing manager was impressed. "You must be fantastically smart," he told the MBA. "The people downstairs in MIS have been trying to do this for years and they haven't gotten anywhere. You did it in a summer."

It was hard for the MBA to reject this assessment out of hand, but he did acknowledge, and this is a key point, that the software world had changed. There are now high level analytic languages available on time-sharing that make it easy to bring up data and start working on it right away.

The MBA and the management scientist, flushed with success, now said to the marketing manager: "O.K. Ask us anything!" (Famous last words.)

The marketing manager thought a minute and said: "I'd like to know how much the competition's introduction of a 40 oz. package in Los Angeles cut into the sales of our 16 oz. package."

The MBA and the management scientist looked at each other in dismay. What they realized right away, and what you might too if you think about it, is that there isn't going to be any number in the machine for sales that *didn't* occur. This isn't a *retrieval* question at all, it's an *analysis* question.

Here then is another point. The marketing manager had no idea the number would not be in the machine. To him it was just one more fact no different in his mind from other facts about the market. Notice also that the question is a reasonable one. One can visualize a whole string of managerial acts that might be triggered by the answer, possibly even culminating in the introduction of a new package by the company.

What is needed to answer the question is a *model,* probably a rather simple model. For example, one might extrapolate previous share and use it to estimate the sales that would have happened without the competitor's introduction. Then subtraction of actual sales would give the loss.

The three discussed possible assumptions for a few minutes and agreed on how to approach the problem. Then the management scientist typed in one line of high level commands. Out came the result, expressed in dollars, cases, and share points.

The marketing manager thought the answer was fine, a good demonstration. The MBA and the management scientist thought it was a miracle! They had responded to the question with a speed and accuracy unthinkable a few months earlier.

The story is simple but contains several important lessons. I see the same points coming up again and again in various organizations, although not always so neatly and concisely:

- *Managers ask for analysis not retrieval.* Sometimes retrieval questions come up of course, but most often the answers to important questions require nontrivial manipulation of stored data. Knowing this tells us much about the kind of software required for an MDSS. For example, a data base management system is not enough.
- *Good data are vital.* If you haven't done your homework and put key data on the system you are nowhere. Thus, a powerful analytic language alone is not enough.
- *You need models.* These are often simple, but not always. Some can be prepackaged. Many are ad hoc.
- *The management scientist is an intermediary.* He connects the manager to the MDSS. The manager does not use the system directly. The management scientist interprets questions, formulates problems in cooperation with the manager, creates models, and uses them to answer questions and analyze issues.
- *Quick, quick, quick.* If you can answer people's questions right away, you will affect their thinking. If you cannot, they will make their decisions without you and go on to something else.
- *Muscular software cuts out programmers.* New high-level languages on time-sharing permit a management scientist or recently trained MBA to bring up systems and do analyses singlehandedly. This makes for efficient problem solving. Furthermore, the problem-solver identifies with and deals directly with marketing management so that his un-

derstanding and motivation are high. Time-sharing costs more than batch processing, but an army of programmers is eliminated and, far more important, problems get solved on time.

Decision Support for the Product Life Cycle: Cradle to Grave Care

Let's look at marketing per se. Over the past 10 or 15 years and continuing unabated, there has evolved from diverse origins a series of tools and techniques for support of the product life cycle.

By product life cycle we mean a sequence of conveniently defined stages that describe the history of a product from conception to possible demise. We do not imply that every product goes through every stage or that any stage lasts some prescribed length of time.

The product life cycle is illustrated in Figure 2. A product starts as someone's bright *idea,* thereby identifying a category. The idea then goes through a stage of concept and product *development and evaluation,* leading to a detailed design and market position. Development and evaluation are closely linked; at various times during development, evaluations of greater or lesser depth will be made and the results fed back to refocus development.

The next step is usually *test market,* although an industrial product will not ordinarily have this step. Then comes national *introduction.* In the *ongoing* stage, the product becomes, one hopes, an established and profitable business. From time to time a product may go through a thorough revamping or "reintroduction." Many at some point go into a *twilight* of obsolescence (the slide rule and the mechanical watch seem headed this way). Finally many products including quite a few former household names, go out of existence entirely. The tombstone in Figure 2 might read: "Chrysler Imperial: 1926–1975, died at age 49 of sales starvation."

The mortality of new products has traditionally been notorious. For example, General Foods reported in *Business Week* (1973) a 15-year history in which 83% of new products did not get out of the idea stage. Of those that did, 60% never reached test market; of those entering test market, 59% failed; and even among those making it to national introduction, 25% were considered financial failures. At the same time, new product introduction is very expensive. For a typical package good of a major manufacturer, the development and evaluation stage might cost $150,000; a test market, $1 million; a national introduction, $5–10 million. A new industrial product would omit the test market expense, but might well spend an equivalent amount on development and evaluation.

Responding to the challenge of the heavy expenses and high profit aspirations of new products, marketing scientists have developed an array of methodologies and measurements to support decision making at various stages of the life cycle.

At the *idea and category selection* stage, systematic search procedures drawn from behavioral science supplement traditional inspiration. Focus groups (Cox, Higginbotham, and Burton 1976) probe customer feelings about needs and perceptions. "Synectics" (Prince 1972) is a technique whereby a group

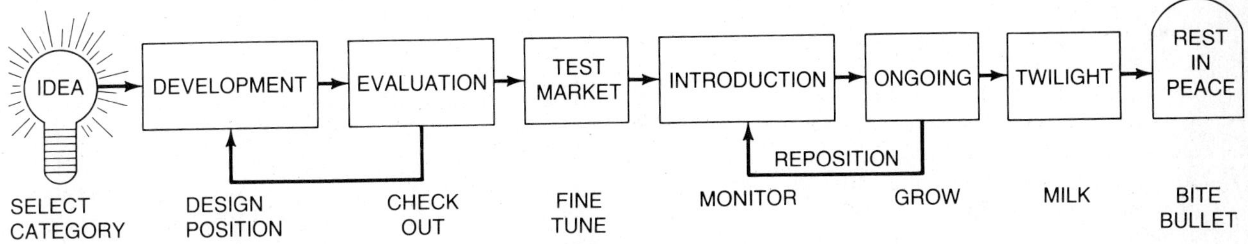

FIGURE 2
Marketing Scientists Have Developed Models and Measurements to Support Almost Every Stage of the Product Life Cycle.

of people seek to solve a problem in an organized way, e.g., conceive of a product to meet a specified set of customers' needs. As demonstrated by von Hippel (1978) customers themselves are an important source of industrial product ideas. Industrial and governmental data on potential markets suggest new product opportunities. Environmental scanning can turn up danger spots for existing products and needs for new ones.

The bulk of the new techniques, however, begins to come into play at the next stage: *development and evaluation.* Value-in-use analysis (Gross 1977) looks at a product from the customer's point of view and asks: "What advantages are there to the customer from using this product? What cost savings? What time savings? What investment would be required to achieve this savings?" By answering such questions for each potential market segment, an aggregate picture of volume versus price can be synthesized.

A particularly well-articulated description of a formal new product design, development, and positioning methodology is that of Hauser and Urban (1977). Their normative design process envisages first finding out the customer's words for talking about the product category. This might be done through focus groups. Then, customer words are developed into psychometric scales. Potential customers use these scales to rate new and existing products in the category. As customers do this, they also express preferences among the products and so generate data that can be analyzed to identify the customers' key utility dimensions. Such information permits the calibration of a model of new product share and sales. A feedback loop between model and manager facilitates the modification of the product and its market position.

Other tools fit in at this stage of the life cycle, some within the Hauser-Urban framework. These include mapping studies, conjoint measurement, and consumer choice models. Mapping is a general term to describe the visual representation of competitive products relative to each other in a space of consumer perceptual dimensions. Conjoint measurement (Green and Wind 1975) presents alternative product features to customers in order to obtain their trade-offs and build new products with high market potential. Consumer choice models (Shocker and Srinivasan 1977; Hauser 1978) relate choice to consumer utility or preference.

A particularly successful blend of models, measurements, and statistical techniques has emerged for *pretest market evaluation.* The best example is Silk and Urban's ASSESSOR (1978). In their method, people passing through a shopping mall are invited to participate in a marketing study. They view competing advertising commercials including one for the new product under test, and then have an opportunity to select a brand from a shelf display containing the new product. Data are taken by a questionnaire during the process and later a telephone call-back determines the customer's likelihood of repurchasing. This type of careful orchestration of psychometric scaling, consumer choice models, trial-repeat purchase models, and statistical calibration has proven extremely useful to marketers of package goods and holds the promise of extension to new areas, e.g., pharmaceuticals and small durables.

As move on to *test marketing* and *national introduction,* the techniques change. The principal tools become trial-repeat models calibrated by store audits, ad hoc surveys, and consumer diary panels. The task is to follow the buildup of consumer trial and repurchase and project to future sales and share. Parfitt and Collins (1968) provide a simple model and Urban (1970) in SPRINTER a comprehensive model for doing this. As pretest market evaluations increasingly eliminate costly failures, test marketing becomes more of a fine-tuning for the marketing mix than a go/no-go test. Therefore, new product tracking models that contain major control variables become most useful.

At the *established brand stage,* the picture changes again. Ongoing brands frequently take a back seat as new products consume managerial attention. Yet for many companies, this is a mistake since major profit opportunities often lie with the old breadwinners. Market response analyses assisted by marketing-mix models like Little's (1975) BRANDAID or Bloom and Stewart's (1977) MAPLAMOD harness major control variables such as price, promotion, and advertising for strategy planning and permit tracking predicted versus actual sales. Discrepancies lead to diagnosis of market problems. Econometric analysis of historical data (Parsons and Schultz 1976; Bass and Clarke 1972) can help calibrate such models. Consumer panel analyses like those of Ehrenberg (1972) can detect customer purchase shifts. Individual models of price, promotion, and advertising are frequently useful for specific tactical problems.

The basic information sources are also different

in the ongoing stage since product management relies more heavily on continuing data: factory shipments; promotion reports; advertising expenses; and syndicated services such as store audits, warehouse withdrawals, and consumer panels. These services are well developed in consumer package goods, spotty in consumer durables, and almost absent in industrial markets.

The *twilight* or obsolescence stage also has attracted effort. For example, Hess (1967) discusses the pricing of new and old products when the new is destined to supplant the old. The final phasing out of a product from a product line is studied as part of product portfolio analyses (Day 1977).

Thus every part of the product life cycle has generated marketing science activity. Some efforts are more extensive and more successful than others in affecting practice, but it is clear that changes are afoot.

Marketing Science: Who Is Kidding Whom?

I like to use the term "marketing science." However, the phrase makes some people flinch and others stir restlessly. Is what we have described an advance in fundamental understanding or is it merely a series of commercial fads? Can we sensibly talk about science in a flamboyant field where the motivation and funding are so far from the usual domain of the natural philosopher? I shall argue that we are indeed engaged in science.

First, it should be observed that most of the actors on the marketing stage are *not* scientists. Many are skillful performing artists and very successful, but not scientists any more than, say, a sculptor is. But when a sculptor hammers a chisel into a piece of marble, he initiates a process that is well described by the laws of physics. In marketing we are not so far along.

Are we anywhere? Natural science is concerned with understanding how the world works. This means models and measurements, the twin engines of scientific advance. Models provide structure for describing phenomena and permit knowledge to be more than an encyclopedia of facts. Measurements separate good models from bad and allow good ones to be calibrated for practical application. It seems obvious that you can make a scientific study of any observable phenomenon and that we are certainly doing that on many occasions in marketing.

Whereas understanding is the province of science, application is the domain of technology. Common usage expands science to cover both. (Thus: "Science put men on the moon, why can't it cure the common cold?") The dividing line is blurred and we shall follow the common usage, but identify understanding as the essential ingredient of science.

Two characteristics of marketing practice tend to obscure accomplishments in fundamental understanding. First, application regularly oversteps knowledge, a situation that makes for confusion, since truths are often proclaimed that are not true. I used to read articles in the business press about marketing successes and marvel that people knew so much more about their markets than I was able to discover by analysis. Eventually I realized that the authors were using different standards of knowing. What was being written reflected the fact that businessmen often make good decisions with relatively poor information. As part of the process, they usually make assertive statements whether or not they possess firm knowledge. In any case, businessmen much prefer to have knowledge and would like us to give it to them wherever possible.

The second point is that, because so much marketing data collection, analysis, and model building is bent toward specific decisions, underlying discoveries are frequently the spinoff of the application, rather than the reverse. On the way to solving a practical problem, people often develop new understanding. This certainly isn't novel in science—probability, for example, was born at the gaming tables. Not all marketing studies produce scientific knowledge—most are not done nearly carefully enough—but the potential is there and sometimes the realization. The marketing papers appearing in *Management Science, Operations Research*, and *Journal of Marketing Research* over the past 15 years demonstrate the quality of the work and the vitality of the field.

Thus, we view marketing science as real. It is an applications-driven subject that is building a base of understanding about marketing processes.

Measurements

Measurements are contact points with reality, they generate the excitement of new discovery and practical payoff more often than models. Companies pay a great deal for measurements. Syndicated services in store audits, diary panels, media ratings, and the like constitute at least a $200 million industry per year in the United States. Ad hoc surveys, copy tests, etc., reach a comparable dollar magnitude.

Measurements motivated by theories and models are most valuable. For example, Figure 3 shows the results of an advertising test. Sales are plotted versus time before, during, and after a heavy-up of advertising.

The results are striking. Notice the rapid-rise, leveling off, and slow decay. The data cry out for a theory—and more measurement. Why do sales go up quickly and down slowly? What would happen if the same test were repeated in the same areas a year later? Clearly Figure 3 has strong policy implications. It appears that much more profit was generated by removing the heavy advertising after six months than would have occurred by continuing it. This is because decay was so slow. However, to determine an optimal, or even a sensible, policy requires a theory of what is going on. This will expose the assumptions that must be made to turn these measurements into decisions. Clearly, there is no shortage of practical and scientific questions here.

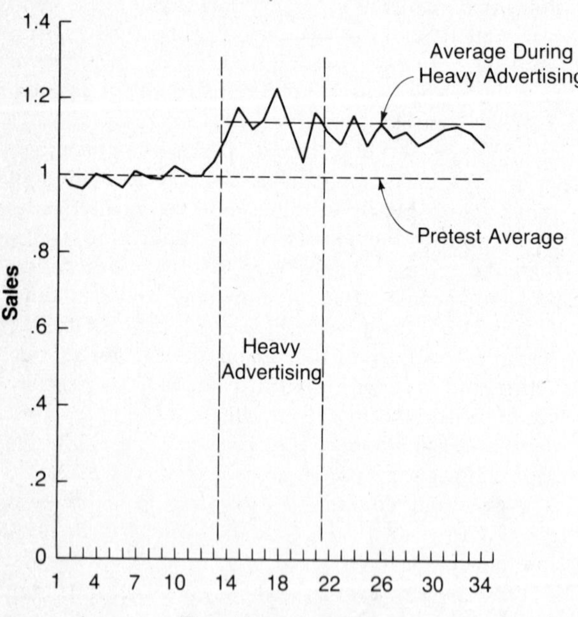

FIGURE 3
Sales Went Up Quickly Under Increased Advertising, but Declined Slowly After It Was Removed. Sales Are Measured as the Ratio of Sales in Test Areas to Sales in Control Areas Not Receiving the Heavy Advertising.

The experiment just described was a project within a marketing decision support operation of a large package goods company. Management asked for the experiment because of concern over advertising budget levels. The sales data used were captured routinely from external syndicated sources and internal company records. Company management scientists analyzed the results using a high level language and wielding a variety of standard and nonstandard statistical tools.

Whenever new measurement technologies appear, they create special opportunities for learning how the world works. Figure 4 shows data of the type that is becoming available through automated checkout equipment in grocery stores. Shown is *daily* market share of two brands of a package good in a supermarket. The bumps are promotions. The speed and precision with which the promotion effect can be read is portentous. Here is an indicator of opportunities for new knowledge that will become possible in the near future.

Models

Models form the other half of the models and measurements team of natural science. They provide theories that seek to bring order to the chaos of collected facts. They are much less well understood by laypeople and, indeed, the word is used in enough different ways by professionals that its meaning is often unclear.

For present purposes, I shall define a model as a mathematical description of how something works. Once upon a time, in a simpler age, scientists thought they were discovering the laws of nature; thus in physics we find Ohm's law, Newton's laws, and the like. Unfortunately, as people subjected these laws to closer and closer examination, they often found unsettling imperfections. These frequently led not to outright rejection, but to deeper, more comprehensive theory. A famous example is Einstein's generalization of Newtonian mechanics through relativity. However, after enough incidents like this, physical scientists became more cautious and often described their theories as models. In more recent times, as social and management scientists have sought to develop mathematical understanding of their worlds,

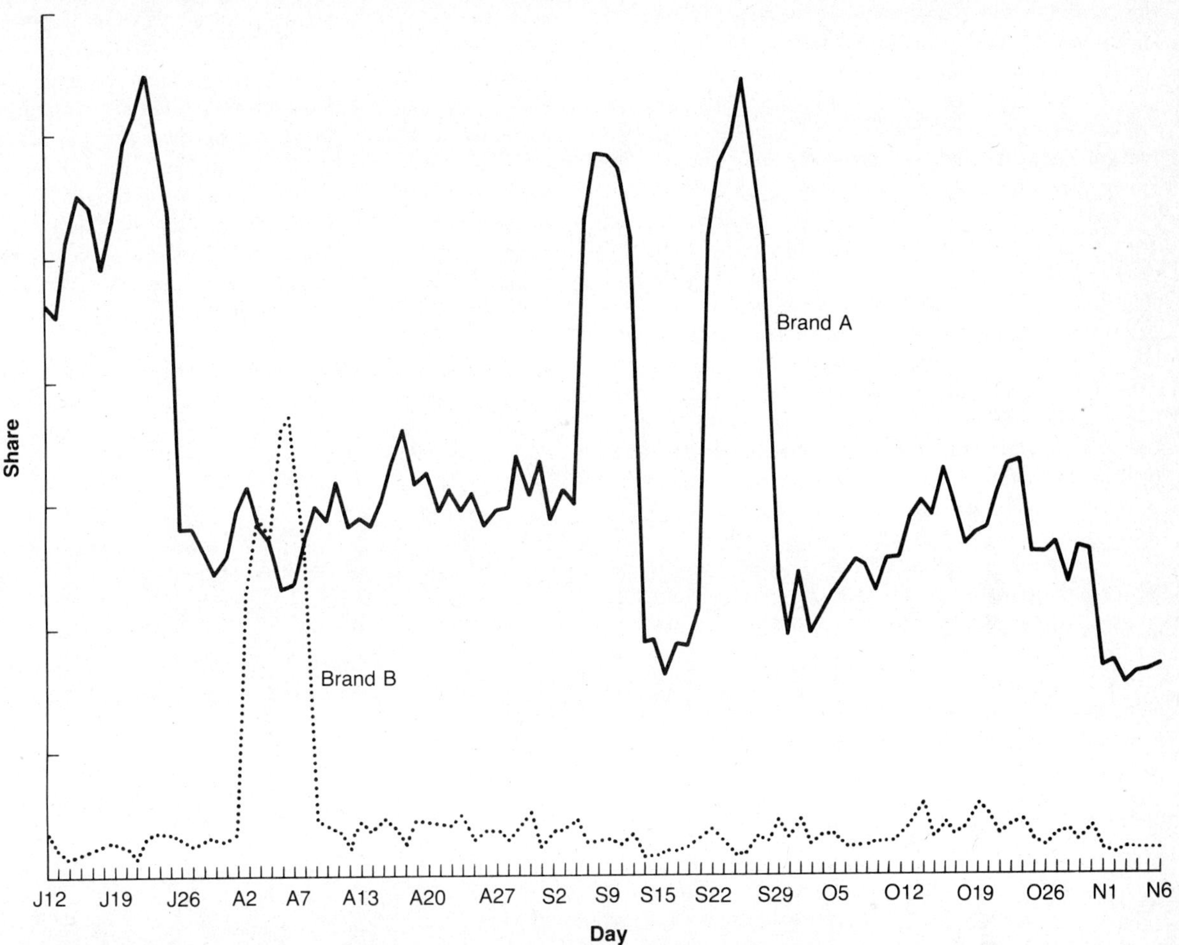

FIGURE 4
Daily Market Shares of Two National Brands in a Supermarket Chain Clearly Show the Effect of Store Specials. Data Was Collected on Electronic Checkout Equipment.

they have entertained few illusions about the exactness of their representations. Consequently, they have readily taken up the term.

There is an important practical advantage to the incompleteness implied by the word model. Consider the construction of a model to help solve a marketing problem. We would wish it to include all the important marketing phenomena required to analyze the problem, but, equally, we would wish it to exclude extraneous complication. This incompleteness is important and desirable. Managers, however, are sometimes nervous about it; they conceive that science is exact (even though science and especially engineering abounds with approximations). If a model is full of art, managers become wary. They say art is just what they were trying to get rid of by hiring expensive, overeducated terminal thumpers.

As something of a corroboration of this mindset, we observe that consulting firms which say they have discovered "laws of marketing" have sometimes had remarkable success with high levels of management.

Managers use models all the time but without the name. Successful management scientists working with managers often deemphasize the word, using models as required for the job but communicating the results as ideas and phenomena, going into detail as requested. One important development in this direction should be noted by those complainers who say models are not used in practice. Management scientists imbed models into problem-solving systems where the models themselves are relatively inconspicuous because they are only a part of the final product. Silk and Urban's (1978) ASSESSOR for evaluating new products is a good example. It employs high technology consumer choice models and statistical calibration, yet the manager-client focuses on the output and its message for his product. A similar situation arises in the models used for audience exposure analysis of advertising media schedules (research and frequency studies). In such cases the client company should, and frequently does, treat the analytic system like any other industrial product and perform a technical evaluation of it before using it routinely.

I would like to distinguish between *model* and *procedure.* If you allocate the advertising budget to major markets proportional to last year's sales in those markets, you have specified a procedure. Implicit in the procedure may or may not be a model. For example, if you hypothesize that advertising response is proportional to last year's sales times a suitably chosen function of advertising dollars, then you can construct a model of market response that will yield as the optimal budget allocation the same results as the described procedure.

Thus a *procedure is a way of calculating a result; a model is a set of assumptions about how something works.* Managers frequently use procedures, usually based in part on implicit intuitive models. Management scientists devise procedures directly, but often try to develop and calibrate explicit models which will generate good procedures.

In my simple world, I like to distinguish between two types of models: good and bad. Bad models include those that are simply wrong. For example, a model with a linear relationship between sales and advertising has to be incorrect. Other models are vacuous. The symbols may not really be defined or the model may merely be a formalistic way of saying something obvious that is better said simply. Still other models are so extraordinarily elaborate that they collapse of their own weight as data and calibration requirements become so enormous that testing and calibration are infeasible.

We have lived through many bad marketing models and, if we are to continue to progress, we will have to live through many more. At least we have good models, too. Fortunately, it is a characteristic of science that once you discover something worthwhile you can use it from then on and make it a building block for continued progress.

Three types of good models are: (1) small models offering insight and structure for thinking, (2) general structures permitting the synthesis of a variety of phenomena, and (3) models of new phenomena. Without trying to cover the whole field, I shall illustrate each of these types.

Small Models Offering Insight. The customer flow model displayed in Figure 5 has very much affected people's thinking about new products in the past 15 years. Here is the basic proposition: A new product has some intended set of customers, called its target

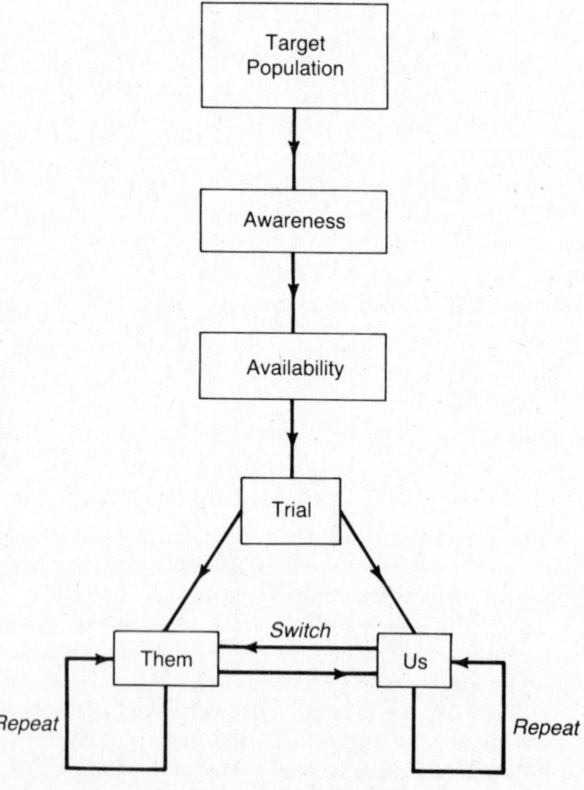

FIGURE 5
A Simple Customer Flow Model Provides a Mathematical Structure for Estimating Future Sales of a New Product.

market. Suppose we have developed an inexpensive gyrocompass for recreational vehicles. Recreational vehicle owners are the *target population.* Before any of them can possibly buy the product they have to be *aware* of it. A company can inform people about the existence of a new product by advertising and, in fact, any advertising agency can produce a reasonable estimate of how much money it will take to do this. For some number of millions of dollars, for example, you can teach 20% of the American public your brand name.

But people cannot buy the product unless it is available. This is a distribution problem. Assuming a company is marketing somewhat similar goods, it will know the appropriate distribution channels and will be able to tell what kind of availability can be achieved for the product.

Once a person in the target market is aware of the product and has a place to buy it, the next question is will that person *try* the product, i.e., buy it once? Involved here is the success of advertising in communicating the product's attributes to the prospective customer and how the customer evaluates the desirability of those attributes. Reasonable estimates can usually be made of trial probability. In some categories of package goods, historical norms are now available. You can also make more refined estimates by taking field measurements with the actual product. Note, however, that even without this, and long before the product has even been made, estimates based on historical norms or managerial judgments will permit useful market calculations.

Given that a person has tried the product, the next question is whether he or she will *repeat* the purchase the next time such a product is needed. Alternatively the customer may *switch* to another brand. Provided that reasonable estimates of switching and repeating probabilities can be made, we can calculate the share of purchases going to the new product among people who try it once.

A straightforward calculation puts together the whole sequence: the number of people in the target market *times* the fraction who become aware of the product *times* the fraction who find it available *times* the fraction of those who try it *times* the share of purchases that triers devote to the new brand *times* the sales rate for the product class, determines the sales rate of the new product.

The notions of awareness, availability, trial, repeat, and switching are fundamental. These processes are obviously going on. The model can be made very elaborate (see Urban 1970), but the basic conceptual structure and the process described above for calculating long-run sales rate are exceedingly simple.

The quality of that calculation will depend on the quality of the inputs, but just using sensible numbers helps keep the new product manager from becoming a total dreamer. Every new product manager is a wild advocate for his or her product. Probably this is necessary since most new products fail and somebody has to be a believer to keep from giving up before starting. The prehistoric way to estimate new product sales was to declare a final number in one judgmental swoop. Amazingly, the number usually turned out to be exactly that value which would justify continuing the development. The discipline of putting plausible numbers into the above calculation restricts answers to a believable range. Then, as the company goes through the new product development sequence, increasing investments in field measurements narrows the uncertainty in the final sales.

Models for Synthesis. Another useful type of model provides a structure for assembling measurements and phenomena from a variety of sources to solve a given problem. An example is the marketing-mix model BRANDAID (Little 1975). BRANDAID, when appropriately calibrated for a product of interest, relates brand sales and profit to major marketing control variables, competitive actions, and environmental influences. The structure is modular so that marketing effects can be added or deleted to suit the application. Each effect is a submodel which can be designed separately. Major control variables such as price, promotion, and advertising are premodeled, but custom versions can be substituted if desired. The number of geographic regions and competitors is flexible, from one to whatever patience will permit.

Model calibration makes the general structure specific to a particular application. Historical data, field experiments, econometric analysis, and whatever else may prove useful are used to develop values for model parameters so that the model becomes a suitable representation of a given market.

Usually a few key variables account for most of the effects on sales. Figures 6 and 7 show an application employing four submodels. The submodel outputs are plotted in Figure 6. These outputs multiply together to give the three-year retrospective tracking shown in Figure 7. Such a model is useful for brand planning and sometimes even more useful for generating an anticipated sales rate. This becomes a standard to be compared with actual sales. Discrepancies trigger diagnosis and feedback to management.

New Phenomena. It is always exciting to discover a new phenomenon and build a model of it. This does not happen often and, because of commercial secrecy, the news sometimes spreads rather slowly. An example that originated a number of years ago, but continues to have ramifications, deals with concentration of retail outlets. The original work was done on gasoline service stations. All the oil companies are familiar with it, but, as with many scientific phenom-

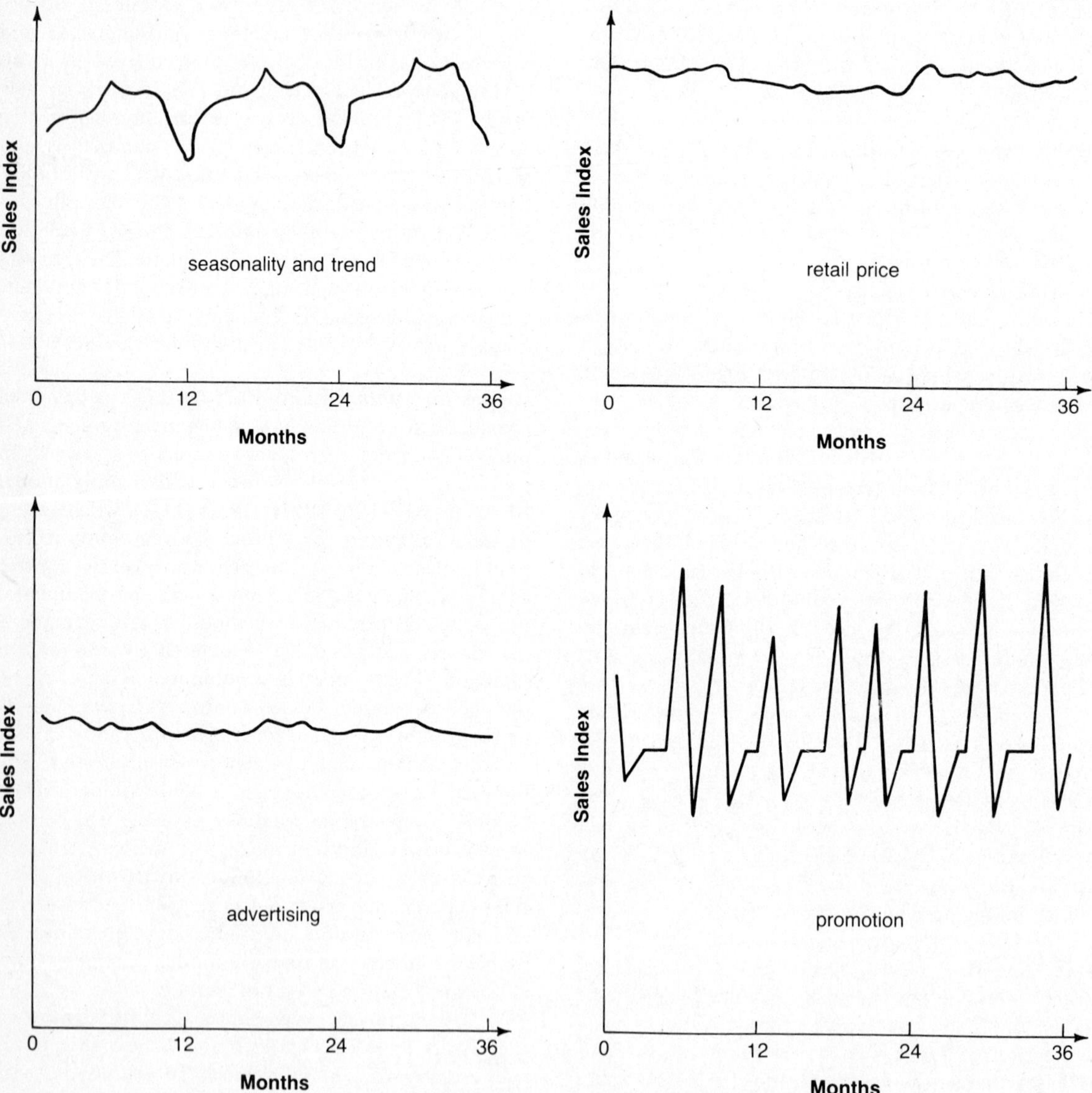

FIGURE 6
An Application of the Marketing-Mix Model BRANDAID. Historical Company Actions and Environmental Conditions Fed into Four Submodels Give the Outputs Shown.

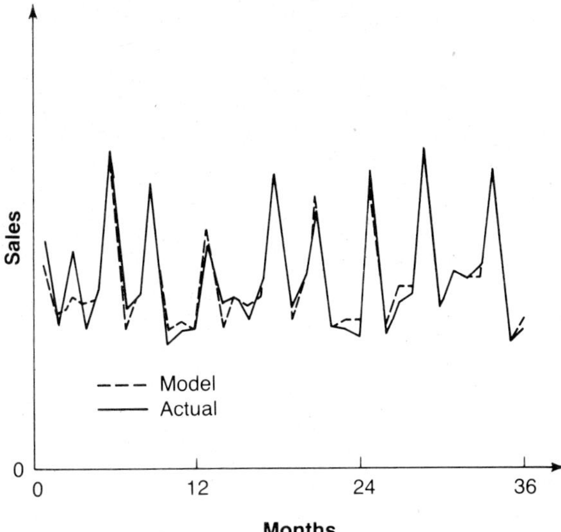

FIGURE 7
The BRANDAID Submodels Are Combined to Track Historical Sales.

ena, the principle is more general. In this case, it carries over into other franchise operations (e.g., branch banks and fast food outlets) and in these industries the idea is just beginning to take hold.

The phenomena deals with competition between outlets in a given city. I recall sitting in the office of a marketing economist from a major oil company and discussing service station site location.

He said, "One thing you have to be careful about is putting two of our stations close together or putting too many stations in the same market. First of all, the dealers will scream, but, in addition, you start running into self-competition. If the company puts new stations in a market where it already has many, it is taking business away from itself."

This point of view is represented in Figure 8 by the curve marked "What people thought" and shows gallonage per station decreasing with number of outlets in a city.

What Hartung and Fisher (1965) and later Naert and Bultez (1975) did was to collect data, analyze it, and build a theory. After filtering out a variety of variables that confused the situation, they found that the curve actually goes *up*. In other words, up to a certain point, stations actually reinforce each other: the more stations the company has, the greater the gallonage *per station*.

To me this is quite surprising, although, once a fact is known, it is easy to offer explanations. For example, stations are outdoor advertisements for the company; the more stations the more people become aware of the brand. In addition, media advertising which is hardly worthwhile for one or two stations in a market becomes economical if there are many. Credit cards become more useful to a customer if the brand has many stations and therefore will enhance total brand sales in the market. Everything makes sense—once you know the answer.

Figure 9 sketches the station reinforcement phenomenon as a plot of market share versus station share. If the effect did not exist, we would expect the diagonal straight line. With the effect, the company does worse than the straight line at low station share, then with increasing station share crosses over the diagonal, and finally bends over to unity as diminishing returns set in.

The strategy implications of the relationship are dramatic and quite opposite to the actions most oil companies were taking at the time. The curve tells a company to add stations where it is already strong, at least up to quite a high level, whereas most companies were trying to reach out geographically as fast as possible to become national companies with the widest possible markets. As we now see, this was not the best way to gain the most new business with new investment dollars. (Notice, incidentally, that the oil industry is characterized by strong regional market-

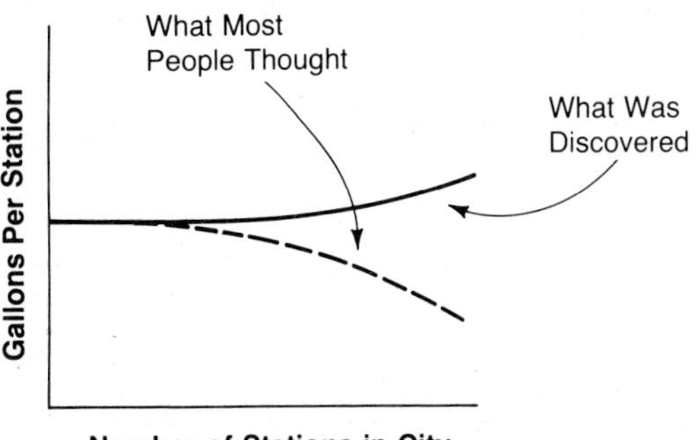

FIGURE 8
Surprisingly, as the Number of Service Stations for a Brand in a City Increases, So Does the Gallonage per Station.

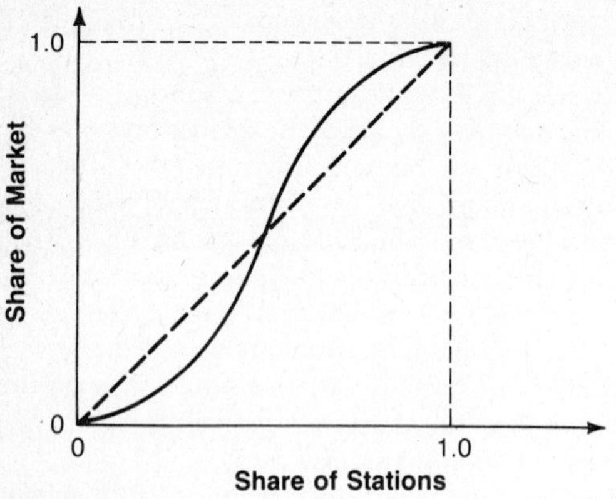

FIGURE 9
The Resulting S-Shaped Relation between Share of Market and Share of Stations Leads to Strong Regional Brands.

ers, a piece of empirical support for the underlying phenomenon.)

Later Lilien and Rao (1976) imbedded the reinforcement model into a financial model that takes into account laydown costs, competitive pricing conditions, building costs, total budget, etc. This provided marketing management with a tool to allocate service station investment dollars to maximize long-run return, thereby reaping the productivity of the basic discovery.

MDSS in Practice: The Bottom Line Is on Top

The best marketing decision support system I know of grew up over several years in the major division of a large package goods company. Although the first big data base came on stream in mid 1972, the system is still evolving. It has become an integral part of marketing operations and has materially affected management style in several ways.

A management science group of two or three professionals and a similar number of clerical and long-time company people run the activity. Their online data base contains internal company sales, records of marketing activities (e.g., advertising and promotion), and a sizeable block of syndicated data (e.g., panel and store audit information). As a rough estimate, 10^6 numbers are online and more can be available with a few days notice.

The system software is a high level, analytic language which offers not only data base management, but powerful manipulative and statistical capabilities. Gradually, many small and large analytic routines and models have been written and incorporated into the system. The computer is in constant use; one or two people are logged in virtually all the time and overnight batch runs ordered online during the day are common.

The bread and butter business of the MDSS consists of responding to a remarkable variety of small requests from brand managers and higher levels of marketing management. Rarely does raw data retrieval provide the answer. Almost always, data are manipulated and presented in a special way because of some issue at hand. Service is sufficiently good with such fast turnaround on short requests that, at one point, barriers had to be raised to reduce requests and maintain quality control on jobs performed. An important block of time goes into data base maintenance and updating.

Changes in Management Style

Two significant changes in marketing management style can be traced to the MDSS. Tendencies toward each had existed previously, but the MDSS permits them to emerge in a practical way.

The first is the growth of a "try and see" approach to new marketing programs. The marketing managers in the company are activists who want to introduce new ideas, but also want to know whether they really work. A miniexperiment program has evolved. The management science group has identified a bank of market areas appropriate for tests. The annual marketing plan includes a set of tests for the coming year. Extra tests can be put in the field quickly. Typical projects are new promotion ideas, packages, product line extensions, and changes in advertising media strategy, copy, or weight. The management science group has developed analytic and evaluative routines for reading the results quickly and efficiently. The detail, flexibility, and rapid turnaround of the MDSS along with the experience and skill of professional people make the operation possible.

The miniexperiment program is the invention of marketing management, not management scientists. This has important consequences. In the first place, the tests are sometimes not very precise. They are often done in single markets and, as any statistician will point out, it is difficult to estimate a standard error from one observation. Nevertheless, the program prospers. Although an individual test may be statistically weak, the whole collection screens a considerable number of new ideas. Real winners stand out. Run-of-the-mill improvements are hard to read but correspondingly less important. As has been shown by Gross (1972) in the case of advertising copy testing, significant gains accrue to creating multiple ideas and screening them, even if the precision is limited. It is doubtful that the management science department would ever have proposed the program on its own. The technical people would have proposed careful multiple market experiments that were more statistically defensible, but then costs would have prevented a really extensive program. As it is, marketing management, having invented the idea, is willing to absorb the uncertainties of the results.

Larger scale, multiple market experiments also are conducted. In fact, a carefully designed advertising weights test analyzed within the MDSS recently led to a major shift in advertising spending strategy.

The second managerial style change is a shift toward regional marketing. Anyone can think up regional strategies, but it is another matter to maintain management control over them and do follow-up evaluations. These are necessary to determine successes and failures and to adjust strategies to changing conditions. The MDSS has been critical in making this possible.

Market Response Reporting

Conventional reviews of brand and company performance stress *status* reporting, i.e., how things are. For example, what are sales, share, price, promotion, and advertising expenditures and what are their trends? Status reporting is characteristic both of standard market monitoring systems like SAMI and Nielsen and of internal company reporting.

A more action-oriented performance review is becoming possible with the evolution of MDSSs. This is market *response* reporting, i.e., how effective marketing actions are. For example, what is price elasticity, how do sales respond to promotion, and what effect will increased advertising have on sales?

The markets of this company have witnessed important competitive changes over the past few years. The historical events captured in company and syndicated data permit extensive analysis of various marketing tactics. Analytic methods have evolved not overnight, but over several years to permit estimates of market response to major changes in marketing actions. These response estimates are the subject of ongoing reviews similar to those conventionally made with static indicators and offer marketing management new and sharper information for decision making.

The market response information also permits projection of future performance by means of marketing-mix models. While this is done for certain purposes, a more important role of models has been in the historical analysis itself. A credible model of the effects of all major marketing variables is essential to performing the market response analysis.

Costs/Benefits

The cost of the MDSS in this company is large in dollars: several hundreds of thousands. As a fraction of sales, however, the cost of the system, the data, and the people who run it is small, perhaps 0.1%. This seems modest considering that marketing budgets run about 5% of sales and, more important, the decisions being affected influence sales and profit by much more. The cost of the system and its operation splits roughly equally among data, people, and computation.

The MDSS did not spring full blown from the marketing vice president's head nor did it evolve without controversy. Its growth has been incremental, moving from the first tentative beginnings and useful initial results, to further extensions, more results, and so on. This has brought certain inefficiencies ("If we'd known then, what we know now . . . "), but the idea of "best" at each evolutionary stage changes considerably by the time of the next one so that a flexible approach pays off.

The MDSS has used outside time-sharing services copiously and so has been a constant target for an inhouse data processing takeover. Yet the power, flexibility, and responsiveness of languages available on external time-sharing has not been duplicated inhouse. Marketing management has insisted on high and increasing levels of service which have only been available externally.

Some payoffs have been explicit. An analysis of

promotion led to a strategy change with a profit increase in seven figures. Such incidents are obviously helpful and may well be essential for survival. However, my own feeling is that the largest benefits have come simply by facilitating good management. Bold changes of direction in a company are infrequent (which is probably good). For the most part management deals with a series of adjustments to conditions, no one adjustment being particularly spectacular nor uniquely traceable to any specific piece of data or analysis. Yet the collection of analyses adds up to influence, decision, and improved profit. Another usually unrecognized role is assistance in preventing disasters. The pressure for improvement in a company turns up fascinating proposals, some of which are bound to be bad. Analyses that lead to recommendations for inaction are not very exciting, but are sometimes more valuable than calls for revolution.

In summary, this particular company has developed an effective MDSS over a multiyear period. The process has been evolutionary with high costs, but higher benefits. Marketing management has become more innovative as it receives more and better feedback from "try and see" operations. The system has encouraged a shift from market status reporting to market response reporting. However, the main point to be made is that effective MDSSs are not "pie in the sky." They are here now.

Problem Solving with Interactive Systems: The Grey Flannel Robot

In the early days of time-shared computers, many people realized that a marvelous invention was at hand. A person could have convenient access to huge computers from any place with a telephone. Without too much difficulty, a computer could interrogate the user in a semblance of natural language, using words and phrases to ask for input and deliver output.

What People Thought

Clearly time-sharing was a breakthrough and the imaginations of the visionaries were stimulated. A new world was forecast in which managers would sit at terminals and formulate their problems. With the help of easy-to-use commands, they would put key assumptions and judgments into the computer. These would be incorporated into models relevant to the issues to be examined. The managers would ask "what if" questions and evaluate various strategies. New ones would be stimulated by the analysis. Finally the managers would select their best alternatives and go off to take action.

What People Found

Managers do not like terminals. They are impatient and busy. They do not formulate problems in model terms because that is not the way they naturally think. They want to think about strategy not analysis. They will propose actions to be analyzed, but they do not want to do it themselves.

Anecdotes to illustrate these points are many. I recall one excruciating incident in the early days of online models when the president of a very large corporation was invited to use the new toy hands-on. Unfortunately, he couldn't type—not even with a tolerable hunt and peck. The situation became embarrassing. Vice presidents fluttered about. Finally a data processing manager took over the keyboard. More fundamentally, however, managers do not go online because of their function and style. As Mintzberg (1973) has observed, the manager leads a high pressure, communications-intensive life which is much more try-and-see than think-and-analyze.

The notion of the hands-on manager is not dead, however. I have rather recently been told that a large computer manufacturer has sold an elaborate information system that will put video terminals on the desks of 10 vice presidents for constant use in running their departments. I am not optimistic about the ultimate level of use. We shall find an occasional top executive who is an avid hands-on analyst, but I feel quite confident the majority will not be for some time to come.

A New Role

All is not lost, however. Interactive systems are definitely the way to go. We need only recognize that managers work through human organizations in this as in most things they do. What we find happening is that individuals are emerging who can be described as *marketing science intermediaries.* They are typically OR/MS professionals or recent MBAs with good technical skills. They are first and foremost problem solvers. They convert managers' questions into models and analyses. They enter into dialogue with managers and others in the organization about what the problems really are. They provide answers to managers' questions and respond to the new questions that the answers provoke. They build portfolios of data bases, models, and systems to solve recurring problems. They do the homework managers lack the time to do. They want the managers' jobs in a few years. For the present they are the organizers and internal consultants who build knowledge and systems to support marketing operations.

Typically, marketing science intermediaries program and use models and systems personally, or with small staffs. However, they are not computer scientists and do not report to MIS. What makes their role possible are powerful new computer languages available on time-sharing.

Hardware and Software: Ready-to-Wear

Computers are impossible to work with, but are getting better. Advances in hardware and software are pushing the evolution of decision support systems. Hardware manufacturing costs are dropping and prices are following at a respectful distance. Some people forecast that hardware costs will eventually become negligible. I am not so sure because we are so good at thinking up big new jobs for computers. However, it is fair to predict that hardware cost will become a negligible part of the computations we are doing today. Software, on the other hand, continues to be expensive but has undergone advances in ways particularly relevant to us here.

The philosophy behind contemporary software is to let the computer solve its own problems. Why should users have to go through elaborate contortions to move data from a statistical package to a marketing model to a report generator? They shouldn't. Good software systems can solve these and many other machine problems, leaving the users free to concentrate on the essence of the analysis. High level commands permit easy plotting, tabling, array arithmetic, statistical analysis, optimization, report generation, and model building, all on the same data base.

As a user, I am most appreciative of "default" options. Thus, if SALES is a defined data variable, I can give a command like PLOT SALES and out comes a plot. It fits on an 8½ × 11 inch page, the curve approximately fills the plot, the axes are labeled, a sensible grid has been selected that has round-number gradations, etc. The computer has finally become a moderately effective clerk. If I want something different from default specifications, I can override them, but most of the time, especially during exploratory work, the automated plot is fine. Furthermore the same commands will work on a dozen different terminals; it is only necessary to tell the computer which one is being used.

High level analytic languages that embody many of these features are increasing in number and scope. An early one with the emphasis on a concise and powerful mathematical notation is APL. A commercial system with a strong business orientation is EXPRESS. Somewhat similar are PROBE, TSAM, and XSIM. Some of the systems are easily extendable so that, for example, FORTRAN subroutines can be easily introduced as new commands. Why reinvent the wheel? Features and degree of power vary, but all these languages try to let the analyst work an order of magnitude faster than a FORTRAN programmer on a bare-bones, time-sharing system.

Most of the observations just made about interactive systems extend well beyond the context of marketing (see for example, Keen and Scott Morton 1978).

Implementation: Which Way Is Up?

Any attempt to install an MDSS has organizational ramifications. Will marketing management's antibodies reject the graft? Will the internal computer establishment gag?

Taking these issues in order, consider Argyris' view (1971) in *Management Science:*

> *If management information systems achieve their designers' highest aspirations, they will tend to create conditions where executives will experience: (1) reduction of space of free movement, (2) psychological failure and double bind, (3) leadership based more on competence than formal power, (4) decreased feelings of essentiality. These experiences will tend to create genuine resistance to MIS.*

Another hand-wringer. I do not agree and will argue otherwise, but first let me give an anecdote to favor Argyris' view. A marketing vice president I know refused to conduct a field experiment which would have sought to measure the effect of advertising on sales. He had various reasons for his position, but I suspect the real reason was that he had negotiated an increased advertising budget with the president. Therefore, if the experiment should confirm the increased budget, it would be redundant and, if not, he would look bad. So why do the experiment? To use Argyris' words, better information only restricted his space of free movement.

I believe that the executive was wrong and that by such actions his company could lose competitive advantage which would eventually reflect on him. However, this type of managerial reaction certainly exists. A better style, in my opinion, is to view the advertising increase as an opportunity for measurement and further adaptation to the market.

Such examples notwithstanding, my main observation is that it takes a first class marketing manager to bring an MDSS into being in the first place and such people are not about to let their systems run them. On the contrary it gives them a feeling of power to act on moderately reliable information for a change.

Let's check other commentators on the MIS scene. Gruber and Niles (1976) write:

> *Understanding what managers actually do and . . . organizing the information they currently use is the only way to build relevancy . . . the biggest mistake in . . . current . . . work is that it . . . builds . . . products that serve some assumed decision making process which real managers do not carry out.*

I agree in part, but we have gone past this stage. To support their point, I recall a director of marketing who was very impressed with computer technology and decided he wanted instant retrieval. His idea was to have a video terminal on his desk so that, if he wanted to know sales last month in Buffalo, he could press a button and, presto, the data would appear.

We told him, "It's not really retrieval you want but models," and explained why.

He said, "OK, you people are the experts not me."

So we gave him models. It turned out that he wanted retrieval. We went back and gave him retrieval. Actually, what we gave him was retrieval plus analysis plus models, and even more important, he hired a marketing science intermediary. This particular marketing director was not about to push any buttons that did not have people on the other end of the wire.

Gruber and Niles' point about doing better and faster whatever is being done now is a good one and an excellent way to build credibility and support for an MDSS. However, we are well beyond that in many areas and have plenty of examples of new and useful analysis, measurements, and models. A variety of these have been discussed already.

A major issue for an MDSS is its relation to inhouse data processing and management information systems. The first 10 years of business applications of time-sharing have been dominated by external vendors. In this period, fixed costs of time-sharing have been high because of hardware, software, communication equipment, and marketing. Much of the marketing has really been low level applications consulting. The costs and required skills have deterred inhouse time-sharing in many organizations. Furthermore, inhouse data processing typically has had its hands full meeting its current operational commitments. As a result, most activities that look like MDSSs have been done on outside time-sharing. Yet, inhouse data processing departments, which typically live in an environment of repetitive batch jobs, frequently consider the cost of commercial time-sharing to be exorbitant. Marketing management, however, has not found the cost high relative to the value of the tasks performed and has preferred to pay an apparent premium rather than wait for specially programmed batch runs or, in some cases, deal with cumbersome, leanly serviced, inhouse time-sharing systems.

The scene continues to change with two rather different patterns now in evidence. On the one hand, central MIS is in some cases becoming a better time-sharing vendor, bringing in good operating systems and languages. It thus becomes a bigger supplier of computations, but one with less concern about the content of the computation, since the usage is decentralized. In our case, this would be done by a marketing science intermediary working for the marketing department.

Another and perhaps more significant development is the decentralization made possible by the increasing power of minicomputers. Small computers with high level analytic languages can be installed in the functional department and only interconnect with MIS to pick up or deposit data. Costs are moderate and technical support requirements manageable. If these machines and their software prove reasonably robust, the growth of decentralized MDSSs seems very likely.

Summary: Whither Decision Support?

The main thrust of this paper is to say that marketing management can, and should, obtain better analytic help for its planning and operations. This can be done by a marketing decision support system that puts the new technology of computers and marketing science to work on increasing marketing productivity. An MDSS means hiring people with marketing science skills. It means organizing data bases and putting them in usable form. It means building a portfolio of models and analytic techniques directed at important company issues. It means integrating problem solving and problem finding within the marketing function using the marketing science intermediary to facilitate the process. A strong system does not spring up overnight. It takes two or three years of evolution and development, but it can lead to new styles of marketing management.

Let's look ahead. In the next five to 10 years, I foresee:

- *An order of magnitude increase in the amount of marketing data used.* Through MDSS development, the internal data of a company will finally become accessible on a rather detailed basis: sales, advertising, promotion, etc. Automatically collected point-of-sale information from the marketplace (e.g., Universal Product Code data from supermarkets) will replace most current store audits. Much better longitudinal data on customers (e.g., panels) will be generally available and will include such currently missing information as media use. The monitoring of competitive advertising, promotion, and price will be vastly improved.
- *A similar tenfold increase in computer power available for marketing analysis.* The hardware is already built; it is out there and purchasable. The price is going to break. The only problem will be for marketing to absorb computer power in a useful way.
- *Widespread adoption of analytic computer languages.* These make data accessible and greatly facilitate analysis. Some exist now, more will be introduced, and all will improve.
- *A shift from market status reporting to market response reporting.* This is an important change. SAMI, Nielsen, and other market monitoring systems, including internal sales reporting, emphasize market status, i.e., how things are: what are sales, share, price, advertising, etc.?

  Tomorrow's systems will report response, i.e., how things react: what's price elasticity, advertising response, promotional effectiveness, etc.? Companies will even do a reasonably good job of monitoring competitor's market response.

  Much work lies ahead for marketing scientists in order for this to come to pass. We need well-designed data sources and many new tools. How do we handle eclectic data sources in developing and calibrating models? What are the best underlying models to represent marketing phenomena? We can expect a flowering of new work.
- *New methodology for supporting strategy development.* Marketing scientists will further advance our understanding of product-market boundaries. Better response measurements will expose more clearly the nature of competitive interaction and give rise to game theoretic strategy development.

And, finally, I foresee:

- *A shortage of marketing scientists.* You know what that means: higher salaries, more fun, exciting new toys. From this I conclude that marketing is the right field to be in.

References

Argyris, Chris (1971), "Management Information Systems: The Challenge to Rationality and Emotionality," *Management Science,* 17 (February), B275–292.

Bass, F. M. and D. G. Clarke (1972), "Testing Distributive Lag Models of Advertising Effect," *Journal of Marketing Research,* 9 (August), 298–308.

Bloom, D. and M. J. Stewart (1977), "An Integrated Marketing Planning System," *Proceedings of ESOMAR Conference,* (February), 168–186.

Business Week (1973), "Ten Year Experience at General Foods," (August 25), 48–55.

Cox, K. K., J. B. Higginbotham, and J. Burton (1976), "Applications of Focus Group Interviews in Marketing," *Journal of Marketing,* 40 (January), 77–80.

Day, George S. (1977), "Diagnosing the Product Portfolio," *Journal of Marketing,* 41 (April), 29–38.

Ehrenberg, A. S. C. (1972), *Repeat Buying,* New York: American Elsevier.

Gorry, G. Anthony and Michael S. Scott Morton (1971), "A Framework for Management Information Systems," *Sloan Management Review,* 13 (Fall), 55–70.

Grayson, C. Jackson Jr. (1973), "Management Science and Business Practice," *Harvard Business Review,* 51 (July-August), 41–48.

Green, Paul E. and Yoram Wind (1975), "New Way to Measure Consumers' Judgments," *Harvard Business Review,* 53 (July-August), 107–117.

Gross, Irwin (1972), "The Creative Aspects of Advertising," *Sloan Management Review,* 14 (Fall), 83–109.

—— (1977), "The Value of 'Value-in-use,'" unpublished note, Wilmington, DE: DuPont Company.

Gruber, William H. and John S. Niles (1976), *The New Management,* New York: McGraw-Hill, 138–139.

Hartung, Philip H. and James L. Fisher (1965), "Brand Switching and Mathematical Programming in Market Expansion," *Management Science,* 11 (August), B231–243.

Hauser, John R. (1978), "Testing the Accuracy, Usefulness, and Significance of Probabilistic Choice Models: An Information Theoretic Approach," *Operations Research,* 26 (May-June), 406–421.

—— and Glen L. Urban (1977), "A Normative Methodology for Modeling Consumer Response in Innovation," *Operations Research,* 25 (July-August), 576–619.

Hess, Sidney W. (1967), "The Use of Models in Marketing Timing Decisions," *Operations Research,* 15 (July-August), 720–737.

von Hippel, Eric (1978), "Successful Industrial Products from Customer Ideas," *Journal of Marketing,* 42 (January), 39–49.

Keen, Peter G. W. and Michael S. Scott Morton (1978), *Decision Support Systems: An Organizational Perspective,* Reading, MA: Addison-Wesley.

Lilien, Gary L. and Ambar G. Rao (1976), "A Model for Allocating Retail Outlet Building Resources Across Market Areas," *Operations Research,* 24 (January-February), 1–14.

Little, John D. C. (1970), "Models and Managers: The Concept of a Decision Calculus," *Management Science,* 16 (April), B466–485.

—— (1975), "BRANDAID: A Marketing-Mix Model, Parts 1 and 2," *Operations Research,* 23 (July-August), 628–673.

Mintzberg, Henry (1973), *The Nature of Managerial Work,* New York: Harper and Row.

Montgomery, David B. and Glen L. Urban (1969), *Management Science in Marketing,* Englewood Cliffs, NJ: Prentice-Hall, Inc.

Naert, Philippe A. and Alain V. Bultez (1975), "A Model of Distribution Network Aggregate Performance," *Management Science,* 21 (June), 1102–1112.

Nigam, A. K., ed. (1975,76,77), Special Issues on Practice, *Interfaces,* 6 (November), 7 (November), 8 (November), Part 2.

Parfitt, J. H. and B. J. K. Collins (1968), "Use of Consumer Panels for Brand-Share Prediction," *Journal of Marketing Research,* 5 (May), 131–145.

Parsons, Leonard J. and Randall L. Schultz (1976), *Marketing Models and Econometric Research,* Amsterdam: North Holland.

Prince, George M. (1972), *The Practice of Creativity,* New York: MacMillan.

Silk, Alvin J. and Glen L. Urban (1978), "Pre-Test Market Evaluation of New Packaged Goods: A Model and Measurement Methodology," *Journal of Marketing Research,* 15 (May), 171–191.

Shocker, A. D. and V. Srinivasan (1977), "Multiattribute Approaches for Concept Evaluation and Generation: A Critical Review," working paper no. 240 (October), Pittsburgh: Graduate School of Business, University of Pittsburgh.

Urban, Glen L. (1970), "SPRINTER Mod III: A Model for the Analysis of New Frequently Purchased Consumer Products," *Operations Research,* 18 (September-October), 805–854.